The Cambridge Companion to

SHOSTAKOVICH

EDITED BY
Pauline Fairclough
and
David Fanning

CAMBRIDGE
UNIVERSITY PRESS

CAMBRIDGE UNIVERSITY PRESS
Cambridge, New York, Melbourne, Madrid, Cape Town, Singapore, São Paulo, Delhi

Cambridge University Press
The Edinburgh Building, Cambridge CB2 8RU, UK

Published in the United States of America by Cambridge University Press, New York

www.cambridge.org
Information on this title: www.cambridge.org/9780521603157

© Cambridge University Press 2008

First published 2008

Printed in the United Kingdom at the University Press, Cambridge

A catalogue record for this publication is available from the British Library

Library of Congress Cataloging-in-Publication Data
The Cambridge companion to Shostakovich / edited by Pauline Fairclough and David
Fanning.
    p. cm.
Includes bibliographical references (p.   ) and index.
ISBN 978-0-521-60315-7
1.   Shostakovich, Dmitrii Dmitrievich, 1906–1975–Criticism and
interpretation. I.   Fairclough, Pauline, 1970– II.   Fanning, David (David J.)
ML410.S53C36 2008
780.92–dc22

                                                    2007050142

ISBN 978-0-521-84220-4 hardback
ISBN 978-0-521-60315-7 paperback

Contents

Notes on the contributors

Rosamund Bartlett's publications include *Wagner and Russia* (Cambridge, 1995), *Shostakovich in Context* (Oxford, 2000) and *Chekhov: Scenes from a Life* (New York, 2004). She has contributed to *The New Grove Dictionary of Music and Musicians* and *The Cambridge History of Russia*, and is editor of the forthcoming *Cambridge Companion to Russian Music*.

Pauline Fairclough is Lecturer in Music at the University of Bristol. She has published on Shostakovich and Soviet culture in *The Musical Quarterly* and *Music and Letters*; her book *A Soviet Credo: Shostakovich's Fourth Symphony* was published by Ashgate in 2006.

David Fanning is Professor of Music at the University of Manchester and has a varied career as scholar, pianist and critic. Author of several books and articles on Nielsen and Shostakovich, his most recent publications include a study of Shostakovich's Eighth String Quartet for Ashgate Press (2004) and a five-volume performing edition of Russian Opera Arias for Peters Edition.

David Haas is Professor of Music at the University of Georgia. His book *Leningrad's Modernists* (New York, 1998) was concerned with the new music and musical thought of Leningrad in the 1920s. His edition of *Symphonic Etudes* by Boris Asafyev (Lanham, Md., 2007) is a translation with commentary of a classic of twentieth-century Russian operatic criticism. He is currently at work on a study of the nineteenth-century Russian symphony and a novel about an American symphonist.

Marina Alexandrovna Ilichova danced with the Mariinsky Theatre before working as a ballet historian and critic. She has taught at the Vaganova Russian Ballet Academy in St Petersburg and since 2003 she has worked at the Russian Institute of the History of Arts. She is the author of many books and articles on ballet, including *Irina Kolpakova* (Leningrad, 1979; 2nd edn, Leningrad, 1986) and *Oleg Vinogradov* (Hamburg, 1994 (in English and German)).

Judith Kuhn teaches at the University of Wisconsin-Milwaukee. She has published articles in *Music Analysis* and in Ernst Kuhn *et al.*, eds., *Dmitri Schostakowitsch und das jüdische musikalische Erbe* (Berlin, 2001). Her book, *Shostakovich in Dialogue: Form, Imagery and Ideas in Quartets 1–7* is forthcoming from Ashgate.

Erik Levi is Reader in Music at Royal Holloway University of London. Author of the book *Music in the Third Reich* (London, 1994) and numerous chapters and articles on German music from the 1920s to the 1950s, he is also an experienced performer and writes regularly for *BBC Music Magazine*. He is currently writing a book about Mozart and the Nazis for Yale University Press.

Gerard McBurney is a composer, arranger and broadcaster. He has made performing versions of many Shostakovich works including a chamber ensemble score of the musical comedy *Moscow Cheryomushki* and an orchestral suite from the music-hall show *Uslovno Ubitïy*. Since 2006 he has been creative director of the Chicago Symphony Orchestra's Beyond the Score series.

Malcolm MacDonald is the editor of a short catalogue of Shostakovich's works (London, 1977; two subsequent editions). His books include the Dent Master Musicians volumes on Brahms and Schoenberg, monographs on Ronald Stevenson and John Foulds and a three-volume study of the symphonies of Havergal Brian. His most recent book is *Varèse, Astronomer in Sound* (London, 2003), and the new enlarged edition of his *Schoenberg* is imminent in 2008.

Francis Maes was artistic director of the Flanders Festival and currently teaches musicology at Ghent University (Belgium). He is the author of *A History of Russian Music, from Kamarinskaya to Babi Yar*, published by the University of California Press (2002).

John Riley is a lecturer, writer, broadcaster and curator. His publications include *Dmitri Shostakovich: A Life in Film* (London and New York, 2005). As a curator he works with various cinemas and produced the first BBC Film Promenade Concert. He wrote, produced and directed *Shostakovich – My Life at the Movies*, which was premiered by the City of Birmingham Symphony Orchestra with narrator Simon Russell Beale. It was then produced at the Komische Oper, Berlin.

Eric Roseberry is a freelance musician and writer who has specialized in the music of Benjamin Britten and Dmitry Shostakovich. His publications include his PhD, *Ideology, Style, Content and Thematic Process in the Symphonies, Cello Concertos and String Quartets of Shostakovich* (New York and London, 1989). He has contributed essays to the Cambridge Opera Handbook series to Britten's *Death in Venice* (1987), Aldeburgh Studies in Music *On Mahler and Britten* (1995), *Shostakovich Studies* (1995) and *The Cambridge Companion to Benjamin Britten* (1999).

Esti Sheinberg teaches Music Theory and Music Literature at Virginia Tech, Virginia, USA. Her publications include *Irony, Satire, Parody and The Grotesque in the Music of Shostakovich* (Aldershot, 2000) and 'Shostakovich's "Jewish Music" as an Existential Statement' in *Dmitri Schostakowitsch und das jüdische musikalische Erbe* (Berlin, 2001).

Chronology

Year	Shostakovich's life and career (works listed under year of completion)	Contemporary political events
1906	(25 September) Shostakovich born	
1909	(24 August) Sister Zoya born	
1914		(August) First World War begins
1915	Begins piano lessons with his mother and almost immediately composes first piano pieces; first visit to opera (Rimsky-Korsakov, *The Tale of Tsar Saltan*); (autumn) begins piano lessons with Olga Glyasser	
1916	Transfers to piano class of Ignaty Glyasser	Murder of Rasputin
1917	'Funeral March in Memory of Victims of the Revolution'	(February) Revolution – overthrow of Tsar
		(March) Formation of Provisional Government; abdication of Tsar
		(October) Revolution – Bolshevik seizure of power
		Formation of People's Commissariats (NKs, i.e. Ministries), including People's Commissariat for Enlightenment (Narkompros) subsuming the arts under education and propaganda, and NKVD (People's Commissariat for Internal Affairs)
		(December) creation of Cheka (Extraordinary Commission for the Suppression of Counter-revolution and Sabotage)
1918	Begins piano lessons with Alexandra Rozanova	(March) Treaty of Brest-Litovsk takes Russia out of War
		(April) Civil War begins
		(September) Red Terror begins in aftermath of attempt on Lenin's life
1919	(Autumn) Enrols at Petrograd Conservatoire – piano under Rozanova, composition under Maximilian Steinberg	(March) Campaign against churches Comintern established
1920	(Autumn) Transfers to piano class of Lev Nikolayev Op. 2 Eight Preludes for Piano (begun in 1919)	War with Poland (November) Civil War effectively ends, with Red Army victorious. Hostilities continue until October 1922
1921	Op. 1 Scherzo in F sharp minor	(March) Kronstadt and Tambov rebellions crushed; New Economic Policy (NEP) introduced at 10th Party Congress; famine in Volga regions (until 1922) kills millions
1922	(24 February) Father dies Op. 3 Theme and Variations for Orchestra Op. 4 *Two Fables of Krïlov* Op. 5 *Three Fantastic Dances* (piano) Op. 6 Suite for Two Pianos	(February) Cheka reorganized as GPU (State Political Administration) within NKVD (3 April) Stalin elected General Secretary of Party (May and December) Lenin suffers strokes (December) Founding of USSR (Union of Soviet Socialist Republics)
1923	(Spring) Operation for tuberculosis of lymphatic system; graduates as pianist (July) Meets and falls in love with Tatyana Glivenko at sanatorium in Crimea (October) Begins works as silent film accompanist Op. 8 Piano Trio no. 1	Formation of ACM (Association of Contemporary Music) and RAPM (Russian Association of Proletarian Musicians)

Year	Shostakovich's life and career (works listed under year of completion)	Contemporary political events
1924	Op. 7 Scherzo in E flat Op. 9 Three Pieces for Cello and Piano (lost) (Autumn) Begins works on First Symphony	(21 January) Death of Lenin; Petrograd renamed Leningrad GPU renamed OGPU and removed from NKVD (Republic level) to SovNarKom (USSR level) (December) Stalin announces policy of 'Socialism in One Country' (as opposed to priority of International Revolution)
1925	(March) Meets Marshal Tukhachevsky, who becomes his sponsor and patron Op. 10 Symphony no. 1 (completed 1 July) Op. 11 Two Pieces for String Octet	
1926	(April) Accepted for postgraduate study at Leningrad Conservatoire (12 May) Triumphant premiere of First Symphony Op. 12 Piano Sonata no. 1	(April) 'United opposition' (opposed to NEP and Socialism in One Country) of Trotsky, Zinoviev and Kamenev formed, but largely defeated by October
1927	(January) Awarded diploma of honour at first Chopin Piano Competition (Warsaw) (February) Returns via Berlin; meets Prokofiev in Leningrad (May) Beginning of friendship with Ivan Sollertinsky (June) Attends performance of *Wozzeck* and meets Berg (Summer) Meets Nina Varzar (future first wife) (Autumn) Meets Vsevolod Meyerhold Op. 13 *Aphorisms* (piano) Op. 14 Symphony no. 2, *Dedication to October* Op. 16 *Tahiti Trot* (orchestration of Vincent Youmans' 'Tea for Two')	(November–December) Expulsions of Trotsky, Zinoviev and Kamenev from Party
1928	(January) Works as pianist and musical director at Meyerhold Theatre in Moscow Op. 15 *The Nose* (opera, after Gogol)	(January) Trotsky exiled to Alma-Ata (May–July) Wreckers' Trial (October) Beginning of First Five-Year Plan
1929	(May) First published article 'On the Ills of Music Criticism' Op. 18 *The New Babylon* (film score) Op. 19 *The Bedbug* (incidental music) Op. 20 Symphony no. 3, *The First of May* (December) Beginning of collaborations with Leningrad TRAM (Theatre of Working Youth)	(November) Defeat of 'Right opposition'; Bukharin expelled from Politburo (December) Stalin's fiftieth birthday marks beginning of 'cult of personality'; he calls for mass collectivization of agriculture and 'dekulakization' (elimination of resistance amongst supposedly wealthy peasantry)
1930	Op. 22 *The Golden Age* (ballet)	(April) Suicide of Mayakovsky; height of cultural domination by Proletarian organizations
1931	Op. 27 *The Bolt* (ballet)	
1932	(13 May) Marries Nina Varzar (August) Joins directorate of Leningrad branch of Union of Soviet Composers Op. 21 *Six Romances on Texts by Japanese Poets* Op. 29 *The Lady Macbeth of Mtsensk District* (opera, after Leskov, begun October 1930) Op. 32 *Hamlet* (incidental music)	(23 April) Central Committee resolution 'On the restructuring of literary-artistic organizations' disbands factions and establishes cultural Unions (Until 1934) Famine in Ukraine and elsewhere kills millions
1933	(November) Elected as deputy to the October district Soviet of Leningrad Op. 34 24 Preludes (piano) Op. 35 Piano Concerto no. 1	(1933–7) Second Five-Year Plan
1934	(January) Premieres of *Lady Macbeth* in Leningrad and Moscow Suite for Jazz Orchestra no. 1 (May) Meets and falls in love with translator Elena Konstantinovskaya (affair lasts until mid-1935) Op. 40 Cello Sonata	(July) OGPU reorganized under NKVD (August) First congress of Union of Soviet Writers proclaims Socialist Realism (December) Assassination of Kirov gives pretext for coming Terror

Year	Shostakovich's life and career (works listed under year of completion)	Contemporary political events
1935	Divorce from Nina Varzar; remarriage following her pregnancy Premieres of *Lady Macbeth* in New York, Czechoslovakia, Stockholm etc. Op. 39 *The Limpid Stream* (ballet)	(4–6 February) 'Discussion about Soviet Symphonism' at Moscow Composers' Union (Shostakovich takes part) Stalin declares 'Life has improved, life has become more joyous' (September) Beginning of Stakhanovite movement (encouraging exceptional feats of industrial production)
1936	(26 January) Stalin attends *Lady Macbeth* production (28 January) *Pravda* editorial article 'Muddle instead of Music' (on *Lady Macbeth*) (6 February) *Pravda* editorial article 'Balletic Travesty' (on *The Bright Stream*) (30 May) Birth of daughter Galina (Galya) Op. 43 Symphony no. 4 (December) Scheduled premiere of Fourth Symphony withdrawn (eventually premiered in 1961)	(17 January) Establishment of 'All-Union Committee for Artistic Affairs' (later to become USSR Ministry of Culture); cultural attacks extended to architecture, literature, film and fine arts (August) Political show trials (Zinoviev, Kamenev and others) (September) Yezhov appointed head of NKVD in succession to Yagoda (December) Stalin constitution promulgated
1937	Spring: Joins staff of Leningrad Conservatoire; begins teaching in September Op. 46 *Four Romances on Texts of Pushkin* Op. 47 Symphony no. 5 (triumphant premiere on 21 November)	Height of Great Terror (until late 1938), millions deported, hundreds of thousands executed (June) Marshal Tukhachevsky (Shostakovich's patron) executed
1938	(10 May) Birth of son, Maxim Op. 49 String Quartet no. 1	Terror continues (1938–June 1941) Third Five-Year Plan (December) Beria succeeds Yezhov as head of NKVD
1939	(23 May) Confirmed as professor at Leningrad Conservatoire Op. 54 Symphony no. 6	(March) 18th Party Congress effectively brings Terror to an end (August) Nazi–Soviet non-aggression pact (September) Nazi invasion of Poland brings UK into War (November) USSR invades Finland
1940	Op. 57 Piano Quintet (March 1941 awarded Stalin Prize, first class) Op. 58 *Boris Godunov* (orchestration of Musorgsky's opera)	(March) Peace treaty with Finland (April) Katyn massacre – NKVD shoots 15,000 Polish prisoners of war (June) USSR annexes Baltic states (August) Assassination of Trotsky in Mexico
1941	(June–July) Volunteers for army service, joins Home Guard, arranges popular songs and opera arias for performance at the battlefront (August) Refuses offer of evacuation (1 October) Evacuated with family to Moscow, then Kuybyshev (arrives 22 October) Op. 60 Symphony no. 7 'Dedicated to the City of Leningrad' (premiere in Kuybyshev, 5 March 1942)	(22 June) Nazi invasion of USSR (July) Beginning of siege of Leningrad (From October) Partial evacuation of Moscow (December) Red Army counter-attacks and drives Nazis back from Moscow
1942	(9 August) Performance of Symphony no. 7 in blockaded Leningrad Op. 62 *Six Romances on Texts of Raleigh, Burns and Shakespeare* Abandons incomplete opera *The Gamblers* (after Gogol)	(May) Anglo-Soviet alliance (August 1942–January 1943) Battle of Stalingrad
1943	(April) Resettles in Moscow, begins teaching at Conservatoire Op. 61 Piano Sonata no. 2 Op. 65 Symphony no. 8	NKGB (People's Commissariat for State Security) split from NKVD (July) Nazis defeated at tank battle of Kursk

Year	Shostakovich's life and career (works listed under year of completion)	Contemporary political events
1944	(11 February) Death of Sollertinsky Op. 67 Piano Trio no. 2 Op. 68 String Quartet no. 2 Completes and orchestrates *Rothschild's Violin* (opera by Shostakovich's pupil, Veniamin Fleyshman, after Chekhov)	(January) Siege of Leningrad lifted (August) Warsaw uprising
1945	Op. 69 *A Children's Notebook* (seven pieces for piano) Op. 70 Symphony no. 9	(February) Yalta conference discusses shape of Europe after War (April) Soviet and US forces meet at River Elbe (9 May) Surrender of Germany
1946	Op. 73 String Quartet no. 3	(1946–50) Fourth Five-Year Plan NKGB becomes MGB (Ministry for State Security); NKVD becomes MVD (Ministry for Internal Affairs) (March) Churchill's 'Iron Curtain' speech; effective beginning of Cold War (August) Beginning of Andrey Zhdanov's anti-formalism campaign in the arts (*Zhdanovshchina* – the Zhdanov business). Central Committee decree attacks writers Akhmatova and Zoshchenko for 'reactionary individualism'
1947	(February) Reappointed professor at Leningrad Conservatoire, though continues to live in Moscow. Moves to apartment on Mozhayskoye Shosse Op. 74 *Poem of the Motherland* (patriotic cantata)	Famine in Ukraine (September) Cominform created (official forum of international communist movement)
1948	(February) Shostakovich condemned in anti-formalism campaign (14 February) Various works included on Main Repertoire Commission list of banned compositions (August) Loses teaching posts Op. 77 Violin Concerto no. 1 Op. 79 *From Jewish Folk Poetry* (song cycle)	(January) Murder of Solomon Mikhoels signals beginning of anti-Semitic campaign (10 February) Resolution 'On the opera *The Great Friendship* by Vano Muradeli' (February) Communist coup in Czechoslovakia (November) Dissolution of Jewish Anti-fascist Committee
1949	(March) Visits USA as part of Soviet delegation to Peace Congress (first of several such duties) (16 March) Ban on 'formalist' works lifted Op. 81 *Song of the Forests* (oratorio; awarded Stalin Prize, first class in December 1950) Op. 83 String Quartet no. 4	Closure of Jewish State Theatre in Moscow (April) Formation of NATO (August) Soviet atomic bomb test
1950	(July) Attends Bach bicentenary festival in Leipzig Op. 84 *Two Romances on Texts of Lermontov*	(June) Korean war
1951	(February) Re-elected Deputy to Supreme Soviet of the Russian SFSR. Many initiatives to help victims of Stalin's purges Op. 86 *Four Songs on Texts of Dolmatovsky* Op. 87 *Twenty-Four Preludes and Fugues* (piano) Op. 88 *Ten Poems on Texts by Revolutionary Poets* (for unaccompanied mixed chorus)	(1951–5) Fifth Five-Year Plan
1952	Op. 90 *The Sun Shines over our Motherland* (patriotic cantata) Op. 91 *Four Monologues on Texts of Pushkin* Op. 92 String Quartet no. 5	Stalin prepares for another purge
1953	Op. 93 Symphony no. 10	(January) Discovery of (fabricated) 'Doctors' Plot' (5 March) Deaths of Stalin and Prokofiev; Malenkov becomes prime minister, Beria head of NKVD, Molotov foreign minister MGB and NKVD fused into new MVD (July) Arrest of Beria (September) Khrushchev appointed first secretary of Party

Year	Shostakovich's life and career (works listed under year of completion)	Contemporary political events
1954	(March–April) Moscow discussion of Tenth Symphony (4 December) Death of Nina (first wife) Op. 94 Concertino for two pianos Op. 96 *Festive Overture* Op. 98 *Five Romances on Texts by Dolmatovsky*	Ilya Ehrenburg *The Thaw* (novella) published, lends name to post-Stalin era (May) Rehabilitation commission established Responsibility for security transferred to KGB (Commission for State Security)
1955	(9 November) Death of mother	(May) Warsaw pact established Bulganin replaces Malenkov as prime minister
1956	(July) Marries Margarita Kaynova (Komsomol activist) (September) Awarded Order of Lenin Op. 100 *Spanish Songs*	(February) Khrushchev's 'secret speech' to 20th Party Congress denounces Stalin's excesses (June) Central Committee resolution 'On overcoming the Cult of Personality and its Consequences' (November) Invasion of Hungary crushes uprising
1957	Op. 101 String Quartet no. 6 Op. 102 Piano Concerto no. 2 Op. 103 Symphony no. 11, *The Year 1905*	(July) Khrushchev crushes 'opposition' and gains supreme power (October) First sputnik launched
1958	(March–April) President of first Tchaikovsky International Competition (May) Records Piano Concertos in Paris. Feels first symptoms of muscular condition, later diagnosed as form of polio or motor neuron disease Op. 105 *Moscow, Cheryomushki* (operetta) Op. 106 *Khovanshchina* (orchestration of Musorgsky's opera)	(February) Khrushchev replaces Bulganin as prime minister (28 May) Central Committee resolution partially rescinds 1948 anti-formalism resolution (October) Pasternak awarded Nobel Prize for Literature for *Doctor Zhivago*
1959	(August) Separates from second wife (November) Visits USA (December) Buys dacha at Zhukovka, near Moscow Op. 107 Cello Concerto no. 1	(1959–65) Seven-Year Plan to regenerate agriculture
1960	(9 April) Elected First Secretary of Russian SFSR Composers' Union (September) Accedes to candidature for Party membership (ratified 14 September 1961) (September) Meets Britten in London, beginning of friendship Op. 108 String Quartet no. 7 Op. 109 *Satires* (song cycle) Op. 110 String Quartet no. 8	Beginning of incarceration of dissidents in psychiatric hospitals (May) American spy plane shot down over Soviet air space
1961	(30 December) Symphony no. 4 premiered Op. 112 Symphony no. 12, *The Year 1917*	(April) First manned Soviet space flight (Yury Gagarin) (August) Berlin Wall erected
1962	(18 March) Elected deputy to Supreme Soviet for Leningrad (April) Moves to apartment on Nezhdanova Street (June) Marries Irina Supinskaya (literary editor) (August–September) Attends Edinburgh Festival as featured composer (1 and 10 October) Meets Stravinsky in Moscow (12 November) Conducts Cello Concerto no. 1 and *Festive Overture* at festival of his music in Gorky Op. 113 Symphony no. 13, *Babiy Yar* (premiere 18 December) Op. 114 *Katerina Izmaylova* (revision of *Lady Macbeth*; unofficial premiere on 26 December)	(October) Cuban missile crisis (November) Publication of Solzhenitsyn's *A Day in the Life of Ivan Denisovich*

Year	Shostakovich's life and career (works listed under year of completion)	Contemporary political events
1963	Attends preparations for various new productions of *Katerina Izmaylova*, including Covent Garden in November	
1964	Op. 117 String Quartet no. 9 Op. 118 String Quartet no. 10 Op. 119 *The Execution of Stepan Razin* (vocal-symphonic poem; awarded USSR State Prize November 1968)	(14 October) Brezhnev replaces Khrushchev as first secretary of Party
1965	Op. 121 *Five Romances on Texts from Krokodil Magazine*	
1966	(30 May) First heart attack, followed by two months in hospital Op. 122 String Quartet no. 11 Op. 123 *Preface to the Complete Edition of My Works and a Brief Reflection apropos this Preface* (song) Op. 126 Cello Concerto no. 2	(1966–70) Eighth Five-Year Plan (February) trial of Sinyavsky and Daniel (dissident writers)
1967	(September) Breaks leg in fall Op. 127 *Seven Verses of Blok* Op. 128 *Spring, spring* (romance to words by Pushkin) Op. 129 Violin Concerto no. 2 Op. 131 *October* (symphonic poem)	Stagnation (*zastoy*) begins
1968	(April) Resigns as first secretary of RSFSR Composers' Union Op. 133 String Quartet no. 12 Op. 134 Violin Sonata *Antiformalist Gallery* (satirical scena, assembled intermittently since ?1948)	(April) *Chronicle of Current Events* launched (dissident *samizdat*, i.e. self-publishing, journal, lasts until 1983) (August) Invasion of Czechoslovakia, crushing attempts at liberal reform
1969	Op. 135 Symphony no. 14	
1970	Op. 136 *Loyalty* (eight ballads for unaccompanied male chorus) Op. 138 String Quartet no. 13	Soviet Human Rights Committee founded by Sakharov *et al.*
1971	(17 September) Second heart attack Op. 141 Symphony no. 15	1971–5: Ninth Five-Year Plan (February) Beginning of large-scale Jewish emigration
1972	(July) Visits Britten in Aldeburgh (December) Hospitalized for treatment for lung cancer	Strategic arms limitation talks (SALT) begin
1973	(June) Visits USA, consults American doctors Op. 142 String Quartet no. 14 Op. 143 *Six Verses of Marina Tsvetayeva*	(3 September) Letter condemning nuclear physicist Andrey Sakharov appears in *Pravda*, signatories including Shostakovich
1974	Op. 144 String Quartet no. 15 Op. 145 *Suite on Texts of Michelangelo Buonarroti* Op. 146 *Four Verses of Captain Lebyadkin*	(February) Expulsion of Solzhenitsyn from USSR
1975	(9 August) Dies of lung cancer (14 August) Funeral at Novodevichy cemetery, Moscow Op. 147 Viola Sonata	(1 August) Helsinki Accord on human rights (October) Sakharov awarded Nobel Peace Prize

Abbreviations

ASM	[*Assotsiatsiya sovremennoy muzïki*] Association of Contemporary Music
DDR	[Deutsche Demokratische Republik] German Democratic Republic
FEKS	[*Fabrika ekstentricheskogo aktyora*] Factory of the Eccentric Actor
GDR	German Democratic Republic
GTsMMK	[*Godsudarstvennïy tsentral'nïy muzey muzïkal'noy kul'turï imeni M. I. Glinki*] Glinka State Central Museum of Musical Culture, Moscow
ISCM	International Society for Contemporary Music
LASM	[*Leningradskaya assotsiatsiya sovremennoy muzïki*] Leningrad Association of Contemporary Music
NEP	New Economic Policy
NKVD	[*Narodnïy komissariat vnutrennïkh del*] People's Commissariat of Internal Affairs
OBERIU	[*Ob"edineniye real'nogo iskusstva*] Society for Real Art
RIAS	Radio in the American Sector (main radio station in Berlin, 1946–89)
RAPM	[*Rossiyskaya assotsiatsiya proletarskikh muzïkantov*] Russian Association of Proletarian Musicians
RAPP	[*Rossiyskaya assotsiatsiya proletarskikh pisateley*] Russian Association of Proletarian Writers
RGALI	[*Rossiyskiy gosudarstvennïy arkhiv literaturï i iskusstva*] Russian State Archive of Literature and Art, Moscow
RSFSR	[*Rossiyskaya sovetskaya federatsiya sovetskikh respublik*] Russian Soviet Federation of Soviet Republics
TRAM	[*Teatr rabochey molodyozhi*] Theatre of Working Youth
TsGALI	[*Tsentral'nïy gosudarstvennïy arkhiv literaturï i iskusstva*] Central State Archive of Literature and Art, St Petersburg

Introduction

PAULINE FAIRCLOUGH AND DAVID FANNING

The first English-language study to attempt a genre-focused overview of Shostakovich's music was published over a quarter of a century ago. Christopher Norris's *Shostakovich: The Man and his Music*[1] was an early attempt to assess the major works (symphonies, operas, piano music and string quartets) by writers from a wide range of backgrounds: music critics, composers, performers, historians and literary theorists. Their retrospective of a composer who had died only seven years earlier captured a moment in time – British Shostakovich reception in the early 1980s – that is fascinating to look back upon. As with much intelligent critical writing about Shostakovich since the 1960s, the best chapters of this collection offered insights that are as valid and appealing now as they were in 1982, regardless of our enhanced knowledge of both Shostakovich and Soviet cultural history. Of particular interest is Robert Stradling's careful bypassing of the assumption that was to dog later popular writing on Shostakovich: namely that he was composing either 'for' or 'against' the Soviet system. In the case of Shostakovich, as of Richard Strauss, he noted, the 'romantic ideology of doomed, suicidal genius is a potent but very partial myth'.[2] Though Stradling's caution was typical for its time, it was soon to be swept away in a tide of startling critical self-confidence concerning Shostakovich's supposed anti-Soviet identity. This mythological dissident Shostakovich has enjoyed two decades of authority in music journalism, popular music writing and on the internet; and it is an accident of the different methodologies and publishing practices of journalism and scholarship that musicologists were apparently slow to counter it.[3]

It is a paradoxical fact that, despite Shostakovich's extraordinary popularity, there was no reliable post-Soviet biography until 2000,[4] and the present collection of essays is the first English-language study that aims for near-comprehensive coverage of his work. That Western musicology has been so late in its engagement with Shostakovich is, however, symptomatic of diverse forces, some specific, some general. Though some of the specific prejudices concerning the quality of his output may be fading today, Shostakovich's belated acceptance into the canon of works for viable musicological study is as much a symptom of musicology's recently broadened cultural remit (popular music, world music, cultural studies) as it is of an enhanced awareness of his wider output and its cultural resonance. There is still a residue of post-Leningrad Symphony disdain among the generation of scholars that came to maturity in the 1960s, a residue that extends to a general suspicion of his concert-hall popularity.[5] There has also been a reluctance to evaluate Soviet music on the same technical and aesthetic levels as Western post-war art music, on the assumption that it must by its very nature be regressive and 'unfree'. More broadly still, the relatively slow pace at which musicology has followed the lead of Slavist literary and historical studies in exploring the complex relationship between Soviet power and artistic creation has meant that Shostakovich has been viewed through a very crude lens (in particular the Manichaean 'for-or-against' syndrome noted above), and this has hardly encouraged a sophisticated understanding of the paradoxical nature of Soviet musical culture and its products.

Even as these issues are being slowly faced up to and addressed, there are other, more practical problems that continue to hamper musicological Sovietologists. The new ongoing 150-volume Shostakovich *Complete Edition* is exclusively prepared by Russian scholars, and access to Shostakovich manuscripts is restricted.[6] On the positive side, there has been a steady stream of excellent Russian source studies, and while it may be frustrating for Western scholars not to be able actively to participate in such work, there is no doubt that high-level research on Shostakovich is now flourishing in Russia.[7]

One consequence of the impracticality (or impossibility) of Western-based source-study research on Shostakovich is that Western scholars have continued to explore the music as analysts and interpreters, much as their Soviet predecessors did, albeit from very different theoretical and critical perspectives. Some of the essays in this collection are clearly analytical in emphasis, most notably Eric Roseberry on the symphonies and *The Execution of Stepan Razin*, David Haas on the Second Piano Sonata and on Shostakovich's harmonic language, David Fanning on the early works, Malcolm MacDonald on the string concertos and sonatas, and Judith Kuhn on the quartets. Others, such as Francis Maes's exploration of Shostakovich's songs, are more contextual in focus, while still others address issues of reception (Erik Levi) or more obscure corners of Shostakovich's output (John Riley on the film scores, Pauline Fairclough on the 'official' works, Marina Ilichova on the ballets and Gerard McBurney on incidental music for the theatre). Rosamund Bartlett's essay on the operas draws on contemporary writings on opera, as well as outlining the twists and turns of Shostakovich's operatic career in the 1930s, taking into account the pioneering work of Olga Digonskaya on the unfinished opera projects *Orango* and *Narodnaya Volya* [The People's Will]. Esti Sheinberg's discussion of Existentialism in the Jewish-inflected works is the only overtly philosophically orientated chapter in the volume, building on earlier work by herself and others on issues of Jewish identity and ethnicity in Shostakovich's music.

Despite a relatively active recording career as pianist (compared, say, to Prokofiev), Shostakovich's own performances of his works have not carried the authority for pianists that they might have done had it not been for the progressive illness that deprived him of normal hand function from the late-1950s onwards. David Fanning's chapter on the composer's recordings does more than chart the decline of Shostakovich's performing powers: it tracks his interpretative decisions in key works (including the Tenth Symphony transcription), suggesting that despite technical deficiencies, Shostakovich's own performances are still invaluable points of reference and may have something to tell us about his attitude to musical structure as a composer. An equally overlooked aspect of Shostakovich's output has been the incidental and 'official' scores. In the case of the incidental scores for the theatre, many languish unperformed. In addition to tracing Shostakovich's recycling of various portions of these scores in other works, Gerard McBurney provides the scenarios to these mostly long-forgotten productions. As with Marina Ilichova's descriptions of the original ballet scenarios and John Riley's pithy descriptions of film plots, this is information not accessible in any other single source, and it reveals more precisely than has been possible up to now the nature of Shostakovich's early artistic collaborations. All three ballets have recently been revived and staged worldwide, and since the mid-1990s the scores and complete recordings have become available.[8] Theatre productions are much harder to revive in the absence of complete scenarios and stage directions, as McBurney's invaluable but necessarily partial reconstruction of the revue *Declared Dead* made clear at its Proms premiere in 1992 under the title *Hypothetically Murdered*. Equally obscure are most of the films to which Shostakovich provided scores, many of them still unavailable on commercial tape or DVD and currently existing only in personal collections or circulated in pirated copies obtained from Russia. Yet the film and incidental scores are far from being the only neglected areas of Shostakovich's music, as Francis Maes's and Pauline Fairclough's chapters on the songs and 'official' works show. Entire vocal and choral cycles and other *pièces d'occasion* remain virtually unknown, or implicitly rejected as not representative of the 'real' Shostakovich. These include the *Ten Poems on Verses by Revolutionary Poets*, op. 88, the two settings of Dolmatovsky poems opp. 86 and 98, *Loyalty*, op. 136, the *Ten Russian Folk Songs*, the *Greek Songs* and the wartime *Torzhestvenniy Marsh* [Ceremonial March]. Shostakovich's two cantatas, *The Sun Shines over our Motherland*, op. 90 and even *Song of the Forests*, op. 81, as well as numerous patriotic songs, languish in neglect, and understandably so, given their poor musical qualities. Revivals of Prokofiev's *Zdravitsa* (his 1939 Toast to Stalin) and 1937 *Cantata for the Twentieth Anniversary of the October Revolution* have been controversial for the obvious reason that their texts extol Stalin and Stalinism – and it can fairly be argued that only a suspension of moral and social standards could find such performances palatable, while the revival of comparable Nazi works would be (rightly) unthinkable.[9] More significantly, perhaps, Prokofiev's Stalinist works are by common consent superior in artistic terms to Shostakovich's; as Pauline Fairclough's chapter on the official works suggests, Shostakovich put far more energy into those works he produced as part of the war effort (and for the highly lucrative Soviet anthem competition in 1943) than he did into those expected of him in the squalid post-1948 climate or, for that matter, in the major anniversary years of the October Revolution in 1957 and 1967. *The Sun Shines over our Motherland*, composed for the 35th anniversary in 1952, cannot bear comparison in compositional terms with Prokofiev's stunning 1937 Cantata, whatever ideological problems both works embody. Texts aside, few concert promoters would be prepared to inflict Shostakovich's work on a paying audience, except perhaps in the context of a festival with didactic as well as artistic aims. But there is less reason for the continued neglect of the 'ethnic' song settings (Russian, Spanish, Greek), which, together with the Dolmatovsky settings, all date from the period beginning with the songs *From Jewish Folk Poetry* (1948–56). In these cases, a prejudice against accepting an apparently 'alien' (Soviet-populist) style as authentically Shostakovich's has arguably led to a tacit ban that is, for political and therefore commercial reasons, as effective as any instance of similarly 'unspoken' Soviet censorship.

Notwithstanding these issues of musical worth, as with all Cambridge Companions this volume seeks to provide an overview that is more or less comprehensive in scope, rather than specific and critical. David Haas's case study of the Second Piano Sonata, viewed against the background of possible models in the sonata genre, is the only exception to this rule. Nonetheless, such a volume would not have been possible without the combination of archival and published source study that is now not only possible but essential to all ongoing research into Shostakovich's music and that of his Soviet contemporaries. The editors would like to take this opportunity to thank Irina Antonovna Shostakovich, Olga Dombrovskaya and Olga Digonskaya from the Shostakovich Family Archive, Moscow, for their generous assistance and cooperation. Levon Hakobian kindly obtained rare scores from the Composers' Union Library in Moscow. But most of all, we thank our contributors, who have shown patience, courtesy and graciousness in tolerating the delays that so often occur with collaborative projects such as these. Will Peters kindly provided a valuable initial translation of Marina Ilichova's chapter on the ballets. We would also like to thank our excellent copy-editor Mary Worthington. Finally, we thank Penny Souster, formally of Cambridge University Press, who took a keen initial interest in this project, her successor Vicki Cooper and Rebecca Jones, whose tact and understanding have made completing this Companion a pleasure rather than a chore.

Every effort has been made to secure necessary permissions to reproduce copyright material in this work, though in some cases it has proved impossible to contact copyright holders. If any omissions are brought to our notice, we will be happy to include appropriate acknowledgements in any subsequent edition.

PART I

Instrumental works

1 Personal integrity and public service: the voice of the symphonist

ERIC ROSEBERRY

To the European mind, no less than fifteen symphonies from the pen of a single composer might seem excessive in the light of a tradition that has taken its bearings from the nine symphonies of Beethoven. But the revolutionary culture that nurtured Shostakovich experienced something of a rebirth of symphonic commitment, and in this connection the ideological climate of Socialist Realism (first proclaimed in 1934) was to prove a potent factor. Far from creatively inhibiting, the Beethoven canon, with its fresh post-revolutionary optimism, could be viewed as positively enabling. The Soviet symphony – a genre that Shostakovich's own Fifth Symphony served memorably to define – became for Shostakovich, as for his colleagues, a medium through which to appear to meet the socio-political expectations of Soviet ideology. At the same time, his symphonies, string quartets and concertos encoded a more personal vision that was to remain suspect in orthodox Soviet circles. As a captive yet independently minded artist working in a totalitarian regime, Shostakovich invented for himself a moral persona that would construct, Dostoyevsky-like, a polyphonic discourse wherein, to quote Victor Terras on Bakhtin, 'multiple individual voices, inner dialogue, parody, inter-textual echoes, irony, and ambiguity interact dialogically, independently of a controlling monologic narrative voice'.[1]

Although not all of Shostakovich's symphonies sit comfortably within the traditional parameters of the genre, taken as a whole his symphonic oeuvre gravitates towards the four-movement sonata-cycle prototype, and embraces the several different types – instrumental/absolute, narrative/programmatic, cyclic, vocal-instrumental – that go to make up the main-stream repertoire of the genre in the post-Beethoven era. The content and form of these symphonies, as well as their social context, are linked to Shostakovich's well-known dilemma as a Soviet composer: the conflict-ridden burden of responsibility he carried towards his genius, his public and, as a professional artist, the Soviet cultural bureaucracy. It was an unenviable balancing act that had to face glaring and indeed frightening publicity, but against all the odds it was accomplished with breathtaking virtuosity and rounded off comprehensively with a work that would appear to have been conceived as a farewell not only to Shostakovich's own cycle of fifteen but seemingly to the symphony as a historical genre. In its extraordinary synthesis of comedy and tragedy, depth and humour, spontaneity and power of calling up the past (the composer's own as well as the established forms and expressive content of the symphony), the last symphony of Shostakovich provides a fitting epitaph both to a life and to the passing of the Classical-Romantic symphony.

Continuities and discontinuities; from the First to the Fifth Symphony (1925–37)

Taking the Fifth Symphony as the crucial turning point in Shostakovich's career as a symphonist, the first four symphonies approach the genre from a number of diverse, seemingly incongruous angles. The brilliant work in four movements that launched his public career was completed in 1925 before the composer was out of his teens. No mere *jeu d'esprit*, it breathes new life into a form that is here taken as standing in need of rescue from academic ossification. The young composer's famous brush with Glazunov before the work was submitted as a graduation exercise at the St Petersburg Conservatoire was in this respect symbolic (see Chapter 3 by David Fanning in this volume). Compared with another famous twentieth-century 'first', the 'Classical' Symphony of Prokofiev, Shostakovich's already goes beyond an affectionate parody of classical models in his provocative mix of the burlesque and the tragic. Though Shostakovich's deeper acquaintance with Mahler's symphonies was yet to come, it is easy to sense here just how much Mahler's ambivalent, highly stylized tone might have appealed to him. The First Symphony was to be followed by two pairs of works, the first of which openly challenges the traditional mould while the second pair (the Fourth and Fifth), for all their disparities, share a realignment with Classical norms. The fascinating duality of the two Shostakoviches – public and private, classicist and modernist, populist and upholder of the high aristocratic tradition in music – is set out with exemplary force and clarity in what is sometimes taken too readily as a journey towards artistic maturity in these first five works. The Second and Third Symphonies are the musical equivalent of brilliantly executed poster art, serving as a reminder of how unshackled the young Soviet Russian composer of the 1920s felt himself to be in his exploration of new avenues of expression before the heavy weight of Stalinism and Socialist Realism fell upon him. Modernism still remains a force to be reckoned with in the violence, the fragmentation and epic scale of the Fourth ('the credo of my creative work'),[2] which nevertheless is not without its pointers to the comparative Classic-Romantic 'sobriety' of the Fifth.

Example 1.1 First Symphony, movement 1, $\boxed{8}^1$, motivic outline

The First Symphony (1925)

The First Symphony proved a highly successful absorption of novelty and tradition. On the traditional side – and Shostakovich, as composer and teacher, was to stand by his grounding in the classics, both Russian and European – it makes bold to link itself with Tchaikovsky, adopting a stance that at the same time caricatures and (in the last two movements) remains respectful of his 'serious', fate-obsessed symphonism. Cast in the key of F minor, it reinforces the association with Tchaikovsky's Fourth in a number of ways: the theatrical-balletic element (introduction, second-subject waltz in the relative major key); the grotesqueries of the scherzo, with the quasi-folk inflections of the trio; the introduction of a 'fate' fanfare motto that permeates the second part of the symphony as a falling/rising minor third; the pathos of the slow movement's opening oboe solo; the unashamed reliance on unvaried and/or sequential repetition as a means of propulsion; and not least the emotionally ambiguous 'resolution' of the finale.

The first movement is preceded by a Petrushka-like introduction, Haydnish in its playful evasion of the main key. It shows a youthful iconoclast at work in producing a carefully crafted cartoon version of sonata form that at the same time – and herein lies its innovative conception – subtly interacts with the introduction from start to finish. But after the further grotesqueries of the scherzo (heightened, as it were, by the arrival of 'the composer' at the piano at $\boxed{3}$), the interlinked slow movement and finale throw off their mask-play in addressing more serious issues, and in so doing make the first of Shostakovich's many memorable cyclic links between movements as well as introducing his lifelong passion for the most extreme contrasts and collisions.

The closely worked thematic unity of this symphony is a feature of particular interest, proceeding in the first place through a very subtle process of thematic transformation of a motto theme from movement to movement, hinging on the crucial motif of a stepwise falling minor third, $\hat{3}$–$\hat{2}$–$\hat{1}$ chromatically arpeggiated to enclose a falling diminished fifth and rising perfect fourth (see Ex. 1.1). David Haas has noted the likely derivation of Shostakovich's first-subject march theme from the scherzo episode of Liszt's First Piano Concerto, and this sheds light not only on the composer's lifelong

Example 1.2a First Symphony, movement 1, $\boxed{5}^{3-4}$
[Allegretto – *più mosso* ♩ = 208]

Example 1.2b First Symphony, movement 1, $\boxed{11}^{1-2}$
[Allegro non troppo ♩ = 160]

'derivative' thematic shapes (breaking out in due course into open quotation) but also on an important historical precedent in Liszt for the composer's own characteristic technique of thematic transformation.[3]

Linked to this is the remarkable adaptability of motivic components of themes, operating in new structural/expressive contexts – to become new 'portmanteau' themes in fact – and for the themes themselves to appear in contrapuntal combination. Unity of a different order is provided by the close integration of the introduction with the main body of the first movement in a number of different ways: structural (notably in the Mahler-like return of the introduction at the beginning of the development section and in the coda), thematic, contrapuntal and harmonic. It is instructive, for instance, to note how the subtly worked harmonies of the introduction continue to serve as accompaniment in the Allegro, or how the top line of the ensuing passage becomes a continuation of the second-subject flute melody (see Ex. 1.2).

The return of the introduction at the end of the first movement points towards the larger key relationships of scherzo (A minor/major) and slow movement (D flat major) to the central F minor tonality of the symphony. A further unifying stroke is the close relationship of the slow movement and finale, in which the slow movement's second subject, a funeral march, is inverted to form the lyrical secondary theme, leading on to the inversion on solo timpani of the slow movement's fanfare motif. The inversion, by the way, does little to dispel a feeling of the triumph of fate – which establishes another (possibly unintentional) link with Tchaikovsky and offers a youthful foretaste of that pessimistic streak in the composer that was to run counter to the officially favoured optimistic endings.

But what of the symphony's modernistic leanings? There is more than a hint of the modish assimilation of 1920s industrial imagery in the First Symphony; this alone marks a stark break with nineteenth-century Romanticism, when rejecting rather than assimilating such imagery was the norm. One could point to the explosive tuttis combining first and second subjects in the first movement or the ostinati, machine rhythms and randomized heterophonic writing in the scherzo. Such characteristics anticipate not only the thoroughgoing modernism of the piano *Aphorisms*, op. 13, and the Second Symphony, but also Shostakovich's attempts to combine such elements with a return to thematic first-movement sonata form on an epic scale in the first movement of the Fourth Symphony. The mechanical ostinato patterns that characterize the first and (more especially) second movement of the First Symphony follow in the footsteps of Stravinsky, in whose early ballets the device becomes a 'primitive' accomplice in the 'downgrading' of functional tonality. Correspondingly, tonal shifts pay scant homage to traditional means of establishing new tonal regions, in what amounts to little more than enharmonic puns: V–I cadences 'pulled out of the hat', and short, sequentially ordered bridge passages. In Shostakovich's use of both chromaticism (via, for example, the frequency of passing augmented triads) and bitonality, the erosion of a traditional harmonic syntax is evident here, if more indebted to the example of Skryabin than Stravinsky in the slow movement.

The frequency of chamber-like textures, with their many soloistic features (especially in the wind department), marks out the sound world of the first two movements of this symphony as typically *à la mode* in its reaction against nineteenth-century tutti-dominated orchestration. The arrival of the solo piano in the second and fourth movements is a further deconstruction of the constitutional norm, the 'Hitchcock touch' of the young cinema pianist-composer, who openly mocks the assertive closing tonic chords of a movement with cheeky finality at the end of the scherzo. There is the heightened role given to percussion, which acquires thematic independence in the dramatic timpani solo of the finale, though it could be argued that in this respect there is no lack of precedent in Beethoven – as, for example, in the Violin Concerto, the Fourth Symphony or in the 'thematic' octave tunings of his Eighth and Ninth Symphonies. Linearity frequently prevails over harmonic considerations, and at the beginning of

Example 1.3 First Symphony, movement 3, [23]
Allegro, ♩ = 192

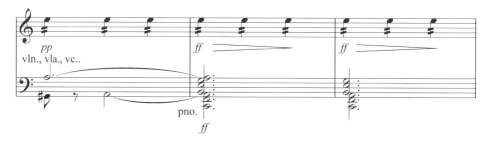

the scherzo we encounter a bold, eccentric heterophony that in the coda finds its harmonic counterpart in Ivesian chord clusters (see Ex. 1.3).

Hand in hand with a linearist's boldness is a caricaturist's heightened sense of dissonance that applies both to the melodic and harmonic dimensions. The sharpness of bitonal harmonic clashes serves both comedy and tragedy. If an intentionally comic, 'Chaplinesque' effect is intended with the oboes' bitonal contradiction of what can be construed as the bassoon/trumpet's enharmonic B flat minor third in bar 5 of the first movement's introduction, then an altogether more threatening expression results from the 'false bass' set against the shifting tremolo string triads beneath the anguished woodwind recitative of flute and oboe in unison that opens the finale. While never completely undermining tonal stability, such passages seriously endanger it, foreshadowing the more ruthlessly atonal techniques of the next symphony.

Modernism as propaganda: the Second and Third Symphonies

The Second Symphony (1927) was originally conceived as a symphonic poem – a 'Symphonic Dedication to October', to give it its intended title – and here we already see Shostakovich stretching the term 'symphony' far beyond its customary application. It is the first of Shostakovich's two symphonic essays in non-thematic (which is not to say unmotivic) composition, whose thrust is dependent on contrasted tempi, changing orchestral textures, an extreme dynamic range, linearity and harmonic tensions that rely on a suspension of tonality that will be corrected only in the final choral section. Up to that point the rationale may, for the most part, be one of organized chaos. Yet a glance at the score will reveal the sheer intricacy of its texture, Ivesian in the boldness of its unfettered linearity, Hindemithian in its motoric energy and application of bustling, neo-Baroque figurations.

In her study of Shostakovich's symphonies, the Soviet musicologist Marina Sabinina asserts that the young Shostakovich relied for his scheme on the revolutionary spectacles of the day, such as open street theatricals in celebration of the Revolution, and that the symphony falls into more or less realistic representations or tableaux. This reading accords well with the composer's involvement in theatrical projects at the time, where staged dramatic situations took the place of 'abstract' symphonic thought. As Sabinina put it, 'at first, there is obscure chaos symbolising the unenlightened past of the working class; then, the awakening of protest, the ripening of revolutionary consciousness; and, finally, glorification of the October Victory'.[4]

A keen dramatic instinct informs the changing scenes and transitions, but this is not, strictly speaking, scene painting – more, to borrow from Beethoven, an 'expression of feeling'. Although the work does include touches of realism – the famous factory hooter summoning the workers, the passages of choral declamation – the Second Symphony is programmatic only in a generalized sense. Its four main episodes proceed from a state of inertia, through purposeful activity followed by laissez-faire freedom (the build-up of the thirteen-part cadenza episode), via instrumental recitative-arioso, to the tonal resolution of the choral denouement. So the question of whether or not this symphony – composed for the tenth anniversary of the October Revolution in 1927 to a text by the proletarian Soviet poet Alexander Bezïmensky – needs a detailed programmatic explanation in order to be fully understood, is perhaps misplaced. A more straightforward approach to its programmatic content is simply to accept its metaphor of chaos to order, darkness to light. Symphonic precedents for such a trajectory are not in short supply – Haydn's *Creation*, Beethoven's Fifth and Ninth, Brahms's First and Mahler's Seventh, amongst numerous others. Nor does Shostakovich's adoption of a one-movement symphonic poem conception rule out their influence; the symphony can be taken as a compression into a single-movement structure of the traditional four-movement sonata cycle: first movement Allegro, scherzo, slow movement and (choral) finale, with episodic links and a slow introduction. The problem here is that unlike, say, Schoenberg's First Chamber Symphony or Sibelius's Seventh, the Second Symphony does not rely on thematic statement, contrast and development for its narrative thrust and cohesion, though certain small motivic shapes – *popevki*[5] – do recur. Only in one place does the transformation of what may be regarded as a recognizable thematic shape occur: where the trumpet arioso that surfaces in the introduction is turned into a thrusting G-minorish march in dotted rhythm as the 'main theme' of the first Allegro. Given its near-palindromic shape, its key orientation and near-twelve-note derivation, it

Example 1.4a Second Symphony, $\boxed{7}^{2-9}$
[Largo $\downarrow$ = 46]

Example 1.4b Second Symphony, $\boxed{13}^{1-4}$
$\downarrow$ = 152

Example 1.4c Fifteenth Symphony, movement 3, bars 1–6
Allegretto, $\downarrow$ = 112

bears a family resemblance to the (strictly twelve-note) principal theme of the march-scherzo (third movement) of the Fifteenth Symphony, with its grotesquely symmetrical inversion, as shown in Ex. 1.4.

With his Third Symphony (1929), Shostakovich retreated somewhat from the uncompromising modernisms of the Second, to proceed as a series of tableaux, filmic in their imagery and continuity content, which in the first protracted march section looks forward to the kaleidoscopic musics of the finale of the Fourth Symphony. As a celebration of the First of May, the physical thrust and energy show a level of stamina somewhat vitiated by a diffuseness of form and content. The overall style of the Third is strongly suggestive of Shostakovich's copious film and theatre music of the period; indeed, it would not be going too far to hear the Third Symphony as an accompaniment to an imagined film script. Correspondingly, a 'symphonic' approach to film music (in, for example, *The New Babylon*, completed earlier in 1929) indicates a cross-fertilization of the two genres. As if to forestall accusations of a film composer's merely scenic, onomatopoeic approach to his subject, Shostakovich wrote of his Third Symphony: 'I tried to convey only the general mood of the International Workers' Day Festival. I wished to portray beautiful construction in the USSR. I would point out that the element of struggle, energy and ceaseless work runs through the whole symphony like a red thread.'[6] Perhaps the first movement of Mahler's Third Symphony, 'Summer Marches In', was a source of inspiration.[7] Light years away from Mahler, however, was Shostakovich's studied avoidance of thematic development or repetition in the Third Symphony. Within this ultra-complex score, however, there are episodes and passages of great freshness and beauty, beginning with the idyllic opening section, with its long-breathed clarinet duet over pulsating cello/bass pizzicato – a genuine symphonic prelude, this, and a demonstration of Shostakovich's capacity to develop and extend an initial melodic cell. There is also an interlude in C major for strings of unexpected sweetness that pre-echoes the almost Gershwinesque lusciousness of the return of the first subject in the recapitulation of the 'Leningrad' Symphony's first movement. Notable, too, is the dramatic episode before the entry of the chorus, with its tutti unisons and passages of hectoring trombone and sinister string glissandi suggestive of an instrumental counterpart to some unspoken revolutionary text. The choral peroration is a bold hymnal setting of some doggerel verses by the proletarian Soviet poet Semyon Kirsanov that finally settles for a heroic E flat coda.

'The two Shostakoviches': the Fourth and Fifth Symphonies (1934–7) – crisis and reorientation

The Third Symphony, with its sunny G major opening, effects a more immediate rapprochement with tonality than does its more hard-line predecessor. It thus provides a transition from the aggressive tonal–atonal confrontations of the Second Symphony to a more thoroughgoing engagement with key as a form-defining agent in Shostakovich's two essays in heroic C minor symphonism: the gigantic post-Mahlerian essay of the Fourth and the no less weighty Eighth. The Fourth was begun some six years after the Third, to be completed in May 1936 when the composer was having to come to terms with the implications of the notorious *Pravda* editorials of 28 January and 6 February. Running for over an hour, this symphony marks in its first movement a return to the sonata principle of thematic content and development on the largest possible scale, encompassing cataclysmic events that are barely contained within the traditionally accepted bounds of sonata form. If the grotesquerie of the first movement of the First Symphony was playful, here it wears an altogether more terrifying aspect. The extremely lengthy first subject (including a dual purpose introduction-cum-prefatory theme) is a menacing caricature of a military march over a pulsating mechanical ostinato. It is the first of many such images in Shostakovich's symphonies, comparable to the images of brutal force in the development of the first movement of the Fifth, the so-called 'invasion theme' of the first movement of the Seventh, or the march theme that opens the second movement of the Eighth. Here, the first movement is an epic instrumental drama, the fruit of Shostakovich's absorption of Mahler, and yet going beyond Mahler in the shock of its collisions, its sudden entrances and exits, its pungent irony and menace, its violence and hysteria. This is indeed a prophetic 'war symphony' of a movement in which we are offered an early glimpse of the composer of the less radical but no less violent imagery of the Eighth.

Only the Fourth Symphony's D minor central movement – a spaciously developed *Ländler* – achieves, through contrapuntal development of its main theme, a measure of the unbroken continuity normally associated with dance forms in a symphony. This is a very Mahlerian movement in a large binary form, its second subject clearly anticipating the sombre descending main theme of the Fifth Symphony's first movement. The two outer movements that frame this intermezzo, on the other hand, are disruptive in the extreme. The vast episodic sonata structure of the first movement, with its splintered central development of material in several episodes, makes a feature of the most disconcerting changes of direction before reaching its ultimate climax in the retransition, with its piled-up dissonances. The twelve-note, multi-intervallic chord that immediately precedes the recapitulation suggests an allusion to the 'crisis' chord of the first movement of Mahler's Tenth Symphony. Now, the compressed and thematically reversed recapitulation effects a radical transformation of its main themes so that the reflective, wandering second subject assumes the relentless martial identity of the first in an overall structural-expressive scheme that served the composer well in his subsequent Moderato first movements.

The third movement combines slow movement and finale in a vast ternary structure. Here a Mahlerian funeral march, returning at the end in an overwhelmingly tragic tutti, frames a central, motorically driven Allegro dominated by the falling minor third in an obsessive rhythm that gives way to a sequence of increasingly fragmented dance episodes, a suite of theatre pieces that are by turns disconcertingly tender and facetious.[8] A brisk mock-military polka in rondo form introduces a lengthy trombone solo that offers its own highly irreverent comments on proceedings, and the music careers on disjointedly in a long diminuendo to its shatteringly loud C major-minor denouement, imperiously dismissive of previous banalities and fading into a twilit coda that suggests a reminiscence of the coda to Mahler's *Das Lied von der Erde* – one of the composer's favourite works. The shock of this movement lies, I would suggest, in the composer's adoption of the most clichéd 'urban' operetta-ish idioms which form a kind of descent into the abyss of the return of the funeral march. As has frequently been noted, some kind of inner psychological upheaval is at work here; the composer's own state of mind after his official reprimands arguably having a bearing on its programmatic implications.[9]

Although the Fourth was withdrawn by the composer and the score apparently lost, Shostakovich made a version for two pianos that was eventually published in lithograph format in 1946. This 'straight' two-piano transcription if anything strengthens the claim of this symphony to be admired as a work of superb musical craftsmanship. If before the first performance of the symphony in its full orchestral glory in December 1961, Soviet musicology tended to approach the work with cautious brevity,[10] regarding it as a cul-de-sac before the magnificent breakthrough of its successor,[11] it was nonetheless studied and admired in professional circles.[11] With the publication of the full score in 1962, it became possible to adopt a more rounded approach; Sabinina's close reading of the symphony, for example, while still viewing it as a work at the crossroads, pays generous tribute to its tragic power. Certainly, the Fourth Symphony was a necessary link in the chain of development towards the Fifth, but this does not lessen the enormity of the extraordinary leap from the wild inner turmoil and 'subjectivity' of expression we encounter in the Fourth to the refinement and concentration of form and content in the Fifth. As in the Fourth, the influence of Mahler remains strong, especially in the second movement Scherzo. But the Fifth Symphony represents an absorption of the high central European tradition that takes in the essence of the sonata-cycle drama in its familiar nineteenth-century aspect while lending an updated twist to familiar tonal/thematic procedures. Thus, in the D minor first movement, the lyrical expansiveness of the two main subject groups is underpinned by a demonstrable thematic unity, while the straight path of the development achieves a directional thrust that was to prove a model for Shostakovich's later first-movement sonata structures. His handling of contrasted tonal regions draws on clearly audible major–minor tensions underpinning the musico-dramatic structure as a

Example 1.5a Fifth Symphony, movement 1, motivic structure of 'epigraph' theme and second subject, $\boxed{9}^{1-9}$

'epigraph' theme, bars 1–3

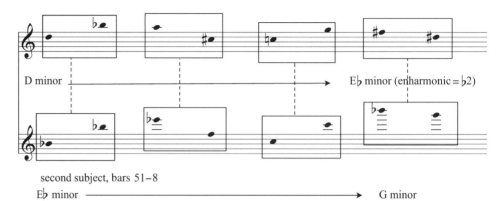

second subject, bars 51–8

Example 1.5b (i) Fifth Symphony, movement 1, first subject, $\boxed{1}^{1-2}$, motivic shape

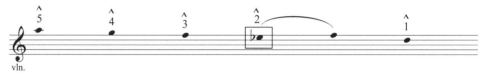

Example 1.5b (ii) Fifth Symphony, movement 1, $\boxed{1}^{3-5}$

Example 1.5c Fifth Symphony, movement 1, Coda, $^{2}\boxed{46}-\boxed{46}^{3}$

whole, with the seminal shift of D–E flat playing a particularly significant role at different structural levels in the first movement, as shown in Ex. 1.5. Also of some significance in the development of Shostakovich's large-scale thinking is his expansion of sonata process through the novel concept of 'forms within a form'. In the first movement of the Fifth the first group of the exposition is considerably enlarged through its expansion into a ritornello-like structure in which the 'epigraph' theme of the opening returns as a kind of refrain.

After the buffoonish, boisterous intermezzo of the Mahlerian scherzo and trio the Largo in F sharp minor explores emotional depths that place this movement at the very heart of the symphony. According to Taruskin, it was readily taken by its first audiences as a Requiem for the victims of Stalin's regime.[12] Its rhetoric draws on a cross-reference to Beethoven's Fifth – the significant motto-motif of three shorts and a long – which corresponds to the striving motto-motif (♪♪ ♩) on a single pitch) of the first movement as well as its recurrence in the finale. The finale's D minor opening chord on winds and percussion strikes a chill after the F sharp major serenity of the slow movement's close. This freely shaped sonata movement *alla marcia* borrows the outlines of its main theme from the first movement of the Fourth and the treatment of the second subject is strikingly similar to the procedure in the finale of the First Symphony, in that the theme is introduced first as part of a torrential allegro, but later begins to play an increasingly nostalgic role as it pulls against the fast current of the main first subject group. And so, counterbalancing the directional thrust of the first movement's development we now have a lengthy episode of reminiscence leading (via the Beethovenian drop of a semitone to a dominant pedal A) into a transformed recapitulation in a long crescendo that develops the main theme with increased animation, winning through to a hard-won D major coda that seems almost to pull the main key out of a tonal impasse. (The struggle to achieve an affirmative D major strikingly compares with that of the finale of Mahler's First Symphony, a plausible influence.)

With this masterly act of symphonic perestroika, premiered in Leningrad on 21 October 1937, the thirty-year-old Shostakovich redeemed himself in the eyes of the Soviet authorities.[13] In fact, Soviet ideology adopted the Fifth Symphony as a model of Socialist Realism. As Taruskin writes,

> With its ample yet conventional four-movement form, even down to an improbably minuettish scherzo, its unextravagant scoring, and its notable harmonic restraint, the Fifth Symphony amounted to a paradigm of Stalinist neoclassicism, testifying, so far as the powers were concerned, to the composer's obedient submission to discipline. It was time to reward him.[14]

Completion of a symphonic trilogy? The Sixth Symphony (1939)

For the time being, the largely favourable reception of the Fifth Symphony effectively consigned the suppressed Fourth to a 'formalistic' limbo in the

Table 1.1 *Structure of Shostakovich: VI/3*

82	96		106	112	122
A	B			A1	B1
Rondo, with secondary theme	Scherzo		Retransition	Recapitulation	Scherzo/Coda
4/4 B minor	3/4 E flat/C minor/major			4/4 B minor	(4/4) B major

public/critical domain; even the composer himself later repudiated what he dubbed its 'mania grandiosa'.[15] If the Fourth Symphony had been received into the canon at the time of the appearance of the Sixth, the later work would perhaps have achieved a more ready critical acceptance; indeed, the two works could have seemed to stand in some kind of complementary relationship. As it was, the Sixth dashed expectations of a return to symphonic normality on Shostakovich's part – further evidence, if needed, of a creative outlook that was not to be hidebound by the constraints of Socialist Realism. As in the Fourth, its three-movement structure may be read as a compression of the traditional four-movement sonata cycle delivered in the Fifth. But whereas the Fourth compresses slow movement and finale into a gigantic ternary finale structure, the Sixth opens with a slow, brooding first movement (compare this with the opening movement of the Tenth, the slow heave of whose expansive motion the Sixth anticipates) that combines the dramatic weight of a sonata-type first movement with the lyrical, reflective depths of a slow movement. Set against this vast and sombre first movement is a crepuscular, demonically exuberant scherzo and – moving into broad daylight – a highly wrought rondo-like finale. Formally considered, there is plenty of structural ambiguity in this finale. Is it a rondo? ABA form or large-scale binary? My own overview is given in Table 1.1, which suggests another of the composer's two-movements-in-one compressions.

In performance, the symphony conveys an overall sense of increasing momentum and rising spirits. The effect – reinforced by a key sequence that moves from B minor through D minor to B major – is a clear 'darkness to light' progression. The first movement begins grandly with a preludial group of themes that serves the dual purpose of introduction and thematic/motivic source for the main body of the movement, yielding a multiplicity of recurring reference points as the movement unfolds. (The opening 'epigraph' theme of the first movement of the Fifth functions in much the same way, and it will be remembered that the 'introduction' to the First Symphony served a similar duality of structural/expressive integration with the rest of the movement.) Following on from the Fifth is that same passionately striving arioso-recitative expansion of the melodic line in the strings; it recurs as a surging melodic current in the first movement of the Eighth and can therefore be heard as a recognizable feature of the composer's 'middle period' symphonism. A long, drawn-out central episode based on a funeral march motif is set up in meditative contrast, losing all sense of motion in becalmed flute cadenzas over static pedal points – a passage that Shostakovich was to recall in the second movement of his Fifteenth Symphony. Conforming to no strict scheme or inherited formal pattern, the first movement of the Sixth Symphony is nonetheless magnificently coherent, requiring no programmatic explanation and achieving a nobility of utterance in its compressed string-dominated recapitulation that all the grotesquerie and high spirits of its succeeding movements do nothing to efface. Here, in essence, is a symphony that treats the Fourth's funeral march finale as unfinished business, taking up its awesome confrontation of the abyss with a consoling nobility of utterance that attains new life and purpose in a freshly minted rethinking of a large three-movement structure. The highly politicized charge carried by the Fifth no doubt proved a hard act to follow. In the Sixth, the composer addresses the perennial problem of human suffering in a totally different spirit – by moving on from the questions raised by its sombre first movement rather than by wrestling with them. The high-spirited finale – precursor of its more emotionally complex counterpart in the Ninth Symphony – provides a lifeline that becomes increasingly farcical, complete with Shostakovich's favourite 'send-up' of the military band.

The Sixth does not wear thematic unity on its sleeve, and this only adds to its frequently disputed claim to true symphonic status.[16] There are no cyclic connections between movements comparable to those in the third and fourth movements of the First or the two-in-one compressed slow movement and allegro finale of the Fourth. The three-movement structure seems a defiant refusal to repeat the conventional four-movement sonata-cycle plan of the Fifth. But a consideration of the various melodic characters across the trajectory of its three movements throws up one of those tiny motivic interconnections in Shostakovich that more openly unify, for example, both the Eighth and the Tenth Symphonies. The saturation of its various themes with the octave leap – whether grandly heroic (as in the first movement), distorted to a seventh or ninth (as in the grotesqueries of the second movement), or perkily capricious (as in the main theme of the rondo-like finale and its various offshoots) is a salient feature of the Sixth's melodic structure.

The 'war' trilogy: the Seventh–Ninth Symphonies (1941–5)

Soviet Russia's Great Patriotic War with Nazi Germany confirmed in Shostakovich a continuing commitment to a type of heroic symphonism

already broached in the Fourth, the Fifth and the first movement of the
Sixth. In both the Seventh and Eighth Symphonies the composer found
himself once more drawn to the key of C major/minor. As in the Fourth
Symphony, the key comes loaded with all the iconic resonance of the
'great' symphonism of Beethoven, Schubert, Brahms, Bruckner and
Mahler.[17] It was, indeed, through his middle-period hugely sculpted
sonata first movements cast in a moderato tempo, with their finely judged
sense of climax and transformed and reordered recapitulations, that
Shostakovich found himself on course for a symphonic breadth on the
largest possible scale.

Familiar though the building blocks may be in the Seventh, there is
nothing commonplace about the grand architectural scheme in four
movements that emerges. Following a classically simplistic exposition
that moves to the dominant and its peaceful mediant 'surrounds', the
first movement daringly challenges conventional sonata form by replacing
development with a mechanical ostinato in E flat, where the brutal repetition of a new theme is carried through to a destructive C minor climax of
long-postponed development. This then overcomes the ostinato's hostile
intrusion, a procedure that renders the eloquent transformations of the
recapitulation all the more beautiful and necessary. The movement offers
an impressive example of the ever-present vocal/operatic element in
Shostakovich symphonies that, it could be argued, runs counter to the
idea of writing a successful sonata allegro first movement. An especially
striking passage is the eloquent bassoon solo in the recapitulation which
transforms the original 'song' of the second subject, breaking it up into a
lament that changes its original diatonicism into a tortured, mixed-modal
expression of personal grief ([60]–[65]). Such a passage exemplifies the
erosion of the distinction between opera and symphony, which in Arved
Ashby's words, corresponds to Mahler's 'conciliation of a symphonic
posture with an operatic inclusiveness'.[18] The ghost of Mahler resurfaces
in the second movement (a kind of gentle *Ländler* in 4/4 time), with a
sardonic mock-triumphant trio that suggests a deliberate debasement of
Beethoven (a parodistic allusion to the 'Moonlight' Sonata's C sharp
minor?) and Bach (the four-note motif tracing the shape of B-A-C-H).
The marvellously expansive slow movement – perhaps the most noble and
grand in Shostakovich's entire oeuvre – with its tempestuous (and openly
Mahlerian) central episode, is founded on the Baroque ritornello principle, drawing on a Baroque-derived recitative-arioso stylization for its
impassioned rhetoric. The finale's tensely suppressed introduction draws
on the experience of the supple lyrical ebb and flow of the first movement
of the Fifth, while at the same time launching the main theme that will
develop the same sustained physical thrust that impels the *alla marcia* of

the Fifth's finale. In its drive and stamina we catch a pre-glimpse of the pounding ostinato imagery so typical of the composer's impassioned scherzos, in particular those of the Eighth Symphony, third movement, and Eighth Quartet, second movement. The slowly gathering intensity of its final moderato section – an intense sarabande prefacing a free passacaglia – completes a huge arc in what is a further instance of Shostakovich's adoption of the idea of a 'form within a form'. Leading from suppressed beginnings through to the triumphant re-emergence of the first movement theme, we have here a powerful metaphor for the expression of human resolve in the face of destructive powers. This warmly humanistic symphony, dedicated to the city of Leningrad and first performed in Kuybyshev on 15 March 1941, gave the tarnished image of triumphalism in the twentieth century a new resonance.[19]

If the Eighth Symphony, completed in the late summer of 1943, surpasses the achievement of the Seventh, its success lies chiefly in the depth of its tragic intensity and its brave rejection of triumphalism at a stage in Russia's Great Patriotic War that would seem to have warranted a glimpse of ultimate victory. As in the Fourth Symphony, Mahler is a presiding influence throughout this epic journey, not only in the bold linearity of its strenuous counterpoint, but also in the cyclic resonance of its now truly terrifying climaxes and collapses. The compelling sweep of the five-movement musico-dramatic structure opens a new chapter in the composer's approach to large-scale symphonic form. The first movement builds especially on the experience of the Fifth: a vast sonata movement in the manner of a funeral march (Mahler again!) beginning with another of those heroic 'epigraph' themes that delivers the same kind of punch as that of the Fifth and Sixth while holding long-term implications for the symphony as a whole. This epigraph theme opens with a simple neighbour-note motif C–B♭–C that forms the motivic cell of the entire symphony, expanding into a motto theme of falling fourths (shades of Tchaikovsky's *Manfred* Symphony) that will return at the three main climactic points. The Fifth Symphony seems a clear prototype for the Eighth, which has the same exploratory, searching line of melody, the same 'brutalized' thematic development and, not least, a superbly organized retransition-cum-recapitulation achieved through the dramatic stroke of a long, drawn-out recitative for solo cor anglais over tremolando strings.[20] Set against this cataclysmic movement is a march in D flat that enshrines all the composer's power of blending destructive force with the grotesque. The most extreme contrasts and collisions of key and expression are embodied in the powerful continuity of the martial toccata-and-trio third movement and the passacaglia fourth movement, ending with a sonata-rondo-like finale, which builds up, via an intense fugue, to a tragic recall of the opening motto theme, before subsiding into the relative peace of a numbed C major resignation. Even if we knew nothing of the Eighth's gestation as a 'war' symphony – and its content certainly suits the appellation – its cogent musico-dramatic unity, the breadth and depth of its dramaturgy and high tragic plane would place it as a symphony for all times, whose impassioned message must go beyond any specifically programmatic interpretation. It is hardly surprising that the symphony – of which the composer was to remain stubbornly proud – was to suffer censorship after being taken to task at the Central Committee meeting early in 1948.

With the end of the war in 1945 came the Ninth Symphony – a Ninth of which Shostakovich's great nineteenth-century predecessors, dogged as they were by the supreme challenge of Beethoven, would never have dreamed. For all its light, 'Haydnish' surface features, this work can be taken as perhaps one of the most caustic utterances to be encountered in the whole of Shostakovich's oeuvre. Although its conception is that of a symphonic burlesque – and as such it marks a long-delayed return to the spirit of the First Symphony – the Ninth plays an altogether subtler game of fractured self-identity and parody of its models. Cast once more in five-movement form, its scherzando-like surface is constantly betrayed by slithers into darkness and a desperate sense of panic and despair. Shostakovich was a master of the long-range accelerando – he had already in the Sixth constructed a whole symphony built on this principle – and here is a work whose two outer movements, but more especially the finale, subject the device to parodistic distortion. The extraordinary collapses and dark, gritty bitonal harmonies of the second movement – a melancholy barcarolle with sinister inflections – are pointed up by a falsely sweet climax (at 44) that is pure saccharin, while the third movement has something of the nervy, menacing instability of the scherzo of the Second Piano Trio. 'Collapse' is the best word to describe what happens at the end of the wild tarantella that is the third movement, as it slides into the ominous brass and bassoon antiphons of the Largo, its solo bassoon recitative already anticipating the twisted smile of the finale's opening in a manner that poignantly echoes the cor anglais recitative at the retransition of the Eighth Symphony's first movement. Indeed, the whole passage could be taken as a deliberate subversion of the message of Beethoven's Ninth. Of the finale itself, anything less like an 'Ode to Joy' would be hard to imagine. As in the case of every one of Shostakovich's symphonies, the 'little' Ninth – the shortest of the composer's purely instrumental symphonies – has its own utterly distinctive sound world, occupying a place in the Shostakovich canon comparable to that of Beethoven's Eighth, with its own playful, yet powerful, agenda.

One of the more searching appraisals of this symphony is to be found in Sabinina's book on the symphonies. She attaches a special significance to this 'symphony scherzo' in Shostakovich's output. Writing from the standpoint of the late 1970s, she considers the work to be a characteristic mix of tragedy and comedy, which, she maintains, is the very stuff of life, relating it to the farce-tragedy of *The Nose*, the tragedy-satire of *Lady Macbeth*, Shostakovich's love for Gogol and the tragicomic art of Chaplin, and the irony of Mahler. In a striking parallel, she further notes the resemblance of the theme of the finale to that of Shostakovich's setting of Robert Burns's 'Macpherson before his Execution' in his *Six Romances on Texts of Raleigh, Burns and Shakespeare*, composed in 1942.[21] And she suggests that, in following the funereal trombones and melancholy bassoon recitative of the fourth movement with this slow change of expression on solo bassoon (as if in the manner of those old-fashioned one-man Shakespeare performances in which the actor would pass his hand over his face as he changed characters), Shostakovich is – like Macpherson in the Burns poem – laughing in the face of death. Viewed in this light, maybe the Ninth is not such an inappropriate sequel to the heroics of the Seventh and the suffering of the Eighth. After the pain and loss of war, its ironic tone can be construed as hopeful rather than bleak, its frivolity genuinely humorous as well as defiantly sarcastic.

Breaking an eight-year silence: the Tenth Symphony (1953)

The Ninth Symphony marked the beginning of an eight-year hiatus in Shostakovich's symphonic output. This was almost certainly the direct result of an ideological crackdown on serious music at the conference presided over by Andrey Zhdanov in 1948, itself part of a far more wide-ranging attack on the arts in the immediate post-war period. The effect of the composer's public humiliation is well known; film music and dutiful cantatas now became his means of professional survival, with two serious works on a symphonic scale – the Fifth String Quartet and First Violin Concerto – withheld for more propitious times. But the premiere of the *Twenty-Four Preludes and Fugues*, op. 87 at the end of December 1952 was an exceptional event during this period. It marked the unveiling of a grandly realized project that – not least in its polyphonic mastery (the work is a genuine cycle) and command of large- as well as small-scale forms – had a direct bearing on the new symphony that was already taking shape in his mind.

Composed in the year of Stalin's death in 1953,[22] the Tenth Symphony stands alone as one of the great masterpieces, perhaps *the* great masterpiece, of the cycle. Quite simply, it is a magnificent re-creation of the Romantic symphony on an imposingly large scale. Its four-movement plan aligns itself strongly with the Classical-Romantic tradition, but it embraces staggering contrasts that throw Classical proportions to the winds. These contrasts range from a vast opening moderato in E minor, through one of the composer's shortest 'rage' outbursts in the polar opposite key of B flat minor, to an allegretto dance movement in C minor which itself is full of the strangest, most personal shifts of mood ranging from uncertainties, and reminiscence through to manic self-assertion. Preceded by a reflective introduction that at the same time contains within it the seeds of what is to come, the finale gains the long-postponed major mode at last in a high-spirited symphonic dance that, in the course of reminiscences both of the second movement and the finale introduction, brings back the composer's musical signature from the alle-gretto in a triumphant unison tutti. If triumph is the message of this finale, then it is a very personal assertion as the timpani hammer home the composer's monogram in the final pages.

Overall, this full-blooded symphony recaptures a neo-Romantic warmth of expression and has in it something of the passion and intensity as well as the lyricism and personal intimacy of Tchaikovsky. Cast in the Tchaikovskian key of E minor (not only the key of that composer's Fifth Symphony, but also of two of the most dramatically intense scenes in *Eugene Onegin*), its 'motto interval' is that of the stepwise rising minor third, permeating its every movement and giving an emotionally ambivalent twist to the tail-end of what can too readily be taken as an optimistic finale theme, while the third movement contains some of the most confessional music the composer was ever to write. Tchaikovskian too are such things as the balletic/soloistic second subject of the first movement (its Jewish *topos* notwithstanding), with its con-stantly shifting tonal ground (compare this with its counterpart in the first movement of Tchaikovsky's Fourth Symphony), the solo woodwind writing, the many thematic transformations, cyclic reminiscences and impassioned rhetoric of its climaxes, the antiphonal scoring and not least the frank harmonic richness and emotionalism of this symphony as a whole.

Despite its epic scale, the Tenth Symphony is not Mahlerian in the way we may view the Fourth, Fifth and Eighth; rather the ambience points towards a re-engagement with the Russian nationalist tradition of the nineteenth century. If Tchaikovsky remains a palpable presence, the brutal scherzo would appear to anticipate a new 'Musorgskian' phase in the composer's development as it reveals itself in the scene-painting of the Eleventh, the realism of the vocal/instrumental Thirteenth and Fourteenth

Symphonies and *The Execution of Stepan Razin*. Orchestrally, the writing luxuriates in a rich foundation timbre of string tone, with woodwind and brass choirs providing Brucknerian antiphons as well as awesome power in the tuttis, not to mention a whole range of memorable solo characterizations. A characteristic feature of the vast first movement is the integration of what could be taken to be an introductory first section with the main body of the movement. As with Schubert's 'Unfinished' Symphony, the opening dark cello-bass ruminations preparing the way for the main theme are destined to play a major role in the unfolding of the drama.

Of special autobiographical significance is the mosaic structure and content of the third movement, with its initially cautious dance steps transforming themselves into manic self-assertion that introduces for the first time the composer's musical signature, the notes that form DSCH. Taken from the German spelling of Shostakovich's name – D. Schostakowitsch – the monogram uses the German convention of spelling B natural 'H' and E flat 'Es' to contrive the motif D–E flat, C, B natural. Since Shostakovich had already paid homage to Bach's own signature BACH in the First Symphony and, as a pianist, was certainly familiar with Schumann's employment of a similar theme in *Carnaval*, Shostakovich was effectively carving out a niche for himself in a distinguished Germanic tradition. The appearance of this monogram marks the emergence of a new referential/quotational authorial stance, developing that already mooted in the recently composed Fifth String Quartet and culminating in the autobiographical Eighth, with its retrospective collection of self-quotations. Featuring in this movement is a five-note horn 'signal' E–A–E–D–A, taken from the name of a young student, Elmira Nazirova, by whom Shostakovich was then temporarily fascinated.[23] The notes of this new element appear as a completely unmotivated event, but then proceed to integrate themselves with the composition as a kind of irrefutable obsession, which in its turn refers to another famous horn call, as shown in Ex. 1.6.

From the completion of the Tenth Symphony onwards, Shostakovich turned his attention increasingly to the medium of the 'private' symphony – the string quartet. Up until then the production ratio of symphony to quartet had been 10:5, and the Fifth Quartet, with its opening sonata allegro, had proved to be a work of symphonic proportions with threads linking it to the Tenth Symphony. Now this ratio was to go into reverse, with certain quartets (for example, nos. 3, 5, 6 and 14) demonstrating that in this medium, the writing of a substantial sonata-allegro first movement – that Classical convention of which in his symphonies he seemed incapable – was no problem. Large-scale cyclic finales, too, became special features of the string quartets, and in the late Twelfth String Quartet, Shostakovich on his own

Example 1.6a Tenth Symphony, movement 3, 114[1–8]
Allegretto

Example 1.6b Mahler, *Das Lied von der Erde*, 'Das Trinklied vom Jammer der Erde', bars 1–3
Allegro pesante

admission produced a true chamber symphony, whose epic – indeed Beethovenian – content and organic conception matched anything to be found in the public domain of the orchestral symphony.[24]

The symphony as programme music: the Eleventh and Twelfth (1957–61)

The Eleventh (1957) and Twelfth (1961) Symphonies mark the rehabilitation of Shostakovich as Soviet composer-laureate, and these two works – his patriotic tribute to the Khrushchev dispensation, one might say – form a diptych which, according to one source, was intended to be performed as a whole.[25] If both works draw on Shostakovich's vast experience as a film composer, they also stand up remarkably well as symphonic 'commentary' on their imagined scenarios, and are not necessarily to be downgraded on that account. As already noted, quotation and allusion, the 'extra-referential' element in Shostakovich, were becoming a more open feature of his style. In keeping with this tendency, the Eleventh Symphony in G minor, subtitled 'The Year 1905', draws its material from popular urban revolutionary song of the nineteenth and early twentieth centuries. The Twelfth Symphony – which Shostakovich allegedly regarded as a deplorable pot-boiler[26] – uses more generalized thematic material, including a thematic cross-reference to the Eleventh in the development section of the first movement, and drawing effectively on the model of Bruckner in the meditative chorale imagery of the second movement. Moreover, it adopts a heroic Russian nationalist style that is launched with a motto theme bearing a strong generic resemblance to the main subject of Borodin's

Example 1.7a Twelfth Symphony, movement 1, bars 1–2
Moderato ♩ = 84

vc., cb.

ff espr. , tenuto

Example 1.7b Borodin, Second Symphony, movement 1, bars 1–3,
Allegro

f

Example 1.7c Twelfth Symphony, movement 1, bars 137–44,
Allegro Più mosso ♩ = 192

vc., cb.

pp

Second Symphony and drawing in the first movement and finale, on the concept of 'the big tune' melodious second subject that is suggestively first presented on cellos and basses, as if echoing the first appearance of Beethoven's 'Ode to Joy' (see Ex. 1.7).

In the Eleventh – as in the Fourth, Fifth and Eighth Symphonies – the influence of Mahler is once more strongly to be felt, in the military fanfares, funeral/triumphant march imagery, conscription of popular idioms, ever-present percussion, and not least sheer epic scale. Memories of the first movements of the Fifth and Eighth Symphonies are evoked in the finale, which features stirring rhetoric in a gigantic orchestral unison alongside a poignant cor anglais threnody. But the real mastery of the Eleventh lies in the composer's absorption of his populist material; the carefully chosen Revolutionary songs, tracking the symbolic victory of the victims of Tsarist oppression, are woven into a cross-referential network of symphonic thought.

The Eleventh and its more compactly organized sequel inevitably invite comparison with one other, and the Twelfth is usually thought to suffer in this respect. Certainly, on the level of identification with its subject matter, the Eleventh would seem to convey a deeper emotional involvement. The wonderfully evocative 'Palace Square' opening movement movingly conveys the spirit of enchainment embodied in its two quoted songs 'Listen' and 'The Prisoner'. Its brooding tension finds release in the ensuing 'scene' of panic and massacre, and its return at the end of the Allegro creates a deep sense of trauma. If no such flashes of inspiration illumine the pages of the Twelfth, nevertheless this work too remains a highly accomplished essay in the musico-dramatic transformation of thematic material from movement to movement, its strong overlapping unity-in-continuity and its highly effective narrative driving the three stages that lead through to a cumulative – if admittedly bombastic – finale. In these respects, the symphony reflects the same processual priorities of the Seventh and Eighth String Quartets (composed between the Eleventh and Twelfth Symphonies), which in their turn lead on to the amazing cumulative drive of the five-movement Ninth Quartet.

Citizen composer: the voice of the symphonist (1962)

A humanist under pressure, Shostakovich in every decade of his career as a Soviet-Russian artist wrote symphonies that in one way or another could not but lend themselves to intense critical debate. But in his Thirteenth Symphony the composer chose for the first time since the oratorical Second and Third to speak directly through the mouthpiece of a poetic text. Of all Shostakovich's symphonies, the Thirteenth is the most heroically outspoken in its bid for freedom of expression – an outspokenness for which it paid in terms of its subsequent neglect.[27] Yevgeny Yevtushenko's poem *Babiy Yar* was published in *Literaturnaya gazeta* in September 1961, in the hopeful years of Khrushchev's 'Thaw'. It took its name from a ravine outside Kiev, where thousands of Jews and native Russians were massacred in one of the worst Nazi atrocities of the war. Along with Alexander Solzhenitsyn, whose short story *A Day in the Life of Ivan Denisovich* was published in the literary journal *Noviy mir* in 1962, Yevtushenko was adopted as the spokes-man of this new critical spirit in Soviet society. After the stifling fear of the Stalin years, Yevtushenko's unprecedented denunciation of the evils in Soviet society (in this case, anti-Semitism) was representative of a younger genera-tion in whom fear of the State was less deeply ingrained and who were desperate for political change.

Shostakovich's symphony had begun as a single-movement setting of Yevtushenko's poem. As with his two previous symphonies, it was a memor-ial piece, this time one in which poet and composer were together able to identify with the victims of persecution. This broader theme of empathy had long held a special fascination for the composer; according to Joachim Braun, the Jewish folk-song element constituted a hidden symbol of protest in such works as the Second Piano Trio, Fourth and Eighth String Quartets and the

First Violin Concerto.[28] But in the Thirteenth Symphony the message is conveyed without recourse to such a borrowed idiom. The single movement grew into a symphonic cantata, with the poet providing further verses that served to shape the work into a five-movement symphony: slow first movement ('Babiy Yar' – B flat minor), vigorous scherzo ('Humour' – Allegro C major – in which 'Macpherson before his Execution' is now openly quoted), two deeply contrasted but conjoined slow movements ('In the Store' and 'Fears' – movements centred around a modal B and A flat tonality) leading without a break into a radiant B flat major rondo finale ('A Career') in which the composer mocks the self-serving careerist and salutes the achievements of great men. The uninhibitedly populist style of this work is a high water mark in the composer's capacity to embrace an audience at many different levels of cultural response, from the sophisticated intelligentsia to the untutored ear of the naive music lover. Its rhetoric responds forcefully to the intonations and inflections of language, and this again brings Shostakovich close to Musorgsky. Textual delivery is sharpened by the choice of vocal means: a (chiefly) unison male voice choir, with its mass-song effect offset by the leadership of a solo bass.

Its companion piece is the vivid vocal-symphonic poem 'in the Russian style' of two years later, *The Execution of Stepan Razin* (1964), enlarging on the theme of the second movement of this symphony – a laughing, scornful contempt of tyranny from the scaffold. *The Execution of Stepan Razin* was initially conceived as the first movement of a further vocal-instrumental symphony along the lines of 'Babiy Yar' but there was to be no continuation in this case and the work became a symphonic poem. *Stepan Razin* marks a further step along the path of Shostakovich's 'style Russe', conspicuously synthesizing elements of both the Eleventh and Thirteenth and looking forward to a later, darker phase that was to bear strange fruit in the Musorgskian 'Songs and Dances of Death' conception of the Fourteenth Symphony. Standing on the threshold of Shostakovich's late period style, *Stepan Razin* gives a clear signal that words and music – even a long delayed return to the 'forbidden' territory of opera – were now at the forefront of his creative preoccupations.

Yevtushenko's poem takes as its subject the historical figure of Stepan Razin, who in the seventeenth century led an unsuccessful rising of the people against the Tsar. It is at once an imaginative reconstruction of particular events and an allegory that as it were stands for the various subsequent uprisings against Tsarist rule in Russian history – Stalin's Communist regime not excluded. Writing for a Marxian society, Yevtushenko presents Razin as a kind of substitute for the risen Christ of religious belief, a saviour of the people who dies on the scaffold and yet rises, like the Thirteenth Symphony's 'Humour', again in triumph over his executioners. Shostakovich's setting of the poem – to which he made certain alterations – falls into several dramatically contrasted parts, following the natural divisions of the poem itself. The whole is unified by what may be thought of as the rough-hewn motto theme that forms the curtain raiser to the first part where the citizens of Moscow rush and tumble through the streets of Moscow, en route for the macabre show. There is a 'close-up' of Razin himself in the cart as he confronts his fate in a monologue (bass solo) and reflects on his career as a doomed revolutionary; his only regret is that he did not go far enough in his harassment of the boyars. As in a dream, he sees the brutish mob transformed into an assembly of human faces and he realizes that he is not after all to die in vain. The execution follows and a pipers' band strikes up. Someone attempts to stir the crowd to rejoice with the pipers in a wild manically repetitive dance (clarinets and oboes in unison against a frozen chord cluster in the strings): but the crowd remains mute in a deathly silence broken only by the hopping of fleas (xylophone) 'from the coats of the poor to the furs of the rich'. Funeral bells toll. In a final horrific episode the staring head of Razin, still alive, spits and mocks defiance at a discomfited and terrified Tsar. Shostakovich's score is unsparingly realistic in its depiction of the details of the whole dramatic scene, featuring a large percussion section that includes bells, xylophone, celeste, harps and piano. The mixed chorus (here deployed with a greater richness and variety than in the purely male voice chorus of the Thirteenth Symphony) functions as both protagonist and commentator, while the bass soloist both narrates and plays the role of Razin. Although the main outlines of the drama can be followed in purely musical terms, such is the composer's fidelity to Yevtushenko's text that only a word-by-word following of the Russian in conjunction with its literal translation will yield the essence of what in effect is an operatic experience. The shock effect of this disturbing piece produced a sensational premiere, yet its critical reception seems to have been cautious during the uncertain period following Khrushchev's deposition in mid-October 1964. It received its first performance on 28 December 1964 in Moscow, given by the Republican State Choir and the Moscow Philharmonic Orchestra conducted by Kirill Kondrashin with Vitaly Gromadsky (bass).

Late style and envoi: the last two symphonies (1969–71)

Shostakovich's penultimate symphony (1969) was originally thought of by the composer as an oratorio, a reminder that for Shostakovich the designation 'symphony' could embrace a wide variety of genres.[29] If to qualify for the title a symphony must embody existential questions in music, then the Fourteenth Symphony seems uncannily to echo the following description of Existentialism: 'man is a temporal being, conscious, through his will, of a future whose only certainty is his own death. To live authentically is to live in the light of this bleak and unrationalizable fact.'[30] The symphony – for soprano, bass, string orchestra and percussion – was dedicated to Benjamin Britten, a composer for whom Shostakovich had the highest admiration, and whose 'War Requiem' of 1962 may well have played a significant role in the gestation of Shostakovich's work, with its opening allusion to the 'Dies Irae' motif.[31] The very term 'late style' lends an anthropological dimension to our consideration of Shostakovich the symphonist, for as physical infirmity overtook him (his first heart attack occurred in 1966), his preoccupation with a sense of his own mortality was increasingly reflected in his work, rising to the surface in a whole sequence of compositions that had begun with his orchestration of Musorgsky's *Songs and Dances of Death* (1962). In the Fourteenth Symphony's powerful theatricality – the vivid contrasts of its images; its transitions and sharp juxtapositions ranging from complete dramatic scene to the most subjectively contemplative; the sudden entrances and exits – we encounter the composer who, but for Stalin's intervention, might have made opera rather than symphony his true *métier*. His chosen poems are Russian translations of texts by Federico García Lorca, Guillaume Apollinaire, Wilhelm Küchelbecker and Rainer Maria Rilke, the Küchelbecker in particular suggesting a direct form of address from Shostakovich to his dedicatee, Benjamin Britten. In fact, the Fourteenth Symphony could be taken as a dark Shostakovichian counterpart to Britten's own *Spring Symphony*. As in the Britten work, its several numbers – notwithstanding their musico-dramatic dependence on the narrative of their texts – create a quasi-symphonic layout that corresponds to the traditional sonata cycle sequence of movements: introduction, symphonic allegro, slow movement(s), scherzo(s), finale. This correspondence is further reinforced by certain recurring intervallic shapes across the whole work, a characteristic that was already replacing conventional thematic unity as early as the Sixth Symphony.

The reinvigorated 'new' twelve-note Shostakovich of the Fourteenth Symphony is a paradox in itself, for here we have a technique imported from central Europe serving a music that is here associated with the idea of death and the powers of darkness, in opposition to life and light as symbolized by tonality. Following the Twelfth Quartet, which epitomizes this conflict, the Fourteenth Symphony would appear to confirm the symbolic association of non-triadic chord complexes of up to twelve pitches with the idea of death – death as it appears in many different guises and transformations.

In defending the symphony against possible accusations of excessive morbidity, Shostakovich commented: 'perhaps, in part, I am following in the footsteps of the great Russian composer Musorgsky. His cycle *Songs and Dances of Death* – maybe not all of it, but at least 'The Field Marshal' – is a great protest against death and a reminder to live one's life honestly, nobly, decently, never committing base acts … [Death] awaits all of us. I don't see anything good about such an end to our lives and this is what I am trying to convey in this work.'[32]

The Fourteenth Symphony had a significant instrumental pendant in the single-movement Thirteenth String Quartet (1970), a work whose twelve-note imagery would seem to echo that of the symphony, and in which the composer would appear to continue his meditations on the theme of mortality. This is surely no less a central preoccupation in his next, and last, purely instrumental symphony, which followed within two years. Although he had four more productive years to live after completing this symphony, with three important chamber works and four song cycles still to be written, the Fifteenth Symphony could well stand as a last will and testament, a consummation of everything he stood for as an artist, far transcending any claim the Soviet authorities could make for him as exclusively 'their own'. This four-movement symphony gathers together in its well-proportioned – even relatively concise – forty-minute span, the experience of a lifetime, offering a retrospective view of the composer's entire development. It encompasses Shostakovich's mastery of traditional (recapitulatory) forms, flexible yet respectful of Classical usage, his acceptance of the nineteenth-century symphony orchestra as an expressive medium in which the percussion department is now to be accorded equal status, his further refinement of a lyrical/contrapuntal voice that absorbs twelve-tone configurations into a tonal context, and his quotation-led blend of the tragic and the burlesque. The retrospective ambience is not simply a matter of the more or less direct self-quotations from previous symphonies, or indeed of the referential nature of these quotations within the symphony itself; rather, it may be perceived as the reflective cohesion of the symphony as a whole across its four-movement span. Thus the burlesque, somewhat sinister character and sound world of the first movement[33] is reflected in the *danse macabre* of the scherzo, just as the funereal aspect of the second movement is recreated in the finale.

With the Fifteenth Symphony, an irresistibly cyclic taxonomy imposes itself on the oeuvre as a whole: central to Shostakovich's output are four non-programmatic sonata-cycle works, numerically spaced at regular intervals and framed at a distance of nearly a quarter of a century by the First and Fifteenth Symphonies. In the same way that Beethoven completed his late, stunningly innovative, cycle of string quartets with a work that was, in Maynard Solomon's words, a kind of 'homecoming',[34] Shostakovich's first and last symphonies define him above all as a composer in the 'Classical' symphonic tradition. As in the First Symphony, a deeply serious funeral march movement (also, be it noted, in the First Symphony's key of F minor and including a spectral celeste allusion to its opening trumpet theme at bar 76!) is juxtaposed with the allegro burlesque of first movement and scherzo. Similarly, again as in the First (and Fourth) Symphonies – the slow movement interacts with the finale in a 'fatalistic' takeover of its final stages. Two chilling 'death chords' on wind instruments, comprising all twelve notes of the chromatic scale, recurrently punctuate the melodic flow of the recapitulation in the finale and continue to haunt its final pages of motivic dissolution, like some fading *memento mori*. The awesome force of the central passacaglia – another of the composer's 'forms within a form'; and climaxing in its dissonant 'crisis' chord – is redeemed, perhaps, by the return of the sad allegretto music of the exposition, but the shadow of death is not to be dispelled. Shostakovich the composer must fade into the unimaginable state of non-existence that awaits us all. Belief in the immortality of great art, however, was another matter – as the composer was shortly to affirm in the *Suite on Texts of Michelangelo Buonarroti*.

Outside Soviet Russia, and following the last symphonies of Mahler, Nielsen and Sibelius, an element of obsolescence has unmistakably attached itself to the genre. One could, perhaps, be forgiven for regarding Stravinsky's two ironic stylizations of the symphony as a fitting farewell salute. And yet the Shostakovich symphonies have, in Philip Larkin's phrase, 'penetrated the public mind' to an extent that has put them on a level with Beethoven. They have proved capable of stirring hearts and minds in an age no longer receptive to heroic triumphalism, still less of the Soviet variety, however ironically meant. As in his First Symphony, so in his last, Shostakovich showed that comedy and tragedy could coexist in a single work, and bringing this Shakespearian dimension to the genre was one of his most notable accomplishments. At the same time, Shostakovich the symphonist was a composer of immense psychological complexity, whose irrepressible penchant for playing the fool, coupled with a mastery of the laconic as well as the rhetorically expansive utterance, saved him from the charge of cultivating an outworn monumentalism. In this respect, his legacy is closer to such grand masters of the genre as Tchaikovsky and Mahler than to Bruckner; at the same time, in their breadth and power the finest of his symphonies represent a true twentieth-century response to the broad historical challenge of this most universal of musical forms.

2 The string quartets: in dialogue with form and tradition

JUDITH KUHN

Shostakovich's magnificent cycle of string quartets has received an exceptionally diverse reception. Soviet commentaries are filled with rhetoric describing the quartets as chapters in the life of the 'positive hero' of Socialist Realist narratives, and writers in both Russia and the West have heard them as vivid narratives, whether confessional autobiography or chronicles of the composer's times.[1] The quartets have also been interpreted as examining major ethical and philosophical issues, including war, death, love, the conflict of forces of good and evil, the nature of subjectivity, the power of creativity and the place of the individual – in particular the artist – in society.[2] This chapter will examine some of the musical features – especially Shostakovich's dialogues with musical traditions both Russian and Western – that have provoked such vivid responses.

Among the most notable of these dialogues is with traditional forms. Non-resolving recapitulations and withholding of harmonic closure are characteristic of Shostakovich's quartets, creating a rhetoric of disintegration, as opposed to the fulfilment characteristic of eighteenth-century formal archetypes. Such strategies are, of course, far from unique to Shostakovich or, within his oeuvre, to his quartets. But they appear here in exceptionally salient and potent guises.

As recent studies have noted, any composer who, for example, refuses to state the second theme in the tonic within a sonata-form recapitulation, in a sense fails to accomplish the generic mission of the sonata archetype – its essential structural closure – and thus creates uncertainty where resolution is promised by the generic model. James Hepokoski has suggested that formal 'failures' of this kind, although recurring from the time of Beethoven, are expressive precisely because of their non-conformity to the structural archetype.[3] From an earlier, sociologically orientated perspective, Theodor Adorno described such expressive distortion in Mahler's music as 'broken-ness' of form, commenting that Mahler's rejection of the organic wholeness of closed Classical forms 'takes up Nietzsche's insight that the system and its seamless unity, its appearance of reconciliation, is dishonest'.[4] A related questioning through formal distortion may be found in Shostakovich's music, nowhere more so than in the quartets, and is particularly striking when contrasted with the 'bright-future' narratives of Socialist Realist mythology.

Quartet no. 1 in C, op. 49 (1938)

In September 1938, during the last months of Stalin's Great Terror, Shostakovich's pre-premiere 'press release' for his First Quartet emphasized its light-heartedness, urging readers not to seek special depth in the work and describing it as 'joyful, cheerful, lyrical [and] ... springlike'.[5]

> I began to write it without special thoughts or feelings, not expecting that it would turn into anything. You know, the quartet is one of the most difficult musical genres. The first pages I wrote as a sort of exercise in quartet writing, not thinking I would ever finish and publish it. ... But then, I found the work on the quartet to be absorbing, and I finished it very quickly.[6]

The First Quartet does indeed appear simpler than its successors; its C major tonality and its rousing triadic conclusion create a frame of reference of childlike optimism. Beneath the surface, however, harmonic ambiguity and formal disintegration undermine the appearance of uncomplicated cheerfulness, presaging techniques that the composer was to use more radically in his later quartets.

The constraints of the work's Soviet context may have had a bearing in its compositional history, which reportedly involved a mid-stream interchange of its first and last movements.[7] As originally conceived and written, it seems that the quartet progressed from a relatively assured and extravert Allegro opening movement to the tentative *meno mosso* and *morendo* ending of the Moderato. As reordered in the definitive version, it moves from the Moderato's fragile lyricism to the Allegro's triumphant C major conclusion. As in the Sixth Symphony that followed in 1939, however, a seemingly optimistic ending is called into question by the work's deep-seated formal imbalance: the First Quartet as we know it consists of two slowish movements, followed by two rapid, relatively short ones.

More subtly, the 'joyful, springlike' tone of the quartet is also undermined by its critique of traditional sonata form. The opening Moderato has no significant development section, and only four bars of the first subject appear in the recapitulation, which fails to achieve the 'double return' of both themes in the tonic key that is sonata form's generic 'task'. The movement ends with a coda based on the second subject, itself the first of numerous waltzes in the quartets built around the melodic interval of the sixth, which commentators associate with Romantic lyricism.[8] Shostakovich's 'sixthy' waltzes are often subject to attack or disintegration in the quartets, and this one, according to one perceptive Soviet critic from close to the time of composition, 'gradually fades, as if it had exhausted its store of energy'.[9]

The second-movement theme and variations, in A minor (Moderato), opens with one of many monologues that give the quartets their confessional character. Its form, in which the melody remains essentially unchanged but the 'background' is varied, is one that Russians have considered peculiarly their own. Although not as starkly emphasized here, the slow dotted-rhythm tread of this movement is surely related to the many funeral marches that populate Shostakovich's works.

The fleeting and urgent Allegro molto is the first of many ambivalent or downright sinister scherzos in the quartets. Here, tension is accentuated by the muted timbre, lightning-quick tempo ($\downarrow$ =96), urgent pulsation in the viola, and an inability to find any resting-point during the first sixty-eight bars. A sixthy-waltz trio section (35) recalls the wistful first-movement coda and prefigures peaceful F sharp major oases throughout the cycle of quartets.

The finale's sonata form, despite its C major optimism, also presents formal peculiarities. Its hearty first theme leads to a surprisingly abrasive transition section (51), where G sharp harmonies over a C sharp local tonic (an unresolved vestige from the previous scherzo?) and a whole-tone scale of major triads (51^{6-10}) create the movement's most disturbing harmonic tension. Although the quartet's first extended development section (from 56) generates a well-defined and satisfying C major arrival (65) at the recapitulation, the music seems to unravel thereafter. Truncated restatements of the primary (65) and secondary themes (67), in C and E major fail to achieve harmonic closure. The disturbing transitional material from the exposition (cf. 51–52), ignored throughout the development and recapitulation, now appears belatedly but forcefully *after* the second subject in the recapitulation (72), serving as transition to the coda rather than to the second theme. Since the music has been unable to achieve full sonata-form resolution within the recapitulation space, the function of this dislocated transitional material seems to be to create a harmonic tension that *can* be resolved. In the coda, the transitional figure is tamed and placed in the tonic against fully consonant C major chords (75). It is a belated 'resolution' of sorts, but one that papers over the movement's formal cracks and prefigures the even more dramatic formal sonata 'failures' that will feature in later quartets.

Quartet no. 2 in A, op. 68 (1944)

The Piano Trio, op. 67 and the Second String Quartet enshrine Shostakovich's apparent response to the Soviet wartime trend for patriotic

folk-music-inspired instrumental works. The Second Quartet is dedicated
to Vissarion Shebalin (1902–63), whose Fifth Quartet ('Slavonic') was one
of the most successful of these folk-inspired chamber works.

Shostakovich's 'twist' on the folk-music trend was to make use of the
inflections of the music of Eastern European Jewry, an ethnic group
historically oppressed within Russia and Eastern Europe. 'Jewish' inflections, whether related to klezmer or to sacred sources, saturate the Second
Quartet with their syncopated rhythms, 'oom-pa' accompaniments,
ambivalent minor-mode dances, and 'oriental' augmented seconds.

The 'laughter through tears' character of Jewish music, with its pre-
valence of minor-mode dances, is a perfect expressive vehicle for the
Second Quartet, which seems to describe a struggle, only partially successful, to move beyond the injuries inflicted by violent trauma and grief.

During the first movement ('Overture'), written in a modified sonata
form, the fragile A major, itself more an aspiration than a presence in the
quartet as a whole, is barely discernible in the opening bars and has
disappeared by [1]. A disruptive tonal challenge with E flat minor inflections ([20]–[22]) occurs during the development section, and its flattened
degrees 'infect' the recapitulation, changing its modality from major to
Phrygian-inflected minor. A major-mode restatement appears only in the
coda ([28]), and as it begins to creep back towards E flat ([30]), the movement ends abruptly, seemingly anything but resolved.

In the second-movement 'Recitative and Romance', the violin's two solo
recitatives seem to mourn the trauma of the first movement. Filled with
Jewish modal inflections, they frame the movement's central Romance,
another sixthy waltz ([35]), which seems at first to achieve a haven of B flat
major, but which soon disintegrates, both tonally and melodically. The
second recitative closes with a gentle cadence in the style of Baroque opera.

The third-movement 'Waltz' is in E flat minor, the 'infecting' tonality
from the first movement's development. The fragile sweetness of the
waltzes in the Overture and Romance here seems to have been contami-
nated by the quartet's E flat minor influence, producing a sinister waltz-
distortion. Its agitated central trio section ([63]) includes an allusion at [67]
to the finale of the composer's Fourth Symphony ([181] in the symphony),
silenced at that time, having been withdrawn by the composer under
pressure in 1936. Quotation of the composer's silenced works will become
an ongoing feature of the quartets.

A slow prologue moves the tonality from E flat minor to A minor for
the concluding 'Theme and Variations'. The theme, heard first on the solo
viola, sounds paradigmatically 'Russian' and is one of many examples of
features in the quartets that display compliance with Socialist Realist conventions. In contour, it resembles the opening of Musorgsky's *Boris Godunov*,

itself a paradigmatic emblem of Russianness. The first three of the movement's thirteen variations (beginning at 93, 95 and ¹97) are in changing-background style, where the theme remains essentially unchanged. From the end of the third variation (99–101), however, the integrity of the form is challenged. The theme is interrupted by challenging motifs that recall the Overture's developmental crisis (compare 103⁸ and 110–116 with 21–22). Fragmented, the theme is rarely able to achieve a complete statement. At 120 the prologue reappears, leading finally to a complete statement of the theme at 123. The movement concludes with a dramatic restatement of the theme, still bearing its minor-mode scars, but nonetheless proudly undefeated.

Quartet no. 3 in F, op. 73 (1946)

The Third Quartet is the first of six dedicated to members of the Beethoven Quartet, who would serve as the composer's faithful advocates for more than thirty years, premiering all but the First and Fifteenth Quartets. Although no subtitles for the quartet appear on the autograph manuscript or any published score, Valentin Berlinsky, cellist of the Borodin Quartet, reports that Shostakovich described his thoughts about the quartet in graphic terms:

> Dmitry Dmitriyevich one day, as we were simply sitting – well, and also drinking a little vodka – said that although there was no programme for this quartet his idea was that the first movement depicted peaceful Soviet life. Nothing was occurring and everything was calm. The second movement was the beginning of the Second World War, although not yet in Russia; still outside the country, in Poland, Czechoslovakia [sings first violin theme from bar 3 of second movement]. The third movement is the tank armada invasion of Russian territory, the fourth a requiem for the dead, and the fifth movement a philosophical reflection on the fate of man.[10]

While the composer's reported description greatly oversimplifies the quartet, the music does seem to tell of a violent struggle and its aftermath, and it has been most commonly heard as a reflection on the impact of war.

The opening Allegretto, in F major, is in modified sonata form. Seemingly carefree at first, it enters a world of dissonance in its developmental double fugue (11), constructed on tritone harmonies between subject and counter-subject. The instruments' arrival at the recapitulation (20–22) is ragged and unsynchronized, and the fugue leaves its mark as the second theme appears (23) not in the tonic, but in B minor, its tritonal opposite (and the same polarity as observed above in the Second Quartet). The recapitulation's thematic restatements are cut short by the expanding presence of an aggressive descending scale motif (25) from the fugue's counter-subject, which the music seems able to contain only by means of a peremptory ending.

Example 2.1 Third Quartet, transition from fourth movement to finale

An uneasy scherzo (Moderato con moto) in E minor leads to a further violent scherzo (Allegro non troppo) in G sharp minor, where the first movement's disruptive descending scale motif and dissonant canonic style reappear.

As so often in Shostakovich's wartime compositions, grief follows violence. Here the fourth-movement Adagio, although not a strict passacaglia, alludes to the similarly placed passacaglia of the Eighth Symphony (1943). As the dirge-like motifs of grief recede, the music seeks shakily to begin again, the viola and cello creating a deeply scarred but just recognizable oom-pa-pa-pa 'new beginning' in the movement's penultimate bar, recalling the opening of the quartet (see Ex. 2.1). Such repeated-note introductory motifs will also open the Sixth, Fourteenth and Fifteenth Quartets, and they seem in each case to serve as a 'new beginning' signal. The cello's dominant-functioning C natural leads *attacca* into the finale, permitting a return to the quartet's F major tonic and seeming – however tentatively – to resolve the deep structural tension of the inner movements' alien tonalities (E minor, G sharp minor, C sharp minor).

Like the finale of the Second Quartet, this concluding Moderato seems to try, with limited success, to re-establish normality. The movement, in a modified sonata-rondo form, is one of the composer's most graphically expressive sonata 'deformations'.

Although the main theme's initial C–G flat–F motif (see Ex. 2.1) seems to encapsulate uncertainty, the D minor second-theme section (91) is

Example 2.2 Third Quartet, finale, attempted transition from development to recapitulation

more assured and harmonically settled. At 97, the music begins to dance, as its third theme appears in A major, its rhythms and its two-bar oom-pa-pa-pa introduction recalling the quartet's opening bars.

The development is, however, haunted by disruptive memories, most explicitly the enlarged reappearance (107) of the fourth movement's passacaglia theme, now in dissonant canon and marked *fff espressivo*. Shortly before 110, the viola's repeated trilled notes seem like an attempt to stimulate yet another new beginning. In a dramatically 'failed' recapitulation attempt, the cello, muted, states a deformed and barely recognizable form of the finale's main theme (110; see Ex. 2.2).

Thereafter all the instruments are muted, and the music moves into a scarred mirror recapitulation, injured by memories. The third theme begins the reprise in A minor (111) instead of its original major (cf. 97). It never appears in the movement's overall F major tonic. The secondary theme appears at 115 in the tonic, but its modality is unclear and harmonies here are far more unstable than in the exposition. As the movement closes, the first violin repeatedly tries to state the main theme (118). Although it reaches higher and higher, ultimately into high harmonics, it remains heartbreakingly unable to complete more than a few bars of the theme. The quartet ends with the three F major chords that have served as signals of a new beginning throughout, but here marked *morendo* and serving as an ending.

Quartet no. 4 in D, op. 83 (1949)

The Fourth Quartet is dedicated to the memory of Pyotr Vladimirovich Vilyams [Williams], a prominent scene designer and painter who died in 1947. He and his family became close friends of the Shostakoviches while they were evacuees in Kuybyshev during the war.[11]

In 1948, the Soviet government's post-war campaign for control of the arts turned its attention to music, condemning Shostakovich and other leading composers for claimed 'formalist distortions'. An official fear of 'Jewish nationalism' also peaked in January–March 1949, with the arrests of hundreds of Soviet Jews. The Fourth Quartet can be heard, at one level, as a reflection on the issues raised by these events, in part thanks to its evocation both of folk idioms in general (drone basses and the like) and of Jewish ones in particular, in part by virtue of what happens to that material in the course of the musical drama. Its four movements struggle to deal with a destructive culmination crisis in the first-movement Allegretto. Occurring during the exposition of its first theme (3–6) – far 'too early' by normative sonata-form standards – this crisis robs the first theme of its beauty and forces it into loud, conventionalized repetition. This violation destroys the balance of first movement's form and seems to constrain the music, which musters neither a clear secondary theme (8?, 9?) nor a significant development section. In the abbreviated recapitulation (from 10^3), the main theme is heard in D minor instead of its original D major, and the basic tonality is further challenged by an E drone in the lower voices. This dissonance is finally dislodged by a miniature hymn-like chorale episode (13) that serves as the movement's tiny 'break-through'. This enigmatic 'hymn motif' becomes a unifying undercurrent within the Fourth Quartet, and it will reappear in later quartets, most notably the Fifth, Ninth, Tenth and Eleventh.

The second-movement Andantino, in F minor, is a fantasia in which the first movement's hymn motif (emerging most clearly at $\boxed{31}$) interacts with motifs from the third-movement passacaglia of Shostakovich's First Violin Concerto, written during the time of the January 1948 denunciations. By comparison with the first movement, its deforming crisis ($\boxed{24}$) is more centrally located (i.e. further on in the structure), less extended and less threatening.

The third-movement scherzo's muted timbre and flat dynamics seem to reinforce an atmosphere of inhibition, as the instruments move in an almost frozen conformity (inner voices at $\boxed{36}$, unison at $\boxed{39}$). It is in the trio section ($\boxed{45}$), with its Jewish folk-music inflections (oom-pa accompaniment, modal characteristics, augmented second at $\boxed{46}^2$) that the music comes alive. Jewish inflections remain a force in the music, as the movement moves without pause into the finale.

The fourth-movement Allegretto, in modified sonata form, opens with a freely improvisational recitative in the viola, which moves into an infectious folk dance ($\boxed{58}$) in D minor. Both recitative and dance are filled with klezmer inflections. The quartet's first real development section now occurs ($\boxed{69}$), building to a more conventionally placed culmination (around $\boxed{82}$, near the end of the development), that mimics the unison and repetition of the first movement's culmination. The recapitulation begins with a transformed restatement of the viola's introductory recitative, its incantation now played *fff*, in brutal parody, by all instruments in unison ($\boxed{84}$). Here, however, for the first time, this distorting 'public voice' encounters a defiant response ($\boxed{86}$) as the solo cello recapitulates the movement's dance-like main theme ($\boxed{87}$, cf. $\boxed{57}$), transforming it into an assertive individual statement.

However, during the reprise of the second subject ($\boxed{90}$ in F sharp major, cf. $\boxed{63}$) the D tonality, which 'should' dominate from this point on, disappears. Yet again the sonata form fails to achieve harmonic closure, and the music becomes more subdued. Earlier movements are recalled by appearances of the hymn motif ($\boxed{98}$) and the second-movement's triadic material related to the Violin Concerto ($\boxed{98}^6$). Three bars before the end, the music finally finds a D major that has been largely absent throughout the work, in a gesture so subdued and fragile that it seems to question the very concept of resolution.

Quartet no. 5 in B flat, op. 92 (1952)

Composed during the repressive final months of Stalin's regime, the Fifth Quartet begins a trend to reflect more personal matters as well as large

Example 2.3a Galina Ustvolskaya, Trio for Violin, Clarinet and Piano (Clarinet in B flat), finale

Example 2.3b Shostakovich, Fifth Quartet, movement 1, development section

social questions. Here Shostakovich's close friendship with his composition student Galina Ustvolskaya is symbolically invoked in the quotation of her Trio for Clarinet, Violin and Piano (1949) (see Ex. 2.3).

A further indication that the Fifth Quartet struggles with personal issues is found in its incipient general 'signature-ness', to coin a phrase *à la russe*. Each of the quartets from the Fourth to the Eighth foregrounds the semitone–tone–semitone melodic cell of Shostakovich's signature DSCH motif. In the Fourth Quartet, the cell appears as the hymn-motif 'breakthrough' in its first movement. In the Fifth, Sixth and Eighth Quartets, the cell appears on 'signature' pitch-level (B–C–D–E flat), although only the Eighth uses the pitches in the definitive DSCH (D–E flat–C–B natural) order. Since the cell in question can result easily from some of Shostakovich's favoured modal inflections, the question of when a modal fingerprint becomes an intentional signature is not an easy one. A similar issue arises with the composer's favoured short-short-long repeated-note figure, which in these middle quartets appears frequently alongside other 'signature-like' indicators. It is precisely this conjunction, however, that encourages reading of signature-like intent.

The Fifth's first movement, like that of the Fourth, reaches an early deforming crisis during the exposition of its first subject (1), but in contrast to the Fourth Quartet it follows this early crisis with a second local crisis (8–11) in the exposition of the second theme, and with a full-scale, conflict-ridden development ([14]–[34]) with its own prolonged culmination zone. The development section's impasse is broken only by the appearance of the Ustvolskaya theme ([29]), which serves, like the hymn motif in the Fourth, as a 'breakthrough' that resolves a conflict in the music. In both quartets, however, the conflict seems to deplete the vitality of the opening theme (see, for example, Fifth Quartet, [6][54] in the viola); it is the Ustvolskaya theme that dominates the Fifth Quartet's first-movement coda.

The passacaglia-like melody of the sonatina-like central Andante in B minor is interrupted repeatedly by allusions to works then languishing unperformed, including Ustvolskaya's Trio ([59], in cello), the finale of Shostakovich's Third Quartet ([60]^5–[61], in viola), the First Violin Concerto ([75]^3 in the quartet, cf. [79]^{19} in the concerto) and the Third Quartet's second-movement F sharp major 'trio' ([76], cf. Third Quartet, [36]). This picture, audibly and symbolically bleak, contrasts with the movement's exquisite second section in B major ([64]), surely one of the loveliest moments in all of Shostakovich's works. Its reprise-echo ([72]) is in F major, creating a tonal tension that had not previously been present in the movement. The movement connects to the finale via a rootless B minor chord, the missing tonic constituting an especially clear demonstration of the lack of formal closure.

After a ruminative introduction, the finale is in a sonata-rondo form. As in the Fourth Quartet, the introductory section precedes a dance-like main theme, which is then followed by a more chromatic second theme. The Ustvolskaya theme from the first movement enters into the furious conflict of the development, where it seems to exert a calming force, as it did in the first movement, until a disordered recapitulation shows the strain of the conflict as themes overlap and intrude upon one another. The subdued coda seems, like the Third Quartet's closing bars, to be about incompleteness, as the first violin and cello seek to restate the subdued material from the introduction but are able to achieve only fragments, the violin coming to rest in the midst of one such fragment on the dominant F. Like the endings of the Third and Fourth Quartets, the final bar is marked *morendo*.

Quartet no. 6 in G, op. 101 (1956)

The Sixth Quartet's most disturbing feature is its repeated 'happy ending' cadence formula, which appears melodically at the end of the first phrase (bars 11–12) and in full at the end of each movement (see Ex. 2.4).

The only variation in this cadence is its transposition, in the second movement, to E flat major, rather than G major. The cadence formula

Example 2.4 Sixth Quartet, movement 1: concluding cadence

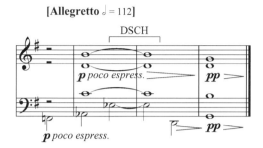

incorporates the composer's initials in vertical formation, continuing the incipient 'signature-ness' already apparent in the Fifth Quartet. Each of the Sixth Quartet's movements ends with a combination of the cadence formula and an augmented form of the short-short-long rhythmic footprint.[12]

Shostakovich advised friends, including members of the Beethoven and Borodin Quartets, that he had dedicated the quartet to himself in honour of his own fiftieth birthday.[13] The signature-ness of each movement's ending, plausibly related to that reported dedication, is only the tip of the iceberg in a work that is filled with possible signatures, beginning with its opening 'D.D' ('Dmitry Dmitriyevich'?), and continuing with Ds and E flats ('S's), juxtaposed and set against one another, throughout the work.

The signatures and the cadential formula also exemplify the harmonic – and therefore emotional – uncertainty in the work, where Ds and 'S's vie consistently with one another as 'alternative dominants', challenging the work's G major tonality. The first movement's opening theme, with its conspicuous display of cheerfulness, recalls the opening innocence of the first four quartets and is closely related to the children's chorus 'Khoroshiy den'' [A fine day] from the 1949 film score *The Fall of Berlin*, sung in a village that is soon to be attacked, and therefore a symbolic paradigm of innocence about to be destroyed.[14]

A halting second theme (⑥) that tries to but cannot cadence introduces uncertainty and leads to a full-scale developmental conflict between G and A flat harmonies (especially involving their dominant Ds and 'S's). As in the Third Quartet, the Sixth's main theme has great difficulty in moving into its recapitulation, emerging (㉑) rhythmically displaced, metrically and harmonically challenged, unbalanced and battered by the conflict, and thereby creating a sense of profound unsettledness at a point where resolution has been promised. The secondary theme, originally in D, is recapitulated (㉕) in E flat minor (more Ds and 'S's), the quartet's disruptive alternative dominant, thus intensifying rather than resolving the harmonic tension. At 30, over ostinato E flat crotchets (in place of the D crotchets of the exposition) the main-theme melody appears in the tonic, without rhythmic displacement. It is only at 31, well into the recapitulation that the tonal centre is able to settle to G major. The influence of the challenging A flat–E flat complex remains present even in the final cadential formula.

The second-movement Moderato con moto is in E flat ('S'), and its main tonal centres of E flat, B minor (42) and D (48) create yet another possible signature (D Sh).

The third-movement Lento, in B flat minor, is a passacaglia, one of many examples of this form in Shostakovich's works. It is interrupted by a dreamy section in G flat (F sharp) major (59). G flat has, in this quartet, generally represented the minor third of the troubling E flat minor tonality. It is especially wonderful to find it transformed here into this briefly radiant oasis of F sharp major.

The passacaglia ends, unresolved, on the DSCH cadence, which sounds especially alien in this B flat minor environment. The music then moves without pause or change of tempo to the G major resolution that begins the finale, marked Lento. The tempo changes to *Allegretto* for the violin's introductory monologue to the finale, which is modelled on the finale of the Third Quartet. Here, as in that work, the return of grieving material from the passacaglia in canon (80) disrupts the development section and seems to injure the music. Shostakovich emphasizes the injury, as he so often does in recapitulations, by directing the use of mutes (84). When the main theme tries to emerge at ^{2}83 and ^{4}84, it is pathetically unable to do so. A mirror recapitulation of sorts is scarred by intruding B flats from the passacaglia, and the first theme is never properly stated. The finale 'proper' ends before 94 on a B minor chord, with the violin's falling D–B melodic thirds unable to complete the movement to the tonic G. In order to reach the tonic, the music must restate the cadence formula. Thus, it ends, as it began, in Lento tempo. The cadence formula is followed by the short-short-long restatement of the tonic chords, concluding *morendo*.

Quartet no. 7 in F sharp minor, op. 108 (1960)

Written in 1959–60, the Seventh Quartet is dedicated to the memory of Shostakovich's first wife, Nina Varzar, who died six years earlier and would have celebrated her fiftieth birthday in 1959. Its dedication may be reflected in F sharp major endings to the first and third movements; F sharp major was the 'love' key in Shostakovich's opera, *Lady Macbeth*, also dedicated to Nina, and the composer often had recourse to it for moments of special tenderness. The second movement's running semiquaver accompaniment recalls the similar figurations in 'Der Einsame im Herbst' [The lonely man in autumn] from Mahler's *Das Lied von der Erde*. Finally, the structural importance of the 'DSCH cell' and the prominent use of short-short-long rhythms throughout the quartet continue the trend of disguised signature-ness, soon to become overt in the Eighth Quartet.

The Seventh is the shortest of Shostakovich's quartets; its three movements are played without pause in less than twelve minutes. Their brevity and cross-movement thematic continuity and development, and the dramatic reprise of the first- and second-movement motifs in the finale ([37], [38]) have all been viewed as aspects of an overarching sonata form, creating a sense that perhaps the music is reaching for, but unable to achieve, sonata form's dramaturgy of conflict and closure. The work is also unified by the gradual emergence of the DSCH cell, which appears mostly in accompaniments in the earlier movements, grows more prominent at the conclusion of the second movement and comes dramatically into its own in the finale, where it is stated emphatically by the viola alone in four semibreves at [23]^4 before lending its profile to the subject for the fugue ([24]).

The first-movement Allegretto is a perfect little AB:AB sonatina form, and its opening notes (F sharp–E flat–D–C sharp) neatly outline the principal tonalities of the first two movements. The first theme's fast anapaest rhythms recall the dance-like rhythms of the Third Quartet, and these seem to converse with the composer's footprint rhythm (the underpinning repeated-note quavers). There is no development, but for the first time in Shostakovich's quartets the recapitulation ([9]) actually resolves the movement's F sharp/E flat harmonic tension, as both themes are heard in the tonic key (the second violin belatedly comes into line after [13], drawing attention to its 'compliance'). The first theme is transformed in the reprise, appearing in 3/8, with all instruments playing pizzicato ([9]). The muted reprise of the second theme and coda lead to an F sharp major *tierce de picardie* in the movement's final chord.

As the second-movement Lento opens, the violin's grieving theme is heard over the second violin's semiquavers. Viola and cello enter at [18] with glissandi in parallel fifths, adding to the sense of strangeness. As in the first movement, a main descending-scale theme is balanced by a rising triadic theme ([20]). In the reprise of the main theme, the viola takes over the running semiquaver accompaniment, and the semitone–tone–semitone motif becomes more prominent. The movement ends uncertainly, with the semitone–tone–semitone motif in the viola's solo B double flat–A flat–G flat–F quavers, moving *attacca* into the finale.

The finale explodes with a furious return of the quartet's opening rhythms, now quasi-inverted in a flattened mode that openly displays its tonal uncertainty. After three bars of *fortissimo* cluster-chord dissonance, the semitone–tone–semitone 'DSCH cell' is heard *pianissimo* in the solo viola in unaccompanied semibreves. This inverted-comma-enclosed declaration echoes and emphasizes the second movement's ending and moves it up a semitone, where it combines with the dotted accompaniment figure from the second-movement trio section to serve as the subject for a raging developmental fugue (24–37). Following the fugue, in a dramatically non-resolving 'mirror recapitulation' of sorts, the second movement's main theme reappears transformed and *fortissimo* at 37, followed by the first movement's main theme in dissonant doubling at 38[4]. If this is intended as a double-function sonata-form recapitulation, in Hepokoski's terms it would surely qualify as a dramatic 'failure', since the dissonance factor is conspicuously increased, rather than resolved.

Finally, there is an extended epilogue (beginning at 41). Two waltzes alternate in this gentle aftermath, the first based on the semitone–tone–semitone fugue subject (41), the second on the first movement's main theme (46). The work ends with a reprise of the first movement's coda, which again concludes on an F sharp major chord.

Dmitry Tsïganov, the Beethoven Quartet's leader, recalls that, soon after the May 1960 premiere of the Seventh Quartet, Shostakovich shared his plans to create a complete cycle of twenty-four quartets, one in each major and minor key.[15] The composer may well have taken this decision much earlier, since he never wrote two string quartets in the same key, but he certainly intensified his composition of string quartets once he had made this intention public, producing nine quartets and only four symphonies in the final fifteen years of his life.

Quartet no. 8 in C minor, op. 110 (1960)

In July 1960, less than two months after completing his Seventh Quartet, Shostakovich travelled to Germany in preparation for composing the soundtrack to *Five Days, Five Nights*, a film about the aftermath of the Allied bombing of Dresden. After viewing the ruins and speaking to survivors, he retired to a nearby spa resort to compose the film music, but instead wrote the Eighth Quartet in three days, between 12 and 14 July 1960.

The immediate impulse for the quartet was probably not the Dresden trip, however, but his own decision to acquiesce in joining the Communist

Party, a step that caused him personal shame and distress. Although the quartet was presented to the public as his response to the Dresden trip, dedicated 'To the victims of war and fascism', Shostakovich informed intimates that the work was dedicated to himself: 'I started thinking that if some day I die, nobody is likely to write a work in memory of me, so I had better write one myself.'[16]

But although the work's prevailing sadness may have resulted from the events that immediately preceded it, the elements of the musical thinking behind it – and quite probably many of the personal issues as well – had been present long before he agreed to join the Party. The signature-ness (and the self-assertion it represents) that peaks in this quartet with the pervasive presence of the DSCH motif, had been growing since the Fourth Quartet. As we have seen, thematic unity, cross-movement development and self-quotation had also been developing during that same time, and these would remain important in the later quartets. In the Eighth and in the later quartets, the composer as it were weaves the fabric of his life through quotations of his own music and the music he loves.

The five movements (Largo–Allegro molto–Allegretto–Largo–Largo) are played without pause, and the double-scherzo format recalls several of the composer's most serious works, including the Eighth and Ninth Symphonies and the Third String Quartet. The first-movement Largo opens in C minor with successive entries of the instruments stating the composer's DSCH signature, creating a fugue-like beginning. The fugue remains unrealized at this time, however, morphing instead into allusions to the composer's First and Fifth Symphonies (1, 4) and (somewhat less clearly) to the first movement of Tchaikovsky's Sixth Symphony (2, referring to Tchaikovsky's first movement second subject) with recurring statements of the composer's signature serving as punctuation.

The frenzied second-movement Allegro molto in G sharp minor culminates in a quotation of the 'Jewish' second subject from the finale of Shostakovich's Second Piano Trio, op. 67 (21). This quotation interacts with the composer's initials and is itself broken off as the music moves into the DSCH-based waltz that opens the third-movement Allegretto. The composer's chronological survey of his works continues here with a quotation of the opening bars of his First Cello Concerto, op. 107 (43).

The fourth-movement Largo opens with two emphatic short-short-long rhythms, followed by a slowed-down version of the Cello Concerto's theme, which identifies its source as 'The Death of the Heroes', from the 1947–8 film score to *The Young Guard*, op. 75. The composer has devised this beginning in such a way that it also alludes to the opening of the finale to Beethoven's Quartet, op. 135, with its three-note 'Muss es sein?'

question and emphatic repeated-note short-short-long response. The strangeness of Shostakovich's music here has inspired extravagant commentaries about the drone of airplanes followed by the explosion of bombs, as well as about KGB knocks on the door.[17]

As the movement develops, the modality becomes, as Fanning describes it, 'flatter-than-minor'.[18] At $\boxed{58}$, after a transposed DSCH motif, Shostakovich quotes the revolutionary song *Zamuchen tyazholoy nevoley* [Tormented by harsh captivity] that was well documented as a favourite of Lenin's. Between $\boxed{61}$ and $\boxed{62}$, the music takes a magical turn as its flattened C sharp minor changes to F sharp major for the quotation of Katerina's love song, 'Seryozha, khoroshiy moy' [Seryozha, my darling] from *The Lady Macbeth of Mtsensk District* (Act 4, $\boxed{479}$; quoted at $\boxed{62}$ in the quartet). The encounter with this aria seems to empower the music, and its finale is now able to present a fully developed fugue on DSCH, with a counter-subject that alludes again to *Lady Macbeth*.

Notable in the Seventh and Eighth Quartets is a new sense that some problem has been worked through and resolved during the course of the work. In this respect, the Seventh and Eighth Quartets, despite continuing many trends from the earlier quartets, seem to live in a different world from that of their predecessors.

Quartet no. 9 in E flat, op. 117 (1964)

The Ninth Quartet had several false starts. In October 1961, Shostakovich told his friend Isaak Glikman that he was writing a quartet 'in the Russe style', but by 18 November 1961, he wrote to Glikman that he had finished the Ninth Quartet but was dissatisfied with it and had burnt it in the stove. In the summer of 1962, the composer told Irina Antonovna Shostakovich, his then new wife, that he was again writing a Ninth Quartet, and on 20 October 1962 he informed a *Pravda* correspondent, 'I am working on the Ninth Quartet. It's a children's piece, about toys and going out to play. I am planning to finish it in about two weeks.' Two autograph manuscripts (an incomplete fair score of the first movement, and the composer's complete rough draft of the movement) discovered in the Shostakovich family archive in Moscow, may represent one or other of these lost compositions. Working with both manuscripts, composer Roman Ledenyov completed a movement, which was premiered in Moscow on 17 January 2005 by the Borodin Quartet.[19]

The definitive Ninth Quartet took little from these early efforts. It was completed in 1964, four years after the Eighth, and two years after the Thirteenth Symphony, Shostakovich's most explicitly dissident work. His personal life had improved in the interim with his marriage in 1962 to Irina Antonovna Supinskaya, the dedicatee of this quartet.

As Khrushchev's 'Thaw' continued in the late 1950s and early 1960s, it gradually became possible to hear twentieth-century modernist music that had been banned in the Soviet Union for over thirty years, and a new generation of composers (spearheaded by Schnittke, Pärt, Denisov and Gubaidulina) was capitalizing on the experience. Shostakovich, for nearly forty years at the leading edge of Soviet music, suddenly needed to revitalize his style in order to avoid seeming out of date. The Ninth Quartet begins this process, trying out ideas that will become fingerprints of the composer's 'late style': oscillating seconds, fourths and fifths, themes based on successive fourths and fifths, chromatic themes based on eleven or all twelve notes of the chromatic collection, pizzicato outbursts and frequent virtuosic cadenzas, along with an increased frequency of quotation and allusion.

The single-movement-ness of the Seventh and Eighth Quartets continues on an even grander scale in the Ninth, one of Shostakovich's great symphonic quartets. Its five movements are played without pause, the centrepiece scherzo framed by two adagios and two faster outer movements. The work is also profoundly unbalanced. Its modest opening Moderato con moto (lasting about four minutes) hardly serves as a counterweight for the massive (roughly ten-minute) recapitulatory finale.

The first movement is in a disintegrating sonata form without development. The second violin opens with an oscillating undercurrent in apparent reference to the theme of Pimen, the monk-chronicler in Musorgsky's opera *Boris Godunov*. Many Soviet critics heard the 'Pimenovsky' accompaniments in Shostakovich's later works as an indication that the composer likewise sought to be a chronicler of his time. The first violin's haunting melody opens on the dominant, moving up a major third and then falling to A natural, the sharpened fourth degree and the music's first chromatic alteration. A natural will serve as a harmonic 'sore' throughout the quartet, challenging the dominant in the first, fourth and final movements and serving as an obstacle to major modality in the middle F sharp-based movements. The movement's secondary-theme dance (④) concludes with a rash of signature-like notes in the viola (the four bars before ⑧) that seem, in turn, to generate a new motif resembling the theme from Ustvolskaya's Clarinet Trio quoted so prominently in the Fifth Quartet (compare Ex. 2.3 with the motif elaborated at ^{8}⑧ to ⑩ of the Ninth Quartet).

The melody of the first Adagio seemingly alludes to Marie's lullaby from the third scene of Berg's *Wozzeck*, a favourite work of both the composer and his new wife. The second Adagio's arch-shaped main melody ([50]), with its 'Pimenovsky' undercurrent, alludes to 'Death of Ophelia' from the film score for *Hamlet*, op. 116, completed immediately before the quartet. The *Hamlet* soundtrack is also the source for the trio section ([37]) of the brilliant centrepiece scherzo.

The finale, a great sonata-rondo form in its own right, also seems to present aspects of development and recapitulation for a larger multi-movement concept, in a manner resembling the finale of the Seventh Quartet. Its first theme ([59]) is a quasi-inversion of the quartet's opening theme, and its second ([69]) transforms the fourth movement's arch-shaped 'Ophelia' theme ([50]). Its developmental fugue (beginning at ^{7}[81]) is followed by a massive mirror recapitulation that restates (and often transforms) the quartet's major themes in reverse order. It ends with a prolonged crescendo lasting almost 200 bars, leading to a triumphant statement of the Ustvolskaya motif.

Quartet no. 10 in A flat, op. 118 (1964)

The Tenth Quartet, written immediately after the Ninth in summer 1964, was dedicated to a composer-colleague and friend, Polish-born Mieczysław Weinberg (1919–96). Since the mid-1940s, the two composers had an ongoing custom of discussing works in progress, and Shostakovich especially admired Weinberg's Jewish-inflected compositions. By 1964, Weinberg had written nine string quartets, and Shostakovich, now on the determined path to his cycle of twenty-four quartets, challenged himself to overtake Weinberg, meeting this challenge with the Tenth and expressing wry satisfaction in having done so.[20]

The Tenth is in four movements, the only quartet after the Sixth to fall into this conventional 'Classical' pattern. Diversity in the number of movements is one of the distinctive features of the Shostakovich's later quartets, which range from one (the Thirteenth) to seven (the Eleventh) movements, making use of every number in between. The Tenth's dramatic trajectory recalls that of the Third Quartet in its progression from a violent scherzo to a grieving passacaglia-like slow movement into an injured finale that seeks to move beyond trauma but stumbles on the memory of the passacaglia. But there is also plenty that is new. The quartet's three- and four-note cells are elaborated by repetition and addition, rather than by the kind of organic thematic development that had been present in Shostakovich's earlier work. Austere simplicity, emotional distance and fragmentation are present here to a new degree, particularly in the first movement, and they will remain characteristic of Shostakovich's late works.

The opening Andante seems oddly stagnant and undirected, its dynamics remaining soft throughout, and its brief sections seem to coexist without emotional connection to one another, creating a chameleon-like shift of moods from one bar to the next. The spiky opening theme borrows inflections first from E minor, and its dual E–A flat focus is important to the quartet's overall structure, although suppressed in the sonata-rondo first movement. In the tiny development section (beginning ²⌐10¬), the primary and secondary themes are heard simultaneously, in a kind of synthesis. A mirror reprise recapitulates both themes in A flat, providing tonal closure, although the secondary theme remains in minor and is now eerily transformed into semiquaver triplets played *sul ponticello*. The movement ends *morendo*, the first movement without an *attacca* marking since the Sixth Quartet's second.

The first movement's restraint – and its tonal conflict – explodes in the second-movement Allegretto furioso, written in a Locrian-inflected E minor. The direct emotional indication in the tempo marking is the only one of its kind in the quartets, and the main theme's four opening whole-tone steps recall the first subject in the opening movement of the Fifth Symphony, previously heard at ⌐4¬ in the Eighth Quartet. The elaboration is repetitive and mechanistic, creating perhaps the most successful and exciting of the composer's attempts to use the string quartet to depict large-scale conflict.

The third movement is a passacaglia in A minor. Its four opening notes outline the semitone–tone–semitone cell, and its E–A flat movement again crystallizes the quartet's broader tonal polarity. As the movement progresses, the first violin's interweaving appoggiaturas and suspensions create a poignant individual voice against inexorable repetitions in the other instruments. In the fifth cycle of the passacaglia theme, the final bar is omitted (¹⌐46¬) to make way for a brief interlude (beginning ⌐46¬) during which the ground bass movement stops. When it begins again at ⌐47¬, it no longer seems quite so inexorable, turning to major at ⌐48¬ and allowing the insertion of added beats and bars in the sixth and seventh cycles. One of these insertions permits quotation of the 'hymn motif' from the Fourth Quartet (⁴⌐50¬). In the passacaglia's coda (⌐50¬), the eighth statement of the ground bass, now in the viola, disintegrates after four bars, as the movement shifts from A minor to A flat major in preparation for the *attacca* transition to the finale.

The finale, filled with folk-dance rhythms and drones, is structured as a sonata rondo. The third-movement passacaglia theme returns *fff* at the end of the development (⌐74¬), weakening the vitality of the music (emphasized by the muted texture from ⌐76¬[9]), which fails to achieve formal closure in the recapitulation, where both themes are restated in their original keys of A flat and D minor. In the coda, marked Andante, motifs from the first movement return ([81], [83], [86]), as if the music has decided to retreat to its original constraint. Reiterations of the finale's two-bar opening fragment sound increasingly irrelevant and forlorn in this first-movement-connected environment, and the music ends, yet again, *morendo*, finding itself in much the same uncertain place as it was at the end of many of the Stalin-era quartets.

Quartet no. 11 in F minor, op. 122 (1966)

Beginning a series of four quartets for the founding members of the Beethoven Quartet, the Eleventh is dedicated to the memory of violinist Vasily Shirinsky, who died suddenly in summer 1965. His death was a crushing blow to the Beethovens, who had worked for over forty years without a change in personnel, and its profound impact can perhaps be 'heard' in the extended second-violin silences throughout the Eleventh, Twelfth and Fourteenth Quartets that contribute to the spare texture of these quartets. It may also be detected in the distinct disarray of the early movements of the Eleventh Quartet, as if the ensemble is trying to adjust to the loss of its colleague. In fact the Eleventh Quartet as a whole has been most commonly heard as a contemplation of death and a deeply felt requiem for Shirinsky, and its structural features can be seen to honour the quartet's dedicatee by portraying the disruption caused by his loss.

The Eleventh consists of seven miniatures, each with a generic title (as often as not sardonically inappropriate) and played without pause. Its thematic unity and the recapitulatory character of its finale have invited commentators to hear it as another single multi-movement sonata form, with the Introduction serving as exposition, the next five movements as extended development, and the finale as recapitulation. The Eleventh is tightly unified thematically, its themes based mostly on a turn-shaped motto theme that appears in the cello at [1] and closely resembles the Fourth Quartet's 'hymn motif'. The opening theme is a decorated example of this contour (see Ex. 2.5a and 2.5b).

In the Introduction, the music seems to struggle with such simple tasks as the statement of a complete triad. The opening theme is a decorated set of open fifths, and parallel fifths accompany the motto theme at [1]; in both cases there are missing harmonic 'middles'. Perhaps as a result of this lack of triadic harmony, the first violin, having stated its opening melody, is unable to find a cadence in the tonic F minor, moving instead up to C sharp and thereby leading the cello to enter on a 'wrong note' F sharp with the

Example **2.5a** Eleventh Quartet, opening theme, aligned to show correspondence with Example 2.5b

Example **2.5b** Eleventh Quartet, motto theme at 1

motto theme. Formally the Introduction is one of the most 'unrealized' of Shostakovich's many provisional opening quartet movements, lacking a contrasting or independent secondary theme (the 'motto theme' is really only an abstraction of the first theme) and a development section. The recapitulation of the opening theme (4) is harmonized in the submediant (D flat major) rather than the tonic. The 'second theme' from 1 is not restated or developed in the recapitulation but becomes the subject for much of the rest of the quartet. Throughout the movement, only the first violin shows any sign of life; the lower voices seem to be unable to make music, woodenly repeating their often inappropriate chords (for example, G major against the violin's F minor melody at 2).

The second-movement Scherzo, a developmental fugue based on the quartet's motto theme from 1, is perhaps a nod to the dedicatee, an active composer who reportedly wrote ninety-eight fugues during his lifetime.[21] The fugue is obstructed by the (untrained replacement?) second violinist, who is six bars late for an entry that should occur at 10, and 'gets stuck' at 11 on a sixthy four-note figure, preventing further statements of the fugal subject during the next three statements of the counter-subject (11, 12 and 13). After one more fugal statement by the first violin on F, the viola enters 'incorrectly' on E flat, effectively stopping the fugue after only two voices have been heard in restatement.

The next three movements – Recitative, Étude and Humoresque – are united by a common metronome marking, and continue the development of the motto theme. The Humoresque has perhaps the most uninteresting second-violin part on record – a G–E 'cuckoo' that repeats idiotically throughout the movement, impervious and unmoving, even when the remaining voices are stating E flat–B flat fifths against it.

In the sixth-movement Elegy, the quartet comes alive as the music is finally able to grieve. The growing assurance of the second violin

([34], [36]) seems to enable the first violin to play a lament against it at [37], the first beautiful music heard in this bleak world since the quartet's opening theme. This exquisite duet leads to a precious F sharp major chord at [38]. The finale, a muted Shostakovichian recapitulation, seems also to 'correct' some of the problems heard earlier in the quartet. Triads are now enabled by the second violin's running figure ([44]), which makes chromatic adjustments in response to the first violin's accidentals; the missing two entries in the Scherzo's fugal restatement are completed ([44], [46]), and the 'incorrect' key of the motto theme at [1] is set aright ([49]). By the end of the work, the ensemble seems once again to be functioning, but the work ends sombrely in F minor, *morendo*.

Quartet no. 12 in D flat, op. 133 (1968)

Shostakovich completed his Twelfth Quartet just in time for the sixty-fifth birthday of its dedicatee, the Beethoven Quartet's leader Dmitry Tsïganov (1903–92). Of the four quartets written for the individual Beethoven Quartet members, only the Twelfth lacks an obvious musical-symbolic connection to its dedicatee. This, instead, is a mighty, experimental quartet, perhaps intended as an ambitious masterwork worthy of the composer's good friend and muse. More than any other Shostakovich quartet, the Twelfth can be viewed as a work about composition and the means of composition, in this respect serving as the composer's contribution to the ongoing Soviet discussion about new music.

The Twelfth is the first of the quartets to make use of twelve-note rows. Shostakovich does not adopt Schoenberg's method of manipulating each twelve-note row as a unit to determine the entire fabric of a piece, but instead uses a number of different rows, related by contour, in both tonal and atonal contexts, freely fragmenting, reshaping and developing them in much the same way as his established practice with other chromatic themes and motifs. Shostakovich's use of twelve-note themes without serial manipulation was part of a flexible approach to twelve-note practices that developed in the Soviet Union in the early 1960s, particularly among a younger group of 'unofficial' composers.[22] This emblematic use of twelve-note themes, without the full panoply of serial techniques, appears in the works of Pärt, Schnittke and others by the mid-1960s.

Even this limited type of twelve-note composition was controversial in the Soviet Union, with twelve-note styles being heard initially as a form of resistance.[23] Although by the mid-1960s twelve-note rows had begun to seep into compositions by older, 'official' composers too, their use remained a sensitive issue, and as late as 1968 Viktor Bobrovsky's *Sovetskaya muzïka* article on the Twelfth Quartet included only a brief mention of the Twelfth Quartet's use of twelve-note rows, buried near the end of the article.[24]

The quartet is in two movements, the second lasting approximately three times as long as the first. But Shostakovich plays here with the concept of 'movement'. On the one hand, although there is no *attacca* marking at the end of the first movement, the work invites analysis as a single-movement structure, since, as in the Seventh and Ninth Quartets, main themes from both the first and second movements are developed and recapitulated in the second movement.

On other hand, however, this two-movement quartet's 'dramaturgy' seems to mimic that of a four or five-movement Shostakovich quartet, with an 'unrealized' first movement, a scherzo, at times violent (beginning of the second movement), a grieving slow movement (45), and a finale with an enlarged return of the Adagio at the end of the development (58) causing a ragged arrival at the reprise of first (61) and second (65) movement themes, and a celebratory conclusion that seems to be crudely insensitive to what preceded it.

The opening twelve-note row itself is clearly tonal in its implications, ending with a classical V–I cadential motion to the tonic D flat major. The second bar continues with an allusion to the subject of the developmental fugue from Beethoven's Quartet in F, op. 59, no. 1 – itself a paradigm of tradition (see Ex. 2.6).

The second subject (4) is also a twelve-note row, and successive rows with clear gestural connections to the first appear as punctuating delimiters of the movement's important sections (see for example, ^{1}4, ^{2}6, 8, 10, ^{1}12, 12^6, 16).

The ABABA first movement (sonatina-rondo? arch-form?) has no development section, only a little tonal 'sigh' as it moves up to D minor for its central A section (8) and back down to the tonic again (10^3). Perhaps 'infected' by the mid-section's minor key, the movement ends in a section that is more D flat minor than major. The cello's D flat–G flat repetitions in the movement's final bars serve as a link to the second movement, which begins in F sharp (G flat) minor with another twelve-note row: a set of three trills passing through the upper voices, followed by a series of stepwise descending-third motifs in the cello (the 'row' – now including an un-Schoenbergian repetition of pitches – continues for just over three bars, ending on the first beat of bar 4). An extensive elaboration includes a thickly scored passage of semiquaver-sextuplet rows (30), heard in canon at 33 and restated *sul ponticello* at 39.

The final theme group in G minor, the quartet's 'slow movement', consists of alternations between dirge-like chorales and recitative

Example 2.6 Twelfth Quartet, movement 1, opening

outbursts, all marked Adagio (45). A brief development section (51) revisits both first and second-movement themes, opening with a remarkable pizzicato solo section for the first violin that incorporates material from the first movement. Tsïganov, whose performances of this section were highly esteemed by the composer, described it as 'ominous music, as if death itself is walking'.[25] The grieving 'slow movement' reappears enlarged at the close of the development ([58]), as slow movements often do in Shostakovich's finales.

The emergence of the music into recapitulation (around [60]) is effortful, and the cello finds the tonic belatedly. The opening note row, from bar 1 of the quartet, appears only at [62], and the first correct statement of the theme fails to synchronize with the first violin's counterpoint, already completed. Recapitulation of the first movement's secondary waltz-like second theme (first movement at [4]; restated at [63]^2) is resisted by continued statements of first-theme material. Around [65]–[66], the mutes are removed, and at [66]^3 the music begins the recapitulation of the second movement's main theme, which builds in assurance towards the quartet's triumphant conclusion, an ending that seems strangely insensitive to the issues left unresolved in the music.

Quartet no. 13, in B flat minor, op. 138 (1970)

The third in the series of quartets for founding members of the Beethoven Quartet was a 'hymn to the viola' dedicated to the Beethovens' violist Vadim Borisovsky (1900–72).[26]

The Thirteenth Quartet shares many musical gestures with the composer's Fourteenth Symphony (1969) and has often been described as its companion. The symphony's texts describe a series of encounters between death and its victims, exploring their implications for the meaning of life, love, wisdom and creativity, and the Thirteenth is typically considered to share its preoccupation with death. The Thirteenth Quartet also borrows directly from a film score completed immediately before the quartet; the wordless '*Plach*'' [Lament] for chorus, from *King Lear*, op. 137, provides most of the music from [1] to [4] of the quartet.

Structurally, the Thirteenth falls into a Bartókian modified arch form: ABCBA plus coda. A single pulse is maintained throughout the quartet, although the composer directs that the three middle sections are to be played twice as fast as the two outer ones. Although the Thirteenth is the composer's only single-movement quartet, it is also, as Laurel Fay points out, a logical extension of Shostakovich's engagement, beginning with the Seventh Quartet, with the idea of creating forms that encompass entire quartets.

Like those in the Twelfth Quartet and the Fourteenth Symphony, the thematic gestures in the Thirteenth Quartet are based on twelve-note rows (as for instance the opening bars, see Ex. 2.7).

Example 2.7 Thirteenth Quartet, opening bars

Furthermore, like the opening row of the Twelfth Quartet, the Thirteenth's clearly defines the home tonality, in this case B flat minor, beginning with a decorated tonic triad and leading back to B flat. Its seven bars divide into three four-note mini-phrases, each ending in a descending semitone sigh. The semitone haunts the quartet on all levels, and the row's contour seems echoed in the quartet's tonal plan.

As in the Twelfth Quartet, the composer treats the row freely, not using strict serial techniques. It is not, strictly speaking, a 'theme', in which intervals are replicated on each appearance, but more of a gesture. As it recurs, its intervals expand and contract, pitches are displaced by octave, and its three four-note groups are reordered in the composer's own free kind of combinatoriality, but its contour and gesture remain recognizable, shaping much of the thematic material of the quartet.

The centrepiece of the quartet ($\boxed{21}$) is a dark dance, where the cello's ostinato pizzicato line bears an incongruous resemblance both to the ground bass of a passacaglia and to the 'walking bass' of jazz. The ghostly quality of this dance is underlined by skeletal clacks as the players tap the wood of their bows against the bodies of their instruments. The quartet then recapitulates the second and then the first sections, to complete its arch. The viola is featured in the fine, lamenting coda. At $\boxed{61}$, the viola states a final twelve-note row, and at $\boxed{62}$ moves up to an extraordinary high Bb'''. One by one, the two violins join the viola on the B flat and the three instruments suddenly crescendo to the ***sffff*** scream that ends the quartet. The Thirteenth's ending, a graphic image of death, recalls the similar crescendo to nothingness that follows Wozzeck's murder of Marie, in Act 3, Scene 2 of Alban Berg's opera.

Quartet no. 14 in F sharp, op. 142 (1973)

As Shostakovich's health deteriorated in the years after the Thirteenth Quartet, a contemporaneous composing block – lasting nearly two years after completion of his Fifteenth Symphony in July 1971 – seemed to cause him even more anguish than his physical problems. He noted that, 'Some kind of spring has broken in my brain. I have not written a note since

Example 2.8 Fourteenth Quartet, opening bars of finale, with 'Seryozha' cryptogram 'solved'

the Fifteenth Symphony. This is a terrible state of affairs for me.'[27] The Fourteenth Quartet, completed in the spring of 1973, broke the composer's creative block and cheered him considerably.[28]

Dedicated to cellist Sergey Shirinsky, the Fourteenth completes the set of quartets dedicated to founding members of the Beethoven Quartet. The familiar form of Shirinsky's first name, Seryozha, is incorporated into the opening theme of the Quartet's finale, where it appears as S – e – re – ë – g – a (see Ex. 2.8).[29] In order to 'solve' this cryptogram, it is helpful to know that

- D sharp = E flat or Es ('S') in German notation;
- 're' is the *solfeggio* syllable for D;
- the Cyrillic letter 'ë' is pronounced 'yo' in Russian; and
- the Cyrillic letter 'ж', pronounced as 'j' in the French 'je' and usually transliterated 'zh', may also be rendered as a Latin-script 'g'.

As the centrepiece of the finale, and in further tribute to the dedicatee, Shostakovich quotes 'Seryozha, khoroshiy moy' [Seryozha, my darling], Katerina's Act 4 aria from *Lady Macbeth* (75, in cello), previously quoted in the fourth movement of the Eighth Quartet.

The Fourteenth shares neither the austerity nor the graphic images of death associated with the other late quartets. Written in the composer's F sharp major 'love' key, the work seems to brim with affection for Tsïganov and Shirinsky, the two remaining members of the original Beethoven Quartet, who can often be 'heard' together in the duets for first violin and cello (see 6, 14, 47, 53). The tuneful themes of the Fourteenth Quartet recall the songs and dances of the composer's early quartets, and the second and third movements have the wistfulness of memory about them. The Fourteenth is in three movements, with an *attacca* marking connecting the second and third. Materials from both the first and second movements return in the finale.

Although the first movement can be viewed as a sonata form (secondary theme at 12³, mirror recapitulation between 27 and 32), it seems rather arbitrary to do so, since variants of the A and B themes simply alternate throughout the movement, even in the 'development' (17–29). By compensation, its thematic processes are unusually subtle. Like the Third and Sixth

Quartets, the Fourteenth opens with the repeated-note introduction that has often seemed to represent a 'new beginning' in the quartets. When combined with the dance-like tune that follows, heard in the cello, it turns out to be full of potential, and Shostakovich develops it freely throughout the quartet, which can be heard as a loosely structured set of continuing variations on aspects of the opening theme, leading eventually to the quotation of the 'Seryozha' aria. For example:

- The first movement's repeated-note opening develops into an E minor lament at ^{2} 44 in the second movement, and seems also to be reflected in the 'Seryozha' anagram that opens the finale.
- The theme's oscillating opening, heard in sequence (A sharp–B–A sharp, G sharp–A sharp–G sharp, F sharp–G sharp–F sharp), with its non-diatonic fourthy centre (bar 6) changes gradually in a series of appearances, eventually emerging as the 'Seryozha' aria in the finale (see, for example, the changes that occur at 14, 53, 62, 69^7, 74^7, 75).
- The theme's stepwise descending thirds, also heard in sequence (A sharp–G sharp–F sharp, G sharp–F sharp–E sharp, F sharp–E sharp–D sharp–C natural) appear frequently as accompaniment, most notably at 47^2 in the second movement.
- A series of triads within the opening theme (A sharp–F sharp–D sharp, G sharp–E sharp–C sharp, F sharp–D sharp–C natural) grows into the first movement's secondary theme (12^3).
- The opening theme's inability to cadence in timely fashion at 1 and complete its overall inverted arch form (moving from A sharp–B down to C and back up to B) provides a kind of engine for the theme's development, at least in the first movement, as it seems to struggle to find a way of completing its arch.

The second-movement Adagio, in AAB bar form, opens with a rising sixth that falls back a semitone, and has been interpreted by some commentators as a reference to the opening motif in the Prelude of Wagner's *Tristan and Isolde*. An alternative source for this opening, possibly related to the composer's satisfaction with the return of his compositional powers, is the 'Heiliger Dankgesang' from Beethoven's Quartet, op. 132, which bears the inscription, 'Holy song of Thanksgiving to the Godhead from a Convalescent, in the Lydian mode'.

During the months preceding his work on the quartet, Shostakovich had been working on an opera (never completed) based on Chekhov's story 'The Black Monk', and in the process had arranged Gaetano Braga's 'Serenade: An Angel's Legend', a popular melody mentioned by Chekhov in his story. The candidly romantic violin–cello duet in the Fourteenth Quartet (53), harmonized in sixths and thirds with cello above the violin, is stylistically similar to the Serenade. Shostakovich was delighted with this section, calling it his 'Italian bit'. In the liquidating coda (57), wisps of the movement's themes return, in new keys, fragmented and out of order, like memories. The Adagio ends *morendo*, its 'duet' played alone in the violin, its key uncertain and its themes reduced finally to repeated crotchets, which lead directly into the finale.

The third-movement Allegretto is a rondo with the 'Seryozha' aria as its centrepiece and the opening Seryozha cryptogram as its refrain. The secondary theme is a lovely F sharp major waltz (62), its oscillation referring back to the second-movement 'Italian bit' and even to the dance that began the quartet. Most of the rondo's episodes recapitulate material from the first and second movements. At 69, a bizarre hocketing episode, dividing a single line between all four instruments, conceals returns of the first (69⁷) and second (71) themes of the first movement, and the opening theme of the second movement (72⁶).³⁰ At 86 the main second-movement theme returns, in its original D minor, in an extended coda that revisits the second movement's themes, perhaps in a second attempt to resolve its uncertain ending. As the movement ends, the music resolves the tension created by the D minor intrusion by incorporating a flattened sixth degree into the F sharp major mode, creating a flattened major mode that perfectly conveys a sense of nostalgia, memory and loss. The quartet ends, like Quartets 3, 4, 5, 6, 7, 8, 10 and 11 before it, *morendo*.

Quartet no. 15 in E flat minor, op. 144 (1974)

The Fifteenth Quartet is the first since the Sixth to lack a dedication, and this feature, along with its valedictory mood, has led many to conclude that it was intended by the composer as his own requiem. Saturated with references to the earlier quartets, the Fifteenth may be read as the grand recapitulatory finale to all the quartets, in the Russian tradition of artistic self-monuments.

Despite the weakness and pain of his final years, Shostakovich continued to set difficult compositional challenges for himself. This quartet, the longest of the fifteen at about thirty-seven minutes, is in six slow movements played without pause, all marked *adagio* or *molto adagio*. In addition, all are in a single basic tonality of E flat minor, although the harmony is far from functional. Generic titles for each of the movements (Elegy, Serenade, Intermezzo, Nocturne, Funeral March and Epilogue) recall similar titles in the Second and Eleventh Quartets and in the composer's early *Aphorisms* for piano, op. 13 (1927).

Like the openings of the Third, Sixth and Fourteenth Quartets, the Fifteenth's first-movement Elegy begins with a repeated-note introduction (bar 1 to bar 3, beat 2), and continues with an incomplete fugue that, in form, recalls the first movement of the Eighth Quartet. The seconds and fourths of its melody seem also to recall melodies from Ninth Quartet's scherzo and the Eleventh's motto theme. But nothing remains constant in this work, and the first violin's 'answer' adds a sixth and a tonic triad ($\boxed{1}^{4-5}$) to the melody, gently altering the melodic contour of the 'subject'. As in the Fourteenth Quartet, a process of continuous change unfolds throughout the work, so that 'themes' are not characterized by any fixed set of pitches, rhythms or intervals, but appear instead as ever-developing gestures, identifiable as much by texture and character as by fixed melodic components.

After all voices have entered, the 'fugue' fades like a memory. The Elegy's triadic secondary theme ($\boxed{6}$), in a surprising C major, seems to return to the relative innocence of the First Quartet. The Elegy's sonata-like form centres around something like an anti-development ($\boxed{11}^{3}$), in which the opening fugue 'subject' ossifies into a chant or cortege, its resemblance to the Eleventh Quartet's motto theme being especially obvious here. The harmonic bases in the movement include D, E flat and C – an unfinished DSCH signature. Although the 'H' never appears, frequent juxtapositions of D and E flat harmonies create a pervasive sense of signature-ness about the work. As recapitulation of the secondary theme concludes ($\boxed{20}$–$\boxed{23}$), the harmony remains unsettled, unable to hold a key even for a few bars. The coda returns to the opening theme, and settles finally ($\boxed{24}$) into E flat minor. Its final eight bars, like the endings of the Sixth and Seventh Quartet first movements, will return to form the conclusion of the work.

A sustained B flat connects the first and second movements, but here, as the second-movement Serenade begins, it grows suddenly from *ppp* to *sf fff*, alluding to the terrifying B flat that concluded the Thirteenth Quartet and serving as a graphic image of death. The title recalls the 'Serenade' from Musorgsky's *Songs and Dances of Death*, and the movement may represent Shostakovich's 'take' on how Death might 'serenade' its victims, as described in that text. The series of dissonant strummed cluster chords ($\boxed{27}$) (Death's idea of a guitar introduction?) serves as a kind of refrain in this movement and the next, leading into a notably un-tuneful recitative by the cello. The whole process of sustained crescendos, strummed chords and recitative is again repeated, its opening crescendo-series now beginning ($\boxed{28}$) with an allusion to the paired semitones that open Beethoven's Quartet in A minor, op. 132. This introductory 'scherzo' is followed by a 'trio' of sorts – a waltz on the paired semitones of the Beethoven motif ($\boxed{30}$) (a dance with Death?). The entire process – crescendos, ugly strummed chords, recitative and waltz – occurs once again in a disintegrating da capo, in what is surely one of the most grotesque double scherzo movements ever written.

The brief Intermezzo alludes to the lamenting recitative from the Second Quartet, now distorted into a vehicle for the expression of rage.

As the Intermezzo concludes, its tonic E flat moves down a semitone to allow the fourth-movement Nocturne to begin over a running quaver figure around a D–A fifth, which moves back ($\boxed{46}^3$) up a semitone to decorate an E flat–B flat fifth, prolonging the DS juxtaposition foreshadowed at the end of the Intermezzo ($^2\boxed{46}$). The fourth movement's melody (in the viola, $\boxed{46}^2$) alludes to the opening song ('Lament for a Dead Infant') of the composer's *From Jewish Folk Poetry*, while the Nocturne's contrasting section ($\boxed{49}$) seems to present a sadly withered version of the Fourteenth Quartet's 'Italian bit' ($\boxed{53}$ in that work). A dotted rhythm creeps in to replace the melody at $\boxed{55}$, prefiguring the fifth-movement Funeral March and recalling similar movements or sections in Quartets 1, 2, 3, 7, 11 and 12.

The opening demisemiquavers of the sixth-movement Epilogue ($\boxed{64}^1$) slightly distort the Twelfth Quartet's allusion to Beethoven's Quartet op. 59 no. 1. The other-worldly patter of this opening serves as a refrain for the movement, which recapitulates the quartet's major thematic gestures. Missing from the Epilogue, however, is any realization of the first movement's fugue, and its absence seems to question the kind of comfort the composer may have depicted symbolically in the Eighth's finale. The profoundly sad *morendo* ending to this last quartet seems valedictory, final and unflinchingly bleak.

Conclusion

The world of Shostakovich's quartets is populated by recurring images: funeral marches, fragile waltzes, violent scherzos, purifying fugues and canons, conflicted and violent fugues and canons, wispy-fragile major-mode endings in overwhelmingly minor-mode environments, forms that struggle towards conventional closure but most often fail to achieve it; themes that are destroyed or robbed of their beauty, tonalities that struggle with malevolent (often E flat-based) challenges, textures that grow ever more austere, and memories that return and disturb.

While the atmosphere of the quartets is often conspicuously bleak, it is not unrelievedly so. Ten of the fifteen quartets bear dedications to valued friends, and many of these dedications are reflected in musical features that convey the composer's deep affection for the dedicatees. Exquisite sharp-key moments appear in bleak flat-key environments throughout the quartets, seeming warmly affectionate. This is also a world of love and deep friendship. Monologues, recitatives, quotations, and a variety of signatures all become means by which the composer can be heard to assert and affirm his own value and that of people he loves, and perhaps by extension, an esteem for individuals in a society that valued them hardly at all.

3 Paths to the First Symphony

DAVID FANNING

Talent is the capacity to learn, genius the capacity to develop oneself.[1]

Symphonic debuts by teenage composers are dotted through the history of Western music from Mozart to Jay Greenberg. Occasionally such works hit the headlines – as in 1882 when the sixteen-year-old Glazunov was hailed as a renewer of the Russian nationalist symphonic tradition – but do not gain a foothold in the repertoire. Occasionally recognition comes belatedly but more firmly, as with Bizet's delectable Symphony in C, composed when he was an eighteen-year-old student in 1855 on the model of Gounod's First Symphony but only premiered eighty years later. It can happen that repertoire status is gradually and unsensationally achieved, as with the nineteen-year-old Schubert's Fifth Symphony, parts of which he closely modelled on Mozart's G minor, KV550. Rarely, however, does such a work both make an extraordinary initial impact and maintain unquestioned repertoire status. Such a case is undoubtedly Shostakovich's First, the work of an eighteen-year-old, and one for which no obvious model can be named, but which itself inspired successors not just among his Soviet elders and juniors but in realms as far-flung as Greece, Finland and Soviet Mongolia.[2]

The piece scored a famous triumph at its premiere under Nikolay Malko on 12 May 1926 in the Great Hall of the Leningrad Philharmonic, an event whose anniversary the composer would commemorate for the rest of his life. His teacher Maximilian Steinberg noted in his diary that evening: 'A memorable concert. Tumultuous success for Mitya's symphony: they encored the scherzo.'[3] The symphony was taken up by Bruno Walter (Berlin, 5 May 1927), Leopold Stokowski (Philadelphia, 2 November 1928), Robert Hager (28 November 1928) and Arturo Toscanini (from 1931),[4] inaugurating an international reputation that has dimmed only slightly as that of Shostakovich's subsequent symphonies has flared. Congratulatory messages came from figures as geographically and artistically distant as Berg in Vienna and Milhaud in Paris.

The sensation of the premiere must have been heightened by the perception that Russia's great symphonic tradition had been in abeyance. Well before the 1917 Revolutions, Rimsky-Korsakov and Skryabin had moved away from the genre of symphony, towards the programmatic symphonic suite and the philosophically orientated poem, respectively. After the Bolshevik coup, many of Russia's symphonists, actual and potential, settled abroad – among them Rachmaninoff, Stravinsky, Prokofiev, Alexander Tcherepnin, Grechaninov, Saminsky and a host of more minor figures. Among those who stayed, some had already given up composing symphonies and were concentrating instead on pedagogy and other activities (Glazunov, Glière, Ippolitov-Ivanov). Still others – such as Steinberg and Vladimir Shcherbachov, also a Steinberg product – put their symphonic output on temporary hold. Of the major symphonists who stayed, only Nikolay Myaskovsky maintained his fluency, grafting elements of Skryabinian ecstasy onto a formal and stylistic orientation fundamentally indebted to Rimsky-Korsakov and Glazunov. Nowhere was there anything remotely comparable to Shostakovich's First Symphony for sheer quick-wittedness, brittleness and the element of surprise. All of those qualities caught the spirit of the age of silent film; but they were also allied to a breathtaking assurance in the juggling of 'genre' idioms (principally marches, waltzes and galops), late-Romantic lyricism, chromatic harmony and large-scale structural checks and balances. The result is a vertiginous balancing act between academic decorum and sheer barefaced cheek.

But where did this music come from? For one thing, it could hardly have been composed without the example of *Petrushka*. Except that in Shostakovich's symphony the self-pitying, frustrated clown seems to have become more hero and animateur than passive victim, immediately setting the tone by his rapid mood-swings, which return as signposts to the various musical situations in the remainder of the first movement. Shades of other *commedia dell'arte* or related characters come and go, as of the Stravinskian milling crowd; and the reckless transformation, juxtaposition and superposition of themes drives climactic sections towards a sense of crisis, easily dispelled by a deft cinematic cut-back to the puppet show.

Equally, Shostakovich's ideas come from the same sources as those of *Petrushka* itself, which is to say from a mix of Russian stage-music archetypes inherited from Rimsky-Korsakov and Tchaikovsky, and from the music hall (especially, one suspects, as adapted in the silent-movie accompaniments that the young Shostakovich was himself supplying at precisely the time he was working on the symphony's first movement). The difference here is that whereas Stravinsky's music feeds off quotation and allusion to actual folk- and art-music sources, for Shostakovich virtually every thematic idea, no matter how vivid its generic profile or how suggestive its resemblance to past models, seems to be freshly minted.[5]

But perhaps the more interesting question is where Shostakovich acquired his phenomenal ability to shape such diverse material into something greater than the sum of its parts. The answer cannot be fully reconstructed, since it must have to do with formative experiences in the classroom, the concert hall and private exchanges, very few of which have been recorded. But we do at least have the evidence of published scores of all Shostakovich's surviving opus-numbered works before the First Symphony except for the Cello Pieces, op. 9, which seem to be irretrievably lost (the slighting reference in Steinberg's diaries to their 'paucity of content' being just about the only record we have of them).[6] And in recent years Russian archives have slowly but steadily been giving up their treasures, one of which throws especially significant new light on the attitudes and techniques of the fledgling composer.

Learning from others

This is a document comprising the composer's responses to a detailed questionnaire 'On the Psychology of the Creative Process', devised by Roman Ilich Gruber of the Department of the Theory and History of the Arts at the State Institute of Arts History in Leningrad and carried out in 1927. Gruber's questions are more penetrating and Shostakovich's answers more revealing, less shaded by politically correct circumspection, than anything in his other autobiographical statements – contemporary or retrospective – published to date.[7] Included is a list of Shostakovich's favourite composers that virtually maps onto the Austro-German canon from Bach up to Schoenberg, Berg, Hindemith and Křenek, and taking in Chopin, Liszt, Verdi (with *Aida* singled out) and Bartók. Wagner is included, even though Shostakovich did not rate him as an operatic reformer, as is Schoenberg, who would soon drop from the list of favourites.[8] French composers are not mentioned at all, and Bruckner only as the object of Shostakovich's 'sharply negative attitude'. The list of favoured Russians is extensive but omits all reference to Glazunov and places Myaskovsky, Medtner, Samuil Feinberg and, first and foremost, Skryabin in the antipathy list (Rachmaninoff appears in the favoured category, however). The list of approved works includes Hindemith's Concerto for Orchestra – only composed in 1925, and therefore hardly a plausible influence on the First Symphony, but certainly a source for some of the crazier linear counterpoint of the Second – and the same composer's String Trio, plus Schubert's last three symphonies, Berg's *Wozzeck* (performed in Leningrad just three months before the questionnaire was carried out), Bach's B minor Mass, Brahms's Second and Fourth Symphonies, Strauss's *Salome*, Wagner's *Die Meistersinger* and *Tristan*. On the long list of Russian works, the non-appearance of *Petrushka* astonishes.

The value of this source is the greater because we have so little information about Shostakovich's early musical development beyond the bare facts.[9] It is not even clear what proportion of his juvenilia is represented by what actually survives. In the 1927 questionnaire Shostakovich mentions '[Hans Christian] Andersen's *The Little Mermaid* (an attempt at a ballet); an "epic poem" on military themes in connection with the World War (*The Soldier* …); a funeral march in memory of the victims of revolution'.[10] That funeral march is a lengthy and musically undistinguished piece. It is presumably the same piece as mentioned in a letter of the ten-year-old Shostakovich to his aunt Nadya as having been composed in memory of Shingarev and Kokoshkin, two individuals identified in Chaliapin's memoirs as ministers of the provisional administration, 'the best representatives of the liberal intelligentsia', arrested and murdered while hospitalized as 'enemies of the people'. Which makes the piece more literally 'in memory of victims of the revolution' than the necessary spin put on it thereafter and accepted until the late-1990s.[11]

But there was clearly much more besides. Shostakovich later claimed that during his post-First Symphony crisis, 'in a fit of disillusionment I destroyed almost all my manuscripts.'[12] His opera on Pushkin's *The Gypsies* is mentioned in this connection, although short extracts did survive and are retained in RGALI: a duet for Zemfira and Aleko, the Old Man's arietta and part of a trio.[13] Various piano miniatures have also come down to us, generally in the personal albums of acquaintances.[14]

At the Petrograd Conservatoire from autumn 1919, Shostakovich studied harmony, orchestration, fugue, form and composition under Steinberg (Rimsky-Korsakov's son-in-law and pupil), and counterpoint and fugue with Nikolay Sokolov. He also attended the history classes of Alexander Ossovsky, and towards the end of his studies he took violin and conducting lessons. Some of his orchestration exercises from this time survive, notably his scoring of Beethoven sonata movements and of Rimsky-Korsakov's song 'I waited for thee in the grotto'.[15] His op. 1 Scherzo for Orchestra was composed, not in late 1919 as Shostakovich's own opus list claimed, but no earlier than spring 1920 and orchestrated sometime between July and September 1921 at the end of his second year at the Conservatoire under Steinberg's supervision.[16]

On the theory side, the Rimskian tradition of rule-bound training in basic disciplines still prevailed, and Shostakovich's ambivalence towards Steinberg's teaching – which made him feel both grateful and stifled – would later be expressed in alternately scathing and respectful terms. In the 1927 questionnaire, writing from the point of view of a young graduate looking to fly the pedagogical nest, Shostakovich refers to his composition training at the Conservatoire in general as an 'unavoidable evil',[17] and in a follow-up comment he describes his resistance to Steinberg's suggestions that he should revise the op. 6 Suite for Two Pianos, and similarly to the advice to correct the Piano Trio, op. 8, the Symphony and the Octet Pieces, op. 11.[18] Steinberg in his turn was vexed by his pupil's interest in grotesquerie.[19] Few details are recorded concerning how much guidance Shostakovich received from his teachers. We know of Steinberg's assistance with the orchestration of op. 1, of his suggestion of additional piano and celesta parts to the op. 3 Variations, and of Glazunov's corrections to the harmony of the introduction to the first movement of the First Symphony which Shostakovich again refused to take on board (see Ex. 3.3 below).

At the same time as going through the prescribed academic hoops, most obviously in his Theme and Variations, op. 3, Shostakovich participated in the 'Circle of Young Composers', consisting of students meeting in the Conservatoire cafeteria (1921–4), and in the Anna Fogt Circle (1921–5), where he made contact with scholar-composer Boris Asafyev, composer-teacher Vladimir Shcherbachov and conductor Nikolay Malko, all of them keen followers of contemporary musical trends in the West. It was in the Fogt Circle that Shostakovich introduced his *Two Fables of Krïlov*, op. 4 and his *Three Fantastic Dances*, op. 5. The appointment to the Conservatoire staff of Shcherbachov (in 1923) and Asafyev (in 1925) eventually provoked reforms, but these were instituted only towards the end of Shostakovich's formal studies, and it is hard to disentangle any influence they may have had from the welter of experience he was gaining from his music-making and concert-going. The stronger catalysts for his absorption of new music from the West, which was flooding into Russia in the mid-1920s, seem to have been his fellow piano student in Nikolayev's class, Mariya Yudina, and the Moscow-based theorist, Boris Yavorsky.[20] Certainly there is no mention of Asafyev or Shcherbachov in the Questionnaire.

Shostakovich's once comfortably off family shared in the deprivations of Russia's Civil War – the 'War-communism' era – and when Shostakovich's father died of pneumonia in February 1922, his mother had to take up typing, and his sister gave private piano lessons (it was only later, from October 1924, that the young composer began to earn pin-money playing the piano for silent films, having previously passed a qualifying exam). Meanwhile he continued his studies and composed his Suite for Two Pianos, op. 6 the month after his father's death, dedicating it to his memory. Ever a sickly child, he developed tuberculosis of the lymph glands, and in the spring of 1923 he had to have an operation. He continued work on his second orchestral Scherzo, op. 7 and began to sketch ideas for what would eventually become the First Symphony, before being sent for a summer sanatorium cure at Gaspra in the Crimea. This trip stimulated a love for travel that lasted most of his life (he generally preferred to travel south in the spring but to spend the summer months in the north of Russia). In Gaspra he met Tatyana (Tanya) Glivenko, daughter of a well-known Moscow philologist and according to some commentators the greatest love of his life. He composed his Piano Trio, op. 8 with his feelings for her very much in mind.

Scherzos in principle and practice

For trainee composers the attractions of the scherzo as a genre are obvious. It invites immediacy rather than profundity of character, and imaginative variety rather than consistency of texture. It also demands strong thematic contrast for a central or trio section. Thanks to the given nature of its sectionalized structure and thematic returns, it poses craftsmanly questions, principally as to how transitions and returns will be handled. At the same time, the very stability of this framework allows for an exhilarating sensation of creative time-moulding within it. Ideally, then, the scherzo offers a testing-ground for characterful invention and sense of form, the two necessarily going hand in hand. And it opens up a path from music as Play to music as Art. It should not be surprising, then, to find that scherzos loom large in Shostakovich's early output, as they do in Stravinsky's and Bartók's.

The orchestral Scherzo in F sharp minor, op. 1, almost certainly an orchestration of the third movement of his recently (partially) rediscovered Piano Sonata in B minor, sounds like a spin-off from almost any ballet in the Delibes or Tchaikovsky manner, though its flexible phrase-structure would hardly make for easy danceability. In its construction it already shows some ingenuity in contrapuntal combination of themes, surely at the behest of Steinberg, and it features a sophisticated retransition, in which the climax of the central lyrical trio section and the return of the scherzo are telescoped into one another. Shostakovich may or may not have realized it, but this synthesis of material already contained the germ of the 'dialectical' approach to structure that he prized in the Questionnaire and towards which he claimed (how genuinely, one wonders?) not to have been guided by his teachers.[21]

The score's professional aspect, not least in its handling of the orchestra, becomes slightly less astonishing now that its compositional history and dating have been revised.[22] The heavy brass are added with discretion, and the greater part of the Scherzo's outer sections could be notated in the treble clef (recall the 'Ouverture Miniature' to Tchaikovsky's *Nutcracker*). Not every detail of the scoring is felicitous (the high oboe writing sticks out, for example). But it is hard not to infer that much of the finely chiselled orchestral detail reflects the careful guidance of Steinberg, and who knows how much of the thematic, harmonic and structural workmanship besides. The initial violin pizzicato counterpoint to the main flute theme takes on a thematic life of its own, particularly at the height of the retransition, which is echoed near the end of the work. And derivations from the scalic material shared by flute and violins are everywhere to be found, with augmentations, inversions and imitations aplenty, all in the service of the hallowed pedagogic principle of making much from little. Whether the fourteen- or fifteen-year-old Shostakovich intuited such subtleties for himself or the paternal Steinberg steered him towards them, the boy composer would hardly have put his name to a piece, or granted it his first opus number, had the essence not been his. And he evidently thought highly enough of the opening thematic idea to reuse it twenty-five years later for the 'Clockwork Doll' movement in his cycle of piano pieces, *A Children's Notebook*, op. 69.

The trio section deftly plays with a theme that suggests duple rhythmic divisions against its triple-metre background, a strategy probably implanted with a view to the dialectical synthesis in the retransition, where the theme combines with the main idea of the scherzo, simultaneously revealing their common motivic source in the ascent through the first five degrees of the scale. In all respects other than that of motivic relationship, this ploy represents a dry run for the second movement of the First Symphony.

The retransition in op. 1 is by some distance the most interesting structural initiative in the piece, since the piece could easily enough have done without it and returned without fuss to the reprise of the scherzo. Its sophistication lies in the fact that the trio section has by this stage not fully unfolded, so that the retransition performs three simultaneous functions: of a withheld trio climax, of a degree of development (by means of thematic and textural intensification), and of retransition. The somewhat over-ingenious motivic recombinations are echoed in the concluding phase of the work, which nevertheless has an ultimate throwaway abruptness not entirely appropriate to the overall proportions or the density of argument. But this is the only conspicuous fault.

Such a brash display of constructional ingenuity is in a way its own critique, since it gives the impression of being an end in itself. It should therefore not automatically be taken for a weakness that the op. 7 'second' orchestral Scherzo, composed in 1923–4 and orchestrated from the second movement of an unfinished Quintet,[23] is both more direct and less subtle. Formally this is anything but an advance on op. 1. It is cast in the most straightforward of ABA structures, with the return of the A section being disappointingly routine. Yet the surface of the music is bursting with life.

For the first time we find here the cheerfulness – never far from rudeness – that will underpin so many of Shostakovich's polkas, galops and cancans in his work for stage and screen, undercut as often as not by mock-seriousness, only to erupt again in more high-kicking japes. The theme of the trio section (marked *più mosso*, though Rozhdestvensky's commercial recording takes it, rather effectively, *meno mosso*)[24] is based on another two-chord alternation, with sly chromatic slitherings underpinned by a vamp bass. This is then seized upon by the full orchestra with the kind of raucous glee that one might attribute to the influence of Ibert's *Divertissement*, were it not for the fact that Ibert's work post-dates Shostakovich's by six years. The prominent piano part is an overt homage to *Petrushka* and the most obvious pointer ahead to the First Symphony.

In op. 7 the transitions from scherzo to trio and back to scherzo, far from being opportunities to showcase structural subtlety as in op. 1, register as a simple running out of steam, and the *Presto* coda is even more perfunctory than the end of op. 1. Not that ingenuity is entirely absent, however. To provide a launch-pad for the piece, Shostakovich deftly turns the short-short-long rhythms of his introductory phrases to the short-long-shorts of his main theme and adds an accordion-like *Petrushka*-style accompaniment, all this neatly disguising the fact that his building-blocks are simply two alternating chords and four-bar phrases. As with op. 1, material from the op. 7 Scherzo was destined for recycling, this time in Shostakovich's first film score, *The New Babylon*.

Pianistic calling-cards

For a young pianist-composer there is nothing more natural than to compose preludes for his own instrument. They can serve as compositional dry runs for more ambitious ideas and idioms, without the pressure of inventing large-scale contrasts and developmental extensions. If successful, they may even be taken up by fellow pianists. If published they may sell in far greater numbers than any orchestral score. Last and not least, they can serve as calling-cards at cultural gatherings where career opportunities may open up.

Shostakovich's *Five Preludes*, survivors from the eight of op. 2 composed as part of a collaborative album of *Twenty-Four Preludes* in all the different keys, are cases in point.[25] Their stylistic debts are not hard to hear: these include Prokofiev's *Visions fugitives* and op. 12 Pieces, Debussy's Violin Sonata (in the closing bars of no. 1), and the soon-to-be anathematized Skryabin in the strenuous 5/8-metre workout of no. 3. At this stage Shostakovich seems to have regarded the prelude as a testing-ground for more or less free forms. Even the piece of this same title from the three miniatures retained in his teacher Alexandra Rozanova's album, and published in vol. 39 of the old Soviet edition of the *Collected Works*, is remarkably free-floating (by comparison, that is, with the well-behaved ABA form of the Menuet and the balanced two-bar phrases of the incomplete Intermezzo from the same source). And there is nothing in the later op. 34 Preludes to compare with the caprice of op. 2 no. 4, whose short-winded ideas, restless changes of tack and pauses for thought come as close as any 'concert' piece of Shostakovich's to an improvised silent-film accompaniment. Similarly open-ended, op. 2 no. 5 could easily be imagined as a prelude to a larger work – a cantata or dramatic scena perhaps – especially given that the main motif is identical to that of the revolutionary song 'Oh, thou, our Tsar, little father', most memorably deployed in the second movement of the Eleventh Symphony.

Equally remarkable, not to say perplexing, in the op. 2 Preludes is the degree of unidiomatic piano writing. Though very little is actually impossible for two hands to perform, the problems posed by the canonic imitation in no. 1, the layered texture of no. 2, the discontinuity of no. 4, and the accumulating strettos of no. 5, are out of all proportion to the effectiveness of the results. In this respect all these pieces have something of the appearance of drafts for orchestral pieces, and no. 2 has a very similar layout to the accompaniment of the second Krïlov Fable, op. 4, which was indeed destined for instrumentation. Paradoxically, the third of the set, whose bouncing chords and chromatic writhings look especially fearsome and whose lead-in to the reprise is particularly tortuous, is actually the most effective pianistically and probably the least susceptible to recasting in any other medium.

In various ways these Preludes are as much composition exercises as they are concert pieces. Witness the strict Mixolydian mode maintained in no. 2, the chromatic maelstrom of no. 3 (one imagines the youngster's brash delight in writing such recherché Skryabinian intervals as augmented sevenths, fully justified by the part-writing), and the claustrophobically close imitations of no. 5. All five could be read as critiques of the miniature ABA pattern that is the default for such pieces. No. 1 achieves an elegant overlap of material, of the kind that would gain a nod of approval from most composition teachers; no. 2 makes a miniature drama out of losing its way, reaching a peak of impotent frustration; no. 3 calls a promisingly dramatic middle section to a premature halt; no. 4 opens up the prospect of atmosphere and eloquence in its *Andante amoroso*, only to brush it aside as though unable to sustain interest in the idea; and no. 5 subordinates ABA form to a design of progressively more intricate imitative writing.

Ultimately, then, these pieces may be little more than teenage doodles. But that little displays an urge to experiment that points ahead, if not to the First Symphony, then surely beyond to the *Aphorisms*, op. 13 and to the orchestral *Fragments*, op. 42 (from 1935, the last time that such relatively inchoate musings would be left so raw and still given an opus number).

The *Three Fantastic Dances*, op. 5 represent a huge advance in terms of idiomatic piano writing, never sacrificing effective textures on the altar of excessive thematic rigour. As with Prokofiev's and Stravinsky's piano idioms, and as distinct from Rachmaninoff's and Taneyev's, it is remarkable how often Shostakovich has the pianist's body displaced towards the right-hand side of the keyboard, as the registral centre of gravity shifts to the treble. At the same time, Shostakovich is at this stage still tied to four-bar phrasing and clear ABA form – unsurprisingly, since dance is the premise. Nor is it any surprise to learn that the pieces were used as accompaniments to ballet by the swimming-champion-turned-acrobatic-dancer Mariya Ponner, whose choreography, so it is thought, offended the composer's mother when she saw it.[26]

Once again the stylistic debts are not hard to spot. The first dance's gestural derivation from Schumann's 'Vogel als Prophet' from the *Waldszenen*, op. 82 has often been remarked upon. But the idea is turned into a miniature Beauty-and-the-Beast *pas de deux*, particularly in the central section. Thematically the third Dance is, wittingly or not, a teasing little skit on the Scherzo head-motif from Beethoven's op. 131 String Quartet, and it ends in a cadence that could have come straight from the second tableau of *Petrushka*. At the same time the detail of Shostakovich's craftsmanship has advanced hugely and succeeds in making the stylistic profile of these pieces entirely his own.

One of the chief delights of the op. 5 Dances is the ease with which they negotiate extended harmonic techniques. Already in op. 1 there were direct modulations from Neapolitan (and in one case the minor-Neapolitan) back to tonic, occurring at significant structural junctures ($\boxed{2}^{7-8}$ and $\boxed{8}^{6}$–$\boxed{9}$). When the first of the *Three Fantastic Dances* is read without accidentals, its conventional three-chord framework and slow harmonic rhythm become apparent. Put the accidentals back, and it is immediately easy to appreciate the mileage Shostakovich derives from his non-systematic flattening of scale degrees, not least when he finally and briefly allows a diatonic version of the theme to appear (bars 25–6).

The second and third dances draw on different harmonic resources – in particular the off-tonic opening. Shostakovich could have learned this procedure from any number of examples, including Beethoven or Chopin, but perhaps most relevantly from Prokofiev's signature-tune

'March' from *The Love for Three Oranges*. His sleight-of-hand as the opening harmony of no. 2 is eventually revealed as a straightforward 'applied' dominant is superb. So too is his simultaneous devising of a melody with as many conjunct fourths as possible. Once again Shostakovich plays with the retransition phase, allowing his chromatic voice-leading to lead him into and back out of a modally inflected submediant. No. 3 is harmonically the closest of all to the *Love for Three Oranges* March, its deceptive A flat opening being revealed as submediant to the tonic of C, which in turn can then be emphasized later in the piece without fear of monotony, indeed to witty effect, precisely because its initial foundation was so rocky.

Scheme and form

Shostakovich's memories of classes on form were principally that he was taught 'scheme', not 'form' at all: on the lines of 'Sonata form consists of (a) an exposition, (b) a development, and (c) a recapitulation. The exposition consists of (a) a principal theme, (b) a subordinate theme, and (c) a closing theme', and that the class was instructed to compose component parts, from which the best would be selected to form some kind of Frankensteinian composite work. He himself, so he claimed, while recognizing the special challenge represented by the development section – which should be 'dynamic and dialectical' rather than 'architectonic' – was looking for guidance on 'the expressive character of the musical line', on matters of 'relaxation, tension, and dialectical development'.[27]

The fact that he could articulate his priorities in that way may reflect the recent impact of Asafyev and Shcherbachov on the composition faculty.[28] Yet as the central section of the op. 1 Scherzo already showed, Shostakovich's instinct for a dialectical approach to form was already in place, if as yet only in somewhat naive terms (superimposition as synthesis). In this and other respects, his progress towards formal mastery – or least self-confidence – in the First Symphony can be traced via his four-movement Suite for Two Pianos, op. 6 and his single-movement Piano Trio (no. 1), op. 8.

The modestly entitled Suite, whose musical content is in fact as beefy as that of many a sonata, styles its first movement 'Prelude' (as does the 1940 Piano Quintet), the second 'Fantastic Dance', the third 'Nocturne' and the fourth 'Finale', as if to confirm a logical progression from the Preludes of op. 2 and the *Three Fantastic Dances* of op. 5, while acknowledging the comparative looseness of internal construction. The Nocturne in particular is a somewhat ramshackle assemblage in its restless changes of tempo. In compensation – perhaps over-compensation – the Suite is thematically one of the most unified of all Shostakovich's multi-movement works. This technique he could have learned from any number of sources, from Schubert through Liszt and César Franck to Rimsky-Korsakov, in whose *Sheherazade* themes first heard as explicit leitmotivs metamorphose into musical storytelling of a more generalized kind. In Shostakovich's case, the opening declamatory theme becomes by inversion the main idea of the Nocturne, reappearing at the central climax of that movement in its original form together with its original counterpoint, which in the meantime has itself metamorphosed not only into the second theme of the Prelude but also into the only main theme of the Fantastic Dance. So potent are the descending fourths of the initial counter-melody that they can also take on a summatory function, returning in canon on the last page of the finale. Thereafter they become one of Shostakovich's favourite motifs, their most poignant reincarnation being on the last page of his final opus, the Viola Sonata, as one of many symbols of retrospection in his late works, in this case possibly to do with the dedication of the Suite to the memory of his father.

If the Suite's themes and their transformations are all highly character-ful, their structural extension is nevertheless somewhat hit-and-miss. Not only do the seams show – to use Tchaikovsky's self-deprecatory metaphor – but needles and thread stick out all over the place. Transitions are especially patchy in the first movement, representing more a failure of the material to find natural means of extension than any lack of ingenuity in the transition itself. Invidious comparisons spring to mind with Rachmaninoff's extra-ordinary ability to spin material out from seemingly unpromising sources, not least in his two-piano Suites, which Shostakovich must surely have known at this time. Nor is the reprise itself convincingly prepared or delivered, and the reliance on rhetoric from here to the end of the move-ment seems like an attempt to cover up the lack of structural tension and momentum. No wonder Shostakovich later bemoaned his lack of guidance in this area.

For all its sharply pointed character, the Suite's Fantastic Dance is still weighed down by its four-square phrase structure, and the fugato in the middle section is rather perfunctory. More interesting is the way the accompaniment figuration springs to life in the first structural return (from bar 50) and actually takes over in a long developmental extension, leading seamlessly through to a *Presto* coda that rounds up the fugato theme as well as the main theme that is otherwise not reprised a second time. This is an innovative, perhaps not yet entirely successful form – one that disdains easy solutions and at least strives to apply dialectical principles.

In its pacific lyricism the Nocturne is a genuine example of the genre, as opposed to the edgy parody in the piece so styled in the *Aphorisms* (no. 3). Here, however, the structure is arguably rather too dialectical for its own good. The theme from the Fantastic Dance recurs at the end of the first contrasting episode (bar 25), while the second episode (bar 42) sees the recall of the opening of the Prelude. The reprise of the first episode is broken off to allow the fugue from the Fantastic Dance to return, initiating a grand résumé apparently rather early in the proceedings and drawing attention to a certain fidgetiness in the changes of tempo. Whether or not the Rachmaninoff two-piano Suites were at the back of Shostakovich's mind, there are still symptoms (as at bar 97 in the Nocturne) of his impatience with devising effective pianistic figuration. That part of his technical armoury he had yet to acquire.

But the finale has several trump cards to play. It opens with the first of Shostakovich's stark fanfare-like calls to attention. An accelerating introduction leads into an attempt at the Rachmaninoff trick of making the main themes out of almost nothing, by means of a curiously jazzy rhythmic animation, culminating in tintinnabulating heights. Then the cyclic-form ingenuity begins in earnest, first with the Nocturne's two main themes, then the Fantastic Dance. A new version of the finale introduction grafts on the first movement theme, and the jazzed Rachmaninoff writing is interrupted, interacts with the first-movement material and sustains tension towards an impressive conclusion.

The one issue still ducked in op. 6 is that of a fully worked-out sonata-form movement. Shostakovich grapples with this in the single-movement op. 8 Piano Trio. In this case, he evidently underwent a Brahmsian uncertainty about the best medium for his ideas. The second subject was derived from an abandoned Piano Sonata, and it also turns up as the main theme for the slow movement of the abandoned Sympfonie [*sic*] originally designated as op. 5.[29] The entire Trio seems to have been destined at one time for the medium of Piano Quintet.[30] Considering all of which, it is rather remarkable that the work as a whole is as successful as it is, not least from the point of view of its scoring. One wonders also whether the missing piano bars in the sources reflect Shostakovich's inability to come up with a definitive texture that satisfied him, though the work was certainly performed on a number of occasions, which means that some such version existed, if only in his head.

Whatever its structural weaknesses – such as the petering-out of the development section and the still perfunctory conclusion, in addition to the occasionally rudimentary piano textures – the Piano Trio has several redeeming features. Here Shostakovich surpassed himself so far as the

Example 3.1a Piano Trio, op. 8, Introduction

Example 3.1b First Symphony, movement 1, opening

off-tonic opening gambit is concerned. As with the second of the op. 5 Fantastic Dances, semitonal voice-leading is the enabling force. But here that voice-leading supplies the thematic substance as well as the harmonic underpinning, initially gliding around in a disembodied state, and gradually taking rhythmically energized shape just as the introduction – a miniature ABA structure – gradually reveals its tonal goal of C minor. The association of two semitone steps with a leap of some kind (most often a perfect fourth), provides the motivic substance and is strikingly prophetic of the principal motif that binds the First Symphony together; the close resemblance at the third bar of the Allegro may be passing and insignificant, but the motivic network of which it is part is by no means a trivial resemblance (see Ex. 3.1).[31]

Thematic economy is once again the watchword. The transition from ⑤ energizes the introduction material, though it leads up a blind alley, and as in the op. 7 Scherzo the approach to the main contrasting theme is compositionally sketchy. The contrasting second subject at ⑦ – the theme derived from the unfinished B minor Piano Sonata and was also orchestrated in the 'pre-First' Symphony – is in the academically conventional E flat major. It is beautiful in a somewhat anodyne Romantic way, with an impressionistic accompaniment in Ravelian parallel triads and rhapsodic extensions reminiscent of Skryabin's Piano Concerto, neither of which styles would remain to Shostakovich's taste for much longer. Within the Russian tradition, the arching thematic outline and its eventual destiny as a

Example 3.1c First Symphony, movement 1, first subject

Example 3.1d First Symphony, movement 2, opening

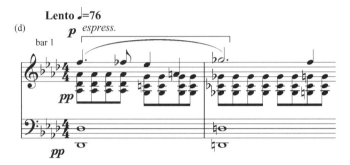

heroic redemptive theme recall nothing so clearly as Taneyev's Piano Quintet (1910–11).

Shostakovich's growing sense of dramatic form can be sensed when the return of the lyrical reverie is cut short at ⑨, and an energetic development section intervenes. His attempt at dialectical development sees the second subject recast in up-tempo guise but in its original rhythmic form, before it is heard in diminution and the up-tempo transition is tentatively touched in as an alternative reading. The first sonata-form reprise in his oeuvre is, significantly, a reversed one. This is a favourite gambit of composers whose instinct is to lead a development section into regions of crisis, and who either lack the technique of a Beethoven (as in the 'Eroica') to rescue it, or realize that the drama and proportions may best be served by keeping the first subject back for later, to supply renewed impetus in the coda. That can be especially effective in cases such as this, where the second subject is cast in a slower tempo.

Text and subtext

The *Two Fables of Krïlov*, op. 4 are the only examples published to date from the 'many songs to words by Pushkin and Lermontov' that Shostakovich composed as a student.[32] Apart from their mild intrinsic charm, their importance for Shostakovich's development is as studies for the kind of free-association text-setting that would be a feature of his operas rather than of his later song cycles. The first adopts the arioso style of Dargomïzhsky (as in the opera *The Stone Guest*) and Musorgsky (as in the song cycle *The Nursery*), with minimal repetition or recursion in the vocal line and maximal responsiveness to verbal imagery in the accompaniment, heightened, naturally, by timbral interest in the orchestral version.

It is in the nature of fables to be applicable to all times and all places, which is itself good reason not to read too much into Shostakovich's choices or settings. Nevertheless it is tempting to detect in the envoi of each song a first exploration of subtextual commentary of the kind that would later flourish in more ambitious compositional environments (subtext being, in essence, a mode of communication that adds to the apparent surface meaning by means of contradiction or association with another less apparent part of it). In the first fable, 'The Dragonfly and the Ant', the feckless dragonfly, who has sung all through the summer rather than laying in stores – ant-fashion – for winter, is heartlessly consigned to oblivion, being told that it may as well dance, since it is doomed anyway. Here a *Presto* coda takes up what is virtually the only thematized motif in the song, originally accompanying the text, '*Vsyo proshlo*' (i.e. everything went [or is] past). Even more suggestive is the conclusion to 'The Ass and the Nightingale.' In this song the ass has a leitmotiv of sorts – a lumbering, yawning figure in the mid-range and bass, reinforced at times by the timbre of the double bassoon – while the nightingale is evoked by scale-based figurations in the treble, related to the dragonfly's music in no. 1. At length the ass declares that the nightingale's song is no match for that of the cockerel, and the ass's motif is piped shrilly in the high treble, as the singer(s) (the orchestral version is designed for performance by a group of mezzo sopranos or contraltos and has been effectively performed and recorded by children's chorus) warn(s), 'God deliver us from judgements of this kind', and the instrumental coda dances blithely off, in a fashion that Shostakovich would recall at the end of the Tenth Symphony.

Conceit and contrivance

It would be hard to point to anything of great significance that carries forward from the *Two Fables of Krïlov* into the First Symphony. However, one final important ingredient was certainly stirred into the mix from his early works, namely an urge to display contrapuntal and variational skill, not least in canonic imitation, which is almost an obsession in his early works. Sometimes, as in the first Prelude from op. 2, imitation is carried through with seemingly reckless disregard for idiomatic texture or ease of performance. But within the larger category of demonstrative skill are also to be found thematic inversion, augmentation and diminution, and stretto – all the devices of fugue, in fact, which he learned as a separate subject at the Conservatoire – plus metrical manipulation and motivic transformation.

In some ways the op. 3 Variations are a diversion from the general trajectory of Shostakovich's large-scale works, in that the formal issues broached in the op. 1 Scherzo carry through to the First Symphony more via the expanding structures of the two-piano Suite and the Trio and the cheeky tone of the op. 7 Scherzo. The Variations, by contrast, take forward op. 1's constructional conceits, arguably driving them into dead ends. The op. 3 Variations for Symphony Orchestra, as they are styled on the autograph, date from his third year at the Conservatoire and carry a dedication to his recently deceased counterpoint teacher Nikolay Sokolov. They are in many ways Shostakovich's most scholastic, and therefore least characteristic, work. There is no trace of a performance in the composer's lifetime, not even of his piano reduction, and Steinberg's diaries, which refer at least in passing to most of Shostakovich's other early works, make no mention of this one (though Steinberg evidently advised on matters of its instrumentation, since at least one of his suggestions – for adding celesta and piano to the fifth variation – is written into the manuscript).

The Theme – in hymn-like four-part string-quartet texture, and vaguely folk-like, thanks to its palindromic main rhythmic cell – is scored for strings alone in chorale style, and might have been conceived as a variant on the main slow movement theme of Beethoven's 'Emperor' Concerto. The cut of the theme and some aspects of constructional ingenuity in the Variations recall another B flat Variation set – Brahms's 'Handel' Variations, which Shostakovich had in his performing repertoire at this time.[33] For a Russian model on the other hand, the slow movement of Glazunov's Sixth Symphony comes close, and the metrical games in the finale of that work bear particular resemblance to Shostakovich's.

The technical inclusiveness and increasing ingenuity of the Variations are impressive in their own right, without, however, suggesting much concern for a satisfying overall design. It is almost as if a class of twelve students had been allocated one variation each, with prescriptions as to desired character and technical feature, but that Shostakovich then decided – *à la* Beethoven in the Diabelli Variations – to do all twelve exercises himself, in the time it took his classmates to do one. At its best his ingenuity is accompanied by a naturalness that points forward ten years to Rachmaninoff's *Paganini Rhapsody* (even in places to that composer's *Symphonic Dances* of ten years later still). Yet even the mention of such pieces brings home that this is essentially the homework of an extremely bright student rather than the creation of a mature artist with something of depth and urgency to say.

The first four variations are comparatively straightforward; they decorate, transpose and truncate the theme and recast its metre, but otherwise stick closely to the given outline. Contractions in the phrase-structure, seemingly accidental in Variation 2, become a main feature of the relative-minor-mode Variation 3 and its waltz-rhythm successor. With the fifth variation Shostakovich begins to experiment with orchestral colour, fragmenting the theme and recombining its elements and exploring various generic types, such as the quasi-tarantella of Variation 9 with its ingenious diminutions and inversions. The three alternating tempi of Variation 7 seem merely fidgety, as though attempting to carry out a prescribed task rather than arising spontaneously. Most ingenious – not to say contrived – of all is the tenth variation, which plays complicated games with quintuple metres (though without straying far from Rimskian principles). Thereafter the eleventh variation defies the listener to detect any trace of the theme (it is there by inversion in the clarinet line, then by diminution in the viola and cello counterpoint). Its extension by means of a central section in a different metre and a cadenza is capped by a finale that throws material from half a dozen preceding variations into the melting-pot, constantly teasing the listener by treating sections as upbeats to other sections, and culminating in a rumbustious revisiting of the rhythmical games of the tenth variation.

Apart from its recherché qualities, the significance of this rarely heard piece could be said to lie in its aesthetic autonomy. Had it been the work of a mature Soviet composer ten years later, it would have been ripe for the charge of formalism, and it could justly have been so charged, had the term by that stage not been so voided of serious content. As the work of a fledgling composer, the last thing the Variations need is over-ingenious commentary. Nevertheless they stand for something in Shostakovich's career beyond their surface preoccupations. Notwithstanding his declaration in the 1927 Questionnaire that 'generally speaking, I composed a lot under the influence of external events',[34] the Variations indicate an ability to disengage from harsh reality that would become as crucial to his art as his ability to engage with it: as crucial a gift, and as communicative to audiences buffeted by the same reality, but also one that has been far less widely acknowledged.

Learning from himself

What can therefore be deduced from all this about the provenance of the First Symphony – this blend, seemingly *sui generis*, of mischief and profundity – and about its uniqueness? The proportions and sharply demarcated sections of its first movement reflect a propensity for episodic form, normally considered the enemy of symphonism. This is apparent too in the stop–start continuity in the op. 8 Piano Trio; and disdain for conventional transition is felt both here and in the op. 7 Scherzo. Yet neither of those criticisms, if such they be, can be levelled against the op. 1 Scherzo. Clearly either Shostakovich could not (yet) expand his forms without recourse to episodic fidgetiness, or if he could do so (having been taught how), he chose not to. In the Symphony's first-movement introduction, however, he spectacularly turns those features to his advantage. Here, stopping to think and taking new turns become of the essence, while *Petrushka*-esque indecisiveness becomes an existential, objectified condition, rather than an inadvertent flaw.

This is in some ways a non-vocal version of the Musorgskian text-shadowing principle seen in the first of the *Krïlov Fables*, and its character also grows out of the op. 5 *Three Fantastic Dances* (compare bar 2 in the Symphony with bar 1 of op. 5 no. 1), while the main motivic content derives from the first movement of op. 8 (and for deeper roots in the Russian operatic and symphonic tradition, see the scene of Boris's death from Musorgsky's *Boris Godunov*, where Boris asks for God's blessing on his children, the Tsar's Cavatina from Act 2 of Rimsky-Korsakov's *The Snow Maiden*, and the finale of Alexander Gedike's First Symphony, which also supplies the F minor tonic and march rhythm for Shostakovich's first subject (see Ex. 3.2). Other motifs reflect the stock-in-trade of late-Romantic/early-Modernist orchestral music, as does the urge to transform by augmentation, diminution and inversion, which is a positive compulsion in all Shostakovich's larger forms – opp. 1, 3, 6, 8. Tonally the symphony's introduction is an expansion of the off-tonic openings explored in opp. 5 and 8, and the tension of the chromatic harmony in bars 5–8 is again prepared by the voice-leading in op. 8.

Incidentally, Shostakovich's memory of Glazunov's corrections to these bars, much cited, seems to have been faulty, or to have exaggerated Glazunov's conservatism.[35] One further striking thing about this progression is that Shostakovich himself 'corrects' it in the movement's coda, where he adds a key signature, as if to show that F minor was the key all along, then allows the chord progression to cadence to A major, before rounding the movement off nonchalantly (see Ex. 3.3).

In the main body of the first movement the propensity for passages of thematic extension to get tied up in contrapuntal knots – a feature of

Example 3.2a Gedike, First Symphony, finale

Example 3.2b Shostakovich, First Symphony, movement 1

opp. 1, 2, 3, 6 and 8 – is also turned to a virtue, first by being objectified and dramatized as a problem, then by forcing the succeeding music to react and derive momentum from it.

The penetration of the main structure by the introduction – for which there is ample precedent in mainstream Classical and Romantic sonata forms – was something Shostakovich had tried out in op. 8. But this time the nature of the linkages yet again turns apparent weakness into strength. Cutting short the form-within-a-form of the first subject serves to question its stability, and this is compensated for, albeit in an anxious way, by the expansion between second subject and development. Here is a fine example of the symphonist's instinct for having the best of more than one world, with intriguing surface incongruities balanced out at a higher structural level.

The second subject itself is again sharply delineated by metre and character, but not this time by tempo. The Taneyevian soulful/heroic tone of the First Piano Trio has now been completely purged in favour of the Stravinskian ballerina. The theme's relation to the introduction is subtle and natural (via the nature of the accompaniment and of the extension to the theme, rather than of the theme itself).

The development section itself achieves a kind of primitive, though stunningly effective, synthesis by forcing the rhythmic scheme of the

Example 3.3a First Symphony, movement 1, introduction, definitive version

Example 3.3b Shostakovich's memory of Glazunov's correction

Example 3.3c Corrections in Shostakovich's piano draft

Example 3.3d First Symphony, movement 1, coda

feminine (*Petrushka*-ballerina-esque) second subject to conform to the masculine (quick march step) of the first. This, together with the plentiful augmentations and strettos, represents the consummation of the scherzo/ trio overlay in the later stages of op. 1 and the ruthless contrapuntal manipulations of opp. 2 and 3.

As with the first movement of Tchaikovsky's Fourth Symphony, the recapitulation of this F minor movement is in D minor and is extremely truncated, so that it feels dramatically still part of the development. Then there is a masterstroke. Having set up the same kind of reversed thematic recapitulation as in op. 8, with the first theme reserved for the coda, Shostakovich runs on into a secondary development-cum-coda extension: another classical procedure in principle, but with the additional virtue of compensating for the contraction of the main development section itself.

The second movement feints at G and D minors (the latter also bringing a feint at the main theme), before establishing its main key as A minor, a move that is also reflected in the theme's extension and is taken a stage further on the circle of fifths by placing the trio section in a modal E minor. The opening gesture guys, perhaps, the student composer's own overdeveloped reliance on imitation, making it into a joke at the double basses' expense. This joke is then turned into a structural *jeu d'esprit*, reinforcing the design by supplying not so much a binding element as an undercutting one. Such a ploy is far more subtle than anything in Shostakovich's preceding scherzos, although the piano obbligato writing comes directly from op. 7, again by way of *Petrushka*. Even the vamping harmony wises up. The nervy and brittle quality is as thoroughly imbued with the spirit of film as the first movement was with that of the puppet ballet. Even the trio section registers as a mock-pilgrims' march, of the kind that might at any moment reveal the face of a Charlie Chaplin or a Buster Keaton under the cowl (the latter being a Shostakovich favourite, along with Lilian Gish). At the high-point of this section comes a colossal orchestral sneeze. An important lesson is carried over from the op. 1 Scherzo, as the trio is notated in 3/4 but sounds closer to 4/4, facilitating its assimilation to that metre in the later stages (and how clearly it derives rhythmically from the 'Spring Rounds' in Part One of *The Rite of Spring*!) where the scherzo's main theme has to bend to the trio's Phrygian mode. Once again light mockery is enjoyed at the expense of mirror-form harmonies and canon, and the cello/bass joke is developed as the cellos defer to the basses' slowed-down equal-rhythm version of the theme, but the basses still cannot fit with it (or they mischievously decline to do so); both instrumental groups adapt, in other words, but in so doing they still fail to coincide, as in corny silent-film comic routines. For the return of the scherzo the bassoon adumbrates the theme, as it does at the opening of the finale of the Ninth Symphony and in the finale reprise of the Tenth.

Much is made by commentators of the apparent change of tone between the first two movements and the last two. Yet motivically there are strong connections, obviously in the relationship of the main theme to the first subject of the first movement, less obviously in the way the trumpet theme from 20 to 21 relates to the first movement's introduction (the trumpet opening, especially in the violins' version at 7). The broad shift from play to lament is arguably less symbolic of marionette to human, or masks to a genuine tone of voice, than of one marionette to another, or from masks to other masks, from Chaplin as a figure of fun to Chaplin as a figure of pathos.

In the slow movement the chromatic shifting harmonies are a natural outgrowth of the introduction to the op. 8 Piano Trio, though without the off-tonic opening. Where Shostakovich might have looked for a model is a

Example 3.4 First Symphony, slow movement, bars 6, 24–5

matter for speculation. The shifting harmonies are often said to come from Skryabin (though they are hardly ever traced to any specific work,[36] and they certainly have nothing to do with the static-ecstatic quality of Skryabin's orchestral Poems). In fact they are stylistically a lot closer to the slow movements of Bruckner's Seventh and Ninth Symphonies, and it may be recalled that Bruckner is named, albeit among the unfavourites, along with Skryabin, in the 1927 Questionnaire.[37] The rootedness of this passage in the tonic, with a highly directional bass-line, is even more like the Adagio from Mahler's Tenth, which it is possible, if unlikely, that Shostakovich could have encountered at this time, since the facsimile of this movement was first published in October 1924 and Ernst Křenek's versions of the first and third movements were performed at almost precisely the same time (his edition of the first movement, prepared that year, followed only in 1951, however). Though Mahler is already mentioned in the Questionnaire as a favourite,[38] this was an affinity that was yet to unfold its full potential. The fateful motif is subtly derived from the diminished octaves of the theme (Ex. 3.4), and the entire extension of this opening section is superbly crafted, both motivically and dramaturgically, instead of being left as a form-within-a-form, as was the case with the first subject in the first movement. In place of a return to the opening theme, the B section is Franckian in its chromatic improvisation, with an unmistakably funereal tread. The return to the A section is inspired, and the restatement itself is a minor masterpiece of adaptation in its short-circuiting of the progress of the A section and superposition of B section material.

The finale introduction again has to seek out the main theme and tonality, bridging the gap from the slow movement. As in the first movement, this introduction is a whistle-stop tour of non-resolved chromaticisms. Beethoven's 'Hammerklavier' Sonata, op. 106 – a piece Shostakovich knew well, having been encouraged by Yudina to add it to his repertoire – is the godfather of such finale introductions. Finally, the rising chromatic scale segment (subtly prepared in the slow movement) sparks off another galop theme, the piano acts as if it has never left the second movement behind, and there are more chromatic knottings-up and orchestral sneezes. Passages that might serve as crude transitions are brushed aside in the onrush, and a breakthrough theme is achieved, a structural ploy that adumbrates, as Eric Roseberry points out in Chapter 1, the finale of the Fifth Symphony, the more so since the new theme then proves to be the basis for a slow episode. The difference is that the theme in the First Symphony is itself an inversion of the slow movement's middle section, again revealing an overpowering urge to tie thematic threads together, even to demonstrate compositional virtuosity. A related urge produces a new wave of developmental combination, at whose peak there is a stretto by double augmentation (from $\boxed{34}$).

It is at this point that something has to be thought out that demands a more imaginative strategy than anything Shostakovich had devised in his earlier works, in order to ground the accumulated force both of the finale and of the symphony as a whole. Here the Fate theme is inverted, just as the funereal one was earlier in the finale (and now all the slow movement's themes have been so treated). The consequences are anything but grandiloquent, however. A kind of redemption is admittedly glimpsed at $\boxed{39}$, with a touch of late-Romantic harmonic richness, but then a reminiscence of the first movement's main theme is grafted onto the head-motif of the main finale theme to form a new entity, which is then laid under the second subject as the radically compressed recapitulation sprints for the finishing line. In textbook terms, the structural grounding may still be far from adequate. But Shostakovich is rewriting the rule-book rather than failing to observe it. In its laconicism his conclusion reflects the quick-wittedness with which the symphony had begun, and which was conspicuous by its absence from virtually any symphonic tradition he could have chosen to emulate. This closing strategy is far and away superior – both in its timing and in its reflection of long-term process – to the superficially similar, peremptory break-offs on the final pages of opp. 1, 6 and 8. The capacity to learn from oneself that this seems to represent may or not be the definitive mark of the genius, as Schoenberg contended in his thinly veiled self-vaunting formulation, quoted at the head of this chapter. But while the first three movements of Shostakovich's First Symphony are the culmination of a learning process that embraced both his teachers, a sizeable number of other role models, and his own music, in the finale it seems that self-reflection was indeed paramount.

For the sake of this chapter's main thrust – to illuminate Shostakovich's path to maturity as a composer – I have not followed a strictly chronological approach. Had I done so, the picture would have been one of constant zigzags, a restless alternation between different layers of creative work. That pattern would remain characteristic of his output, at times heightened, it might be thought, almost to the point of multiple personality disorder, were it not more plausibly diagnosable as a necessary coping strategy. Following the First Symphony, Shostakovich's career vacillated alarmingly. There was a short-lived but intense creative crisis, during which he later claimed to have destroyed a number of childhood scores; there was a frantic and almost as short-lived sowing of modernist wild oats in the First Piano Sonata, the piano *Aphorisms* and *The Nose*; there was a prolonged phase of work for stage and screen (described in the chapters in the present volume on theatre music, ballet, film scores and opera); and there was a gradual return to traditional forms and language via the First Piano Concerto, the Piano Preludes and the Cello Sonata, all of which pick up where the First Symphony left off so far as ambivalence of tone and permeability of emotional states are concerned. This prolific and unpredictable path was undoubtedly provoked by the artistic and political currents that seethed around him. But it was also prophesied by his artistic development as a teenager, when the dictates of personality and individual professional development were paramount.

4 Shostakovich's Second Piano Sonata: a composition recital in three styles

DAVID HAAS

Since composers in the Soviet Union were routinely urged to devote themselves to increasing the production levels for the officially sanctioned mass genres of patriotic cantata, opera and programmatic symphony, Shostakovich had little professional incentive to compose chamber and solo works. But as all artistic celebrities come to realize, inattention can spell relief and freedom for creativity and the artist's conscience. While it would be simplistic to claim that Shostakovich's smaller-scale compositions are more personal, more revelatory, let alone superior to his symphonies, it is nevertheless certain that most were written with a different kind of performance and performer in mind. Following a notable Russian precedent, Shostakovich routinely released new works of this sort that were not dedicated to the 'tsars, kings, and emperors' of the world, nor to his inescapable employer and patron – the Soviet State – but to individual musicians, living or dead, who had attained a level of artistry commensurate with the music's demands.

Leonid Nikolayev: pianist, composer, pedagogue

Shostakovich dedicated his Second Piano Sonata to a Conservatoire mentor whom he revered throughout his career: Leonid Vladimirovich Nikolayev (1878–1942). Begun in early 1943, just four months after Nikolayev's death in Tashkent, this sonata stands apart from later works dedicated to Rostropovich, Oistrakh and the Beethoven Quartet when they were quite active as performers. In style as well as the circumstance of its composition, the Second Sonata encourages a retrospective glance back to the 1920s, when Nikolayev was the renowned head of the Leningrad Conservatoire's piano faculty, Shostakovich was a precocious multi-talented student, and all of the musicians of post-revolutionary Russia were struggling to establish an identity for themselves and a relationship to the past, present and future. But before more specific questions can be posed, let alone meaningful responses given, it will be helpful to review Nikolayev's own musical background and achievements, his musical priorities and their effects on his musical progeny.

A native of Kiev, Nikolayev began his professional studies there, before transferring to the Moscow Conservatoire, from which he graduated in 1902. Biographical notices typically name Vasily Safonov as his major professor in piano and Mikhail Ippolitov-Ivanov as his primary composition teacher. Nikolayev also benefited from considerable contact with the multi-faceted musical mind of Sergey Taneyev, under whom he studied counterpoint, fugue and form. Upon graduating, Nikolayev was appointed to a teaching position at the Moscow Philharmonic School; in 1909 he then moved to the pre-revolutionary capital, St Petersburg, where he became a junior member of the Conservatoire's piano faculty. From then until the end of his life, Nikolayev allowed himself to be publicly recognized as concert pianist and piano pedagogue, thereby accepting the general assumption that composition was secondary to him. In other words, on the basis of comparable conservatoire training, Nikolayev chose a career trajectory that was the mirror image of his future student's.

In the belated Festschrift dedicated to Nikolayev that came about due to the persistent efforts of Shostakovich and other famous students can be found a considerable quantity of information about his secondary career.[1] An impressive list spanning the years 1886–1942 contains 144 original works, representing all the traditional genres. More noteworthy than the three-act *Manfred* opera (1890), the early-career cantata settings of Romantic poetry and the later ones on Soviet-sanctioned topics, the single Symphony in A minor (1901) and the single Piano Concerto in C minor (1900) are the four Scherzos for orchestra, the cluster of chamber works from the pre-revolutionary years, the run of independent fugues and a 'Fugue-nocturne' for piano. Among the works that earned Nikolayev recognition as a composer were the First Quartet in A major (revived by the Auer Quartet for a commemorative concert on 9 March 1942 during the Tashkent evacuation), the Second Quartet in D (completed in 1942, then performed at the March concert), and the Suite in B minor for Two Pianos (published by Jurgenson and popularized in the West by Alfred Cortot).

If the compositional side of Nikolayev's career can be surveyed through scores and work lists, assessing his pedagogy is more problematic, first because he rarely made public statements of much specificity, and, secondly, because his teaching produced players distinguished by markedly different temperament, tone and repertoire. It is hard to imagine what shared cardinal principles could have shaped such disparate careers as those of Mariya Yudina (1899–1970, a virtuoso of timbres and polyphony, renowned for her Bach, late Beethoven, Mozart, Berg and Stravinsky), Vladimir Sofronitsky (1901–61, a romantic poet of a player, specializing in Schubert, Chopin and Skryabin) and Alexander Kamensky (1900–52, a pioneer of the new music – Russian and foreign – of the 1920s).

Nevertheless, in an essay of 1935, Nikolayev identified six 'theses' that he considered fundamental to his pedagogy. Of greatest significance to young composers in the studio were his affirmations of the role of *intellect* (Thesis no. 6: 'Talent alone counts for little. Intellect and enormous effort are required in addition') and *individuality* (Thesis no. 4: 'The teacher should attempt to develop and expand [the student's] individuality, not permitting the student to rely on what has already been accomplished').[2] Thesis no. 5 charges the student to use his intellect to accomplish a specific task: 'In the handling of music, one must remember that a nuance is not merely an ornament; just as in conversational speech, it is not an ornamental, but an essential component of what is being communicated. The task of the performer is to *seek out the nuances that emerge from the musical content of the work*' (my italics).[3]

One especially important category of nuances was those that served as the building blocks of discrete musical styles. According to Lev Barenboim, a mature conception of historical styles was of paramount importance to Nikolayev, who included it in his idea of the 'basic grammar of piano playing'. Nikolayev's short list of essential styles ran as follows: 'Bach, the French claveçin composers, Mozart, Beethoven, Schumann, Chopin, Liszt, the impressionists, Russian composers and Soviet composers'.[4] On this basis, he envisioned a special course for performers on the elements of pianistic styles, taught not by the theory or history faculties, but by the piano pedagogues.

Even though a comprehensive knowledge of styles was held to be foundational, Nikolayev's intention was never to suppress the pupil's own individuality, but to incorporate this knowledge into the process of developing that voice. Reviews of Shostakovich's piano playing provide examples of how a performance of his own or another's music could be enhanced and individualized by a sophisticated knowledge and innovative (to a purist, anachronistic!) application of the elements of style. Nathan Perelman suggested that Shostakovich's Chopin was marked by the anti-Romantic and contrapuntal-linear trends of the 1920s:

> [Shostakovich's] Chopin playing didn't resemble anything I have heard before or since. … He never allowed himself the slightest hint of 'Chopinesque ' sentiment, and this in its own way had much charm … Shostakovich emphasized the linear aspect of music and was very precise in all the details of performance. He used little rubato in his playing, and it lacked extreme dynamic contrasts. It was an 'anti-sentimental' approach to playing, which showed incredible clarity of thought.[5]

Erik Tawaststjerna detected other discrete historical styles when he heard Shostakovich perform his Second Sonata in 1947:

> When Shostakovich began performing the figurations in the first
> movement, I remembered the descriptions of Mozart's murmuring
> *non legato*. The descending third of the main theme was interpreted by
> him with a restrained melancholy, the majestic octave theme being tinged
> with the colour of steel. … The melodic line [of the second movement]
> evolves in an endlessly subtle rubato. … In the recapitulation,
> Shostakovich reveals all of his pianistic brilliance to the fullest. With the
> melody being woven into cascading arpeggios, the sonority becomes
> absolutely impressionistic.[6]

Reviews such as these suggest that Shostakovich was not only capable
of assembling the elements necessary to mimic a particular style, but that
he could then apply them in a variety of contexts as a means of making
his interpretations distinct and memorable. At a time when the historio-
graphy of musical styles – Guido Adler's grand project – was still in its
infancy, when the six great style periods (of late twentieth-century par-
lance) had not even been labelled, let alone codified, when trafficking in
musical styles was entrusted primarily to concert artists, critics, dance
studio accompanists and cinema *illyustratori* – at such a time, Nikolayev's
pedagogy of style and Shostakovich's creative applications of it must
surely be deemed progressive.

In the absence of readily available textbooks of style, we must assume
that knowledge of it was acquired piecemeal, from encounters with individual works that had established themselves in the concert-hall canon:
in private study, in master classes, in the audience, and in front of an
audience. Since no ordinary researcher could seriously expect to match
wits with the quick ear and phenomenal memory of Shostakovich decades
after his death, he or she is obliged to seek for clues, both intrinsic and
extrinsic to the score. In the case of the Second Sonata, the dedication is
the first clue, but since Nikolayev is at issue, this creates a dilemma: Would
Shostakovich likely have been more interested in Nikolayev as composer
or as interpreter, or as teacher of interpreters … or of composers?

Setting forth on the first line of enquiry, I turned up two likely quotations from among published works by Nikolayev. The falling D–B third
that spawns the first subject of Shostakovich's first movement was used by
Nikolayev in the finale of his last instrumental work, the Second String
Quartet in D (1942), where it serves both as germinal motif and as
challenge to the tonic key (see Ex. 4.1).

The contour of the four-note (B, F sharp, B, E) motif that begins the
sonata's third movement theme and variations, resembles that of a motif
(B, F sharp, C sharp, F sharp) used in a counter-melody in the second
movement of Nikolayev's First Quartet in A (1901), which is also a theme
and variations (see Ex. 4.2).

Example 4.1 Nikolayev, Second String Quartet, finale

Example 4.2a Shostakovich, Second Piano Sonata, finale

Example 4.2b Nikolayev, First String Quartet, movement 2

There is a further equally striking parallel: both theme and variation movements begin with an unaccompanied statement of an extensive theme.

Although Shostakovich performed at least one Nikolayev work[7] and had perhaps read through others, without question teacher and student would have devoted considerably more time to discussing more familiar works of the concert repertoire. A sense of the young pianist's stylistic breadth can be gained from the programmes he chose for his graduation recitals. For the first of the requisite pair of recitals (on 28 June 1923), Shostakovich performed Bach's Prelude and Fugue in F sharp minor from Book One of *The Well-tempered Clavier*, Beethoven's 'Waldstein' Sonata, Mozart's Variations on 'Ah vous dirai-je, maman', Chopin's Third Ballade, Schumann's Humoresque, and Liszt's *Venezia e Napoli* (from the *Années de Pèlerinage*). For the second recital, Shostakovich fulfilled the concerto requirement by playing Schumann's A minor Concerto.[8]

Could Shostakovich have viewed the composition of the Second Sonata as an opportunity to demonstrate the extensive stylistic knowledge he had developed at his mentor's prompting? Anyone at all familiar with the work will likely suspect the presence of borrowed styles and idioms in each of the movements. The first movement contains a march, the next two feature waltzes, and the work as a whole presents a marvellous variety of textures, easily traced to four historical style periods. To go further than this, to name either specific composers or works as primary to understanding the sonata may seem a risky venture, since Shostakovich was always capable of combining *multiple* borrowings in a single work, none of which need be more significant than the others.

Difficult or not, I consider this line of enquiry to be necessary if we are serious about exploring why the Second Sonata resonates with so much piano music of the past. For this enterprise, the analysis of harmony, form or any other 'element' in isolation can contribute little. Neither would an unfocused collection and tallying of data for *several* elements be all that useful, even if dozens of works were similarly scrutinized. (Sophisticated comparative stylistic analysis differs categorically from market research!)

Instead I propose that the most direct approach to questions of stylistic influence is to compare a work, a movement, or a cluster of style traits within a movement with works of the past held to be exemplary of a particular keyboard composer or group of composers. The intent is not to prove that the examples selected by the analyst actually served as the chief model, but rather to demonstrate that a carefully chosen work can serve as a convenient touchstone for appreciating Shostakovich's style-combinatorial virtuosity. Should the rationale for the choice be questioned, then the most beneficial mode of challenge would be a counter-claim, in the form of a more representative example of another potentially germinal or contributory style that was unfairly ignored. If, on the other hand, the choice might be defensible in advance and subsequently revelatory, then a portal would have been found into a set of stylistic attributes that both this composer and his dedicatee believed to be essential components of the 'basic grammar' of musicianship.

A dark 'Waldstein'

It is not merely the first movement's key signature (of two sharps) that should inspire reflection about Shostakovich's referencing one or another style of the past, since so many Soviet composers and – if the truth be told – a significant number of composers in the West were also still writing in keys during the 1940s. Nor is Shostakovich's choice of B minor crucial, even though this key had previously been employed by Chopin, Strauss and Berg in their piano sonatas, as well as by Nikolayev in his Suite for Two Pianos, op. 13 (1908). Far more significant than these coincidences is the first movement's opening gesture: an unaccompanied ribbon of rapid scalar

Example 4.3 Second Piano Sonata, movement 1, opening

semiquavers, commencing in the soprano and dropping to the tenor range, where it changes into a standard arpeggiated accompaniment of the late eighteenth century (see Ex. 4.3). Evidence of this type is frequently offered up as sufficient grounds for labelling an instrumental work as neoclassical and gathering up all the other gestures and devices that are consistent with eighteenth-century norms. I believe, however, that a significant number of the first movement's defining traits are grounds for considering the possibility of an association with a more specific composer, style and work.

If that ribbon of notes initially calls to mind certain works of Mozart (such as the Sonata in F, K332), the broad dimensions and developmental coda suggest Beethoven far more strongly. Is there a particular sonata at issue? Leonid Gakkel cited the use of a prominent triadic motif with a dotted rhythm, together with the movement's unmistakable tragic tone, as grounds for naming Beethoven's 'Appassionata' as an influence.[9] Had Shostakovich realized his initial intention of composing a four-movement work that would conclude with a fugue, then the 'Hammerklavier' would unquestionably have been an inspiration. In order to posit a link from the B minor work that he *did* write, one must be prepared to look beyond the distinctions in key choice and the general contours of the themes and instead consider such factors as the grand proportions, the deep-seated harmonic and motivic interrelationships underlying thematic groups that contrast so sharply in affect, the presence of a substantial developmental coda, and the parallels between main and secondary key choices (i.e. from tonic B minor up to the *raised* major-mode mediant D sharp (=E flat)). When all of these factors are given their due, both the previously considered Beethoven sonatas are eclipsed by the 'Waldstein', a work that, as noted above, Shostakovich had included in his graduation recital and that Yudina had played in the 1920s and later recorded. Whether or not Shostakovich consciously chose this work as a touchstone for his B minor Sonata, it remains, to my mind, the best foil for appreciating a series of broad strategies and defining moments of the later work.

At the broadest level, the 'Waldstein' is linked to Shostakovich's Second Sonata by the quality of breathless momentum spanning the entire first theme group and the transition to the second. In the Beethoven, thirty-four bars of steady quavers then semiquavers (foregrounded to become a defining trait, described by Rosen as 'an energetic hardness, dissonant and yet curiously plain, expressive without richness'[10]) are broken only by a single fermata. In the Shostakovich, steady semiquaver motion persists until the last four bars of the transition. As Shostakovich's opening run completes its staggered descent, it outlines first-inversion triads from the keys of B minor, G minor, and E flat minor. Once the run subsides into an accompaniment, a leisurely first subject appears. Its head-motif (mentioned above as a probable Nikolayev allusion) is expanded into a fourteen-bar theme that is economically structured from a dotted rhythm, falling thirds and ascending scalar segments that can be heard as a development by inversion of a segment taken from the opening run.

While Shostakovich's *semplice* theme differs considerably in affect from the 'Waldstein' Sonata's opening phrases, the development of motifs and chromatic incursions within the former theme count as an affinity. More significant than the mere presence of chromaticism in each of the sonatas is its dual function: in each case the non-diatonic pitches chosen both enrich the harmonic content in the immediate context and establish a significant link to a key introduced later. While a harmonic reduction revealing semitonal voice-leading in Beethoven's Sonata can be used to explain away the pitches and triads that are foreign to C major, critical harmonic information is lost in the process, concerning specifically the first of a series of steps taken to prepare and justify the eventual modulation to E major. As it happens, the E minor run of the transition is slyly presaged by that scale's first five pitches, which appear in the melodic line, crowning the opening phrase's tonic-to-dominant progression. In Shostakovich's theme, the B flat that is first heard in bar 7 is not the only pitch introduced to move the key away from B minor, but it is the most prominent, most frequent, and most significant for the remainder of the movement. Moreover, the pitch sequence F sharp, G, A, B flat, first introduced (in reverse order) in bar 1, will travel from the first subject (bars 6–7) to the second (bars 63–5; 66–8), after appearing in the transition between the two. By the same token, Shostakovich's chromatic alterations to B minor and to the following transition can be seen as steps to prepare his modulation to E flat. Although that moment arrives with a shock, the key, salient pitches and prominent motifs have all been carefully prepared.

In both sonatas, the brusque endings of the transitions lead unexpectedly to second subjects with affects markedly distinct from all that has preceded them. While change of affect can produce effective contrast, contrast at the level of style can communicate jarring affective conflict.

Beethoven's simple homophony, minims-and-crotchets rhythmic profile and expressive marking of *dolce e ligato* constitute contrast of the former type: change of affect without a marked 'breach' of style. Nevertheless, the relaxation of pace and stabilization of dynamics provide a respite from the previously relentless intensity. Though scored in an equally simple homophony, Shostakovich's second subject has nothing to do with Beethoven or the eighteenth century, nor does it offer any degree of relief, once attention is given to all of its defining traits. With one exception, Russian writers have unfortunately placed too much emphasis on only one of those traits: the sounding of a sprightly melody in a major mode. Leonid Gakkel's reading differs because he rightly takes note of three additional factors: the crudity of the 'flute-and-drum' scoring, the key choice of E flat, which corresponds to that of the Seventh Symphony's 'invasion' episode (as well as to the coda of the *1812 Overture!*), and the subsequent 'struggle' between the first and second subjects in the recapitulation. As a result, his interpretation pointedly contradicts Delson's view of the theme as 'exceptionally radiant', Alekseyev's impressions of 'courageous qualities' and 'lyrical character', and Moshevich's labelling of it as a 'victorious E-flat theme'.[11] 'To be frank, with every fibre, we must protest against such a characterization. So sharply does the second theme contrast with the first that the imagination cannot help but escape the confines of the musical collisions and enter into the broad reality of life in the years 1942–43.'[12]

Whether or not one concurs with all of Gakkel's inference, the fact remains that Shostakovich here shows himself capable of maximizing contrast to such an extent that the traditionally positive associations attending a shift to a major key and a simpler texture do not register in the normal manner. Quite the reverse.

At the end of their respective expositions, both sonatas underscore the considerable amount of surface contrast and conflict between their two subjects with tightly integrated developmental strategies. How, then, can yet more conflict be generated and musical interest maintained in the development section proper? Beethoven relies on the typical procedures of his middle period: by developing thematic fragments in faster juxtaposition than in the exposition, by increasing the level of chromaticism and by avoiding tonic-reinforcing gestures. The *dolce* second theme is notably absent. All of these procedures are echoed in Shostakovich's Sonata, albeit deployed in a more attenuated texture that rarely attains four independent lines. Neither Beethoven nor Shostakovich allowed any key to be established for long in their development's opening sections, although G as a pitch centre emerges briefly in both (Beethoven: bars 95–9; Shostakovich: bars 155–60). Slightly after the midpoint, Shostakovich allows the key of B flat major to stabilize long enough for a brief reprise of a variant of the first subject, which is restored with both its lyrical character and 'eighteenth-century' accompaniment intact. The unusual key choice is surely another nod to Nikolayev, who resorted to that key at the centre of his B minor Piano Suite's first movement (at 6–8). The use of the sonata's opening run to introduce the passage gives it the character of a false reprise. After the expansive B flat section, both hands cooperate to establish G minor, as important motifs from the run and first subject return in non-imitative polyphonic counterpoint.

While Shostakovich's developmental material and procedures are all consistent with those of middle-period Beethoven, it could be argued that a full tally of keys and motif choices would show many more differences from than similarities with corresponding aspects of the 'Waldstein'. However, when focus is shifted to the employment of rhythm as an agent of long-range structure, significant parallels emerge. Briefly stated, Beethoven's attention to animation levels produces a compelling tripartite structure from a metrical standpoint: a progression of quaver and semi-quaver motion, to triplets, then semiquavers again. Shostakovich achieves the same goal of increasing the animation but through different means. In the first half of his *binary* organization scheme, the animation level is stalled at a crotchet pace, with the more rapid motion of the various recurring motifs unable to take hold for more than a few beats. The sudden shift is made in bar 140, when the semiquaver motion of the opening run is transferred, as at the beginning of the sonata, into the accompaniment. Semiquaver motion continues in the development for a total of thirty bars, as compared to fourteen in Beethoven. Hence, after a slower start, Shostakovich pointedly outstrips Beethoven in this respect.

Two correspondences between the respective retransitions bear mentioning. The first has to do with the relationship between tempo and animation level. If Shostakovich's exposition presented considerably more semiquaver motion, he nevertheless opted for a slower tempo (*Allegretto*, as opposed to Beethoven's *Allegro con brio*). Having attained something closer to Beethoven's tempo – with a jolt! – at the beginning of the second subject, he maintains it throughout the development. Therefore, when the semiquavers return for the second half, they must now be played at the speed of the 'Waldstein', a circumstance calling for Czerny-like dexterity in view of the greater difficulty of the passage work. The second correspondence involves a gradual ascent into the high treble range (f''' in Beethoven, $f\sharp'''$ in Shostakovich), from which point the respective lines plummet in scalar fashion, two octaves and more, down into the tenor range to launch the recapitulations.

Two strategies set Shostakovich's recapitulation on a different course from Beethoven's: first, the fragmentation of his lyrical first subject into segments, which are used to create two lines (bass and extreme soprano) in canon at the minim, then dotted minim displacement; and secondly, the restatement of the first subject, still in the tonic, in counterpoint with the second subject, still locked in its original key of E flat, resulting in the bitonal clash that Gakkel termed a 'struggle' between themes. By comparison, Beethoven's recapitulation appears more conventional, with the main novelties limited to a recomposed transition that does not lead back to the tonic and a second subject that is stated first in A major, before progressing – via a brief feint towards A minor – to the tonic C major.

If the most obvious justification for an extended coda be the existence of unfinished harmonic or thematic business, then the decisions to prolong these sonata movements make perfect sense. Equally obvious is the decision to pattern sections of the respective codas after their developments. As stated above, Beethoven finally restores his tonic C in the second theme group, but harmonic stability is weakened by a penultimate swerve towards the subdominant in bars 235–48. Thus the recapitulation ends as it began, with the establishment of C as tonic still contested. Beethoven then begins his coda with a brief pocket of motivic development and semitonal voice-leading within the lines, followed by some more extended 'white-key' passage work that is more diatonically conceived. After a cadenza-like run and extended half cadence, the second subject makes its final return (bars 284–94). Although the tonic now reigns unopposed, the diatonicism even here is not pure. Semitonal inflections involving the pitch G sharp (and its enharmonic twin) are final echoes of previous audacities, which now appear as early signs of the pervasive chromaticized C major that Beethoven invented for the 'Waldstein'.

Shostakovich's coda, no less than Beethoven's, both parallels the course of his development and concludes epigrammatically with a passage containing a pitch foreign to B minor conceived as a diatonic key. The main sections of his coda are a tonally unstable section of motivic development, a reprise of first-theme-group material with harmonic content pointing towards the relative major D, a reprise of the opening of the first subject in B minor, in the variant first heard in the development, and a final combination of the scalar run and motifs from the first subject.

What is the key of this fourth section? As in Beethoven, the preponderance of harmonic evidence points to the tonic. In tonal music it would be difficult to counteract the cumulative harmonic reinforcement of two pedal Bs and unconflicted first-beat Bs in one or both hands for nine bars in a row. Nevertheless the tonic is strongly challenged – much more than in Beethoven – by the accumulation of E flats and E flat triad arpeggiations appearing on the *third* beats of six of the nine bars. Whereas Beethoven's foreign pitch G sharp was ultimately reduced to a mere chromatic inflection in the melodic line, Shostakovich's E flats remain strong due to the metrical placement and repetitions. The penultimate bar holds the key to interpreting much that has gone before. The six pitches of the chord struck on the third beat consist of three Bs and three E flats (respelled as D sharps). Through the brevity, sharp accent, timbral crudity, and cross-relation (with the B minor thirds that frame it), Shostakovich reveals a darkly tragic poetic content: the garish quick-tempo march was more than a refreshing change of pace from the gentle lyricism of the first theme group. The conflict of key and affect that Shostakovich presented in his exposition is resistant to the final reconciliation that Beethoven achieved for his. The final bars reaffirm the grim message of the recapitulation: bitonal juxtaposition is a far cry from harmonious coexistence.

Second movement: shards of a waltz

The realization that the second movement Largo is, at root, a waltz in A flat of the simplest sort is hampered because the necessary musical clues emerge successively, not simultaneously. Furthermore, as new ones emerge, previous ones disappear. Meanwhile, the quite audible implementation of the centuries-old technique of canonic imitation (for the reprise of the main theme) and the less obvious but more pervasive manipulation of a three-note chromatic idea – a more modern technique redolent of the twin New Viennese values of motivic economy and developing variation – both vie for attention as they also obscure the waltz and contribute directly to the movement's high dissonance level. When further note is taken of Shostakovich's liberal use of legato lines, the indication *espressivo* and other expressive markings, one can reasonably conclude that this simple sentimental waltz returning in fragments and obscured by present-day complexities is a fitting musical record of a deeply personal loss and the struggle to retain the object lost in memory.

The ultimate point of origin of this movement's waltz couplets (see Ex. 4.4a) would be difficult to pinpoint, thanks to the combined effect of distortion, fragmentation and contrapuntal accretions. And even if something approximating a source phrase could be reconstructed, it might just as likely originate in a generic dance hall number as in a specific work of Lanner, Chopin, Tchaikovsky or the Strausses. On the other hand, certain of the compositional techniques can at least be traced to two earlier waltzes composed by Shostakovich. A two-beat ('oom-pah?') accompaniment suggesting a sarabande rhythm matched to a disjunct melodic line for flute create the second subject of the First Symphony's first movement (see Ex. 4b). Fragmentation was present there as well: three bars of bare accompaniment

Example 4.4a Second Piano Sonata, movement 2, opening

Example 4.4b First Symphony, movement 1, second subject

Example 4.4c Prelude, op. 34, no. 17

precede the theme and full triadic harmony is not maintained. The disassociated accompaniment in Prelude no. 17 of the op. 34 set is, by contrast, of the oom-pah-pah sort and triadic (see Ex. 4.4c). Here the main distortions occur in the metre (added beats, fermate, rubato, and eventually a brief 'recitative', whose slow tempo and equal note values remove it from the written metre) and in the eclectic assemblage of melodic phrases, featuring intra-phrase modulations hinting at distant keys, jagged contours, pianistic figurations, trills, and a keyless stretch of sevenths for the recitative.

With these precedents in mind, one is well prepared to reassemble the waltz of the sonata's second movement. Shostakovich allows a mere two bars for the establishment of the metre and a two-beat accompaniment, but he withholds both a full tonic triad and any dominant at all. The missing C of the tonic triad does not appear with the remaining notes until bar 12, by which point the periodicity and metric stability are lost. By the time the metre is restored, Shostakovich has also returned to his main theme, albeit with some pitches missing and the direction of the three prominent fourths reversed.

Phrase periodicity finally emerges within the trio section that begins at bar 45 (*Meno mosso*); meanwhile, short spans of bars at phrase beginnings establish C major through repeated chords in the bass as a harmonic point of departure. Though the conjunct intervals sound new, the initial G, F sharp, F motion is traceable to the movement's opening theme. (An inversion of the motif (C, C sharp, D) later accomplishes a modulation to D minor.) The strict canon that marks the onset of the reprise of the waltz also obscures it by forcing the expansion and truncation of the bar length and the splicing of the line with crotchet rests. For the remainder of the waltz, the changes occur mainly on the surface. The waltz ends with the barest of dominant-to-tonic gestures: the dominant pitch struck in the tenor range underscoring an odd whole-tone melodic descent is answered (after a gap in which the chromatic motif sounds one last time) by a tonic in the bass on the second beat of the penultimate bar and by an unharmonized alto-range tonic with octave doublings in the last.

Third movement: Schubert (and Nikolayev) made symphonic

The finale of the Second Sonata is launched with a monophonic melody, thirty bars long, in the soprano register. For the listener or critic accustomed to the thickly textured piano works of the years prior to the First World War (Rachmaninoff, Skryabin, early Prokofiev) or the typically dense linear counterpoint of the 1920s, there can be no talk of a 'rich' experience, let alone a 'symphonic' one. As before, the proper course towards an appreciation of this movement's specific anomalies is to speculate on precedents until a context emerges that can account for choices made.

With respect to the monophonic opening, the most obvious possibility of continuation proves incorrect (fortunately!): the opening theme is not destined to serve as a subject for a sprawling fugue, nor even for a more compact fugato, as for example in Schubert's 'Wanderer' Fantasy. If we extend the range of enquiry beyond the specific genre at hand (as is always necessary with Shostakovich), several alternative precedents leap out. The second movement of the First Quartet, op. 49 (1938) begins with an unaccompanied theme in the viola. The openings of that movement and the sonata's finale are quite likely the belated offspring of Nikolayev's own First Quartet in A major (1901): an Allegretto, in which the violin plays an unaccompanied theme of twenty-three bars, to be followed by seven variations.[13] A second reference to Nikolayev has to do with keys: the gradual establishment of B flat as a rival tonic, to which Yury Kholopov has drawn attention,[14] reflects both a key choice made in the first movement and, therefore, once again, to Nikolayev's Piano Suite in B Minor.

While Nikolayev's gambit of launching a variation set with a monophonic theme quite likely inspired the opening of Shostakovich's finale, the similarity ends there, since Nikolayev's seven variations soon enough betray the older composer's typical caution and conventionality with respect to key choices (never in doubt), form (authentic cadences and rests breaking up the movement) and character (restricted rather than expanded, due to the uninspired academic counterpoint of the inner voices).

When the course of the entire movement is taken into account, another work emerges as worthy of consideration: Schubert's Impromptu in C minor (D899, 1827). Though I have found no evidence that Shostakovich himself programmed this piece during his brief career as a performer of other people's music, Sofronitsky and Yudina both performed and recorded it, which constitutes a rare convergence of their generally disparate repertoires. The initial grounds for relevance are once again Schubert's monophonic presentation of a minor-key theme of the same character and in the same range. After playing through thirty bars of the impromptu, one may well claim to observe more differences than similarities: for example the call-and-response texture instead of pure monophony, greater periodicity, common-practice harmonic and a modulation only to the relative major of E flat. Yet if one can look beyond such predictable Classical or post-Classical traits, another set of characteristics emerges, with potentially greater appeal to Shostakovich's post-Romantic sensibility than what he would have seen in Nikolayev.

The most striking facet of Schubert's theme (see Ex. 4.5a) is the incipient chromatic bent, resulting from the B to C and D to E flat motion (perhaps not coincidentally, another precedent for the DSCH monogram!). Semitonal motion implants Schubert's unaccompanied lines with gravitations towards multiple goal tones, while postponing the definitive assignment of tonics and tonalities until accompanimental triads appear as harmonic reinforcement. While Shostakovich's melodic line (see Ex. 4.5b) exhibits considerably more intervallic variety, nearly all the phrases play upon semitonal motion in the pitch range B to E flat.

Throughout the remainder of Schubert's Impromptu (which takes the form of a small rondo), the repeated crotchets and semitonal inflections of the initial theme are utilized as linking devices to balance the contrasts in key, contour and character that emerge with the advent of new melodic material. Shostakovich's employment of theme and variations as the underlying structure of his finale would seem to impose limitations on the nature of his sectional contrasts. Yet as the movement unfolds, he not

Example 4.5a Schubert, Impromptu in C minor, D899

Example 4.5b Shostakovich, Second Piano Sonata, finale, opening

only provides variety in character and tempo but also departs considerably from the movement's tonic and the theme's melodic and rhythmic profile. The following commentary on Shostakovich's series of variations is offered as a case study of how a post-tonal composer born over a century later could commence in the compositional footsteps of Schubert and, in the end, produce a piece whose scope and audacity are worthy of comparison with the grander inventions of Beethoven.

For most of the movement, discrete variations can be grouped in pairs on the basis of a compositional technique. The technique that pairs the first two is centuries old and quite prevalent in Schubert: that of increasing the animation level of the accompaniment. Variation I is cast in an impoverished first species counterpoint, wherein the four sounding voices of the thickest passage are distinguished mainly by range and rhythm, but are not awarded the usual degree of melodic independence due to the use of pedal points and ostinati in lieu of competing melodic contours. In Variation II, continuous triplets animate the lone accompanimental voice, a staple technique of the post-Classical variation set, which Schubert introduces in his Impromptu to coincide with the appearance of a second theme. Shostakovich's application of the procedure is distinguished by a greater degree of contrapuntal dissonance and an accompanimental line that migrates from the soprano to the bass range.

Schubert was obviously forgotten for Variations III and IV. Both the key and the original succession of pitches are retained, but the melodic line is subjected to a pair of quasi-isorhythmic procedures that obliterate the theme's original metrical accents and strain the relationship between theme and metre. In Variation III, the theme, still in the tenor voice, is dissected into cells of three staccato quavers separated by quaver rest, with a note in the bass register placed, hocket-like, to fill the gaps. For Variation IV, the theme itself drops to the bass range, and all of the rests are removed. When the goal tones of the original theme are somehow emphasized (as in Yudina's memorably ferocious recording of 1960), the latent non-periodicity of the melodic line is brought to the fore, creating sharp metrical dissonance with the brusque accompanying chords that *do* conform to the printed metre.

At the beginning of Variation V the original *moderato* tempo is restored and the animation at the quaver level removed. The block chords that accompany the theme are both a carry-over of the previous variation and another point of comparison with Schubert, who had introduced them already in the second period of his Impromptu's theme. If Schubert used a subsequent string of block chords to interject chromaticism and the prospect of modulation, Shostakovich uses the accretion of chromatic (semitonal) inflections within the individual lines to intensify further the dissonance level. A new tempo of *Allegretto con moto* marks the beginning of Variation VI. A new key is introduced by means of a kind of harmonic pun, traceable to an internal phrase found in the theme of the movement. In bars 21–2, a tritonal transposition of the opening motif had been followed by a modulation to B flat. When the pitches in question (C, G, C, F) recur at the juncture between Variations V and VI, however, their purpose is not to prepare the internal phrase, but to launch the new variation (marked Allegretto) and the new metre (3/4) in the new key of F minor. With respect to genre, this variation brings yet another waltz into the sonata (the fastest yet). Curiously enough, by the time the presence of the waltz has registered (through newly periodic phrasing and harmonization in parallel sixths), the integrity of the theme has been compromised due to fragmentation and phrase repetitions.

The change from triple to duple metre signals the end of Variation VI and the beginning of a pair of extended variations (nos. VII and VIII) that, for different reasons, register as developmental. The first is structured as a strict canon at the diminished octave, in which four-note or two-note segments in dotted rhythm chase each other without pause and without overlapping. The rapidity, the fragmentation into motivic cells, and the chromaticism resulting from the interval of canonic imitation all coordinate to simulate a particularly intense development of the sort found in the Beethovenian first movement. In the next variation (no. VIII, marked *poco meno mosso*), the prescribed metrical slackening is enhanced due to the emergence of sustained octaves and chords in various registers, a tarrying over a nine-note segment of the theme (in inversion), and a motivic offshoot turned into an accompanimental ostinato. Underneath the broad phrases and the persistent ostinato, the pitch A resounds throughout most of the variation. Through these very means, which collectively could result in the celebrated 'heavenly lengths' in many a work, Schubert brought his Impromptu to a gentle close over the span of forty-five bars. In Shostakovich's case, however, what might seem to be a penultimate achievement of stasis leads not to a subdued final cadence, but proceeds, unexpectedly and without pause, into new musical terrain: to a grand Adagio (Variation IX), which serves as pinnacle to the work simultaneously capping off the progress of the work, while encouraging reflection over broader musical horizon.

Prior to my commentary on the Adagio 'movement', it will be beneficial to review the factors that ally the finale as a whole with the stylistically limited variation sets of Schubert and Nikolayev and those that already call to mind the more elaborate musical edifices of Beethoven. The first indicator of significant influence from the former type was the monophonic presentation of a long lyrical theme. For the first two variations, Shostakovich did not tamper with the slow metrical pace of the theme but instead animated the accompaniments. In the two 'isorhythmic' variations, nos. III and IV, there is little sense of Schubert beyond the obsessive rigidity of rhythmic patterns. The block chords of Variation V are Schubertian in their chromatic inflections but are carried to a dissonant extreme in Shostakovich. With the polyphonically scored waltz and the two subsequent developmental variations, however, Shostakovich moved the work closer to the more 'symphonic' conceptions of Beethoven (such as the Piano Variations, op. 35 and 120 and the finale to the Third Symphony). By relinquishing pitch centricity, the preservation of the theme's full length and contour, and the usual stratification of texture (melody, inner voice chordal figurations, bass), Shostakovich ventured beyond the conventions of the early nineteenth-century keyboard variation set. By the end of Variation IX, he will have transcended the limits of the medium as well.

As noted above, the potential parallel with Schubert suggested by the relaxation (expansion) of theme and slowing of pace in Variation VIII vanishes at the outset of Variation IX. The listener is right to suspect a Baroque reference when a double-dotted rhythmic gesture and semi-hemidemisemiquaver triplets appear to ornament the theme. The allusion, however, comes by way of Schumann, who used both features in Etude VIII of his *Symphonic Etudes*. In this way Shostakovich gains a double resonance. Of equal significance is the dramatic expansion of purely acoustic factors: for twenty-seven bars, a dynamic of *forte* or above is maintained, as six octaves of the keyboard are engaged. Altogether these factors create an unmistakable tragic culmination for both movement and work, as they awaken resonances with the passacaglias of *Lady Macbeth* and the Eighth Symphony.

The tension that accumulates from the Adagio's many powerful gestures demands a release. To produce it, Shostakovich responds to the implications drawn from a wide range of intertextual associations: Schubert, the earlier course of the movement and work, his symphonies, others' symphonies, and, in one way or another, some portion of the broader pantheon of tragic art. At bars 414–15, the dominant resolves, for the first time in a very long work, to the tonic major, which Shostakovich then sustains through the use of pedal points, ostinati, and long note values – until the impact of the unexpected brightening registers. The extended delay of tonic major – hardly coincidental – not only solidifies the impression of cyclic structural planning but also invites consideration in the context of numerous works in the Beethovenian tradition, most obviously his Fifth and Ninth Symphonies. Leonid Gakkel was justified in sensing a musical premonition of the hushed ending of the finale to Shostakovich's Eighth, to be completed later in the year.[15]

The belated yet unhurried revelation of tonic major in Variation IX represents a crossroads for the sonata's emotional trajectory, evoking resonances with penultimate junctures in Schubert's Impromptu, Tchaikovsky's Piano Trio (in which the tonic major had rather successfully supplanted the minor mode throughout much of the finale), and Shostakovich's as yet unwritten Second Piano Trio. What is the outcome to be?

After a short reminiscence of Variation V, Shostakovich provides his answer. By restoring the tonic minor, he pointedly rejects the Beethovenian *per aspera ad astra* aesthetic (to which Shostakovich's Eighth Symphony certainly cleaves) and follows instead the path of Schubert and Tchaikovsky. With the change of tempo to *moderato* (bar 446), the heavenly vistas just opened disappear and Shostakovich collapses the scale of the music: acoustically, stylistically and formally. Gone are the tonic major, the quasi-orchestral range and the grandeur of the preceding adagio. The reappearance of semiquavers in the accompaniment signifies a return to the medium of piano music, specifically to the conventions of the late eighteenth and early nineteenth century, which had been used so prominently in the first movement. For the final variation, the theme that was heard in soprano is now passed among all four conventionally singable ranges, before descending into a fifth: the contrabass register of Russian Orthodox choristers (and the final bars of Tchaikovsky's 'Pathétique' Symphony).

From a harmonic standpoint, the coda revisits the B–E flat polarity left unresolved at the end of the first movement; however, the roles are here reversed. In the last eleven bars, there are now five E flats and four Bs assigned to first beats. Strangely enough, the last full triad to sound has E flat, not B, as its root. When that chord's two E flats fall in parallel motion to Ds, the influence of this work-spanning irritant finally wanes, and the elegiac tone first suggested by the dedication can finally prevail unopposed.

At the end of many a Shostakovich work, it is a temptation for all in the audience – awestruck initiate, seasoned ticket-holder and cagey scholar alike – to ponder the issue of extra-musical meanings, personal and collective experiences, and the possibility of articulating a philosophical underpinning. In the Second Sonata, there is enough affective and stylistic variety, enough harrowing excess, enough stasis and peripeteia to launch a number of distinct, perhaps contradictory hermeneutic projects. The focus might be given to personal grief over the loss of an artist and friend, or to a nation whose recent past, present and foreseeable future in 1943 seemed inescapably defined by a culture of suffering, sacrifice and loss, regardless of whether Hitler, Hitler's SS and Wehrmacht, Stalin, the NKVD, death in general, or something else, or nothing at all be considered the source of the evil. At such moments, it bears reminding that Dmitry Shostakovich had acquired his characteristic reluctance to divulge specific extra-musical meanings long before the War and 1936. In the person of Leonid Nikolayev – a kindred spirit in this regard as well – verbal reticence was more than a personality trait. In his studio he not only discouraged the use of poetic imagery but was capable of satirizing it.[16] In this he remained loyal to an aesthetic tradition that Lev Barenboim has traced back through Taneyev to Taneyev's own teacher: tone poet Anton Rubinstein's more analytical and programme-*averse* brother Nikolay.[17] For such as these, the deepest riches of a musical work are inaccessible to metaphorical approximations, but are instead best appreciated upon the completion of a proper apprenticeship in other styles and other works.

5 'I took a simple little theme and developed it': Shostakovich's string concertos and sonatas

MALCOLM MACDONALD

The seven works to be considered here – Shostakovich's concertos and sonatas for violin and cello, and his sonata for viola – occupy a special place in his output. While the two Piano Concertos, despite their manifest differences in style and orientation, are essentially lightweight (if masterly) exercises in entertainment, the string concertos and sonatas all carry a very powerful expressive charge and speak to us with a distinctive eloquence. There is a sense in which they (the earliest-composed, the Cello Sonata, partly excepted) may be regarded as confessional works. The ability of the string soloists to sustain an immense melodic line, independent of the act of breathing, paradoxically lends their music a profoundly vocal quality, and whether their accompaniment is orchestra or piano, the opportunities for both dialogue and monologue are brilliantly exploited. Indeed all three sonatas possess 'concerto-like' elements, not least in the fact that they all contain 'cadenza-like' instrumental solos at crucial junctures of the argument.

Yet in these works' powerful emotional life what is 'confessional' is – perhaps even more than in Shostakovich's symphonies – far removed from any programmatic critique of external conditions. In so far as we seem to hear the composer's personal voice with a particular clarity, and in so far as that voice laments or protests, we may attribute such expressions to the political pressures and constraints that encompassed him. But the contrast of the individual against the collective is a condition of the concerto form itself, without necessary political implication. In Shostakovich's concertos and sonatas, as in most of his other works, the politically subversive and the directly critical are subordinate to the obligations that an artist feels to his materials and to the necessity to work out a large and taxing design with the highest exercise of craft and the accurate reporting of personal emotional truth. Above all, these are magnificently composed works of distinct and memorable expressive affect, which attempt to create something contemporary and authentic in venerable genres whose repertoires are already generously supplied with masterpieces.

Like Mozart, Shostakovich evolved a mature language in which not a note is wasted, and every note is exposed. Like Mozart too, he excelled at comedy and developed an essentially comic vocabulary as the basis for a style encompassing tragedy. The *opera buffa* elements in Mozart's concerto finales, and the more generally operatic gestures in their first and slow movements, have long been noted. Shostakovich was a somewhat similar case. With the First Symphony, the future composer of *New Babylon* and *The Nose* was already learning to turn the satirical elements in his musical personality – evident as early as the op. 5 *Three Fantastic Dances* and the op. 7 Scherzo – to heightened expressive effect. Here they are less obviously humorous and anecdotal than their ultimate sources in Stravinsky (and, perhaps, Prokofiev); they have been purified to a point where they could be made the basis of an ongoing argument. The *buffo* elements remain prominent in the first of all Shostakovich's concertos, the First Piano Concerto of 1933 (more correctly designated Concerto for Piano, Trumpet and Strings). But in the Sonata for Cello and Piano, op. 40, of one year later these have been rather effectively sublimated into something less obviously humorous and much more classically poised, and this signals the beginning of a process of stylistic retrenchment and osmosis that would soon make possible the apparently unified, developmental, highly expressive idiom of the Fifth Symphony.

The Cello Sonata: prophetic retrospection

The Cello Sonata has proved a durable addition to the recital repertoire, yet is seldom accorded the importance that it can be seen (retrospectively) to possess. The twenty-seven-year-old Shostakovich composed it in August and September 1934, in the aftermath of the premiere performances of *The Lady Macbeth of Mtsensk District*, around the time of the ballet *The Bright Stream* and just before he began work on the Fourth Symphony. Superficially, the sonata has little in common with any of these works, or indeed with anything much that Shostakovich had written before. Compared especially with *Lady Macbeth* and the Symphony – both in their different ways works of excess and extravagant emotion – its relative poise and economy seem isolated qualities indeed. For in this sonata his musical language has already been purged of everything inessential to its expressive point. On the one hand without any hint of experimentation, on the other devoid of that partiality for the grotesque which to a greater or lesser extent had marked nearly all his previous works, it is by some distance the most 'Classical' composition Shostakovich had so far essayed. It is, in fact, a harbinger of the composer's mature development, and especially of the Fifth Symphony, with which that period sets in. The Fifth's apparently sudden stylistic shift to a more immediately comprehensible and classicizing tonal language, often seen as a response to the *Pravda* denunciations of early 1936, is in fact fully anticipated in the Cello Sonata, which may therefore be taken as evidence that Shostakovich was already developing in this direction.

As is now well known, the sonata was written at a painful juncture in Shostakovich's personal life. He was in the midst of an affair with the translator Elena Konstantinovskaya; he and his wife Nina had decided on a temporary separation, she going on to Leningrad while he remained in Moscow, and the sonata was begun just after she left. Soon after he completed it Shostakovich asked Nina for a divorce, but in fact they were reunited in 1935. While these circumstances hardly explain the work's form, they may have something to do with its emotional directness and unashamedly lyrical stance.

Shostakovich dedicated the sonata to his long-time friend Viktor Kubatsky, cellist of the Stradivarius Quartet (and previously principal cello of the Bolshoy Theatre); they gave the first performance together in the Small Hall of the Leningrad Conservatoire on 25 December 1934 and subsequently toured as a duo, with a programme that also included the sonatas of Rachmaninoff and Grieg. The Rachmaninoff apart, there were very few notable Russian predecessors in the cello/piano genre, so it was perhaps inevitable that Shostakovich should avail himself of Classical models; and it is apparent that while writing the sonata he had Beethoven's sonatas very much in mind. The 'Classical' aspects extend far beyond the finely balanced four-movement structure,[1] to take in parallelisms and even aspects of melodic phraseology. On the other hand it is not fanciful to hear connections between this sonata and Shostakovich's First Piano Concerto, his most recent preceding instrumental work – not only in the humour of the second and fourth movements but also in the lyricism of the first and third, already partly adumbrated in the concerto's slow movement.

Yet the tune that opens the Allegro non troppo first movement (whose composition apparently took just two days) sounds neither like Beethoven nor, it must be said, particularly like Shostakovich himself.[2] It has such eloquent urbanity it might almost be by Fauré. With this melody the cello, accompanied by gently flowing piano arpeggios, dominates the proceedings from the outset. Nevertheless this is to prove a real 'duo sonata' with a prominent role for the piano. In fact, after helping to drive the first theme to an urgent climax, it begins the songfully lyrical second subject with its unusual tonal shift to B major. This theme, by contrast, may remind us of Rachmaninoff; but we should note as characteristic the emergence, under this tune, of a march-like ostinato that soon becomes a spiky rhythmic underpinning for the start of the development: another strategy that foreshadows the Fifth Symphony. March-rhythm and opening theme are heard together in the Largo coda, the most prophetic portion of the movement, where after the impressive fluency of invention that has prevailed up to this point, the pinched tone of the muted cello, against the piano's awkward octaves, suddenly looks forward forty years to the emotional no man's land of Shostakovich's Viola Sonata.

The A minor scherzo, which also anticipates that of the Fifth Symphony in several features (key being one of them), has the character of a perpetuum mobile that is also a wild oriental dance, opening with sinewy cello scales and giving the piano the eldritch main theme, which includes a repeated-note idea irresistibly prophetic of Khachaturyan's 'Sabre Dance' from *Gayaneh*. The cello switches to phosphorescent glissandi in harmonics as the setting for the gentler second theme, assigned again to the piano in octaves. As this theme (whose working-out corresponds to a trio section) is developed against triadic harmonies in the piano's left hand, the music begins to sound increasingly Beethovenian, or rather it adopts a Prokofievian 'Classicism' in which familiar gestures are set askew by sudden tonal swerves. It is a reminiscence of this passage that Shostakovich uses to bring the movement abruptly to a close after a return of the opening scherzo material.

A melancholic solo from muted cello, rising from the deepest register, begins the Largo slow movement; it seems to be searching for its theme, only finding it as the music settles into B minor and the three-note ostinato in the piano's left hand imparts a sinister hint of march-time to the rhythm. Altogether this sombrely passionate movement has a quality of raw emotion not admitted by the poise of the other three. The solo ascent from the start of the movement proves capable of development; the piano provides a quietly dissonant bell-like accompaniment and then takes up the big theme itself, high and icily *espressivo*, against restless cello figuration. The melancholic rising theme provides the coda, a desolate sound in what seems a wide and empty landscape.

The opening theme of the finale is the nearest the sonata has got to a Classical formula: one could imagine it as a variation-subject for Mozart or Beethoven. There are many such 'Classical' allusions in the movement; and after the cello's restatement (itself a variation) Shostakovich takes off in a *buffo* outburst of piano chords and cartwheeling cello triplet figuration. Returns of the theme are separated by contrasting episodes, mostly displaying a caustic wit, such as the contrapuntal galop that succeeds the first return; and, in the work's frankest, irreverent evocation of Beethoven, the piano embarks on a busily virtuosic cadenza in the manner of the famous 'Rage over a Lost Penny' Rondo, which had been the subject of deliberate quotation in the last-movement cadenza of the First Piano

Concerto. The cello joins in, but the piano's bravura is seemingly unstoppable until the cello takes over its buzzing semiquavers, freeing the pianist to return to the main theme with recovered aplomb. The coda is a charming quiet variation of it on the piano combined with guitar-style pizzicati from the cello, and a final cadence, caustically abrupt.

Sublimation of the comic to the elegiac

Despite its significance for Shostakovich's output, the Cello Sonata stands somewhat apart from the other works to be discussed here, which belong to the post-war world and appeared after Stalin's demise (though op. 77 was written during his last years); they represent a later stage in compositional evolution and they form a more homogeneous group, even sometimes seeming to explore common material, growing out of a nexus of characteristic motifs (labelled *a* to *q* in Ex. 5.1) that seem to mirror and reflect each other in different aspects in different works. Nevertheless the two earliest of these pieces – the First Violin Concerto and the First Cello Concerto – remain somewhat separate from the other four. Much more so than the Cello Sonata, they trace the development, and sublimation to increasingly elegiac ends, of the comic style.

The comic style – any comic style – depends not particularly on jokes but on the unexpected: surprises, reversals, incongruities, double-takes; and, of course, the timing of these things. While the string concertos and sonatas are not, on the whole, humorous works – rather the reverse – they manifest the sublimated comic style as fully as any other mature work of Shostakovich: and more graphically than most, in so far as the dialogue of contrasted forces, solo/accompaniment, affords such increased opportunities for argument and confrontation. Thus while their general discourse is just as concerned as are the symphonies with the ongoing development of thematic elements and the inevitable building of climaxes through long, coherent spans, there is a countervailing sardonic, sometimes even anarchic impulse that undercuts such processes, or sets them in relief, or in an alienated perspective.

An important aspect of this impulse – found throughout Shostakovich's oeuvre but with some special pungency (and poignancy) in the later concertos and sonatas – is his use of materials that seem a little alien to the habitual flow of his discourse: *objets trouvés*, so to speak. Two such radically different elder masters as Mahler and Stravinsky, both revered by Shostakovich, pioneered their own forms of this technique, and presumably provided suggestive guidance. By *objets trouvés* I do not merely mean quotation and allusion – Stalin's favourite Georgian folk song 'Suliko' in the First Cello Concerto, the street-vendor's cry 'Bubliki' in the Second, Beethoven's 'Moonlight' Sonata op. 27 no. 2 in the Viola Sonata and so on – but motivic entities that flit from work to work (DSCH and its derivatives) and particular motivic formulations that present themselves as impervious

Example 5.1 Motivic saliencies in Shostakovich's string concertos and sonatas

Example 5.1 (cont.)

Example 5.1 (cont.)

Viola Sonata, movt.1

to change, such as the twelve-note elements in the Violin Sonata (Shostakovich's rows, being coextensive with themes in a way they seldom are in Viennese School twelve-note method, have a pointedly self-contained, anti-developmental, solid-object quality). There is also the very physical impression created by certain instrumental protagonists – the horn in the First Cello Concerto, the tom-tom in the Second Violin Concerto – on which one metaphorically stubs one's toe. And what might more solidly and graphically qualify as a 'found object' than a thirty-year-old opera score (*The Gamblers*), long unseen by its composer, from which he was able to lift the materials for the scherzo of the Viola Sonata?

Violin Concerto no. 1: symphonic architecture

The First Violin Concerto is the least affected by these elements, and at first glance might seem to be as 'Classical' a piece as the Cello Sonata. It was composed between July 1947 and March 1948. By the time it was completed, the notorious *Zhdanovshchina* against 'Western-style formalism' in Soviet music had begun, and Shostakovich was under the darkest cloud of his career. He accordingly withheld the concerto – which he had intended to be his op. 77 – until 1955, when it was premiered by the dedicatee, David Oistrakh, in Leningrad on 29 October with the Leningrad Philharmonic Orchestra conducted by Yevgeny Mravinsky. It was published as his op. 99, only regaining its original (and chronologically correct) number many years later.

In all Shostakovich's string concertos the orchestral line-up has unorthodox features, usually displayed in a (carefully considered) reduction in the numbers of the brass. In the First Violin Concerto he calls only for four horns and tuba, the latter instrument lending much of the 'symphonic' sense of weight to certain tuttis, and otherwise functioning as a bass to the horns. 'Symphonic' is not a lightly chosen epithet in regard to this work. While in every bar a true concerto, the large-scale four-movement form, with passacaglia for slow movement, and the predominant seriousness of tone, align it with his symphonic output of recent years – with the significant exception of the short and 'lightweight' Ninth Symphony, to which the concerto seems to stand in possibly deliberate contrast, reaffirming the expansive profundity of the Eighth Symphony (and at the same time at certain points clearly anticipating the Tenth). In this respect it continues the expressive line of the comparably 'symphonic' Third String Quartet (1946).

Shostakovich's interest in passacaglia form had already produced such powerful examples as the tragic entr'acte between Scenes 4 and 5 of *The Lady Macbeth of Mtsensk District* and the fourth movements of the Eighth Symphony and Third Quartet. But in the First Violin Concerto the passacaglia is unmistakably the heart of the entire work and extends its influence forward and backward through the other movements. In any case the process of solo decoration over an orchestral bass is one highly amenable to the concerto genre.[3]

The main element which tells against a purely 'symphonic' interpretation of this concerto – and runs equally counter to Classical concerto form – is the absence of a true sonata first movement. Instead Shostakovich writes a 'Nocturne' with some sonata features but more obvious departures from any norm. This is a movement of singular refinement and intensity; no previous creation of Shostakovich is quite like it in its cataleptic, almost mystical calm. Instead of sonata-style contrast we have unanimity of themes in a noble, deeply thoughtful and intensely felt soliloquy. In spirit it seems to anticipate by nearly thirty years the exquisite ninth movement, 'Night', of the *Suite on Texts of Michelangelo Buonarroti*, which contrasts Giovanni

Strozzi's praise of the sculptor's statue of the figure of Night with his world-weary response: 'Sleep is dear to me; and still more being made of stone / When shame and crime are all around: / It is a relief not to feel, not to see.' These lines might well have summed up Shostakovich's mood at the height of the *Zhdanovshchina*.

The undulating line in broad dotted rhythms that rises and falls on low strings at the concerto's outset is less than a theme, but more than an accompaniment to the immensely long melodic line that the violin expounds: rather it is a kind of germinal ritornello, restlessly reshaped by the soloist. Though other instruments make their contributions, the first half of the movement is mostly an aria for the violin, the woodwind adding a kind of codetta. The sonorities are predominantly dark and brooding, the registers generally low; a change of colouring signals the movement's second half. When the violin re-enters, it is very high, muted and *pianissimo*, its line now elaborated into triplet figuration. There is an ecstatic moment at 13, *meno mosso*, when the tuba enters with a deep pedal far below the soloist (the instant quietly reinforced by timpani and tam-tam) while the celesta, which has already varied the ritornello in tandem with the harp, begins a plangently descending bell-like chime. Shostakovich often uses the celesta's distinctive sonority to signal a move to a new expressive level, but this moment of high and low *tessitura*, with a gaping void in the middle register, creates an unearthly quality rare in his work. The violin's restless triplets flower into a passage of deeply disturbing *fortissimo* polyphony: two of the several simultaneous lines here are in the solo part, in violin writing of great difficulty. The whole span seems to express pain and constriction, but eventually resolves onto the tonic D. The coda returns bleakly to the fretfully twisting triplets, spiralling up into the stratosphere while celesta with harp harmonics point fragilely to dissolution on a soft tam-tam stroke.

To the near-stasis of this remarkable first movement the scherzo poses a familiar Shostakovichian profile of capricious yet obsessive busyness and goblin energy. It is a kind of tarantella, its B flat minor pungently opposed to the first movement's A minor, whose humour runs a malicious gamut from sarcasm to savagery. The hectic main dance tune on woodwinds is elaborated from the motivic kernel (a) that the violin jabs at. This is the source of most of the movement's themes, though general shape is more important to Shostakovich than precise pitch or note order. Before long it gives birth to a four-note figure in the woodwind, taken up by the violin in fiercely proclamatory octaves: a figure with which we are now very familiar. For though it never appears at its 'autograph' pitch, this new element (b) approximates to Shostakovich's famous DSCH monogram, foreshadowing its first overt use in his Tenth Symphony. Further development in 2/4 time leads to a raucous, raffish peasant dance in G, a kind of demonic Gopak, but clearly derived directly from (a). This forms the scherzo's central episode – one can hardly call it a trio. The violin is scarcely silent throughout the movement, but careers on in a sustained display of hard-driven virtuosity to the explosive bravura of the coda.

Gravity of mood, and the specific gravity of deliberate pace and profound emotion, are restored by the Andante slow movement, a passacaglia in F minor on an extended seventeen-bar theme. The theme itself is principally an elaboration of a three-pitch (but four-note) motif (c). This majestic and impassioned movement manifests a noble purity of language. There are nine variations in all, the statement of the theme on cellos and basses being in effect the first of these, as horns and timpani already provide a stern counterpoint notable for its fanfare-like triplet rhythms. The theme passes from player to player, featuring different orchestral choirs, while the violin and other instruments weave expressive and progressively more eloquent counter-melodies around and above it. Wide-ranging arpeggios over a pedal F in low strings and timpani lead into the cadenza, one of the longest and most elaborate in the concerto repertoire.

In fact in this concerto (as also the First Cello Concerto written over a decade later) the cadenza assumes an importance quite beyond that which it has in a Classical concerto scheme. Shostakovich's treatment of the cadenza may indeed count as his principal innovation in concerto form. In the Classical and Romantic three-movement design the principal cadenza almost invariably occurs towards the end of the first movement, usually prefacing the coda.[4] But in Shostakovich's four-movement concertos the cadenza in both cases prefaces the finale, forming a structural link from the slow movement.[5] It thus becomes a decisive stage in the overall form of the work. While it performs the time-honoured function of displaying the soloist's virtuosity to the utmost level, it is largely devoid of mere decoration. It also, as is customary, recapitulates and develops previously heard themes; but since it is placed so late in the evolution of the design, the materials it has to work upon are numerous, and the cadenza becomes a substantial structure with an overall shape and several contrasted spans. Moreover, it may adumbrate elements yet to be heard in the concluding movement – certainly the First Violin Concerto's cadenza exposes at least one of the themes of the ensuing finale. Beginning on D in the third movement's funereal triplet rhythm, and including a transposed foreshadowing of the DSCH motif and the scherzo's Gopak, it works round, with an impression of effort and constructive power, from D minor to the dominant of A, the work's home key, in which the finale begins.

The finale itself, which Shostakovich entitled 'Burlesque', is comparatively short, with similarities of mood and texture to the scherzo. It too exploits a Russian dance character, one reminiscent of the finale of Tchaikovsky's Violin Concerto, though more hectic and defiant. Though the feeling is implicitly of A major, Shostakovich at first leaves the confirming major third unsounded and it is only really in the final bars that the major mode is explicitly embraced. Before then, the passacaglia has made its presence felt again, only to be neutralized and co-opted into the general bustle. Just before the coda the entire passacaglia theme is heard, acerbic, brittle and hilarious on woodwind and xylophone; and the violin then kick-starts the coda with a burlesque version of that same theme (see Ex. 5.1c). The theme's final appearance is in the headlong, tumultuous closing bars: (c) only, but in grand augmentation on horn.

This 'triumphant' ending (perhaps the epithet is best left in quotes, to acknowledge the movement's ambiguities) allows us, in retrospect, to see the Violin Concerto as conforming in its own way to the 'heroic' pattern of post-Beethovenian symphonism: the pattern of minor-key striving and sorrow resolved at last in a joyous and confident finale. A structural cliché – and, for that very reason, capable of infinite variation in the right hands – this was the pattern adopted by Tchaikovsky, in for example his Fifth Symphony, and the formula much beloved of Soviet musical orthodoxy in the Stalin years. Shostakovich's personal adaptation of the design tended to involve a slow or moderately paced first movement rather than a sonata allegro, and so it is here: in a sense the whole concerto embodies a struggle against stasis, negativity, despair. Despite its extreme beauty, the first movement's frozen, numbed calm is close kin to black depression; the second movement's cruel mockery is in the tradition of a *scherzo diabolico* and Death as a fiddle-player that runs from Tartini to Mahler's Fourth Symphony. These are forces enough to contend with, and the passacaglia, for all its constructive power, has the funereal ring of 'the hero borne to his grave' familiar from the 'Eroica' to Mahler's Fifth. It is in the way things are worked out in the cadenza – one has a mental image of the violinist/hero, abandoned by his accompaniment/mourners, raising himself up out of the grave by sheer will-power – that earns the qualified triumph of the finale.

Cello Concerto no. 1: the hunted soloist

A minor is not traditionally a heroic key, though it is powerfully associated with the 'negative heroism' of Mahler's Sixth Symphony. The classic key for heroism is the E flat major of Beethoven's 'Eroica', and this is the tonality of Shostakovich's next major solo string work, the First Cello

Concerto. But before that, Shostakovich's Ninth Symphony had shown that he tended instead to find an earthy, humorous quality in it: evidently he considered E flat major to be a good tonality for mockery and rude gestures. There is something of that in the Cello Concerto: as in the Symphony, the musical ideas have an intensely physical, even theatrical quality. The humour as such is pretty acerbic, but it is certainly possible, especially in the first movement and finale, to see how the music has evolved from what could be called a comedic style. There is a sense of following the protagonists in a stage dialogue, and to facilitate this Shostakovich promotes one instrument – the horn – to the status of a subsidiary soloist, an obbligato interloper who claims a part of our attention. Such attention-seeking behaviour within the constraints of a solo-accompaniment genre usually has a humorous effect: think of the over-eager trombone in Nielsen's Flute Concerto, or the raffish trumpet in Shostakovich's own First Piano Concerto (and of the trombone's disconcerting contributions to the first movement of the Ninth Symphony). But in the Cello Concerto the stentorian horn sometimes seems like a voice of conscience, calling the cello stubbornly back to the principal topic of argument.

The work was composed in 1959 for Mstislav Rostropovich, who premiered it in Leningrad on 4 October of that year with the Leningrad Philharmonic Orchestra under Mravinsky. Apparently Shostakovich was spurred to write it not only out of admiration for Rostropovich but also from his esteem for another work dedicated to the great cellist, the Symphony-Concerto of Prokofiev. In fact Shostakovich's concerto was soon referred to in the Soviet press as a 'symphony with obbligato cello', in acknowledgement of its concentrated thematic writing. Unlike the Prokofiev, which is in three movements with a central scherzo, Shostakovich's concerto is laid out on a four-movement plan superficially similar to that of the First Violin Concerto, but in this case it is a four-movement work *manqué*, in so far as the third movement is the cadenza, which occurs at the analogous place – bridging the gap between slow movement and finale – to the Violin Concerto (whose cadenza is no shorter and merited no separate numbering). Compared to the Prokofiev, the work manages to be both terser and more extrovert in expression. And whereas Prokofiev employed a full symphony orchestra, Shostakovich's orchestra is small – a carefully chosen ensemble of woodwind, a single horn, timpani, celesta and strings. As already noted, the horn has an especially important role, promoted on occasion to the status of co-soloist, a sonorous, breathy extension of the cello.

In this, his second major work for cello, Shostakovich projects a mood very different from the poise of the Cello Sonata. In the outer movements especially, the agile, voluble soloist seems constantly on the run – pursued and harried, rather than supported, by the orchestra. The cello seems engaged at all such times in a struggle to assert and maintain its individual voice: the task is not made any easier by competition from the horn. But cello and orchestra (sometimes, it seems, cello, horn and orchestra) are united in an ongoing and strenuous process of motivic development. Shostakovich's reported comment apropos the concerto – 'I took a simple little theme and tried to develop it'[6] – though in one sense a flippant, throwaway piece of misdirection, is entirely relevant to the way this strain of musical argument proceeds, and can be taken in a wider sense to describe some of the underlying processes of all the works described in this chapter.

The first movement (Allegretto) has tremendous rhythmic drive: it is largely concerned with a pithy four-note theme (d) announced at the outset by the solo cello – a theme rhythmically related to Shostakovich's favourite anacrusic deployment use of his DSCH monogram, which itself feigns to make an appearance in various guises. The orchestral accompaniment is at first for wind instruments alone, the mood being both pawky and determined. Timpani and sniggering woodwind introduce the second subject, an impassioned, high-lying melody based on a chant-like figure (e). This idea is very similar to the tune in 'Trepak' from Musorgsky's *Songs and Dances of Death*, where Death invites the wandering, drink-sodden peasant, worn out by work and sorrow, to dance the eponymous dance. If Shostakovich intended a deliberate reference to this tune – and we know that an even more oblique allusion to a different tune is embedded in the finale – that may help account for the intermittent feeling of a *danse macabre* both in this movement and the last. The solo horn only enters later, taking up the four-note theme (d). The entire impression conveyed by the movement is taut and urgent, a *tour de force* of epigrammatic concision; at the end a return of the 'Trepak' second subject is only hinted at before the brusque closing bars.

By extreme contrast, the following Moderato, a slow movement in all but tempo marking, is a point of rest, even exhaustion, after this manic activity. Set, as mentioned, in A minor, a tritone away from the first movement's E flat, it begins with an almost mystical refrain on the strings, suggestive of a sarabande. Its main melody – which could well be considered a close variant of the first movement's 'Trepak' theme (see e) – is instilled with the spirit of Russian folk song in its quiet melancholy. The horn remains prominent as a kind of 'subsidiary soloist'; but now its function is to provide romantic calls to which the cello responds with melody. And the cello has the last word, in an eerily beautiful transformation of the movement's main theme into high, plangent harmonics accompanied by the celesta, here making its sole appearance in the work.

The ensuing brilliant and extended unaccompanied cadenza is here accorded the status of an entire movement in its own right.[7] Bridging the gap between slow movement and finale, it starts by ruminating on the previous movement's themes but becomes progressively faster and more strenuous, full of hair-raising challenges to the soloist's technique, not least in its allusions to scalic figures from the First Piano Sonata. At its peak the finale (Allegro con moto) bursts out in a spirit of rather malevolent folk-burlesque, with a raucous, hurdy-gurdy-like woodwind theme. At the end of this theme, both at its first statement and later when the cello takes it up, is a brief, apparently related figure (f): Shostakovich pointed out to Rostropovich that this is in fact a reference (tart and sarcastic, in contrast to its sentimental original) to the Georgian folk song 'Suliko', notorious as Stalin's favourite tune.[8] Whatever ironic or satirical purpose it serves here – and it recurs in a variety of contexts and scorings – the figure immediately gives birth to the movement's second main subject, another headlong tune suggestive of a chase. The movement keeps up a parade of boisterous yet increasingly frenzied ideas, the pulse changing to 3/8 and introducing a sinewy tune in fast waltz time. The sharp-eared may detect the four-note theme (d) of the first movement folded into this melodic line. The horn engages the cello in baleful counterpoint, and the first phrase of the second theme shrieks stubbornly in high clarinets, a Mahlerian ostinato. At the climax of this passage, (d) reannounces itself with a vengeance, recalling the music to the mood and pace of the concerto's opening, with the figure proclaimed *ff espressivo* by the horn in a near-verbatim reprise of its initial first-movement appearance. Thereafter first-movement material combines with the folk-burlesque theme and the most dazzling display of solo pyrotechnics in the entire score, driving to a curt, splintered ending. There is no sense of exhilaration, as there is at the end of the Violin Concerto; but there is certainly one of finality, painful or otherwise.

The late sonatas and concertos: shared concerns

The three compositions so far discussed are all cast in four movements (though the third movement of the Cello Concerto, being the cadenza, is a kind of movement *manqué*: Shostakovich would not feel it necessary to separate off a cadenza in this way again). The remaining four works – the Second Cello Concerto, op. 126, Second Violin Concerto, op. 129, the Violin Sonata, op. 134 and the Viola Sonata, op. 147 – are all in three movements, which is a sign of their greater concision, although apart from op. 129 the disposition of the movements bears no relation to the Classical archetype. Opp. 126, 134 and 147 all place the scherzo at the middle of the scheme; their first movements are slow or moderately paced; and the two sonatas conclude with a very slow finale, lasting approximately as long or longer than the other two movements combined. In all three works, the expressive trajectory closes out the possibility of or justification for a fast fourth movement; each of their finales conveys a sense of farewell, of epilogue, of energy and perhaps hope running down. Formal parallels might be sought in Mahler (above all the Ninth Symphony) and Tchaikovsky (the 'Pathétique'); but if Shostakovich was thinking of any specific models, at least for the general outlines of his works, the late Beethoven sonatas, perhaps especially opp. 109 and 111, are most likely candidates.

Cello Concerto no. 2: obliqueness as style

The Second Cello Concerto was begun in the spring of 1966 in Moscow and finished during April at the Oreanda Sanatorium, Yalta, in the Crimea, where Shostakovich had gone for treatment of the heart condition that was slowly undermining his health.[9] This work too was dedicated to Rostropovich, who had already proved himself a peerless interpreter of its predecessor. Rostropovich was the soloist in the premiere, given at the Great Hall of Moscow Conservatoire with the USSR Symphony Orchestra conducted by Yevgeny Svetlanov on 25 September 1966 – Shostakovich's sixtieth birthday. Ten days later Rostropovich introduced the new work to the UK at the Royal Festival Hall, with the BBC Symphony Orchestra conducted by Colin Davis.

Critical reaction in the UK was, at that time, fairly muted. Whereas the First Cello Concerto was already popular as a spiky, pithy, extrovert modern concerto, the Second perhaps marks the beginning of Shostakovich's 'late style': oblique, intimate, elegiac, filled with painful radiance, bizarre humour, nostalgia and regret. In all this it anticipates his next major utterance, the *Seven Verses of Alexander Blok* (dedicated to Rostropovich's wife, Galina Vishnevskaya, and featuring substantial roles for Rostropovich's cello and Oistrakh's violin). It has taken many years for the manifold beauties of this remarkable concerto, so powerfully and personally expressive, to be valued at their true worth. The scoring is for a curiously balanced orchestra of double woodwind (though with a third bassoon or double-bassoon), two horns, timpani, harp, strings and a fairly large and colourful body of percussion. Its three-movement shape alluded to above, with the scherzo placed at the centre of the scheme, more strongly recalls the Prokofiev Symphony-Concerto than the design of the First Concerto. Also it was one of two pieces – the other being the sardonic *Preface to the Complete Collection of My Works* – that Shostakovich said he had written as a sixtieth birthday present to himself, which suggests that the music contains particular personal resonances and, like the *Preface*, takes a critical stance towards life.

This concerto is generally described as being in G, though the first movement has an almost stronger D minor feel to it. It grows out of the lowest register of cello and low strings, a desolate music whose principal motif (g) is centred around a lamenting, drooping semitone interval. As the melodic line rises, harp and upper strings impart a cold, wintry colouring to it. A subsidiary theme involves a three-way dialogue between cello, horn and harp. The tempo seems to speed up (the pulse remains the same but with quicker note values) in an unexpectedly bright, mechanical texture for woodwind, xylophone and harp, something like the sound of a clock mechanism. The cello part becomes more capricious and virtuosic and soon takes the lead in the fun. But this is an increasingly grim sort of fun, building to a climax that is brutally cut short by the impact of a bass drum, which then engages in grotesque dialogue with the cello. The coda passes various elements of the movement in curtailed review, the bassoons croaking like frogs. The horn, muted, winds the gloomy falling semitone to end the movement.

The scherzo, in F sharp, follows the familiar Shostakovichian pattern of a pawky, sardonic folk dance, with flamboyant glissandi from the cello and throwaway rhythmic quips. It is fascinating to learn that the principal subject of the movement (h) is based on a folk song from Odessa that was popular in the 1920s: 'Bubliki, kupite bubliki' (Bubliki, buy my bubliki), the *bublik* being a type of bread roll in the shape of a ring, akin to a bagel.[10] The tune had apparently been on Shostakovich's mind some months before he wrote this movement. It also fits with his liking for using Jewish-style melodic material, as for example in the Second Piano Trio, Fourth String Quartet and the song cycle *From Jewish Folk Poetry*.

Even on its initial appearance there is something both defiant and wheedling about the tune, and as the movement proceeds the mood becomes increasingly saturnine and wild, with pungent interjections from horns, timpani and bassoons. This darkening tendency climaxes – it is actually the seamless start of the finale – in a baleful fanfare for the two horns against a militaristic side-drum roll that introduces the main cadenza of the work. This is more recapitulatory than in the previous two concertos: the cello reviews all the material against a continuous shake on the tambourine. As the keening semitone returns in more sustained melodic writing, we find ourselves already embarked on a finale that contrasts an ambling, lyrical tune, accompanied by harp, against a more rhythmic, scurrying music in which the cello is partnered by percussion and pizzicato strings. The horn fanfare also returns as another element. But time and again the music is punctuated by a sighing, falling figure (i) that suggests infinite nostalgia.

An angry cello solo with side drum brings back the fanfare as a wrathful tutti outburst that suddenly breaks into the scherzo's 'Bubliki' theme, grown enormous and transformed into a baleful, frenzied dance. This cuts off to leave the cello sounding the fanfare in solo double-stopping, from where the music winds down to a long coda of regret and long-drawn-out farewell, a Mahlerian *ewig* (eternally), even recalling the concerto's opening theme against meditative strings and harp before another 'clock mechanism' starts up again in the percussion, finally dissipating into silence against the cello's low, long-sustained D. This kind of ending – other examples are the second movement of the Fourth Symphony and the finale of the Fifteenth – seems to symbolize for Shostakovich both the heedless passage of time and the extinction of the individual life. Thus it does not seem improper to guess that the Second Cello Concerto is one of the various late works in which he seems to foresee his own death.

Violin Concerto no. 2: dancing on the abyss

Only a year separates the Second Cello Concerto from the Second Violin Concerto, op. 129, in C sharp minor, composed rapidly in May 1967 and dedicated, like the First, to Oistrakh. Shostakovich intended the work as a sixtieth-birthday gift to the great violinist, but he was a year out in his calculations: Oistrakh was only fifty-nine in 1967. He duly gave the unofficial premieres – on 13 and 26 September in Bolshevo and at the Great Hall, Moscow Conservatoire, respectively – with the Moscow Philhamonic under Kirill Kondrashin; and also the official premiere in Moscow on 26 October.

In some respects the Second Violin Concerto is more intimate in expression and also more orthodox in form than the First, and when it appeared it was viewed in the West – like the Second Cello Concerto – as a comparative disappointment. Appreciation of this bleak and subtle work has been slow to grow. Certainly of all the string concertos it has, outwardly, the most conventional three-movement shape: a moderate-paced first movement with an Allegro feel to much of it is followed by a deeply lyrical Adagio whose tempo persists for a few bars of recitative-like preparation, linking into a superficially skittish and lively Allegro finale. The main cadenza (there is a shorter one in the first movement, preceding the recapitulation) occurs about two-thirds of the way through this concluding movement, here having an orthodox summing-up function. But beneath its surface (and openly, in the Adagio) the entire work is suffused by the profoundly elegiac tone that assumed ever greater prominence in Shostakovich's last years; even the most vivacious passages communicate a curious sense of dancing on the edge of an abyss.

Once again the orchestra is restricted in order to produce an individual colour palette: double woodwind (but with piccolo and double bassoon), four horns, strings and, apart from the timpani, a single percussion instrument – the tom-tom, which adds a hollow, surreal edge to a part that might more conventionally have been assigned to a side drum, not least in the several passages in the work that have a somewhat 'military' flavour. The principal key is C sharp minor – an unusual one for a violin concerto, but one with illustrious Beethovenian associations.

Above an uneasy quaver figure in the low strings, almost as if the cellos and basses were muttering in their sleep, the violin enters with the first movement's principal subject, which springs from a typically inward-turned motif (j) narrowly spanning the interval of a fourth that the cellos and basses have delineated. This motif, which might be regarded as a reluctant expansion of the DSCH monogram, resounds almost continually throughout the movement. There is a sense of self-referential monologue about these opening moments, the intervals gradually opening out as the soloist ascends to higher registers, there to take over and develop the quaver figure as the woodwind and strings take over the evolution of the main line. Percussive pizzicato writing for the strings and barking dactylic rhythms in the violin power an increasingly angry transition.

A new section begins, *più mosso*, with a double idea: an incisive motif in flute and piccolo, while the dactylic rhythms broaden into a new snatch of tune (k). Played off against a disarmingly melodic canon between piccolo and violin, the tune develops, with some help from the horns, into a kind of strutting 'recruiting dance' (the hint of the first movement of Bartók's *Contrasts* may or may not be purely coincidental). The development section grows grotesque in a dialogue of violin and bassoons, then increasingly sinister with the entrance of the tom-tom, with its heavy, hollow resonance. To its grim jocularity Shostakovich adds other elements of almost Stravinskian discontinuity: a fierce and plangent woodwind tune, like a folk song from *Les Noces*, and a further self-reference in the citation of the four-note kernel (d) of the First Cello Concerto, literal except for transposition. Every motif mentioned so far is pressed into service to create the movement's climactic paragraph, while the cadenza takes the place of a formal recapitulation by recreating the movement's opening as two-part counterpoint on the solo violin. When the orchestra strikes in again, violin in dialogue with horn, we are embarked on what feels like an extended coda, and eventually the music is liquidated down to the (k) motif's nagging dactyls in violin and tom-tom.

The violin begins the central Adagio (pitched a tritone away from the first movement, in G minor) with an uneasily flowing cantilena over a chromatically moving bass. A flute counterpoint immediately alludes to the first movement's figure (j), and the violin takes it up in inversion, so that the shape rises, with some attempt at aspiration, instead of its habitual downward droop. But though this carries the soloist to a higher register, the music loses itself in withdrawn meditation; the opening cantilena sounds now in the bass. The soloist's musings high above it issue at length in a wide-spanned E minor melody of exquisite simplicity and refinement, accompanied only by strings. Its wide open intervals (fourths, mainly) bring a sense of cool fresh air to the proceedings, but uneasy semitonal movement is increasingly felt in the accompaniment, taken over by paired bassoons and oboes. The music subsides to a timpani roll, over which the violin plays a biting triple-stopped figure, closely related to (j). This provokes a brief, angry cadenza-like flurry, a gypsy moment that becomes a lamenting theme over tremolo strings and proves a lead-back to a much-varied reprise of the opening materials. The violin now has what was the flute theme, chilled by eerie glissandi in the violas.

As the soloist falls silent, a horn takes up the movement's opening cantilena, turning it into a kind of 'Last Post' (with hymnic string harmony), in D flat. Its last notes are stopped to create a ghostly echo. This links straight into the finale, where the violin initiates proceedings with voluble solo recitative, then swaps three-note semitonal quips with the four horns, muted, in unison. The D flat of the end of the Adagio persists, and indeed throughout the movement this is how Shostakovich respells the tonic C sharp. The three-note figure proves to be the basis for the main subject of the rondo finale, a vivacious but slippery *Allegro* tune in mainly dactylic rhythm, whose capacity for generating humour is continually undercut by its tricksy chromaticism. Allied to it is an epigrammatic woodwind figure, descending through a fourth that could be considered a reformulation of (j) from the beginning of the work. In its *scherzando* character and somewhat edgy élan, the movement is clearly closer to the model of a high-spirited concerto finale than that of the First Cello Concerto. Within that overall conception, Shostakovich alludes in the episodes to a number of first-movement elements: not by direct quotation or resumption of their development, but – as with the woodwind figure, which becomes increasingly important – by generating fresh melodic materials with strong mutual similarities, either in intervallic content, in texture or in rhythm. Thus a duet between horn and pizzicato violin at 77 prompts memories of the 'recruiting dance' theme, while high rhythmic violin writing against emphatic oboes and clarinets (85) parallels the first movement's '*Noces*-folk' episode.

The music's fleet-footed progress is increasingly disrupted by battering attacks of the three-note figure in winds, timpani and tom-tom, and at the end of a big tutti these prompt the return of the violin's initial recitative as the lead-in to the work's principal cadenza. Possibly the most difficult of all Shostakovich's concerto cadenzas, this is at least as full of substance and expressive contrasts as its predecessors. An *espressivo* counterpoint from oboes and clarinets in unison provides the lead-back to the *Allegro* character and, at length, to a substantial coda in which – as in the First Cello Concerto – the soloist is subjected to a sustained battering from the disruptive three-note figure, but all ends in a certain acrid unanimity.

Violin Sonata: radical bleakness

In some respects the Violin Sonata, op. 134, which Shostakovich composed from August to October 1968 and dedicated to Oistrakh on his sixtieth birthday (thus rectifying his error of the previous year) suggests a continuation of the argument of the Second Violin Concerto, though with new elements, notably the twelve-note row so prominent in the first movement. Oistrakh first played the work at a private audition for the Union of Soviet Composers on 8 January 1969, the pianist being the composer Mieczysław Weinberg.[11] The public premiere followed at the Moscow Conservatoire on 3 May; on this occasion Oistrakh was partnered by Sviatoslav Richter.

Shostakovich originally gave the three movements the titles: 'Pastorale', 'Allegro furioso' and 'Variations on a Theme', but he withdrew these to leave the bare tempo markings Andante, Allegretto, and Largo – Andante. Notwithstanding reports that the first movement is based on a sketch dated June 1945 (whose eventual publication in the *New Collected Works* should either confirm or scotch the notion), the music throughout is utterly characteristic of his bare and essentialized late style, and it is difficult to see how even some of the basic material – the twelve-note row and its thematic derivatives, for example – could have been conceived a quarter-century earlier.[12] Even if Shostakovich was returning to a long-abandoned project, he completed it in a manner wholly concomitant with his compositional concerns at the end of the 1960s. On all levels, this is one of his most uncompromising works; gaunt to its very marrow, but laid out on an ample scale, two very large movements enclosing a substantial central scherzo. (There is a hint, in this formal plan, of Beethoven's *Sonata quasi una fantasia*, op. 27 no. 2. Both the late string sonatas, like the Cello Sonata, make significant references to Beethoven, both formal and symbolic.)

The brooding first movement turns out to be full of subtle echoes of the Second Violin Concerto, but generally recalled in a more fragmented context.

This is a bleaker conception than the Concerto, more radical but also more obsessive in its processes. Its many beauties illuminate a mood of elegy and frustration. The piano's stealthy, wide-stepping twelve-note theme ascends and descends in bare two-octave unisons over almost the entire range of the keyboard. The rise and fall seems to describe an expressive arc of aspiration and decline, hope and despair. Fourths – perfect, diminished and augmented – are almost a trademark of Shostakovich's personal idiom, but this row places them – the tritone most of all – squarely at the core of the sonata's thematic essence; the anapaestic rhythm of the second bar will also engender much of the sonata's material.

This 'row-theme' is illustrated in Ex. 5.1 at its second, verbatim statement (which will be followed by another, and then an augmented version: the procedure immediately hints at the passacaglia principle that the finale will embrace). True to his practice in other works, Shostakovich is much more interested in its identity as a theme than in its unifying essence as a row. It can be seen from (l) that the violin's first entry, with a counter-theme in conjunct motion, is, virtually, an explicit statement of the DSCH motif.

The row-theme, on its many appearances, is seldom transposed, thus functioning as a kind of 'solid object' within the argument. But it prompts the growth of other melodic lines: these are not its retrogrades or inversions but more generally mimic its shape and encompass the twelve notes, in other orders, with as little note-repetition as Shostakovich allows himself in it. The piano maintains its stark octaves for a considerable time, but the violin continues with keening, dissonant double-stopping.

When it arrives, the contrasting material makes a kind of second subject. This has a more diatonic feeling, and supplies the only possible 'pastoral' associations in the movement. The open fourths and the anapaest rhythm – prone now to collect a second or third 'long' – seem about to break into the Second Violin Concerto's 'recruiting dance', but prove instead to be the starting point for a different reminiscence (m). The almost perky ascending idea reminds us of the opening theme of Shostakovich's Fourth Symphony, and in fact seems designed to. The development section works with all these elements, until an eloquent chorale-like episode and a *forte* restatement of the row-theme – at its original pitch, in the piano's left hand against nebulous right-hand harmony – lead into a mysterious and miasmic *tranquillo* of violin arabesques descending from high to low against deep, resonant chords and plangent, chorale-like harmonies. Trills, alternating a fourth apart, emerge on the piano. The row-theme is left behind and it is this trill motif, becoming increasingly sinister as the violin takes it over *sul ponticello*, that comes to dominate the fragmented coda, along with the 'recruiting dance' rhythm, now (see m) in the guise of two quavers plus four crotchets.

A form of this rhythmic figure, turned into a motif (m(ii)), is the obsessive motor of the ensuing scherzo. There is nothing gentle, and not much that is witty, about this deceptively marked Allegretto: the original Allegro furioso describes it better. This is one of the most strenuous movements in the whole of Shostakovich's chamber music, a furiously athletic toccata for the two instruments with rather the character of a moto perpetuo. The mood parallels that of the 'Malagueña' of the Fourteenth Symphony. Just as there is no relaxation, there is nothing resembling a trio section; rather the movement, in an implied E flat minor, opts for the approximately ternary shape of a vestigial sonata form, with two principal subjects, of which the second (announced by *fortissimo* repeated chords in pizzicato violin and piano in 3/4 metre) is a kind of brutal, hard-edged waltz-serenade. Twelve-note formulations with prominent fourths abound, especially in the piano part, though the first movement's row-theme plays no explicit role.

The finale begins with a grim dotted-rhythm fanfare in the piano, itself a twelve-note succession that foreshadows the bleak fanfares of the *Suite on Texts of Michelangelo Buonarroti*, op. 145 and once again gives prominence to fourths, both perfect and augmented. The fourth is equally central to the theme that now emerges pizzicato on the violin. This eleven-bar idea, which encompasses eleven of the twelve chromatic pitches but with sufficient repetitions to make it sound securely tonal, is the subject of the extended and grimly majestic passacaglia, which occupies most of the movement.

Chaconne and passacaglia, used as large-scale instrumental forms, generally impress by their demonstration of cumulative constructive power (as in Bach's D minor Chaconne – which seems to be invoked occasionally here – Brahms's Fourth Symphony and Shostakovich's own First Violin Concerto). So, on one level, does this one. But there is also the possibility to express, through the unwavering recurrences of the ground, barrenness and constriction: the imprisonment of the constructive impulse, rather than its liberation.

The variation process proceeds in two similarly set-up large spans, progressing from bare two-part textures to fuller harmonies and simultaneously diminishing note values in order to create a sense of increasing activity. The fanfare's dotted rhythms are briefly drawn into the process, and the first span subsides with some pastoral writing that lightens the mood. When the second span begins (at 68, the subject once again pizzicato) the violin soon produces a warmly expressive counter-theme in high register. But development becomes increasingly strenuous, with a sense of sustained effort that rises eventually to a violent cadenza-like solo from the piano. We may remember the 'Rage over a Lost Penny' moment in the finale of the Cello Sonata, but this is an infinitely darker and more painful outburst; and it serves to introduce a furious solo from the violin, *fff* in coruscating tremolo writing, transforming the counter-theme into a protest. As it builds in intensity, the piano re-enters with the fanfare, and together they sweep to the movement's climax, the violin proclaiming the passacaglia theme in sonorous triple-stopping.

Sombrely flowing development of the counter-theme dissolves what remains of the variation process. The coda harks back to the ending of the first movement, recalling verbatim its spectral violin arabesque passage. Then, with a parenthetic reminiscence of the fanfaring fourths in the piano, it repeats the first movement's closing bars (also based on fourths, but with trills that chill to the bone) almost literally, with some slight intensification of effect. We can understand the gesture as a 'cyclic' return, binding the sonata more closely into an expressive unity. But in thus abandoning the passacaglia process in favour of a reprise of previous material, Shostakovich seems to have despaired of the attempt to provide a resolution of the work's expressive conflicts. A circle is closed – the rising fourth which was the work's very first gesture is mirrored in the falling one which is its last – but so, it seems, are the gates that might offer a way out of frustration and melancholy. There is no escape, and the violin's last stertorous tremolandi, *sul ponticello*, sound eerily like a death-rattle.

Viola Sonata: radical retrospection

The possibility, at least, of expressive resolution was reserved for Shostakovich's final work for a solo string instrument, the Sonata for Viola and Piano, op. 147. Composed from April to July 1975, it was, in fact, the last music that Shostakovich completed. Like the Violin Sonata, this too, and in the profoundest sense, is a 'Sonata quasi una Fantasia'. All three movements – an 'Aria' marked *Moderato*, a central scherzo and a concluding Adagio – end with the performance direction *morendo* ('dying away'), though it is probably misleading to think of the work as a whole as a deliberate gesture of farewell. Shostakovich had known for years that his crippling heart condition and now cancer were slowly killing him, and the sense of pain and valediction runs through all his late works – as well as defiance, a sardonic humour, and a constant concern for moments of beauty. If the work *is* to be considered a farewell, however, it is but one farewell in a long series; as long as he remained alive the compositional urge seems to have persisted in him, and if he had been granted some more months, perhaps there would have been more music (there were rumours, shortly after his death, of a projected Sixteenth Symphony).

He lived long enough to correct the proofs of the Viola Sonata in his hospital bed, four days before his death. The work is dedicated to Fyodor Druzhinin, who had been the violist of the Beethoven Quartet since 1966 and was a long-time friend of Shostakovich. Shostakovich consulted Druzhinin on technical points while completing the sonata. Druzhinin, with the pianist Mikhail Muntyan, played the sonata for the first time in a private performance at Shostakovich's home on 25 September 1975, which would have been the composer's sixty-ninth birthday. Among other remarks, Shostakovich had told Druzhinin that the first movement should be considered a 'novella' and that he intended the concluding Adagio as a homage to Beethoven. Though in essence a late work, the Viola Sonata contains some music earlier than anything discussed in this chapter apart from the Cello Sonata, making it something of a *Rückblick* to distant times.

As befits such a late utterance, the musical texture is spare and austere, refined down to essentials. Shostakovich's characterization of the first movement as a 'novella' seems to imply a certain narrative quality, which can certainly be sensed behind the formal paragraphs. The music begins with a repeated, almost indifferent, pizzicato phrase (n) in fifths for unaccompanied viola, which will recur at various parts of the movement, sometimes almost like an out-of-tune guitar. The first 'de-tuning' of the phrase's blank C major (see (n)) is the substitution of D flat for the bottom C, and when the piano enters at the fifth bar there is a momentary feeling of bitonality, for the suggestion is again of D flat. The viola is continually forced back to the 'impersonal' pizzicato pattern, however. The instrument's open strings tend naturally to formations in fifths, swiftly to be inverted to fourths; gradually other pitches are introduced by semitonal inflection, and from these skeletal beginnings most of the sonata's material is generated. The piano's right hand exploits the fourth at once, in melancholic fanfare and carillon. The fourth – this time more often perfect rather than augmented – is the Viola Sonata's key interval: that and the semitone, which allows stealthy stepwise movement and contradiction of tonal implication, the agent of tonal instability and the search for the next tone on which to rest, in a process as fluid and potentially endless as any Bachian Chromatic Invention. The main material unfolds in uneasy lyric style, the viola's sometimes melancholic, sometimes passionate melodic line contrasted with plangent double-stopping and supported by a slow-moving piano accompaniment. Melody and harmony are drawn out, stretched thin and sere by the bare textures.

The first movement has a kind of sonata-form outline, with a slightly more lyrical C sharp-ish tune for second subject starting at [4] and a chorale-like fragment in the piano for codetta. An extensive and passionate development, whose triplet rhythms hint at waltz-time, appears to be altogether quicker, though there is no specified tempo change and the impression of rapid motion is entirely a product of shorter note values (unless, of course, the performers change the pulse, as some do), which eventually settle and slow upon an oscillating fourth, a near-featureless figure we could regard as a slowed-down version of the Violin Sonata's expiring trills. It signals a 'recapitulation' transfigured by spectral *sul ponticello* tremolo writing in the viola and thoroughly infiltrated by motivic material from the development. This leads to an unaccompanied 'cadenza' for the viola, which evolves a triplet figure (o) that corresponds to nothing so far heard but looks towards the coda of the entire work. Then the chorale-fragment returns to preface the driest possible ending, the viola's pizzicato against hollow staccato octave jabs from the piano.

The sardonic grotesquerie and manic energy of the ensuing scherzo may remind us of an earlier Shostakovich, and rightly so. He noted on the manuscript a line of Pushkin: 'The work of long-ago days'. In fact for the substance of this movement he went back to the unfinished opera, *The Gamblers*, a setting of a comedy by Nikolay Gogol, which he had abandoned in 1942 after several months of work. The fragment of *The Gamblers* has since been performed and recorded, but in 1975 this operatic torso (it consists of nearly fifty minutes of music) was entirely unknown – Shostakovich had given the manuscript to his former close friend and pupil Galina Ustvolskaya, but he requested its return from her in 1974. By adapting his thirty-year-old score into the Viola Sonata Shostakovich may or may not have intended to allude to the story of *The Gamblers* – a gallery of cheats and liars – as such, but he may well be paying a last private homage to the wit and irreverence of Gogol, one of his favourite writers and, for him, a characteristically Russian genius.

The sonata's scherzo thus begins with an arrangement of the opera's short overture and continues (at a slower pace, with strummed viola chords and a broad tune) with part of the ensuing scene, in which one of the main characters, arriving with his manservant at an inn, extravagantly praises his packs of cards ('They represent real capital! It's something one can bequeath to one's children!'). This passage – remarkable for its writing for viola and piano both in their lowest registers, the piano returning to the nagging semitone oscillation – functions as a kind of trio; Shostakovich completes the form with a varied repeat of the scherzo music, and a quiet coda, in which the piano's bass appears to quote the fugue subject of the twenty-fourth and last of the op. 87 Preludes and Fugues, that links directly into the finale.

The movement jolts us by its radically different manner – not so much the sardonic humour as the sheer brilliance of its address and sure-footed continuity from idea to idea, which makes an almost shocking contrast with what may seem to be the outer movements' painful groping for the next note, where the music is almost palpably feeling its way step by step. The contrast extends even to the look of the page. The minutely phrased and accented music of the scherzo, so scrupulously annotated with staccato dots, *sforzato* wedges and so on, in the manner of a younger Shostakovich, does indeed appear to have strayed from a different piece to sit between the outer movements, whose text is in many places so deliberately – provocatively – nude of definition or inflexion, as if these things scarcely mattered any more to a composer for whom meaning was now entirely entrusted to his brute material of tones and the intervals between them. There is, however, one inserted passage, forming the transition from the trio to the reprise of the scherzo, which serves to bind the scherzo more tightly into the sonata's overall scheme. This sequence of falling fourths (p), so apt for purposes of lament, comes into its own in the finale.

Indeed this sequence is the basis of the viola monologue with which the finale opens, along with references to the first movement's second subject and the strummed chordal figure of the scherzo, making this prefatory string solo a brief summation of the work so far, before it embarks on the finale proper. The ensuing Adagio – the sonata's longest and most substantial movement, beginning like the first with the viola unaccompanied – is imbued with a spirit of homage. Yet the composer told Druzhinin that, though in this finale he wished to honour Beethoven, 'don't let that inhibit you. The music is bright, bright and clear.'[13] Unlike the finale of the Violin Sonata, this movement is not a strict design but a kind of elegiac fantasia on a number of evocative elements. Evidently Beethoven was much in Shostakovich's thoughts towards the end of his life: the last number of the *Suite on Texts of Michelangelo Buonarotti*, written the previous year, is based on a toy-like transformation of the finale theme of Beethoven's Fifth Symphony.[14] Now, with the entry of the piano, the music recalls – not exactly, but unmistakably – the opening theme of Beethoven's Piano Sonata in C sharp minor, op. 27 no. 2 (the 'Moonlight'). Shostakovich does this (q) by isolating two elements that are fused in Beethoven: the sequence of rising arpeggios, like slowly spreading ripples across the surface of a lake, and the tolling dotted rhythm that is the head-motif of Beethoven's theme and which, transferred to the viola, gives the impression of painful, stuttering attempts at speech.

Through a combination of passionate soliloquy, wandering piano figuration, gravely meditative double-stopping and dramatic chordal writing for the viola, Shostakovich conjures up a unique spiritual landscape.

Accruing emotional gravity as it progresses, in its central span the movement arrives at an extraordinary passage of intense lyricism ($^1\boxed{70}$–$\boxed{73}$). Not at first sight or hearing much different from the music so far encountered in this finale, the apparent plasticity and freedom of the viola's line at this point has been shown to encompass a grand roster of achievement: motifs from the first movements of Shostakovich's Symphonies 1–12 are explicitly quoted, in numerical order, with the piano's bass supplying motifs from nos. 13–15 once the viola has lapsed into its semitonal oscillations.[15] Not only is this passage a *ne plus ultra* of Shostakovich's powers of using short motifs to generate musical meaning, but despite its meditative tone it is clearly penned with pride: perhaps a Shostakovichian equivalent, emptied of all hubris, of 'The Hero's Works of Peace' in *Ein Heldenleben*. It motivates a long solo for the viola, developing the all-important sequence of perfect fourths: a last 'cadenza' that builds to a monumental climax and then gradually winds down, over a development of the semitonal figure (o) in the piano's deep bass, to a painful but intensely lyrical recapitulation of the 'Moonlight' theme, which fragments and eventually gives way to the falling fourths from the movement's outset. In a sepulchrally tender coda the elements of light and dark (the C–D flat opposition, and the emptily oscillating fourths, evoking the op. 6 two-piano Suite dedicated to Shostakovich's father), reach some kind of resolution on the viola's final, long-held C. This is marked *morendo* – dying away – as are the endings of the other two movements (and the first and last movements of the Violin Sonata, for that matter) and the silence that succeeds it did indeed prove to be final. Yet the Viola Sonata's finale has a spiritual quality and an astonishing, serene fluidity of thought and motivic content that make it a fitting full stop to almost sixty years of continuous creativity.

I observed above that the Viola Sonata was not necessarily intended as Shostakovich's last work – but he was realistic enough about his health to have known that it might well turn out to be just that, and the 'hidden' tapestry of symphony quotations, awaiting only the right pair of ears to hear them, certainly has the character less of a testimony than a testament. Doubtless, also, he chose its genre with care. And a moment's thought suggests that apart from the wish to write a piece for Druzhinin this was a very unusual genre to select. In fact as a genre the viola sonata hardly existed in Russian music, for Glinka's unfinished sonata and the two then unpublished and unknown examples by Roslavets are unlikely to have been present to Shostakovich's mind. What drew him to a medium whose most stalwart practitioners were Brahms, Hindemith and, perhaps, Ernest Bloch? To some extent, his choice must have been determined by the instrumental timbre, the peculiarly vocal qualities of the viola. That instrument may lack the clarion soprano bite and sweetness of the violin, or the cello's rich warm tenor-bass-baritone, passionate and melancholy. Yet perhaps even more than those more glamorous instruments it evokes a querulous, lamenting, stressed yet defiant speaking voice – a voice, moreover, that can sometimes assume the rasping edge of the lifelong chain-smoker.

Shostakovich was a pianist, not a string player. Yet he clearly valued above all that vocal quality in string instruments that allowed them to stand as surrogates for the composer's personal voice, in quartet, concerto or sonata, evoking public debate or private soliloquy. These confessions without words were conceived with some of the Soviet Union's most eloquent exponents in mind; they continue to present challenges to technique, rhetorical power and nerve, and to live on in the playing of all those violinists, violists and cellists who themselves have something to say. Here, if anywhere in Shostakovich's output, we really do seem to discover his innermost feelings; and in giving them voice he was able to speak for all who experienced the most tragic years of the twentieth century.

PART II

Music for stage and screen

6 Shostakovich and the theatre

GERARD McBURNEY

In the first twenty years of his career, Shostakovich wrote a dozen incidental scores for the theatre. In length and variety they represent a substantial part of his output, yet they are surprisingly little known. There are practical and historical explanations for their neglect, but also good reasons why they are worth looking at. In the first place, Shostakovich's early theatrical experience was in so many ways the key to his rapidly evolving artistic character and technique. By contrast with his music of later years, his output through to the first half of the 1930s was overwhelmingly dominated by drama of different kinds, including two full-length operas, a third uncompleted opera, three full-length ballets, a score for the live accompaniment of a silent movie, three or four of his finest sound-movie scores, an unfinished musical comedy, a full-length show for the music hall and his first six sets of incidental music. As the conductor Gennady Rozhdestvensky has observed, for Shostakovich at this time the theatre was a 'laboratory' in which he could experiment and develop his skills in an abundance of ways. If these incidental scores do not have the mastery and finish of the operas or the brilliance and span of the ballets, they still reveal much about what went on in that laboratory. Writing at speed and usually under harsh conditions, he was forced to invent weird vocal and instrumental combinations, to set sometimes preposterously improbable texts and, more generally, to hone his quickfire ability to solve dramatic and creative problems thrown in his way not by the demands of his own imagination, but by the day-to-day requirements of those in charge of the productions he was working on.

We can also find many fascinating links between these little-known incidental scores and the more familiar masterpieces of the same period. The incidental music of 1931–2, in particular, has an especially close relationship with his hugely successful second opera *The Lady Macbeth of Mtsensk District*, op. 29, 1930–2), composed in parallel with it. The theatre scores of this time frequently leak into the opera or, alternatively, parasitize it. In the process they illuminate Shostakovich's distinctive methods of reusing material, especially his cool-headed grasp of the way the same music could bear different meanings in different contexts – something of a heady issue in recent critical engagement with this composer.

Different but equally intriguing are the early incidental scores, which contain music like no other he ever wrote: at some moments aggressively experimental and modernist, at others outrageously political and deliberately primitive in a propagandistic manner ('agitprop'). Here we see the young man's alertness to the multifarious stylistic and dramatic tendencies that swirled around him at that time, and sense something of musical paths he could have pursued further but chose not to.

Beyond the music, examination of the background to these theatrical scores helps us place the young Shostakovich in his cultural and historical context, to see something of the complex web of writers, actors, directors, painters and designers with whom he was closely involved. Their work can shed fascinating light on his, and vice versa.

Shostakovich's professional involvement with the theatre declined steeply in the later 1930s, a fact seen by some as a direct effect of the public and official campaign against him begun early in 1936 with the publication of two notorious articles in the newspaper *Pravda*. The first, 'Muddle instead of Music' ('Sumbur vmesto muzïki', 28 January), attacked *Lady Macbeth*, while the second, 'Balletic Falsehood' ('Baletnaya fal'sh', 6 February), took him to task for his ballet *The Limpid Stream* (op. 39, 1934–5). It is certainly possible to imagine that such violent assaults on two of his most substantial theatrical scores would have left the composer with little inclination to pursue this applied side of his talent, and a greatly increased desire to concentrate on more 'abtract' and less word- and plot-dependent forms, such as the string quartet, symphony and concerto.

In fact, the evidence is rather less clear than that, and it is important to be careful about how we interpret what happened. In the first place, although it is true that Shostakovich never returned to full-length ballet after 1936 and never completed another serious opera, he did not give up working for the theatre. His later output includes a large part of an unfinished opera, *The Gamblers* (1941–2), a full-length operetta *Moscow, Cheryomushki* (op. 105, 1957–8) with extended ballet sequences, new orchestrations of Musorgsky's two most famous operas (*Boris Godunov*, op. 58, 1940, and *Khovanshchina*, op. 106, 1958), and a new version of *Lady Macbeth* (*Katerina Izmaylova*, op. 114, 1954–63), as well as a scattering of further incidental music from the war years and just after. He also gave family and friends fairly frequent indications up to the end of his life that he was still searching for operatic subjects (see Chapter 7 by Rosamund Bartlett in this volume).

At the same time, there were signals from well before 1936 that Shostakovich was already frustrated with his theatre work and with the amount of 'applied' music (incidental music or scores for other people's dramatic projects) that he was required to produce in order to earn a living. Writing such material was time-consuming and artistically constricting, and it left precious little time for more concentratedly musical undertakings. At the end of 1931, he gave vent to his feelings by publishing a substantial article in a left-wing Leningrad magazine with close links to the various 'proletarian' organizations in the arts, *Rabochiy i teatr* (The Worker and the Theatre).

'A Declaration of a Composer's Duties' is a remarkable document, and one of the most striking of any of Shostakovich's public pronouncements. In it he inveighed passionately against the tawdriness and crudeness of many of the projects he had been involved in, and made a plea for 'the composer' to be given time and support to engage in serious and substantial works where the music would take pride of place rather than being simply a handmaid to someone else's drama. He even went so far as to vow that he would accept no more theatrical commissions for the next five years (he did not stick to this).

The 'declaration' opens: 'Being on a two-month break, I have thought a great deal about my compositional work. From the beginning of 1929 to the end of 1931, three years in total, I have worked only as an 'applied' composer.'[1] To make his point, Shostakovich supplies a list of his recent pieces, all of which are theatrical apart from his Third Symphony, the 'First of May' which he calls his only worthwhile contribution of this period 'to the development of Soviet musical culture':

> It is no secret to anyone that on the 14th anniversary of the October
> revolution the situation on the musical front is catastrophic. It is we
> composers who are responsible for this situation … And I am deeply
> convinced that it is the mass flight of composers into the theatre that has
> created such a serious situation.[2]

For almost a page of close-typed print, Shostakovich surveys his own and others' work, and deplores the demands of theatre directors, producers and purveyors of frivolous entertainment, and their effect on composers:

> The composer strives with all his strength for a 'temporary theatrical role'
> [*k 'gastrolerstvu'*] in the dramatic theatre and the cinema, and not for long-
> term work. And this when the composer ought to be putting all his strength
> into the creation of a symphony, an opera, a ballet, a sonata, a song, a
> cantata, a fugue, etc.

At the end of the 'Declaration' he unleashes his proposal:

> *A banner should be hung up to direct the role of music in the musical theatre.*
> A soviet musical show capable of serving as a spur to the transformation of

musical theatres will be created without connection to the theatre, as the
directorate and workers of the musical theatre are in no condition to give
help to the creation of a musical soviet show [*sic*].

I sum up.

Let music play the leading role in the musical theatre! Down with compositional
shabbiness! Leave behind the dramatic theatre and sound cinema! Leave
behind musical theatre in the creation of musical shows! [italics in the
original]

Like any piece of written evidence, 'A Declaration of a Composer's
Duties' should be read with a sense of the shifting context. There is also the
question of authorship, of course, as with all of Shostakovich's published
articles. It is known, for example, that most of his later articles were
written by a variety of other hands. His published correspondence with
Isaak Glikman routinely reveals him requesting Glikman to write journalistic pieces on his behalf, which were then printed under his own name. It
is true that 'A Declaration of the Composer's Duties' reads strangely to
those familiar with Shostakovich's private letters and other writings, but
its manner is not so peculiar in the context of the rhetoric employed at
that time in such journalistic debates, and there is no specific evidence to
suggest that it was *not* written (or in some sense dictated) by Shostakovich
himself. Several friends and colleagues could have helped him with this
exposed and politically sensitive piece, however; perhaps the most obvious
candidate would have been Ivan Sollertinsky, a brilliant writer who no
doubt had a sharp grasp of what would have been appropriate on this
occasion and a more confident sense of journalistic politics than the
composer himself. This matter needs more research. The bald and sometimes incoherent words certainly suggest that Shostakovich was genuinely
irritated at what he felt to be the demeaning of his gifts, and was also trying
to defend himself against some of the harsh press criticism that had
already been levelled against him, not least and in fiercely ideological
terms by the journalists of the very magazine in which he was now writing.
And predictably, these same journalists were now swift to respond to 'A
Declaration', accusing Shostakovich of trying to evade responsibility for
his own failures.

However, the composer very probably had other intentions behind this
article as well. After all, at the moment when he wrote it he was in the midst of
Lady Macbeth, which he no doubt hoped would prove beyond dispute that
he – 'the composer' – could be in total dramatic and artistic control; and he
had plans for a new symphonic work on a far larger scale than he had
previously attempted (this project, after a false start in the early 1930s,
came to fruition as the Fourth Symphony, op. 43 in 1935–6). From this

angle, 'A Declaration' reads as though he was deliberately preparing his public for a change of direction, something further borne out by the fact that he proudly sent copies of the article to a number of colleagues.[3]

At the same time, the openness and forcefulness of this 'declaration' of private intentions and frustrations, published in a leading theatrical journal of the still powerful 'proletarian' movement (the proletarians were hardly his natural artistic allies), reflects Shostakovich's alertness to deeper shifts of power in official Soviet culture at this time. One of the most important of these was being driven by determined pressure from the highest authorities to move the public's attention away from the experimental and volatile theatre and towards other more fixed art-forms where it was easier to control the content. Shostakovich must have known what was happening (the issue was widely discussed at the time) and it would undoubtedly have been exceedingly important for him to make clear his relationship to what was likely to be the new order. As Katerina Clark has established in her magisterial study of the arts in Leningrad at this period, up until this point theatre had played the leading role in the creation of the whole of early Soviet culture, from the vast pageants of revolutionary Petrograd to the rich variety of political theatres and avant-garde tendencies that flourished through the 1920s and up to the early 1930s.[4] All the other arts were affected by dramatic performance, as innumerable productions of the young Shostakovich and most of his contemporaries make clear. But now in the early 1930s, matters were changing and it was the solid and non-performative art of prose literature – especially of the more monumental kind – that was moving into prime position, with epic cinema, grandiose sculpture and architecture, and traditional symphonies and oratorios not far behind. This was the moment when Socialist Realism put forth its first shoots.[5]

For a whole variety of reasons, therefore, it is hardly surprising that the composer's impressive early output of incidental scores for theatrical productions and revues has been neglected. In a sense, history passed these pieces by. Never intended to last for long even on their own terms, they were simply occluded by other more important works composed at the same time, by cultural and political events and by the composer's own changing attitudes and interests.

In addition, there are practical reasons why they have not received much attention. Most obviously, there is a considerable problem with access to materials. One score, *Virgin Soil* (*Tselina*, op. 25, 1930) was considered lost outright, until materials were discovered in 2004.[6] Several others also survive only in sketches or in fragmentary form (the most comprehensive published source being volumes 27 and 28 of the old *Collected Works* edition, Moscow, 1987, 1986). Even those that do survive in a more or less playable form pose performance difficulties. Music of this kind was so closely tied to its original theatrical context that reviving it independently of that context can make little sense. Short of reconstructing the original production (a dubious proposition even if it were possible), anybody putting on this music has to take many decisions about what bits of the score to play, in what order and with what other music. And there is always the risk, as with any composer's theatre music, that playing it out of context will risk making it sound odd and unbalanced, or plain inconsequential.

It requires imagination, curiosity and sympathy to get the most out of these pieces. And for that reason it is probably best to begin not with the scores, especially when they exist only in scraps, but with the historical context of the original productions for which they were written, with what those were about, what they looked like and who were the other artists involved. Viewed this way, Shostakovich's first attempt at incidental music for the theatre, *The Bedbug*, op. 19, immediately leaps out as among his most interesting and revealing.

A baptism of fire: working with Meyerhold

The text of *The Bedbug*, by one of the most successful writers of the period, Vladimir Mayakovsky (1893–1930), is itself an important literary artefact (something that cannot be said for certain of some other plays and scripts for which Shostakovich supplied music). It was written in 1928, at a time when the poet's personal and political life, despite his immense public fame, was in turmoil. After extended visits to the USA and France, he was finding it ever harder to keep up his strident appearance as the bard of the new Workers' Paradise. He was also in the grip of an amorous obsession with a young White Russian émigrée in Paris, a girl of a kind scarcely approved of in the new Soviet order. He was torn between two worlds, and *The Bedbug* reflects this.

The play, which Mayakovsky himself described as 'an extravaganza in nine scenes' and a 'magical comedy', is in two contrasted halves. In the first, set in the present day of the late 1920s, the author vents his spleen against the supposed moral and political decadence encouraged by the New Economic Policy (NEP) and practised by the Soviet regime between 1921 and 1928. A once-authentically proletarian Communist, Ivan Prisïpkin, has greedily abandoned revolutionary principles and gravitated towards a life of petty bourgeois luxury. In the process, he has thrown over his previous girlfriend in favour of a vulgar and flighty mani-curist, whom he marries at a celebration held amid the gaudy surroundings of the beauty parlour where she works. The party leads to a drunken fight which in turn leads to a fire, and the shop and wedding guests are burnt to ashes.

In the second half, set fifty years later in 1978, we wake to an antiseptic revolutionary future, a scene from science fiction in which everything is controlled by electricity, regimentation and automation. An excavation on the site of the old beauty parlour has revealed that one person miraculously survived the fire: Prisïpkin himself, cryogenically frozen in the water from the firemen's hoses. With immense scientific skill, Prisïpkin is unfrozen, revived and transferred to a zoo where he is exhibited as 'bourgeoisius vulgaris' alongside 'bedbugus normalis',[7] these two revolting creatures serving to remind visitors of primitive life-forms now otherwise happily extinct.

The mockery and sarcasm of this knockabout tale are unmistakable, especially in the lethal description of the moronic revolutionary paradise to come, and it is some tribute to Mayakovsky's immense reputation that he was allowed to get away with it (though there was apparently official anger behind the scenes, and the play marks the beginning of the poet's slide into difficulties, leading eventually to his suicide in 1930). To produce such a piece in 1929, as Stalin was gradually unwinding NEP and consolidating a new kind of grip on the country, was an act of daring. Perhaps this was exactly what fired the great theatre director Meyerhold to take it on.

Vsevolod Meyerhold (1874–1940) is one of the most important names in the history of twentieth-century theatre and someone whose influence extended far beyond the specific domain in which he practised his art. He was a force in Russian culture before the 1917 Revolution, but assumed his true significance in the early Soviet years as a prophet and leader in the battle to create a new modernist culture. He was also someone who took on protégés among prominent younger artists, forming almost familial relationships with them. The great film director Sergey Eisenstein, for instance, was briefly one such protégé, and Shostakovich became another when he spent a couple of months early in 1928 living in Moscow with Meyerhold and his wife, the celebrated actress Zinaida Raikh (1894–1939), and working for his eminent protector as the resident pianist in his theatre. This was the young composer's first experience of day-to-day theatrical life, and it was also the very time when he was working on his first opera, *The Nose*. Although Shostakovich may later have minimized Meyerhold's specific influence on this piece, its revolutionary approach to musical theatre and to the Gogol-based story and text of the libretto are inconceivable without Meyerhold's example. It is true that Shostakovich only met Meyerhold after he had begun the opera, but like everyone in his artistic milieu he was already well acquainted with Meyerhold's style and influence, and with the innovative theatrical approach that he was pioneering.

Meyerhold began preparing for *The Bedbug* in the autumn of 1928, assembling a powerful team for a show that was bound to be controversial. One striking idea was to allot the sets and costumes of the two halves of the play to different artists. The first-half designs, in a part-realistic, part-expressionist manner, were done by a brilliant young trio calling themselves the Kukrïniksï (a sobriquet derived from their three names); the futuristic second half was given to the celebrated photographer, painter and theorist Alexander Rodchenko (1891–1956), who came up with a bleakly amusing spectacle of machines, brightly-lit sterility and automation. Meyerhold's first choice as composer was Prokofiev; when Prokofiev declined, the director turned to his young friend Shostakovich.

Thus Shostakovich, for his very first attempt at incidental music, found himself at the creative centre of Soviet theatre, working with some of the most prominent figures of the age. Surviving sketches and performing parts from the original production show that the experience was a far from easy one.

The first thing these materials reveal is a difference between what was much later published as music from *The Bedbug* (a seven-movement suite of characteristic dances arranged for piano, beginning and ending with a march, and including a foxtrot, waltz, galop, etc.)[8] and what was actually played in the theatre. Some numbers of this suite (possibly including the foxtrot and the waltz) appear not to have been used at all in the final production, even though their intended dramatic relevance is clear. Waspish and colourful parodies of popular dance idioms, somewhat *à la* Kurt Weill, they evoke the Westernizing commercialism and self-indulgence of the NEP era that so entrances the anti-hero Prisïpkin in the opening four scenes. On the other hand, some similarly parodic numbers from the suite, including a half-jazzy 'Scene on the Boulevard' and 'Intermezzo', were used several times and in different ways. The surviving piano part from the orchestral materials shows a mass of repeat marks, cuts, verbal cues and other indications, all suggesting that as the show evolved Meyerhold was furiously recomposing Shostakovich's music to his own directorial ends. The two marches from the suite, wittily scored for small brass band and certainly played more than once in the production, are the pieces that most obviously reflect the musical import of Shostakovich's oft-quoted anecdote of an uncomfortable meeting with the famous poet: 'Mayakovsky asked me: "Do you like firemen's bands?" I said that sometimes I do and sometimes I don't. And Mayakovsky answered that he liked firemen's music best and that firemen's music was the kind I should write for *The Bedbug*.'[9] This anecdote should be placed alongside the fact that, as contemporary reports and photographs illustrate, onstage brass bands were a regular feature of the modernist theatre style in the Soviet Union in the late 1920s and might well have been requested by Meyerhold even without Mayakovsky's comments.

Just as important as these marches and dance numbers were several large-scale (and by the look of Shostakovich's handwriting hastily rewritten and expanded) passages for voices and instruments created to accompany the riotous wedding scene, the fire and the arrival of the firemen. Here the dramatic style begins to resemble opera, with recitatives and instrumental outbursts, and much manuscript evidence of moving bits of music from one place to another, all again showing how Meyerhold as much as Shostakovich was the driving creative force here (the artificiality of opera was an important part of Meyerhold's directorial style). Evidently the end of the first act was intended by the director as a musical climax as much as a dramatic one. At the moment when the petty-bourgeois world of the 'NEPmen' in their beauty parlour goes up in flames, and the firemen arrive with their hoses, the action segued into a purely instrumental outburst (to judge by the performing parts this was created by splicing together and repeating sections of Shostakovich's music for the fire with earlier passages from the wedding music and parts of the number in the suite called 'Intermezzo'). Meyerhold was apparently pleased with the outrageousness of the overall effect, exclaiming 'That'll clean out brains!', while someone else observed: 'The cacophony was indescribable! Some people covered their ears from such music, others – they were in the majority – construed the intermezzo[10] as a purely comic effect and laughed wholeheartedly.'[11] What comes across most obviously from the musical evidence for this scene is that Meyerhold showed a distinct preference for Shostakovich's more avant-garde numbers (atonal, dissonant, wailing and thumping) over the more subtle and enjoyably jazzy parodies. Perhaps he felt that the latter would make the audience take too much pleasure in the spectacle. At all events, as he kept cutting and reinserting the cruder and harsher material into the show, this will have been, to say the least, a sharp lesson from a mature artist to a young one on how music so often has to serve non-musical functions in theatrical circumstances.

According to Shostakovich, reminiscing later in life, Mayakovsky (who was encouraged by Meyerhold to take a prominent part in the production of his own play) asked for the music in the dystopian second half to be 'as simple as mooing',[12] which if true gives an amusing impression of the poet's dramatic intentions. Quite a bit of the surviving music for this part of the play is associated with the final scene at the zoo, when the stage directions call for a group of musicians standing centre-stage around Prisïpkin's cage, and there are also march-like entries by groups of young Pioneers, the Soviet City Fathers, and other regimented crowds of the citizens of the future. Shostakovich's music for this zoo scene, if not exactly 'mooing', is a blatant and far from subtle parody of the bald, crass and lumpen style favoured by the so-called 'proletarian composers'. Given that this was the musical and dramatic note on which the play ended, it is no wonder that among its loudest critics, in the furious discussions that followed the premiere, were what the composer's biographer Laurel Fay calls 'the proletarian cultural watchdogs'. They can hardly have been pleased to see themselves the butt of such contemptuously knockabout humour on the part of such a distinguished team as Mayakovsky, Meyerhold, Rodchenko and Shostakovich.

Years of tumult: from TRAM to Shakespeare

It is curious, therefore, that Shostakovich's next excursion into the theatre saw him moving towards rather than away from the dreaded proletarians. TRAM, the Theatre of Working Youth (*Teatr Rabochey Molodyozhi*), was founded in Leningrad in the mid-1920s by Mikhail (or Misha, as he preferred to be called) Sokolovsky (1901–41), whom Katerina Clark describes as 'one of those Komsomol activist firebrands who refused ever to wear a tie'.[13] The 'acknowledged godfather' of the enterprise was the fascinating Adrian Piotrovsky (1898–1938), a now forgotten but then influential and radical figure in the theatre, a writer, director and theorist, described by Clark as one of those who 'saw themselves as cultural ecologists who were ahead of their time because, they believed, they had divined the formulae that might transform Man'.[14] Although he had distanced himself from Meyerhold by the late 1920s, in earlier years Piotrovsky had been a pupil and disciple of 'the master' (as everyone seemed to call Meyerhold) in the theatre studio that the great director founded in Moscow in 1913, and, as with so many important figures of this time, Piotrovsky was someone whose work cannot be understood without the example of Meyerhold.

The original idea of TRAM was to create a truly proletarian theatre on the basis of amateur groups of young actors drawn from among factory workers, but the project was so successful with its audiences that it swiftly evolved into something rather different. By the later 1920s, although still espousing the same politics, TRAM was established on a more or less professional basis, with a theatre of its own in Leningrad and something resembling a repertory company (a mixture of professionals and amateurs with the professionals becoming ever more important). The Leningrad centre also spawned other TRAM theatres in different cities.

Music was central to TRAM productions. There seems to have been a general principle, quite typical of modernist theatre of the time, that songs and instrumental numbers were to be performed primarily by the actors themselves, although Shostakovich's contributions assume the presence of a pit band as well (another sign of the evolution of TRAM from amateur to professional). Contemporary photographs of TRAM productions, including those with music by Shostakovich, regularly show onstage musicians as part of the acting ensemble, often as uniformed brass bands, with ostentatiously optimistic smiles on the faces of the other actors standing nearby. There are also photographs of crowd scenes that are evidently rousing chorus numbers.[15] For the most part, the favoured musical style at TRAM was the very one Shostakovich parodied at the end of *The Bedbug*: the authentically proletarian 'placard' manner of rousing workers' songs and marches, heroic fanfares and onstage brass bands. If other musical styles were present, they were there (again to judge by Shostakovich's scores) mostly for purposes of sending up the despised and decadent petty bourgeoisie (by means of jazzy and sentimental numbers, as well as noise effects of one kind and another). At the same time it should be stressed that, unlike some other versions of proletarian art, TRAM had by no means cut its links to the earlier experimentalism of the avant-garde.

Several composers were associated with TRAM. Of these, the most prominent was Vladimir Deshevov (1889–1955), a now forgotten pioneer whose brief railway-inspired piano piece 'The Rails', was hailed by one hyperventilating author in 1927 as the perfect music for the new revolutionary era on the grounds that 'the proletarian masses, for whom machine oil is mother's milk, have a right to demand music consonant with our era'.[16] Deshevov is sometimes referred to in press reports and advertisements of the time as the 'musical director' of TRAM.

Shostakovich joined TRAM in the autumn of 1929 for what Laurel Fay describes as Sokolovsky's first ever production of 'a play by a professional dramatist', *The Shot* by Alexander Bezïmensky (1898–1973). Perhaps Sokolovsky's idea in importing the already famous Shostakovich was to emphasize on all fronts a greater professionalism in the expanding company.[17] Bezïmensky had been known for some time as a poet and a leading ideologue and practitioner of proletarian literature. Shostakovich had already worked with him, for it was this author who provided the coarsely uplifting verses about the 1917 Revolution that the composer set at the end of his Second Symphony (op. 14, 1927). Of that earlier poem, the conductor Nikolay Malko commented, 'One must admit that Bezymensky's words were bad. Shostakovich did not like them and simply laughed at them.'[18]

By the time Bezïmensky wrote *The Shot*, he was seeking to distance himself from other members of the proletarian movement. His new play was a verse drama which, as a modern scholar puts it, 'demonstratively rejected the psychological realism favored by the leadership of RAPP (the Russian Association of Proletarian Writers, *Rossiyskaya assotsiatsiya proletarskikh pisateley*) and dealt directly with shock workers and bureaucrats, exposing hindrances to production and offering heroic remedies to remove them'.[19] In other words, Bezïmensky was already seriously engaged in the aesthetic shift that was to lead only a year or two later to the creation of Socialist Realism, as was disarmingly revealed when Stalin wrote a fan-letter to Bezïmensky in 1930 to tell him that *The Shot* 'should be considered as a model of revolutionary proletarian art for the present day'.

An early participant in TRAM, Pavel Marinchik, gives a curious sketch of the plot: Prishletsov, a bureaucrat in charge of a tram park, and Gladkikh, a party official and lackey, poison a Komsomol member, Mitya Korchagin, who leads the youth shock brigade. Unable to endure the experience, Korchagin dies. The struggle is continued by the youth workers and communists in the tram park, who defeat their enemies and organize a new shock brigade.[20]

Critical reaction in Leningrad to TRAM's production of *The Shot* was noisy with controversy. Some were for and some against, and that applied also to the reception of Shostakovich's score. But the main critics and other proletarian contributors to the debate that raged in various publications from the end of 1929 throughout the first half of 1930 directed their harshest fire at Bezïmensky himself, who responded by publishing several angry and defensive letters in *Rabochiy i teatr*,[21] disowning the TRAM approach and accusing the theatre of a travesty of his intentions. At this time, Meyerhold was engaged in his own production of the same play in Moscow, and the author wanted to make clear that he considered Meyerhold's version the correct one. From the point of view of the later attacks on Shostakovich in 1936 and 1948, it is interesting to note of this debate (which on the whole mentioned Shostakovich's music more often positively than negatively) that the word 'Formalism' was already and habitually being flung around as catch-all insult. Everybody seemed keen to free themselves from this label and to apply it to their opponents.

As for the score, although what survives may be incomplete, it is enough to reveal one of Shostakovich's oddest creations. The instrumentation is weird: apart from the obligatory onstage brass band, there was an orchestra of three woodwind and four brass, a considerable amount of percussion, two balalaikas and a piano, and a whole section of violins but no other stringed instruments. For this eccentric ensemble the composer wrote some of his harshest and most brutal music. Everything is in hammering march rhythms, including instrumental fanfares, transitions and a forceful little tune for the balalaikas entitled 'Enter the technical secretaries'. A couple of numbers are for chorus and instruments. In one, to angular and almost atonal melodies (extremely difficult for amateurs and actors to sing) and with dissonant and harmonically contradictory instrumental accompaniments, the chorus hurls insults at the betrayal of revolutionary ideals ('The flag of the working classes has been NEP-ized'). In another, the massed chorus shouts over the thundering orchestra: 'We have the power! Do not wait for permission to enter the struggle. Raise the fury of the masses against the accursed bureaucrats!' Some idea of how the original cast received this uncompromising music, and of the music's place in the struggle between the different branches of the proletarian movement, may be gauged from Katerina Clark's comment that 'Shostakovich ... had to work overtime on the worker youths of TRAM to persuade them that the new music was more truly proletarian than the more melodious and schmaltzy revamped Tchaikovsky and Mussorgsky peddled as "revolutionary music" by RAPP's counterpart in music, RAPM [the Russian Association of Proletarian Musicians]'.[22]

The only charm and relief comes in a parody cabaret romance for the show's MC, a character called 'Dundi' (i.e. 'Dundee'), whom we are evidently meant to find despicable (like Prisïpkin in *The Bedbug*) on account of the fact that he appears on stage in top hat and tails and carries a file under his arm labelled 'Business'.[23] According to a contemporary photograph,[24] in the scene with his song the actor accompanied himself on a guitar, leaning out of a window while cardboard cherubs swung above his head, and beneath him four couples danced in an absurdly lackadaisical manner. The song itself is in a sugary nineteenth-century style, of the kind popularly perpetuated (to the wrath of the proletarians) in the NEP-men's favourite drinking-holes and restaurants, and entirely appropriate to Dundee's mood as he whines on in E minor about the boring demands of the revolutionaries: 'They keep telling me I have to think, but thinking's not my thing ... The happiest creatures on earth are fishes; they don't speak.' Whatever the political intention, this song is said to have had a 'popular' success.[25]

Shostakovich's next TRAM score, *Virgin Soil*, op. 25, was for a play about the ideological struggles of collectivization by Arkady Gorbenko and Nikolay Lvov, whom Katerina Clark describes as 'young authors ... [their] names not to be found in any literary encyclopaedia – [who] allegedly came from a worker milieu and were completely inexperienced as writers'.[26] As Shostakovich's score was lost until recently and is still awaiting publication, there is little information about this music, apart from production photos with yet another onstage brass band. But in a major feature on the show in *Rabochiy i teatr*, published on 16 May 1930 in the week following the first performance, Shostakovich was singled out from the rest of the production team for praise in the highest terms, and over the next few months his score for this play was referred to quite frequently in reviews in the same magazine of other shows and in debates as though everyone had agreed that it had been a notable achievement of the theatrical year. Even the distinguished conductor Nikolay Malko praised it. The only other reference to it after that comes at the end of 1931, when in a hostile review of *Declared Dead* (*Uslovno ubitïy*, op. 31), the critic (again in *Rabochiy i teatr*) angrily objected to the way Shostakovich had carelessly reused a march from *Virgin Soil*. There it had spiritedly accompanied the appearance of heroic soldiers of the Red Army, but now it had become comical and undignified. The march in question is presumably the one called 'Camouflage' in op. 31 and subsequently further reinvented as 'Fortinbras's March' in Shostakovich's music for Akimov's production of *Hamlet*, op. 32.

Shostakovich's final TRAM contribution came a year later in May 1931 when he wrote music for a production of *Rule, Britannia* (*Prav', Britaniya!*, op. 28), a play about 'the class war abroad'.[27] The author was the theatre's *éminence grise* and principal ideologue, Adrian Piotrovsky, who had spent much of the previous autumn publicly defending TRAM against mounting criticism and hostility, and the inevitable accusations of Formalism from journalists and rival proletarian establishments. The situation had become critical. At one point, TRAM itself had been forced publicly to disown its connection to Piotrovsky. A certain amount, therefore, hung on the success of this production.

The results were not happy. By this time TRAM was fast losing power and influence, and the public attacks on it and on Piotrovsky were growing ever shriller. It was clear that the theatre's days were numbered, and, well before the official dissolution of proletarian organizations early in 1932, there was little the champions of this organization could do to keep it going. To judge by Shostakovich's scathing references to this production and to TRAM in general in his 'A Declaration of a Composer's Duties', published only six months later, we may assume that the experience was artistically and politically disagreeable to him.

A handful of musical numbers survive, scored for a relatively conventional theatre orchestra (three woodwind, five brass, percussion, piano and a normal string complement). There is no evidence of onstage bands or other quirky items. This suggests that all pretence that the actors would be playing instruments on stage had now been more or less given up. TRAM was now struggling to show that it could be a more conventionally acceptable theatre. The manner of Shostakovich's orchestral writing and the musical style of certain passages is close to that of his ballet *The Bolt*, op. 27, which had received its unsuccessful premiere just weeks before the production of *Rule, Britannia!* The harmonies are still sometimes densely dissonant, and there are heavy marching rhythms in the older approved TRAM manner, but the tunes are now more obvious and straightforward, and some of them are simply reworkings of familiar pre-existing songs. For example, an imposing and vigorously aggressive orchestral introduction (which may have been an overture) leads into a massed unison rendition of the 'Internationale' in D major. Another choral-and-orchestral number, 'On the Soviet road', is a D minor anthem in the familiar four-square manner of the mass song or marching song. More interesting is a catchy 'Infantry March', which Shostakovich recycled early in 1932 in his music for *Hamlet*.

Political pressure on TRAM was but one part of the larger story of mounting tensions in Soviet culture throughout 1931. Cultural journalism of the time (including Shostakovich's own 'Declaration' at the end of the year) vividly suggests an atmosphere of turmoil in which almost everyone was jockeying for position and fighting to preserve their own way of doing things. It was a situation that would suddenly end on 23 April 1932 when, following decisions taken only weeks before at the 17th Conference of the Soviet Communist Party, the Central Committee would abolish all prole-tarian organizations in the arts, close down their magazines and offices and those of other independent organizations, and inaugurate the process of centralizing all Soviet cultural life into carefully controlled Unions. Before this happened, however, Shostakovich would complete two more theatre scores whose stories vividly reflect these changing times.

The first was the music-hall show *Declared Dead* op. 31.[28] In the period of the pre-revolutionary and early Soviet avant-garde, the idea of music hall, along with circus and other lowbrow forms of entertainment, had played a prominent role as a theoretical model in the imagining of a new and modernist culture. From around 1910 onwards, it became almost commonplace for artists to refer to the example of the music hall when justifying or explaining artistic innovations. In this, most were following the lead of Filippo Tommaso Marinetti, whose first Futurist manifesto makes much of the necessity to replace highbrow models with lowbrow ones such as music hall and circus. This manifesto had been published in Russia in 1909 and Marinetti himself had visited the country in 1914.[29] At the time there were no actual Russian institutions called 'music halls', and so fashionable Russian artists simply appropriated the English term, speaking of '*myuzik-kholli*'.

Real theatres called music halls appeared in the Soviet Union slightly later, in the mid- to late 1920s, and, while a few of them were founded by avant-garde experimenters, most were simply a product of the energetic culture of commercial entertainment that flourished in the larger Soviet cities under the New Economic Policy. As places of lighthearted and comical diversion, these Soviet *myuzik-khollï* successfully pandered to popular tastes of the time and made a good deal of money, but that did not make their position easy, for they had many critics. There were committed revolutionaries on the far left who disapproved of such dens of frivolity on principle because they were squalid emblems of petty-bourgeois vulgarity, and others who were prepared to tolerate them but only if they could be turned into workshops of propaganda, expressing or idealizing authentically proletarian and revolutionary tastes, and indoctrinating the politically ignorant. So a strident press campaign began, emanating from the circles of RAPP and with the stated intention of solving what was often called 'the problem of the music halls'. Attacks of this kind, and using this or similar phrases, can be found in the pages of *Rabochiy i teatr* throughout 1929 and 1930. This meant that the music halls had to defend themselves.

The resulting tension came to a head in the autumn of 1931 when the Leningrad Music Hall announced a series of productions designed to answer its enemies. One such was *Declared Dead*. Two young writers, Vsevolod Voyevodin (1907–73) and Yevgeny Rïss (1908–*c*.1970),[30] were chosen to provide a script with a clear political message, which, as the Music Hall itself proudly announced, would illuminate 'the defense capability of our country, the connection between the work of front and rear, the goals of Osoaviakhim and PVO'.[31] These last two organizations were formed to train the Soviet population for self-defence in the event of, respectively, a chemical attack and an aerial bombardment, and at this period they regularly staged elaborate practice exercises, compulsory for everyone and usually taking place at a weekend.

Voyevodin and Rïss came up with a shaggy-dog story about an idle young NEP-man called Stopka Kurochkin. At the start of the show, Stopka is walking down the street with his airhead girlfriend Mashenka, when he is stopped and told that a hypothetical air raid is in progress and that as a result he has now been 'declared dead' (i.e. he has been given the role of an imaginary casualty). He refuses to play along with this game and runs away.[32]

Act 1 depicts the practice manoeuvres in the countryside outside Leningrad and Stopka's adventures as he tries to evade his civic duties. Act 2 takes us into the city and contrasts the frivolous petty-bourgeois lifestyle of a NEP-ster (cue for a comical scene in a restaurant with dancing waiters and waitresses) with the ferocious political dedication of one Comrade Beyburzhuyev (Mr Beat-the-bourgeois), who is desperately worried that revolutionary values are being undermined and betrayed.

In Act 3 we are transported to Heaven and treated to a rambunctious atheist cabaret with God, the archangel Gabriel, Mephistopheles and other angels and devils, all of whom spend a ridiculous amount of time dancing. Atheist cabarets were a popular draw in many shows at this time, as they combined entertainment and political correctness, thus pleasing everyone.

Into this loose frame, the Music Hall poured a huge selection of its favourite acts designed to appeal to its regular audience, including comic recitations, light songs, ballet dances, jazz numbers, a performing dog and acrobatics.

What made the show remarkable was the amazing line-up of artists who took part in what was, after all, just a short-lived popular divertissement. The team was headed by the theatre's music director, the well-known light-music composer Isaak Dunayevsky (1900–55), and by the jazz-band leader and star, Leonid Utyosov (1895–1982), already and for half a century afterwards the most famous and best-loved entertainer in the USSR. Naturally Utyosov played the comical role of Stopka, thereby immediately undermining the show's supposed political message by making Stopka the character with whom the audience was most likely to sympathize. Other prominent light entertainers also took part.

At the same time a remarkable list of figures from the world of serious theatre and music were also added to the mix. The inevitable connection to Meyerhold was emphasized by the hiring of two of his most distinguished pupils, the director Nikolay Petrov (1890–64) and the designer Vladimir Dmitriyev (1900–1948), who had already done the original sets for Shostakovich's opera *The Nose* and would shortly go on to design one of the first productions of *Lady Macbeth*. Equally impressive was the participation of another leading designer, Nikolay Akimov, who would work with Shostakovich several times in the future, and the outstanding choreographer Fyodor Lopukhov (1886–1973), who had earlier that same year choreographed Shostakovich's *The Bolt* and would later script and choreograph Shostakovich's third ballet, *The Bright Stream*.

And then there was Shostakovich himself. Evidently, Utyosov and Dunayevsky felt that bringing on board the famous young composer would help to give the show some cachet. For his part Shostakovich, at least to begin with, was wildly enthusiastic about Utyosov. He had first met the older man in the summer of 1930 while both were staying in the same hotel in Odessa. In a letter to his friend Ivan Sollertinsky, he was sceptical about the combined music and movement of Utyosov's famous *Tea-Dzhaz* Ensemble (Theatrical Jazz) but wrote that he was enjoying meals in Utyosov's company and that Utyosov was 'without doubt the best performer in the USSR that I have seen. He reminds me of Meyerhold. I am really pleased with my new friendship.'[33]

The lengthy score Shostakovich produced in the autumn of 1931 for *Declared Dead* is one of his most variegated and splendidly silly productions, stuffed full of delightful jokes. Act 1 includes two naughty cabaret-style songs for Stopka's girlfriend Mashenka (played by the subsequently very famous popular singer Klavdiya Shulzhenko), as well as a brilliant Offenbach-like cancan and a sugary parody of a Chopin waltz. In Act 2 hilarity is created by introducing a 'chastushka' tune familiar to most Russians for the way it is usually sung to obscene lyrics, while Act 3 includes the Tsarist national anthem, 'Bozhe tsarya khrani' ('God save the Tsar') turned into a foxtrot, and a number where the Devil begins by singing the 'Song of the Golden Calf' from Gounod's *Faust*, before launching into a string of silly dances including well-known tunes like *Chizhik-pizhik* ('Birdie, birdie!').

Understandably, given pressures of time, the composer recycled some music from earlier works. The noisy overture of *Declared Dead* is a cut-down version of the overture from *The Bolt*, and, as mentioned above, the 'Camouflage' march from Act 1 probably began life as a Red Army march in *Virgin Soil*. In Act 3 a dance number for 'the Archangel Gabriel' reworks a cheeky popular song that Shostakovich first used in op. 23 (music for insertion into an opera, *Poor Columbus* by the German composer Erwin Dressel) and then recycled into the ballet *The Golden Age*, op. 22.[34]

To balance that, a large amount of the new music for this music-hall show was then reused by Shostakovich in later works. This somewhat gives the lie to his impatient dismissal of *Declared Dead* in his 'Declaration of a Composer's Duties' as 'plain bad and shameful'. Whatever he thought of the production, he did not throw away what he had written. The Poor Columbus/Golden Age/Archangel Gabriel music resurfaces as a comical stunt in the last movement of the First Piano Concerto, op. 35, and other dances and instrumental pieces make reappearances in such varied pieces as *Hamlet* (1932), the unfinished operetta *The Big Lightning* and the unfinished opera *Orango* (both 1932), the film score *The Tale of the Priest and his Servant, Blockhead* (1934), the ballet *The Bright Stream* (1935), the operetta *Moscow, Cheryomushki* (1958) and, remarkably, the last movement of the Fourth Symphony (1936).

Most fascinating are the various connections between *Declared Dead* and *Lady Macbeth*, which Shostakovich was composing more or less simultaneously. In the absence of a detailed chronology of their composition, it is hard to be absolutely sure whether the music-hall version or the operatic one came first, especially in the case of the innumerable small details and motifs that almost seem to be bouncing between the two works. But what is easily established is that the most important *Lady Macbeth* moments in *Declared Dead* belong to Act 1 of the opera. These include a striking sequential passage from the dance from Act 2 of *Declared Dead* called 'Jugglers and Waitresses', which appears in Act 1, Scene 3 of the opera at the moment when Sergey forces Katerina towards the bed, and a blasphemous 'Bacchanalia of John of Kronstadt and Paraskeva Pyatnitsa' from Act 3 of *Declared Dead*, which is the same as the orchestral accompaniment to the molestation of Aksinya in Act 1, Scene 2 of *Lady Macbeth*. Most of the scribbled piano sketch of the *Declared Dead* version is – in key, chord-spacings and many other details – the exact twin of the composer's version of the same music in the first published piano score of the opera, except that in the opera there is no reprise of the opening and there are voices superimposed above the instrumental rumpus:

> *Aksinya*: Help! He pinched me! Ow! Ow!
> *Sergey*: Look out! Stop! Hold her!
> *Labourers*: Ha, ha, ha! What a fine little voice! Keep still, Aksinya! Hold her, Seryozhka!

Shostakovich never attended the premiere of *Declared Dead* on 2 October 1931. Some time before, having completed what he had to do on it, he set out for the Black Sea to recuperate from his recent frenetic output of commercial music and push on with *Lady Macbeth*. He returned home only in mid-November, just in time for the final performances. Perhaps he managed to see the show around this time, as only a few days later on 20 November he published his petulant repudiation of it in his 'Declaration'. It is possible, however, that his scorn sprang as much from his experience of working on the production two months earlier.

The last paragraph of the 'Declaration' begins:

> I will finish this article with a fact from my biography: with a heavy heart I assure the Vakhtangov theatre that I will write the music for *Hamlet*. As far as concerns [the projected operetta] *The Negro* and [the projected film score] *The Cement Hardens*, in the next few days I will cancel the contracts and return the advances. I have no strength left to 'depersonalize' myself and write mechanically ['*obezlichivat'sya' i shtampovat'sya*]. By doing this I will clear the way ahead of me for a great symphony dedicated to the 15th anniversary of the October Revolution. And I declare to all my future 'commissioners' from the dramatic theatre and the sound cinema that I am breaking with this musical front for the next five years.

And so, within days of returning from the Black Sea with part of an opera in his case and publishing these words, Shostakovich began work on the music for Nikolay Akimov's production of *Hamlet* at the Vakhtangov Theatre.

Akimov (1901–68) was an important figure in Soviet theatre in the 1920s and 1930s, a director and designer, and an active polemicist. He was also an artist with a gift for caricature, which strongly marked his memorable costume designs.[35] Like many of his generation he worked in both popular and serious theatre. He was one of the designers of *Declared Dead* and responsible for several entertaining shows at the Leningrad Music Hall, but at the same time he participated in important avant-garde productions of classic texts, most famously a 1929 production of Molière's *Tartuffe*, in which prominent world leaders of the time, wearing grotesque masks designed by Akimov, clambered out of a sewer,[36] as well as experimental agitprop shows.

The Vakhtangov Theatre in Moscow was founded by the remarkable Yevgeny Vakhtangov (1883–1922), a loyal Stanislavsky disciple who absorbed much from Meyerhold. After his early death, it remained a noted centre of experimental productions, and was therefore a dangerously exposed place to put on a show that was intended to be controversial but unfortunately turned out to be a downright fiasco.

The historian of Soviet theatre, Konstantin Rudnitsky, has proposed that a principal reason for the failure of Akimov's *Hamlet* was that it was a show too late for its own time.[37] In style it belonged to the mid-1920s, when, after a period of directing mostly new and avant-garde plays, Meyerhold had broken new ground by going back to classic writers such as Ostrovsky and Gogol, but deliberately staging them in a distorted and shockingly modernistic way. For example, in his famous 1926 production of Gogol's *The Government Inspector*, Meyerhold hugely extended the original text by introducing material from other places, stretching and exaggerating every theatrical gesture that could possibly be made more absurd and more grotesque (it is from this specific tradition of treating Gogol that the libretto and music of Shostakovich's *The Nose* took its cue). The ostensible purpose was to force specifically contemporary relevance on a work of art from the past, but really it was the antinomian excitement of doing violence to a classic that gave this performance its astonishing appeal.

Akimov now attempted exactly the same thing with *Hamlet*, adding texts from elsewhere in Shakespeare and, strangely, from Erasmus. He also demanded nearly an hour of music from Shostakovich. The result was intolerably long and offensively incomprehensible. Akimov's clunkily obvious intention was to turn *Hamlet* on its head. Hamlet himself was to be 'an obese glutton', a liar cynically attempting to dethrone his uncle, and the actor had to deliver famous monologues such as 'To be or not to be' in a deliberately boring or 'mercenary' monotone. Claudius was 'a timorous neurasthenic (played … in a sharply grotesque manner)'. There was no ghost but only Hamlet himself shouting into a clay pot as a practical joke. 'Ophelia looked like a dissolute wench, and in her madness scenes she seemed frankly tipsy.' 'Akimov's production', notes Rudnitsky, 'more than anything else resembled a parody.'

To judge by surviving photographs,[38] and as one would expect from a talented artist such as Akimov, the look of the show was impressive. Unfortunately neither this nor Shostakovich's vigorous and witty music could save the production from devastating criticism after its first performance on 19 May 1932. In the now swiftly changing climate of the times, this *Hamlet* was, as the film and theatre director Grigory Kozintsev put it, 'an unholy anachronism'.[39] It was even more so because this was only four weeks after the Central Committee of the Communist Party had overnight changed the entire cultural landscape of the country with its publication of the resolution 'On the Reconstruction of Literary-Artistic Organizations', abolishing proletarian and other avant-garde and freewheeling societies and magazines, and launching the epic journey towards high-Stalinist cultural consolidation. Under the circumstances, Shostakovich, who broadly supported the new resolution as freeing him from recent persecutors, must have been relieved that his music was on the whole praised when so much else about this *Hamlet* was unreservedly condemned.

In later years, the émigré musician Juri Jelagin, who had played violin in the pit band at the Vakhtangov, related in his personal memoirs that:

> The music [Shostakovich] wrote for *Hamlet* was exceptional … [and] much closer to Shakespeare … than anything else in Akimov's production. Of course there were moments of great eccentricity in the music which were in the style of the production; for instance, at the ball, under a biting, spicy jazz accompaniment, the drunken Ophelia … sang a jolly song with a frivolous text in the style of German chansonnières from the beginning of the century.[40]

Jelagin is right about the cheap song – a waltz which sounds like a quotation of a nineteenth century melody – but wrong about the words, which are genuine Shakespeare ('Take O take those lips away' from *Measure for Measure*; although, for good measure, Akimov added Beaumont and Fletcher's smutty but lovely second verse continuation, 'Hide O hide those hills of snow').

Jelagin also notes:

> It was interesting how, in the famous scene with the flute, Shostakovich angrily mocked both the Soviet authorities and a group of proletarian composers who at that time were at the height of their power … In this scene, Hamlet held the flute to the lower part of his torso, and the piccolo in the orchestra, accompanied by double-bass and a drum, piercingly and out of tune played the famous Soviet song 'They Wanted to Beat Us, to Beat Us' written by the composer Alexander Davidenko, the leader of the proletarian musicians.[41]

Here too Jelagin's memory is playing tricks. It may indeed have been that the actor did rude things with his instrument, but the opening phrase of Davidenko's pompous song is allotted not to the twittering piccolo (or flute, as it is marked in the score) but to a tuba playing in the flatulent lowest register and accompanied not by a drum but by a tambourine. Evidently there were meant to be two schoolboy jokes at this point, not one.

As a whole Shostakovich's entire score for Akimov's *Hamlet* is probably his most brilliant and fully achieved incidental music, funny and touching, sharp-edged and memorable. It is not surprising that, despite the vicissitudes of the production, he himself thought well enough of what he had done to extract a thirteen-movement concert suite, which is still sometimes performed and therefore the only part of his output of incidental music that is more or less familiar to concert-goers. It begins with a march ('Night Watch') which reworks to splendid effect the 'Infantry March' from *Rule, Britannia!* from the previous year. Other recyclings include a sprightly cancan, called 'The Feast' in the original production and curiously renamed 'Pantomime' in the suite; this is adapted from the blistering cancan that ends the music-hall scene in *The Golden Age*. 'Fortinbras's March', the suite's conclusion, is, as previously noted, a variant of the 'Camouflage' march from *Declared Dead*, which may itself have begun life in *Virgin Soil*. And once again there are many connections to *Lady Macbeth*. Another cancan, renamed 'The Feast' in the suite (there are several such curious shifts of title between the original theatre score and the concert suite), as well as the 'Hunt' and two or three other dance-like movements show marked resemblances to important episodes from the opera including several of the famous and indeed very cancan-like entr'actes.

There is also an orchestral reworking in the suite of a cheap and catchy cabaret song, 'Ophelia's Ditty', originally sung in the production in the madness scene when, in Akimov's version, the heroine 'seemed frankly tipsy'. Here we find the strangest connection to the opera. The words are taken from Ophelia's sex-haunted song in Act 4 Scene 5:

> Tomorrow is Saint Valentine's day,
>   All in the morning betime,
> And I a maid at your window
>   To be your Valentine.
>
> Then up he rose, and donned his clothes,
>   And dupped the chamber door;
> Let in the maid, that out a maid
>   Never departed more.

In the last scene of *Lady Macbeth*, Sergey, wishing to seduce a fellow convict Sonetka, returns to his erstwhile lover Katerina and begs her to give him her stockings. He wheedles and lies that he needs the stockings to keep his legs warm and protect him from his leg-irons. Katerina yields helplessly to his sentimental entreaties: 'You want my stockings? Why didn't you say before, Seryozha? Here are the stockings, take my stockings.' The skipping refrain-like phrase to which she sings these words in this agonizing moment of self-delusion is taken from the very moment in Ophelia's song when she sings:

> Then up he rose, and donned his clothes,
> And dupped the chamber door ...

The parallels between these two moments, contained within a mere three bars of music in a flagrantly cheap style, are rich, poignant and alluring. In both cases Shostakovich is dealing with a sinister mesh of lying and seduction, with despair, madness and death as the consequence. In both cases, articles of clothing are involved. But there are also differences hidden within these parallels which shed intriguing light on why this scrap of the *Hamlet* score should have come into Shostakovich's mind when he was composing this moment in *Lady Macbeth*: Ophelia sees the story she is telling as explaining to all around the disaster that is overwhelming her; by contrast, Katerina is either horrifyingly ignorant or desperately trying to avoid looking the truth in the eye. The sudden surfacing of the Ophelia phrase would suggest that the latter explanation is more plausible.

The smaller movements from the *Hamlet* music – the melodramas, fanfares, songs and interludes – are also full of delights and deserve to be heard. Indeed, taken as a whole this entire score suggests that, despite the 'heavy heart' spoken of in his 'Declaration', the composer was still riding high on the excitement of the compositional discoveries he had made writing the opening scenes of *Lady Macbeth*. Everywhere in *Hamlet* there is a remarkable sense of dramatic control.

Into the cold: from Balzac to Shakespeare

In November 1931, well before the public failure of Akimov's *Hamlet*, Shostakovich had ended his 'Declaration of a Composer's Duties' with a vow to renounce writing incidental music for the next five years. This undertaking was soon broken, however. By the end of 1933 he was back in the Vakhtangov, this time providing music for a much less provocative enterprise. *The Human Comedy* (*Chelovecheskaya komediya*, op. 37) was a loosely gathered medley of episodes drawn from the stories of Balzac by the minor writer Pavel Sukhotin, otherwise only vaguely remembered as a literary collaborator with Count Aleksey Tolstoy.[42] The directors, A. Kozlovsky and Boris Shchukin, were talented and longtime Vakhtangov actors who had played prominent roles in *Hamlet* two years earlier, Kozlovsky as Horatio and Shchukin as Polonius.[43] Shchukin later migrated into the cinema, where he made a name for himself playing Lenin in Stalinist biopics.

Sukhotin's literary confection may not have been particularly daring, but it was a decided success with the public, and after its premiere in April 1934 it ran for many performances. A contemporary Muscovite who saw it in her youth remembers it being much talked about, for its nostalgic evocation of French life (something most of the audience were unlikely ever to experience), for the stress it predictably laid on the corruption and exploitation of a capitalist society dominated by material greed, and for the dramatic staging of the suicide of one of the main characters (perhaps Guillaume Grandet?).[44]

It is immediately clear both from this private account and from Shostakovich's score that the glory days of avant-garde theatrical experiment were now well over. The surviving music is sweet, memorable and atmospheric, but mostly clever pastiche calculated to suit the occasion. Shostakovich gets good mileage out of his 'Paris theme', an attractive barrel-organ tune in waltz rhythm and plausibly French in manner, cunningly varying it and twisting it to provide scene-setting entr'actes in several moods ('Happy Paris', 'Cruel Paris', 'Panorama' and so on). There are lively numbers for moments of greater drama ('The theatre', 'Panic on the stock-exchange') and a fine cancan-like march and a waltz, both of which recall passages from Shostakovich's first film score, *New Babylon*, also a drama set in nineteenth-century Paris. Most attractive are two cod eighteenth-century (or perhaps Delibes-like) dances for strings alone, a pizzicato gavotte and a gentle sarabande. In later years three movements from *The Human Comedy*, including the Gavotte, were expanded and heavily reorchestrated by Lev Atovmyan, for inclusion in the 1951 Ballet Suite no. 3.

No incidental music followed in 1935 as Shostakovich was absorbed in his ballet *The Bright Stream*, his Cello Sonata and then, in the last part of the year, the start of his new Fourth Symphony. In early 1936, while he was still only halfway through that monumental work, he found himself the victim of a shattering public campaign of hostility, beginning with the two notorious *Pravda* articles.

The subsequent course of the symphony and of the composer's political difficulties has been well chronicled, but only slight attention has been given to the fact that, in the midst of these events, in the autumn of 1936 he wrote some incidental music to a play by Alexander Afinogenov, *Salute,*

Spain! (*Salyut, Ispaniya!*, op. 44). The story of this forgotten music is more intriguing than might first appear.

Afinogenov (1904–41) was a major figure of left-wing theatre in the early Soviet period and known to Shostakovich. In the composer's 1931 'Declaration', in a passage fiercely defending the right of artists to write plays and operas without directorial interference from what he contemptuously refers to as 'the musical theatre', he noted: 'After all, Afinogenov and Vladimir Kirshon [1902–38] created the best examples of proletarian theatre without the "help" of the theatre!' What he had in mind here were Kirshon's play *Bread* and Afinogenov's *Fear*, both successfully staged earlier in 1931. *Fear*, in particular, had been given a prominent production at the Leningrad Academic Theatre directed by Nikolay Petrov and designed by Nikolay Akimov, both of whom shortly afterwards joined Shostakovich in the Music Hall as part of the team for *Declared Dead*.

By 1936, times had changed and Stalin's grip on all aspects of life was growing daily stronger and more muscular. But there were also other issues in the world, not least the Spanish Civil War, which started in the summer of 1936. Within weeks of its outbreak, Stalin made the decision to involve the Soviet Union, sending armaments and manpower. One immediate result was a stirring of Soviet press interest in Spain, including reports of battles and ideological interpretations of the ongoing struggle.

It was against this background that in three weeks Afinogenov knocked off an uplifting drama of Spanish heroism and sacrifice. The evident purpose was to sell to the Soviet theatre-going public the moral rightness of active solidarity between the USSR and Spanish republicans. The main characters of the play included the real-life figure of Dolores Ibárruri, 'La Pasionara', then at the height of her international fame, and a fictional 'mother', happy to give her three daughters Lucía,[45] Concha and Rosita to the revolutionary cause. On 26 October the Leningrad City Council instructed the Academic Theatre to mount this play and specifically mentioned that the directors should be the celebrated Sergey Radlov (1892–1958)[46] and, once again, Nikolay Petrov. The composer, said the order, should be Shostakovich.[47] Akimov was, also once again, brought in as designer. Within a month the music was written, the sets built and the show was on.

As it happened, Shostakovich had a personal interest in the events in Spain. Two years earlier he had met and fallen in love with a twenty-year-old student and translator called Elena Konstantinovskaya. The episode nearly wrecked his marriage to Nina Varzar, and Konstantinovskaya remained an important element in his emotional life for several years thereafter.[48] By the autumn of 1936 she was far away from the composer, working in Spain as a translator for the newly arrived Soviets. These last included the distinguished documentary film-maker Roman Karmen, to whom she was for a brief while thereafter married.[49] Recent scholarly investigation has revealed a curious connection between the amorous triangle of Konstantinovskaya, Karmen and Shostakovich, and the composition of the Fifth Symphony which was begun in April 1937, only a few months after *Salute, Spain!*[50]

Apart from its other implications, this previously unknown personal story lends a curious tinge to the most attractive music from *Salute, Spain!*, the 'Song about Rosita'. In the play, this song was sung by a man grieving for the beautiful Rosita who has been killed in battle and become a martyr for the republican cause:

> Time and life haste along,
> Much in our life will be forgotten,
> But we will never forget your name,
> Rosita, Rosita.

In the pleasingly sentimental style of Stalinist popular music, but with a lightly Spanish feel and several unexpectedly haunting harmonic moves, this fugitive piece evidently meant something to Shostakovich. Three years later he wrote it out again, transposing it from its original key of B minor into F sharp minor and giving it to one of his sisters as a birthday present.[51]

The rest of the score is somewhat less remarkable. According to the composer's Soviet biographer Sofya Khentova, both Shostakovich and Akimov were required to make something of the play's Spanish flavour. Akimov responded with picturesque backdrops of sea, landscape, military buildings and so on, while Shostakovich emphasized the connections between Spanish- and Soviet-style politics by providing arrangements of Spanish revolutionary songs. These last are not found in the surviving score. What we have are fanfares, a military march (quoting from the Rosita song), a shortened instrumental version of the Rosita song, and a grandiose funeral march unexpectedly suggesting the funeral march from Beethoven's 'Eroica' Symphony. The composer evidently made this reference on purpose, for the ending of the play depicted the funeral of Rosita's equally heroic sister Lucía, with a scenic panorama of Madrid in ruins in the background and Beethoven's famous music resounding from the pit.[52] If Shostakovich's march came earlier in the play, it was presumably intended to anticipate this corny finale.

Several years passed – and the composition of the Fifth and Sixth symphonies – before Shostakovich returned to incidental music. The occasion was a production of *King Lear* early in 1941 by the film-maker Grigory Kozintsev (1905–73). Kozintsev was one of Shostakovich's most constant collaborators, from the silent movie *New Babylon* in 1929 through seven other films to a cinematic version of *King Lear* in 1970. Along with his colleagues Leonid Trauberg and Sergey Yutkevich, in 1922 he founded the experimental theatre company FEKS (the Factory of the Eccentric Actor),[53] and he returned to the theatre at several further points in his career. Twice, Shostakovich wrote stage music for him.

Kozintsev's 1941 *King Lear* was for the large stage of the Bolshoy Dramatic Theatre in Leningrad, with designs by the erstwhile constructivist painter Natan Altman (1889–1970), and conceived on a grand scale. Shostakovich provided suitably meaty music, which gives a vivid impression of romantic and epic aspirations and, more interestingly, at several points anticipates a work the composer was to begin only a few months later, his vast Seventh Symphony, the 'Leningrad'.

The quasi-symphonic atmosphere of the *King Lear* music is set in the opening bars of the 'Introduction', a stormy funeral march in D minor, fading to a pulsing accompaniment, and the voice of Cordelia singing a folkish, Mahlerian 'ballad' in G minor. The so-far unidentified words of this song (complete with a reference to Arthurian legend) are unrelated to the opening of Shakespeare's play but may have something to do with the various (mostly inauthentic) ballad texts subsequently associated with Edgar's famous line in Act 3, Scene 4: 'Child Roland to the dark tower came':

> Beyond the dark sea on a cliff stands a high house,
> Birds nest on the high cliff but it is empty in that house.
>
> Long ago the hearth was extinguished, no voices are heard,
> And only the wind, a wild guest, disturbs the quiet owls.
>
> He brought news from afar that the lord had disappeared,
> That beyond the sea and the clouds Merlin had taken him away.
>
> In a green and distant place on a ghostly black steed,
> He prances in golden armour, but sees his home in dreams.
>
> The wind flies and sings and sobs around him,
> No one answers and empty is the high house.[54]

Some numbers from what was originally an extensive score now appear to be missing,[55] but five unusually evocative fanfares and seven purely orchestral movements survive, again in a grand manner and Mahlerian almost to the point of quotation. For example, the 'Scene in the Steppe', another tramping funeral march, carries echoes both of the funeral march from Mahler's First Symphony and of 'Der Abschied' from *Das Lied von der Erde*. These crude references look forward to the dense and far more subtle web of Mahlerian suggestions found all over the 'Leningrad'

Symphony. In addition, there are movements in *King Lear* that more directly anticipate the 'Leningrad' Symphony, especially 'The Approach of the Storm', which is like a sketch for some of the high-points in the symphony's first movement.

More unexpected and offbeat is a group of ten tiny 'Songs of the Fool'. Musically interconnected in the style of a self-contained orchestral song cycle or even a set of variations, these miniatures were written to be scattered throughout the relevant scenes in the first half of *King Lear*. They set clever verse translations of the fool's original lines by the well-known children's writer Samuil Marshak (1887–1964)[56] and, somewhat oddly to English-speaking ears, make extensive use of the American Christmas song, 'Jingle Bells'. Perhaps Shostakovich thought 'Jingle Bells' was a folk song. It was in fact written by James Lord Pierpoint (1822–93).

King Lear was also the occasion for Shostakovich to publish an article in the programme containing his first extensive thoughts about working in the theatre since 'A Declaration of a Composer's Duties' ten years before. Naturally he made enthusiastic and suitably modest observations on the problems of writing music for Shakespeare: 'The author of *Hamlet* and *King Lear* absolutely does not tolerate banality. It seems to me that when one speaks of the magnitude of Shakespeare then one needs to keep in mind the inner magnitude and the breadth of spirit, not the external pomp and circumstance.'[57] Words like these may seem windy at first sight, but in the context of Socialist Realism's relentless assertion of the primacy of external 'reality' and its monotonously aggressive assault on the right to personal and internal experience, they carry a certain defensive poignancy that is worth remarking on.

The composer also took the opportunity to complain in this article about directors' tendency to saturate their productions with too much music simply in order to underscore and heighten their intentions. Here again we feel him quietly pushing against the tedious restrictions of Socialist Realism:

> I remember a show in the old Alexandrinsky theatre. The hero was in doubt and suffering. The author put a fairly modest text into his mouth. The director decided to come to the aid of the suffering hero and underline, as it were, his experience. He placed a violinist backstage who played a very sensitive and very sweet melody, and then, as I remember, a storm broke out and the whole effect – that is to say, the traditional music and the traditional storm – gave the whole scene an utterly vulgar and tasteless quality.

He added: 'In a great tragedy music ought, I think, to appear only at moments of highest tension … It is not the composer's job to be a musical illustrator … That work can be done by a musical librarian.'[58]

On 22 June 1941, only months after the premiere of Kozintsev's *King Lear*, Hitler invaded the Soviet Union. Suddenly, musical illustration became after all very important, and musical propaganda too, as we can vividly hear in the composer's next three incidental scores: *Native Leningrad* (*Rodnoy Leningrad*), op. 63, written in 1942 as a suite within a larger show *Fatherland* (*Otchizna*), *Russian River* (*Russkaya reka*), op. 66 in 1944, and *Victorious Spring* (*Vesna pobednaya*), op. 72 in 1946.

Apart from his wartime concert-party pieces (innumerable arrangements of folk songs, popular dance tunes and snatches of operetta), these three items are the most obscure music of Shostakovich's war years. They were written for the Song and Dance Ensemble of the NKVD (*Narodnaya komissiya vnutrennïkh del*, the People's Commissariat of Internal Affairs, i.e. the secret police, the predecessor of the KGB and one of the primary agents of Stalinist terror and repression). The unspeakable Lavrenty Beria, then the NKVD's head, created this unlikely outfit in 1940 for the entertainment and encouragement of his men during the war against Finland.[59] Evidently he considered its work important enough to be continued through the much larger conflict that followed. Probably what is most interesting about these NKVD shows, as with *Declared Dead*, is the remarkable roster of artists who took part in them.

The director of the Ensemble was Sergey Yutkevich, a theatrical pioneer from the early FEKS years and a fine film-maker for whom Shostakovich had already provided three movie scores, *The Golden Mountains* (1931), *The Counterplan* (1932) and *The Man with a Gun* (1938). The scenarios were the work of a team of three: Iosef Dobrovolsky, Mikhail Volpin and Nikolay Erdman. While little is known of Dobrovolsky, Volpin (1902–88) and Erdman (1900–70) are significant figures. Volpin started in the first post-revolutionary years as a poet and satirist, and then in the later 1920s fell into the avant-garde orbit of Mayakovsky.

Erdman began his career close to Meyerhold, for whom he wrote two of the most important and outrageous plays of the early Soviet period, *The Mandate* (1925) and *The Suicide* (1932).[60] He also turned out many music-hall shows and several famous film scripts, including *Happy Fellows* (*Vesyolïye rebyata*, 1934). Volpin and Erdman were both arrested in the early 1930s, imprisoned and exiled. It was during exile that they met, which led to their working together for much of the rest of their lives, beginning with the script for one of Soviet cinema's most enduring comedies, *Volga-Volga* (1938), directed by Grigory Alexandrov. In 1941 Volpin and Erdman were drafted into the army together and sent to the NKVD Ensemble as principal writers for their shows.[61]

The choreographer was Kasyan Goleyzovsky (1892–1970), a brilliant inventor of ballet from the immediately pre-revolutionary era and a pioneer of new Soviet dance styles in the 1920s.[62] Goleyzovsky had a considerable success in those years with his Chamber Ballet, and some flavour of his work can be gleaned from accounts of a 1923 show advertising itself as 'eccentric erotica'.[63] He was also director of movement on some of Meyerhold's most avant-garde productions of the mid-1920s. Presumably all such modernist aberrations were now left far behind when he went to work for the NKVD.

Finally, the designer was Shostakovich's 'close friend', the Leningrad painter Pyotr Vilyams (1902–47). At this period the Vilyams and Shostakovich families were both living in evacuation in Kuybyshev, and Vilyams was earning his living designing sets not only for the NKVD Ensemble but also for the Bolshoy Theatre. What this suggests is that the NKVD Ensemble unexpectedly brought together a number of experienced and talented people, many of whom knew one another from earlier times and all of whom shared artistic roots in the pre-Socialist Realist time of experiment in the 1920s.

Not much is known or published of what the NKVD audiences actually saw at these shows. One account speaks vaguely of *Fatherland* as:

> Something new in the genre of synthetic art. The public were supposed to be presented with, as equal partners, a symphony orchestra, an orchestra of Russian folk instruments, a light-music orchestra, a large choir with soloists, a group of theatrical actors, a large ballet troupe consisting of young dancers of the most varied types from classical to folk-style.[64]

The performances took place in the Dzerzhinsky Club in Moscow,[65] which must have had a large stage and pit to accommodate such lavish forces.

For *Native Leningrad*, his suite for the first show in 1942, Shostakovich provided a beefy choral and orchestral 'Overture', featuring two well-known nineteenth-century revolutionary songs, the 'Varshavianka' and 'Bravely, Comrades, Step Forward!', both of which he later incorporated into the Eleventh Symphony. He also added two ponderous vocal and orchestral anthems with tunes of his own and, more interestingly, a whirlwind 'Dance of Youth' for orchestra, which was presumably the occasion for some spirited choreography from Goleyzovsky. Though somewhat blander in style, this amusing item is filled with nostalgic echoes of the wild cancans and galops of Shostakovich's youth and specifically recalls a number from *Declared Dead*, suggestively entitled 'The Dance of the Temporary Victors'. Khentova tells us that he also contributed a number of songs to *Fatherland*, mostly with words by the Socialist Realist poet Yevgeny Dolmatovsky, and that at some point there was a declamation based on a text by the notoriously bogus Kazakh 'folk-poet', Dzhambul Dzhabayev.[66]

Table 6.1 *Shostakovich's Theatre Scores*

Title	Theatre company, and place, date of premiere	Author	Director
The Bedbug (Klop), op. 19	Meyerhold Theatre, Moscow, 13 February 1929	Vladimir Mayakovsky	Vsevolod Meyerhold
The Shot (Vïstrel), op. 24	TRAM, Leningrad, 14 December 1929	Alexander Bezïmensky	
Virgin Soil (Tselina), op. 25	TRAM, Leningrad, 9 May 1930	Arkady Gorbenko and Nikolay Lvov	
Rule, Britannia! (Prav', Britaniya!), op. 28	TRAM, Leningrad, 9 May 1931	Adrian Piotrovsky	
Declared Dead/ Hypothetically Murdered (Uslovno ubitïy), op. 31	Leningrad Music Hall, 2 October 1932	Vsevolod Voyevodin and Evgeny Rïss	
Hamlet (Gamlet), op. 32	Vakhtangov Theatre, Moscow, 19 May 1932	William Shakespeare, trans. Desiderius Erasmus	Nikolay Akimov
The Human Comedy (Chelovecheskaya komediya), op. 37	Vakhtangov Theatre, Moscow, 1 April 1934	Pavel Sukhotin (after Honoré de Balzac)	A. Kozlovsky and Boris Shchukin
Salute, Spain! (Salyut, Ispaniya!), op. 44	Leningrad State Academic Theatre, 23 November 1936	Alexander Afinogenov	Sergey Radlov and Nikolay Petrov
King Lear (Korol' Lir), op. 58a	Gorky Bolshoy Dramatic Theatre, Leningrad, 24 March, 1941	William Shakespeare trans. Mikhail Kuzmin, Anna Radlova and Samuil Marshak	Grigory Kozintsev
Suite *Native Leningrad* (Rodnoy Leningrad) for the revue *Native Land* (Otchizna), op. 63	NKVD song-and-dance ensemble, Dzerzhinsky Central Club, Moscow, 7 November 1942	Mikhail Volpin and Nikolay Erdman	Sergey Yutkevich
Russian River (Russkaya reka), op. 66	NKVD song-and-dance ensemble, Dzerzhinsky Central Club, Moscow, 17 April 1944	Mikhail Volpin and Nikolay Erdman	Sergey Yutkevich
Victorious Spring (Vesna pobednaya), op. 72	NKVD song-and-dance ensemble, Dzerzhinsky Central Club, Moscow, 8 May 1946	Mikhail Volpin and Nikolay Erdman, with lyrics by Mikhail Svetlov	Sergey Yutkevich
Hamlet (Gamlet), without opus	Pushkin Theatre, Leningrad, 31 March 1954	William Shakespeare	Grigory Kozintsev

Even less information survives about the remaining two NKVD shows. *Russian River* (1944) was evidently intended as a celebration of victory at Stalingrad on the river Volga, and the surviving score includes perhaps the most primitive march Shostakovich ever bothered to write down, two more choral and orchestral anthems in a dirge-like style, and another lively orchestral cancan, this time with the suggestive title, 'Football', and close in several details to the lively 'Russian Dance' from *The Bright Stream*. For his final outing with the NKVD Song and Dance Ensemble, *Victorious Spring* (1946), Shostakovich apparently recycled some music from *Russian River*,[67] but also composed two sweet if innocuous settings of verses by Mikhail Svetlov (1903–64), a poet very popular at the time and still remembered for his ballad 'Granada'. In 1970, presumably with the composer's permission, the conductor of the original NKVD shows, Yury Silantyev, recycled much of their music into a patriotic oratorio.

These three curious outings marked more or less the end of Shostakovich's career as a composer of incidental music for the theatre. Only one small addition followed. In 1954 his old friend and colleague Grigory Kozintsev staged *Hamlet* at the Pushkin Theatre in Leningrad. With the composer's permission, Kozintsev recycled most of the music Shostakovich had written for his 1941 production of *King Lear*. All he asked the composer to add were two more short orchestral movements. One is a strangely 'oriental'-sounding gigue. To judge by a stage cue in the score, it was probably played during the play-within-a-play and was interrupted in the middle by Hamlet's gleeful comment on the effect of 'The Mousetrap' on his uncle Claudius: 'Wormwood, wormwood!' The other new piece was a brief but touching Finale, serious in tone and distinctly recalling Shostakovich's Tenth Symphony, composed in the autumn of the previous year.

Such was the understated ending of a career as a composer of incidental scores that had begun a quarter of a century before in the great and noisy years of the 1920s when drama was the dominant art-form of the still young Soviet Union.

7 Shostakovich as opera composer

ROSAMUND BARTLETT

Shostakovich's musical genius was protean, but it was with opera above all that he wanted to consolidate the dazzling international reputation he established when Bruno Walter conducted his First Symphony in Berlin in February 1928. He was thus following in the footsteps of his nineteenth-century forebears Musorgsky, Tchaikovsky, Rimsky-Korsakov and Borodin, whose gravitation towards opera was a reflection of its central importance within Russian musical and cultural life. Somewhat surprisingly, opera continued to be a high-profile musical genre after the Revolution, despite its bourgeois associations, and new Soviet operas were actively sought for the main stages of Moscow and Leningrad, earmarked to become traditional symbols of national prestige as before. Shostakovich therefore had every reason to feel confident and optimistic when beginning his first opera in 1927.

After completing *The Nose* before he even turned twenty-two, Shostakovich embarked on what he planned to be a tetralogy of operas about women – a kind of self-styled Soviet *Ring of the Nibelung*. His *Rheingold* equivalent, *The Lady Macbeth of Mtsensk District*, was a huge success when it was first performed in 1934. Two years later, however, Shostakovich was stopped in his tracks by a savage denunciation of his new work in the Soviet Union's premier newspaper *Pravda*, following an infamous performance attended by Stalin. Quite apart from the fact that *Lady Macbeth* did not exemplify the principles of Socialist Realism, which had been launched in 1932 as the monolithic and conservative new style for Soviet artists to follow, this was the period marking the start of the 'Great Terror' – a time of mass arrests and summary executions. Shostakovich may have been the most brilliant composer of his generation, but he was clearly not immune, and suddenly the kind of public exposure to be gained from writing for the theatre no longer seemed such a good idea. Although he toyed with many other possible subjects after 1936 (see the chronological listing at the end of this chapter), and made orchestrations of Musorgsky's *Boris Godunov* (1939–40) and *Khovanshchina* (1958), Shostakovich was unable to complete another opera.

With only two operas and an operetta to his name, it might seem far-fetched to regard Shostakovich even potentially as the Verdi of the twentieth century. This is, after all, a composer better known for his impressive corpus of instrumental works. But for the traumatic events of 1936, however, this appellation would have been fully deserved, for Shostakovich, apart from being well read, had an acute literary sensibility, and shared with Verdi an innate and brilliant dramatic talent. He never had the chance to fulfil his ambition to write a string of large-scale, genuinely popular works. Despite still trying to write an opera in the last days of his life, his unfinished *The Gamblers*, begun in 1942, remains his last and most substantial attempt to reclaim his rightful inheritance. Prefaced by a brief discussion of the 1920s debates about the problem of Soviet opera, this chapter will provide an overview of Shostakovich's career as an opera composer. While the main focus will be on the composition history of *The Nose* and *Lady Macbeth*, other unfinished operatic projects such as *The Gamblers*, *Orango* and *The Black Monk* will also be discussed.[1]

Shostakovich and opera in 1920s Soviet Russia

Shostakovich was nine years old when he was taken to see his first opera, Rimsky-Korsakov's *The Tale of Tsar Saltan*, in 1915.[2] The fact that the following day he was able to recite and sing most of the opera to his family confirms that this first visit to the opera was indeed one of the 'strongest musical impressions' of his childhood, as he later attested: 'When I first heard an opera I was astonished. A new world opened up before me.'[3] Shostakovich had the fortune to be born in St Petersburg when it was still the capital of Russia, and thus the centre of the nation's musical life – which in the years immediately leading up to the Revolution happened to be extremely rich. Standards at the Mariinsky Theatre, Russia's premier stage for opera and ballet, in particular, had never been higher, and inspired Shostakovich to plan an opera based on Pushkin's narrative poem *The Gypsies* even before he wrote his First Symphony.[4] And despite living through the vicissitudes of the First World War, and then the upheavals that accompanied the 1917 Revolution and the ensuing Civil War, Shostakovich also had the good fortune to reach adulthood during the period of the New Economic Policy (NEP), when, despite many privations, the arts in Russia were at their most vibrant. It is telling that in a letter to his mother during a period of recuperation in the Crimea in September 1923, he should write of his longing to be at the Mariinsky Theatre (aware that he was missing the opening of the new season).[5]

The fact that opera survived is partly due to two key people: Lenin, who did not favour the wholesale abolition of pre-revolutionary culture, and his first Minister of Culture, Anatoly Lunacharsky.[6] With half the windows of the Bolshoy shattered by artillery fire during the Revolution, there were many who felt the rest of the theatre should simply be blown up.[7] But opera became very popular, with new audiences thronging theatres every night with free passes from their trade unions. Lenin ordered work to begin on the Bolshoy's reconstruction in 1919. But that still left the problem of the repertoires, which were to be bitterly argued about. Should not the theatres be presenting works by Soviet composers? The answer was a resounding 'yes', but where were these Soviet composers in the early 1920s? Prokofiev, Rachmaninoff and Stravinsky were all in emigration, and Shostakovich was, of course, still a teenager. Another problem was the uncertainty about the nature of the putative new Soviet operas. In the meantime, extensive contacts were renewed in the 1920s with the West, made possible by the relatively liberal conditions introduced by the New Economic Policy.

Several composers visited Russia in the 1920s, including Milhaud, Berg, Bartók, Hindemith and Schreker, as well as numerous conductors and performers, amongst them Bruno Walter, Erich Kleiber, Otto Klemperer, Joseph Szigeti and Artur Schnabel.[8] These contacts led to the Soviet premieres of many contemporary avant-garde operas, including those by émigré Russian modernists such as Prokofiev. It was certainly in Leningrad, Shostakovich's home city, that the most exciting productions took place in the 1920s. Here a major role was played by the critic Boris Asafyev, later to become the *éminence grise* of Soviet musical life, and an important and complex figure in Shostakovich's life.[9] Asafyev was at the centre of the new music group that formed in Leningrad, and with which Shostakovich was affiliated. It was officially launched as the Leningrad Association of Contemporary Music in 1926, the year of Shostakovich's debut as a symphonic composer and graduation from the Conservatoire. The Association of Contemporary Music in Moscow was loosely affiliated to the International Society for Contemporary Music, and several Soviet composers were invited to represent their country at the Society's festivals in the 1920s. Alexander Mosolov, for example, was chosen to go to the Society's Frankfurt Festival in 1927, which led to his receiving the commission to write his opera *The Hero* for the opera house at Baden-Baden.[10] Levon Hakobian speculates, with justification, that Shostakovich's operatic ambitions were partly fuelled by the spirit of competition with the Moscow-based Mosolov, six years his senior. *The Nose*, after all, dates precisely from this time.[11]

The Leningrad Association of Contemporary Music was also generally modernist in orientation, but much more active in promoting the work of Western composers. It became directly involved with the productions of contemporary operas in the city's two main theatres. Following the

Russian premiere of Strauss's *Salome* in June 1924 at the former Mariinsky, the theatre stepped boldly into new territory the following season by staging Schreker's *Der ferne Klang*. Then in 1926 the theatre produced Prokofiev's *Love for Three Oranges*.[12] In 1927, the former Mariinsky staged its most spectacular production yet: the Russian premiere of *Wozzeck*, which had been first performed in Berlin only two years earlier. Berg travelled specially to Leningrad for the occasion,[13] and the twenty-one-year-old Shostakovich was introduced to him at the premiere.[14] From 1927 onwards it was the smaller Maly Theatre, where both Shostakovich's operas were first performed, which carried the torch of the Western avant-garde in Russia. The theatre's experimental orientation had been made clear from the time it opened as an opera house in 1918, and it also had a commitment to contemporary works. March 1926 saw the premiere of *Mona Lisa* (1915) by Max von Schillings, and a few weeks before the premiere of *Wozzeck* it staged a critically successful production of Křenek's *Der Sprung über den Schatten*, premiered only three years earlier in 1924. This was followed by another Křenek premiere: the wildly popular *Jonny spielt auf*.[15]

In many ways, this can be regarded as one of the most exciting times in the history of Russian operatic life. For a few years it was opera houses in Soviet Russia that led the world in daring productions of contemporary operas that Western theatres shrank from. The impact of all these productions on Shostakovich's own operatic writing was naturally overwhelming, and no doubt whetted his appetite to write for the stage. Indeed, Valeryan Bogdanov-Berezovsky, the author of a book about Soviet opera published in 1940, and someone who knew Shostakovich very well, states baldly that *The Nose* was his answer to *Der Sprung über den Schatten*.[16] And in 1927, Shostakovich responded to a questionnaire in which he declared that his attitude to contemporary opera was extremely negative, with the exception of *Wozzeck*.[17] Apart from Berg, Shostakovich also at this time came into direct contact with Schreker, Milhaud, Honegger and Bartók,[18] who all visited the former imperial capital before the centre of gravity shifted permanently to Moscow.

Avant-garde productions constitute one side of the story of opera in the Soviet Union in the 1920s. The other side concerns the performance of new operas by Russian composers and the political pressures brought to bear by militant factions on both composers and theatres in the race to create proletarian Soviet opera, amidst increasing hostility towards the Western European operas staged. Shostakovich was in a fortuitous position by being sympathetic to modernism in his musical orientation, and sympathetic politically to the Bolshevik cause (he accepted the commission to write a symphony to celebrate the tenth anniversary of the

Revolution, after all), but hostile to the proletarian musical fraternity. Opera certainly remained central to the debates about musical modernity in the 1920s. Asafyev was keen to champion the Western avant-garde, but he was also anxious to promote native talent. In an article of 1924, entitled 'Composers, hurry up!', he urged Russian composers to stop believing that writing on revolutionary topics was somehow vulgar and trivial, and to write operas on contemporary topics, since this medium provided them with the simplest way of engaging with their new social environment.[19] Until there was an abundance of revolutionary operas in the repertoire, theatres were faced with the problem with finding suitable works for performance that could accompany the popular revivals of classic works, and works by the Western European avant-garde, which were at least revolutionary from a formal and aesthetic point of view. The revolutionizing of old operas was proposed as an interim solution.[20] Matters were also taken in hand to produce new Soviet operas in Leningrad in 1924 with the creation of a Workshop of Monumental Theatre. One of its first projects was Pashchenko's *The Eagle's Revolt* [*Orlinnïy bunt*], a work that was heralded as the first serious attempt to revolutionize opera, but that had serious flaws and did not survive long in the repertoire. The revolutionary opera *For Red Petrograd* [*Za krasnïy Petrograd*], by the young Leningrad composers Arseny Gladkovsky and Yevgeny Prussak, which was staged at the Maly in April 1925, was also rushed into production, and also did not fare well. One of its many alleged artistic weaknesses was the disparity between its revolutionary subject and the conservative idiom of its score, which preserved the arias and duets of operatic convention.[21]

Theatres began to attract the charge that they were out of touch with their public. In Leningrad at least there was a solid core of modernists ready to defend the productions of contemporary Western operas, but there was also a phalanx of militant proletarian musicians who still felt there was no place for opera at all in the new regime, and began to subject the opera houses to relentless attacks in the press and accusations that it did not meet the needs of the new audiences. Throughout the 1920s, the two main Soviet arts journals, both based in Leningrad, were filled with articles about the 'Sovietization' of opera.[22] In early 1926 there was a heated debate on the topic,[23] and the theme of the 'death' of opera was revived a few months later,[24] followed by another debate.[25] Shostakovich did not participate directly in these debates, but it is unlikely they would have passed him by, not least because his own name started occasionally to be mentioned in them from as early as 1925 onwards.[26]

Just as Shostakovich was beginning *The Nose*, the battles about contemporary opera became more highly charged, particularly when the Russian Association of Proletarian Musicians (RAPM) began to take a more militant stance. Exemplary of their aggressive new attitudes is a substantial article on the opera 'crisis' published by Lev Lebedinsky, a key member of the organization, in the journal *Sovetskoye iskusstvo* in May 1928. Insisting that opera was 'sick' and needed to be treated, and that Soviet opera houses did not know how to create a suitable new repertoire, he nevertheless affirmed its topicality and the great demand for it 'amongst the broad sections of workers'. In Lebedinsky's view, the basic function of opera was to educate people 'in accordance with the ideology of the proletariat'. Shostakovich figures as a composer whose impact was as yet still untested on the 'mass audience', and who is thus given a temporary reprieve from excoriation.[27]

At the start of the First Five-Year Plan, the state theatres inevitably came under close scrutiny, with numerous articles referring to the 1928–9 season as a turning point (*perelomnïy*).[28] By June 1930, when art was included in the Plan, the important performing arts journal *Zhizn' iskusstva* [Art Life] had been shut down, and the headlines in the surviving *Rabochiy i teatr* were 'The Reconstruction of Art', 'On the Musical Front', 'To War! To War', and 'State Theatres under Attack'.[29] And yet this was the time that the first modernist Russian operas reached the stage. Shostakovich's *The Nose* and Deshevov's *Ice and Steel* were premiered in January and May 1930 respectively. Like his colleagues at the Maly, Shostakovich could not but be aware by this time that it was no longer enough to be radical from an artistic point of view. From the outset, Shostakovich had resolved to write a satirical opera, and he believed that a work of classical literature would provide the best material. Accordingly, he considered works by Saltykov-Shchedrin and Chekhov as well as Gogol.[30] In fact, as he was to find to his cost, it turned out that by this time it was also no longer enough to be satirical.

The Nose

Shostakovich began work on his first opera a year after the triumphant premiere of his First Symphony, in the summer of 1927, and he completed it a year later, when he was still only twenty-one years old. By common consensus, it is the most important work of his early period.[31] He chose as its subject Nikolay Gogol's 1836 short story *The Nose*, and wrote his own libretto, with the assistance of Georgy Ionin, Alexander Preys and Yevgeny Zamyatin. Bearing in mind its surreal events (concerning the nose of an unprepossessing government functionary in St Petersburg, which literally takes on a life of its own),[32] the story did not exactly lend itself to operatic treatment. But this was grist to Shostakovich's mill. By mixing the musical ideas of the Western avant-garde with the artistic innovations of the most radical figures in Soviet culture he had also come into contact with, including Meyerhold and Eisenstein, his aim was to write a truly revolutionary opera, laying at last a foundation stone for Soviet opera which would stand the test of time. In a 1928 letter he explained that he had been attracted to this particular story because of the realistic and serious way in which Gogol relates its fantastic events. Accordingly, as a composer, he did not feel the need to insert irony or parody into his score.[33]

An extravagantly experimental work whose only nod to convention seems to be its nominal three-act structure, *The Nose* certainly was an assault on traditions. Calling for a cast of at least seventy-eight singing roles (which, the composer conceded, could be doubled and tripled, as indeed they have to be to make any performance feasible), the opera is audaciously scored for a very small chamber orchestra (following Křenek), which nevertheless includes fourteen different percussion instruments, plus four domras and two balalaikas – the first time Russian folk instruments had been ever been used alongside conventional strings in a work of this kind. Another first is the inclusion in the first act of a five-minute-long interlude for unpitched percussion, the first of several instrumental interludes that bear witness to the powerful impact on Shostakovich of *Wozzeck*, whose musical influence is readily apparent (along with those of Schreker, Křenek, Prokofiev and Stravinsky).

As Laurel Fay has summarized, the music Shostakovich wrote for *The Nose* is largely non-tonal and non-lyrical, and makes 'extensive use of the parody of familiar genres and the grotesque, highly differentiated juxtaposition of tone colours'.[34] It also interacts with the text in a novel way. In a *Krasnaya gazeta* [Red gazette] article published two days after the premiere, Shostakovich explained that he had not approached his opera primarily as a musical work, and had in fact regarded the drama as equally important (although he took pains to disassociate himself from Wagner):

> Neither one nor the other dominates. I was thus trying to create a synthesis
> of music and theatrical action. The music is not written in numbers, but
> in the form of a seamless symphonic flow, but without a leitmotif system.
> Every act is part of the unified musical and theatrical symphony.[35]

Such a conception owed a great deal to Shostakovich's attraction to Gogol's rhetorical gifts, and, more generally, to his own acute literary sensibilities (his knowledge of Russian and world literature was extensive, and combined with an astonishing ability to remember what he read). It also bears witness to the fruitful time he had spent under the tutelage of Meyerhold, having been employed by him as pianist and composer in Moscow in 1928, while he was writing *The Nose*, and even housed by the great director for a time. Music had been integral to Meyerhold's radical theatrical vision since the outset of his career, when, as an actor in Stanislavsky's Moscow Art Theatre in 1904, he had written to Chekhov about the symphonic qualities of his play *The Cherry Orchard*. By the time he came to found his own company after the Revolution, Meyerhold had several years as a director of opera productions at the Mariinsky Theatre behind him (including *Tristan und Isolde* and Gluck's *Orpheus*), and he ploughed that experience into the revolutionary theatre of stylization that he now continued to develop, turning his back on the hyper-realist naturalism championed by Stanislavsky. His most celebrated (and typically controversial) production was his radical reinterpretation of Gogol's *The Government Inspector*, premiered in 1926. Its influence on the composition of *The Nose* becomes immediately apparent when bearing in mind the fact that Meyerhold structured his production in the form of fifteen episodes, and incorporated a sophisticated musical score designed to be 'one element in an over-all rhythmical harmony designed to reveal the "subtext" of the drama'.[36] When Shostakovich wrote to his friend Ivan Sollertinsky from Meyerhold's flat in Moscow in January 1928, he singled out *The Government Inspector* as the production that had made the greatest impression on him: at that point he had seen it seven times.[37] Another probable source of influence on Shostakovich's conception of Gogol's story, which aligns it with the literature of the absurd, was the Leningrad 'Oberiu' group, with whose eccentric activities and writings he seems to have had some familiarity.[38]

The Nose was put into production as soon as it was completed in the summer of 1928, but its musical and scenic complexities – including extremes of register, abrupt changes, naturalistic imitation of people shaving or yawning – dictated a long and careful rehearsal period. In preparation for the premiere, Nikolay Malko conducted a vocal and instrumental suite from the opera in Moscow in November 1928, extracts were performed for groups of composers, and articles about the opera began appearing in the press, some by the composer himself.[39] Recently published minutes of an extended plenary meeting of the Artistic Council of the Maly Theatre held on 20 May 1929 regarding the planned production confirm the new note of defensiveness that was occasioned by the changing political climate. The director Nikolay Smolich found himself having to justify the selection of this particular opera to the sixty people present, arguing that the creation of genuine Soviet opera would be impossible if the theatre did not nurture its composers, even if their works were difficult.[40] Two months later, on 16 July 1929, a concert performance of the entire work was given at a national music conference in Leningrad, despite Shostakovich's misgivings (precisely because of his having given equal weight to music and dramatic action). The opera's style and subject were roundly condemned by the proletarian faction, who predictably found fault with its failure to cater for the working masses. Four days before the stage premiere, a few scenes from the opera were actually tried out on some workers. Shostakovich declared he was ready to be deported should his opera not be comprehensible to them, while Sollertinsky went one step further by maintaining that only those used to Italian opera would really find it a challenge.[41]

Opinions divided sharply about the *The Nose* when it was finally premiered on 18 January 1930. The opera was hailed by Sollertinsky as showing the way forward out of the impasse in which Soviet opera already seemed to find itself, and as the first original opera written in the Soviet Union by a Soviet composer. Shostakovich, he argued, had managed to do away with old operatic form by writing a score based on rhythm and timbre, in which the stage became dynamic, and characters spoke in a living language rather than in arias. It might be only a 'long-range missile', but surely it was a work that was central to the development of Soviet opera?[42] Another critic argued that *The Nose* was actually more like a hand grenade, and that, like an anarchist, Shostakovich was bringing panic to the front line of musical reaction and so clearing the path for Soviet operatic construction.[43] But there was also an opposition already marshalled, and the opera was damned as being the product of too much Western avant-garde music. The Maly may have believed it was firmly on the road to the Sovietization of the operatic repertoire, but this was not how the theatre should be reconstructed, according to the proletarian critics who now had taken ideological control of the Soviet musical establishment, and who were insisting that opera could no longer be apolitical.[44] As theatre employees were dragooned into going to the collective farm 'front', and shock brigades from Leningrad theatres were dispatched to Moscow to challenge the torpidity at the Bolshoy Theatre, articles in *Rabochiy i teatr* called for an end to Formalism and proclaimed Soviet Opera to be at 'crisis point'.[45] Shostakovich was challenged by his opposition in the Russian Association of Proletarian Musicians to write on a contemporary topic rather than a literary classic, and to become more politically engaged. Typically, it was a challenge Shostakovich simultaneously answered and turned his back on. There is plenty of political engagement in *Lady Macbeth*, but the source for the libretto, a short story published in 1865 by Nikolay Leskov, was just as much a literary classic as *The Nose*. The latter survived in the repertoire only until the following season, and then disappeared completely from Soviet theatres until it was revived, with the assistance of the composer, in a celebrated production conducted by Gennady Rozhdestvensky at Moscow's Chamber Opera in 1974.

The Lady Macbeth of Mtsensk District

Shostakovich had just turned twenty-four when he began work on his second opera, *The Lady Macbeth of Mtsensk District*, in the autumn of 1930. The defiant young composer was aware that the political climate in Russia was changing, but he still had no intention of capitulating to that kind of political pressure, nor did he think he had anything to fear. With hindsight, he might have rued the naive confidence of the article he published about opera composition in the journal *Rabochiy i teatr* in November 1931.[46] The appearance of 'Declaration of a Composer's Duties' nevertheless indicates Shostakovich's awareness of how much was expected of him with his second opera, which was from the outset intended to be more accessible in idiom.

He conceded that the situation on the 'musical front' was 'catastrophic', but avoided advocating anything other than the supremacy of music in Soviet music theatre, and avoided the issue of political commitment and alignment with the proletariat.[47] Shostakovich's article drew forth a barrage of attacks in the very next issue of the journal from composers who lambasted his 'vacillation', the 'emasculated formalism' of *The Nose*, and his 'individualism'.[48] The issue of *Rabochiy i teatr* that printed Shostakovich's article 'Declaration of a Composer's Duties' in late November 1931 also carried articles entitled 'The War on Stagnation and Conservatism', 'In Support of Bolshevik Criticism of Proletarian Creativity' and 'Expose the Idealists, Formalists and Vulgarizators'. Little did Shostakovich know, when blithely writing about the 'catastrophic situation on the musical front', that in just a few years' time he would be the one to be unmasked as the arch-Formalist.

Shostakovich began work on *The Lady Macbeth of Mtsensk District* on 14 October 1930, and completed the opera on 17 December 1932, working as librettist again alongside Alexander Preys, whose literary talents he valued.[49] If he had taken liberties with Gogol's story in *The Nose*, he made some fundamental interpretative changes when it came to setting Leskov's story to music, as he made clear in an article published in *Sovetskoye iskusstvo* [Soviet art] in October 1932, which he embellished upon in a further essay published in 1934 at the time of the opera's premiere. Leskov's heavily ironic attitude towards his protagonist Katerina Izmaylova is clear from the title of the story, which takes place in a nondescript town in the middle of the Russian provinces. He describes Katerina's heinous crimes in an objective and detached way, furthermore depicting her as a cruel and thoroughly repellent individual. In Shostakovich's opera by contrast, Katerina emerges as a true heroine, who is not only a sympathetic character, but in fact the only sympathetic character – 'a talented, clever and exceptional woman perishing in the nightmarish conditions of pre-revolutionary Russia'.[50]

It was Shostakovich's contention that Leskov could not provide a correct interpretation of the story's events because he was a pre-revolutionary writer. In his task to 'justify' Katerina, according to a new 'critical', and 'Soviet' perspective, and render her as a 'positive' character, Shostakovich therefore decided to 'discard' the murder of her young nephew. Via the intensely lyrical music written for her in the score, which Shostakovich now defines as playing the 'principal' role in the opera, Katerina is fashioned into a warm, suffering person, whose fate as an unloved wife in the dark patriarchal kingdom of reactionary Russian merchants is genuinely tragic (the analogy with Ostrovsky's play *The Storm* (better known via Janáček's opera *Katya Kabanova*) is intended). Shostakovich also depicts in a tragic vein the convicts marching to Siberia in the opera's final act, which is far more reminiscent of Dostoyevsky's *Notes from the House of the Dead* than of Leskov's pithy tale.[51] Otherwise the characters are treated satirically. In his 1934 article, Shostakovich declares that it was his task 'musically to unmask the essence of each of the main characters'. He was careful to stress the importance of the secondary characters, and also that of the orchestra, which he regarded as playing a role that was perhaps even more important than that of the soloists and chorus.[52]

In its exuberance, caricature and riotous grotesque, *The Lady Macbeth of Mtsensk District* certainly bears the stamp of Leningrad's vibrant operatic life in the 1920s, but the political changes wrought by Stalin's 'Cultural Revolution' also left their mark. Thus the atonal writing and tragicomic farce of *The Nose* gives way to a more conventional and accessible musical language in *The Lady Macbeth of Mtsensk District*, and also to a simpler, black-and-white plot of good and evil. Just as Shostakovich was beginning the third act of *Lady Macbeth* in the spring of 1932, the Central Committee decided to deal with the insubordinate and dictatorial proletarian arts organizations by summarily liquidating them. The Party Resolution 'On the Reconstruction of Literary and Artistic Organizations', issued in April 1932, at one stroke initiated the establishment of single creative unions, and with them a new era of ideological conformity and artistic conservatism. In some respects Shostakovich was clearly undeterred by the new ideological pressures. In a revealing article published in March 1933, he declared that socialist construction and five-year plans made poor subjects for operas, and that their 'anaemic, impotent' heroes were incapable of arousing strong feelings, unlike those of classic writers like Gogol and Leskov, who provoked laughter and 'bitter tears'.[53] Shostakovich was drawn to Leskov's story in particular because, at a time when he was about to marry for the first time (Nina Varzar, in May 1932) he was captivated by the idea of a love that knew no compromise. What he projected on to Leskov's Katerina, therefore, was the idea of her embodying a passion so strong that she would sacrifice everything to pursue it. In the article that Shostakovich published on the day of the opera's premiere, he acknowledged that justifying Katerina's crimes was not easy, although the fact that her unappealing lover Sergey is so patently unworthy of grand passion does not make his task any easier. As Richard Taruskin has argued, however, there was a sinister undertow to the whole enterprise. Shostakovich may not have capitulated to the demand to write an opera on an explicitly proletarian subject, but he nevertheless did react to the introduction of Stalin's new cultural policies by grafting the topical theme of class warfare on to his plot. Thus in his quest to portray Katerina as a 'positive' heroine at all costs, her victims are consequently dehumanized, since they are class enemies who deserve to be exterminated.[54] The last act of the opera, furthermore, was written after the 1932 Party Resolution was issued, and thus perhaps under the impact of its ideology.

With the Party's attention initially being focused on troublesome poets and politicians, *The Lady Macbeth of Mtsensk District* was wildly successful when it was first performed in January 1934, but it was only a matter of time before it came under scrutiny. By 1936, when Stalin decided to see *Lady Macbeth* for himself, the unbridled sex and violence of Shostakovich's opera, and the biting satire of the police and other authority figures, not to mention the musical complexity of the score, sat uncomfortably with the wholesome family values the Soviet leader was now cynically promoting while prosecuting his campaign of terror. If the young composer's international fame protected him from being purged, he could nevertheless be brought to heel by being publicly denounced in the nation's central newspaper *Pravda* for writing 'Chaos instead of Music'.

It is not within the scope of this chapter to explore in detail the performance and reception history of *The Lady Macbeth of Mtsensk District*, which has been well documented.[55] It is necessary to comment briefly, however, on Shostakovich's reworking of his opera, a process that began as early as 1935, but was undertaken in earnest soon after his wife's death in 1954. As well as making revisions to the score, in 1955, following a successful private performance, he set out to tone down what he now regarded as the 'vulgarity' of the language in the libretto and its 'naturalistic excesses' in advance of a proposed new production at the Maly Theatre (the notorious trombone glissandi that follow the lovemaking scene had already been removed in 1935).[56] Shostakovich also composed two new interludes. This new version, however, under the name *Katerina Izmaylova*, was not performed until 1963.[57] In 1956, Shostakovich played it through on the piano to a Ministry of Culture commission, whose members decided it was not yet fit for public performance. Only after another private audition was the opera officially rehabilitated and passed for performance. Shostakovich took an active role in his opera's revival at the Nemirovich-Danchenko Theatre in Moscow,[58] and subsequently endorsed the revised version as definitive.

The Gamblers

The public attack on Shostakovich in the pages of *Pravda* had dire consequences for the rest of his musical career, not to mention his plans to write further operas. In 1937 he managed to regain official favour with his Fifth Symphony without compromising his artistic integrity, and in 1940 this was consolidated when he was awarded one of the first Stalin Prizes for his immediately popular Piano Quintet. A few months later Hitler invaded the Soviet Union, and Shostakovich was evacuated to Kuybyshev. It was here on 27 December 1941 that he completed his Seventh Symphony, begun in Leningrad six months earlier. According to some sources, Shostakovich started work on *The Gamblers* the very next day, although there is some evidence that he had been mulling it over as a possible project for several years already.[59] Reading about the 1938 Munich Agreement, for example, had apparently made him draw an analogy between the characters in Gogol's play and the European politicians who had appeased Hitler.[60] For Shostakovich, Gogol's play clearly had a universal meaning beyond its nineteenth-century Russian context: in this case, it was Chamberlain, Mussolini and Daladier playing a high-stakes card game against Hitler, who of course a year later started gambling the entire future of Eastern Europe with Stalin.

The world of tawdry pre-revolutionary provincial Russia, and Gogol's inimitable satire on the morals of its equally tawdry inhabitants, provided the composer with a welcome change of scene in between the epic Seventh and Eighth Symphonies. Isaak Glikman was surely right to see the context of this work in Shostakovich's career at this time in terms of a light interlude in a Greek tragedy.[61] Interestingly, Shostakovich himself encourages such an interpretation by using the orchestra in *The Gamblers* as a kind of Greek chorus, which emerges as a character in the drama in its own right and comments on the nefarious exploits of the characters on stage.

The film-maker Grigory Kozintsev said of Shostakovich that he had the ability to adopt as his own Gogol's maxim that the Russian language has the potential to transform itself within a single sentence from the elevated to the everyday, from the frivolous to the tragic.[62] We might further say that it was a propensity for the grotesque that attracted Shostakovich to Gogol in the first place, not least because it was a quality he himself possessed in the highest degree. Who else could have switched overnight from writing a tragic symphony to embarking on a comic opera complete with bass balalaika? That Shostakovich did so says something about his desperate need to escape during the long months of evacuation in wartime, and about his confidence at the time, bearing in mind the absence of any kind of commission.

In turning once again to Gogol, Shostakovich was of course already taking a gamble, bearing in mind the hostile reception given to *The Nose* eleven years earlier. But as Gogol's last play *The Gamblers* is altogether more down to earth than the surreal world conjured up in *The Nose*, so Shostakovich's operatic treatment of *The Gamblers* was infinitely more straightforward and conventional, in keeping with the idiom of the music he composed after the 1936 watershed. If *The Nose* was complex, atonal and extreme, *The Gamblers* was going to be far more linear and measured, with only the occasional evocation of the exuberant earlier work. And Shostakovich deliberately wanted to work differently with the text of *The Gamblers*. If he had used *The Nose* as little more than a point of departure, his game plan with *The Gamblers* was the opposite: to set every single word in the play just as Gogol wrote it, using continuous recitative. Partly Shostakovich was being pragmatic here, since his regular librettist Alexander Preys was not at hand, having been evacuated elsewhere, but partly he was following an important precedent, for this had been Dargomïzhsky's tactic in turning Pushkin's play *The Stone Guest* into an opera, and also that of Musorgky, who was a composer very close to his heart (indeed, he had just completed a new orchestration of *Boris Godunov*).

Musorgky had attempted to make an opera out of Gogol's play *The Marriage* without changing a word in the text, but had given up. Shostakovich also believed Gogol was the best librettist, but the problem he soon encountered was that the resulting opera threatened to become unwieldy, and he eventually gave up too. As he wrote in November 1941 to his friend Vissarion Shebalin, some six months after first mentioning this new operatic project: 'I am still composing the unrealistic opera *The Gamblers*. I call it unrealistic for reasons of its unreality: I've composed thirty minutes of music already, and this is only about one-seventh of the whole work. It's too long.'[63] The following month he decided to call it a day, yet in March 1943 he informed his closest confidant Ivan Sollertinsky that he was making a piano score and continuing the opera, despite not really believing he would finish it. To the three Moscow Conservatoire students for whom he played through the work he gave the lack of female parts as a further reason for stopping work on *The Gamblers*[64] – somewhat ironic given that Shostakovich had originally planned to write a whole tetralogy of operas about women. If completed, *The Gamblers* may have taken over three hours to perform, but the quality of the first act alone suggests that the audience's interest could have been sustained.

Like many Russians, Shostakovich had an impulsive streak, and was fond of gambling himself. But he was not a very proficient at it. In fact, he invariably lost – as he confessed to his friend Isaak Glikman soon after beginning his new opera.[65] When it came to real life, however, political circumstances had forced Shostakovich to learn a painful lesson about expediency and restraint. If he never finished his experiment to turn Gogol's play *The Gamblers* into an opera, was it not partly because he realized he was perhaps staking time and energy on a work that might never work on the stage? And maybe he felt he should also hedge his bets regarding the darker side of Gogol's mordant satire, and its resulting musical embodiment, fearing the authorities would swiftly veto any performance: Stalin was still Soviet leader, after all, and the creative climate might have become slightly easier as a result of the war, but not much. The ultimately bleak vision contained in Gogol's work summed up by the often-quoted notion of 'laughter through tears' was not exactly consonant with the tenets of Socialist Realism, which demanded that art should be both uplifting and politically engaged. As a result, what we are left with is a tantalizing and powerful first act. The score for *The Gamblers*, comprising approximately two hundred pages of inspired writing, was the closest Shostakovich ever came to completing an opera following the removal from the repertoire of *The Lady Macbeth of Mtsensk District* in 1936.

The strength of Shostakovich's own attachment to this incomplete work can be ascertained from the fact that he poignantly incorporated the themes of its opening bars into the second movement of his last work, the Viola Sonata, which he completed days before he died in August 1975. It was Gennady Rozhdestvensky who had boldly rescued *The Nose* from nearly half a century of oblivion by conducting the revival at Boris Pokrovsky's enterprising Chamber Theatre in Moscow in 1974, and it was consequently Rozhdestvensky to whom the composer's widow, Irina Antonovna Shostakovich, entrusted the score of *The Gamblers* after his death. The work was first given in a concert performance in September 1978 in his home city of Leningrad, where his two previous operas had received their premieres in much more optimistic times.[66]

Other operatic projects

Shostakovich never completed his planned tetralogy of operas on women, his Soviet *Ring of the Nibelung*, having in 1934 outlined in *Krasnaya gazeta* his intention to follow *The Lady Macbeth of Mtsensk District* with an opera about a pre-revolutionary political activist linked to the People's Will organization, another featuring a woman from the twentieth century, and a final instalment in which he would create a Soviet heroine who embodied characteristics from the present day and the future. Some of these ideas found expression in the score Shostakovich wrote for Lev Arnshtam's 1968 film *Sofya Perovskaya*.[67] He never completed any other opera following the events of 1936 (although in 1944 he finished the opera *Rothschild's Violin* begun by his student Veniamin Fleyshman).[68] Yet he never ceased to conceive new operatic projects, and it is worth at least detailing them (in the absence of any substantial documentation in most cases), as well as other earlier projects that did not materialize. Certainly the range of subjects Shostakovich considered was very broad, including *The Adventures of Pinocchio* and *Crime and Punishment*, and a plan to create a 'film-opera', a new genre that would enable him to set the action in Moscow, in New York and on Mars. He also considered writing an opera about Pushkin, which would be based on Bulgakov's *Last Days*.[69]

1930

The Carp: commissioned in 1929 by the Maly Theatre to a libretto by Nikolay Oleinikov, which like that for another opera, *Zaton*, was never written, despite a contract being drawn up for production also with the Bolshoy Theatre.[70]

1932

The Big Lightning: comic opera, commissioned by the Maly Theatre, with a libretto to be written by Nikolay Aseyev. Nine numbers were written before Shostakovich abandoned the project due to lack of confidence in the libretto.[71]

Orango: incomplete 'opera-bouffe' projected for performance at the Bolshoy Theatre during the 1932–3 season, with a libretto commissioned from Aleksey Tolstoy and Alexander Starchakov. Shostakovich started writing this opera at some point in the first half of 1932, while he was still composing

Lady Macbeth. According to an announcement in the journal *Rabochiy i teatr* in June 1932, the opera, which was to be based on Starchakov's novella 'Karyera Artura Kristi' [The Career of Arthur Christie], was conceived as a 'political pamphlet targeted at the bourgeois press'. Excerpts were to be performed at the Bolshoy Theatre to mark the 15th anniversary of the 1917 Revolution. According to Olga Digonskaya, who first brought the fragments of this unfinished score to light, observes that the theme of mocking the capitalist West was one explored in the ballet *The Golden Age* and the unfinished opera *The Big Lightning*, and shared some textual and situational similarities with Mayakovsky's play *The Bedbug*. The overture and other parts of this unfinished opera were taken from the score of the ballet *The Bolt*, after it had been removed from the repertoire, while other parts of the score came from *Declared Dead*, having first been transferred to *The Big Lightning*, before work on that opera was halted. Neither the libretto nor Starchakov's novella have been located, which Digonskaya speculates is probably because they were destroyed by the conformist Aleksey Tolstoy after Starchakov was shot in 1937.[72]

With a view to possible collaboration on an opera, Shostakovich also met with Eduard Bagritsky in 1932, having been impressed by a libretto the poet had written for his friend Vissarion Shebalin. Aleksey Tolstoy wrote at this time a libretto for Shostakovich on a contemporary theme, but no opera was written.[73]

1934 (?)

Opera about members of the 'People's Will': Shostakovich planned the second part of his projected tetralogy (following *Lady Macbeth*) to focus on the 'Narodovoltsi' – activists of this late nineteenth-century revolutionary organization. Olga Digonskaya has speculated with justification that this opera, to be written to a libretto by Alexander Preys, remained unfinished because the assassination in December 1934 of Sergey Kirov, officially recorded as a Trotskyist terrorist act, rendered its subject matter politically unacceptable. The 122 extant bars are for a soprano role, with the name 'Yelena' indicated.[74]

1936

Two months after the *Pravda* editorial was published, the Maly Theatre announced that Shostakovich would write an opera about the Baltic Fleet's role in the 1917 Revolution.[75]

1937

Volochayev Days: commissioned by the Kirov Theatre in 1937 while he was writing the score for the film of the same name. The contract was broken in 1940 due to the unsatisfactory libretto.[76]

1938

Hero of Our Time: novel by Lermontov on which Meyerhold planned to write a libretto for a projected collaboration with Shostakovich, who a few months later contemplated writing an opera on Lermontov's *Masquerade*.[77]

Poet of the People: libretto by R. Benyash for a proposed opera by Shostakovich, which he approved but did not set to music.

How the Steel was Tempered: projected opera commissioned by the Maly Theatre to be based on Nikolay Ostrovsky's novel. Shostakovich returned the advance to the theatre.[78]

1939

Libretto for an opera set in the Civil War by V. Bragin, to which Shostakovich contemplated writing music.

The Great Citizen: Shostakovich wrote music for this two-part film, and toyed with the idea of writing an opera about its subject: Sergey Kirov.[79]

1940

The Snow Queen: agreement reached with the Kirov Theatre, but Yevgeny Shvarts did not complete the libretto.[80]

Katyusha Maslova: opera about the heroine of Tolstoy's last novel *Resurrection*, commissioned by the Kirov Theatre in March 1941 and begun in 1940; libretto by Anatoly Mariengof. In May 1941, however, the libretto was banned by the Repertoire Committee.[81]

1948

The Young Guard: opera to be based on Fadeyev's novel of the same name.[82]

1963

Matryona's house: plan by Shostakovich to write an opera based on Solzhenitsyn's story after reading it when first published in *Novy mir* in January 1963.[83]

1964

Quiet Flows the Don: plan to construct an opera from episodes from Sholokhov's novel, with libretto by Yury Lukin and Alexander Medvedev. Perhaps as much as half of the score was written before Shostakovich decided to destroy it.[84]

1972

The Black Monk: Shostakovich's last operatic project. He had been interested in Chekhov's unusual 1894 story since at least 1925, and was particularly struck by the apparently musical properties of its construction: he was convinced it was written in sonata form. Like many of Chekhov's stories, it is a morbid work that explores sickness, death, hallucination and madness, and so had a particular resonance with Shostakovich at the end of his life. In 1972 he completed an arrangement of the Gaetano Braga *Serenade*, which features prominently in the story, for soprano, mezzo-soprano, violin and piano (echoing the themes of the story, it tells of a sick girl who experiences hallucinations). He heard the first performance of his transcription down the phone from his hospital bed: the musicians made a tape recording of it in his flat. It was approximately at this time that Shostakovich completed an outline for a two- or three-act opera, but by 1975 he had evidently given up on this plan when he asked Alexander Medvedev to write a libretto for what he now decided should be a one-act opera. Shostakovich was inspired by his conversations with Medvedev, but all that was ever completed by the composer, apart from his transcription for the *Serenade*, was one manuscript sheet of music for the first scene of his planned opera, plus a few exchanges between the two central characters, Kovrin and Tanya, relating to the beginning of the story, and probably dating from 1973.[85]

8 Shostakovich's ballets

MARINA ILICHOVA

Dmitry Shostakovich wrote three ballets: *The Golden Age*, op. 22 (1929–30), *The Bolt*, op. 27 (1931) and *The Bright Stream*, op. 39 (1935). Despite the fact that Shostakovich, though young, was already well known and showing great promise, the brief initial stage life of these scores meant that they were for a long time not properly appreciated or studied. Officially, they were identified as 'formalistic' and alien to Soviet art, which is partly why they remained 'the least explored part of his musical legacy'.[1] However, a quarter of a century after these unsuccessful premieres, fragments of Shostakovich's ballet music began to be used quite widely. Three ballet suites for small symphony orchestra were often performed at concerts and individual numbers from the scores were included in ballets subsequently created from their music from them, as will be seen.

In the 1920s and 1930s, the former Imperial Ballet went through a period of transition. Its nineteenth-century repertoire, along with its content and aesthetics, was regarded as antiquated and inappropriate for a revolutionary era. To encourage the creation of new works, at the beginning of 1929 the Leningrad Theatre of Opera and Ballet (formerly the Mariinsky) announced a competition for a new ballet scenario, set in the present day. Its demands were typical of the late proletarian period: 'Themes must be predominantly contemporary ... subject matter could be the Civil War or socialist construction ... [it must be] formed from everyday material and, in part, from ethnography ... [from] the peoples of the SSSR ... The spectacle must make use of mass movement.'[2] Among the genres envisaged were the lyrico-heroic poem, comedy, satire, the contemporary fairy tale, survey and even the Soviet revue.

Shostakovich had completed the piano course at the Leningrad Conservatoire by the age of seventeen. To continue to study in the composition department there, he had to begin earning money, and it was in three Leningrad cinemas – 'The Bright Reel', 'The Splendid Palace' and the 'Piccadilly' – that he created musical accompaniments for silent films of various types. These included films of 'everyday life' that called for music of the street, of the restaurants for the new 'NEP-men', and of the music hall. The repeated illustration of the same scenes and the montage of individual episodes gave rise to distinctive intonational formulae that were linked to particular genres. Shostakovich's ability to pick out the most characteristic intonations of a particular environment is widely recognized; it drew inspiration from the full range of his musical interests, which famously spanned all music 'from Bach to Offenbach'. The 'Bright Reel' cinema housed the Choreographical Institute of the famous ballet theoretician and critic Akim Volinsky. Shostakovich earned money there both as an accompanist and as a pianist for classes in 'listening to music'.[3]

The second half of the 1920s was later called the 'golden age' of innovation in the arts. It was the time of Vsevolod Meyerhold and Alexander Tairov in the theatre, of Vladimir Mayakovsky in poetry and of Sergey Eisenstein in the cinema. By this period, the young Shostakovich was regarded as one of the Soviet Union's outstanding composers. His First Symphony, premiered when he was just nineteen years old, proclaimed the arrival of a composer attracted to monumental forms. In his early compositions, a vividly expressed theatricality was observed: even a significant degree of musical illustration, arising directly from the influence of the cinema and theatre. Very soon, Shostakovich was invited to Meyerhold's theatre, and in 1929 he composed music for the show *The Bedbug*, based on Mayakovsky's play. Meyerhold made wide use of the devices of social caricature, pantomime, circus and street theatre, which certainly had an impact on Shostakovich's illustrative devices, and which also played a crucial role in experiments in dance, as choreographers sought to free the medium from the outdated conventions of pre-revolutionary ballet.

No one thought that it would be an easy task to create a new 'Soviet' art, particularly because the first attempt to express the struggle between the proletariat and the bourgeoisie – Fyodor Lopukhov's 1924 ballet *Bolsheviki*, or 'Red Whirlwind' – had turned out to be a failure. The music, by Vladimir Deshevov, made use of revolutionary songs and everyday intonations, including a rendition of the 'Internationale' in the finale. The ballet itself, 'a synthetic poem in two processes with a prologue and an epilogue', consisted of two acts: the first act, or 'process', was based on mass dances and presented the Revolution in terms of the conflict between the forces of reaction and revolution, as embodied by different dancers. The second act showed the reaction to political events of the ordinary 'riff-raff' of society: all social types from ladies with parasols to the 'drunken rabble'. Lopukhov's ambitious programme for the ballet ran as follows:

> Act One: 1. The accumulation of the elements of the socialist worldview without nationalist coloration. 2. The accumulated musical energy is transformed into light energy, reflecting the ever-growing complex of socialism. 3. The further transformation of energy from music to light and then into the form of a living organism. 4. A classical choreographic adagio characterizing socialism. 5. The monolith of socialism. 6. The beginnings of

the schism. 7. The schism. 8. Revolution and counter-revolution (two themes). 9. The affirmation of the star. Act Two: 1. Musical Call. 2. The Citizens Awaiting the Revolution. 3. The Revolution. 4. The Entrance of the Plunderers. 5. The Entrance of the Supporters of the Revolution. 6. The Anguish of the Citizens and the Entrance of the Drunken Rabble. 7. The Dance of the Drunken Rabble and their Arrest. 8. The Entrance of the People Cracking Sunflower Seeds.[4]

The difficulty of portraying such abstract concepts as the 'monolith of socialism' and the 'socialist worldview' proved the downfall of this production, which received only one performance and was never repeated. Even over forty years later, Lopukhov himself described it as his greatest failure.[5] Perhaps most unfortunately of all, the most memorable dances in the ballets were those given to the most negative characters – the 'positive' revolutionary characters were little more than cardboard cut-outs, as critics were quick to point out. Also, in his desire to avoid using any of the gestures of the imperial ballet style, Lopukhov attracted criticism for simplifying dance into a series of marches and gymnastic exercises.[6] But his idealistic scenario, eccentric though it seems today, exemplifies the spirit of experimentation that was thriving in all the arts. To rejuvenate Soviet ballet and create a new kind of dance that was appreciably distinct from the old 'Imperial' style, choreographers turned naturally enough to forms of agitprop such as poster art, street theatre and circus, just as Meyerhold was doing in the theatre and Eisenstein in the cinema. And though *Bolsheviki* was deemed a failure, elements of Lopukhov's 'poster' style found their way into his scenario for Shostakovich's *The Bolt*, as will be seen.

The Golden Age

In 1929, The Leningrad Theatre of Opera and Ballet announced a competition for the best ballet libretto, which was won by the film scriptwriter Alexander Ivanovsky for his libretto *Dynamiada*. This was subsequently taken up by the theatre and recast as *Zolotoy vek* [The golden age], with a score by Shostakovich. It was set in the form of a revue, intended as a striking spectacle rather than as a drama in ballet form: 'The authors wished to contrast Soviet people and Soviet relationships with bourgeois ones. This ballet was characterized by the theatre's management as a "transitional style in Soviet ballet".'[7]

The production of *The Golden Age* was entrusted to the young choreographers Vasily Vaynonen and Leonid Yakobson, who had already revealed their talents in single concert items. Vladimir Chesnakov supplied a few of the dances. The opera producer Emanuel Kaplan was enlisted as director, marking the beginnings of the collaborations between opera producers and choreographers that subsequently, in the era of Soviet ballet-drama, became normal practice. Valentina Khodasevich, well known in the field of agitprop theatre, was the show's designer, and she created a stage background with constructivist buildings and factory chimneys.

The scenario related the visit of a Soviet football team to an industrial exhibition called 'The Golden Age' in an unnamed capitalist city. The Soviets' hostile reception there is contrasted with the warm reception for the fascist team. The appearance of the fascists embodying all the evils of capitalism in a 1929 ballet scenario can scarcely be attributed to the prescience of its author, foreseeing the future course of history. It is more plausible to suppose that this new political development in the West seemed at that time to be an exotic phenomenon, on a par with the depraved temptations of the music hall.

The plot contained various symbolic elements. The transformation of an Indian conjuror into a 'gentleman' at the end alluded to the absorption of national individuality in the capitalist world. A boxing contest between a black man and a fascist is rigged so that the fascist wins, in turn provoking the anger of local workers who are thrown out by the police. Moving to a dance hall, the scenario then shows a sequence of dances: the 'golden youth' dance a foxtrot (devised by Yakobson); the Diva (performed by Yelena Lyukom and Olga Iordan) and the Fascist perform an Adagio, followed by the Diva's solo variation (both devised by Vasily Vaynonen). In sharp contrast to this bizarre 'Western' choreography was the 'Soviet folk dance', full of life and healthy energy, 'characterized in music by contemporary Soviet songs, whose colours were expressed in the orchestra by the bayan'.[8] Vaynonen attempted to combine the movements of Russian folk dance with acrobatics, but this synthesis proved mechanical rather than organic.

In contrast to the Diva, imbued with all the pernicious spirit of the tango and foxtrot, a positive heroine was presented – a sportswoman: indeed, a Komsomol member, with the elastic body of a gymnast and a crystalline soul. Her role was performed by Galina Ulanova and Olga Mungalova, but the anti-heroine Diva, sketched far more vividly, had a greater success with audiences. She was particularly dazzling in the shape of Olga Iordan, a dancer of striking beauty and elegance, whose dance style was a conscious imitation of the famous black American singer and dancer Josephine Baker's angular, plastic movements. Iordan's success severely weakened the denunciatory spirit of the Diva's role. The other dancer of this role, Yelena Lyukom, had a less controversial, more lyrical style; her heroine – pampered, languid, frail, surrounded by servile attention – expressed indifference and boredom. Vaynonen's wife, Klavdiya Armashevskaya, wrote in defence of the choreography,

> The movements of the tango and the foxtrot of the NEP period, crammed with the choreographer's innovations, became especially 'stylish' and acquired virtuosity. In the distinctive Adagio there were even elements of classical ballet, coloured, however, by elements of the atmosphere of modernistic salons. The Diva executed the typical movements of the foxtrot on points. The supports devised by Vaynonen displayed a certain disruption of 'beautiful' stage composition. The producer had no desire at all to force the public to admire the extravagance of this dance, but tried to express in it a sarcastic attitude to the characters.[9]

In Act 1, the captain of the Soviet team refuses to drink the health of the fascists; as they attack him, he raises his hand, holding a football. Taking the ball to be a bomb, the fascists fall to the ground; the Soviet team leave the stage and there ensues the episode 'A Rare Case of Mass Hysteria'. The female dancers were seated in armchairs along the proscenium, wringing their hands and making convulsive movements with their legs, while the male dancers twitched in balletic 'hysterics'. The police rush in, and the episode ends with the 'Bacchanalia of the Foxtrot'. All these scenes were provided by Yakobson, with his characteristic inventiveness.

In Act 2, the Soviet 'action' continues. The captain, the *Komsomolka* and the Negro are strolling in the city, when they are suddenly arrested; fascist agents have secretly planted leaflets on the Soviet captain. The Negro rescues the girl from the police and escapes with her. The subsequent action at the workers' stadium was also devised by Yakobson, and Shostakovich recalled his choreography with pleasure:

> This composition made a great impression through its originality. The pioneers' dance was vividly memorable. The pupils of the famous Leningrad choreographical academy ... thought up a game in which one dancer portrayed a capitalist. He was dressed in a tailcoat and top hat and suddenly merged into the crowd, when suddenly and unobtrusively his costume was plucked from him, revealing a Pioneer underneath. The full-throated laughter of the audience in the hall was the reward for this artifice. But what particularly stuck in the memory was the massed panorama of sport, with Khodasevich's stage scenery and costumes, yellow like pools of sunlight. Here were all types of sport, which Yakobson represented choreographically. Everything that was presented was brought together into a single whole so harmoniously that when after unusually vigorous action the whole ensemble suddenly stopped and floated slowly, as in a slow-motion cinema scene, I could no longer hear the music on account of the ovation of the audience in the hall, directed at the choreographic device (called the 'magnifying-glass of

time'). It was an unforgettable evening. It seemed to me that Yakobson and I had been born in art for the first time, and my music sounded in a new way through its choreographic interpretation.[10]

The music in the dance of the Western pioneers was reminiscent of Soviet songs. A large 'football' tableau, complete with an imaginary ball, showed the Western and Soviet workers in competition, each represented by their own characteristic dances; at the same time, the fascists were shown to be playing cards while the workers engaged in sport. After the football, there followed a quintet of dance and acrobatics, performed by the *komsomolka* and four worker-sportsmen, in which the girl was lifted and thrown from one to another, sometimes vertically, sometimes horizontally and sometimes from above to below with a somersault in mid-air. An orchestral entr'acte, whose main theme was Vincent Youmans' well-known foxtrot song 'Tea for Two', was performed before Act 3. As Alexander Gauk, who conducted the first performance, recalled, during this music 'the public always responded enthusiastically and demanded a repeat'.[11]

In Act 3, the action was again set in the hall for the 'Golden Age' Festival. It opened with a *chechotka*, danced by the Negro advertising a 'superior brand of shoe-polish'. As Armashevskaya recalled, 'it was not a genuine negro dance. Rather, it was a stylization, syncopated, with vigorous rhythm and with an abrupt and disjointed depiction of its movements'. It was so effective that, once again, the audience insisted on a repeat. Then comes the satirical polka 'One Day in Geneva', depicting the 'chatter of the bourgeoisie about peace, disarmament and other fine things'. But the central number was a highly effective pas de deux performed by the Diva and the Fascist, dressed in the Soviet captain's clothes, symbolizing the fascists' false portrayal of a touching unity of capitalism and socialism. As Armashevskaya noted, 'The character of these numbers ... was determined to a significant extent by Shostakovich's exceptionally interesting music'.[12] To conclude this divertissement, a cancan took centre stage, while to the side a jail was shown, in which workers were freeing political prisoners and moving to surround the hall. In the finale the workers and Soviet footballers perform their 'Dance of Solidarity', described in the libretto as 'a dance of labour processes'. Shostakovich later wrote about this: 'The dance of enthusiasm, or the pantomimic representation of a work activity (striking an anvil with a hammer) reveals an inadequately thought-out approach to the problem of a realistic balletic display constructed on a Soviet theme.'[13]

The ballet was warmly received by the public; one reviewer noted that 'the long-continuing calls and tempestuous ovations that greeted the performance speak for themselves'.[14] In the 1930–1 season the ballet was performed nineteen times, and its success was at first officially acknowledged, as is evidenced by the intention to show one act at a ceremony dedicated to the annual anniversary of the Revolution. But soon reactions to the ballet changed. The fate of *The Golden Age* was preordained by its appearance at the end of the 1920s and beginning of the 1930s. The NEP period had come to an end and the 'Great Breakthrough' proclaimed by Stalin had begun.[15]

Of course, the plot was naive and there were weaknesses in the ballet, but in Yury Brodersen's devastating review in *Rabochiy i teatr* [The worker and the theatre] the emphasis was on something else: 'How could it happen that the ideology of the bourgeois music hall, that urban mongrel, that ideology hostile to the Soviet theatre, could penetrate, and to such an immodest degree, the stage of the State Ballet Theatre?'[16]After that article, in which the music was not discussed at all, *Rabochiy i teatr* published the distinctive programme of the Russian Association of Proletarian Musicians (RAPM): 'We shall totally unmask bourgeois ideology in music', in which it was asserted that 'the class enemy is trying to penetrate into the everyday life of the workers'.[17] The entr'acte (*Tahiti Trot*) from *The Golden Age* was cited as an example of such 'bourgeois ideology'. Following these negative official articles, individual numbers gradually began to be removed from the show. Some of the acrobatic elements were curtailed, the *chechotka* at the start of Act 3 was dropped, and after that the whole ballet was withdrawn. Even so, *The Golden Age* was later staged in Kiev and Odessa, here under the title *Dinamiada*, or the *Way of Europe*, with different producers and choreographers.[18]

Notwithstanding either its initial success or the hostile criticism it later attracted, Shostakovich evidently had doubts about *The Golden Age*. Though he staunchly stood by his own score, he was at least for a time unhappy with the production as a whole, perhaps feeling that he had been pressurized into it. Egged on by *The Nose*'s director Nikolay Smolich and his friend Sollertinsky, Shostakovich had collaborated in a ballet that he went so far as to describe as 'anti-artistic', blaming those who had encouraged him to pursue it against his own judgement.[19] The problem for Shostakovich seemed to lie in what he perceived as a lack of unity between the music and the staging, and in the fact that he felt the music had not played the primary role he believed it should have done. Still, his memories of *The Golden Age* could not have been completely negative, given his warm recollection of Yakobson's staging in the 1960s. And any doubts he may have had about *The Golden* Age did not prevent him from continuing to work with choreographers on further projects; indeed, he might conceivably have continued to work with ballet had it not been for the brutal curtailment of any such plans by the *Pravda* article 'Baletnaya Falsh' [Balletic falsity] in February 1936.

The years passed, and Shostakovich's music for ballet remained a legacy of incontestable artistic value and a vivid testimony of its own time, which attracted the attention of later choreographers. *The Golden Age* was the first of Shostakovich's three ballets to be revived, when Yury Grigorovich devised a new production at the Bolshoy in 1982. In an attempt to overcome the weaknesses of the original scenario, Grigorovich, in collaboration with Isaak Glikman, composed a new libretto, though this arguably failed to strengthen the drama. And by inserting other works by Shostakovich into the score, Grigorovich further damaged the integrity of the original ballet. Shostakovich himself had argued that,

> A ballet, just like an opera, should be staged using the actual score, and not an 'imaginary' one. Furthermore, in the choreographic world the approach to ballet is still rather like the approach to a 'semi-finished' product at a factory, that is not deserving of any particular respect ... Respect for the composer's work should be the first commandment for interpreters, be they choreographer, producer, conductor or designer. No distortions of the composer's text must be allowed – that is a rigid rule.[20]

The Bolt

Almost at the same time as the *The Golden Age* was originally staged, the Opera and Ballet Theatre were rehearsing *The Bolt*: a choreographed show in three acts, also to Shostakovich's music. Even before its premiere on 8 April 1931 (after which it was immediately withdrawn) it could have been suspected that the ballet was doomed to failure owing to its weak scenario, written by Viktor Smirnov, who at that time held the post of Director at the Moscow Art Theatre. In other respects, however, the brightest and best names in Soviet ballet were collaborating on the project. It was choreographed by the innovative Fyodor Lopukhov, with sets by the young artists Tatyana Bruni and Georgy Korshikov. *The Bolt* was the first experiment in ballet on the theme of industrial production, to which at that time drama and even opera were making their due contributions. Despite the ballet's dangerously topical subject of criminal conflict (factory sabotage), Shostakovich and Lopukhov devised a cheerful, satirical comedy show in the style of the post-revolutionary theatrical productions of the young workers' theatres. However, Shostakovich was scathing about Smirnov's scenario, writing to Sollertinsky:

> Comrade Smirnov has read me the libretto for a ballet, *The New Machine*. Its theme is extremely relevant. There once was a machine. Then it broke down (problem of material decay). Then it was mended (problem of amortisation),

and at the same time they bought a new one. Then everybody dances round the new machine. Apotheosis. This all takes up three acts.[21]

However embarrassingly banal Shostakovich and Lopukhov may have found the scenario, *The Bolt* might have been salvaged by its characteristically witty choreography and scoring if it had been shown for more than a single night. As it was, it would be seventy-four years before it received a second performance, this time with radically different sets and designs.[22]

The scenario was set in a factory, whose workers included Olga, the secretary of the Komsomol organization, Boris, the team leader, Kozelkov, the chief clerk (but in reality a ne'er-do-well) and a number of drunken workers. The factory management sack one worker, Lyonka Gulba, for drunkenness and absenteeism. He then forces the young apprentice Goshka to place a bolt in the machinery in order to cause an accident. But Goshka's revolutionary conscience triumphs; he tells all, and 'justice' wins the day. The first two acts were devoted to presenting the 'positive' and 'negative' characters. On the one hand, there were the Komsomol workers; on the other, Lyonka and his drinking companions, Kozelkov, the priest and some 'god-worshippers'. The choreography, in line with the music, was linked with the genre of Soviet song, with fitness-promoting marches and everyday dances (waltz and polka). Examples include the exit march from the first act, 'To Work with Gymnastics', 'Checking the Installation of Machines', 'Quadrille of the Komsomol Members' and 'Start-Up at the Workplace'. These scenes formed a satirical general revue on an industrial theme, in Lopukhov's best vaudeville style. This time – in contrast to his earlier *Bolsheviki* – even the positive characters were portrayed in a playful manner, in a style originating in the spirit of the old folk street theatre. The blacksmith, dancing with two little hammers, was presented in this humorous way, as were the cavalry, where chairs served as 'horses', something that went down especially badly with the Soviet press, as will be seen.

The workers' music developed actively, while the themes of the saboteurs remained almost unchanging. In Lopukhov's characteristic 'poster' style, both musical and choreographical images of the negative characters were realized exclusively in brightly satirical colours. The first appearance of Lyonka was accompanied by a languid waltz, reminiscent of the Viennese waltzes that were recognized as symbols of bourgeois contentment. Kozelkov entered to the melody of a tango, with the same 'bourgeois' Strauss waltz-like 'caprices'. Similarly, the god-worshippers, the priest and the sacristan were sketched with prayerful, doleful intonations. As their hypocrisy is unmasked, the priest – forgetting the dignity of his office – breaks into a dance and blesses the group of saboteurs.

The 'production' dances had a special place in the ballet, drawing their animated character from the urban art that had sprung up in the West. Reproducing the movements of a 'lifting dance', a 'tractor' and, most memorably, a 'loom', twenty-four ballerinas were arranged in two lines, in which the front row now sank to their knees, now rose and almost straightened up, while their arms kept moving, representing the flicking of the shuttles and threads of a sewing machine.

It is now hard to establish what was successful for the producers and what was not. It could be guessed that, as with Lopukhov's *Bolsheviki*, many of the satirical portraits of the negative characters were successful, since the reviewers, while accusing Lopukhov of relishing depictions of drunken revelry, nevertheless observed that this action had been well devised in a variety of episodes. *The Bolt* was a veritable collection of clear and cheerful youthful themes, several of which Shostakovich recycled in later works: the cantata *Song of the Forests*, the Ninth Symphony, the score of the film *The First Echelon* ('Song of Youth'), in the Second Piano Concerto and in the operetta *Moscow-Cheryomushki*.

In the press, *The Bolt* was discussed solely from an ideological point of view, with predictable criticisms concerning Lopukhov's stark divisions into 'goodies and baddies' and vulgarized use of music and dance: 'A class-based disposition of forces has been replaced by a simplified division of all characters into the good and the bad.'[23] The satirical presentation of the positive characters, specifically the blacksmith's dance, was perceived as slanderous: 'The disgraceful smith's dance with two little hammers is close to parody ... The Red Army dance (a race on chairs) is an insult to the Reds' Cavalry, and all the Red Army dances discredit the Red Army.'[24]

In May 1931 Lopukhov decided to rework *The Bolt* in accordance with these criticisms, but it made no further appearances on the stage. Nonetheless, Shostakovich's association with Lopukhov continued. Although Lopukhov's career with the Leningrad Theatre of Opera and Ballet came to an end after *The Bolt*, he was subsequently invited to create a second ballet company in the Maly Opera Theatre, with a repertoire distinct from that of the Theatre of Opera and Ballet. Inspired by the founder of realistic ballet comedy in the time of the French Revolution, Jean Doberval, the Maly Opera Theatre struck upon the idea of shaping their productions along comedic lines, as a genre close to the masses and well liked by them. They began by presenting reworkings of Drigo's *Harlequinade* and Delibes's *Coppelia*. The characters of the *commedia dell'arte* and the *Tales of Hoffmann* were turned into real people: Columbine became a daughter of the bourgeoisie, Harlequin a poor student, and the mythical Coppelius was recast as the owner of a travelling puppet theatre. Lopukhov sought an everyday, social 'concretization', conveyed not in the libretto, nor through pantomime, but in dance, which he regarded as the principal medium of artistic expression. In their work on these ballets, Lopukhov and his associates had in mind a performance dedicated to the contemporary world, in which, having learned the lessons of *The Bolt* and *The Golden Age*, they wished to avoid both crude propagandizing, or the conventional 'exotic' portrayal of the West.

The Bright Stream

Lopukhov's collaborator Adrian Piotrovsky proposed that the action of their next Soviet comedic ballet should be transferred to a southern *kolkhoz* (collective farm) at the colourful and joyous harvest festival, whose images of village youth, milkmaids and combine harvesters would be revealed – images that would bring to the show distinctive, lively dance styles. Such a setting would enable them to use the best of traditional choreography in a faultlessly contemporary setting, circumventing the problems of 'cardboard' goodies and baddies as well as avoiding the difficulty of expressing essentially abstract ideological notions in dance. As Lopukhov declared in his introductory essay to the production of *The Bright Stream*, 'the basis of the art of ballet in our times remains classical dance, as a means of expressing emotions in their utmost intensity, as a language of lyricism and passion'.[25] As he recalled in the 1960s, however, looking back on the 1930s, 'we were unable to overcome, by direct means, the contradiction ... between classical dance and the real life that surrounded us'.[26] It proved necessary, rather, to resort to various dramatic subterfuges. Whatever criticisms Lopukhov expressed about his own work, however, he was full of generous praise for Shostakovich's score:

> For the creation of the music we were able to attract a young composer whom we loved and whom we had admired from his first beginnings.... I refer to D. Shostakovich.... In *The Bright Stream* we wished to show that the mistakes of *The Bolt* were a stage that we had left behind us; we wished to devote music and dance to positive heroes, to proclaim the joyfulness of their lives, their work of clear purpose, foreshadowing the joy of labour. Shostakovich wrote inspiring, tuneful music of great humour and lyricism ... His outstanding talent, illuminated by his contemporary sensibility, allowed Shostakovich to rise above our naive and clumsy venture.[27]

In turn, Shostakovich supported Lopukhov's experiments and was truly fascinated by the creation of this new ballet: 'It is a hard and responsible task to create a major ballet on a Soviet theme. But I am not afraid of difficulties,' he wrote in the collection of articles issued for the first performance. 'To stick to the beaten track is, perhaps, easier and "safer", but boring, uninteresting, purposeless.' Shostakovich saw the failure of his first ballets as lying in the fact that the producers, in showing contemporary life, did not take the specific nature of ballet into account, introducing a pantomimic representation of work processes. 'I cannot ordain', he concluded, 'that the third attempt should not also turn out to be a failure, but even then this will on no account turn me away from the intention of undertaking, even for a fourth time, the composition of a Soviet ballet.'[28]

This time, the plot focused on romantic situation comedy rather than politics. For the kolkhoz harvest festival, a team of performers arrives from the city, and are met by a student agronomist, Pyotr, and his wife Zina, an old *kolkhoz* activist, Gavrilich, and a girl, Galya, and her friends. Among the performers Zina recognizes an old ballet class friend; though she has concealed her professional training in the *kolkhoz*, she has not forgotten it, and when the others leave, the two girls dance together. Unfortunately, Zina's husband is already fascinated by the newcomer (who has arrived with her partner), and Zina is immediately jealous of her friend.

Evening comes and work is finished. The performers bestow gifts on the *kolkhoz*, and the dancing begins. The old men and the girls from the amateur dramatic society perform, the farm labourers dance an antique chaconne, a milkmaid (in a dress given her by the visiting performers) dances with a tractor driver. The professionals perform in an improvised way, without stage costumes. Pyotr is increasingly drawn to the ballerina. The Kuban cossacks and the Caucasians perform a spirited dance, and the festivities reach their climax. As everyone disperses, an old labourer invites the ballerina to meet him, while his wife invites her partner. But Pyotr, upsetting Zina, will not leave the ballerina alone. When the ballerina comes to reassure Zina that she has no intention of responding to his advances, she suggests that Zina reveal her past training, and the girls then dance, astonishing Zina's fellow villagers. They then plot to trick Pyotr and the labourers by swapping clothes and going to meet them as planned. The whole of the second act is occupied by this comic rendezvous, which prompts a mock duel before the inevitable cheerful country dance and reconciliation of all parties.

Such is the scenario of *The Bright Stream*, full of absurdities. However, its plot was hardly without precedents in the history of world theatre (*The Marriage of Figaro* being the most obvious). And the first performance of *The Bright Stream* was a complete success. Among its stars were well-known dancers of the former Mariinsky Theatre who had worked closely with Lopukhov: Pyotr Gusev (Pyotr), Feya Balabina (Ballerina), Nikolay Zubovsky (Dancer) and Andrey Lopukhov (mountain-dweller). The music of the new ballet was based on material from *The Bolt* and, like the earlier scores, it was constructed on the principle of montage of lyrical and comic episodes, of classical dance and specific 'character' dances. There was a marked absence of any kind of unifying, developing idea; both Shostakovich and Lopukhov emphasized the accessibility of the music. 'The music of the ballet … is cheerful, easy, entertaining and – the main thing – is for dancing to', wrote Shostakovich. 'I deliberately tried here to find a clear and simple language, equally intelligible for the audience and for the performers.'[29] Still, Ivan Sollertinsky, one of the most prominent musical figures of those years, had mixed praise for it. He considered the music to be 'lively, spirited, not very complex in construction, orchestrated always with virtuosity, sometimes biting and malicious, sometimes gently humorous, at times sinning in repetitiveness and a certain crude simplification, but always engaging and cheerful. *The Bright Stream* is not one of Shostakovich's best ballet scores and, generally speaking, falls short of *The Golden Age*, which is remarkable in its mastery.'[30]

The premiere was a huge success, and the ballet quickly became popular. Lopukhov was invited to stage it at the Bolshoy Theatre, where its success again exceeded all expectations. He was duly appointed as the artistic director of the ballet company of the Soviet Union's leading theatre. But the articles in *Pravda*, with their criticisms of Shostakovich's opera *Lady Macbeth* and *The Bright Stream*, cut short the stage life of these works; *The Bright Stream* was removed from the ballet repertoire as swiftly as *Lady Macbeth* was taken off the opera stage, and it remained unperformed until its revival in 2003.

Reinventions and revivals: symphonic ballets

Today, Shostakovich's creative work has come to be more fully valued. Figures in the world of ballet, both in Russia and abroad, have again become interested in music that is expressive, flexible and full of danceable ideas. Leonid Massine was the first to turn to Shostakovich's music, albeit to symphonies rather than to ballet scores. On 4 May 1939 in Monte Carlo he produced *Le Rouge et le noir* ('L'Étrange farandole'), a ballet composed from the First Symphony, with scenery by Henri Matisse. Its New York premiere took place on 27 October at the Metropolitan Opera. In the summer of 1945, Massine directed the New York production of *The Leningrad Symphony* given by the 'Ballet Russe Highlights', a ballet set to the first movement of the Seventh Symphony. In this way Massine was in the forefront of those choreographers who interpreted Shostakovich's symphonic music.

In 1961, the famous dancer and choreographer of the Kirov Ballet Igor Belsky returned to this idea. He too produced the first movement of the 'Leningrad', which reflected on events of the war.[31] Musical imagery was his ally in opposing the choreodrama that then dominated Soviet ballet. On the advice of Shostakovich he created his choreography on the basis of the musical score and so established the genre of the 'ballet-symphony'. Belsky's experience of symphonic ballet continued on the stage of the Maly Theatre of Opera and Ballet in the production *The Eleventh Symphony* ('The Year 1905')'. Through songs the epoch of the first Russian Revolution was presented as the tragedy of the events of 1956.

Following Belsky's work with Shostakovich's symphonies, in 1977 the choreographers Natalya Rïzhenko and Vladimir Smirnov-Golovanov staged a production entitled *Symphonic Revolution* to music from the Eleventh and Twelfth Symphonies in the Odessa Theatre, while Svetlana Voskresenskaya devised the ballet *Dangerous Shadows* (1985) to musical fragments from the First, Second and Seventh Symphonies for the Stanislavsky and Nemirovich-Danchenko Theatres.

In the 1960s, ballets set to Shostakovich's music were staged at many of the Soviet Union's theatres. In 1959 the balletmaster Aleksey Varlamov produced *Dance Suite* at the Bolshoy, comprising the numbers 'Introduction', 'Spring Waltz', 'Polka', 'Elegy', 'Gavotte', 'Waltz', 'Galop and Coda'. The balletmaster Vladimir Varkovitsky produced *Flowers* at the Maly Theatre in October 1961. In December 1962, the Maly put on three one-act ballets by Konstantin Boyarsky to Shostakovich's music: *The Lady and the Hooligan*, *The Directive Bow* ['Direktivnïy bantik'] and *The Meeting*. The first of these, composed for a film scenario by Mayakovsky, was revised for the ballet stage by Belsky and became very popular. *The Directive Bow* was choreographed as a satirical sketch, while *The Meeting* was set to music from the Tenth Symphony. In 1975 the Stanislavsky and Nemirovich-Danchenko Theatres produced the premiere of Rïzhenko and Smirnov-Golovanov's ballet *The Dream*, which was set to music from *The Bolt* and *The Golden Age*.

Another choreographer to have used Shostakovich's music extensively is Leonid Yakobson. For his group 'Choreographic Miniatures' in June 1962, he produced a choreographed 'poster' in two acts on Mayakovsky's *The Bedbug* with Shostakovich's original score for Meyerhold's 1929 production.[32] For the Kirov Theatre, Yakobson created remarkable shows with music from various Shostakovich works: *The Favourite Absinthe* (1959), *Flying Waltz* (1960) and *Carters' Dance* (1964). Shostakovich's symphonic poem *The Execution of Stepan Razin* inspired the balletmaster Konstantin Rassadin to create a unique ballet, again for the group 'Choreographic

Miniatures' in June 1977. More recently in 1982, Yury Grigorovich staged *The Golden Age* at the Bolshoy, with a new scenario, while Aleksey Ratmansky, the head of the Bolshoy Theatre Ballet Company, re-created *The Bright Stream* in 2003 as well as staging *The Bolt* in 2005. *The Golden Age* was revived again at the Mariinsky Theatre in 2006 with a new scenario and choreography by Konstantin Uchitel (libretto) and Noah D. Gelber.[33]

9 Screen dramas: Shostakovich's cinema career

JOHN RILEY

By the time Shostakovich's opera *The Lady Macbeth of Mtsensk District* was condemned in 1936,[1] over half of his forty numbered opuses were dramatic works: two operas, three ballets, seven theatre scores, and nine film scores. His juvenilia include dramatic and programmatic pieces and throughout his career he continued to write such works. But after 1936, for a variety of reasons both political and practical, his dramatic output fell away, often leaving him collaborating on politically acceptable work with friends: he seems not to have enjoyed theatre work, his ballets had been negatively received, and after the mauling of *Lady Macbeth* he did not complete another opera (only the operetta *Moscow, Cheryomushki*). His film music was left as the only outlet for his dramatic talent.[2]

His professional introduction to cinema came in 1924, as he helped support his family by becoming a cinema pianist. His enthusiasm soon waned: not only did this hackwork compete with his conservatoire studies, but there were few opportunities for him to develop new approaches to dramatic music. Happily, the First Symphony's success allowed him to drop the work in 1926, but he was lured back to the cinema when the Leningrad studio Sovkino commissioned a score to be performed live to *New Babylon* (1929),[3] a film about the Paris Commune. The directors, Grigory Kozintsev and Leonid Trauberg, led FEKS (acronym for Factory of the Eccentric Actor) and, with their desire to shock and surprise the audience, they offered just the sort of freedom Shostakovich had craved in the cinema pit.

Each reel of *New Babylon* formed a single 'act' of around ten minutes, and Shostakovich followed this structure, though the music sometimes ran contrary to what was on screen so violently that Shostakovich, with the directors' approval, prepared the ground with an explanatory press article.[4] He highlighted the way he used operetta music for the scenes on the barricade, and music associated with the Prussian cavalry for a scene in a deserted Paris restaurant, to remind us of their continuing approach.

But the intended effect was completely ruined when the film was massively re-edited under instruction from the studio after he had completed the music. As best he could, Shostakovich reworked the score and corrected the parts to match the new version, but it defeated the performers, who in any case would have preferred to play the usual concoctions of popular hits. *New Babylon* was a notorious scandal, though in fact Shostakovich's score was positively received by some critics. With only silent prints extant, revivals still rely on a live orchestra, and the exact synchronization of music and action is still a matter of debate[5]

As state control over the cinema industry tightened, scrutiny increased and film proposals had to include the names of all major collaborators. So when, despite *New Babylon*'s problems, Kozintsev and Trauberg kept faith with Shostakovich, they had to include his name in the proposal for their next film, *Alone* [Odna, 1931], in which the teacher Yelena Kuzmina (played by the actress of the same name) is assigned to the remote Altai. Contrary to Kuzmina's claim,[6] *Alone* was planned as a sound film from the beginning, and the studio approved Shostakovich as the composer, so long as he understood that he was to refrain from writing anything like his iconoclastic early opera *The Nose* or *The New Babylon*. Rather than matching each reel with a complete musical structure and risking a rerun of *New Babylon*'s frantic re-editing, Shostakovich wrote a mosaic of small pieces that could be cut, repeated or edited to match the film on its way to completion. Not only did this pragmatism make synchronization easier, but it also suited *Alone*'s shorter scenes. With full control over the synchronization, it would be clear that the strange effects that had puzzled *New Babylon*'s audience were deliberate. One of these occurs when the petit-bourgeois teacher and her fiancé go shopping and end up duetting on cello and kitchen implements, while the score itself ignores their music, instead commenting on their hopes through the song '*How Good Life Will Be!*' [Kakaya khoroshaya budet zhizn'!]. With few sound cinemas in the USSR, synchronized speech and sound effects were used sparingly and written intertitles still appeared on screen to report speech and explain the action for the still-silent cinemas. In fact, *Alone*'s almost continuous music gave Shostakovich essentially the same task as he had had with *New Babylon*. But unlike the earlier film, *Alone* adds speech and sound effects to the music so that the relationship between the three had to be decided. So, as Kuzmina does her morning exercises, a hurdy-gurdy man's music and other street sounds are made to accommodate each other while her movements constantly miss the beat, implying either that she is oblivious to it or that this particular synchronization was a late decision. In *Alone*, the makers deliberately blur diegetic and non-diegetic music in a way that extends their earlier approach in *New Babylon*. There, the score falls away at one point to make room for a poignant moment of nostalgic calm as an old man plays the melody that Tchaikovsky adapted as his *Old French Song* on a piano that has been piled onto the barricades. In *Alone*, the directors used the recording of a real shaman to cut short Kuzmina's reminiscences of Leningrad, symbolized by the theme that first accompanied shots of the city at the beginning of the film. This prescient view of music and sound remains important in film-making today, and while it was appreciated on a technical level, *Alone*'s negative outlook made it only slightly less politically contentious than *New Babylon*. It was held back for a few days by the studio, a particular problem being the song '*How Good Life Will Be!*' – perhaps perceived even then as an ironic provocation, as it was claimed that it would 'put the viewer in an undesirable state of mind'.[7] But from the point of view of Shostakovich's cinema career, the song was the most important feature of the film: up to this point he had not written many songs, least of all in a popular style. After Shostakovich's death Trauberg claimed to have dictated it to the composer.[8] But whatever its origin, it opened up another flank in his film music writing, and from now on he would often pursue the symphonic and the song score in parallel, most notably in his next film *Golden Mountains* [Zlatïye gorï, 1931].

In the 1930s, industrialization was a popular theme in much Soviet art and *Golden Mountains* is one such example. In 1914, the peasant-farmer Pyotr comes to Petrograd to earn the money to buy a horse, and the song 'If Only I Had Mountains of Gold' reflects his dreams of wealth. The bosses bribe him to strike-break, but he recovers his class-consciousness and sides with his fellows. Though *Alone* and *Golden Mountains* were made at around the same time, the latter has more synchronized speech while still using intertitles for silent cinemas. Again the music moves in and out of the narrative: Pyotr is bribed with a chiming watch whose catchy waltz becomes the theme of the duplicitous bourgeoisie and appears both diegetically and non-diegetically. Ironically, the waltz's political implications were overlooked when, divorced from its context, it became popular in its own right: there were several piano reductions,[9] and Shostakovich is seen playing it in the short film *Concert Waltz* [Kontsert-Vals, 1940]. A suite from the film score was published in 1935,[10] and the film was re-released a year later, though this may have been because dozens of other films were being stopped in production as both scripts and films at various stages of completion, together with their directors, were re-examined for their political orientation. As Yekaterina Khokhlova notes, 'in 1935 about 2,700 films made between 1922 and 1935, including newsreels, shorts, animated films and around 500 full-length feature films were banned ... By 1935 the majority of films made in the 1920s and many of those made in the early 1930s had been taken out of distribution.'[11] As with *Alone*, the division between music and sound effects is subtly blurred: the strike-planning scene in the toilets uses a tolling harp and celeste, both to mark the slowly passing time and to evoke the sound of dripping water.

Whatever their quality, sound films were still a novelty and would have attracted audiences; but all the same, Soviet cinema was falling embarrassingly behind the West. By the time of *The Counterplan*'s [Vstrechniy] release in 1932, Western cinemas were almost all equipped for sound, whereas the Soviet Union's sheer size and the levels of investment necessary meant that the majority of cinemas were still mute. Nevertheless, *The Counterplan* went further than its predecessors in dispensing with intertitles, its particularly complex soundscape intermingling music and effects in even more advanced ways. And, building on the success of his previous two film songs, Shostakovich wrote the hugely successful 'Song of the Counterplan'. Though mass songs have sometimes been unfairly stereotyped as simple, repetitious songs sung in unison at great length by untrained proletarians, they could be more complex. Shostakovich had up to now avoided the genre entirely; but his film songs did conform to the mass song ideal by at least being catchy and popular. *The Counterplan*'s opening credits are accompanied by a rendition of this infectious song's early morning call to work, repeated by choir, orchestra and, as the film opens, the heroine, as she and her husband get up. But the film also marked a further advance in the coupling of music and sound effects as the factory noises and score occasionally interweave, making it difficult to tell where one ends and the other begins.

Inevitably, some of Shostakovich's film scores were written either after the film was complete or late in production, but his next film, a version of Pushkin's *The Tale of the Priest and his Servant, Blockhead* [Skazka o pope i ego rabotnike Balda] was animated, so that the images and music were planned in parallel, with the music being written first. But work proceeded haltingly, and in 1936 the director Mikhail Tsekhanovsky was sacked with the film still unfinished. Though he claimed that it was Shostakovich's involvement that led to its being canned, this may have been an excuse for his own dilatoriness.[12] Some of what was completed was destroyed in the wartime bombing of Leningrad, but what survives looks like animated *luboks* (folk woodcuts).[13] To match this, Shostakovich produced a score full of grotesquerie that harked back to his earliest works, but which may not have been in keeping with the reverence with which Pushkin was held in the approach to his centenary year of 1937.

After *Pravda*'s condemnation of *Lady Macbeth*, Shostakovich's income fell dramatically. During these years, and those immediately post-dating the *Zhdanovshchina* of 1948, Shostakovich worked extensively in the cinema, for the practical purpose of earning much-needed money and using politically acceptable projects as a route to rehabilitation. As he worked on *The Tale of a Priest*, the doctrine of Socialist Realism was unveiled at the Writers' Congress of August 1934. Perhaps in part because the tenets of this new aesthetic were as yet not fully formed, for a time it seemed possible to interpret it according to one's own creative ideas, Shostakovich's next two films, *The Youth of Maxim* (1935) [Iunost Maksima] and *Love and Hate* (1934) [Lyubov i nenavist], show little of what we might today perceive as Socialist Realism's direct influence. However, he soon began simply to provide diegetic music or to use the score unequivocally to mould the audience's emotions. Rather than penning new songs, he often relied on existing popular and revolutionary songs such as 'Be Brave, Brothers' [Smeley, druzya] and 'You Fell as a Victim' [Vï zhertvoyu pali], which would play an important role in several future works.

One of the last exuberant moments in his film work for some years was the Prelude from *The Youth of Maxim*, with its cunning interweaving of three popular melodies: *Oira Polka*, the *Krakowiak* and *Dark Eyes* [Ochi chornïye]. Kozintsev and Trauberg's Maxim Trilogy charts a simple worker's progress from joining the Party in 1910 to becoming head of the National Bank in 1918. Maxim is identified by variants on the folk song *Whirling and Twirling* [Krutitsya-Vertitsya]. So strong was the association between Maxim's character and this song, that Shostakovich used it to identify Maxim when he returns, disguised, in the first part of Fridrikh Ermler's two-part film *The Great Citizen* (1937) [Velikiy grazhdanin] which, though apparently unrelated, does have some links to the Maxim Trilogy.

Despite the poorly defined but palpable restraints of Socialist Realism, production continued on Albert Gendelshteyn's *Love and Hate*. The setting of the Civil War-torn and occupied Donbass certainly provided an opportunity to celebrate the country and its people with appropriate revolutionary fervour; but the women in the film manage their affairs largely without the Party's help and their men are 'saved' by the Red Army's arrival only at the last minute. Although the women's work songs suggest a more overtly populist approach, the film remains strikingly dark, its expressionistic photography complemented by Shostakovich's turbulent score. His now-familiar trick of diegetic/non-diegetic ambiguity is here found in his use of the gramophone, which comments on the action whilst being part of it, as when a soldier uses a recording of a sleazy waltz to seduce a woman.

With Lev Arnshtam's *Girlfriends* [Podrugi, 1936], Shostakovich moved back to a more purely 'musical' score. Starting with music for string quartet (foreshadowing his great cycle), he thickens the texture with piano and trumpet, echoing the texture of his recent piano concerto and later introduces full orchestral cues. He was also able to include the revolutionary song 'Tormented by Harsh Captivity' [Zamuchen tyazholoy nevoley] without it seeming forced, and it would reappear in the Eighth String Quartet (1960). Like most of his previous films, *Girlfriends* was distributed in the West, but with only moderate success both there and at home, it was soon relatively forgotten: a pity, since it was Shostakovich's last consistently interesting film score for some time.

The crisis of 'Chaos Instead of Music' seems to have prompted Shostakovich to turn more urgently to revolutionary themes. After 1937's *The Return of Maxim* [Vozvrashcheniye Maksima], 1938 marked a high-point in quantity if not in quality with five films: *Volochayev Days* [Volochayevskiye dni], *Friends* [Druzya], *The Man with a Gun* [Chelovek s ruzhyom], part one of *The Great Citizen* (part two followed in 1939) and *The Viborg Side* [Vïborgskaya storona]. In this work his style was noticeably more 'comprehensible', in response to official criticism of 'formalist' music. Calls for comprehensibility were not limited to composers, and film was especially vulnerable to the demands of the concept of 'reality' contained within Socialist Realism's phrase 'reality in its revolutionary development'. As early as 1928 a cinema conference had called for films that were 'intelligible to the millions'.[14] Rather than truly depicting current reality, art was now expected to portray the world that socialism would bring in the future. Shostakovich would have to control his exuberance, experimentation and satire. It was time to sing a new kind of song.

Shostakovich's involvement with some of the more propagandistic films of the immediate pre-war years was fairly minimal. For *The Man with a Gun* (1938) he wrote just ten minutes of music, but though most of it is standard issue, there is a clever interlude to transport the hero from the First World War trenches to Petrograd, using clock chimes to move us through various locations. *Volochayev Days* also has some interesting musical moments, including a curiously comic battle scene that looks forward to the finale of the Sixth Symphony. He had very little to do on Ermler's two-part epic *The Great Citizen*, which clearly echoes the assassination of the Leningrad Party chief Sergey Kirov and explains the need for retribution. The title music's rising motif is reminiscent of the finale of the Fifth Symphony, which might in retrospect imply some ambiguity, but it is also the 'optimistic' opposite of the falling melody of the old Russian revolutionary song 'You Fell as a Victim' which forms the basis of the final funeral march. Ironically, the people who were being proposed as 1930s counter-revolutionaries were the very ones who were being extolled as the builders of the Revolution in the Maxim Trilogy.[15] The continuation of Maxim's story (*The Return of Maxim* and *The Viborg Side*) was similarly light on original music, though there were a number of arrangements of various pieces including the ubiquitous *Whirling and Twirling* and, for the anarchists, Kurt Weill's *Cannon Song*. Of the films from this period, *Friends* has more music than most, but hardly any of it is distinguished or even identifiably by Shostakovich.

Though none of these films involved a great deal of work, like many Soviet citizens, Shostakovich must have been exhausted by the general atmosphere of the Terror. The years preceding the Soviet Union's entry into the Second World War in June 1941 had been so bleak that the conflict itself may actually have come as a kind of relief, since Hitler's forces represented a real, firmly defined, external enemy onto which the regime could turn its fire, rather than the imagined one within. With the Seventh Symphony announced and in hand, Shostakovich was able to work on less propaganda-saturated films, and these years saw just three releases: a children's film, a comedy and a war film.

The Story of the Silly Little Mouse [Skazka o glupom mïshonke, 1940] marked the return of the animator Mikhail Tsekhanovsky after the debacle of *The Tale of the Priest*. Since the mid-1930s, his style had become softer and more Disney-like, and Shostakovich matched it with a gentle evocation of evening and a charming portrayal of the various animals who try to persuade a baby mouse to sleep. Shostakovich followed that with the slapstick comedy *The Adventures of Korzinkina* [Priklyucheniya Korzinkinoy, 1940], following a hapless singer, obviously modelled on Chaplin, who was as great a cult in the Soviet Union as in the rest of the world. It was planned as the first of a series of films, presumably with Shostakovich as composer for all of them, but in the event only the first was completed. Both *The Mouse* and *The Priest* allowed Shostakovich a closer cooperation with the film-makers than he had been accustomed to. In order to ensure the synchronization of music and image, Tsekhanovsky's film was animated to Shostakovich's pre-written music, and the synchronization in *Korzinkina* makes it clear that parts of the film were edited to fit the score.

Given Shostakovich's love of Chaplin, he could well have enjoyed this commission, but his most substantial wartime film score was for Arnshtam's *Zoya* (1944), the mythically expanded true-life story of Zoya Kosmodemyanskaya, a partisan who was hanged by the Nazis aged eighteen. Some of the fanfares have an unusual and appropriate tenderness, though later parts of the score tend to bombast. There are about twenty-five minutes of music in the film – Shostakovich's lengthiest for some time – but it is very fragmentary; he seems to have had difficulty composing extended cues and the occasional uncertainty as to whether or not the music is part of the diegesis does not appear to be wholly deliberate. A 'growing-up' fanfare accompanies Zoya at various points in her life, but when she dreams of taking part in a Red Square parade the orchestration seems relatively light for such an event, leaving us momentarily uncertain as to the music's role.

After the war Shostakovich continued to compose film scores, starting with *Simple People* [Prostïye lyudi], which was in production from 1944 to 1946 but was only released in 1956 in a version so mangled that the makers disowned it. Like *Love and Hate*, it is a dark story, this time set in Uzbekistan, and Shostakovich wrote an equally tortured score with an 'optimistic' end that seems forced and half-hearted – its echo of the finale of the Fifth Symphony may not have been accidental. Like the earlier *Friends* it has 'ethnic' music, but it is much better integrated and rather than simply forming background colour it does move the story forward, underlining the differences between the Uzbeks and the immigrant Russians. But the Kozintsev–Trauberg partnership was suffering internal strains, which increased when Trauberg was accused of 'cosmopolitanism' (a common euphemism for being Jewish) in the late 1940s,[16] and *Simple People* was their last collaboration. Many of the major Soviet directors (including Kozintsev) were Jewish or part-Jewish, but for reasons that remain unclear Trauberg was particularly targeted. Most of the regular team (including Shostakovich) who had worked with them for nearly twenty years continued with Kozintsev rather than with Trauberg, who broke with the composer in about 1950 in a misunderstanding over a planned operetta.[17]

The late 1940s and early 1950s saw a rash of biopics extolling great Russians who had paved the way for the Revolution, be they composers, scientists or military heroes; contemporary figures were generally avoided for fear of creating a rival personality cult.[18] Shostakovich contributed to three: celebrating the Crimean surgeon Nikolay Pirogov (1947), the agronomist Ivan Michurin (1950) and the literary critic Vissarion Belinsky (1950, released 1953).[19] Though they were exceptional people, in these films the important point was that they were completely focused on their work in which they were inspired by the concept of *narodnost* [being for or of the people]. This had been a central tenet of Socialist Realism since the 1930s, but it was more rigidly enforced after the Decree of 1948 in which Shostakovich, Prokofiev, Myaskovsky, Shebalin and Popov were accused of 'formalism' and 'anti-people' tendencies. Accordingly, choral music and folk songs became very popular in the post-1948 cultural climate, and as well as ensuring that he included them in the three biopics, Shostakovich produced several such works for the concert hall, including *Song of the Forests* (1949) and, in 1951, *Ten Poems on Texts by Revolutionary Poets* and *Ten Russian Folk Songs*.

Pirogov was Kozintsev's first post-Trauberg project, and it seemed to be continuing on the same road as *Simple People* with its dark, expressionist photography and questionably 'positive' climax. Shostakovich's music echoed this ambiguity, wavering between bombast and uncertainty. The setting made it easy to include fanfares and military music, but the music often fails to convince, sounding more pompous than genuinely grand. Unlike *Simple People*, *Pirogov* was at least released at the time of its production, but Kozintsev was less than satisfied with the result despite its winning a Stalin Prize.

After the relative failure of *Pirogov*, Kozintsev turned to the nineteenth-century literary critic Belinsky who was then being assiduously promoted as a proto-Revolutionary. Unsurprisingly, his Westernizing views were being played down, and he was made more of a Slavophile who found the source of his inspiration in 'the people'. Just as the film flatters the Soviet official mood of post-war xenophobia, so Shostakovich follows suit: the broad theme that opens the overture is reminiscent of *kuchkist* depictions of Rus and of the Russian landscape (and so evokes a kind of *narodnost*), and the same theme often recurs *sotto voce* against rural scenes. But though completed in 1950 and apparently toeing the post-*Zhdanovshchina* line, the film was repeatedly rejected by the studio and only released in June 1953. Kozintsev later disowned it.

The last of the three biopics, *Michurin*, was the most ill-fated: Popov's score was rejected and the director Alexander Dovzhenko had his health broken by almost five years' work on the project, which was eventually completed by his wife. Though Shostakovich did not rate Dovzhenko particularly highly as a director, he admired the photography, even if he felt that his music had been drowned out by the dialogue and sound effects. In a letter to Trauberg, Shostakovich wrote

> I heard only 20 per cent of my music. Possibly even less ... It was drowned out either by conversations or by the running commentary or by the noise of cement-mixers and electric threshers, not to mention locomotive whistles and such like ... Music is the mother of all arts. So it must not be reduced to a background role or to music accompanying recitation, whether the person reciting be the announcer or People's Artist [actor Nikolay] Cherkasov or a cement mixer.[20]

Some of the music is less pastoral than the agriculturalist's story might have implied, stressing Michurin's struggles with the uncomprehending Tsarist regime and backward-looking Church.

While the biopic genre continued onwards and downwards, Shostakovich's cinema career took a new direction with the onset of the Cold War and developing Stalinist monumentalism. *Meeting on the Elbe* [Vstrecha na Elbe, 1949] is one of the most extraordinary examples of the former, as the real-life friendly post-war encounter between US and Soviet troops in the town of Torgal is rewritten to include American spying. Shostakovich's contribution includes his most authentic jazz music to date, accompanying the drunken brawling of degenerate Americans, while Germany is symbolized by extracts of Beethoven played by the town band.

Around this time film resources were being concentrated on a few 'super-productions' (output in some years fell to single figures) and Stalin began to feature more prominently. Shostakovich, temporarily sidelined in his concert career after the 1948 Decree, turned to the cinema for some desperately needed political credibility and money. He produced scores for two extraordinary films: *The Fall of Berlin* [Padeniye Berlina, 1950] and *The Unforgettable Year 1919* [Nezabïvayemïy 1919-iy god, 1952]. Innumerable cameramen and extras were involved in these grandiose productions, and Shostakovich was expected to create weighty scores worthy of their genius. In the case of *The Fall of Berlin* he padded things out with a predictable chunk of the Seventh Symphony for the Nazi invasion but was able to find an outlet for his wry sense of humour in a march for the entrance of Hitler, which puts him on a par with Adenoid Hynckel, the hero of Chaplin's *The Great Dictator* (1940). Of course there could be no such satire in the musical depiction of Stalin, complete with the uninspiring lyrics of Yevgeny Dolmatovsky, in the (entirely fictional) scenes of Stalin at Berlin airport and his final speech, with 'Slava' chorus.

If Hitler's march was an unexpected moment of levity in *The Fall of Berlin*, Shostakovich excelled himself in *The Unforgettable Year 1919* (1952). Indeed the tone of the entire film – a hugely fictionalized vision of Stalin's exploits, the Soviet-Polish War and the Versailles conference – borders on the grotesquely comic. Western leaders are depicted as infantile incompetents accompanied by a galumphing march, while Lenin and Stalin are sanctified with pompous music that Shostakovich must have written with either pain or his tongue firmly in his cheek. The apotheosis of inappropriateness is the battle scene, for which Shostakovich wrote a miniature Soviet piano concerto in Rachmaninoff style (The Assault on Red Hill), that is unceremoniously cut off in mid-flight. Naturally the 'people' also appear in the film, in the form of the sort of choral songs that he had used before. This is the Shostakovich film score that has suffered most misunderstanding: divorced from the film, the suite's puzzling exaggerations, silliness, bombast and inappropriateness become merely tiresome. However the interaction of the music and the images leaves one more confused about the intended tone, and there is an unsettling feeling that the confusion was not entirely unintended. For instance, the overly simplistic use of melodies such as the 'Marseillaise', the Tsar's Hymn and 'God Save the King' seems to mock their role as musical symbols by pointing to their own redundancy in the very obvious contexts in which they appear.

The Thaw years and after

The death of Stalin in 1953 caused an immediate decline in propagandistic films and, accordingly, a rise in the number of non-political films.

However, Shostakovich's first post-Stalin film was a co-production with Soviet-friendly East Germany. In what was a completely new departure for Shostakovich, Joris Ivens's *The Song of the Rivers* (*Das Lied der Ströme*, 1954) became his first (and only) documentary film score, though many others had used his pre-existing music. A compilation of largely mute footage shot throughout the world, it could have allowed him a greater degree of freedom with the commentary written to accommodate his music. However, as it was overseen in East Germany, this was not entirely the case.[21] Perhaps Shostakovich sensed this lack of influence, or perhaps he was out of sympathy with the subject (the 1953 congress of the film's commissioners, the World Federation of Trades Unions), since the score comprises much recycled material, including music from his Eighth Symphony and the Maxim Trilogy. This seems particularly strange since some of the original music in the film, including violent outbursts at the activities of the Ku Klux Klan, and Egyptian cotton barons, ranks amongst the strongest of his film scores, though the half-hearted setting of a text by Brecht is his most cursory film song.

As a propaganda film, *The Song of the Rivers* was seen by millions over the globe, but Shostakovich's next film, *The Gadfly* [Ovod, 1955], based on Etel Voynich's romantic fiction about Italian unification, was more explicitly populist. Though inevitably political – anti-church, pro-revolutionary unity – it was also a melodrama about a nineteenth-century Italian revolutionary and his girlfriend. Now under less pressure, Shostakovich produced one of his most effective recent film scores, adding some local Mediterranean colour, though there was some confusion as to the precise source.[22] When compiling the well-known suite, Atovmyan changed the score extensively and in the process created the popular *Romance*, a portrayal of the ardent young hero.

Khrushchev's 'Virgin Lands' policy, turning the steppe into farmland in an echo of the industrialization of the 1930s, was the setting for Mikhail Kalatozov's *The First Echelon* [Perviy eshelon, 1956]. Appropriately, Shostakovich returned to the film song, an idea he had largely abandoned over recent years. But despite several repeats through the film and the almost immediate publication of the music, its hit song 'Children's Song' [Molodyozhnaya] did not manage to repeat the success of 'The Song of the Counterplan'. *The First Echelon* is a conventional score in other ways as well, and Shostakovich mostly avoided the innovative soundscapes of his earlier films, preferring to write large-scale mood pieces. There is just one quietly satirical moment when, depicting a failed tractor, Shostakovich quotes a fanfare from *The Counterplan* to link the concepts of industrial and agricultural failure.

At the same time another film project was developing. While working on her 1955 film of Musorgsky's *Boris Godunov*, director Vera Stroyeva invited Shostakovich to prepare the score of *Khovanshchina* for a film that would eventually be released in 1959 using Rimsky-Korsakov's orchestration rather than Shostakovich's. From editing and orchestrating the torso, his enthusiasm for Musorgsky led him to co-write the screenplay. Around this time Shostakovich came under intense pressure to join the Communist Party, finally succumbing in October 1961. At the same time he was becoming increasingly ill and a form of nervous degeneration (much later diagnosed as motor neurone disease) forced him to give up playing the piano in public by 1966.

Despite Shostakovich's late conflict with the Soviet authorities over his Thirteenth Symphony (see Chapter 1 by Eric Roseberry), he still accepted more conventional Soviet assignments, arguably as much to support his director friends as to earn money for himself. Throughout his career, both in the cinema and the concert hall, Shostakovich preferred working with friends, a tendency that became even more pronounced in later years. Though he worked with more than twenty directors, a third of his films were by Kozintsev, Trauberg and Arnshtam.[23] One of the best of these is his score for Arnshtam's *Five Days, Five Nights* [Pyat dney, pyat nochey, 1960], which tells the story of Soviet troops' help in saving artworks from Dresden Museum during the war. Despite the mendacity of the story (Soviet help was far less than the film claims and to the USSR's benefit as many of the art-works stayed there far longer than necessary), Shostakovich produced some evocative music, often avoiding the military bent that the story might have implied, though he fell back on quoting Beethoven's Ninth Symphony to symbolize Germany (as Beethoven's Fifth had done in *Meeting on the Elbe*) and international (Eastern bloc) cooperation. One benefit of the project was that during the visit to Dresden he wrote his Eighth String Quartet, originally dedicated to 'the victims of fascism and war'; but that work has perhaps obscured a film score that is better than its reputation implies.

His next film assignment was less onerous – an adaptation of the operetta *Moscow, Cheryomushki* (1962), necessitating a few changes to the libretto (mostly carried out by Isaak Glikman, who proposed the idea) and some cuts and extra music. Though Shostakovich began by doubting the value of the project, he came to prefer it to the stage version. But his next film would be one to which he was committed from the start. Kozintsev had been planning *Hamlet* [Gamlet, 1964] for some time: he had originally wanted FEKS to produce it in the late 1920s. He then staged *King Lear* (1941) with music by Shostakovich, which he reused (with new material) for their 1954 staging of *Hamlet*. Shostakovich had written music for Nikolay Akimov's iconoclastic stage production of *Hamlet* in 1932, but, even ignoring questions of changing artistic politics, this would have been wholly inappropriate for Kozintsev's film, and so he wrote completely new music for the film, in the shape of a large, powerful score contrasting the muscular music of the hero and his ghost father (perhaps the most corporeal to appear in any film) and the more fragile textures associated with Ophelia.

After his enjoyable work on *Hamlet*, Shostakovich was plunged again into cinematic drudgery with Grigory Roshal's *A Year is Like a Lifetime* [God kak zhizn, 1965], the first Soviet biopic of Karl Marx – the subject's importance had made earlier attempts hazardous. Kozintsev and Trauberg's 1940 planned biopic was stopped at the last moment, and Eisenstein's plans to film *Das Kapital* came to nothing. Shostakovich's lack of engagement with this new project is evident not only from his letters, which record his despair of ever finding inspiration, but also in the result: the poorest of his late scores, doing little to enliven a leaden film. Predictably pious, the revolutionary philosopher's story made recourse to the 'Marseillaise' and 'Ça ira' almost inevitable, and though the diegetic music is pleasant enough – for example, that played by street performers – elsewhere some of the score has so little to do with the onscreen events that it is hard to understand the makers' intentions. The worst of it neither illuminates the characterization nor illustrates external events. Thankfully, it was the last film that would be devoid of interest for the composer, and from now on to some degree or other he would be more fully engaged.

In January 1963, *Katerina Izmaylova*, Shostakovich's revision of his banned opera *The Lady Macbeth of Mtsensk District*, was premiered in Moscow. The film version of the same title was released to coincide with Shostakovich's sixtieth birthday celebrations in 1966. Obviously the full-length opera was too long for a film, and so Shostakovich, who collaborated on the script, made some cuts – notably eliminating the police station scene – and wrote a couple of new interludes. But despite his involvement, his attitude to the result was exactly the reverse of what had been the case with *Moscow, Cheryomushki*. The project started hopefully for Shostakovich but ultimately he was dissatisfied with the result, at least as far as the sound recording was concerned.

His next collaboration was on Arnshtam's biopic of the would-be assassin of Alexander II, *Sofya Perovskaya* (1968), but during pre-production the director's wife died, and by the time Shostakovich came to write the score he himself was in hospital. Nevertheless, as a favour to his old friend he agreed to do it without viewing the film, basing his music on the script and list of timings for each scene. Despite this lack of direct engagement, the result is very satisfying, combining the finely etched textures of *Hamlet* in a series of fragments that could be shuffled around to fit the film in his absence. Not only was this a return to the technique of *Alone* but it also provided an opportunity for Shostakovich to recapture some of the satirical brilliance of his youth, even in the snippets of diegetic military music. The score features some interesting orchestral colours and effects, including two pieces for four solo timpanists, one with the addition of a trumpet, while the explosion itself brings a cliff-edge cut-off so synchronous with the images that it is almost certain that the freeze-frame was edited to the music.

Shostakovich's long collaboration with Kozintsev came to an end with *King Lear* [Korol Lir, 1971]: the director died in 1973 whilst working on a script based on Gogol. There is about half an hour of music in the film, though Shostakovich wrote far more, probably to cover for the fact that illness prevented his visiting the set. Many of the cues are aphoristic in the extreme: fanfares, the fool's pipe, and so on. But the proliferation of brief pieces (many of them diegetic) makes the larger ones stand out, and 'The People's Lamentation' is the climax of one of his most telling scores, a sarcastic reminiscence of the choral songs in the 1940s biopics, filtered through his long career and flavoured with the bitterness of Brezhnev's stagnation. It also provided the material for the opening of one of his most desolate creations, the Thirteenth String Quartet.

With the deaths of so many of his cinema collaborators and his own increasing frailty, Shostakovich withdrew from the cinema and spent his last four years working on a dozen or so masterly final works, which, taken together, give a concentrated view of his later style and concerns. Having drawn away from ballet and incidental music for the theatre, and with his operatic career hobbled by 'Chaos instead of Music' Shostakovich's only consistent outlet for dramatic music from 1936 onward had been the cinema. His early dramatic works, particularly the operas *The Nose* and *Lady Macbeth* were full of satire, and in later years he worked hard to revive some of them. He described *Lady Macbeth* as 'tragi-satirical',[24] but despite the condemnation of the work the satirical vein continued throughout his life and is most clearly seen in vocal works such as *Five Romances on Texts from Krokodil Magazine*, op. 121, the *Preface to the Complete Edition of my Works and a Brief Reflection on this Preface*, op. 123 and *Four Verses of Captain Lebyadkin*, op. 146 and of course *Satires (Pictures of the Past)*, op. 109 (see Chapter 10 by Francis Maes in this volume).

His cinema work was more populist than satirical, but even so, his familiar humour finds its way into the film scores. There his satire is often put to the service of the state and aimed at predictable targets such as the Church or pre-revolutionary reactionaries (*The Gadfly* scores heavily on both counts). During the Thaw this extended to works such as *Moscow, Cheryomushki*, where criticism of minor local officials was allowable. These examples of 'acceptable satire' extended throughout the arts, but there are other, more cutting comments, though these are often necessarily more subtle, even covert. These include his reuse of the pompous fanfares from *The Counterplan* in *The First Echelon* and, even more secretly, in *Rayok*, the contrasting uses of 'You Fell as a Victim' in the Maxim trilogy and *The Great Citizen*, and perhaps the slightly hollowly victorious endings of films such as *Pirogov* and *Simple People*. Thus, the undercurrent of satire that had run through his work from the start comes to the surface in some unexpected places.

PART III

Vocal and choral works

10 Between reality and transcendence: Shostakovich's songs

FRANCIS MAES

Although reception history has given pride of place to Shostakovich's impressive double set of fifteen symphonies and string quartets, he was anything but a genre specialist. On the contrary, he adhered more strictly than any of his contemporaries to the traditional role of the composer as competent and active in all genres and modes of expression. Song writing was an area for which he showed special affinity. With twenty opus numbers devoted to solo vocal pieces (including the Fourteenth Symphony, which is a song cycle in all but name), a handful of unnumbered songs, and a significant element of vocal writing in his theatre and film scores,[1] his place in the history of twentieth-century song can hardly be questioned.

Shostakovich wrote songs throughout his career, with a particularly high concentration in his later years. It has rightly been observed that 'from 1960 until his death the relationship between vocal and instrumental music is virtually in balance',[2] and in this latest phase of his development he turned the genre of the song cycle – without ever using that specific term – into a flexible and multi-layered means of expression for his autobiographical and philosophical musings. But it should come as no surprise that the earliest work to show signs of his distinctive musical voice is also a set of songs: *Two Fables of Krïlov*, op. 4. Composed during his student years, these were a logical outcome of his conservatoire training, in which exercises in word-setting on the basis of the Russian literary classics were normal practice.

The songs in criticism

The songs that Shostakovich composed before the onset of his late style have received relatively little critical attention, the only exception being the cycle *From Jewish Folk Poetry* of 1948. However, interest in this work has been provoked in the first place by its highly charged symbolic status in the context of the last years of Stalin's regime. This is an extreme example of a tendency, especially in the West, to approach the songs mainly with a desire for unequivocal answers to vexing questions of meaning in Shostakovich's music as a whole, based on the tacit belief that words should provide a stable conceptual framework that is lacking in instrumental music. This belief has resulted in an unfortunate, if understandable, tendency to take literally a highly debatable remark in Solomon Volkov's *Testimony*, where he has Shostakovich declare that 'when I combine music with words, it becomes harder to misinterpret my intent'.[3] Music with words is thus interpreted as a 'message in a bottle', floating on an ocean of hypothesis and doubt, and awaiting only a reader with eyes to see. By extension, Shostakovich's songs have become a reference point for the interpretation of his instrumental works, particularly in the German Shostakovich literature, reinforcing even more dubious approaches to musical understanding. This is exemplified in the following statement about the late masterpiece, the *Suite on Texts of Michelangelo Buonarroti*: 'Between the bare melodic lines are introduced echoes of Shostakovich's great works, above all the symphonies. Michelangelo's words give these echoes the concrete meaning of a moral-ethical message – this is how Shostakovich wanted his oeuvre to be understood.'[4] Similarly Kadja Grönke reads the late song cycles as confessional works, in which Shostakovich measured his own artistic achievement against the highest ethical, in his case unobtainable, standards of artistic duty.[5] And Sebastian Klemm developed this approach further in his detailed analysis of the Michelangelo Suite, arriving at an endorsement of the confessional nature of the work, albeit complemented with existential generalizing as an additional layer of meaning: 'In Shostakovich's late works he trusts the power of the poetic word more and more as a self-sufficient level of expression ... At the same time it must be said at the outset that the meaning and content of a text-based composition is never merely identical to the text.'[6]

But song criticism can easily become reductive when applied with exaggerated hopes for uncovering unequivocal meaning. Can it really be that Shostakovich only composed his setting of Shakespeare's Sonnet no. 66 (the fifth of the *Six Romances on Texts of Raleigh, Burns and Shakespeare*, op. 62) because of the line 'And art made tongue-tied by authority' (the expression has even been turned into a symbolic summary of Shostakovich's career)?[7] Or that he turned to Michelangelo's poetry only because he could thereby project his experiences with Stalinism onto the relationship of the Florentine sculptor with Pope Julius II? Such an approach not only denies the multi-layered meanings in the texts and music's capacity to enrich their content, it even tends to regard only selected sentences from the poems as significant for the meaning of the songs.

The dangers of reductive literalism are exemplified in certain critical readings of the first of the Pushkin Romances (*Four Romances on Texts of Pushkin*, op. 46). Since Shostakovich composed the set in 1936–7, it is logical to presume a connection with the dramatic events of January 1936, when *Pravda*'s denunciation of his opera *Lady Macbeth of the Mtsensk District* precipitated his public disgrace. This would appear to explain the choice of a poem whose first line reads: 'An artist-barbarian with his sleepy brush blackens over a picture of a genius.' The moral of this song is certainly located in the belief that true genius will prevail. In Pushkin's poem, in fact, the added layers of paint disappear with the years. And the allusion to the song in the finale of the Fifth Symphony prompts a reading of that work as the expression of the moral superiority of the true artist over his detractors.[8]

Two problems should warn us against an overly literal reading, however. Firstly, the so-called song quotation hardly deserves that label. What is actually quoted does not extend to more than a bar and a half and applies only to the lilting accompanying figure at the beginning of the last quatrain. One could argue with equal justification that the passage at Fig. 120 of the symphony's finale is a new composition based on a similar idea.

A second problem is the fact that Pushkin's poem is not about art at all, let alone about some moral superiority of the artist. The image of the distorted and restored painting serves as a metaphor for something else: the distortion and recovery of the pristine purity of the youthful mind. As a literary contour for an interpretation of the symphony, this idea may still be useful, but only if confined to a far more general level than a literalistic reading would have it. A more obvious case of song quotation in a symphonic work occurs in the second movement of the Thirteenth Symphony at the thought that humour is executed. At that point, Shostakovich quotes the song 'MacPherson before his Execution' from his op. 62, another defiant dance in the face of death. On the other hand, the allusion to the Pushkin monologue on the text 'What does my name matter to you?' (the second song from op. 91), which Elizabeth Wilson detects in the Tenth Symphony, is too vague to carry much critical weight.[9]

Song criticism that focuses on unequivocal meaning in this way denies the defining quality of the genre. Meaning in song is multidimensional by nature, resulting as it does from a subtle interplay between two discrete, autonomous modes of expression, whose combined content is always hard to paraphrase and partly elusive. The multidimensional quality of song has been accepted in song criticism in general as one of the glories of the genre, but it is all too often neglected in the case of Shostakovich.

A reading of Shostakovich's songs that aims to be more integrated and multidimensional should therefore respond to the central challenge of all Shostakovich criticism, which may be expressed as follows:

(a) The dramatic and charged context in which Shostakovich's art came into
   existence makes it unthinkable to view his legacy in purely aesthetic terms,

since such an approach would amount to irresponsible escapism, a denial of the weight of history.

(b) On the other hand, Shostakovich criticism all too often demonstrates a failure to grasp the fact that the meaning of a work of art cannot be confined to a more or less veiled message responding to specific circumstances. Such readings tend to deny the metaphorical resonance of great music.

(c) The tension between the concepts of art as concrete message or as a wide metaphorical realm is present in the work of many great artists, but it becomes extreme in the case of Shostakovich. Instead of limiting the interpretation to one side or the other, criticism should endeavour to define the creative tension that lies at the basis of each of his works, negotiating between the poles of the weight of reality and the transcendent calling of art. This goes for his songs too, even though their texts may seem to pull the reader/listener towards one or other pole.

Periods of song production

It is customary to divide Shostakovich's career according to the tremendous ordeals he had to face: his condemnation in *Pravda* in January 1936, the horrific siege of Leningrad and his evacuation, and the charge of Formalism in the 1948 campaign spearheaded by Andrey Zhdanov (commonly known as *Zhdanovshchina*, the Zhdanov business). In the domain of song writing, however, this entire period could be seen as a first wave, extending from the adolescent *Two Fables of Krïlov* of 1922 to *From Jewish Folk Poetry* of 1948.

Shostakovich's spectacular early development in large-scale symphonic and theatrical works was interspersed with efforts in more intimate genres. After the first important essays in piano music – the first Piano Sonata (1926) and the *Aphorisms* (1927) – Shostakovich turned to solo vocal music in 1928–32 with the *Six Romances on Texts by Japanese Poets*, preceding his first masterpiece of chamber music, the Cello Sonata of 1934. *From Jewish Folk Poetry* of 1948 is usually discussed in the context of the anti-Semitic repressions that began in earnest later that year, but Shostakovich's interest in the Jewish idiom and Jewish themes goes back at least to 1944, to his completion of the opera *Rothschild's Violin* by his pupil Veniamin Fleyshman[10] and his acquaintance with the Jewish composer Mieczysław Weinberg. Apart from the Jewish colouring, in its subject matter the cycle is closely linked to the preceding one, the *Six Romances on Texts of Raleigh, Burns and Shakespeare* of 1943.

A second period may be identified from 1948 until 1966. As a result of the 1948 anti-formalist campaign, Shostakovich focused for some years on songs with popular appeal. Later in this period his civic persona showed the other side of the coin, in a renewal of his satirical mode, with the *Satires* of 1960 and *Five Romances on Texts from Krokodil Magazine* of 1965.

Shostakovich's illness in 1966, following his first heart attack in May that year, marks the beginning of the third period, which continued until his death in 1975. This last period is particularly rich in vocal cycles, including the Fourteenth Symphony (1969). Infirmity and frequent hospitalization constitute the personal background of these works, through which shimmer the philosophical and retrospective concerns of an artist in the autumn of his life.

The path to (Socialist) Realism

Shostakovich's adolescent *Two Fables of Krïlov* reveal a debt to the naturalistic text-setting of Musorgsky – in which the verbal content is shadowed by a constant freely structured arioso – and to the brilliant, evocative tonal magic of Rimsky-Korsakov's operas, while adding the first glimpses of Shostakovich's peculiar talent for irony.[11]

The *Six Romances on Texts by Japanese Poets* are the only other songs before the dramatic turning point of 1936. Composed between 1928 and 1932, they are still conceived within a spirit of youthful vigour and self-reliance. The set is dedicated to Nina Varzar, Shostakovich's future wife, and the multiple facets of love constitute its thematic coherence. The first three poems were taken from the 1912 collection of Japanese lyric poetry by A. Brandt – *Yaponskaya lirika* – also used by Stravinsky for his *Three Japanese Lyrics* of 1912–13. The chief appeal of these songs lies in the delicate atmospheric suggestion that Shostakovich weaves around the poetic imagery. He conceived them as orchestral songs from the outset, and the suggestive colouristic quality of the orchestral writing plays its most significant part in the first three songs, in which natural and atmospheric imagery dominates.

In the first romance, 'Love', the theme of erotic love at night leads to a continuous, atmospheric and delicate tone poem. In the second, 'Before Suicide', the hopelessness of unrequited love is also expressed through natural imagery: the fog over the forest and the cries of the wild geese over the lake. The poet ruminates that he will no longer be there to hear them next autumn. The expression in the voice part is more direct than in the first song, not eschewing passionate climaxes. The third song, '*An Indiscreet Glance*', has a light and airy quality. Here the music responds to the playful eroticism of the text. The playfulness of the wind, exposing the legs of the beloved to the poet's eye, is imitated by the woodwind.

The illusion of artistic freedom in the USSR was shattered by the events of January/February 1936. The earliest work – after the completion of the Fourth Symphony later that year – to document Shostakovich's artistic response to the attack by the Party Leadership is the set of *Four Romances on Texts of Pushkin*. The choice of song composition on poetry by Russia's most beloved classical author has been explained as a kind of private retreat into the everlasting values of lyrical introspection.[12] There is, however, a more likely explanation. Most probably, Shostakovich wanted to be ready for the official Pushkin celebrations that were planned for 1937. The fact that he did not submit the songs for performance during the Pushkin year does not preclude the possibility that he may have considered the event initially as an opportunity to rehabilitate himself.

The Pushkin Romances were followed in 1942–3 by the *Six Romances on Verses by Raleigh, Burns and Shakespeare*, and in 1948 by *From Jewish Folk Poetry*. All three post-1936 song sets have a specific feature in common, namely Shostakovich's response in one way or another to official expectations. In the Pushkin Romances the music displays a classicizing tendency, functioning as a musical correspondence to Pushkin's stature as the timeless Russian classic *par excellence*.[13] Classicizing restraint is most obvious in the first and second songs. The first, 'Rebirth', is cast in a standard ternary form, with a simple tonal resolution from minor to major conveying the positive evolution of the poem. The opening melody resonates in its contours with classic examples of the genre, such as the opening phrase of the *Four Serious Songs* of Brahms, with which it shares its reflective tone. The thinly scored, sonatina-like texture of the second song alludes to an eighteenth-century character piece on the harpsichord or pianoforte. This musical characterization parallels the classical allusion of the poetry, taken from Pushkin's translations of Anacreon. The music underlines its character of a gallant vignette. The *Six Romances on Verses by Raleigh, Burns and Shakespeare* meet official expectations in so far as the poetry of Robert Burns could be assimilated to the standard proto-revolutionary narrative of the fate of the common people and their resistance throughout history. The background to the poem by Sir Walter Raleigh, 'To his Son', is different, however, where the poet's warning of the threat of the gallows comes from a Renaissance courtier who knows the dangers of courtly intrigue. *From Jewish Folk Poetry* responds, in its outward characteristics, to official demands for vocal music based on folklore, as formulated during the anti-formalist campaign of 1948. During the collective process of recantation and atonement of all reprimanded composers, Shostakovich dutifully pledged to devote himself to song writing in a melodious and folkloristic style, accessible to the masses. *Prima facie* at least, *From Jewish Folk Poetry* meets all these requirements.[14]

Notwithstanding their apparent adjustment to official standards, however, the three song sets transcend, or even contradict, these demands in specific ways. The creative tension of the Pushkin Romances reveals itself in the contrast between classicizing appearance and their focus on the unpredictable nature of life. The central idea that unifies the four songs is a theme crucial to Pushkin's poetry: the instability of Life through the workings of Time. The classicism of the songs does not function as the expression of a timeless state of a perfected society. On the contrary, expression is centred on feelings of change, loss and decay.

In the first song, 'Rebirth', Time distorts but also contributes to spiritual healing through memory. The music suggests this healing process through carefully chosen details, such as the ingenious rhythmic variations on Pushkin's uniform iambic pattern (see Ex. 10.1), and the exquisite lightening of the texture in the setting of the last quatrain (see Ex. 10.2).

The poems 'Foreboding' and 'Stanzas' count among the most memorable poetic expressions of Time's hold on human destiny. 'Foreboding' (1828) conveys Pushkin's anxiety over the possible outcome of the Senate investigation on the publication of his poem 'André Chénier'. The poet reflects on impending destiny and doubts whether he could still face an ordeal with the pride he had in his youth. Shostakovich responded to the image of time through the continuous motion of a Mahlerian scherzo. 'Wandering the noisy streets' (1829), re-titled 'Stanzas' by Shostakovich, offers a most profound meditation on the passing of the years. The inevitability of change and decay is expressed with a mixture of religious awe and a sense of nature mystique. Shostakovich underlines the gravity of Pushkin's meditation through the use of a walking bass, allusions to the *Dies irae* motif, and the suggestion of a Baroque passacaglia, in spirit if not in technique.

The *Six Romances on Verses by Raleigh, Burns and Shakespeare* display a comparable tension between official Soviet criteria and personal nuance. In Shostakovich's response to the poems of Raleigh and Burns, the emphasis is on the idea of oppression and tyranny. The clearest examples of this are the first poem, 'To his son', and the sarcastic gallows humour with which the condemned MacPherson faces his ordeal in the third. The suggestive setting of Shakespeare's Sonnet no. 66 puts the songs in a philosophical perspective, stating that life's countless ordeals could only be softened through the value of true friendship. The last song, 'The King's Campaign', is a sarcastic afterthought. Through its use of a children's game and its naive setting, Shostakovich exposes the lie of war.

The imprint of the music of Gustav Mahler makes itself felt already in the third of the Pushkin Romances. The beginning of the Raleigh setting,

Example 10.1 *Four Romances on Texts of Pushkin*, op. 46, no 1: Rebirth, rhythmic organization of the text setting

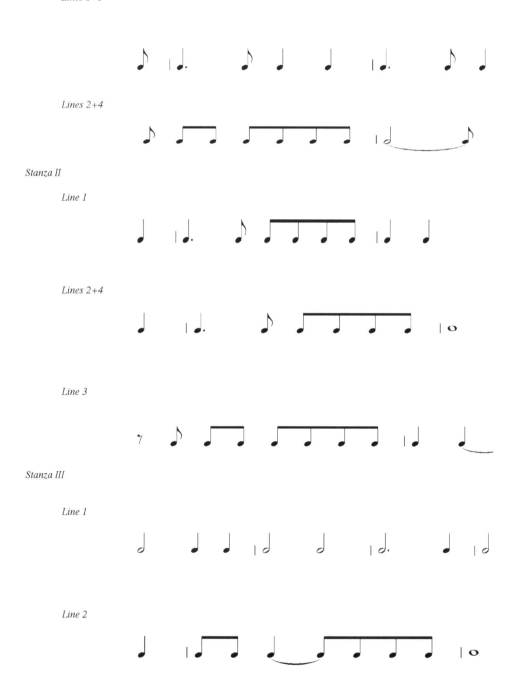

Example 10.1 (cont.)

Line 3

Line 4

Example 10.2 *Four Romances on Texts of Pushkin*, op. 46, no. 1: Rebirth

(a) bars 1–7 'An artist-barbarian with his sleepy brush blackens over a picture of a genius and senselessly sketches over it his own illicit drawing.'

Example 10.2 (b) bars 18–23 'So do the delusions vanish from my tormented soul …'

'To his son', also resonates audibly with Mahler's songs. The opening phrase, scored as a flute solo in the op. 140 chamber orchestral version of 1971, alludes both to the *Kindertotenlieder* and *Das Lied von der Erde*. The connection to Mahler, however, applies mainly to the content of the set. The songs on 'English' (i.e. British) poets deal with problems of oppression and freedom, as experienced by simple people, bandits and children. These ideas run parallel to Mahler's *Lieder aus des Knaben Wunderhorn*.

The same thematic cluster links the 'English' song set to the cycle *From Jewish Folk Poetry*. The poems depict genre scenes, portraying characters that suffer from hunger, poverty and injustice: the birth and death of a baby, a cradle song for an infant with a father in Siberia, the painful parting of lovers, a desperate father's warning to his daughter not to shed her Jewish identity, a merry dancing song that bravely laughs away the despair of poverty, winter without food or hearth. The mood changes in the ninth and tenth songs: misery is exchanged for the happiness at the *kolkhoz* and the relative success of a cobbler's family. Taken together, the *Six Romances on Verses by Raleigh, Burns and Shakespeare* and *From Jewish Folk Poetry* form an impressive artistic response to Mahler's *Wunderhorn* Songs.

The tension between official criteria and subversive content has elicited most commentary in the case of *From Jewish Folk Poetry*. There is no disagreement on the meaning of the cycle as a monument to the sufferings of an oppressed people – both literally and metaphorically as implying all victims of Soviet rule. Controversy comes in with the question whether this interpretation was deliberately invested in the cycle by the composer, or whether it came about through the forceful way in which the historical circumstances of Stalin's anti-Semitic campaign impelled a specific and inescapable reading. The debate is exemplified by Esti Sheinberg's response to the sober view that Laurel Fay expresses in her biography:

> [Fay] raises the options that the composer wanted to express compliance with the party's demands for simple, folk-like music, and that he made a simple mistake by choosing the 'wrong ethnic group'... This assumption is not only unsubstantial, but also unconvincing: Shostakovich was not as stupid as to believe that 'a folk is a folk is a folk, and it doesn't matter which folk idiom you choose for your works as long as it is a folk idiom'. He knew what would be perceived as a 'right ethnic group' and what would not. He knew Stalin was Georgian and was familiar with his likes and dislikes.[15]

In such a polarized formulation, the debate about the intentions behind Shostakovich's use of the Jewish idiom seems unresolvable. To enter an artist's mind is beyond any methodology of historical research. A possible way out, however, could be reached by considering the three vocal cycles Shostakovich composed after 1936 as a group. The Pushkin Songs, the English and the Jewish cycles all betray the same tendency in Shostakovich's approach to consider aesthetic choices and matters of content as an indivisible whole. The same goes for the remarkable fusion of official criteria with personal content. The three cycles all in a way fulfil official expectations, while being critical at the same time. The dissection of these pieces into layers of meaning remains an interpretative act, with a legitimacy of its own. If it is our goal, however, to define the specificity of Shostakovich's approach, this unity of aesthetic construct with personal utterance seems fundamental for his art since 1936. As we shall see, the events of 1948 would divide Shostakovich's song production more than ever before into clearly delineated categories – the officially acceptable and the critical. Although composed after the disturbing events of 1948, the Jewish cycle still thrived on the composer's élan of the previous years. Shostakovich encountered the texts in a collection of Jewish Folk Songs, compiled and translated by Y. M. Dobrushin and A. D. Yuditsky.[16] He completed eight settings for three voices and piano between 1 and 29 August 1948, unveiling them in a private gathering on 25 September. Subsequently, Shostakovich added three more settings, to arrive at the cycle as we know it on 24 October.

The start of Stalin's ruthless anti-Semitic campaign in January 1949 made a public unveiling chimerical. However, the work did not remain in the drawer, and the score circulated among musicians both within and outside Shostakovich's inner circle.[17] Nevertheless public disclosure had to wait until after the death of Stalin.

The music of the cycle is thoroughly infused with the idiom of East European Jewish music. Joachim Braun's pioneering study has revealed the details and the scope of the conscious stylization effected by the composer.[18] The first level of this Jewish colouring consists of borrowings of, or allusions to, existing melodies. On a second level, Shostakovich makes intensive usage of stylistic markers, such as the *freigish* mode (the 'altered Phrygian' – as in white notes on E but with a raised third) and the Dorian with a raised fourth (as in white notes on D but with G sharp for G). The typical feature of the iambic prime (note-repetitions in unstressed–stressed rhythmic units, chained together in descending scalar figures) makes its appearance in most of the songs. Shostakovich combined features of both modes and the iambic prime into a series of related characteristic phrases with the function of a leitmotiv.[19]

On a third level, the forms and accompaniment formulas represent the simple song forms and instrumental practices of Klezmer bands. Finally, the cycle as a whole refers to the defining genres of Jewish folk music: lamentation, lullaby, dance songs (*freilekhs*) and genre scenes.

Critical opinion on *From Jewish Folk Poetry* has always struggled with the three songs that Shostakovich added after the private performance of the cycle in its original form. They are usually viewed as inferior, as paying mere lip-service to Soviet ideals.[20] Whatever Shostakovich's intentions, it remains hard to conceive that he would have written inferior music on purpose. A likely stimulus for the happy songs of nos. 9 and 10 was given by certain Jewish intellectuals themselves. Before the anti-Semitic campaign, some of them – including the Jewish actor Solomon Mikhoels, who was murdered in January 1948 – expressed optimism in a better future for the Jews in the new Soviet society.[21]

However much discomfort these songs may cause to those who would prefer Shostakovich to have been an uncompromising anti-establishment critic, it would be going too far to call them neutral in character. 'The Good Life' is close to the model of Soviet Realist classicism, featuring as it does a diatonic lyrical melody and an Alberti bass-like accompaniment. This type of song was designed to express the timeless and collective qualities of a society that had overcome the evils of the past. The tenth song, 'A Girl's Song', is a Soviet pastoral, in which the classical imagery of the bucolic genre scene conveys the blessed state of Communist life. The pastoral imagery is probably the reason why Shostakovich changed the gender of the character from the original male. The crystalline voice of a shepherdess is more consonant with Arcadian imagery than a sturdy tenor.

Ethnic markers are not entirely absent in these added songs. In 'The Good Life', the iambic prime surfaces through the idealized classicism. In 'A Girl's Song', the imitation of the little pipe of the shepherdess remains in the compound Jewish idiom of the *freigish* mode combined with the altered Dorian mode, bringing the cycle full circle. The closure arrived at in the penultimate song is dissolved again in the last one, however. Here the music turns the words of the cobbler's wife into satire, suggesting that the happiness portrayed is shallow at best, fake at worst. The music could also stand as a critique of the bourgeois attitudes and pretences that the cobbler's wife seems to cherish.

From Socialist Realism to critical realism

After the resolution of 1948, as part of what he judged to be a necessary demonstration of contrition, Shostakovich composed film music and Socialist Realist cantatas, alongside instrumental masterpieces such as the Fourth and Fifth String Quartets that would have to await more favourable times for their performance. His song output at this time contains surprisingly anachronistic settings of verses by the Soviet poet laureate Yevgeny Dolmatovsky and folk-song arrangements. Later in this period, Shostakovich produced two remarkable sets of satirical songs: *Satires (Pictures of the Past)*, op. 109 and *Five Romances on Texts from Krokodil Magazine*, op. 121. In his song writing of the 1950s and early 1960s, Shostakovich gave a different artistic response to his anti-formalist condemnation than he had done after the *Pravda* scandal of 1936. Instead of writing works that would combine official expectations with personal conviction, he now reacted by dividing his output in two, the songs representing a thorough adjustment to official aesthetics. This artistic accommodation to Soviet reality was eventually paralleled in his life with his acquiesence in candidature for the Communist Party in 1960.

At the same time as that traumatic event, however, Shostakovich channelled his feelings of unease or discontent into a satirical pose. The satire in the two mentioned sets is not so much directed at the unmasking of specific Soviet societal ills as it is an outlet for suppressed feelings in a period of intense human and artistic constraint.

In 1949 Shostakovich made the acquaintance of Evgeny Dolmatovsky, who was a reliable partner for the composition of cantatas and songs along accepted ideological lines. Shostakovich composed two sets of songs on his verses: op. 86 (1950–1) and op. 98 (1954). The first of the op. 86 songs, 'The Motherland hears', acquired legendary status because Yury Gagarin is supposed to have sung it during his space flight on 12 April 1961.[22] Dolmatovsky's poems glorify the great deeds of the Soviet people and paint an idyllic picture of life under Communism. Shostakovich's settings are uncomplicated, straightforward and easy to remember. The second set is more elaborated than the first, which consists mainly of strophic songs.

Shostakovich's settings of Dolmatovsky's romances amount to undisguised pastiches of early nineteenth-century song types or character pieces. Nevertheless, he approached the task with undeniable sophistication. Some examples possess a naive beauty, which ensures their survival among the generally forbidden fruits of conformist Soviet music. One example may suffice: 'Rescue me', the second romance of op. 86. The poem conveys a Soviet girl's dream of a young Soviet soldier who would save her from the misery of the past, like a knight in shining armour. The anachronistic setting highlights the timelessness of the fairy-tale imagery. In veritable Schubertian fashion, Shostakovich employs the ambiguity between the keys of F minor and A flat major to distinguish between mourning and expectation. The vision of the knight is highlighted by a change from duple to triple metre, comparable to German romantic songs of an archaizing type. The subtle simplicity of these songs places them in the line of romantic children's songs or piano pieces, such as Schumann's *Kinderszenen*. In their stylized timelessness, the best of the Dolmatovsky songs could be seen as a musical parallel to the sometimes equally exquisite illustrations in Soviet children's books.

In this period, Shostakovich composed two sets of folk-song arrangements: the *Greek Songs* (1952–3) and the *Spanish Songs*, op. 100 (1956). The Greek songs are arrangements, either of folk songs, or of popular songs by the Greek composers A. Xenos and A. Tzakonas. Shostakovich received the melodies from the Soviet folklorist Lev Kulakovsky. The *Spanish Songs* were composed at the demand of the mezzo-soprano Zara Dolukhanova. They are simple arrangements of folk tunes, employing stock-in-trade hispanicisms.

Most of the songs in the two satirical sets are hardly seditious in content. The *Satires*, op. 109 are based on poems by the *fin-de-siècle* poet Sasha Chorny (1880–1932), whose favourite targets were the trendy habits among the Russia intelligentsia after the 1905 Revolution. The subtitle *Pictures of the Past* was added at the suggestion of the dedicatee and first performer, the soprano Galina Vishnevskaya, in the hope – so she reports – of circumventing likely objections of the authorities.[23]

Most of the poems are too closely linked to the atmosphere of the *fin de siècle* to arouse suspicion. In 'Kreutzer Sonata' (no. 5), for instance, Chorny targets idealists who preached that intellectuals should mingle with common people. His little scene depicts an impoverished intellectual whose passion is aroused by the legs of a plump laundress. Symbolist imagery of rays of sunlight and a new colour shining on everything appears to be the result of the prosaic cleaning of the window. The sexual act is elevated by the intellectual into a lofty communion of two classes.

The two songs that could be understood as references to Shostakovich's own time are 'To a critic' and 'Descendants'. The first ridicules the philistine who cannot even fathom the difference between the person of the poet and the character he creates. Shostakovich's use of this text could be read as a critique against the pettiness of official Soviet criticism. The contemporary relevance of 'Descendants' is more far-reaching. The poem is a bitter critique of any rhetoric that justifies actual hardship with the promise of a better future for the next generations. The poem makes a powerful statement about the individual's right to happiness: let the descendants care for themselves... Official reluctance to approve of the song revealed itself in the prohibition of a television broadcast.[24]

The source of the second series of satirical songs was the 30 August 1965 issue of the satirical periodical *Krokodil*. The magazine was created by the Soviet authorities to channel discontent into accepted lines, a clear example of what is called 'repressive tolerance' in the critical social sciences. Shostakovich selected five anecdotes of ordinary life: the attack of a pensioner on a bus driver, the despair of a bachelor who cannot find a wife who would not ask for money, mistrust in the police, the yearnings of a girl for a cowherd, and a paean to a fresh piece of bread from the first harvest.

In his satirical songs, Shostakovich takes as his model the naturalistic songs by Dargomïzhsky and Musorgsky, and much of the humour in the *Krokodil* set derives from the odd combination of a nineteenth-century type of vocal music with contemporary anecdote. In the *Satires*, an additional layer of parody is added through the quotations and allusions in the music: Rachmaninoff's song 'Spring Waters' in 'The Awakening of Spring', or the real 'Kreutzer' Sonata by Beethoven at the outset of 'Kreutzer Sonata'. The portrayal of the intellectual by a waltz in the same song (starting in bar 16) is introduced in bars 14–15 by a quote of the viola motif that sets the scene for Lensky's Act 2 aria in Tchaikovsky's *Evgeny Onegin*.

Shostakovich made his most personal contribution to satire in the song *Preface to the Complete Edition of My Works and a Brief Reflection apropos this Preface* for bass and piano, op. 123. He composed it in view of the sixtieth-birthday celebrations that were being prepared for him. In anticipation of lofty official congratulations, Shostakovich chose to remind his listeners of the ephemeral status of music, paraphrasing an epigram by Pushkin, 'The Story of a Versifier'. Parallel to Pushkin's original, Shostakovich states that his music is only good to torment audiences and will soon be forgotten. The setting of the text emphasizes the one-syllable last word of every line with a sudden *fortissimo*: *list, svist, slukh, bukh*. In the second part, the Brief Reflection states that the Preface would fit the collected works of many composers, Soviet or otherwise. Shostakovich finally signs the statement with his name and some of his honorary titles. As could be expected, the signature appears in musical form in the notes of his musical monogram, DSCH. Shostakovich extends the in-joke by punningly emphasizing the notes E flat and D (the latter usable for 'R' because of the French designation *Ré*) in RSFSR (Russian Soviet Federation of Soviet Republics) and SSSR (Soyuz, i.e. Union, of Soviet Socialist Republics). As a musical performance of a prosaic statement, this *Preface and Brief Reflection* has a precedent in the Russian repertoire: Rachmaninoff's sung letter to Stanislavsky, congratulating him on the tenth anniversary of the Moscow Art Theatre in 1908, complete with signature, date and postscript.

Besides his official works and their satirical reverse, Shostakovich continued the series of Pushkin settings that he had started in 1936. Later, in 1967, Shostakovich would add one more song: 'Spring, Spring'. He labelled the set of four new Pushkin settings monologues (op. 91), instead of romances (op. 46) or songs. The choice is usually explained by the predominance of syllabic, declamatory text-setting. This character applies especially to the first and third numbers. In the second and fourth, the lyrical impulse remains. The most remarkable of the series are the first, 'Fragment', and the third, 'In the depths of the Siberian mines'.

The first monologue is based on an untitled poem of 1826, relating the story of a Jewish family struck by fate. Pushkin's poem constructs a sophisticated poetical image, set in a Rembrandt *chiaroscuro* fashion. Pushkin sets the scene around a lamp shedding its dim light on a Bible. The characters and their drama remain in the shades. The poetic image resonates with powerful religious symbols: Rachel's lament, Jeremiah bemoaning the fate of Israel, the angels visiting Abraham and Sara, Elijah, Christ at Emmaüs … Shostakovich paints the darkness and stillness of the scene with a continuous rhythmic pulse (see Ex. 10.3). The

Example 10.3 *Four Monologues on Texts of Pushkin*, op. 91, no. 1: Fragment bars 1–13. 'In a Jewish cabin the dim light of a small lamp glimmers in a corner. In front of the lamp an old man reads the Bible.'

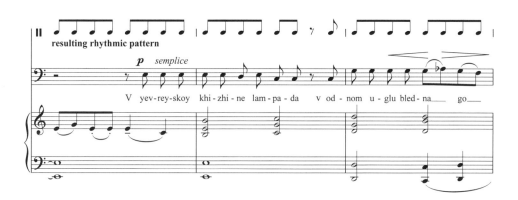

pulse is subtly interrupted at expressive moments, such as the tolling of the bell from the church tower and the knock on the door. The change of metre to the unusual 11/8 in the postlude suffices to suggest the possibility of a new beginning.

'In the depths of the Siberian mines' was Pushkin's word of support and solace to the condemned Decembrists (members of the intelligentsia who took part in the unsuccessful revolt against Tsar Nicholas I in December 1825). The poem is replete with weighty romantic imagery: the toil that is not in vain, the everlasting value of ideals, the awakening of hope, and the promise that all yearnings will be fulfilled. Whatever contemporary relevance the poem may have had for Shostakovich and his audience – as an allegorical reference to the Gulag – the musical setting stays within the romantic contours of the poetry.

Towards the transcendence of art

The *Seven Verses of Blok* for soprano, violin, cello and piano, op. 127, signify the start of Shostakovich's late style. Written after his first heart attack on 3 February 1967, the Blok cycle opens a series of works that were composed against a background of constant illness and infirmities. Initially, ailment gave rise to a feeling of creative burn-out. Conceived in hospital, the Blok cycle meant nothing less than a return to creative life.

The concept of a late style is generally understood as an art mirroring feelings from the autumn of the artist's life. The Blok cycle heralds a retreat from civic action into contemplation and introspection. Traces of civic commitment do not disappear entirely in the late vocal cycles: consider the fierce protest against tyranny in 'The Zaporozhian Cossacks' Reply to the Sultan of Constantinople' in the Fourteenth Symphony. Such instances are, however, embedded in a larger and more abstract process of philosophical contemplation.

The Blok Verses open up new dimensions in Shostakovich's songs. Nowhere else did the composer glorify to such a degree the transcendent value of the art he had practised all his life. Besides being a recurring image in the poetry, Music is also the title Shostakovich gave to the last poem (the Blok original being untitled). Music counts among the central themes in *fin-de-siècle* symbolist poetry, serving as an image for the theurgic power of art to transcend life. Shostakovich turned to this comforting view in a time of illness, confronted with his own vulnerability. Considered in a wider cultural and historical context, however, the cycle acquires special significance as an expression of a belief in music's transcendental power.

In the Blok cycle, Shostakovich found words to make explicit a spiritual thread that runs through his output.

Such a statement remains surprising when applied to a composer who made no secret of his atheism and who created his output in the context of a materialistic and immanent artistic ideology, which as a composer he both endorsed and resisted. His enormous talent for satire, for instance, is a clear demonstration of the immanent vision of the function of art. To manipulate the material features of a given type of artistic expression serves to unmask the pretensions behind those artistic utterances. On the other hand, Shostakovich developed in his instrumental music a line that could be considered an impressive continuation of the principles of absolute music. The extent to which he attached any significance to the spiritual and metaphysical foundations of the concept of absolute music in its nineteenth-century meaning remains a matter of conjecture. The Blok cycle, however, makes explicit the fact that Shostakovich valued the idea of music's spiritual potential, if not in an overtly metaphysical sense, then certainly in the sense of beauty transcending the conditions of every-day life.

It is well known that Shostakovich composed the work in response to a request from Mstislav Rostropovich for a vocalise for cello and soprano, a work the great cellist could perform with his wife, Galina Vishnevskaya. Shostakovich expanded the idea in two ways: firstly in dimensions and form, adding two instruments to make the form expand while retaining the idea of interplay between voice and instrumental cantilena, secondly in providing words to the vocalise. The chosen words, however, stay as close to the wordless voice as could be possibly achieved by poetry.

Voice is an essential theme in the poetry of the first three songs. In 'Ophelia's Song' (no. 1), Shakespeare's unfortunate heroine sings of memory and premonition beyond the dimension of rationality: 'Her speech is nothing, yet the unshaped use of it doth move the hearers to collection', as Shakespeare puts it in *Hamlet*. Ophelia's voice became a theme in symbolist poetry, for example in poems by Blok, such as 'Ophelia in Flowers and Adornments', 'Ophelia's song' by Pasternak, and 'Lessons in English' of Bryusov, responding to the cycle *To Ophelia* by Afanasy Fet. The prophetic voice of the mythical bird Gamayun (no. 2) also comes from another dimension – hard for humans to decode, it contains the totality of human destiny, just as the bird's shining face radiates with the light of spiritual love. The third poem introduces a more realistic, human level to the imagery, enshrining the memory of a lost love encounter against the wordless voice of a nocturnal violin.

The second group of three songs exchanges the image of music for visual symbolism: the city, the glimmers of dawn, the mysterious signs on the wall, nocturnal caverns, the bright heavens ... These visions appear in silence. Only the fifth song returns to the wordless voice with the image of the howling wind. Shostakovich's title for the seventh and last poem, *Music*, focuses attention on the image of the music of the world that reveals itself during the silence of the night. In choosing this title for the untitled poem, Shostakovich emphasizes the connection between Blok's romanticized vision of the Music of the Spheres in the first stanza with the concept of the supernatural 'Mistress of the Universe' in the last.

For each poem Shostakovich devises a powerful image in the instrumental writing. The cello part in 'Ophelia's Song' is pure cantilena, predominately diatonic. The unearthly voice of Gamayun is invoked through dispassionate declamation in the voice and octatonic lines (based on tone–semitone alternations) in the piano. In 'We were together', the image of the violin in the distance is elaborated in a violin cantilena, turning into virtuosity. 'The city sleeps' suggests the silence of the night through a harmonious and warm texture in piano and cello. 'Storm' turns the feelings of fear and the howling wind into tone painting through *sul ponticello* figures in the violin. In 'Secret Signs', the hieroglyphs of the other world are turned into musical symbolism by the use of twelve-note rows. Finally, 'Music' employs a beautifully static texture of sustained notes and highly resonant chords. A last outburst of passion coincides with the words 'accept ... this last foaming cup of passion from your unworthy slave'. To conclude, however, the music returns to cantilena in the two string instruments.

The quest for transcendence in art, begun in the Blok cycle, receives an impressive continuation in the *Six Verses of Marina Tsvetayeva*, op. 143 (1973). In the Blok cycle, music was the central means to explore art's transcending powers. In the Tsvetayeva verses, it is poetry that elevates humans above earthly reality. The poetess, who lived from 1892 until her suicide in 1941, was convinced that true poets gained access to a timeless plane, where they could communicate with other poets from all times.[25] Tsvetayeva's artistic vision dealt with 'the poet's translation between a limited physical world and an abstracted "elsewhere" for which the poet longs. The ideal "elsewhere" is defined as the absence of commonly construed boundaries or limitations which fragment that wholeness of vision the poet seeks to recover and to make endure.'[26] The task of the poet is therefore no less than the Orphic mission of counteracting death.

The first romance is based on a poem from Tsvetayeva's adolescence, written in 1913, in which she expresses her confidence in the survival of her art. The second she wrote for Osip Mandelstam after a summer spent together in 1916. Nos. 4 and 5 belong together and relate the story of Pushkin's death in a widespread but unhistorical version accusing Tsar

Nicholas I of his murder. The last poem belongs to a series of odes that Tsvetayeva wrote in 1916 in honour of Anna Akhmatova.

The third poem, 'Dialogue of Hamlet with his Conscience', is not devoted to a poet, but to a fictional character. However, Hamlet performs in Tsvetayeva's poetry the specific role of the poet's antithesis. While symbolist poetry used the Hamlet-Ophelia pair to express the poet's sense of guilt before the demands of his female muse, Tsvetayeva identifies with Ophelia. Her Ophelia reproaches Hamlet for his rejection of eros. Being incapable of erotic love, Hamlet becomes a symbol of the lack of generative, transcendent longing, which should be the mission of a true poet. In Tsvetayeva's poem, the voice of Ophelia is replaced by Hamlet's own conscience, confronting him with his guilt.

Shostakovich's setting of the 'Dialogue' for one singer indicates that the voices of Hamlet and his conscience are part of the same person. A second musical choice is the construction of the core of the song according to a rhythmic pulse. From bars 6 to 27, all rhythmic movement is structured as a succession of quavers, divided in irregular patterns over voice and accompaniment, a technique that comes close to the ancient principle of hocket. A precedent for this procedure can be found in the first of the Pushkin Monologues (see Exx. 10.3 and 10.4). In the 'Dialogue', the device suggests the perpetual present of Hamlet's guilt. His mind turns past events – the drowning of Ophelia and his own conduct that caused it – into a mental state.

In the structure of the work as a whole, the 'Dialogue of Hamlet with his Conscience' forms the middle part, around which the expressions of poetical communion are symmetrically structured (at least if one takes the two poems about Pushkin together, as the *attacca* indicates). If Hamlet stands for the anti-poet, the other songs glorify poets who did not shrink from their mission.

In these songs, the concept of synchrony – of the ever-present in the poetical communion – is expressed musically in different ways. In the first song, this is done through the coupling of adolescent verses to the mature voice of a contralto. Here the twelve-note rows stand for eternal truth. In the second song, the extensive reference to the circle of fifths in the accompanying figures also alludes to a static concept of time. The concluding ode to Akhmatova is constructed as a sacred icon in tones, replete with suggestive bells in the orchestral version. In the Pushkin episode, Shostakovich's bitterness towards tyranny flares up in the satirical idiom that magnifies the sins of the Tsar and his entourage. Shostakovich's musical monogram lurks below the surface in this work. It suggests, if not identification, then certainly the composer's wish to take part in the community of poets.

Example 10.4 *Six Verses of Marina Tsvetayeva*, op. 143, no. 3: Dialogue of Hamlet with his conscience bars 6–11. 'She is at the bottom where the silt and weeds are ... She went there to sleep, but there is no sleep even there!'

Tsvetayeva's thinking about poetry contains a certain resemblance to the ancient creed of Neoplatonism. Both a continuation and a critique of Plato's ideas, this philosophical tradition originated in the Roman period, but was most influential on the humanists of the Renaissance. The main point that distinguishes Neoplatonism from the original Platonism is its monistic principle. Neoplatonism recognizes a level of reality that is higher than the visible and sensible things, but by contrast with Plato himself it asserts that these two domains are linked by the same identity. The theory was especially appealing for artists, because it defined their work in the sensible realm as a means of contact with the supernatural ideal. As Tsvetayeva puts it in *Les Nuits Florentines* (1933): 'a great master can create something in its ideal form, for he is creating that which ought to be: reality in potential.'[27]

The greatest master of all times to preach and practice Neoplatonist ideals was, of course, Michelangelo, and Shostakovich's preoccupation with Tsvetayeva's ideas finds a logical continuation in his *Suite on Texts of Michelangelo Buonarroti*, op. 145 (1974). Although Shostakovich approached Michelangelo through his verses, it is mainly as a sculptor that the artist speaks to the imagination. Of the eleven poems that Shostakovich selected, two speak directly about his work as a sculptor. 'Creation' deals with the Neoplatonic concept of creativity as a reflection of the creative act of God; and 'Night' recalls the famous dialogue in quatrains with the Florentine academician Giovanni di Carlo Strozzi on Michelangelo's allegorical sculpture of *Night* in the Medici Chapel.

Michelangelo considered art essential as a weapon in his vision of the conflict between love and death, since it plays a significant role in the task of defeating the destructive power of time over all things.[28] The Suite continues the vision that Shostakovich had been developing since the Blok cycle. In that work, music was the main transcendent force; in the Tsvetayeva cycle it was poetry; in the Michelangelo Suite, it is visual art. In the texts Shostakovich selects, art joins love in the Neoplatonic quest for eternal truths. Nos. 2 to 4 of the Suite are devoted to love. The second song, 'Morning', is based on a poem as sensual as Michelangelo's poetry can possibly get, whereas 'Love' conveys the Neoplatonic vision of beauty, where the sight of beauty does not stay in the sensual realm, but is absorbed and spiritualized by the soul. The fourth song, 'Separation', rounds off this subsection with a poem about unrequited love.

A second subsection in the Suite meditates on the value of creativity. It begins with the story of Dante in nos. 6 and 7 and culminates in no. 8, 'Creativity'. The Dante episode points the contrast between the poet's heavenly vision and the blindness of his fellow citizens. Michelangelo elevates Dante to the rank of an artist who fully realized the calling of art: to gain insight into the eternal 'true light' and bring it back to earth. Michelangelo would take Dante's exile gladly, if he could achieve the same lofty ideal. The text of no. 7, 'To the exile', repeats the same line of thought about Dante's greatness contrasted with the ungratefulness of the city of Florence. This episode echoes the one about Pushkin in the Tsvetayeva cycle. In the eighth number, 'Creativity', Michelangelo turns to his own art as a sculptor in order to convey his conviction that the artist's hand is guided by the divine creator.

The last subsection, comprising songs nine to eleven, deals with death. In the ninth number, Michelangelo's allegorical sculpture of *Night* in the Medici Chapel confesses that she loves her sleep because it frees her from the wickedness of the world. The next setting, 'Death', is again infused with Neoplatonism: the world delights the senses but is not the real home for the soul. The final song, 'Immortality', fuses two separate epitaphs, written for Cecchino Bracci, the deceased nephew of Michelangelo's 'agent' Luigi del Riccio. After the death of his sixteen-year-old nephew, del Riccio requested from the sculptor a portrait for his tomb. Michelangelo wrote a series of fifty poems instead. Like most of those poems, the pair that Shostakovich selected deal with the triumph of love over death. Although the tomb to which these poems refer is deprived of the soul of the deceased, he continues to live in the souls of those who loved him.

In true Neoplatonic fashion, the succession of themes in the Michelangelo Suite deals with the role of love and creativity in the transcendence of death (in which sense it could be regarded as a commentary on the Fourteenth Symphony's insistence on the finality of death). The entire cycle, however, gains a further perspective through the more mundane concerns of the artist's struggle with authority and power. The idea is touched upon in the Dante episode but receives its full expression in the first and fifth numbers: 'Truth' and 'Anger'. The poem that opens the Suite resulted from precise circumstances in Michelangelo's career. The artist is annoyed by the preference of his patron, probably Pope Julius II, for the services of his competitors over his own. In the sonnet of the fifth number his annoyance at the pope's policy turns into a bitter attack on the bellicosity of Rome.

As a whole, the Michelangelo Suite expresses the Neoplatonist idea that love and creativity may transcend man's mortality, but it sets this lofty calling against the tensions of the world.

The question about autobiographical identification in Shostakovich's choice of texts looms large. A resonance of Shostakovich's own ordeals may readily be detected in the pieces about the artist's tensions with patrons and politics, in the episode about the ingratitude of the Florentines towards the genius of Dante, or in the petrified image of Night accusing the world of injury and shame. The Dante episode has often been heard as a reference to the exile of Alexander Solzhenitsyn.[29] Whether or not Shostakovich intended the episode as such, the allusions to the tribulations of an artist are set in an abstract philosophical frame.

More important than hypothetical references to Shostakovich's own biography may be the question why the composer aligned himself with a Neoplatonic vision on the meaning of art, hinted at in the Blok cycle and fully developed in his settings of Tsvetayeva and Michelangelo. Nothing indicates that Shostakovich's turn to Neoplatonism was premeditated. His allegiance to its lofty ideals was probably an emotional release of his creative tensions, rather than a systematized set of beliefs. The force of the transcendent image of art in his late works indicates how vital it became for him to validate the importance of the art he had been practising all his life. This quest for ultimate validation indicates, if anything, how deeply the real-life tensions experienced on his thorny path had descended into the deepest realms of his being. In this way, in the three vocal cycles of Shostakovich's late period the tension between reality and transcendence in art received its most pronounced expression.

Yevgeny Shenderovich, the pianist who premiered the work with Yevgeny Nesterenko, recalls a conversation with the composer about the monothematic principles of the structure.[30] It would be more appropriate, however, to call the structure cyclic, because of the recapitulation of the opening statement in the tenth movement. This theme comes close to an allusion to a two-part trumpet toccata in the vein of Gabrieli or Monteverdi. It has been labelled 'truth motif' because it introduces the first line of the text, highlighting the word 'truth'. But it could equally be understood as suggestive of the atmosphere of grandeur at the papal court, of which the poem speaks, or as a sonic image of power *tout court*. Its recurrence in the tenth song, in the context of a poem about death, may then indicate either that death is the ultimate truth, or that the worldly trumpets may easily be turned into their apocalyptic counterparts.

The fifth number, 'Anger', uses Shostakovich's technique of the uninterrupted rhythmic pulse in a particularly aggressive way (see Ex. 10.5). Besides this unified pulse, the texture is for large stretches reduced to unison or octaves. The interruption of the aggressive pulse occurs on sensitive words, such as God and Poverty (bar 42). The aggressive *topos* is even more graphic in the piece on the work of the sculptor, 'Creativity'. Here Shostakovich paints the heavy blows of the earthly and divine sculptors with rhythmically unpredictable strokes. The music for 'Sleep' follows the characteristics of a romantic nocturne in its texture of steadily flowing broken chords. The melody employs a quotation from the Trio for clarinet, violin and piano by Galina Ustvolskaya, previously quoted by Shostakovich in his fifth String Quartet.[31]

The structural and emotional closure achieved in the tenth song is broken up again in the childlike ultimate setting of the two closing epitaphs, whose opening theme comes from a piece that Shostakovich composed as a nine-year-old. We owe this information to a comment by Shostakovich himself after a Moscow performance of the work on 8 January 1975, as related by Shenderovich.[32] The original has not come down to us.

Invincible scepticism

In his large vocal cycles with an eleven-part structure, including the Fourteenth Symphony, Shostakovich moves beyond the closure arrived at in the penultimate song by means of a contrasting or ironic final song. This procedure serves to express a fundamentally sceptical world-view, calling hard-won certainties into question.

Example 10.5 *Suite on Texts of Michelangelo Buonarroti*, op. 145, no. 5: Anger, bars 5–13. 'Here they make swords and helmets from chalices and sell the blood of Christ by weight. His cross and thorns are made into lances and shields, yet even so the lips of Christ remain patiently silent.'

Example 10.5 (cont.)

The same pertains to his vocal oeuvre as a whole. After the weighty ideas and emotions of the Tsvetayeva and Michelangelo cycles, Shostakovich composed his most compelling exercise in the grotesque: the *Four Verses of Captain Lebyadkin*, for bass and piano, op. 146 (1974). The cycle employs verses scattered over the novel *The Demons* by Dostoyevsky, rearranged into four songs. Songs one to three are based on verses composed by Ignat Lebyadkin, retired captain. This grotesque character is a scoundrel, violent and permanently drunk, who acts as a buffoon and recites his own clumsy verses. His poetry is characterized by a mixture of imitation and parodies of eighteenth-century Russian classics, with signs of illiteracy. The fourth song in the cycle is not taken from verses by Lebyadkin, but from a parody of a famous nihilist poem.[33]

The first song, 'Captain Lebyadkin's Love', is derived from three separate poems in the novel. Lebyadkin is in love with Elizaveta Tushina, and the opening verses are delivered by him on the street at night. The exaggerated imagery of love as an explosion of a cannonball on the battlefield of Sebastopol is countered immediately by the prosaic remark that he had never been present at the battle in question. The second idea is taken from a love letter written by Lebyadkin to Lisa, entitled 'To the Perfection of the Maiden Tushina', in the style of eighteenth-century amateur verses. The final part is inspired by Lisa's horseback riding. The idyllic image turns sinister at the words 'if this beauty of beauties broke a leg, she would be more interesting than before'. Lebyadkin's self-confident but nearly illiterate performance is excellently imitated in the voice part, for instance in his stumbling over the word 'aristocratic'. The music alludes to the curse motif from *Rigoletto* and, at the pathetic climax, to Prince Yeletsky's aria from *The Queen of Spades*. In a *jeu d'esprit* of self-deprecation, Shostakovich signed the last lines – 'composed by an untutored man during an argument' – with a transposed version of his monogram.

The second song, 'The Cockroach', parodies the genre of the fable. The story about a cockroach who falls into a glass full of flies and is finally dumped into a tub by a certain Nikifor, is interrupted with responses by Lebyadkin's audience and his insistence not to interrupt him anymore. Characteristically, the performer repeats the beginning in a higher tone and louder voice. Lebyadkin lapses into a prose clarification of his fable, stating that Nikifor represents Nature. The musical pattern of the song is derived from a Russian children's piano tune, *Chizhik*, playable with one finger (see Ex. 15.1, p. 358).

The third song, 'The Governesses' Benefit Ball', turns an ode to the governess into a provocation. In the novel the song is not performed by Lebyadkin but by the fool Liputin. The strategy behind the performance is to turn the guests at a ball into a mob as a cover-up for murders. In Shostakovich's setting the song alludes to the beginning of the tragic outcome of the novel's plot. The music refers to the style of a classical ode in its use of stylistic markers, but with 'wrong' notes and a disturbing asymmetrical quintuple metre. This metre continues to distort the pompous laudatory phrases in the voice part, adding rhythmic monotony to the ensemble of Shostakovich's satirical devices.

The final song, 'A Beacon to Humanity', is a parody of 'The Student', a poem by Nikolay Ogaryov (1813–77). The original was dedicated to Sergey Nechayev, a disciple of the famous anarchist Mikhail Bakunin. Dostoyevsky was horrified by the news of a murder engineered by Nechayev. Shostakovich's setting presents it as a simple strophic song with a little piano refrain. The melodic writing is deliberately monotonous and uninspired. The subtext of the Nechayev episode and its counterpart in the novel's sinister plot turn this final song into a thinly veiled allusion to infamous political murders engineered by the Soviet regime. The song is written as a bleak afterthought on Soviet history and the discrepancy between it and the ideals on which the new state had been built.

The tension between reality and transcendence runs through most of his song output. In the late cycles, the quest for transcendent values became especially pronounced. The higher the hopes set on the redeeming quality of art, the more violent the backlash of scepticism. The darkness of the Lebyadkin cycle counteracts the elevated hopes hinted at in the Blok, Tsvetayeva and Michelangelo cycles, and Shostakovich himself sensed that it had turned out a rather sinister composition.[34] His world-view remained a sceptical one to the end.

11 *Slava!* The 'official compositions'

PAULINE FAIRCLOUGH

The notion that after the 1948 *Zhdanovshchina* Shostakovich's output divided into two halves – official and non-official – is almost a truism in Shostakovich studies. Yet though it clearly drew considerable sustenance from *Testimony*, the idea that he had composed music to placate the Soviet authorities was mooted in the West as early as the 1960s – the decade when the West first began to be more widely aware of the growing wave of Soviet dissidence. Perhaps more surprising is the discovery that those works that were initially perceived as so compromised were not the choral pieces written soon after the events of 1948 – the cantata *Song of the Forests*, op. 81 and the oratorio *The Sun Shines over our Motherland*, op. 90 – but rather his symphonies, in particular the Eleventh and Twelfth. In fact, not one of the 'official' works to be discussed in this chapter was widely known in the West during Shostakovich's lifetime, for the obvious reason that they were not readily exportable. Since Western audiences rarely heard Shostakovich's more overtly political works – and since he was not generally regarded as a 'dissident' composer during his lifetime – they had to assume that works performed in the West such as the Fifth Symphony, the 'Leningrad' Symphony and the Eleventh and Twelfth Symphonies were all, to greater or lesser degrees, pleasing to Communist officialdom, as was in fact the case (that the Fourth and Thirteenth in particular had not been equally pleasing was acknowledged in the West too). But if Western audiences suspected that some of Shostakovich's symphonies were less well received than others in Russia, they did not perceive an actual split in Shostakovich's output, merely ranking some works lower than others and regarding Shostakovich as an 'uneven' composer.[1] Until the 1980s and 1990s brought some of Shostakovich's more obscure music into broader circulation on CD, including the two choral works mentioned above, it had been only Soviet audiences who might have perceived this stark division between 'official' and 'non-official' musical categories that is now so entrenched a part of the West's view of Shostakovich's music.[2]

Evidently, the West's perception of what should be termed 'official' has never been set in stone. However, since *Testimony*'s publication, the assumption that Shostakovich consciously wrote 'official' music that was not truly representative of his creative persona has gained strength. And while it is possible to wrest some works from this inglorious category with relative confidence – for example the beautiful *Ten Poems on Texts by Revolutionary Poets*, op. 88 and the unfairly maligned Twelfth Symphony, op. 112 – much of the music to be discussed here is so overtly political that its rehabilitation as a valid part of Shostakovich's output is still a very remote prospect, and arguably not even desirable. To probe this issue in the depth it requires would involve a wide-ranging discussion of Shostakovich's film and incidental music alongside his political songs and choral works that is plainly beyond the scope of a single chapter; but illumination of intersecting aspects of Shostakovich's 'popular' and 'official' style may be found not only in this chapter but also in Chapters 6 and 9 by Gerard McBurney and John Riley in this volume. Like any composer, Shostakovich wrote differently in each genre, and it is absurd to compare a film or incidental score with a song cycle or symphony and declare that the one is the 'real' Shostakovich and the other is not. Therefore, it is simply not possible to set apart the music Shostakovich composed (for example) for the three stage plays of the NKVD Song and Dance Ensemble during the 1940s from all his other incidental scores, any more than it is possible to divide his scores to the Stalinist *Meeting at the Elbe*, *The Fall of Berlin* and *The Unforgettable Year 1919* from those for other, less overtly politicized, films. It must also be remembered that a topic striking a contemporary Western listener as crudely political may have been very differently perceived by Shostakovich's Soviet contemporaries. While Elizabeth Wilson, in the first edition of her indispensable collection of memoirs, classed the *Ten Poems on Texts by Revolutionary Poets* as 'official',[3] Isaak Glikman thought them moving and powerful;[4] and Henry Orlov asserted that Shostakovich's many works on revolutionary themes (including his film scores for the Maxim Trilogy and the *Ten Poems on Texts by Revolutionary Poets*) were composed from genuine ideological conviction rather than from a cynical attempt at political rehabilitation after the harsh attacks on him in 1936 and 1948.[5] It would certainly be facile to assume that any work with the word 'revolution' or 'Lenin' in its title must have been either covertly subversive or overtly placatory, and hence to be relegated to the 'official' category. Matters are further complicated when dealing with Shostakovich's wartime propaganda works, since these fulfilled a genuine social function in keeping up troops' morale in the face of Nazi aggression and as such should not necessarily be perceived as a cynical paying of state dues.

Example 11.1 *Ceremonial March*, bars 8–12

Contributions to the war effort

Ceremonial March **sans op. for wind band**[6]
There is still disagreement over the exact dating of this piece, but it was
certainly composed between 1939 and 1941. Like the much later *March of
the Soviet Militia*, it is written for a standard military band of wind, brass
and percussion and shares the same cheerfully bombastic tone. While
March of the Soviet Militia is little more than an extended fanfare, the
Ceremonial March is a full-length (approximately three minutes) military
march. Even for Shostakovich's 'populist' style, it is clumsy, with an
absurd galumphing main theme (Ex. 11.1) that is heard three times in
all, courtesy of the march's exasperating da capo form. Since Shostakovich
wrote almost nothing further in this genre, it is not possible to evaluate it
on the basis of stylistic fingerprints; certainly, nothing in the *Ceremonial
March* is recognizably Shostakovichian.

Songs
That Shostakovich, like many of his Soviet colleagues, threw himself into
wartime work with genuine patriotic zeal has never been questioned. He
twice attempted to join up, but was rejected both times. Even after joining
the Home Guard he was only allowed 'safe' jobs such as building defences
around Leningrad; unbeknown to him, as soon as any real danger threatened, Conservatoire officials conspired to have him moved to safety.[7]
Soon after Hitler's forces invaded the Soviet Union, Shostakovich became
involved with popular musical activities, including the theatre of the
Home Guard, of which he was made musical director. In fact, the Soviet
authorities took crucial steps to ensure the participation of prominent
composers in such activities: as early as September 1941, the organiza-
tional committee of the Composers' Union announced its first competition for popular war songs, with the promise of 500 roubles for each
'acceptable' entry.[8] In addition to setting twenty-seven popular songs

and arias for solo voice with accompaniment, Shostakovich composed several popular songs of his own. One of these, 'The Great Day has Come', or 'Oath to the People's Commissar',[9] was one of the most popular songs of the early war years. It was even published in America as 'The Song of Liberation'.[10] Set to a rousing text by Vissarion Sayanov, the song itself is actually not one of Shostakovich's best efforts in the genre, scarcely venturing beyond its tonic C major and its melody almost too short to merit the name. The solo/chorus format within a three-verse strophic song quickly feels stale, and though Shostakovich defended the exaggerated simplicity of the song by claiming that he wanted everyone to be able to sing it, the fact that it was his first attempt in the mass song genre might also have had something to do with the fact that it is far less appealing and singable than its companion pieces. 'The Fearless Regiments are on the Move' (or 'Song of a Guard's Division'), for example, is far more attractive, and written in a more complex harmonic and rhythmic language. It was composed to a text by the Soviet sports journalist Lev Rakhmilevich, whom Shostakovich knew from the Leningrad Home Guard. Though it is also in a solo/chorus, three-verse form, rhythms are sometimes quite substantially altered to fit the text, making it less pedestrian than the 'Oath', and the accompaniment is also far more varied. Additionally, its overall character – quiet minor-key verse followed by louder, major-key chorus – is not only more interesting, but also more dramatically effective.[11]

Shostakovich's forays into the mass song genre took a more serious turn in 1943, when a competition was announced for a new Soviet national anthem to replace the 'Internationale' that had been used since 1917. By this time Shostakovich had been appointed professor at the Moscow Conservatoire, moving from his wartime base in Kuibyshev to Moscow in the spring of 1943. Shortly after beginning work on his Eighth Symphony that summer, he laid it aside to take part in the competition, writing three anthems on texts by Yevgeny Dolmatovsky ('Patriotic Song', or 'Glory to our Soviet Homeland') and Mikhail Golodny (two versions of 'Song of the Red Army'[12]). Both versions of 'Song of the Red Army' to Golodny's words were collaborative efforts written with Aram Khachaturyan, though only one is available in a published version. According to Khachaturyan, it was Marshal Voroshilov who suggested that he and Shostakovich compose an anthem together.[13] There are two variants of the song they collaborated on, one of which Khentova states is in Khachaturyan's hand with additional markings by Shostakovich.[14] Apparently, Khachaturyan wrote the first eight bars, and Shostakovich orchestrated it. All three songs went through to the third and final round at the Bolshoy Theatre, where the five songs that were admitted

Example 11.2a Shostakovich/Khachaturyan, 'Hymn to the Bolshevik Party', bars 1–8 (*source*: Khentova, *D.D. Shostakovich*, p. 177, text not given)

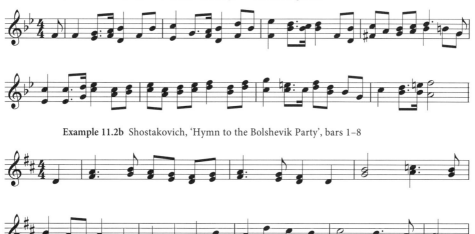

Example 11.2b Shostakovich, 'Hymn to the Bolshevik Party', bars 1–8

to the final round (by Alexander Alexandrov, Khachaturyan, Shostakovich, the Shostakovich/Khachaturyan collaboration and Iona Tuskiya) were performed by the Red Army Chorus and the Bolshoy Theatre orchestra. Then, in December 1943, according to Khachaturyan, a new text by Sergey Mikhalkov and Gabriel El-Registan, entitled 'Hymn to the Bolshevik Party', was pronounced the basis of the new national anthem. Shostakovich made two versions of this song: one, with Khachaturyan, was a reworking of one of their Golodny settings, the imposing 'Song of the Red Army'.[15] The other version used music composed just by Shostakovich, who reused it in its entirety in his NKVD stage work *Russian River*, op. 66 (1944), and its opening melody in the 1950 'Our Song' (text by Konstantin Simonov), in the 1957 hymn 'We Sing Glory to our Motherland', to a text by V. Sidorov and in *Novorossiysk Chimes* (1960, text Kira Alemasova) (see Ex. 11.2).[16]

Shostakovich reused both the Golodny and Mikhalkov/El-Registan National Anthem entries in other works, though he most frequently returned to his own version of the Mikhalkov/El-Registan song. He also rather cheekily reused the Khachaturyan/Shostakovich song in 1957 as 'October Dawn', with new lyrics by Vladimir Kharitonov as the first of a group of three songs written for the fortieth anniversary celebrations for the October Revolution. Of the three songs from 1957 (discussed below), the by then fourteen-year-old hymn 'October Dawn' is by far the most successful, thanks in part to Shostakovich/Khachaturyan's judicious use of first-inversion chords and ready substitutions of major chords for minor, especially at melodic ascents and peaks. The dominant seventh pedal for the chorus delays the final cadence to stirring effect, and despite its

Example 11.3a 'A Toast to our Motherland', bars 11–19 ('Whatever you love, whatever you breathe, whatever is in your soul')

Example 11.3b *Moscow, Cheryomushki*, op. 105, Boris's Serenade, [64]–[65] ('My love is for you alone in all the earth/You alone fill my soul, ehey, nanina, nina!')

pompous anthem style (marked 'Grave'), it manages to avoid the leaden feel of many Soviet anthems.[17]

Marking the national change of mood as victory over the Nazis seemed certain, 'A Toast to our Motherland' (text by Iosif Utkin) is strikingly different from the preceding songs, suggesting that Shostakovich's confidence in the mass song genre had increased considerably. After his Eighth Symphony had been criticized for its gloomy tone, by October 1943 Shostakovich declared that his Ninth Symphony would be 'about the greatness of the Russian people, about our Red Army liberating our native land from the enemy'.[18] And just as the solemn Seventh and Eighth Symphonies sit naturally alongside Shostakovich's popular contemporary works, this song is wedded to the perky tone of the Ninth Symphony's opening movement. Set in a cheery 3/4 and marked 'Presto', it bears a stronger resemblance to Shostakovich's 1930s incidental music style than to the grandiose pretensions of 1940s Soviet hymns. More bizarrely, it bears a marked resemblance to Boris's 'Serenade' from *Moscow, Cheryomushki* of 1957–8, sharing its initial triadic shapes and its jaunty waltz character (Ex. 11.3).

Like its predecessors, 'A Toast' is cast in the familiar solo/chorus mould, but instead of following a purely strophic form, the solo melody is different for the second verse, moving from G major to B flat major, switching back rather awkwardly to G major for the chorus.

'The Black Sea' was the last of Shostakovich's wartime songs, and like 'The Fearless Regiments are on the Move', it is a minor-key march with a major-key chorus. But it differs from all the songs discussed so far in that it is modal rather than diatonic, centred on a Phrygian D. Moreover, in addition to its flattened second degrees, the opening two phrases harp on a tritonal A/E flat, making the already exposed sound of the open bass fifths, sixths and octaves even starker. In the second half of the verse, the sharp mediant F sharp minor/major acts as a temporary centre around which parallel chromatic shifts back to D and E/E flat sound disorientating, until A major signals a return to D minor just before the G major opening of the chorus. Unlike 'The Fearless Regiments', however, this chorus is never firmly in any key: piano triads descend stepwise from G–F sharp–E before moving to the tonic major (D) ending.

From victory to the *Zhdanovshchina* and its aftermath: 1948–60

Poem of the Motherland, op. 74

Scored for soloists, choir and full orchestra, *Poem of the Motherland* [Poema o rodine] was written for the 30th anniversary celebrations of the October Revolution in 1947. Remarkably, given his status in the Soviet Union, it was the first such 'official' work composed by Shostakovich, then at the height of his post-war (and pre-*Zhdanovshchina*) standing. It set six popular Soviet songs, appearing in chronological order until the last song:

> Anon., 'Bravely, comrades, to arms'! [Smelo, tovarishi, v nogu]: pre-revolution-ary song (c.1897)
>
> Ilya Aturov, 'Through valleys and over hills' [Po dolinam i po vzgoryam]: civil war song (1920s)[19]
>
> Shostakovich, 'Song of the counterplan' [Pesnya o vstrechnom] 1932
>
> Alexander Alexandrov, 'Arise, mighty land' [Vstavay, strana ogromnaya] 1941
>
> Vano Muradeli, 'Banner of victory' [Pod znamya slavï v groznïy god] 1945; victory song
>
> Isaak Dunayevsky, 'My broad homeland' [Shirokaya strana moya rodnaya] [from the film *Circus*, 1936][20]

Opening with a quiet C minor march, the entry of 'Bravely, comrades!' swings into C major for the song itself, which is stated in full; after slight

Example 11.4a First Cello Concerto, movement 1, bars 1–2

Example 11.4b Poem of the Motherland, $\boxed{29}^{1-4}$

orchestral variation, the music anticipates the second song: a typical minor-key (F sharp) revolutionary march. Again, after variation the music moves towards the third song (in F major), Shostakovich's own 'Song of the Counterplan' on which he dwells for some time, there being three verses rather than two, and each verse itself being fairly long. For variety, Shostakovich moves into A flat for the third verse. After rounding off triumphantly, the mood darkens with the threat of war: the orchestration and instrumental writing here is characteristic of Shostakovich's wartime symphonic style, with agitated, repetitive writing for strings, wind and percussion, underpinned by a bass march. At the climax comes Alexandrov's song 'Arise, mighty land!' in an ear-splitting *fff* tutti for full choir and orchestra. As the song finishes, there is a striking pre-echo of the First Cello Concerto's opening theme (Ex. 11.4).

This motif, together with Alexandrov's song, is developed further, moving through a repeat of the 'warning' music heard before the entry of the song, here denoting the war itself. Then (at $\boxed{34}$) Muradeli's 'Banner of Victory' enters with a baritone solo in a broad D minor. The final song, Dunayevsky's upbeat 'My broad homeland', is anticipated in gentle wind solos and a general softening of mood. Sung by solo bass, it begins with a low-key delivery over a string chorale texture that only gradually fills out to admit all four soloists and eventually the choir, ending with an inevitable full-scale tutti for the final verse. Unsurprisingly, the ending itself is overtly triumphal, extending a grandiose IV–♭VI–V7–I cadence over twenty-two bars of repeated *ff* unison tutti chords. It is an odd companion piece to the notably non-triumphant Ninth Symphony which preceded it by two years, and in fact it anticipates the post-*Zhdanovshchina Song of the Forests* and *The Sun Shines over our Motherland* in the skill with which Shostakovich adapts to the clichéd bombast of the Soviet cantata style. There is no evidence to suggest that Shostakovich composed this upbeat choral fantasy under any duress other than the inevitable expectation of a celebratory work for the anniversary celebration. Rather, it seems a natural outcome of his extensive experience of writing and arranging Soviet popular songs during the war. Though *Poem of the Motherland* was subjected to criticism for being insufficiently weighty,[21] it seems likely, given the ensuing events, that even the most committed post-war choral work would not have been enough to save Shostakovich from the repression that swiftly followed.

The Central Committee's Resolution 'On V. Muradeli's opera *The Great Friendship*' was published on 10 February 1948. The document criticized Muradeli along with Shostakovich, Prokofiev, Khachaturyan, Shebalin, Popov and Myaskovsky, for showing 'formalist tendencies and antidemocratic tendencies in Soviet music that are alien to the Soviet people'.[22] The publication of this infamous decree was preceded by a three-day conference of musicians in January 1948, headed by Andrey Zhdanov, Stalin's Minister for Cultural Affairs, after whom the label 'Zhdanovshchina' was coined.[23] The immediate consequence of the Resolution was Shostakovich's removal from his position in the Composers' Union and, in September that year, being stripped of both his teaching positions in the Leningrad and Moscow Conservatoires. Several of his works, including the Sixth, Eighth and Ninth Symphonies, were placed on a blacklist, which effectively prevented him from earning any performance royalties at all.

Though Shostakovich completed his First Violin Concerto in March 1948 and even presented it to its dedicatee David Oistrakh later that year, he decided not to have it performed, and it was premiered only in 1955. The Concerto was only the first in a series of works that Shostakovich wrote between 1948 and 1950 but kept from public performance: the song cycle *From Jewish Folk Poetry*, op. 79, the Fourth Quartet, op. 83 and the *Two Romances on Texts of M. Lermontov*, op. 84 were all kept back until after Stalin's death (according to Derek Hulme, the Lermontov songs were not performed until 1984).[24] However, he continued to work publicly on film scores, writing music for *Michurin*, op. 78, *Meeting on the Elbe*, op. 80, *The Fall of Berlin*, op. 82, and *Belinsky*, op. 85, all between 1948 and 1950.

Affairs took an unexpected turn early in 1949 when Stalin phoned Shostakovich and asked him to visit the United States as part of an official Soviet delegation at the Cultural and Scientific Congress for World Peace, held in New York in March 1949. It was during this conversation that Shostakovich apparently informed Stalin that his works had been blacklisted in the Soviet Union, with the immediate result that the ban was lifted on Stalin's orders.[25] Thus, on his return from America, Shostakovich's personal situation had eased slightly, though one former student recalled that until the premiere of his Tenth Symphony his music was very rarely performed.[26] Nevertheless, he remained under pressure to show public compliance with the Resolution and to compose something appropriately optimistic and 'democratic'. The result was a seven-movement oratorio on texts by the officially 'approved' poet Dolmatovsky on the subject of the post-war reforestation scheme. Shostakovich commissioned Dolmatovsky to write the verses, and once he had received them, composed *Song of the Forests* in the summer of 1949. Though Shostakovich began work on the oratorio without a contract from the Committee for Artistic Affairs, it moved swiftly through the proper channels, receiving its premiere on 15 November 1949 and being performed again at the November–December Plenum of the Composers' Union that year, where it was extravagantly praised as evidence that Shostakovich had overcome his 'formalist' tendencies.[27]

A certain amount of mythology has spread around this particular work, started by Shostakovich himself. Evidently embarrassed by both the work and its success, Shostakovich 'confessed' to his former student Elmira Nazirova that 'I sat down one night and in a few hours dashed off something "with my left hand". When I showed them what I had written, to my astonishment and horror, they shook my hands and paid me.'[28] Another student from that period, Galina Ustvolskaya, attended the premiere with Shostakovich and reported that afterwards, back in his hotel room, Shostakovich buried his face in a pillow and sobbed – before getting very drunk.[29] Nonetheless, the oratorio relieved his poor financial situation. It was awarded a Stalin Prize (first class) the following year, worth 100,000 roubles. Perhaps partly because of the disproportionate amount of praise and largesse heaped upon him for composing the oratorio, neither Shostakovich nor his friends and pupils have ever had a good word to say about it. Flora Litvinova, an old family friend, dismissed it as 'insignificant'. A former violinist of the Leningrad Philharmonic classed it with *Moscow, Cheryomushki* as an example of 'occasional weak works in his output … But written under particular circumstances … and they can be discounted. Dmitri Dmitrievich didn't care to talk about them.'[30] Isaak Glikman, Shostakovich's close friend and confidant, takes care, in his commentary to the collection *Pis'ma k drugu* [Letters to a friend] to inform us that 'Shostakovich considered Dolmatovsky at best a professional versifier'.

> Shostakovich wrote the oratorio *The Song of the Forests* at great speed and with great technical mastery … [it] was nominated for a Stalin Prize first class, but Shostakovich was not particularly fond of it and was uncomfortable at all the praise that was heaped upon it. He had a particular aversion to the passages in the text that mentioned Stalin. … I said to

him: 'Suppose, instead of Stalin, your oratorio had featured, for example, Queen Wilhelmina of the Netherlands? She is said to be a keen forester.' Shostakovich exclaimed, 'Oh, how wonderful that would be! I do take responsibility for the music, but the words???'[31]

While it is understandable that Shostakovich and those close to him should have sought to downplay *Song of the Forests* as an atypical work composed under unimaginable political pressure, the fact is that, though it does not sound much like the Shostakovich of the mid-period symphonies and quartets, it *does* sound like another Shostakovich with whom we are currently less familiar: the composer of several film scores and popular songs of the late 1940s and 1950s; and it is by no means as dismally tokenist as might be expected. Moreover, its intonational sphere overlaps with that of works such as the Seventh, Eighth and Ninth Symphonies, the *Ten Russian Folk Songs*, the better film scores (such as *The Gadfly*, op. 97, composed six years later), and even the early incidental score *Hamlet*, op. 32 as well as borrowing certain nineteenth-century nationalist fingerprints. This last point is hardly surprising given Zhdanov's demand for composers to write in the style of the Russian classics.[32] Though anachronistic by 1948, these intonations are subtly utilized and successfully blended with those of contemporary Soviet music, including those of popular song as well as art music. It might fairly be argued that precisely such intonational/historical merging had been a feature of Shostakovich's mature style since the Fourth Symphony, with its powerful echoes of Mahler, Tchaikovsky and Musorgsky. If the Mahlerian influence on Shostakovich became less overt after the Fifth Symphony, Tchaikovsky's loomed rather larger. From 1948 until approximately 1962, Shostakovich moved closer to his nineteenth-century compatriots than he had been before, as can clearly be seen in such works as *Ten Poems on Texts by Revolutionary Poets*, op. 88, the *Ten Russian Folk Songs*, sans op. and the Eleventh and Twelfth Symphonies (1957, 1962), not to mention films on Russian topics such as *Belinsky*, op. 85 and his orchestration of Musorgsky's unfinished opera *Khovanshchina*, op. 106.

Song of the Forests, op. 81

The first movement's spacious C major opening evokes a similar expansive pastoralism to that of the 'Leningrad' Symphony; in its return in the sixth movement in wordless chorus, it has more obvious echoes with the 'Vocalise' set in Stalin's garden from the contemporaneous *Fall of Berlin* and is more closely associated with a pastoral theme (see Ex. 11.5).

The 'planting' of this motif in the first movement, and its recurrence and interweaving with others in the sixth and seventh movements suggests

Example 11.5a Shostakovich, *Song of the Forests*, movement 1, 'When the war was over', bars 1–6

that Shostakovich planned this work more carefully than he was prepared to admit. For instance, just before the wordless choir enters at 71, the cor anglais pre-echoes the opening motif of the 'Slava' finale, and the two versions of motif 'x' (see Ex. 11.5a and b) are closely allied to the finale's opening theme (see Ex. 11.6).

Even more dramatically effective, though rather less subtle, is the first movement's rapid introduction of the finale's closing peroration: an intonation that recurs in numerous Shostakovich scores in the post-1948 period, complete with the hackneyed lurch from the tonic to the major submediant (and also sometimes the major mediant) that appears frequently in Shostakovich's Stalinist paeans, including the cantata *The Sun Shines over our Motherland* and the 'Vocalise' from *The Fall of Berlin* (see Ex. 11.7).

The nineteenth-century Russian influence is most obvious in the second movement's robustly folky introduction, which, giving way to a more typically Soviet-style melody, nevertheless retains a nineteenth-century flavour in its closing phrase that becomes more evident with the entry of the chorus. Here the phrase 'odenem Rodinu v lesa!' [let's clothe the Motherland in forests!] ends on the octave unison typical of Russian folk song, to which Shostakovich returned more explicitly in his 1951 *Ten Russian Folk Songs* (especially in 'The Match'). Following the third movement's solemn French Overture-style orchestral introduction (powerfully reminiscent of the opening of the Eighth Symphony as well as of the slow movements of the Ninth Symphony and the First Violin Concerto), the

Example 11.5b *Song of the Forests*, movement 6, 'A Walk into the future', $\boxed{71}^{1-4}$

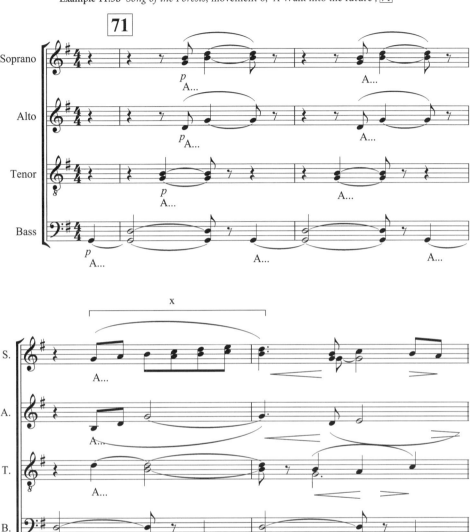

bass solo prefigures one of the most beautiful of Shostakovich's *Ten Russian Folk Songs*: 'The Cuckoo's Cry' (Ex. 11.8).

With the entry of the chorus, the tone veers between that of *Boris Godunov* and contemporary Soviet choruses; but at its second entry at $\boxed{37}$, an agitated string figure strongly recalls the crowd's anguished cries in the St Basil's scene from Musorgsky's *Boris Godunov*. Given the text at this point – 'the drought spreads over the villages / begging for bread. The fields are suffering from the cheerless heat / their paths are open to the hot winds. Give us just a little relief / people, save us!' – the intonational

Example 11.5c *The Fall of Berlin*, 'Vocalise', bars 1–4

Example 11.6 *Song of the Forests*, movement 7, 'Glory', $\boxed{81}^2$ ('Along the kolkhoz fields')

Example 11.7a *Song of the Forests*, movement 1, 'When the war was over', [2]^1-4 ('The bright days came')

Example 11.7b *Song of the Forests*, movement 7, 'Glory', [103]^5–[104]^5 ('Truth and happiness are with us. If only Lenin could see our Fatherland now.')

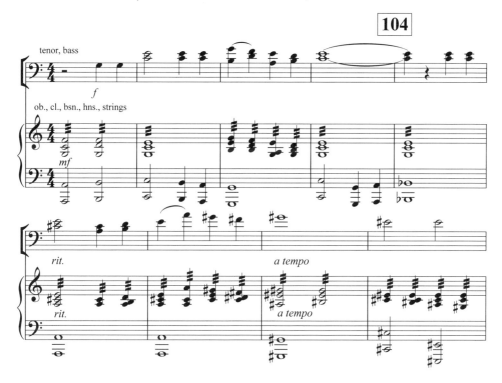

connections with the St Basil's scene are almost inevitable; and since the text refers to the ravages of war inflicted on Russia by the Nazis, evoking Musorgsky's powerful depiction of the starving crowd does not suggest analogous criticism of Stalin. Drawing the listener back to the happier intonations of contemporary Soviet life, the fourth movement 'Pioneers Plant Forests' is a cheerful pioneer song in the same vein as the successful 'Khoroshiy den' [A beautiful day] from *The Fall of Berlin*. With the opening of the fifth movement, 'Komsomols, forward!', Shostakovich evokes a quite different link: to his comic incidental score to Nikolay

Example 11.8a *Song of the Forests*, movement 3, 'Reminiscences of the past', $\boxed{30}^{1-4}$ ('We did not forgot our bitter lot')

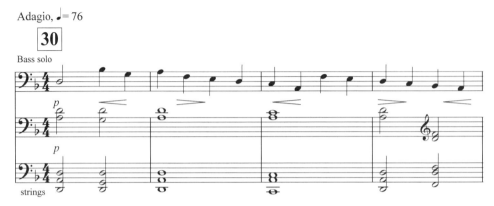

Example 11.8b *Ten Russian Folk Songs*, sans op., 'The Cuckoo's Cry', bars 1–6 ('Akh, cuckoo')

Example 11.9 *Song of the Forests*, movement 5, 'Komsomols, forward!', $\boxed{54}^{1-5}$

Akimov's 1932 *Hamlet*, using the same abrupt V–I punctuation and skittering strings as can be found in 'Banquet', though the links with 'Tournament' are perhaps even stronger (see Ex. 11.9). The 'wrong-note' pungency of the earlier score is abandoned in favour of a more straight-forward tone: but that is also the case in later film scores such as *The Gadfly* (in particular, 'Folk Festival' and 'Galop') and need not be directly attributed to Shostakovich's attempt to compose in a straight-laced Soviet-festive vein.

Returning to a vaguely nationalist style – here Rimsky-Korsakov rather than Musorgsky – the sixth movement 'A Walk into the Future' opens with a touching, old-fashioned cor anglais solo before moving back to more 'Soviet' intonations with the wordless chorus (see Ex. 11.5b). Shostakovich opted for a part-fugal finale, opening with an extremely accomplished five-voice fugue for both choirs (mixed and boys'), complete with augmentation (from $\boxed{92}$). It is with the return of the 'big tune' at 103 that the finale deteriorates into the worst excesses of the Soviet-*pompeznïy* style, with an execrably sentimental tenor solo repeated by the chorus from $\boxed{108}$. The motivic seed 'x' planted in the first movement (Ex. 11.5a) is also grotesquely over-exploited and inflated in these final pages.

The network of intonational connections between *Song of the Forests* and contemporary film scores and songs demonstrates that *Song of the Forests* was by no means an atypical work for Shostakovich. Though it undoubtedly lacks the subtlety of his major instrumental works – the ambiguity of tone and mode that is such a vital ingredient in his musical language – it does share features of works that are far removed from its shameful role as a rehabilitation piece after the disgraces of the *Zhdanovshchina*. Accordingly, it might be more appropriate to see *Song of the Forests* as the work that prompted Shostakovich to follow a new path, during the course of which he developed a genuine interest in precisely the kind of 'Russian' materials he had thus far ignored: peasant

Example 11.10a Alexandrov, Hymn of the Soviet Union, bars 9–10 ('The glorious union of free peoples')

Example 11.10b *The Sun Shines over our Motherland*, ⑨¹⁻³ ('Under the banner of Lenin march the generations')

and revolutionary folklore. While it is undeniable that these works have little in common with those that he withheld until after Stalin's death, on which he worked at the same time, they do not inhabit completely alien intonational spheres, even if their shared ground tended towards the wartime symphonies and the Violin Concerto rather than to the more obviously controversial Jewish-coloured Fourth Quartet and *From Jewish Folk Poetry*.

The Sun Shines over our Motherland, op. 90

Mounting any sort of defence for the cantata *The Sun Shines over our Motherland* is a fairly thankless task. Despite its one-movement form, it is less engaging than the much longer *Song of the Forests*, mainly because it lacks any genuinely appealing tunes, merely recycling clichés from the earlier work without adding anything substantial of its own. There are echoes of Alexandrov's Soviet national anthem as well as of *Song of the Forests* (Ex. 11.10). But there is also a fleeting, but thrillingly Musorgskian moment at 15 that briefly lifts the cantata from its otherwise mundane musical plane. This is very distantly echoed in the Twelfth Symphony finale (bars 89–141 and 220–46), in the larger context of a passage written almost exclusively in a nineteenth-century nationalist style. These connections suggest not so much that *The Sun Shines over our Motherland* formed a repository for popular 'Soviet' intonations in the same way as did *Song of the Forests*, but rather that Shostakovich, either deliberately or intuitively, drew upon the same nineteenth-century intonational

Example 11.11a 'Our Song', bars 4–6 ('From the cruel steppes of Pryazov')

Example 11.11b 'Lyubit ne lyubit', bars 1–3 ('There are many girls in our town')

reservoir when composing the symphony (in 1961) as he had done in both the oratorio and the cantata, in the Russian revolutionary and folk songs and in the film scores of the late 1940s and early 1950s. When the British critic Peter Heyworth commented that the Twelfth Symphony would have 'gladdened the heart of Zhdanov',[33] he was absolutely right: this symphony, together with a large body of works beginning with *The Fall of Berlin* and *Song of the Forests*, fulfilled with masterful precision the (by then) late Zhdanov's demands for composers to form a 'Soviet Kuchka'.[34]

Songs

Only three songs date from the years 1948–50. According to the editorial introduction to vol. 34 of the Muzïka *Collected Works*, the chorus of the unpublished song 'Hymn to Moscow' (subtitled 'Stand Fast, our Inviolable National Shrine') dating from 1948, shares the same music as that of 'Song of Peace' from *Meeting on the Elbe*.[35] Of all Shostakovich's patriotic songs, this one is arguably one of the best. Though the introduction is flat-footed and its ending is weak, it has a very singable, if ordinary, melody. The last line of each verse concludes unconventionally (if sentimentally) with a gentle suspension to the dominant (C) before picking up for the more grandiose chorus 'Our cornfields gleam'. The other songs, 'Our Song' and 'March of the Defenders of Peace', were probably composed around the same time: the editorial introduction states that the date of composition of 'March of the Defenders of Peace' is not known but that musical similarities between them suggest that they were contemporaneous. 'Our Song', originally composed for chorus and orchestra, shares its introduction with 'Lyubit ne lyubit' [Loves me, loves me not] from the Four Songs on words by Yevgeny Dolmatovsky, op. 86, written between 1950 and 1951 (see Ex. 11.11).

The introduction of 'March of the Defenders of Peace' also faintly echoes the introduction to 'The Battle of Stalingrad' from *Russian River*,

Example 11.12a 'March of the Defenders of Peace', bars 1–3

Example 11.12b 'The Battle of Stalingrad', bars 1–3

itself a recycling of Shostakovich's National Anthem entry 'Hymn to the Bolshevik Party', and reused in several songs (Ex. 11.12 cf. Ex. 11.2b above).

The year 1957 was the fortieth anniversary of the October Revolution, and alongside his Eleventh Symphony, Shostakovich ostensibly produced three more Soviet hymns to mark the occasion. Not a single one of them, however, was original. As discussed above, 'October Dawn' was the Shostakovich/Khachaturyan collaborative effort from 1943, set to a new text. The music of the second song, 'We Cherish the October Dawns in our Hearts' also dated from 1943: as stated in note 14, this song is a variant of the unpublished Shostakovich/Khachaturyan 'Hymn to the SSSR' located in the Glinka Museum. It sounds weary from the start, opening with a clichéd drumroll-style piano tremolo marked 'Maestoso' ('Grave' in the 1943 score) and plodding through to the end, weighed down by an excess of root-position chords and a clumsy bass-line. But a new nadir in Shostakovich's anthem writing is reached with the third song, 'We Sing Glory to our Motherland'. This is by far the weakest of the three songs, again opening with a 'Maestoso' tremolo, and scarcely moving beyond the most elementary chord progressions. There are no spicy substitutions: no submediants, major or minor, in place of the tonic E flat, and weak chord movements such as V $^6_4$–I give the song a trudging – even amateurish – feel. This song contains very little original material, since most of it was lifted from the by now familiar introduction to 'The Battle of Stalingrad' from the NKVD show *Russian River* (see Ex. 11.12). The leaden style of this song strongly recalls the satirical skit *Antiformalist Rayok*, to which Shostakovich returned in 1957: its banal fanfares and tremolos are all echoed in the second and third songs. It is worth pointing out the poor quality of these songs, since the likely reason was that Shostakovich had used either obscure or rejected material from the 1940s that audiences would not readily recognize. What is certain is that Shostakovich could have written successful songs, as he did on other occasions, but did not this time – something that suggests a distinct lack of enthusiasm for the project.

The final song from this period is *Novorossiysk Chimes* (text by Kira Alemasova), a short chorus for male-voice choir and piano. Shostakovich explained the motivation for this work in a short article for *Izvestiya*: 'The defenders of Novorossiisk covered themselves with glory during the Great Patriotic War and I was honoured to compose music for the Fire of Eternal Glory burning at the memorial in Heroes Square. The city's authorities applied to the RSFSR Union of Composers to commission a piece of music to commemorate the heroes of Novorossiisk. That is how my *Chimes* came into being.'[36] The precise date of composition is not known, though the premiere was 27 September 1960. But whatever the date it was written, Shostakovich's 'late' period had effectively begun the previous summer with his First Cello Concerto, the work which, together with the Seventh and Eighth Quartets and the song cycle *Satires*, op. 109, marked a change in his style.[37] The 1950s were characterized for Shostakovich by uncertainty: starting with 1948 and the real beginning of his role as a composer of 'official' music, the decade also saw the deaths of Stalin, his wife Nina and his mother and his short-lived second marriage. He was fêted abroad with honorary degrees and memberships[38] and increasingly secure in his official roles at home as People's Artist of the USSR, election to the secretariat of the Composers' Union and as deputy to the RSFSR Supreme Soviet for Leningrad's Dzerzhinsky District. But a remarkable total of twelve compositions – not counting film scores, mass songs/hymns or children's pieces – from a work list of twenty-four pieces between 1948 and 1959 are today almost completely neglected: a proportion far higher than that of any other decade in Shostakovich's life. It was during this decade, more than in any other, that Shostakovich seemed to falter in his vocation as a composer, suffering writer's block after Stalin's death and the completion of the Tenth Symphony and fearing that he would be like Rossini, drying up in his forties.[39] But by 1959 this uncertainty was over, and regardless of the civic worthiness of Shostakovich's comments about *Novorossiysk Chimes*, the fact remains that he did not trouble to compose original music for it. Around the same time of its composition (which could hardly have taken more than a few hours, if that) he was composing his haunted Seventh Quartet, the song cycle *Satires* and the tragic Eighth Quartet, written as the formal procedures confirming his membership of the Communist Party were going through, an event that brought about a near breakdown. Given these circumstances, it is perhaps not surprising that *Novorossiysk Chimes* sounds less than freshly inspired, opening with the ubiquitous introductory phrase of the Mikhalkov/El-Registan National Anthem song that Shostakovich had already recycled four times, having only to think of a new way to round off its second phrase and a new second half.

Three late works: *October,* op. 131, *Loyalty,* op. 136, *March of the Soviet Militia,* op. 139

Shostakovich's last three 'official' works date from the three-year period between 1967 and 1970. The first of these, the symphonic poem *October,* op. 131, was especially composed for the fiftieth anniversary celebrations of the October Revolution. The most obvious and striking feature of the work is the affinity between its first theme and that of the Tenth Symphony's first movement. Though *October* has none of the brooding quality of the symphony, its opening rising minor third shape, initially traced (as in the symphony) in slow-moving crotchets, immediately connects with the intonational sphere of the symphony. As in the symphony, it proves highly generative, with four main variants of the theme (at figs $\boxed{7}$, $\boxed{48}$, $\boxed{51}$ and $\boxed{55}$) both proceeding from, and giving rise to, fairly intensive development. This alone makes *October* feel strikingly active, compressing motivic development on an almost symphonic scale into a twelve-to-thirteen-minute span. Its second theme, though, was the initial impetus for the work's composition. In 1967, Mosfilm was preparing for the re-release of the Vasiliev brothers' film *Volochayevskiye dni* [Volochayev days], for which Shostakovich had written the music in 1937. Shostakovich's 'Partisan Song' – a catchy tune that lies somewhere between an English sea shanty and a Russian folk song – was the main theme of the score, recurring throughout the film. Writing popular tunes proved surprisingly difficult for a composer who worked so extensively in film, ballet and incidental music, and the 'Partisan Song' required ten drafts before Shostakovich was satisfied with it.[40] Laurel Fay records that when he heard his score again in the Mosfilm studio, it gave Shostakovich a starting point for his new work.[41] The 'Partisan' theme – happily appropriate for an anniversary piece – contrasts with the opening theme in being almost entirely non-generative, sharing some materials with the first theme (chiefly, its counter-subject at $\boxed{1}$, which becomes the accompaniment to the song theme at $\boxed{49}$ and the main shape of its accompanying counterpoint at $\boxed{50}$) but never directly engaging with it. After the main climax at $\boxed{45}$, the alternation between the two themes becomes more rapid; but it is the Partisan Song that concludes *October,* at double speed, with its opening shape cheerfully reiterated over a triumphant dominant–tonic bass.

Loyalty, op. 136 was another anniversary piece, this time written for the centenary celebrations of Lenin's birth in 1970. The set of eight ballads for a cappella male chorus was the last of his collaborations with Dolmatovsky, whose patriotic and popular poems had served Shostakovich well since 1943. It was dedicated to the conductor of the Estonian State Academic Male Voice Choir, Gustav Ernesaks, who gave the premiere and, together with the Fourteenth Quartet, the cycle was awarded the Glinka Prize in 1974. As with all his 'official' works since Stalin's death, Shostakovich was by no means obliged to compose a special piece to mark any anniversary, and, at least after Stalin's death, he had generally managed to do so on his own terms, composing his Eleventh Symphony as the main work of 1957 and the fine symphonic poem *October* in 1967. But *Loyalty* stands slightly apart from these other works, being rather less distinguished in content, not least because of Dolmatovsky's ludicrous verses which compare Confucius, Buddha and Allah, no less, unfavourably with the man who 'gave us belief in mankind' – Lenin. Shostakovich's exhortation to composers to commemorate the Lenin centenary was possibly no more than an automatic fulfilment of his official role as the Soviet Union's leading composer; but all the same, it is intriguing to speculate on the conversation between Shostakovich and Dolmatovsky that the poet later 'distilled' into the poems.[42] In a television interview, Shostakovich remarked that the poems 'contain serious, very heartfelt lyrical reflections about Lenin, about the Motherland, about the Party. This is not the first time I have treated this theme ... And I think it will not be my last work about Vladimir Ilyich. In the future I will most certainly strive to embody the image of this great man.'[43] The motivation for Shostakovich's collaborations with Dolmatovsky after 1953 remains intriguing; all his other songs, with the exception of his folk-song settings and deliberately off-beat or bad poems such as the *Five Romances on Texts from Krokodil Magazine*, op. 121 and *Four Verses of Captain Lebyadkin*, op. 146, were settings of verses by distinguished European poets: Shakespeare, Alexander Blok, Michelangelo Buonarroti, Marina Tsvetayeva, Pushkin, Guillaume Apollinaire, Rainer Maria Rilke, Wilhelm Küchelbecker, Federico Garcia Lorca and Lermontov. But though at first glance Shostakovich's turning to Dolmatovsky's sentimental and propagandistic verses appears anomalous, it would seem that literary quality was not necessarily the most important factor for Shostakovich when selecting verses for musical setting. His defence of the young Soviet poet Yevgeny Yevtushenko in 1965 against those who attacked him for superficiality and moralizing, is telling. In 1962 Shostakovich had selected some of his verses for his Thirteenth Symphony, most famously the poem 'Babiy Yar'. When the composer Boris Tishchenko criticized the poems as 'moralizing', Shostakovich claimed not to understand: 'As for what "moralizing" poetry is, I didn't understand. Why, as you maintain, it isn't "among the best". Morality is the natural sister of conscience. And because Yevtushenko writes about conscience, God grant him all the very best.'[44] Though Shostakovich regarded Yevtushenko as talented rather than a genius, he treasured his poems precisely for the moral content that provoked squeamishness in others.

Though *Loyalty* is hardly a companion piece for the Thirteenth Symphony, the two works do share some common features: both are written for male-voice choir, with verses whose political appeal overrides their relative weakness as poetry. Both Yevtushenko's and Dolmatovsky's poems convey a sense of immediacy, almost intimacy, that stems from addressing the Soviet listener exclusively and personally. Although Shostakovich would inevitably have expected his symphony to be performed internationally, he would hardly have expected the same of *Loyalty*; and in fact its overtly 'domestic' *topos*, combined with the challenge of a cappella writing, prompted a return to the 'Russian' style of the *Ten Russian Folk Songs* and *Ten Songs on Verses by Revolutionary Poets*, op. 88. Dolmatovsky's verses will strike many twenty-first-century readers as laughable; but Shostakovich's committed setting of them invites deeper reflection.

The question of why Shostakovich, entirely of his own volition, chose to set Dolmatovsky's romanticized propaganda is no more answerable than a host of others relating to Shostakovich's personal and professional activities during his last decade. Once he had joined the Party in 1960, he took his official duties seriously to the point of endangering his own health as he grew increasingly frail, and of alienating his friends and colleagues as he went through the motions of the loyal Party servant, refusing to ally himself with prominent dissidents such as Solzhenitsyn or Andrey Sakharov.[45] It is of course possible that, having composed nothing for *a cappella* choir since his two Russian folk-song arrangements, op. 104 (1957), the prospect of writing for male-voice choir again held genuine appeal for Shostakovich, regardless of how bad the texts themselves were. In April 1969, with the centenary of Lenin's birth approaching, he made public his intention to compose an oratorio.[46] The fact that he had publicly declared a forthcoming work celebrating Lenin several times during the 1930s (after the premiere of the Fifth Symphony, and again shortly before Russia entered the war in 1941) does caution us against taking Shostakovich's word at face value. But this time the work duly materialized, perhaps aided by the prospect of performance by the excellent Estonian State Academic Male Choir. Despite the weakness of the poems, *Loyalty* is not the cheap throwaway work that some writers have assumed. It bears comparison with both choral works of 1951 (the *Ten Russian Folk Songs*, sans op. and the *Ten Poems on Texts by Revolutionary Poets* op. 88) in the skill and beauty of Shostakovich's choral writing, its homophonic passages occasionally reminiscent of Russian Orthodox or folk music, chiefly in the first and last verses. Inevitably, musical illustration of the verses sometimes feels mawkish, as for the recurring line 'Like a banner of the Revolution' in the fourth song and the climactic line 'It is for us to open the weighty doors of communism' in the second.

But elsewhere even the most sentimental verses are set to beautiful music; the intimate sixth. poem, 'I want to learn all about him', for example, is tenderly lyrical, while the ambivalent passage beginning 'Life is a difficult search for beauty' ends with an especially lovely evocation of Russian Orthodox singing on the sentimentally patriotic line 'there is none better [than the Motherland]'.

Shostakovich's final 'official' work was the short *March of the Soviet Militia* op. 139 for military band. Perhaps because of its brevity, this second of Shostakovich's military marches is a notable improvement on the first. Dedicated – surely with extreme irony – to the satirical writer Mikhail Zoshchenko, it is no more than a lightweight function piece, written in appropriate marching style, with none of the brash clumsiness of the *Ceremonial March*. Its late position in Shostakovich's complete works list is characteristically paradoxical; but then the curious *Four Verses of Captain Lebyadkin* sit equally oddly alongside such works as the Viola Sonata and the Fifteenth Symphony. Shostakovich's cheerful miniature *March of the Soviet Militia* might well serve as a closing reminder of his multi-layered personality and creative legacy: one with which the world is still coming to terms, and one in which those 'official' opuses must still take their full place.

PART IV

Performance, theory, reception

12 A political football: Shostakovich reception in Germany

ERIK LEVI

From my previous money I still have forty dollars, so I decided to go to Berlin. I persuaded Oborin to come, too. He can speak the language, albeit not too well. Berlin is an enchanting city. I couldn't imagine anywhere like it.[1]

Judging by the excitable nature of the letter that Shostakovich wrote to his mother from Berlin on 8 February 1927, the young composer's eagerness to expend precious financial resources on a week-long trip to the German capital was merely an act of impulse born out of frustration at his lack of success at the Warsaw Chopin Piano Competition. On further reflection, however, there seems to have been a much greater degree of calculation in his behaviour. No doubt, like many other young Soviet composers, Shostakovich was fascinated by the increasing amount of new German music that was being performed in his native country in the mid-1920s. For this reason he would have seized any opportunity to experience at first hand the cultural environment from which such compositions emanated. Perhaps his desire to visit Berlin was also stimulated in the previous month by the invitation to play through his First Symphony to the conductor Bruno Walter, who was giving concerts in Leningrad at the time.

Shostakovich's encounter with Walter proved particularly decisive. Although an arch conservative when it came to the promotion of contemporary music, Walter was evidently so impressed by the qualities of the symphony that he agreed at once to programme the work in his next season of concerts with the Berlin Philharmonic Orchestra. The auspicious German premiere took place on 6 February 1928, its overwhelming success serving to launch Shostakovich's name in the West as a composer of extraordinary promise.

The triumph of the Berlin performance can only have strengthened Shostakovich's initial enthusiasm for the city. Later he would return there and to other parts of Germany on a number of occasions that were to prove crucial for his own development as a composer. Throughout his life he continued to venerate Austro-German composers, professing particular enthusiasm for Bach, Beethoven, Mahler and Berg. Indeed, according to Hilmar Schmalenberg, 'Germany represented for Shostakovich the next most important cultural tradition after that of his homeland'.[2] To what extent, however, the Germans reciprocated Shostakovich's devotion to their country in the reception of his music is a more complex question. All too often, any serious critical engagement with Shostakovich's output was obfuscated by arguments of ideology, the main preoccupation being the potentially positive or harmful impact that political interference might have exerted upon the development of his musical language.

A man for all seasons – Shostakovich in the Weimar Republic (1928–33)

At the outset of Shostakovich's career, ideological controversies were rarely brought to the fore in German discussion of the composer's music. Despite the highly polarized cultural debate between the Left and Right that ravaged the Weimar Republic, critics from a wide spectrum of opinion managed to find something positive to say about the First Symphony – a point emphatically highlighted by Shostakovich's publishers Universal Edition, whose advertisement for the symphony, published in the March 1928 edition of their house magazine *Musikblätter des Anbruch*, included enthusiastic appraisals of the work from the conservative Max Marschalk and the more progressive Walter Schrenk. Remarkably, in subsequent performances of the symphony, the composer's Soviet origins proved not to be a hindrance for right-wing critics. For instance, the anti-Semitic musicologist Alfred Heuss, an active proponent of Alfred Rosenberg's *Kampfund für deutsche Kultur* with a long-standing hatred towards any manifestations of *Musikbolschewismus*, endorsed Shostakovich's talents when, in November 1930, Walter presented the work for the first time with the Leipzig Gewandhaus, the orchestra of which he had become chief conductor the previous year. Writing in the proto-nationalist journal *Zeitschrift für Musik*, Heuss regarded Shostakovich's symphony far more favourably than a recent novelty by Křenek, praising the composer for the rare understanding with which he manipulated orchestral colour and for the seriousness of purpose demonstrated in his symphonic writing.[3]

Given that the First Symphony attracted a number of other distinguished conductors, including Robert Heger, Karl Böhm and Leopold Reichwein, and that it was performed to almost unanimous critical and audience approval in various cities, it seems curious that none of the many German music journals of the period sought to publish a detailed profile of the composer. One possible explanation for this seeming lack of interest may have been that Shostakovich appeared on the scene almost at the very end of a period in which new Soviet music had been given a sympathetic platform in the Weimar Republic. The origins of this process can be traced back to 1925, the year in which the influential Viennese publishers Universal Edition had taken the financially risky step of signing an agreement to act as agents for the burgeoning catalogue of music issued by the Russian State Publishing House. Yet the promotion of relatively unknown repertoire in the German-speaking world proved a challenging task, requiring a good degree of intensive propaganda. To enhance this objective, in March 1925 the *Musikblätter des Anbruch* published the first of three special issues focusing on musical life in the Soviet Union. The main purpose of the articles, written primarily by Soviet musicologists, was to provide detailed commentary on the work of a number of emerging composers. Although Shostakovich was briefly mentioned in the publication, it would have been impossible to present a profile of his work, since at this juncture he had not even completed his First Symphony.

By the time Shostakovich's First Symphony was heard in Berlin, however, interest in new Soviet music had reached its peak. In the interim period, Universal Edition appears to have singled out Alexander Mosolov as the Soviet composer most likely to appeal to progressively minded German audiences. Intensive campaigning on his behalf soon paid dividends, with some of his most recent works receiving performances in Berlin and at the 1927 ISCM Festival in Frankfurt. But while there was a healthy awareness of Mosolov's piano, chamber and orchestral works, apart from the First Symphony, little was known about the rest of Shostakovich's output.

During the early 1930s there were some sporadic attempts to broaden the picture. In June 1930 Franz Osborn performed the First Piano Sonata at a Berlin ISCM concert, but judging by the comments of the critic Karl Westermeyer, writing in the journal *Die Musik*, the work failed to make much of an impact. Westermeyer's principal complaints were that the Sonata suffered from an excessive striving for effect and was deficient in terms of establishing a clearly defined musical style.[4] A more favourable response to a recent work by Shostakovich appeared in the same journal in February 1931 with regard to a performance of the Suite from the opera *The Nose* given by the Berlin Radio Orchestra under Nikolay Malko.[5] The critic's enthusiasm for the brittle Russian humour projected in this score suggests that under different political and economic circumstances, some theatres might have been tempted to introduce the complete opera to German audiences. But once again, the timing for such an event was not advantageous. Following the Wall Street Crash in 1929, almost all opera houses were forced to make a drastic reduction in the performance of contemporary repertoire. Thus despite publishing Eugen [Yevgeny] Braudo's positive and detailed review of the Leningrad premiere of *The*

Nose in April 1930, a journal such as *Die Musik* was unable to influence public opinion to the extent that a German staging of Shostakovich's opera could ever have been realized during this period.[6]

Shostakovich and the Third Reich

In the turbulent political environment of 1930, it was still possible for a nominally independent journal such as *Die Musik* to publish a laudatory critique of Shostakovich's opera without risking the accusation that it had pandered to the propaganda of Bolshevism. Needless to say, the situation three years later was rather different. Following the anti-Communist denunciations unleashed in the early months of the Third Reich, it was obviously much more hazardous for music periodicals to make any mention of musical developments in the Soviet Union, on the basis that presenting such information could be construed as potentially subversive. For the next twelve years, therefore, Shostakovich was effectively ignored, his music no longer finding any place in German concert programmes. Interestingly, in the light of Nazi censorship directed towards Hindemith and other composers, German music journals were careful to avoid any discussion of the 1936 *Pravda* crisis, the last detailed reference to Shostakovich appearing in the August 1933 issue of *Die Musik* in relation to the first performance in Chicago of the Third Symphony.[7] Following the new critical orthodoxy of the Third Reich, the Chicago correspondent peddled the predictable argument that the composer's promising talents had unfortunately been undermined by strange influences and constrained by the necessity to follow the Soviet Union's idiosyncratic political and cultural policies.[8]

The Nazi ban on Shostakovich was sufficiently resolute to have withstood the impact of the Hitler/Stalin pact of 1939, which brought an unforeseen, if temporary, possibility of cultural rapprochement between the two nations. To complement this unlikely political alliance, the Nazis made a sudden and cynical move to incorporate far more Russian music into German concert and operatic programmes than in the previous six years of the Third Reich. Yet despite an attempt by the Leipzig publishers Breitkopf & Härtel to make some gain out of the pact through securing the performing rights for a number of recent orchestral works, including the Sixteenth Symphony by Myaskovsky, the First Symphony of Khachaturyan and Shostakovich's Fifth Symphony, the performance of Soviet music remained strictly off-limits. This explains the strange situation that occurred in 1940 when the conductor Albert Bittner managed to challenge the status quo by securing the German premiere of Shostakovich's Fifth Symphony at an orchestral concert in Essen on 3 December. Although Bittner had evidently been able to overcome any potential objection to the performance by the local state music functionary, intervention at a higher level must have prevented the work from being heard. At the concert in question, the Shostakovich was replaced by Rimsky-Korsakov's *Sheherezade*, the dubious justification for its substitution being that the orchestral materials could not be made available in sufficient time.[9]

Post-war revivals (1946–9)

When the Fifth Symphony eventually secured its German premiere on 6 July 1946, with the Berlin Philharmonic under its new principal conductor, the Romanian Sergiu Celibidache, the Allies had already started to rebuild musical life out of the ashes of the Third Reich. Although the four occupying powers were by no means in total agreement as to ways in which this might be achieved, they all supported the principles that lay behind presenting such a work so soon after the end of the war. In essence, the prime objective was to re-educate the German public to embrace a repertoire which, in the opinion of the Americans, was 'designed to restore the exchange of ideas between Germany and the world outside it'.[10] At this stage, the rhetoric of the Cold War had not yet taken root, and the accessible and humanitarian message of Shostakovich's music was regarded as particularly effective in the drive to inspire empathy and fraternity amongst different nations.

The impression that the Fifth Symphony could help to heal wounds was forcibly conveyed by the critic and composer Siegfried Borris. In his review of the Berlin performance in the *Tägliche Rundschau*, Borris responded particularly effusively towards the work, praising its strength of personality and expression, and claiming that it occupied an essential point of reference for the development of new music. At the time of writing, Borris was reacting with genuine enthusiasm for Shostakovich's achievement. Yet with the benefit of hindsight he may well have regretted that his remarks, originally published in a newspaper controlled by the Soviet military authorities, were to be taken out of context many years later at a time when the German Democratic Republic was engaged in a bitter propaganda war against the perceived decadence of Western avant-garde music.[11]

While in 1946 Berlin audiences responded warmly to the Fifth, which was programmed again on the 10 and 11 August, it must have been much more difficult for them to have to come to terms with the 'Leningrad' Symphony. This work was given its first German performance at the Admiralspalast in the Eastern Sector of the German capital on 21 December 1946, also with the

Berlin Philharmonic under Celibidache. Although later in life Celibidache strongly denied the suggestion that the decision to perform such a work barely a year after the cessation of hostilities had been imposed upon him by the occupying powers, there is little doubt that the concert provided a very compelling public demonstration of German atonement for the atrocities recently committed against the Russians – a point underlined not only by the thunderous reception to the work, in which the conductor was recalled to the podium more than twenty times, but also by the speech of thanks to the artists delivered after the performance by Berlin's Russian military commandant.[12]

If, as Celibidache argued, it was purely on the strength of its music that he chose to conduct Shostakovich's 'Leningrad' Symphony, the first German performance on 9 July 1947 at a Berlin Philharmonic concert of the composer's wartime orchestration of Eight British and American Folk Songs must be regarded as a more unequivocal political gesture, particularly since the conductor on this particular occasion was the American John Bitter, formerly in charge of the Miami Symphony Orchestra but currently a US military officer whose principal occupation was to coordinate the de-Nazification of German musical life. Yet setting aside the motives that lay behind such events, there seems to have been a genuine desire in the immediate post-war era to catch up with other works by the composer that had not yet been heard in Germany. Thus the concert season from 1946 to1947 also included performances of the Sixth Symphony in Berlin under Artur Rother on 3 August 1946, the Eighth under Herbert Albert in Leipzig on 7 November 1946 and the Ninth on 28 February 1947 in Dresden under Heinz Bongartz and later on 31 August in Berlin under Celibidache. In conjunction with these premieres it is interesting to note that in 1947 the Leipzig publishers Breitkopf & Härtel also secured the copyright for the Eighth and Ninth Symphonies. There was further evidence of the Shostakovich revival in the more unlikely surroundings of the contemporary music festival in Donaueschingen on 28 July 1946. In a programme that also featured compositions by Walter Piston and Stravinsky, the First Piano Concerto received a particularly warm reception. It was the first and only example during Shostakovich's lifetime of his music's being heard within the context of a German festival normally associated with the avant-garde.

The consensus breaks – Shostakovich and the German Democratic Republic

The spirit of nominal cooperation between the occupying powers soon fell apart, with profound consequences for the long-term development of German musical life. In this context, the subsequent reception of

Shostakovich's music came to be determined not so much by questions of musical quality as by political allegiance either to the West or the East. The arguments became even more polarized in the wake of the 1948 Zhdanov decrees and the composer's much publicized appearances at the World Peace Conference in New York. Contrasting positions were crystallized by the 1949 division of Germany into two separate countries, one controlled by the Russians, the other by the Western powers. In the newly created German Democratic Republic the effects of Stalinism were all too visible in the cultural sphere. The opening pages of the first issue in 1951 of the official journal *Musik und Gesellschaft* underlined the link, with a large photograph of GDR State President Wilhelm Pieck alongside a delegation of Soviet composers, including a grim-faced Shostakovich, taken in front of the Bach monument in Leipzig at the time of the anniversary celebrations. This visit inspired Shostakovich to compose his *Twenty-Four Preludes and Fugues*, but for the moment the major preoccupation for GDR musicians seems to have been with the oratorio *Song of the Forests* that had secured the Stalin Prize in 1950. Writing in the April 1951 issue of *Musik und Gesellschaft*, Carl Friedrichs lavished this work with extravagant praise, drawing specific attention to its monumental greatness and sublime beauty which speaks 'with a warm heart to all peoples'.[13] Friedrichs's motive for drawing attention to this work was unequivocal: namely, that Shostakovich's oratorio should act as a spur and inspiration for GDR composers to follow suit with their own politically conceived contributions to the choral literature – a tactic that soon paid off, judging by the enormous number of cantatas by the likes of Ernst Hermann Meyer, Johannes Thilman and Ottmar Gerster that were subjected to extensive review and analysis in subsequent issues of the journal.

During its early years, *Musik und Gesellschaft* mirrored the twists and turns of Soviet musical policy with an almost inflexible fidelity. As far as Shostakovich was concerned, this meant an exclusive concentration on his political music. In September 1952, for example, the journal carried a German translation of Marian Koval's extremely detailed appraisal of the recently composed *Ten Poems on Texts by Revolutionary Poets*, op. 88, which had originally appeared in *Sovetskaya muzïka*, and the highlight of the following month was a review of the Leipzig radio broadcast of *Song of the Forests*. Naturally, after the death of Stalin the focus shifted far more towards Shostakovich's abstract works, though often replicating the same caveats that had been raised in the Soviet musical press. The first GDR performance on 12 May 1954 of the Tenth Symphony by the Leipzig Gewandhaus Orchestra under Franz Konwitschny occasioned a lengthy, if somewhat cautious, appraisal from Eberhard Rebling. Noting that the work was received with a strong ovation, Rebling nonetheless followed the line of some Soviet commentators in suggesting that its emotional contradictions had not necessarily been resolved, and that the symphony required further discussion and dissemination before its true stature could be assessed.[14]

From 1953 onwards, reviews and articles of Shostakovich's new works became a regular feature of the GDR music journals *Musik und Gesellschaft* and *Musik in der Schule*. Three GDR musicologists, Heinz-Alfred Brockhaus, Karl Laux and Siegmund Schultze developed research specialisms in the composer, publishing some of the first substantial if politically correct appraisals of the composer's output in the German language. The process of Shostakovich dissemination was further enhanced by regular performances and recordings of his music by GDR orchestras, conductors and performers and by the publication of many works under the aegis of the Leipzig branch of Edition Peters.

If one of the principal motives that lay behind all this active promotion of Shostakovich in the GDR was to bolster the cultural policies of the regime, the composer himself was portrayed as a willing accomplice to its stance. Two examples in particular served these objectives admirably. First, there was Shostakovich's work on the anti-fascist film *Five Days, Five Nights* (1960), a joint project between the GDR and Soviet Union that necessitated the composer's high-profile visit to the country. Although Shostakovich's visit is best remembered nowadays as the time when he worked on his Eighth String Quartet, it was the film music that initially attracted most attention. Second, both *Musik und Gesellschaft* and *Musik in der Schule* were especially proactive in publishing German translations of articles written by the composer that toed the party line with regard to issues of music and ideology. For instance, Cold War rhetoric undoubtedly prompted the publication of 'Eine Mode ohne Zukunft' [A fad without a future] in the February 1960 issue of *Musik und Gesellschaft* – a reprint of an interview Shostakovich had given in *Sovetskaya muzïka* in connection with the programme of the 1959 Warsaw Autumn festival.[15] The main purpose of his argument was to launch a savage attack against the proponents of dodecaphony and other vestiges of musical experimentation, both of which were described as sterile. In particular, Shostakovich argued that composers such as Boulez and Varèse were merely intent on destroying the basic aesthetic principles of music.[16]

Shostakovich and the Bundesrepublik – a victim of anti-Soviet propaganda

Whether or not Shostakovich sincerely believed in these remarks, his reactionary statements proved par for the course so far as those steering

musical life in West Germany were concerned. If Shostakovich was cano-
nized in the GDR, his position in the West was much less assured.
Undoubtedly the most hostile response to his work emanated from contemporary music circles. Composers and performers allied to the modernist
avant-garde attitudes generated at places such as Darmstadt considered
Shostakovich's adherence to traditional compositional techniques a mere
irrelevance and a sad reflection of the ways in which political authori-
tarianism had quashed creative individuality. On the other hand, for
Theodor Adorno the problem with Shostakovich was not so much his
fractured relationship with the state as his compositional naivety and technical flaws – deficiencies he apparently shared with Britten and Stravinsky.[17]

Other West German musicians were less hidebound by such objections. A consultation of orchestral programmes during the 1950s and
1960s reveals that a number of the composer's symphonies were heard,
albeit on a far less regular basis than in the GDR. Indeed, irrespective of
the political climate at the time, some performances achieved considerable
profile, one example being the Berlin Philharmonic's rendition of the
Tenth under Herbert von Karajan on 1 March 1959, an interpretation
that was to enjoy permanency and much critical acclaim in two commercial recordings on the Deutsche Grammophon label released in 1966 and
1981. Karajan's motives for presenting this work were purely musical, for
it was one of the few mid-twentieth-century orchestral pieces for which he
felt a particular affinity. Likewise, the decision of other prominent conductors, such as Rudolf Kempe and Wolfgang Sawallisch, to perform
Shostakovich's symphonies from time to time was determined purely by
admiration for the music. One should contrast these sporadic attempts to
accommodate Shostakovich into the symphonic repertoire with the rather
more controversial and contrived performance of the Suite from *The Lady
Macbeth of Mtsensk District*, given by the Berlin RIAS Orchestra under
Ferenc Fricsay in Berlin and Paris in 1952. In presenting a work that was
ostensibly banned in the Soviet Union, orchestra and conductor were
willing collaborators in an act of deliberate provocation against the
Stalinist regime. The mastermind behind this particular salvo was the
composer and US intelligence officer Nicolas Nabokov, who had discovered the score in Vienna and wanted to challenge the notion that the work
could never again be played 'in spite of Stalin and the verdict of the
commissars'.[18]

A remarkable feature of Shostakovich reception in West Germany was
the singular reluctance amongst its academics and musicologists to engage
on any serious critical level with Shostakovich's music, a situation that
persisted until the early 1970s. One looks in vain for any substantial
articles on the composer's work, and the few critiques of performances

that were published in contemporary journals such as *Musica* and *Neue Zeitschrift für Musik* were reserved and locked into the notion that his musical invention had been suppressed by the impossible demands of the Soviet regime to compose music that should be immediately understandable to the masses.

Reconciliation and resolution – the 1970s and beyond

The first breakthrough against this trend of silence and disengagement in West German academic circles took place in 1974, the year before the composer's death. In the prestigious journal *Archiv für Musikwissenschaft* the Cologne-based academic Klaus Körner devoted forty pages to examining the cultural and musical context of the Fourth Symphony, one of the most controversial and problematic of the composer's works.[19] Marshalling an impressive knowledge of the relevant literature in English, German and Russian, Körner's article appears to have acted as the model for a more analytical article on Shostakovich that appeared in 1978 in the journal *Melos/Neue Zeitschrift für Musik* by the distinguished academic Hermann Danuser. Following very much the trend of the period, which sought to re-examine much of the long-forgotten avant-garde repertoire of the 1920s, Danuser provided a detailed exploration of the tensions between progressive and traditional features in the First Piano Sonata and the Second Symphony, works that dated from Shostakovich's experimental phase, which he had largely disowned later in his life.[20]

These apparently isolated examples of Shostakovich scholarship in the 1970s suggest that irrespective of political agendas, Shostakovich was gradually being readmitted into the canon of twentieth-century composers deserving of more objective appraisal. To what extent this process of acceptance was intensified by the German translation of Volkov's *Testimony* in 1979 is not entirely clear. Undoubtedly, Volkov's portrayal of the supposedly 'dissident' Shostakovich offered Cold War apologists an admirable justification for making a critical volte-face and pursuing a 'revisionist' interpretation of the composer's output. But two other factors should also be taken into consideration. First, in the political sphere, there was a noticeable increase in cultural cooperation between the West German and Soviet governments. This was manifested in concrete terms by the increased activity of the Hamburg-based publisher Hans Sikorski, who cornered the market in the distribution of previously inaccessible Soviet music, and in publications such as the 1982 *Beiträge zur Musikkultur in der Sowjetunion und in der Bundesrepublik Deutschland*, a book jointly edited by Carl Dahlhaus and Giwi Ordschonikidse,[21] which included detailed exploration of each country's musical life and even featured chapters by Party apparatchiks such as Khrennikov and Kabalevsky. With respect to Shostakovich, the process of cultural exchange inspired notable events such as the Duisburg Shostakovich Festival of 1984 and the Internationales Dmitri Schostakowitsch Symposium, which took place in Cologne in 1985.

Arguably more significant than these gestures of collaboration was the changing post-modernist artistic climate of the 1980s, which enabled composers such as Shostakovich to be reappraised in the context of a much wider, stylistically pluralist context. Perhaps the most tangible evidence of this re-evaluation was provided not so much by the burgeoning number of books on Shostakovich published in West Germany during the 1980s, as by the 1985 publication of Wolfgang Rihm's essay *Zur Musik von Dmitri Schostakowitsch*, essentially a copy of a speech that had been delivered at the Duisburg Shostakovich Festival.[22] That a young composer, most closely associated with the avant-garde and active as a professor of composition in Darmstadt, could now openly demonstrate his admiration for Shostakovich, proclaiming him alongside Berg and others as a legitimate inheritor of the Mahler tradition, suggested that even before the dismantling of the Berlin Wall, the Adornian and total serialist prejudices of an earlier generation were now merely a distant memory.

13 The rough guide to Shostakovich's harmonic language

DAVID HAAS

Points of origin

However diverse the influences on Shostakovich's idiosyncratic harmonic language, and however ambivalent his attitude to the tradition in which he was schooled, he was ineluctably a descendent of the Rimsky-Korsakov school. There is good reason therefore to launch this survey with a paradigmatic example from the master pedagogue, its symbolism forming as much a part of Shostakovich's inheritance as the technical aspect.

The first evidence for the existence of the Devil in Rimsky-Korsakov's Gogol opera *Christmas Eve* is to be found in bar 6 of the Prelude to Act 1. Here the preceding pattern of major triads descending by thirds (E–C sharp – A–F sharp – D–B–G) would suggest one last fall to E to close the circle of this D major diatonic collection of chord roots. Instead the G falls only to F, which forms a tritone with the still sounding B of the G triad (see Ex. 13.1).

Over the course of the next four acts, numerous tritones will follow as the Devil purloins the moon and stars, cavorts with the witch Solokha, and attempts to catch and then escape from his nemesis, the icon painter Vakula, who has confined him to a burlap sack and ordered that the Devil fly him from Dikanka to St Petersburg and back. In both nocturnal voyages (Act 3, 6th tableau; Act 4, 8th tableau) Rimsky-Korsakov expands the tritone count from one to four. From this he creates passages that evoke the disruptive, nihilistic influence of dark powers by means of rootless diminished-seventh chords and linear segments, in which the four tritones interlock to create the eight-note 'octatonic' scale (see Ex. 13.2, where all pitches belong to the scale of semitone–tone alternations upwards from E).

Demonic octatonicism eventually dissipates, tentatively so with the celestial union of the two pagan deities Ovsen and Kolyada, more conclusively with the dawning of Christmas morning (Act 3, 8th tableau, bars 38ff.), when the last demonic B–F tritone is pointedly resolved into a C major triad of church bell pealing and chanting choristers. From then until the end of the opera, 'human' diatonicism prevails, and the few tritones that do appear function not to confuse or oppose, but to strengthen tonal centricity.

Example 13.1 Rimsky-Korsakov, *Christmas Eve*, Act 1, Prelude, bars 1–6

Example 13.2 Rimsky-Korsakov, *Christmas Eve*, Act 3, 'Demonic Carol', opening

While Rimsky's unusual treatment of commonplace harmonic materials in *Christmas Eve* and subsequent operas is broadly relevant to Shostakovich (and unquestionably a departure from what was going on in Western European conservatoires), its function in the grand-pupil's hands is radically altered. There is no mistaking Rimsky's intent – at both the structural foundations and the perceptual surface – to use a dichotomous harmonic language to establish distinctions between the opera's parallel worlds. His goal, in effect, is to represent a cosmic opposition between benevolent and malevolent entities and elements. And meanings can be further specified thanks to a generous quantity of surviving documents: original literary texts, libretti, annotated musical sketches, Rimsky's practically minded 'chronicles' of his projects, and even a handful of transcribed comments in which he shared his understanding of the musical languages he employed. With few exceptions, Rimsky-Korsakov painted his tonal landscapes, mimicked speech patterns of character types and social strata, and depicted events both supernatural and mundane, all with the intent of conveying specific emotions, impressions, and conceptual content as vividly and directly as he was able. The contrasts between this attitude and Shostakovich's could hardly be greater, whether one is considering authentic explanatory texts from the composer, the use of texts in the music, or the use of distinctive motifs and harmonic systems to establish psychological or stylistic contrast.

In fact the conceptual and perceptual clarity of the Korsakovian polarities had already largely vanished with the harmonic innovations of the intervening generation. Both Alexander Skryabin (1872–1915) and Igor Stravinsky (1882–1971) abandoned the pure diatonicism of Rimsky-Korsakov's folk heroes rather early in their compositional careers, opting instead for the 'expanded' (i.e. chromatically inflected) harmonic possibilities of the post-Wagnerian, post-Tchaikovskian, and late-Rimskian epoch, whose allurements beckoned to them even as their respective teachers (Taneyev and Rimsky-Korsakov) attempted to inculcate a solid grounding in the common-practice harmony as taught at Russia's twin conservatoires.

The harmonic languages of such breakthrough works as Skryabin's orchestral *Poèmes* and Stravinsky's *Petrushka* and *Rite of Spring* cannot be satisfactorily explained with reference either to a diatonic framework wherein one or two tritones communicate tension and point towards a triad to dispel it, or to Rimsky's brand of octatonicism, in which a ubiquity of at least four tritones and the inevitable chains of diminished seventh chords would temporarily suspend perceptions of a tonic as well as traditional harmonic tension and release. Skryabin's 'Mystic Chord' contains two tritones, not four, as well as other harmonic tendencies that have resulted in competing theories of its origins and the salient consequences for his music.[1] As a protégé of Rimsky-Korsakov, Stravinsky gained direct knowledge of the octatonic scale and its properties. Yet after *The Firebird*, he employed it only in piecemeal fashion and, therefore, usually in conjunction with other harmonic materials (pitch collections such as diatonic, whole-tone or pentatonic), which both complicate the task of analysis and again give rise to competing theories. Thus, while it is apparent to most listeners that both Skryabin and Stravinsky abandoned the harmonic certainties of common practice diatonicism, wherein chord progressions and tritone resolutions eventually reveal both the tonic and the tonic triad, it takes an extensive background in theory, deep knowledge of the music itself, and probably acquaintance with a few theoretical monographs as well, to gain a proper understanding of the new languages that they developed as alternatives.

Those detailed monographs were a long time coming, both inside and outside Russia. On the other hand, two Russian theorists should be credited with making significant first steps before the First World War that would later condition theoretical investigations of Shostakovich's music as well.

The two points most Western scholars recall about Leonid Sabaneyev's essay on Skryabin, printed in *The Blaue Reiter Almanac*, are first his claim for a six-note Mystic Chord (C, F sharp, B flat, E, A, D in Sabaneyev's ordering) as the main generative pitch collection for late-period Skryabin, and secondly the more questionable claim that Skryabin created the chord from the 8th, 9th, 10th, 11th, 13th, and 14th partials of the harmonic series.[2] (Subsequently, those six pitches, together with the 'missing' G, would be termed the 'acoustic scale', when ordered F sharp, [G], A, B flat, C, D, E.) Though it is true that certain of these partials do not exist in the equal-tempered keyboard instruments of Skryabin's day and thus were an unlikely influence, Sabaneyev's theory was nevertheless valuable for drawing attention to a salient feature of the Mystic Chord: its ability to coexist and intermingle with the materials of late nineteenth-century expanded or extended tonality. By identifying a specially generated six-note chord, he established a theoretical precedent for postulating a harmonic language based not on a tonic-centred scale or mode, but on an unordered collection of pitches.

Like Skryabin himself, composer-theorist Boleslav Yavorsky (1877–1942) was a graduate of the Moscow Conservatoire and a student of Taneyev. By the 1920s, Yavorsky had not only eclipsed Sabaneyev (whose full Soviet fall from grace occurred in 1926 when he emigrated) in scholarly and musico-political influence but had risen to become the most prominent theorist of his day. Yavorskians believed his ideas to be nothing less than a theory of all music. At the very least it was unrivalled in Russia as a 'unified field theory', with a potential range of applications extending from folk modes to post-tonal languages. In essence, Yavorsky advocated a dynamic conception of pitch structures in which the dissonances (specifically one or more discrete tritones) generate tertian consonances (i.e. a major or minor third, a triad, or a larger stack of thirds). For Yavorsky, scales, melodic phrases and chords were secondary in significance; they were merely surface manifestations of the dynamic process of tritones resolving to thirds. At the not-so-simple foundation of Yavorsky's postulates, one learns that the tonic triad of the C major scale consists of a lower major third produced by the contraction through contrary-motion semitonal voice-leading of a B–F tritone into a C–E major third. So far so good. The explanation of the E–G upper dyad is more problematic: Yavorsky saw it as resulting from the contraction of two tritones, each of which is formed by one pitch found in the C diatonic collection and one that is not. Each of these two tritones only contributes a single pitch (see Ex. 13.3).

In progressing through Yavorsky's explanations of the theory, one encounters increasingly complex pitch structures with potential relevance to music composed with various diatonic modes, octatonic and whole-tone collections, and various other pitch vocabularies.[3] The paradigm of tritones resolving to thirds (or sixths) was potentially applicable to the

Example 13.3 Yavorsky's tritonal derivations of minor and major thirds

music of Skryabin, Stravinsky, Strauss and others whose training included guided study of common-practice part-writing as well as direct encounters with the heavily chromaticized major–minor system of the post-Wagnerian epoch. Subsequently, Yavorsky's theory would be admired for its positing of functional relationships between pitches of a dissonance–consonance paradigm normally regarded as distantly related to one another, if at all. In this it was clearly applicable to various musical repertoires, and for his ultimate concerns as much as for his specific analyses, Yavorsky has received serious attention from later generations of Russian theorists. And even though no extensive attempt to apply his theory of 'modal rhythm' (*ladovoy ritm*, roughly speaking, the unfolding of modal properties over time) to Shostakovich exists, the quest for the mode or modes that define Shostakovich has been the dominant concern for a half century and more of Russian-language theorists.

When Dmitry Shostakovich entered the Petrograd Conservatoire in the autumn of 1919, Rimsky-Korsakov and Skryabin were deceased (but by no means forgotten!), Stravinsky abroad, and Yavorsky not yet as influential in Petrograd as Moscow. That Rimsky-Korsakov should be seriously considered as a primary influence on the thirteen-year-old prodigy is beyond dispute. Soon Shostakovich was regularly entering the 'Rimsky-Korsakov' classroom to receive training in theory and composition at the hands of Rimsky-Korsakov's son-in-law Maximilian Steinberg, consulting the explanations and illustrative examples excerpted from Rimsky's music that appeared in Rimsky's harmony textbook (*A Practical Manual of Harmony*, first published in 1886), and absorbing the messages from numerous edifying anecdotes taken from the life and career of the all-but-canonized master. There was also quite a bit of Rimsky's music to be heard at the State Academic (formerly Mariinsky) Theatre, where nearly all his fifteen operas were in the repertoire. Meanwhile the Petrograd State Orchestra (renamed Philharmonia in 1921) was showcasing the music of Rimsky-Korsakov's friend and successor as Rector of the Conservatoire, Alexander Glazunov, by programming concert cycles of his eight symphonies, along with similar cycles devoted to Beethoven, Tchaikovsky and Skryabin.

The modernist-minded critic Boris Asafyev complained about programming of this kind, which he considered antiquated, and set about increasing his musico-political clout so as to initiate change. By the mid-1920s Asafyev had become the city's leading music critic and main musical power-broker, thanks to which he was able to see many of his projects come to fruition. The combination of a Party Resolution of 1925 advocating tolerance for diversity in the arts, the rise of a Soviet bourgeoisie with an appetite for the arts, trade agreements with the Western powers, and a rise of performance standards turned Leningrad into a centre for a wide variety of recent compositional trends, both domestic and foreign. The period in question overlaps with Shostakovich's years of graduate study at the Leningrad Conservatoire (1925–30) and, not coincidentally, with his most overt rebellion and rejection of a previous set of influences. The rejected aesthetics and style were those of his teacher and his teacher's teacher. The new inspirations are a bit more difficult to delimit, given the plethora of available choices. A repertoire list for the theatres and concert halls of Leningrad would be studded with twentieth-century titles such as Strauss's *Salome* and *Rosenkavalier*, Berg's *Wozzeck*, Křenek's *Jonny spielt auf*, Stravinsky's pre-war ballets, *Les Noces* and recent chamber instrumental works, Prokofiev's *Love for Three Oranges* and concertos, chamber works of *Les Six*, Hindemith and Bartók . Much research remains to be done before anyone can state with confidence which of these mattered most in the development of Shostakovich's own harmonic vocabulary. The process is further complicated by the fact that a number of the performed works that are emblematic of one trend or another are themselves notoriously difficult to analyse and have therefore either been ignored or are still subject to theoretical debate.

As all commentators on music in the 1920s have to acknowledge, there was no mainstream with respect to harmonic language. The same was true for the resident composers of Leningrad, even though no composer of Shostakovich's prominence vacillated quite as much as he did. Nevertheless a number of scholars have been tempted to explore the affinities between certain of Shostakovich's compositional priorities in the years 1926–9 and those espoused by a quartet of new appointees in the Conservatoire's theory-composition department, headed by Vladimir Shcherbachov. In a previous study I identified three cornerstones of the new pedagogy: (1) *linearizm*, that is, the concern with the shape, tensions and goals of melodic motion, approached one line at a time, (2) the examination of the devices and procedures responsible for *form as a process*, and (3) the full endorsement and exploration of *stylistic heterogeneity*.[4] Shcherbachov's fascination with unusual melodic structures of indeterminate harmonic implications is already evident in the opening bars of his Nonet (1919) (see Ex. 13.4).

Without the key signature and the sustained dominant A in string tremolo (not shown), one could not identify either the mode or the tonic

Example 13.4 Shcherbachov, Nonet, movement 1, opening

of this passage, not least because the full set of pitches includes three tritones (G–C sharp, E–B flat, A–E flat). But neither could one deny the intervallic pull of the opening tritone and the subsequent semitonal motion, or the sense that all but a few pitches correspond to a single mode: D minor. It is the kind of uneasy situation that occurs frequently in Shostakovich, where a soft pedal point provides the only tonal mooring, and even that perhaps only briefly.

Problems

It is much simpler to chronicle the wide range of potential influences on Shostakovich in the late 1920s than it is to specify those most significant to him at the time he began graduate study in 1926. Already in his first semester, he was composing in a manner guaranteed to estrange Steinberg, who was once again his assigned mentor. The First Piano Sonata, the *Aphorisms*, portions of the Second and Third Symphonies, and virtually all of the comic opera *The Nose* are paradigmatic of contemporary international trends, thanks to pages and pages of dissonant, chromatic (to varying degrees), atonal, non-periodic and mainly non-repetitive linear counterpoint. Although the very consistency of the negations of common practice might still coax a theorist to conceptualize a harmonic language in one or other composition, to date no rigorous analysis has appeared, most likely because the distinct voice that can be recognized in the music of the next four decades had not yet fully emerged.

The healthy conditions for artistic experiment in Leningrad were not invulnerable to the economic and societal pressures of the late 1920s, particularly when RAPM's Leningrad branch infiltrated the Conservatoire and the repertoire committees of the city's theatres and performing ensembles. During the turbulent period of the so-called 'Cultural Revolution' (1928–32), which coincided with Stalin's First Five-Year Plan), Shostakovich established a long-term habit of pursuing dual compositional careers: one devoted to substantive stand-alone works for the concert hall, the other to the realm of incidental music, film, musical comedy and satire. His opera *The Lady Macbeth of Mtsensk District* (composed 1930–2), the masterpiece from this period, draws heavily on influences from *both* concurrent careers, as one already senses from the designation *tragediya-satira*. The work is a hybrid with respect to musical style as well as genre, for the composer resorts to a broad assemblage of styles and devices to express the opera's disturbing juxtapositions of burlesque comedy and graphic violence. Qualities of dualism, ambiguity and eclecticism are also evident in the harmonic language. Though dauntingly complex if approached from a common-practice standpoint, this language nevertheless hints at a coherence more compelling than the non-tertian dissonant counterpoint of *The Nose*. Among the distinctions: the occasional return of key signatures (e.g. for Katerina's F sharp minor aria in Act 1, the F minor entr'acte between the second and third scenes, or the B flat entr'acte between the sixth and seventh scenes), triadic harmonization, an ebb and flow of dissonance, and extended sections framed by pitch centres. The combination of factors that would seem accessible to some type of systematic analysis, the prominence of untexted 'symphonic' interludes (especially, the passacaglia between the fourth and fifth scenes, with its eight-bar bassline), and finally (of course), the historical significance conferred on the opera by its fall from grace in January 1936, have made the work appealing to theorists, even in the 1940s, when simply to mention this banned 'anti-human' work was to risk bringing disfavour onto one's own career.

For several decades the initially unaccompanied eight-bar theme of *Lady Macbeth*'s passacaglia (see Ex. 13.5) would figure prominently in the investigations of *modality*[5] in Shostakovich's music, which for much of this time was the main and largely unrivalled concern of Russian theorists. There are two problems with assigning such a central role to the music of this opera. The first concerns chronology: its completion date of December 1932 raises a valid suspicion that it could well be a transitional work, revealing some qualities that point backward as well as forward in the career. The second problem relates to genre: both immediately before and after the banning of the work in 1936, Shostakovich concentrated on the composition of instrumental, not texted, music, and he would continue to do so until the 1960s. While the passacaglia itself is for orchestra alone, Katerina's aria 'The Foal Runs after the Filly' (which has also been examined by several theorists),[6] by virtue of its text could open up special analytical concerns not shared with the movements of symphonies and quartets.

The instrumental career of Shostakovich's middle years began less than a year after the completion of the opera with a trio of small-scale and unpretentious works: the *Twenty-Four Preludes*, op. 34 (1933), the First Piano Concerto in C minor, op. 35 (1933), and the Cello Sonata in D minor, op. 40 (1934). Irrespective of their lesser dimensions and celebrity,

Example 13.5 Shostakovich, *The Lady Macbeth of Mtsensk District*, passacaglia theme, entr'acte between Act 2, Scenes 4 and 5

these works of the early 1930s constitute a measurable stylistic break with *Lady Macbeth* and already embody the set of compositional techniques that would serve Shostakovich until well into the 1960s. While analysts may suggest a number of reasons for defining that career on the basis of one or another extended work, there are no compelling reasons for excluding the Preludes, Concerto and Sonata from consideration.

What then do the Preludes reveal from a harmonic standpoint, and what questions do they raise? To begin with, Shostakovich allowed key signatures to return. The Preludes complete a cycle through the keys, in Chopin's ordering based on relative major and minor pairs arranged in the circle of fifths. With the exception of nos. 3, 13 and 17, all conclude with the tonic or a simple tonic triad, the majority by means of a perfect cadence. From tracking key areas one quickly discovers that most of the Preludes are tripartite in form, albeit quite varied in both sectional proportions and the design of the melodic-harmonic reprise. The major analytical challenges arise as soon as one decides to go beyond crude reductions or three-sentence descriptions in order to explain the inner modulations (most of which are accomplished without three- or four-voice cadences), the whole-tone passages, the dissonance treatment, or simply the function of all the pitches that conflict with the key signature.

As a case study illustrative of the essential analytical problems found in numerous passages, we can turn to Prelude no. 5, bearing a key signature of two sharps. In the first bar, the left hand's D and the right hand's D major scale unambiguously establish the key; the perfect cadence in the last bar is further confirmation. The problems – and they are formidable – lie in the middle, the nineteen bars that make up 90 per cent of the piece.

At least two solutions involving established methodologies are tempting. The first is to conclude, with Detlef Gojowy, that the Prelude's relentless, mainly scalar right-hand passage work makes of it a romp through a surprising number of keys in close proximity, a feat comparable to, and conceivably inspired by, Beethoven's two Preludes through all the Major Keys, op. 39 and other works of that sort. Proceeding scale by scale, Gojowy produced an analysis involving nearly a dozen inexplicably juxtaposed scale designations.[7] In opposition to this approach, Schenkerians would insist that priorities must be set, patterns found, structural bulwark pitches be

Example 13.6 Shostakovich, Prelude, op. 34, no. 5, opening

proposed, and the hundreds of notes *reduced* to several dozen, which can then be graphed in such a way as to demonstrate a hierarchy, according to which more prominence is given to the seven diatonic pitches of the D major scale than to the five pitches that do not belong.

Clearly a case can be made for extending the graphing procedures that Schenker formed on the basis of the common-practice music he preferred, so as to accommodate the compositional style of a composer whose music he would likely have disdained. In embarking on such a course, however, the analyst would quickly encounter a host of problem spots, resulting either from too much or too little harmonic data. The main difficulties are already present in the Prelude's first four bars (see Ex. 13.6).

The most immediate challenge stems from the texture of two rather than four parts, which occurs in so much of Shostakovich's music. Moreover, in the present example the melody is scalar, not arpeggiated or triadic. The succession of bass notes – also scalar – does not amount to a common-practice chord progression. And if the tonality is indeed D major, as conceptualized in the common practice established in European conservatoire teaching, then the analyst must confront a series of anomalies including: the parallel D–E flat octaves leading into the first beat of the second bar, the melodic peak on B on beat 3 of bar 2, the inexplicable C major scale fragment (or Locrian mode) in bar 2, the left hand's six-note whole-tone segment, and a generous quantity of dissonances and cross-relations. Recalling the Yavorskian interest in patterns of tritone resolution, one may wonder if this traditional dissonance might reveal the structure of the harmonic language. Unfortunately, after the first bar, a full five out of six possible tritones can be found in close proximity, yet not employed in such a way as to substantiate the claim that Korsakovian octatonicism or Glinka–Dargomïzhsky–Debussy whole-tone-ishness has superseded the D major diatonicism.

Eschewing the tritone-based paradigm of Yavorsky, one might instead take note of how one or more other intervals are employed. Certainly the raw count of dissonances and the laxity in applying traditional techniques of dissonance treatment are sufficient to allow one to deduce that this conservatoire graduate not only received his training in the twentieth century, but that he had still not made a rapprochement with the strict academic norms of his mentors. From that perspective, Shostakovich, no less than Prokofiev, was prone to write 'wrong' notes, even within the tradition-bound genre of the twenty-four-key cycle of preludes. But are the traditional dissonances of Western European common practice truly emancipated? One suspects not, based merely on the fact of their consistent exclusion from final cadences. In addition, there are numerous examples in Shostakovich's works of the 1930s and later wherein dissonances are deployed in conjunction with expressive markings and surface gestures, in a manner clearly reminiscent of Tchaikovsky, Mahler and Strauss. Two striking examples are already present in the Preludes. The crude interjection of minor seconds and an out-of-key C sharp minor triad marked *fff* in the G major Prelude may be indebted to *Salome*. An unresolved five-note dissonance in the G minor Prelude heightens through contrast the poignancy of the frail unaccompanied G minor scale that descends into the final cadence.

With these works of 1933–4 in mind, we can now formulate several essential questions for theorists intent on explaining Shostakovich's harmonic language. First, what theoretical approach best serves a compositional idiom in which significant modulations from or alternations to the keys implied by the key signatures occur rapidly, sometimes inconclusively, and often within a single line – modifications that may be unaccompanied or may conflict with the pitch content of other lines? Secondly, are modifications to an initial tonality used with enough frequency and in a sufficiently circumscribed manner as to allow the pitches of a mode to be named, that mode itself labelled, and some degree of function or hierarchy assigned, as is possible in Rimsky-Korsakov's frequently sectionalized harmonic practice? Thirdly, do the traditional tendency notes (leading-notes, Neapolitan seconds) and intervals (for example, tritones, sevenths and seconds) maintain their implications in passages where Shostakovich has deviated from the traditional diatonic modes? Fourthly, if not Rimsky-Korsakov, are there other composers whose music may have been a shaping force on Shostakovich's harmonic practice and therefore relevant to the formation of an analytical approach? Finally, when certain harmonic ambiguities or contradictory implications cannot be resolved, is it still possible to delimit or restrict *most* of a passage's pitch content in some analytically significant way?

Responses in Russia

Although we may safely assume that theoretical minds of sufficient calibre to confront these questions have existed both inside and outside the Soviet Union, conditions were such – again, both inside and outside the Soviet Union – that meaningful responses emerged quite sluggishly. Nothing about the Stalinist 1930s was conducive to new initiatives in the analysis of twentieth-century music. While the academic fields of music theory and history had outlasted the tumult of the RAPM years, Shcherbachov, Asafyev, Yavorsky and other seminal thinkers were under considerable pressure to distance themselves from their earlier advocacy of the Western modernists and to align themselves instead with Socialist Realism's principle of 'party-mindedness'. When it eventually became possible for Soviet theorists to write on contemporary music, their efforts typically took the form of programme notes illustrated with a handful of thematic incipits, perhaps with the keys named in the accompanying prose.

From this category emerged the earliest essays on Shostakovich by Lev Mazel. Building on the precedent of his landmark intertextual and multi-dimensional essay on the style and structure of Chopin's F minor Fantasy, Mazel focused his attention on individual themes of Shostakovich's Fifth Symphony. In a prefatory comment to the 1986 reprint of these essays of the late 1930s and 1940s, he recollected just how novel it had been to discuss music in such note-to-note analytical detail.[8] That these attempts were published at all was due to the fact that the analytical detail was recruited to establish thematic links to non-controversial canonic works of the nineteenth century and earlier.

From a harmonic standpoint, the essay devoted to the opening thematic material of the Fifth's first movement is most significant for broaching the subject of modality. Already in the first subject (bars 6–13), Mazel finds a mixture of modes: 'Phrygian D minor', a Dorian C minor digression ('a possible subdominant to G minor'), Phrygian E flat minor, and finally A minor.[9] All of the preceding point to a 'tentative conclusion', which takes the form of a 'tone–semitone' (i.e. octatonic) scale that gives further metrical salience to the aforementioned C, E flat, and A, as well as the minor thirds built on them. Is this reason enough to consider Shostakovich's harmonic language octatonic? Should the octatonic collection be assumed whenever accidentals proliferate and support for a previously established tonic key is withheld? Mazel leaves these specific questions unanswered. Instead the more general conclusion emerges that in a mere twelve bars in which primary themes are first introduced, phrases in the melodic line occur that are not in the tonic key, not octatonic, not trivially chromatic, and in fact, not governed by anything beyond *tetrachordal fragments* of modes. Most provocatively of all, Mazel maintains that a single pitch (here, the cadential D sharp on the downbeat of bar 3) can be deployed in such a way to communicate multiple contradictory harmonic implications, none of which can be cancelled out by appealing to prior or subsequent events. On the contrary, 'this pitch is consequently perceived as extremely unstable and pointing in various directions'.[10] How frustrating when the contextual reading only complicates matters!

In an essay drafted in 1944–5, Mazel risked more.[11] Its publication having been delayed initially for unspecified reasons, the essay then became a casualty of the wave of career-damaging vilifications initiated by Andrey Zhdanov and carried through by the young Tikhon Khrennikov after Zhdanov's death. Overlooking the gap between the writing and the delayed publication date of 1966, we can still use this essay to gain perspective on how matters of harmony in Shostakovich were approached by an eminent contemporary. Mazel's typical breadth of approach is evident in the essay's organization into separate sections allotted to the intervallic properties of melodic lines, modal-harmonic content within the melodic line, rhythm, phrase structure and form, generously illustrated with thirty-seven musical examples. As in the previously discussed essay, he focused his description of harmony on the activity of melodic lines, which emerge as fully capable of absorbing modal material and harmonic functions – including sophisticated modulations – with little or no assistance from the bass-line and other voices. The examples draw attention to a variety of traditional (church) modes and modal inflections that can hint at a mode. Mazel rejects the notion that Shostakovich ever abandons the 'classical foundations' in the major-minor system, but he allows that these foundations can be obscured by 'complexity'. The main new finding has to do with a particular recurring alteration to a traditional mode. Terming it an 'intensified Phrygian', Mazel describes it as a 'minor mode in which not only the second, but also the fourth degree is lowered'.[12]

Independently of Mazel, Alexander Dolzhansky conducted his research into Shostakovich's harmonic language during the 1940s, based on such prominent works as the Fifth, Sixth and Seventh Symphonies, the Piano Quintet and the Second Piano Sonata, with a further two musical examples boldly drawn from the now banned opera *Lady Macbeth* (whose printed vocal score was nevertheless still circulating). This is the first attempt at a systematic theory well deserving of its eventual repute, both for its pathbreaking status and for the conceptual clarity with which certain issues are raised and addressed.

Like Mazel, Dolzhansky makes most of his points based on the pitch content of the melodic lines, which for one reason or another deviate from common-practice major and minor. His first set of examples can be classified according to the Renaissance modes (Phrygian, Locrian, Lydian, Mixolydian). Mixed usages follow. The article's main thrust, however, concerns 'new modes', which he conceptualizes as altered versions of older modes, such as his own version of a 'lowered Phrygian', which, as in Mazel's discussion of the Fifth Symphony, incorporates an additional lowered fourth scale degree. His 'double-lowered Aeolian' mode is most striking, due to the combination of lowered fourth and eighth scale degrees, for example, B–C sharp – D–E flat – F sharp – G–A–B flat (used in the theme of the Second Piano Sonata finale, wherein both B and B flat function as tonics).[13] From Katerina's Act 1 aria in *Lady Macbeth*, Dolzhansky extracts a 'lowered Phrygian' mode whose defining trait is the pair of complete minor triads separated by half-step, built on the first two scale degrees.[14] Refusing to limit himself to a single mode, he nevertheless makes a significant generalization: 'A tendency toward the lowering of scale degrees, i.e., to moving nearer to the lower tonic as they distance themselves from the upper tonic – is the fundamental structural principle of these modes.'[15]

The remainder of Dolzhansky's article is chiefly concerned with consequences for triad formation and modulations. His system of paired altered modes was intended to correlate with the oppositions that exist between major and minor triads distributed among the scale degrees of the major and minor scales. The alterations of scale degrees also affect modulation patterns. Dolzhansky responds by redefining 'parallel' modes as those that share a majority of pitches but have tonics separated by a semitone, and 'relative' modes as those separated by a diminished fourth (e.g. B and E flat), as opposed to a minor third.[16]

Although Dolzhansky's essay did make it into print, neither his ideas nor any other theoretical investigations of Shostakovich's music were destined to bear fruit in the short term. As a result of a third wave of the ideological perestroika of Soviet musical life and institutions in 1948, both Dolzhansky and Shostakovich lost their positions. In the aftermath of Stalin's death in 1953 and the Twentieth Party Congress in 1956, both were reappointed. Meanwhile Shostakovich had resumed composing sophisticated works in a harmonic language clearly related to those of the 1940s. Published theoretical investigations, however, had to wait until the 1960s; their proliferation at that time may owe something to

Example 13.7 Dolzhansky's 'Shostakovich mode' (11-pitch variant spanning major ninth)

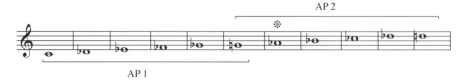

Shostakovich's new public prominence, resulting from his being appointed president of the Russian Republic's Composers' Union and his coincident entrance into membership in the Communist Party.

The shelf of 1960s publications relating to Shostakovich included biographical studies, handbooks to the symphonies by Mazel and Genrikh Orlov, and two edited volumes with a substantial amount of theory and analysis. In the 1962 volume, the showpiece was a reprint of Dolzhansky's essay from 1947. In the 1967 volume, Mazel's article of 1945 finally appeared, along with a new essay by Dolzhansky – his last – in which he presents a significant means for conceptualizing Shostakovich's untraditional modal usage. As before, Dolzhansky claims that the best approach is to view Shostakovich's modality as the result of a compressing or lowering of intervals with respect to the tonic. Now, however, the lowering of intervals results in a change to the traditional parity (within the diatonic system) between the number of pitches and number of scale degrees. To be specific, the lowering of the fourth scale-degree of a Phrygian pentachord (e.g. B–C–D–E flat–F sharp) results in an augmented second, which Shostakovich avoids by inserting a sixth pitch, namely the F natural, thus producing a six-pitch 'fill' of the B to F sharp fifth, involving the double usage of one scale-degree. His term 'Alexandrian pentachord' refers to a fifth-spanning scalar segment of *six* pitches. After noting the complete identity between the most common type (B–C–D–E flat–F–F sharp) and a six-pitch segment of the octatonic scale, he claims a distinction for the 'Shostakovich modes', owing to a different pattern of extension beyond the initial fifth. According to Dolzhansky, the mode used most often by Shostakovich in its most complete version conforms to the pattern shown in Ex. 13.7.

The starred A flat marks the break from the octatonic pattern. Dolzhansky maintains that the G that tops the original (lower) 'Alexandrian Pentachord [AP]' also functions as the bottom pitch of a second (higher) 'AP', which extends the total number of pitches to ten and the range to a major ninth. Unfortunately he does not substantiate his assertions that this 'decachord' or the shortened version spanning a diminished octave (i.e. C to C flat) has 'predominating significance' for the music of Shostakovich.[17] In the remainder of the essay he expands on the basic premises to consider gapped occurrences (i.e. with one pitch missing), fully chromatic variants, and, most intriguing of all, the possibility that Shostakovich's use of the six-pitch pentachord constitutes an abandonment of the seven-scale-degree system of diatonicism.

Without question, Dolzhansky deserves credit for bringing focus to a series of melodic patterns that most listeners would recognize as being characteristic of Shostakovich. While we may question how often and how fully the six-pitch AP actually occurs, the theory is an improvement over Mazel's ad hoc comments applied to alterations of individual scale degrees. Dolzhansky's nine-pitch extended version is also more successful at capturing that balance of octatonic, minor, and whole-tone qualities found in many a melodic line than an analytical approach that favours one of the three over the other two. Finally, the AP provides precision and delimitation as to linear-modal intervallic structure, without making the naming of a pitch-centre obligatory.

For the next two decades, a number of other Soviet theorists took up Dolzhansky's line of thought. Since their contributions have already been summarized, evaluated and compared by Ellon Carpenter, my commentary here can be brief. Like the pioneers, the mode investigators of the 1960s and 1970s focused their attention on passages not explainable in terms of major and minor keys or the traditional diatonic modes, with the goal either of refining the basic taxonomy of intervallic structure or of investigating how certain pitches function. Carpenter identified as common ground the assumptions that Shostakovich's modes (however conceived) are 'linear and melodic, diatonically based, and varied, representing different diatonic categories and subcategories'.[18] Considerable divergence in detail results from disagreement over the count of pitches, the range of the modes, whether or not the tonic can shift, and whether some of the pitch content is variable. As implied above, the investigation is typically confined to melodic lines, with the goals of extracting a pentachord, filling it in (cf. Dolzhansky), and then extending the mode to the span of an octave or diminished octave.

Those familiar with the important and multi-faceted career of Yury Kholopov at the Moscow Conservatoire would likely be curious as to which approach to Shostakovich he advocated and why. In fact his three essays on Shostakovich display a range of approaches. The case study of Shostakovich's Eighth Symphony in his landmark monograph *Sketches of Contemporary Harmony* (1974) brings attention to the full breadth of the composer's harmonic practice, ranging from tertian sonorities to reinforce the main tonality in the opening and closing of the first movement, to the proliferation of dissonant counterpoint in the development, wherein full triads vanish and harmonic instability reaches the point where a hierarchy between 'central and peripheral elements' cannot be established, a condition that 'approximates atonality'.[19] Nevertheless, even when a definite tonality and supportive triads are absent, there is harmonic logic to be found, according to Kholopov. Bars 145–52 of the Eighth Symphony's first movement development section have a modal stability resulting from a fusion of the octatonic mode and a prominent 'plagal' linear emphasis on an A to E motion.[20] Later on in the movement, the dissonant five- and six-pitch chords from the retransition (bars 258–82) are 'verticalizations' of melodic gestures previously heard.[21]

Although form is the central concern in Kholopov's essay for David Fanning's *Shostakovich Studies*,[22] the nomenclature he employs to explain it involves a revealing eclectic mix of traditional key designations, modes, altered modes, figured bass, and the familiar T, D and S symbols of Riemann-inspired Russian functional harmony. The transitional passages that manifest an unresolvable harmonic ambiguity are analytically rendered with his own kind of graphic reduction, serving chiefly to highlight prominent pitches and recurring motifs in various melodic lines.

In a third essay, Kholopov weighed in on the matter of 'Shostakovich modes', grounding his response to Dolzhansky in a conception of Russian music as being conditioned by Graeco-medieval modality as well as common-practice triadic harmony. Specifically, he argued that the Shostakovich modes should be conceived as a scalar fifth range consisting of six pitches (the Alexandrian Pentachord) that overlaps with a scalar third placed above or below, thus resulting in a seventh (or 'diminished octave') as framing interval.[23] In claiming that Shostakovich was not unique among twentieth-century composers in exploring an 'individual modus', he again insisted that the defining traits might occur in a span of pitches much smaller than an octave.

Responses in the West

We may turn now to the relatively few theoretical studies on Shostakovich published outside Russia that can be considered attempts at generalizing his harmonic language. Prior to the publication of *Testimony*, for reasons still not entirely explored, there appears to have been an unwritten, unopposed ban on such investigations within the academic community, of greater consequence than the shorter-lived repressions within the Soviet Union. Prior to *Testimony*, one mainly finds only actual programme notes, expanded programme notes, and collected programme notes, in which more musical detail on the harmonic language is likely to be found in the musical examples than in the prose. The brief set of generalizations in Norman Kay's short book would be the exception. But since his essential point is to substantiate his view that Shostakovich be viewed as a fundamentally conservative composer, the harmonic materials he extracts are the familiar building-blocks of centuries-old tonal practice: octave, fifth, fourth, and the major and minor thirds. By means of the latter, according to Kay, 'ambiguity was introduced in the works of the fifties. Over the static tonic a fleetingly interchangeable situation could occur, so that sometimes it was impossible to say which species of triad – major or minor – was taking precedence. But ... the all-important root remained in evidence.'[24]

Within a decade after *Testimony*, the status of Shostakovich studies had risen and with it a climate for deeper investigation of theoretical matters. David Fanning must be considered the earliest academically trained champion of Shostakovich as a master composer, willing to argue his case based on the sophistication of his musical language and formal structures. That viewpoint is amply substantiated in his extended analysis of the Tenth Symphony, published in 1988.[25] In essence, the analysis is transmitted as prose narration, illustrated with excerpts and charts, and periodically interrupted with explorations of matters of psychology, structure, style, or harmonic language. In a work as multi-faceted as the Tenth, there are many issues competing with harmony for the analyst's attention, but Fanning returns to it frequently, often in reference to passages of unquestionable significance to the form yet prone to a range of theoretical interpretations.

The Tenth Symphony's challenges to the analyst emerge early on: the unaccompanied theme for basses and cellos commences with a tonic downbeat E but establishes neither E minor nor any other common practice key convincingly. From the standpoints of genre and Shostakovich's own previous practice, this is not a problem: the symphonic tradition includes many cases of non-tonic and disputed tonic introductions. Moreover, the reassuring dominant-to-tonic gesture eventually does appear at ⑤. But what precisely is going on prior to that moment? Since the diminished intervals in conjunction with the chromatic inflections are enough to rule out common-practice E minor and the other diatonic modes, the solution must involve an altered mode. Pervasive tone–semitone scalar segments might point to octatonicism, but if so, the usage is not pure: the D, B and F of bars 7–14 are all foreign to that scale. One could instead conclude that the tone–semitone motion only creates a five-pitch filled-in diminished fifth, which is transposed twice to other pitch levels. Meanwhile, Dolzhansky would have found his pentachord (D sharp, E, F sharp, G, A, B flat (=A sharp)), extended by B and D to create the diminished octave, lacking only a C sharp (see Ex. 13.8a). Later on, at ②–⑤, all the pitch content of the

Example 13.8a Shostakovich, Tenth Symphony, movement 1, bars 1–8

Example 13.8b Shostakovich, Tenth Symphony, movement 1, decachord collection at ②–⑤

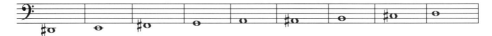

bass-line can be traced back to a complete 'Alexandrian decachord', built on D sharp (see Ex. 13.8b).

One's preference among these and other options has much to do with one's broader analytical and interpretative goals. Whatever the choice, it bears repeating that Shostakovich's harmonic language differs markedly from Rimskian absolutes. Though one may begin by favouring either a diatonicism that becomes chromatic or an octatonicism that becomes diatonic, the notes on the page bring into being a mixed harmonic realm that cannot conclusively be labelled one or the other. Can one conceptualize harmonic ambiguity or open-endedness with precision? Can one accept the existence of a temporary modality that deserves definition on its own account yet can also function as an incipient stage in a subsequent establishment of another modality? These would seem to be the central questions raised by the opening bars of the Tenth Symphony.

Fanning's gambit is consistent with his goal of revealing the large-scale tonal coherence of a symphonic movement: he proposes logical key centres and then quite properly draws attention to the pitches and gestures that complicate matters. Initially, E minor is unopposed, yet the 'dominant degree ... is withheld and the next phrase does not acknowledge the tonic at all'.[26] In that following phrase, G can be claimed as a new pitch centre, but the modality it establishes is less a scale of fixed identity and more a 'harmonic field' (to use a term that Fanning employs elsewhere). In this case, the 'field' involves 'variable third, sixth, and seventh degrees, and then, in the context of subdominant regions, also touching on flat second, flat fifth, and flat octave, cadencing onto a pivot back to E minor'.[27]

In venturing further into a work such as the Tenth Symphony, one knows to expect new textures and new information relevant to harmony. In some cases, such as the commencement of the first subject (as I hear it) in the clarinet, the additional lines bring clarification: here, a pedal E gives further reinforcement to the clarinet's E minor theme and establishes E minor as a primary tonality – in fact the main key – of the first movement.

Yet in so many other cases, the additional lines complicate matters. For example, the chromatic second subject ($\boxed{17}$–$\boxed{28}$) suggests either G or E as pitch centre but lacks the additional pitch information needed to fix the mode. The resonantly scored accompaniment presents a host of further difficulties: ostinati instead of progressions, cross-relations, non-tertian sonorities, chromatic bass-lines, and reharmonizations. Whereas the recurring pitches, chromatically filled minor thirds and triads offer audible links with the past for most listeners, Shostakovich's ingenious arrangement of his harmonic materials results in a calculated ambiguity that somehow manages to be both distinctive yet maddeningly resistant to analytical precision. In his harmony no less than in his public pronouncements, Dmitry Shostakovich refuses to be pinned down.

While no analyst can relish writing prose or making charts fraught with unresolved ambiguities, these are precisely the challenges that Shostakovich's music presents time and again. Are there any satisfactory options? Glossing over the difficulties is obviously unacceptable. So too is any reductive technique so rooted in common practice that withheld dominants must be written in, altered pitches explained away as local phenomena, or modulation within single lines dismissed as superstructure (i.e. confined to the Schenkerian foreground). It bears repeating that Russian music from its earliest phase to the present has always laid claim to the rich possibilities of continuity, discontinuity, variation and development, expression, and musical individuality offered by the melodic line sufficient unto itself.

To his credit, Fanning is both aware of the Russian concern with the modality of lines and sensitive to the kind of passage deserving of special scrutiny. He responds to the undeniable harmonic eclecticism at the surface of the music with something of a 'combined arms' approach, generally involving both charts and commentary. At least seven distinct tools are employed in the analyses: the naming of definite and indefinite pitch centres; traditional scale-degree tonal analysis; use of the chord symbols of expanded tonality; the extraction and taxonomy of special modes (e.g. the 'hyper-mode characterized by the organizing power of its third steps' applied to the opening thematic paragraph of the first movement);[28] the definition of 'harmonic fields', wherein one or more scale degrees fluctuate (e.g. 'G aeolian … with Neapolitan inflections', at $\boxed{8}^{4}$–$\boxed{9}^{2}$);[29] extraction of motifs and intervals that retain 'autonomy, even to the point of conflicting with the tonal implications of accompanying voices' (e.g. Fanning's 'motif x', (E, F sharp, G), whose superimposition atop an arpeggiation of a G triad 'colours the ostensible G major in unexpected yet logical ways',[30] and diastematic charts of linear, mainly chromatic, motion (e.g. the reduction of the development's bass-line in the first movement (p. 25) or the long-range melodic ascent in the second movement (p. 42). Although competing analytical strategies may arise, for the time being Fanning's combination of charts and prose remains the most comprehensive exploration of the harmonic language of the Tenth Symphony's many 'ill-defined regions', wherein the 'profound relationship between harmony and structure in Shostakovich's music resides'.[31]

In the years since the appearance of the Tenth Symphony monograph, Fanning has explored an eighth methodology: neo-Schenkerian voice-leading reduction. The qualifier 'neo-' is well justified, since Shostakovich's attenuated textures and post-tonal dissonance treatment result in some markedly unusual graphs. In an all-too-brief analysis of the Boris Izmaylov material from Act 2 of *Lady Macbeth*, the reduction highlights the role of subdominants, of four chromatic linear motifs at the foreground level, and, more generally, of the extensive non-functional diastematic activity in the bass and other lines.[32] In the introduction to *Shostakovich Studies* Fanning offers an even briefer analysis (thematic incipits, a chain of 'modal pentachords', Schenkerian background reduction) of the Fifth Symphony's first movement that still manages to point towards a workable synthesis of phrase-level modal analysis and anomalous static (from a common-practice standpoint) movement-spanning tonal plans.[33] In his monograph on the Eighth Quartet, the five graphs of the quartet's five movements function chiefly as an index for assessing how much Shostakovich has departed from common tonal practice. It is a wide spectrum indeed, ranging from a fourth movement in which the main musical interest lies outside the scope of the Schenkerian model (since it involves modal transformation within the melodic line) to a second movement in which the graph reads like a log of the tonal system's near meltdown! Clarity is restored, fittingly enough, in the finale. The firm restoration of a C minor tonality, coupled with a compendium of traditional procedures of modulation, counterpoint, and the treatment of dissonances in this fugal finale are duly noted by Fanning and central to his interpretation of the quartet as a whole. Shostakovich's sustained contrapuntal writing and lowering of the count of non-diatonic pitches allow Fanning to produce a middleground reduction sporting a level of detail that one sees in graphs of older tonal masterworks. However, in the section that Fanning labels 'Exposition 2: Climax Zone' (i.e. ^{4}[69]–[70]), the striking modulation to the 'outlandish looking key of F flat minor', deviates markedly from common practice.[34] If the reprise of an F flat-major triad and a cadential DSCH motive at [69]^4 establish overt links to the first movement, both the modal flattening procedure utilized and the pitch content of the DSCH motif point to quite a number of seminal works of Shostakovich.[35] Moreover, if indeed, following Fanning, we are to comprehend this quartet's finale as Shostakovich's manifest attempt to transcend the 'self-referential tone' of his previous movements, and achieve a 'world of pure musical thought', then we must acknowledge that the feat was accomplished, in part, on the basis of his own prior innovations in the realm of harmony.[36]

In the wake of Fanning's pioneering work, there have been precious few attempts to address even form, let alone harmonic language, in detail. Interrelationships of expression and form were at issue in Patrick McCreless's essay on the Second Piano Trio, but they precluded extensive speculation on harmony.[37] Movement design, expressive tropes, and cyclic – mainly thematic – processes are the main concerns in two British dissertations published in the late 1980s. Nevertheless Richard Longman's includes a concise yet meaty chapter devoted to harmony. The all too familiar conclusions that Shostakovich, in comparison to Schoenberg and Stravinsky, cannot be considered a harmonic innovator[38] and must especially be considered conservative on account of his use of the materials of tonal music (e.g. major, minor, diminished, and augmented triads)[39] are pointedly contradicted by the variety and complexity of harmonic examples that Longman discusses. His general approach is one of prose description, much of it phrased with admirable sensitivity to nuance and the telling detail. But since he proceeds under the assumption that the traditional terms of tonal analysis are generally applicable until the emergence of twelve-note lines in the 1960s, his selected passages are mainly classified by the degree to which they conform to or deviate from common-practice norms. Consequently, the possibility of a unique and coherent harmonic language is not seriously considered. Eric Roseberry chose not to devote a special unit in his dissertation to harmonic matters. Those of his musical descriptions that reference harmonic problem spots involve a similar incorporation of traditional terms and ad hoc accounts of the specific deviations, as can be seen in his interpretation of the first subject of the Cello Sonata's first movement: 'This witty theme, beginning in D minor, makes a round trip of an implied (but impishly unstated) F minor (bar 7), E flat major (bar 9) and a C minor with second degree characteristically flattened (hence the ambiguous D flat-major diad at bar 11) before it slips back bitonally (D flat/A natural – bars 15 and 16) into the home key.'[40]

Beginning in the latter half of the 1990s there have been a series of American attempts to define Shostakovich's harmonic practice (or part of it) that have appeared with the kind of geographical proximity that usually justifies conjecture about a school of thought, but whose premises and conclusions suggest quite the opposite. In an MA thesis focusing on the relationship between a harmonic language consistently applied and the composer's generic designation of the Fourteenth Symphony, John Moraitis argued for a pervasive octatonicism, which for the most part operates without tonal moorings. Since the analysis actually depends on the prominence of subsets of the octatonic collection, as opposed to full presentations, his approach can easily be reconciled with the Alexandrian Pentachord (which is a six-note octatonic segment) or any extension of it that would contain a further (seventh) pitch. Numerous musical examples, including his discovery of an arresting string tutti presentation of the contour of the DSCH motif (seventh movement, bars 65–71, shown as Ex. 8 on pp. 61–2), and other occurrences of octatonic subsets are discussed.[41]

My own previous response to the issue of modality commenced with some speculation on the possibility of antecedence, not in the ancient modes of Western Europe or Russia's folk modes, but in a harmonically innovative masterwork of Shostakovich's own day – Berg's *Wozzeck* – whose premiere in Leningrad on 11 July 1927 caused a sensation. My paradigm of the 'Shostakovich mode' was a collection of seven pitches sometimes known as the 'acoustic scale', an astonishingly flexible collection containing a five-pitch whole-tone segment, a six-pitch octatonic segment, and numerous possibilities for modulating to traditional keys, especially minor ones.[42] That ability to mimic tonality with its characteristic seconds, thirds, fourths, and fifths, together with its incorporation of the full six pitches of the sonority that George Perle has called the 'principal referential chord of the work as a whole',[43] gave me reason to posit a link. At the transposition level used by Berg (C sharp, D, F, G, A, B), the collection carries strong D minor implications, and this key is foregrounded by Berg in *Wozzeck* and employed prominently by Shostakovich in three major scores of the 1930s (the Cello Sonata, the Fourth Symphony and the Fifth Symphony).

My term 'vagrant mode' was introduced as analogous to Schoenberg's 'vagrant sonorities', suggesting that the mode lacks a tonic and exists 'between, two or more keys, a condition prolonged until one of its pitches is altered or one of its tendencies somehow reinforced'. Although one could argue over whether it is more scale or mode, it is certainly something other than an unordered pitch collection, since it tends to occur in melodic lines, commencing with stepwise motion that fills in a diminished fourth. For the frequently recurring transposition level commencing on C sharp, the pitches are: C sharp, D, E, F, G, A, B (C sharp). A possible reconciliation between this proposed 'Shostakovich mode', and Dolzhansky's Alexandrian Pentachord would be to consider the missing pitch (here, G sharp) as an added dominant, introduced to transform C sharp temporarily into tonic and then discarded when this function is no longer required. The scale's intervallic properties make other tonicizations possible without the need for added pitches. For example, in the final bars of the Fifth's finale, a reordering of the transposition spelled F sharp, G, A, B flat, C, D, E provides all the necessary pitches for a major-mode peroration of the movement's opening theme, harmonically grounded in D major thanks to pedal Ds and the infamous hammered As in the upper strings. The surprising discovery of this most characteristic of Shostakovich's pitch sequences not only attests to its ubiquity but begs for a re-examination of those tiresome entrenched opinions about banality and acquiescence to Socialist Realism. At the very least, the consistency of the harmonic language underlying surface-level impressions of the antipodal contrast between conflict-ridden D minor passages of the first movement and the celebratory coda of the finale offers a dissenting (yes!) subtext to what might otherwise have been only a *staged* progression from tragedy to triumph aimed at a broad audience.

When a composition unfolds for much of its duration under the governance of tonally ambiguous or 'vagrant' sonorities or modes, one may reasonably doubt the perceptual relevance of the short tonally centred passages that bookend the large middle. Whenever the sway of the tonic is so limited, it is reasonable to suggest that an atonal analytical system has as much to offer as one grounded in common-practice tonality. Focusing on the *Twenty-Four Preludes*, op. 34, Jason Solomon has proposed a methodology based on a combination of pitch-class sets and voice-leading, specifically the 'parsimonious' voice-leading of late Romanticism, grounded in common tones and semitonal motion. This enables him to chart not only the occurrences of the acoustic collection at various transposition levels, but also the 'hypermodulations', by which it is transformed – usually with alterations of merely a single pitch – into whole-tone or octatonic collections. Although merely a page in length, the C major Prelude displays considerable harmonic variety:

> Minimal sense of departure accompanies a hypermodulation in which a high number of common tones are maintained. In fact, the shift from A0 [i.e. the acoustic collection at its initial transposition level] to O1,2 [the octatonic collection beginning with a semitone, then tone] could easily be considered a prolongation rather than a progression. A transformation or hypermodulation with the least amount of common tones establishes the greatest sense of progression and a mounting tension. In Prelude No. 1, this occurs in bars 11–12, when a chromatic pentachord briefly touches on the white-key diatonic collection that then transforms into the four-flat diatonic collection[44] [see Ex. 13.9].

As Solomon observes, a further examination of voice-leading procedures would also provide a theoretical basis for discussing types and degrees of Shostakovichian musical contrast: from the barely discernible flickering of a

Example 13.9 Solomon's analysis of Prelude no. 1 (op. 34), bars 11–13

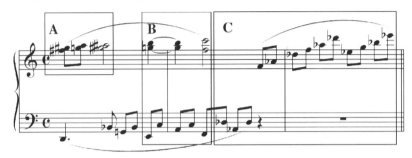

scale degree to the grating clash of sonorities whose juxtapositions have in the past been dismissed as crude, unsystematic local-level special effects, unworthy of serious analytical interpretation.

Conclusion

Having surveyed some seven decades of analytical attempts, we can now return to several of the questions first raised in connection with the compositional style that Shostakovich consolidated with *Lady Macbeth* and the instrumental works of the early 1930s. The first challenge taken on emanated from Shostakovich's exploration of the melodic line as a sophisticated locus of musical structure. With Dolzhansky in the forefront, Russian writers drew attention to the characteristic intervals and scalar shapes that lay outside diatonic common practice, setting the ultimate goal of identifying a characteristic Shostakovich mode or modes, together with its functional properties. Although no single mode has gained widespread theoretical acceptance, Dolzhansky's six-pitch Alexandrian Pentachord, spanning a fifth instead of an octave, successfully encompasses the widely recurring diminished fourth gesture (and, therefore, the DSCH monogram), points to some of the properties for interfacing or mimicking tonal, whole-tone, or octatonic languages *within the melodic line alone*, and neatly skirts the problem of naming a local tonic or pitch centre with minimal supporting evidence. When the music dictates that the conceptual model be extended beyond a fifth, both Dolzhansky and Kholopov offered useful reminders that, in Russian music, pentachords and tetrachords can be adumbrated without being bound by an octave as delimiting interval. Kholopov and Fanning, in their reductions, also raised the possibility of large musical spans in which directed long-range motion is dictated not by a succession of pitch centres supported by harmonic progressions but instead by a purely 'diastematic' scheme of salient pitches in either the treble melodic line or the bass. The main risk attending further application of these and other possible contour analyses would be the loss of the directionality or tendency of individual intervals and of their potential for behaving in accordance with some old or new paradigm of tension and release.

If the analysis of common-practice works often relies on the composer's addition of a chordal accompaniment or counter-melody to clarify tonal ambiguities in the melodic line, in the case of Shostakovich, the additional lines instead tend to complicate matters. Although Kholopov, for one, has tabulated intervals up from Shostakovich's bass-lines, his intent was to chart the voice-leading, not to assemble and label chords. While various voice-leading reductions will continue to be useful for explaining tonal moorings and large-scale form, by themselves they cannot fully explain Shostakovich's harmonic language. For reasons cited previously (two-voice textures, rapid yet inconclusive modulations, and lines of conflicting pitch content), the study of Shostakovich's devices for achieving harmonic stability and instability might benefit the most from an investigation of the pitch-content within phrases and the pitch behaviour at cadences. In the Preludes and in the expositions of themes in larger works there is enough periodicity and guidance from score markings to determine the *locations* of the cadences. While so much of his treatment of harmony departs from common practice, his heavy reliance on cadences to articulate lines and to register degrees of tension and release is quite traditional. An extensive investigation of the occurrence and functioning of cadences might lead to clues about the structure and harmonic function of any and all alternative scales and eventually contribute much to a general theory of the function of both lines and chords in Shostakovich's harmonic language. It also bears repeating that *linear analysis* would be consistent with the new theoretical concerns that emerged at the Leningrad Conservatoire in the 1920s, when Shostakovich as a graduate student launched his rebellion against the traditional training in composition that he received as an undergraduate.

There remains the problem of the unresolvable harmonic ambiguities that arise when too much corroborating evidence for a particular key centre or mode is left out. When Rimsky-Korsakov made his harmonic forays into non-diatonic modes, he attempted to make the break with diatonicism a clean one. Thus the typical Korsakovian village youth who can be observed to discover a vastly different plane of existence or order of being on stage, can also be *heard* to 'leave' diatonicism to travel into an octatonic sea kingdom or demonic gale (in *Sadko*). Eventually those experiences will end, and the character can return to home and to the diatonically represented discourse of the human community.

In Shostakovich's instrumental works, by contrast, good and bad, good and evil, individual and community, cannot entirely be separated from each other. The anonymous *lyrical persona* inhabits a musical universe wherein the extremes of experience may be presented sequentially but will continue to register simultaneously, in a tense coexistence fraught with ambiguities. Hence the experiences, if taken collectively, lose all black-and-white definition to take on the proverbial shades of grey, producing a psychological environment quite different from Rimsky-Korsakov's, one not unlike the 'Greeneland' one comes to expect in work after work of Shostakovich's novelist contemporary, Graham Greene.

As we enter into the second century of Shostakovich studies, scholars should accept as a central challenge the search for an analytical approach that is both comprehensive and subtle enough to respond to the highly allusive, familiar-yet-uncanny harmonic language that undergirds, synchronizes, and, in fact, is directly responsible for producing the realm of *Shostakovia*: that agglomeration of affective states whose peculiar organization of familiar tropes and distortions and lingering unease renders it easy to recognize yet difficult to characterize in words and charts. Reasonable though it may appear in the short term, a powerful 'all-explanatory' analytical system, when imposed too broadly and unilaterally, ultimately disappoints. As F. Scott Fitzgerald (a slightly older contemporary) put it: 'The test of a first-rate intelligence is the ability to hold two mutually opposed ideas in the mind at the same time, and still retain the ability to function.' The same holds for anyone seriously wishing to engage with the music of Dmitry Shostakovich and has informed the best analytical investigations of it to date.

14 Shostakovich on record

DAVID FANNING

With the completion of his First Symphony on 1 July 1925, two months before his nineteenth birthday, Shostakovich had already travelled further in stylistic terms than many composers do in a lifetime. Yet such was the pace of his artistic development and his urge for self-realization that he ran headlong into a crisis of confidence, from which he emerged almost as precipitately:

> Starting in the autumn of 1925 and continuing to December 1926, I kept trying to compose, but unsuccessfully … [M]y creative consciousness could not escape the bounds inculcated by academic canons. From autumn 1926 I turned to the study of contemporary Western composers (Schoenberg, Béla Bartók, Hindemith, Krenek), which apparently provided the immediate stimulus for 'liberating' my musical faculties: my first compositions from this new period were composed in white heat (from the end of 1926 through 1927).[1]

And there was another change of direction that Shostakovich had to negotiate at this time. In January 1927 he took part in the first Chopin Piano Competition in Warsaw, where he was one of eight finalists but not a prizewinner (his Moscow-based friend Lev Oborin won first prize, and the now legendary Grigory Ginzburg came fourth). He put the outcome down to a combination of pain from appendicitis and chauvinism on the part of an all-Polish jury. Be that as it may, it was a disappointment that was to mark the end of his serious aspirations as a concert artist, and his solo appearances gradually reduced in number. He continued to advocate his own works in performance, however, and the piano was central to his extensive activity as a composition teacher from 1937. Snippets of his playing may be seen on film,[2] and from 1946 to 1958 a number of his interpretations were recorded. These were almost entirely confined to his own music, the exception being a one-off contribution to Bach's triple-keyboard concerto BWV1063 at the 1950 bicentennial celebrations in Leipzig, where he deputized for Mariya Yudina, playing alongside Tatyana Nikolayeva and Pavel Serebryakov, with Kirill Kondrashin conducting the Berlin Radio Symphony Orchestra, in a performance whose evident ad hoc nature and chunky textures are compensated for by powerful rhythmic energy.[3] Already in 1958 a mysterious muscular weakness of the right hand, compounding his proneness to stage fright, served further to curtail his concert appearances, the last of which took place on 28 May 1966, the evening of his first heart attack, at the age of fifty-nine. The onset of that condition – eventually tentatively identified as a form of polio but now understood to have been motor neuron disease[4] – also put paid to his visits to the recording studio, and only one private recording, of a pre-premiere run-through of the Violin Sonata with David Oistrakh, post-dates it. His one and only public appearance as conductor – in his *Festive Overture* and First Cello Concerto on 12 November 1962 at the festival devoted to his music in Gorky – was not recorded.

A full account of Shostakovich's pianistic training and concert activities, together with a survey of the reception of his public and private performances and a near-complete list of recordings, is provided in Sofia Moshevich's painstakingly researched book.[5] It is not my intention to paraphrase that study or to supplement it with the ample evidence of Shostakovich's professional encounters with other performers of his music.[6] Nor will I speculate on the relationship between his activities as performer and composer, beyond suggesting that, as for many composers, the physicality of performance surely had some general bearing on certain basic creative instincts, in his case notably exuberance, quick-wittedness, impatience, and – more objectively quantifiable – structurally conceived *accelerandi*. As that physical dimension became gradually more impaired from the late 1950s, so a sense of loss became ever more palpable in Shostakovich's music; inwardness was enhanced, but often in the form of a lonely, fretful brooding, interrupted by explosions of pent-up frustration. Of course there were other reasons, but the forced abandonment of a huge part of his musical identity must have left scars.

The main point of this essay is to probe the recorded evidence of Shostakovich as performer, since this is an area in which Moshevich's commentaries are shaded by hagiography. Her initial claim that 'Dmitry Shostakovich was not only a great composer of the twentieth century but also an outstanding Russian pianist, one of the best of his generation'[7] is already an optimistic one, given that 'his generation' included the likes of Yudina, Oborin, Ginzburg and Vladimir Sofronitsky (a fellow student in the Petrograd Conservatoire class of Lev Nikolayev), with Emil Gilels and Svyatoslav Richter being only nine or ten years younger. And Moshevich's closing statement – 'with Shostakovich's death, the galaxy of the century's most important composer-pianists lost its last star'[8] – also smacks of special pleading, even though a number of Shostakovich's friends and contemporaries may have endorsed it. A more realistic assessment comes from Vladimir Ashkenazy, whose credentials as pianist and admirer of Shostakovich can scarcely be questioned: 'My teacher, Mr. Oborin, knew him very well. He played terribly dry and not very well prepared. So I'm not sure that he was really an outstanding pianist … I don't think you can compare those performances [Shostakovich's recordings] with those by professional pianists. It's not really that great.'[9]

My purpose is nevertheless not so much to demythologize or dethrone as to probe Shostakovich's recordings sympathetically for what may be of interest to listeners and performers. In so doing, I have in mind as points of comparison Rachmaninoff, Prokofiev and, to a lesser extent, Stravinsky, all of whom were, like Shostakovich, concertizing pianists whose legacy of recordings likewise shows at least one way in which their music might 'go'. Of course to infer from any composer's recordings how the music 'should', 'must' or 'was intended to' go is another thing altogether, since the very act of recording is contingent on so many potentially non-ideal conditions. Even in hypothetically ideal circumstances, recording serves only to fix one among numerous valid interpretative viewpoints at a given moment in time. To find excellence in any composer's recording of their own work is therefore never tantamount to holding it up as a model. On the other hand, finding serious flaws in it is not the same thing as saying that valuable lessons may not be learnt. To take a famous example, Rachmaninoff's adoption of swift tempos and substantial cuts in his sole recording of his Third Piano Concerto may be thought of as a salutary corrective to self-indulgent lingering and excessive reverence for the printed page; but on what logical basis would a pianist nowadays adopt those tempos without the cuts, or (more to the point, since it has become fashionable) reject the cuts while still insisting on the tempos? Just so with Shostakovich: any of the features in his playing that set it apart from later norms of recorded pianism may betoken either straightforward weaknesses, given that his technique was by no stretch of the imagination in the Rachmaninoff class, or straightforward strengths, indicating possible ways in which the evidence of the published scores may be enriched. Equally, those same features may be regarded as a combination of strength and weakness, inviting debate. Furthermore, close attention to the evidence of Shostakovich's recordings should yield information about his attitude as an interpreter of his music that is at least as important as his often reported remarks to individual performers, refracted as those remarks invariably are through the vagaries of memory and claims to privileged understanding. Above all, if there are correctives to be entered, then let them be in the spirit of opening up avenues for understanding and interpretation, rather than of narrowing them down. In this respect I take the opposite view from Moshevich, who not only commends Shostakovich's recordings for their intrinsic qualities but, as in the case of op. 5, for instance, considers them 'helpful for determining authentic tempos'.[10] Whereas I do not believe that any such things exist, much less that they should be recommended for thoughtless emulation.

The issue of metronome marks will nevertheless loom large in the following discussion, and with good reason: the closeness or otherwise of a performer's adherence to the text is one of the more quantifiable aspects of musical interpretation, and there is an apparent contradiction in the fact that Shostakovich could occasionally berate other performers for 'incorrect' tempos in his music and yet take very different tempos in his own performances of the same work – different from the text, and in some cases wildly different from one recording to another. The mere discrepancy between metronome markings and the tempo adopted is not in itself necessarily a remarkable point. It arises partly from the extra time that music takes to register properly in concert-hall performance as opposed to in a studio run-through at the piano – something that composers routinely underestimate, so that the norm is for 'real' tempo to be slower than notated. Moshevich's comparison of Shostakovich's recorded performances with the notated metronome marks demonstrates, unsurprisingly, that in 45 per cent of cases his initial tempos were slower than indicated, 40 per cent were within one notch on the metronome, and only 15 per cent were faster.[11] Far more revealing is the kind of variation in tempo that Shostakovich allowed himself in the course of a movement, irrespective of his notation.

As for other parameters, I have chosen to concentrate on Shostakovich's departures from the letter of his scores that would not easily be predicted, with some consideration also given to cases of surprisingly literal adherence. For the most part I have avoided discussion of detailed discrepancies between score and recording unless they have escaped Moshevich's attention.

In terms of repertoire, what we lack – frustratingly – is recordings of Shostakovich in either of his Piano Sonatas. This is hardly surprising in the case of the First, which was stylistically beyond the pale in the early years of Soviet recording, and tacitly ruled out until the 1960s (in fact there seems to have been no recording of the piece made anywhere in the world before 1969), by which time Shostakovich's infirmity would have ruled out the possibility of his relearning such an athletically demanding score – one he had probably not played for close on thirty years. Any pianist who has grappled with the First Sonata would be fascinated to know whether the composer ever took the main tempo at anything close to the marked $\downarrow = 104$. The $\downarrow = 84$ generally agreed upon as a maximum in recorded accounts already sounds fairly headlong, even before the texture becomes denser and most pianists are forced to compromise still further.[12]

The absence of a recording of the Second Sonata is less easily explicable and in many ways even more regrettable, since this was a work for which

Shostakovich reportedly harboured special admiration, and a recording of it by him might have told us – uniquely – something about his interpretative approach to a multi-movement structure, in a solo context rather than as accompanist or concerto soloist. Also to be lamented is the loss of the recording with Mieczysław Weinberg of the op. 87 Preludes and Fugues in the composer's duet arrangement.[13]

Yet we are fortunate to have as many recordings as we do. We can hear Shostakovich as pianist in the *Three Fantastic Dances*, the two Piano Concertos,[14] the Cello Sonata, the Piano Quintet and the Second Piano Trio (each in two versions), twelve of the *Twenty-Four Preludes* (two of them in alternative versions), the song cycle *From Jewish Folk Poetry*, seventeen of the *Twenty-Four Preludes and Fugues* (six of them in alternative versions), the duet transcription of the Tenth Symphony, the two-piano Concertino, and miscellaneous scraps including the Polka from *The Golden Age*, the *Children's Notebook*, and a movement from the soundtrack to the film, *The Gadfly*.

Miniatures and mixed fortunes

Some of these recordings are admittedly negligible. What should we make, for instance, of Shostakovich's scrappy accounts of the *Three Fantastic Dances*, virtually a signature piece for him and one he must have played hundreds of times? Certainly the Dances are trickier to bring off cleanly than they look, and if the better-known May 1958 Paris version was hampered by his incipient hand weakness, that might account for the stressful agitation in the central Allegretto of no. 2 and in the tricky bars 13–20 of no. 3; these same shortcomings were less pronounced, though already present, in his 1947 recording, which overall is far superior to the 1958 remake. Yet harmonic blend and synchronization of chords are fairly haphazard in both recordings. Technical finish apart, it is evident that some features of the score are more strictly adhered to than might expect be expected, while others are more loosely treated. For example, both recordings feature a rhythmically aberrant version of bars 10 and 12 in no. 1 and a curious variant in the left hand of bar 4 of no. 3, which are hard to explain away as mere accidents (Exx. 14.1, 14.2). Similarly, Shostakovich evidently favoured a romantic flurry in the main figure of no. 2, rather than a strictly rhythmical rendition, as he did an occasional Viennese lilt (especially in the reprise of that piece) and unwritten arpeggiatos at least in 1947 (as in no. 3, the section from bars 21 to 30). In both recorded accounts, tempo changes tend to be abrupt rather than smoothly negotiated, though whether out of technical

Example 14.1 *Three Fantastic Dances*, no. 1, bars 10, 12, score; recordings

Example 14.2 *Three Fantastic Dances*, no. 3, bar 4, score; recordings

anxiety or from a disinclination to linger it would be hard to judge. On the other hand a *ritardando* may take place much earlier than marked (end of no. 3, 1947 recording). As for character, rather than charm, which might be most pianists' instinctive aim in these pieces, there is an underlying sense of subdued mischief, especially in the earlier recording.

As for the *Children's Notebook*, the impression is mainly of throwaway impatience. Could it be that the composer's clipped verbal announcements, the absence of thirteen bars of the final piece, and the generally brisk, businesslike approach – the 'Sad Tale' taken at a remarkably un-*Adagio* ♩ =112, for example – are all to do with bringing the whole thing within the bounds of a single 78 rpm side (timing at 4′33″)? On the matter of alternative readings, at bar 30 in 'Sad Tale', Shostakovich takes the last note in the right hand as F natural, rather than the printed D sharp, which corresponds to the main motif of the piece rather than with the variant established at bar 26.

The *Golden Age* Polka, recorded in Prague on 26 May 1947, on the same day as the *Three Fantastic Dances*, eight of the op. 34 Preludes, the *Children's Notebook* and the Second Piano Trio, is once again fast and impatient, but not without a certain attractive impishness in its quiet shadings. This is a really tricky arrangement, and the fact that Shostakovich could get as close as this to playing it cleanly shows that his technique must have been in pretty good shape. If the performance is again somewhat rushed, that may again have been in order to accommodate it on the same side as the *Three Fantastic Dances*, which together make for a duration of 4'24".

With the op. 34 Preludes there is a clearer sense of the composer's doing himself and his music justice. In fact these are in many ways his most impressive solo recordings. They are technically well prepared, nimble-fingered, harmonically and melodically well blended, and the characterization is sensitive, charming, and laced with dry wit. The score itself is studded with *espressivo* and *ritardando* markings, *espressivo* being interpreted by the composer sometimes as a licence to hold back, sometimes merely as a reminder to take enough time for the notes to speak, while his *ritardandi* are never constrained to the exact point in the score where the marking appears. Where common sense dictates, Shostakovich observes an unmarked *a tempo*, and his dreamy – again unmarked – rubatos on the second page of the E flat major Prelude, no. 19 are more or less what any sensitive pianist would apply. It is hardly possible to legislate for his attitude to conclusions, which may either relax, as in no. 14, or ease forward, as in no. 15. The three recordings of uncertain provenance, apparently dating from 1950, are duplicates of nos. 8 and 22 and a unique one of no. 23; where comparisons can be made, these later recordings are significantly more spacious.

Certain departures from the text of the Preludes are of the kind that a responsible critical edition would routinely note, allowing performers to weigh the options. These range from passing details – for instance in no. 8, bar 25, at the second beat in the right-hand part, where both recordings have dotted quaver, semiquaver instead of the notated two quavers – to discrepancies that would be dubbed cavalier were it not the composer who was responsible for them (though they are, as a rule, perfectly in accord with common practice among concert pianists of the time). Perhaps most startling is Shostakovich's reversal of the dynamics in no. 16, which begins with a pounding *forte* instead of the notated *piano*. And in the F minor Prelude, no. 18 – one of several polkas in the set, and pleasingly reminiscent of Gottschalk's once-famous novelty piece, *Le bananier* – he takes the marked *Allegretto* ♩ =126 closer to *Allegro vivace* ♩ =168. Perhaps most suggestive in its implications for Shostakovich's attitude to large-scale structure is his performance of the E flat minor Prelude, no. 14 – a prototype for several of the philosophically brooding slow movements in his later works – which features a dramatic *accelerando* towards the main climax, through bars 20–5. On the other hand, there are Preludes where close attention to the text is the order of the day. The slightly tipsy, late-night-café-strumming mood of no. 17, only hinted at in the score, is brought out exquisitely, and the recording indicates that Shostakovich clearly meant exactly what he wrote in the flurry of diminutions in the middle of no. 24 (bars 27–30).[15]

Shostakovich's accompaniment to the song cycle *From Jewish Folk Poetry*, recorded on 16 January 1956, again shows his pianism in a good light. Inflections here are subtle, the tone beautifully shaded, and ostinatos flexible but without a trace of self-indulgence, while the fact that the tricky figuration of no. 7 is negotiated without a flicker of distress is a good indication of his technical facility at this date. If the discreet relation of the piano to the voices is a true reflection of the performance, rather than the work of the balance engineer, then that too is greatly to Shostakovich's credit. Once again he is not bound by the placing of *ritardando* markings in the score, as the last verse of no. 2 shows. On the other hand, where no *ritardando* is marked at the end of a song, as in no. 3, then generally none is forthcoming. Tempos in the darker first eight songs tend to be two or three notches below those marked, though those for nos. 2 and 6 are virtually spot-on. However, the last three songs – added later and widely considered to be tokenistic in their depiction of a happy life for Jews in the Soviet Union – are all taken a good deal faster than marked (respectively ♩ =108 rather than 92; ♩ =120 rather than 112; and ♩ =100 rather than 80). In this respect no. 10, depicting a girl happy to be on her collective farm, deserves especially close attention. The very fact that the song – exceptionally for Shostakovich – ends in the relative minor key, serves to add a question mark to the text; and his shading of the piano part does much to enhance a subtext of this kind. Set off strikingly from the faster-than-marked initial tempo, bars 50–61 are suddenly and without licence taken *meno mosso*, where the text runs: 'the feeling of great joy flashes into my heart like a spark. Sing, then, my simple pipe! How easy it is for us to sing together!' However one chooses to read or reread the text in this light, the effect is again to place a question mark or aposiopesis (three dots …) at the end.

Structural accelerations: beneath or beyond competence?

Confronted by a difference of opinion about ways of playing Bach, Wanda Landowska is famously supposed to have retorted: 'You play Bach your way, I'll play Bach *his* way.' For her reputation's sake one hopes that this crass remark is either a legend or was said tongue-in-cheek. But many pupils of strong-minded teachers will have encountered similar sentiments, voiced without irony. The problem is not just the arrogance of presuming to know and to be able to reproduce a composer's 'way', but also the assumption that there is any such thing in the first place; and even if there was such a 'way', would there be any merit other than historical curiosity in trying to reproduce it? Composers vary in the amount and kind of latitude they favour from performers, as they do in the amount they grant themselves (as may be evident when they themselves make more than one recording of a piece). In Shostakovich's case we are fortunate to have two examples of his recorded performances of several major works. In the case of the two Piano Concertos these demonstrate no especially significant deviations, but in the Cello Sonata, the Second Piano Trio and especially the Piano Quintet there is much to ponder.

By contrast with the Preludes and *From Jewish Folk Poetry*, Shostakovich's two recordings of his Concerto for Piano, Trumpet and Strings crave the listener's indulgence for their obvious technical shortcomings. The November 1954 account with Samuil Samosud is live, and full of rushed fences, some of which are less pronounced in the 1958 studio remake with André Cluytens in Paris. But by that time Shostakovich's hand weakness was starting to become apparent, and it is hard to think that this recording is in any way representative of his playing at its best, although the film clip of the end of a performance of uncertain date suggests that a hectic sprint finish was always a higher priority than clean negotiation of technical obstacles.

Along with the *Twenty-Four Preludes*, the First Concerto, composed in the first half of 1933, marked Shostakovich's return to instrumental composition after a frenetic period of film scores, ballets and incidental music for the theatre. The fruits of that writing for stage and screen are to be seen in the Concerto's reckless hurtling from one idea to another, covering a welter of styles from Prokofiev, Stravinsky and Ravel back through thinly veiled parodies of Rachmaninoff to riotous send-ups of the Viennese Classics. In his recorded performances Shostakovich generally lets the slapstick take care of itself, to the extent of playing some of the apparently comic ideas dead straight; and for all his reputation as a reckless speed merchant, his tempi in the first movement at least are consistently below the metronome marks. Noteworthy departures from the score are his taking of the right-hand octaves at bars 36 (last quaver) to 37 (second crotchet) an octave higher than marked in both recordings (the first two right-hand notes of bar 49 in the finale are also played up an octave). The notated *rit.* at ⟨10⟩ is not observed, perhaps ill-advisedly, given the mess that ensues two bars before ⟨11⟩. The second movement is a melancholy slow waltz, framing a cadenza-like outburst played by the composer with defiant steeliness. Here the heaviness of Shostakovich's *ritardando* two bars before ⟨27⟩ and his (mock-pedantic?) spelling-out of the scale figure at ⟨28⟩ with 'long' staccatos come as something of a surprise, as does his retention of pedal through the *diminuendo* from the main climax after 32 (not to mention the massive *forte espressivo* treatment of the *pianissimo* strings passage thereafter, in the earlier recording only). In the uproarious finale, Shostakovich goes full tilt, disregarding the notated holding-back for the first solo passage after 52. For the 1958 studio recording, the mini-cadenza at 71 brings an apparent change of acoustic – a sure sign that it was recorded separately for the sake of accuracy. In the final solo from 76 – a frenetic parody of hit-and-miss pianistic vamping – Shostakovich disregards his own *meno mosso* marking in both recordings. In 1958 he still emerges remarkably little scathed: so remarkably in fact, given his technical distress early on, that one could almost believe that his place had been taken by a stunt double (or that an assistant had been drafted in for a few bars of duetting, of the kind Rostropovich reports in his recording of the Cello Sonata with the composer[16]). In this respect the uninhibited approximations in the 1954 account feel much more real.

The less virtuosically demanding Second Concerto allows for an assessment of Shostakovich's interpretative temperament less clouded by issues of pianistic fallibility. The piece was composed for his son, Maxim, who at the time was completing his pre-Conservatoire studies at Moscow's Central Music School and who gave the premiere on 10 May 1957, the day of his nineteenth birthday. Despite the composer's occasional remark to the effect of the Concerto's lacking all artistic merit,[17] his recordings pay it the respect of special attention to the dramatic structure, above all in the long passage of accumulating tension at the heart of the first movement. Beginning with a sense of subdued threat at 10, Shostakovich pushes the tempo in the four bars before 18 where many others yield to the obvious temptation to rhetorical grandiosity, thereafter maintaining tension through the climax itself and surfing the same wave into the cadenza. The extra notes that bulk out the octave tremolos at 22^{3-4} could be viewed as part of a related concern to project a large-scale arc of dramatic tension. Hearing the movement performed this way, it is hard to return to more score-bound readings without some lingering sense of dissatisfaction, and also hard not to conclude that Shostakovich may well have had similar priorities in mind with many of his symphonic first movements, whether or not he prescribed an acceleration or a terracing of tempos in the score. Several of his recorded chamber performances point to the same conclusion, as will be seen.

The *Andante* slow movement is a gentle sarabande that suggests another Rachmaninoff parody (this time of the Second Piano Concerto, slow movement), and here Shostakovich provides an object lesson in non-sentimental, even anti-sentimental, lyricism. He then immediately puts a personal stamp on the finale's opening anapaest figures, taking the crotchets short and in the main theme fractionally elongating the ties so as almost to convert the three concluding semiquavers into triplets. As for the subsequent imitation-Hanon exercises – the kind of thing he might well have heard his son hammering away while he tried to compose – it is a cruel irony that these patterns, designed to develop pianistic technique in the young, reveal just how badly the fifty-one-year-old composer was beginning to labour under his physical difficulties. He all but gives up on the repeated chords at $^{3}\boxed{44}$, and approaching the point of recapitulation in both recordings he keeps $\boxed{55}^{6-7}$ at the higher octave and at $^{4}\boxed{56}$ seemingly plays clusters rather than dyads, to no obvious musical purpose.

Shostakovich's two recordings of the Cello Sonata and of the Second Piano Trio are understandably diverse, given the different artists involved; but the same may be also said of the two he made of the Piano Quintet, both featuring the Beethoven Quartet. The range of tempo these alternative recordings display is one indication of the breadth of readings his works allow.

There is no way of telling whether the relatively leisurely tempos Shostakovich adopted with Daniil Shafran for the Cello Sonata in 1946 are closer to his original conception than the relatively urgent ones with Rostropovich in 1957, though in the first movement it is certainly Shafran who is closer to the score.[18] One consequence of Rostropovich's initial haste is that he has to slow considerably for the second subject, whereas Shafran can continue at something like the same pulse (Rostropovich moderates his tempo considerably for the exposition repeat).[19] In general there is equal force of personality behind Shafran's pliancy and Rostropovich's directness. In the cello-led continuations of the second subject, for instance, Shafran broadens earlier than Rostropovich; likewise he begins the *accelerando* seven bars earlier than Rostropovich and twelve bars before it is marked. But it is Rostropovich who finds the more dramatic contours for the development section by beginning more stealthily and with more shadowy tone – an especially effective contrast after his relatively brisk and direct account of the exposition.

In the Scherzo Shafran is once again on the measured side compared to Rostropovich, and once again closer to the score. In both recordings the composer is in good technical shape for the awkward hand-crossings and the fiery closing phrases, whereas the manic etude-like episode in the middle of the finale is very approximate, either because he simply could not cope with it or because he preferred to leave it ragged for the sake of its out-of-control character. In the slow movement Shafran sets out in extremely lugubrious manner, necessitating a two-bar anticipation of the *accelerando* marked at $\boxed{42}^{6}$. Two details in Shostakovich's playing are especially worth noting: his beautiful lyrical spreading of the demisemiquavers between ⑮ and ⑯ – taking a crucial fraction of extra time – and his placing of the *pp sub.* at ⑰ on the half-bar, rather than the beginning as printed. Shafran's steady tempo for the finale lends a sly, humorous quality to the main theme, but it also means that he has to make a colossal unmarked *accelerando* towards the second theme, in the seven bars leading up to ⑭ (Rostropovich pushes forward even more urgently at this point).[20] Both performances settle back in the eight bars before ⑰. Whoever was the driving force behind the structural accelerations in these performances, they fall into a consistent pattern of Shostakovich's attitude to his large-scale structures, especially his finales.

Shostakovich's two recordings of the Piano Quintet with the Beethoven Quartet are so different that it is hard to believe that the same pianist was involved. In 1940 – just months after the premiere – tempos are consistently on the slow side, though close to those in the autograph score, whereas the faster tempos in the 1955 recording correspond fairly closely to those prescribed in the first publication of the score in the following year One wonders whether Shostakovich was encouraged in this general geeing-up of tempos by the temperament of the Borodins, with whom he had performed the piece in the interim.[21]

Yet as with the Cello Sonata the flexibility of tempo within movements – especially in the lengthy Fugue and Finale – is at least as revealing as the initial pulse, going far beyond the score, and beyond 'normal' allowance for instinctive musical licence. Since these gradations are not recorded in Moshevich's tabulation of tempi in the Quintet,[22] I include them in the expanded display shown in Table 14.1.

In the opening Prelude, Shostakovich does play for the most part strictly in tempo, creating a fine sense of continuity and disdaining all temptations to point harmonic tensions by rhythmical means. Arpeggiating the initial octave grace-notes, as he does in 1955 but not in 1940, is evidently the kind of routine option that he would not have thought worth notating (though how many teachers or chamber music coaches would allow it, much less encourage it, nowadays?). At the lead-back to the opening theme there is an unmarked *stringendo* through the first two bars of ⑫, the full tempo being reached in the third bar then maintained despite the following *poco rit.* In both recordings of the Fugue, Shostakovich subtly holds back for his entries at ㉑ and ㊲, lending them an impressive, dark-hued gravity. Having gradually returned to the main tempo by ㉔ he drives a further *stringendo* between ㉘ and ㉚ (from ㉕ to ㉘ in the 1940 performance) and the quartet continues the process between ㉚ and ㉜, at which point Shostakovich holds back again (these variations are generally less marked in the 1940 account). Between his two

Table 14.1 *Tempo Schemes in Shostakovich's recordings of the Piano Quintet (units assimilated to crotchets per minute)*

	Prelude			Fugue						Scherzo	
Rehearsal nos.		[3]	[12]	[16]	[21]	[23]–[24]	[25]–[28]	[28]–[30]	[30]–[32]	[45]	[55]
Manuscript	58	83		72						160	
Printed score	72	108	58	84						252	
Recording 1940	54	66	56	58			(→)			228	→
Recording 1955	72	100	63–80	72	60	→72		→ 80	→69	276	→
Duration 1940	4′ 56			12′ 25″						3′ 44″	
Duration 1955	3′ 41			10′ 27″						3′ 04″	

	Intermezzo	Finale								
Rehearsal nos.	[68]	[80]	[81]	[84]	[88]	[90]	[96]	[101]–[102]	[103]	[104]
Manuscript	72	144								
Printed score	72	192								
Recording 1940	54	→	152	168	232	→	276		←	152
Recording 1955	72	→	192	216	224	264	276	←		192
Duration 1940	8′ 12″	7′ 22″		Total: 36′ 39″						
Duration 1955	6′ 25″	5′ 55″		Total: 26′ 32″						

recordings, Shostakovich had evidently incorporated the imitation point between viola and cello at [43]³⁻⁴ accidentally discovered thanks to Rudolf Barshai's false entry in rehearsal.[23]

The Scherzo is jet-propelled in the 1955 recording, with a concomitant minor messiness but a hugely compensating no-nonsense energy, and the composer pushes the opening tempo even faster from [55]. The Intermezzo emerges very differently in the two recordings, the earlier one giving due weight to the piano's five *espressivo* markings and having a strongly romantic-melancholic atmosphere, with abundant portamento glides from Dmitry Tsïganov's first violin. By 1955 the only *espressivo* marking to engender a holding-back is at ³[74], just before the return of the opening theme; by this time the violin line from [72] is in false harmonics and the pervasive portamentos have been eliminated; the resulting mood is now more restrained and stoical, almost to the point of indifference.

The finale of the Quintet is far and away the most interesting movement from the point of view of tempo giving contour to the musical drama. From the outset it is evident that the notated *rit.* stands (exceptionally) for *ritenuto* rather than *ritardando* – a slower tempo (than the basic *Allegretto* still to come) rather than a gradual slowing down from the end of the Intermezzo – and the *poco a poco a tempo* begins almost immediately, the effect being of an initial reluctance to arrive at full tempo. In both recorded interpretations, seemingly driven by the composer's initiative at the piano, the tempo increases incrementally up to ⟨96⟩ with a compensating massive, and likewise unmarked, *ritardando* from ⟨101⟩ to ⟨102⟩. Yet again the structurally conceived *accelerando*, akin in many ways to the carefully marked gradations in many of Shostakovich's symphonic movements, seems to have been an instinct so strong as to have been more or less taken for granted; either that, or its metronomic fixing was not something the composer wanted or was able to do. This *accelerando–ritardando* arc is not the only way to get round the interpretative problem of tone (is the innocent surface genuine or deceptive?) in this finale; another option is to keep the tempo grindingly slow, resisting the temptation to let it flow forward, and to derive dramatic tension precisely from that resistance: literalism as bloody-mindedness. But that would certainly fly in the face of the composer's example in his recorded performances.

The Second Piano Trio poses similar problems of structural tempo as the finale of the Piano Quintet, but it does so from the very outset as well as in its finale. In the first movement the score suggests a terraced accumulation of tempo more or less to the mid-point, and that scheme can work well enough when literally adhered to. But it was not Shostakovich's way in performance. Both his recordings suggest that he thought once again in terms of a more or less continuous, albeit subtly graded, *accelerando* (see Table 14.2) that extends beyond the point where the score ceases to indicate an increase in tempo. On the other hand his consistent avoidance of conventional *ritardando* at the end of the movement is a strong indication of his preference for the letter of the score at this point. Ever since the appearance of the old *Complete Edition* in 1983, and the spin-off publications from it made available in the West, performers have wrestled with the $\bemol = 132$ marking for the Scherzo, which is hard enough for the violin and cello to negotiate in the key of F sharp major, and even harder to combine with the opening instruction to play *marcatissimo, pesante*. In both his recordings Shostakovich in fact takes a tempo just a little above the first edition's specification of *Allegro non troppo*, $\bemol = 108$, which few successors have dared to surpass. Both performances push forward at various points in the movement, and the 1946

Table 14.2 *Piano Trio no. 2, first movement, tempo schemes in*
Shostakovich's recordings

Rehearsal nos.		6	11	14	17	18	20
Score	69	96	120	160			
Recording 1946	60	120	156	172	208	*Ritardando*	*Stringendo*
Recording 1947	76	100	152	200	208	*Ritardando*	*Stringendo*

account in particular conveys a superb overall sweep. Whereas this recording barges straight into the G major contrasting theme at 45, in 1947 there is an equally effective agogic slowing into the new idea.

The passacaglia slow movement is often heard virtually twice as slow as the notated ♩ =112, and a judgement has to be made in performance as to how broad a pulse the violin and cello can sustain tonally while balancing depth of feeling against stoical resignation. Shostakovich himself shows two alternatives for the pianist at the opening: in 1946 he sets a pulse of around ♩ =76, which is then held back a fraction more at the violin entry (Dmitry Tsïganov); in 1947 he abandons the attempt to match his tempo with that of the strings and sets off at ♩ =126, which David Oistrakh then immediately adjusts to 76/80.

The finale once again poses an acute problem. As in the Quintet, a fairly rigorous adherence to the markings can produce a tremendous effect of resistance and of going against the grain. But this is a hard policy to agree on between three players, and especially hard to reconcile with the sudden increase of tempo marked at 71, from the initial ♪ =144 to 168, which is not modified at any point thereafter until the chordal return of the passacaglia theme on the last page. In both recordings Shostakovich himself builds in a steady *accelerando*.[24] The sense of delirium generated at the cyclic return of the first movement's main theme is hard to read from the printed page but unmistakable in both of Shostakovich's recordings and much heightened by the muting of violin and cello (a marking disregarded by many modern performances, presumably in the interests of dramatic immediacy, but in fact with catastrophic loss of character). The final return of the passacaglia theme at 105 is marked ♩ =96, in effect more than twice as fast as the corresponding statement in the slow movement (♩ =48 versus ₒ. =19). But to stick rigidly to this prescription is clearly not compulsory, given that Shostakovich corrects the discrepancy by playing at less than half the notated speed in both recordings. His avoidance of a final *ritardando* in the 1946 recording – with only the last chord slightly 'placed' – works as well as the slightly more flexible 1947 conclusion.

In many ways the single most revealing document of Shostakovich as performer is the piano duet version of the Tenth Symphony – curiously so for a transcription which he in all probability never performed in public and which was only made and recorded for utilitarian purposes, to assist conductors in getting to know the work. Its extraordinary value comes not directly from the pianism it displays, though the collaboration with Mieczysław Weinberg, who took the treble part, was evidently a congenial one, and the playing is far more carefully prepared than the ad hoc nature of the project might suggest. Nor could it seriously be suggested that the transcription represents a viable alternative in the concert hall, in the way that Prokofiev's *Romeo and Juliet* or Stravinsky's *Petrushka* movements and even his duet version of *The Rite of Spring* do. But the inestimable value of this recording lies in what it suggests about the composer's views on large-scale dramatic structure in general. It is, in fact, the nearest thing we have to the kind of interpretation he might have given as a conductor, or at least to the framework for such an interpretation. Yet again, structurally conceived acceleration is the most compelling feature, and it operates in all four movements.

By common consent one of Shostakovich's finest compositional achievements, the first movement of the Tenth Symphony presents a challenge to any conductor in terms of organic progression of tempo and character. Shostakovich and Weinberg begin significantly slower than marked and creep towards the notated speed, showing yet again that Shostakovich's metronome marks within movements need not (and arguably should not) denote instantaneous steps to a new level at the exact point marked. The tempo continues to edge forward through both first and second subject areas (as in most performances with orchestra), and it does so again through the development section and on into the early stages of the recapitulation. In compensation, a number of framing sections – including the very opening and the transitions to the development and second subject recapitulation – recede to a point slower than the marked tempos (see Table 14.3).

The second movement begins at almost precisely ♩ = 176 (as opposed to the piano score's ♩ = 116 and the orchestral score's presumably misprinted ♩ = 176), gathering speed thereafter through the quaver-two-semiquaver figures through to 192 for the trio section at 79, driving further forward after the reprise of the scherzo up to 212 by 91 and bringing the movement home in a breathless 3′46″, roughly ten seconds shorter than the fastest orchestral performance known to me (the Czech Philharmonic Orchestra in 1955, conducted by Karel Ančerl, on DG 463 666).

The third movement begins, like the first, a few notches steadier than the marked ♩ = 138. The central horn theme is immediately slower (around ♩ = 88, adjusted to 92 where the strings enter and the score marks 96).

Table 14.3 *Tempo scheme in Shostakovich's piano duet recording of the Tenth Symphony, first movement*

Rehearsal nos.	4^9	5	14^8	17	24	29	32^6	35	37	40	47	56	57	65	68
Piano score	96	108		120		108						104	120	96	
Orchestral score	96	108		120	108									96	
Recording	76	80	108	116	126	152	92	112	120	152	144	152	88	138	80 108
Structure	intro.		first subject		second subject	development						recapitulation		coda	

Table 14.4 *Tempo scheme in Shostakovich's piano duet recording of the Tenth Symphony, third movement*

Rehearsal nos.	100	114	115	116	117	117^6	118	122	127	129	130	131	132	137	139	141
Piano score	138		96	120	96	80	108	138			Poco accel.		240		108	
Orchestral score	138		96	120	96	72	96	138				accel.	240		108	
Recording	126	88	92	96	84		96	108	152	160			180	rall.	152	112
Structure	exposition	horn theme						development							recap./ coda	

Succeeding tempos are as shown on Table 14.4. Most interesting is the central development section, where Shostakovich and Weinberg yet again begin considerably below the marked tempo and advance far beyond it well before the marked *poco accelerando* but still fail to reach anywhere near the marked ♩ = 80 at the apex of the movement. The coda, played with breathtaking sensitivity by Weinberg, incidentally, is interesting for the missing bar in the piano score and recording at 142^8.

The finale begins with a superbly judged, flexible yet sinewy, account of the introduction, the tempo kept fluid between an opening ♪ = 108 and a basic 126. Shostakovich and Weinberg's ♩ = 176 for the insouciant first subject is spot on the notated marking, but once again the tempo is pushed significantly through the development section. The reprise of the introduction is a genuine *l'istesso tempo*, a marking not present in the duet score but added in the orchestral score, presumably because Mravinsky either succumbed to – or maybe himself noted – the danger of slowing down at this point. The structural push forward in Shostakovich and

Table 14.5 *Tempo scheme in Shostakovich's piano duet recording of the Tenth Symphony, fourth movement*

Rehearsal nos.	144	153	170	173	184	185	194
Piano score	126	176					
Orchestral score	126	176					
Recording	108/126	176		→	192		200
Structure	intro.	exposition	development			recapitulation	

Weinberg's performance continues even beyond this point, being sustained virtually without relief until the end of the movement, which thereby registers as though in one gigantic breath (see Table 14.5). As with all Shostakovich's performances, the point is not to measure other interpretations by its yardsticks; it would be possible to argue that the structural *accelerandos* work partly as compensations for the lack of orchestral colour and would be vulgar, even nonsensical, if transplanted literally into orchestral performance. Equally, however, if conductors' instincts impel them towards such unnotated deviations, then it is worth knowing that they have the composer's implied assent.

Other works where Shostakovich's attitude to large-scale structure might be expected to have come through in his playing prove less revealing. The Concertino, op. 94, is a frankly pedagogic exercise: a kind of single-movement sub-concerto, and as such doubtless well adapted to the developing pianistic skills of Shostakovich's teenage son, with whom he recorded the work in February 1956. This is one of the few scores from Shostakovich's maturity to lack metronome marks, perhaps suggesting that he (accurately) did not foresee much of a life for it in the concert hall. The recorded performance is well prepared and efficient, without being especially noteworthy.

The 1969 recording of the Violin Sonata is an exceptional case. This was taken from a private rehearsal with Oistrakh, presumably made for the violinist's benefit in learning the piece and later donated by him to the State recording firm, Melodiya. It post-dates Shostakovich's last concert appearance by three years, and it precisely reflects his comments to Isaak Glikman: 'I could manage the easy passages well, but the difficult ones were awful.'[25] At this stage Oistrakh himself was still, as Shostakovich noted, 'getting to grips with the sonata',[26] and his vagueness in the first movement's eerie arpeggiato figuration (indebted, as are so many of the textures in this work, to Prokofiev's Violin Sonata no. 1) throws the composer off the scent. After 36 in the Scherzo, Oistrakh skips a bar, and Shostakovich catches up a couple of bars later as he spots the inadvertent elision. Shostakovich himself miscounts at ³[40] but soon recovers. And so on. The wild, semi-random piano cadenza in the finale could almost have been conceived as an enraged protest at the infirmity that had reduced his piano technique to tatters; certainly Shostakovich gets nowhere near the notes on this recording. Yet for all the technical approximation there is much to admire and learn from in the performance, for instance in the prowling character of the first movement's second theme (from [10]). Tempos in the first two movements are fairly close to the notated markings, suggesting, perhaps, that other published metronome marks in Shostakovich's scores may have been derived from similar private performances. However, the basic tempo for the third movement is rather faster (♩ =100, rather than 88).

The Preludes and Fugues: archetypes and nuances

The cycle of *Twenty-Four Preludes and Fugues*, op. 87 was composed in the aftermath of Shostakovich's visit to Leipzig in July 1950 where he attended the Bach bicentenary celebrations and served as jury member for the First International Bach Competition. They appeared over a period of four and a half months, and from modest beginnings the decision to produce a complete cycle covering all the major and minor keys only took shape as work progressed, as it did with the String Quartets. Since early 1948 Shostakovich had been suffering from the fallout of the 'anti-formalist' campaigns spearheaded by Andrey Zhdanov. His most serious works from this time – the First Violin Concerto, the song cycle *From Jewish Folk Poetry* and the Fourth String Quartet – were languishing unperformed, and his ability to teach, to influence his country's musical life, even to earn a living, had been severely curtailed. A glance at the music he was able to get performed in these years – chiefly the oratorio *Song of the Forests* and the film scores *The Fall of Berlin*, *Belinsky* and *The Unforgettable Year 1919* – points to a deep-seated psychological *raison d'être* for the Preludes and Fugues: as a project undertaken to restore the balance, for the sake of his creative sanity and self-esteem. In submitting the cycle of prima facie formalist (in the sense of autonomous and self-sufficient) music for peer review by the Composers' Union in March 1951, he was pushing at the vaguely defined boundaries of the permissible, on behalf of himself and his composer colleagues, even, perhaps, on behalf of artistic standards in Russian cultural life in general. Compositionally the Fugues tend to follow the textbook pattern of tonic–dominant–tonic–dominant exposition, with middle entries in related keys and strettos in the later stages; but on the basis of that template Shostakovich maximizes variety by all manner of means.

Shostakovich recorded seventeen of the cycle of twenty-four over three sessions in 1951, 1952 and 1958. All but one of the eight Preludes and Fugues recorded in 1958 (no. 18) is a duplicate (the version issued on Revelation RV70003 being a misattribution;[27] the performance of no. 17 on that disc is also not by the composer). For the most part these later readings are marginally less fluent and display fewer interpretative refinements than the earlier ones. As a performer Shostakovich could never claim to command either the lucidity of part-playing he admired in the likes of Yudina or the rock-like steadiness of a Richter. But what does emerge from his accounts is a clear sense of a number of archetypal characters binding the cycle together: renewal, playfulness, meditation and grandeur.

The clean C major of the very first Prelude and its white-note Fugue has the air of a tribute to the first Prelude of Bach's *Well-Tempered Clavier* and to the contemplative modality of the late Renaissance. The fugue is an unobtrusive compositional *tour de force*, in that it covers all the diatonic pitch-levels with its entries, and therefore by definition all the different white-note modes including the theoretical Locrian (with tonic on B). In the context of the post-Zhdanov, late-Stalin era, this unfolding of a realm of pure untainted musical thought is tantamount to making a political statement by not making one. In the context of Shostakovich's output as a whole, it echoes the first of the op. 34 Preludes and the first String Quartet, each of which in its own way made a manifesto of artistic renewal – respectively, a return to instrumental composition after a spate of works for stage and screen, and a turn to the most elevated medium of high-art music in the aftermath of the 1936 *Pravda* denunciations. In the Preludes and Fugues this sense of personal artistic renewal is echoed at the quarter-way point in the broken chords and arpeggio figurations of A major, no. 7, and again at the half-way point in the rocking motion of the F sharp major Prelude, no. 13 (which has been related by more than one commentator to Chopin's Barcarolle, in the same key). In performances of the complete cycle these are islands of repose where the pianist and audience can mentally draw breath.

The other character types that recur throughout the cycle are set out in the second, third and fourth Preludes and Fugues. Playfulness is to the fore in the A minor, and it is to be found also in the immediately following G major Fugue (Shostakovich orders his keys sharpwards in major and relative minor pairs), in the D major Prelude and Fugue, no. 5 (a minuet and humoresque, respectively), in the two-part invention of the E major Fugue, no. 9, in the following C sharp minor Prelude, in the lightly tripping B major Prelude, no. 11 and its robust Fugue, in the rough-and-tumble D flat, no. 15, in the mischievous A flat, no. 17, and in the étude-like B flat Prelude, no. 21 with its skipping Fugue. The counterbalance to playfulness is the sober meditation of several of the slow-moving, mainly minor-key pieces, beginning with the E minor Prelude and Fugue, no. 4, and continuing through the B minor Fugue, no. 6, the Fugues in C sharp minor (no. 10) and F sharp major (no. 13, the only five-voice fugue in the set), the brooding E flat minor and C minor Preludes and Fugues, nos. 16 and 20, and the G minor, no. 22. There are overlaps in character between these meditative statements and the final archetype of grandeur (which is at its strongest in the G major Prelude, no. 3) accumulates through the G sharp minor Prelude, no. 12 (actually a full-blown passacaglia) and its convoluted 5/4 metre Fugue, culminating in the massive final D minor Prelude and Fugue, no. 24, during whose course much of the thematic material for the first movement of the Tenth Symphony, composed two years later, seems to be forged. It goes without saying that these character archetypes are nuanced by the nature of the themes in each instance, as is the default fugue-structure template already noted. It is these nuances and certain other details highlighted in the playing that the following comments seek to highlight.

Shostakovich projects a wise simplicity in the first Prelude and Fugue, with a chaste beauty of tone that few if any future interpreters have rivalled, plus a touch of stoicism by means of dynamics that are acknowledged rather than highlighted, so that, for instance, the pronounced *diminuendo* into the reprise of the Prelude stands out structurally (in 1958 the *pianissimo* markings are more pointed). His tempo for the fugue confirms that the printed crotchet unit for the metronomic unit should be a minim.

By contrast, it is hard to mount much of a defence of the composer's playing of the neo-Baroque (and somewhat César Franckian) A minor Prelude, or of its playful Fugue. Rather than bringing out any hidden part-writing or phrasing in the Prelude, Shostakovich applies a haze of impressionistic pedal, with many crushed notes and no attempt to stabilize the texture at the level of half-bars or crotchet beats. The Fugue, on a subject borrowed from his as-yet-unperformed Fourth Symphony (which in turn borrows it from a fugue composed at that time as an exercise), is played not just spikily and caustically, as one might expect, but as though being chased and anxious not to be caught up from behind. Technically the performance is something of a mess, the impression being of a top-rank pianist given about twenty minutes to learn and record the piece from scratch. The counter-subject that could easily stabilize the tempo is habitually rushed, and whenever the main anapaest figure begins off the beat, the rhythm wobbles alarmingly.

In the G major Prelude Shostakovich survives the tricky semiquaver octaves by means of a slight broadening, a modicum of pedal and a lighter touch. For the most part his playing has an admirable fullness of tone, with a stern *sempre marcato* that exults in its own power. The gigue-style Fugue includes that comparatively rare feature in fugal composition, the *stretto maestrale* (close imitation of the subject in all the voices). Here Shostakovich makes no compromises over tempo and as a result gets into something of a panic in the later stages. First beats are often unclear, and many semiquaver figures are 'swallowed'. Viewed more positively, it is as though the fugal structure has become incidental to the general character of urgency and, again, of being chased; it could be said that the way the composer grits his teeth and simply gets through imparts a character all its own.

The E minor Prelude supplies a calm counterpart to the manic G major Fugue. It is laid out rather like a trio sonata, but its limpidity also recalls the Mozartean slow movement of Ravel's G major Piano Concerto, offering a glimpse of a better world in the contrasting chords, which are then beautifully integrated back into the texture. Shostakovich's performance is considerably slower than marked and more sorrowful than might have been predicted, but with fine flexibility in its *rubato*, and wonderful timing of the chordal theme. The Fugue is a long-breathed lyrical meditation, its sigh figures clearly derived from the Prelude; it is a double fugue, with overlaying of subjects and eventually superimposed strettos. In the beautiful counter-subject, Shostakovich does not lighten the second note of the two-note slurs as one might expect. More predictable is his somewhat spasmodic acceleration through the *più mosso*. His technique cannot quite stand the pressure of the structural accumulation he seeks to project thereafter, but the expressive design emerges with exemplary clarity.

Shostakovich takes the minuet-style D major Prelude quite fast, with a strong sense of forward motion, the character being simple, unsentimental and almost happy, like another evocation of a better world. The fugue subject is as playful as a children's chorus, even when it is put through the mill of another *stretto maestrale*. The tempo pushes forward with real urgency, each entry seemingly more insistent than the last, with no *ritardando* at all on the last page (though a modest one may be heard in the 1958 remake); as a consequence the texture does not bear close scrutiny.

The neo-Baroque B minor Prelude (no. 6) recalls the eighth variation in the Second Piano Sonata finale and their shared model in Schumann's *Études Symphoniques*. Here Shostakovich's severe delivery gives some idea of how he might have played those works. Rhythms are less sharply defined here than the score would suggest, and evidently the composer had not gone to the trouble of finding the ideal fingerings that would have clarified them. The Fugue is altogether more successful, showing great breadth of conception and a wonderful transparency of tone at the major-mode counter-exposition. As at several points elsewhere in the cycle, Shostakovich tends to accelerate through certain entries and episodes, then to point the next by a *diminuendo* or a slight holding-back for the strettos.

The Prelude and Fugue in F sharp minor is one of the minor compositional miracles in Shostakovich's oeuvre. His account of the Prelude points its daintily despairing, klezmer-inflected mood by rushing the acciaccatura figures and making the semiquavers expressively uneven. For compositional subtlety, the Fugue is in a class of its own. The diminished seventh in its subject already registers as a logical reaction to the modality of the Prelude, and the middle entries respond in their turn with statements based on the diminished fourth and diminished octave degrees. Following the same train of thought, the fugue subject returns with the diminished fourth degree newly incorporated, eventually to be enharmonically transformed into a *tierce de picardie* as B flat is re-spelled as A sharp. Shostakovich's pianistic delivery of the long subject is masterful, and throughout he registers not only the modally flattened notes but also the calls of pain in the tritone figures of the second half of the subject with the utmost sensitivity.

The G sharp minor Prelude and Fugue, no. 12 is a grand summatory piece for the first half of the cycle. The Prelude is already something of a *tour de force*: a passacaglia that ends with a canon and evolves the Fugue subject towards the end, as the final D minor Prelude will do. Each of these Preludes is strongly related to the first movement of the Tenth Symphony, both in thematic terms and in the broader sense of conveying the power of musical thought to transfigure suffering. In his recording Shostakovich does superb justice to the long dynamic contours of the passacaglia. But the Fugue is a huge test for the pianist, both intellectually and pianistically, and here his performance can only really be called a sketch. Twice it goes seriously off the rails, the first time as the composer virtually skips a line from bar 14 to bar 17, the second time from bars 56 to 58, where he is reduced almost to busking. It is hardly surprising, then, that he did not attempt it again in 1958, even though by that stage he could more easily have availed himself of the technology of retakes. Noteworthy, since it goes against pianistic instinct in favour of the letter of the score, is Shostakovich's minimal *rallentando* into the *Andante* near the end.

It is great pity that he never recorded the D flat Prelude and Fugue, no. 15 – one of the most popular of the set – to let us hear his take on its cheeky waltz and headlong chromatic brainstorm. But his account of the

B flat minor, no. 16, offers rich compensation. Up to the short coda, the Prelude is another passacaglia, but here camouflaged by variational figuration. This is another of Shostakovich's subtlest performances, the passacaglia theme always taken in one breath and the coda registered with touching reluctance. The Fugue takes up the Prelude's idea of ornate decoration of a hidden line, the long-limbed subject being based more or less on the same head-motif as the passacaglia, though following the usual pattern of the minor-key fugues in having a re-exposition in the major mode, followed by middle entries and strettos. Shostakovich's recording is the acme of patient structuring. The demisemiquavers are inflected with yearning *rubato* stretches before each new entry, and the arrival of the re-exposition is carefully pointed. It may be noted that his reading in bar 14 (middle voice, second and third notes c″, d flat″) is not reflected in any edition to date. As Moshevich notes, he is happy to retake tied notes when they have faded (as, for example, in the last six bars), and this is a recurring feature of his recorded legacy.[28]

The recording of the A flat Prelude and Fugue credited to Shostakovich is clearly not by him, as the technique is too professionally finished and the characterization too bland. The same goes for the version of no. 18 on Revelation RV70003.[29] The 1958 recording of the F minor Prelude and Fugue, first issued on Columbia FCX 771, is the only one not to have appeared on CD, and it has so far eluded all my efforts to find a copy.

With the beautiful F major Prelude – a neo-Baroque aria over walking bass, laid out rather like a Bach–Busoni transcription – Shostakovich's playing reaches extraordinary heights, worthy of some unknown marking beyond a mere *espressivo*. This performance is like a benediction, its solemnity emphasized by a surprisingly slow tempo ($\quarternote = 36$ rather than the marked 48). Curiously, Shostakovich reads bar 8, alto voice penultimate note, as b flat rather than d′, but in the 1958 remake he plays according to the printed score. In both performances the notated comma in bar 24 is scrupulously observed. The Fugue adheres closely to the basic structural pattern, as though saving virtuosity and concentration and epic dimensions for the D minor Fugue to come. Shostakovich's performance is surprisingly urgent, as if responding to an unmarked *poco agitato*, even though this tends to make the stretto phase almost nonsensical, its confused textures being compounded by an evident refusal to devise an optimum redistribution of wide intervals between the hands.

The final D minor Prelude and Fugue is the strongest of many pointers forward to the Tenth Symphony, and Shostakovich rises magnificently to its pianistic challenges. The grand, sarabandish, somewhat César Franckian Prelude seems to cast a wise glance back on the entire set, even as it prefigures the Fugue theme. Shostakovich's *maestoso* within *piano* where the fugue subject is proposed, is especially impressive, and this time the final *espressivo* and *diminuendo* markings come with the unmarked *ritardando* that most pianists would add in any case. The double fugue (mirroring the design of the E minor Fugue) is an immensely complex construction. The first exposition already has two redundant entries, serving to establish the expanded time-scale, and the counter-exposition features Mixolydian alterations, as if recalling and building on the possibilities of modal reconfiguration proposed in the F sharp minor Fugue. The second fugue is placed in A flat, a tritone distant from the home key, and it is given an additional middle-entry sequence. It develops a tremendous rhetorical force. The subjects are then combined, with a much-delayed stretto of the first appearing only after the mode has been colossally affirmed as major, as if to turn the questionable triumph of the last pages of the Fifth Symphony into one really earned. The Phrygian inflections on the final pages are by now as natural to Shostakovich as subdominant leadings in a common-practice era coda. In his performance Shostakovich tends to apply *inégalité* to the paired quavers in the opposite way to Baroque performance practice, leaning towards a scotch-snap (short-long) distortion. Disregarding incidental details (the divergent readings on Shostakovich's two recordings may be purely accidental), by far the most interesting structural feature in the composer's interpretation is the impression of a continuous *stringendo* through the second fugue, well past the point where a literal view of the *più mosso* marking would dictate stabilization, with little *ritenuto*s as momentary holds. The 1958 performance is less ethereal in the Prelude but achieves a less panicky *stringendo* in the fugue.

That was not quite Shostakovich's last visit to the recording studio, and one suspects it must have already cost him a good deal of anguish because of his muscular distress. But it stands as a magnificent capstone to a chequered performing career that, whether or not it deserves a place in the pantheon of Russian pianism as some would have us believe, offers far more insights, both into the works being performed and into the creative processes informing those works, than many a more impeccably grounded pianism.

15 Jewish existential irony as musical ethos in the music of Shostakovich

ESTI SHEINBERG

Irony is a key element in the music of Shostakovich. Its presence is so conspicuous and varied that it allows the creation of a taxonomy of sub-types: satire, parody, the grotesque, and even a new type that has been tentatively described as existential.[1] Shostakovich used satirical irony to criticize; parody as a compositional device; the grotesque as a quasi-philosophical statement on human nature; and, possibly, existential irony to present an ethical approach to life, embracing the amalgam of both dysphoric and euphoric aspects of human existence as a source of our aesthetic experience.[2] Although some of the composer's output has been interpreted as existentialist in other sources,[3] no systematic analysis has been offered to explain how existential ideas, let alone existential irony, are correlated with the music itself.

Existentialism is a rather vague concept that includes literary, philosophical and psychological writings whose common denominator is a concern with human existence and the search for its significance.[4] Its vagueness and the variety of approaches to it make the detection of its musical correlations problematic, because such correlations require a semantic correlative sufficiently characterized to allow a direct, reasonably undisputable interpretation.[5] In spite of this difficulty, there are still several traits of existential thought that are agreed by most writers on the subject: above all, a generalized dysphoric approach to human existence and a strong feeling of its senselessness and lack of direction. Both these traits correlate easily with musical elements: the dysphoric mood has a long line of musical correlations, such as slow motion, descending pitches, minor and/or inflected modes, and so on; disorientation is often correlated with long melodic phrases, lack of harmonic resolutions and the lack of clear rhythmic patterns. The Prelude to Wagner's *Tristan and Isolde* and more or less the entirety of Debussy's *Pelléas et Mélisande* are prophetic of a whole flood of musical works expressing similar meanings, not least those that make use of twelve-note elements, as Shostakovich did precisely with the aim of expressing chaos and disorientation (as in his Violin Sonata, op. 134 and his last four string quartets).

Although a major philosophical movement in the West, twentieth-century existentialism was far from popular in Soviet Russia. In that country, existential *angst* was not an intellectual pose but a daily struggle, and the people involved in that struggle, while deeply committed to the Russian tradition of life directed by ideology, had to confront the constant presence of meaningless Evil. In such circumstances, existential ideas did have a special significance.[6] Shostakovich's literary interests, evident in his choices of poetic and dramatic texts, show a continuous interest in philosophical issues related to human existence. In fact, two issues seem to have been of great concern to him in his musical works: the nature of morality, and the phenomenon of happiness within a context of a miserable life. And for both issues he seems to have preferred existential answers. His two favourite dramatic works, *Hamlet* and *King Lear*, are perhaps Shakespeare's most 'existential' plays, in that they focus most explicitly on moral dilemmas concerning the meaning and value of human life; Gogol's *The Nose* is, in fact, a study on the essence of being human; the Jewish folk poetry that Shostakovich set for his op. 79 song cycle deals with the relativity of human happiness; the texts of Lorca, Apollinaire, Rilke and Küchelbecker in the Fourteenth Symphony form a chilling document of existential pessimism; finally, the composer's two last vocal works, the *Four Verses of Captain Lebyadkin*, op. 146, to texts from Dostoyevsky's *The Possessed*, and the *Suite on Texts of Michelangelo Buonarroti*, op. 145, focus on existential themes. In a letter to Isaak Glikman of 23 August 1974, Shostakovich specified the 'essence' of his Michelangelo Suite as 'Wisdom; Love; Creation; Death; Immortality'.[7] A comparison of these settings with the Lebyadkin verses reveals the same subjects, only in grotesque guise in the later cycle.

Although there is no direct evidence, it is likely that Shostakovich was aware of existential philosophy. His general – rather than specifically musical – cultural background, particularly since 1927, was closely related to his intimate friendship with the musicologist Ivan Sollertinsky, whose influence on the composer was immense.[8] Sollertinsky knew the writings of Schopenhauer, Kierkegaard and Nietzsche and thus was familiar with the sources of existentialist thought.[9] Moreover, the ethical ambivalence of Shostakovich's interpretation of Leskov's story *The Lady Macbeth of Mtsensk District* strongly recalls Nietzsche's outlook on love in his 'The Case of Wagner', and the essence of human moral values in the same author's *Beyond Good and Evil*.

To consider *Lady Macbeth* as advocating Nietzsche's moral ideas requires both a careful comparison between Leskov's story and the Shostakovich–Preys libretto, and a scrupulous analysis of the opera, as performed by Caryl Emerson.[10] Here it should suffice to observe that Shostakovich made significant changes in the original story, mainly by excluding parts that would indict Katerina (the murder of an innocent child, her husband's nephew, is completely ignored) and adding scenes that enhance her emotional distress, her romantic feelings towards Sergey, and her high moral stand (for instance her 'sermon' aria to the male workers following Aksinya's molestation in Act 1, Scene 2). Another indicator is presented by the additional scenes that create moral confusion in Soviet terms: beyond the obvious satire on authority (one that few Soviet citizens in 1934 would likely have interpreted as an unambiguous reference to Tsarist times) there is the satire on the *folk*, the *crowd of Russian people* presented as a stupid, cruel herd, as in the molestation scene, the wedding and its aftermath, and the mockery of Katerina in the last act. To see in this amalgam of ideas just an attempt to present an allegedly objective picture of reality that is congruent with Marxist ideology is not entirely convincing.

The chapter in *Testimony* that begins with a discussion of *Lady Macbeth* opens with a series of paraphrases of the composer's former statements about the opera. However, in an apparently unexplained way, Solomon Volkov juxtaposes the famous paragraph where Shostakovich allegedly states that he dedicated the opera to his future wife (Nina Varzar) with a paragraph that speaks about Sollertinsky and focuses on the latter's interest in love:

> Love was one of Sollertinsky's favorite themes. He could speak for hours on it, on the most varied levels: from the highest to the very lowest. And Sollertinsky was very supportive of my attempt to express my ideas in *Lady Macbeth*. He spoke of the sexuality of two great operas, *Carmen* and *Wozzeck*, and regretted that there was nothing comparable in Russian opera. …
>
> Sollertinsky believed that love was the greatest gift and the person who knew how to love had a talent just as does the person who knows how to build ships or write novels. In that sense Ekaterina Lvovna is a genius. She is a genius in her passion, for the sake of which she is prepared to do anything, even murder. [11]

Assuming this citation to be more or less accurate – whatever its provenance – Sollertinsky's reliance on Nietzsche is quite obvious. In his 1938 article on *Carmen* he describes the scenery as populated with a 'colourful, diverse public, feeling the tinge of expectation for a *Corrida*. All this is alive, moving, turbulent, speedily frantic, full of unrestrained joy, filled with feverish Southern warmth.'[12] 'Southern joy' is the expression used by Nietzsche to describe the same opera.[13] In an earlier article about *Carmen*, Sollertinsky stated that the title-character symbolizes the 'sweeping, fateful power of Eros'[14] and described Bizet's music in the opera as having in its basis an anarchistic approach to love.[15] In similar vein, Nietzsche, when speaking about *Carmen*, exclaimed:

> And finally love, love translated back into *Nature*! Not the love of a 'cultured girl!' – no Senta-sentimentality. But love as fate, as a fatality, cynical,

innocent, cruel, – and precisely in this way *Nature!* … I know no case in
which the tragic irony, which constitutes the kernel of love, is expressed with
such severity, or in so terrible a formula, as in the last cry of Don José with
which the work ends. … Such a conception of love … [is] the only one
worthy of a philosopher.[16]

Echoes of these words can be found not only in Sollertinsky's 'fateful
power of Eros', but also in Shostakovich's article from the same year, where
he describes Katerina Izmaylova as a 'vigorous, talented, beautiful woman'.
A few lines further she is described as 'a complex, earnest, tragic character.
She is an affectionate, sensuous woman, devoid of sentimentality.'[17]

However, the word 'genius' – let alone the combination 'genius in
love' used by Volkov in *Testimony*, does not occur, to the best of my
knowledge, in Shostakovich's 1933 article, nor in Sollertinsky's relevant
writings. 'Genius' in connection with someone who, due to his creative
talent, is above normative moral considerations is a Nietzschean usage.
Moreover, according to Nietzsche, the only other quality that, beyond
being a 'genius', allows disregard of normative morality, is *love*: 'Whatever
is done from love always occurs beyond good and evil.'[18]

In 'The Case of Wagner' Nietzsche speaks about the true 'essence' of
love as selfish, and as demanding complete possession and subjugation.
Nietzsche then speaks about the *selfishness* of love in that it wants to
'*possess* the other creature', a rule to which 'even God is no exception …
He becomes terrible if he is not loved in return.'[19] Love, then, becomes a
moral criterion. And not just love in general, but rather the specific love
between man and woman: not the Platonic, 'mystical' or 'sentimental'
love, but love that is part of *Nature*. This Nietzschean approach, while
non-existent in Leskov's story, is quite explicit in Shostakovich's *Lady
Macbeth*. Katerina's lust, her 'mate-yearning' aria in Act 1, Scene 1, the
'naturalistic' intercourse scene, her complete obliviousness to any person
or any value beyond Sergey, the subject of her love, absolutely blind to
his many weaknesses and faults, all classify Katerina as a Nietzschean
'genius' – a talented, complex, tragic and unique individual who follows a
set of personal ethical criteria rather than the social contract of the era.

Moreover, Katerina's behaviour and personality point not only to
Nietzsche's perception of Genius but also to his opinion on the Feminine.
The closing paragraph of the section entitled 'Our Virtues', in *Beyond Good
and Evil*, reads almost as a critical analysis of the personalities of both
Carmen and Katerina Izmaylova:

What inspires respect for woman, and often enough even fear, is her *nature*,
which is more 'natural' than man's, the genuine, cunning suppleness of a
beast of prey, the tiger's claw under the glove, the naïveté of her egoism, her

uneducability and inner wildness, the incomprehensibility, scope, and movement of her desires and virtues –

What, in spite of all fear, elicits pity for this dangerous and beautiful cat 'woman' is that she appears to suffer more, to be more vulnerable, more in need of love, and more condemned to disappointment than any other animal. Fear and pity, with these feelings man has so far confronted woman, always with one foot in tragedy which tears to pieces as it enchants. [20]

The imagery that associates women with beasts of prey recurs, and probably not coincidentally, in *Beyond Good and Evil*, where Nietzsche refers to music in general, and particularly to the music of the South (i.e. by implication, to *Carmen*). Moreover, the language he uses strongly suggests the sensual art with which Shostakovich was familiar: Boris Kustodiev's drawings for Leskov's *Lady Macbeth* .[21]

Suppose somebody loves the south as I love it, as a great school of convalescence, in the most spiritual as well as the most sensuous sense, as an uncontainable abundance of sun and transfiguration by the sun that suffuses an existence that believes and glories in itself … If such a southerner, not by descent but by *faith*, should dream of the future of music, he must also dream of the redemption of music from the north, and in his ears he must have the prelude of a more profound, more powerful, perhaps more evil and mysterious music, a supra-German music that does not fade away at the sight of the voluptuous blue sea and the brightness of the Mediterranean sky, nor does it turn yellow and then pale as all German music does … A music whose soul is related to palm trees and feels at home and knows how to roam among great, beautiful, lonely beasts of prey –

I could imagine a music whose rarest magic would consist in its no longer knowing anything of good and evil, only now and then some sailor nostalgia, some golden shadows and delicate weaknesses would pass over it – an art that from a great distance would behold, fleeing toward it, the colors of a setting *moral* world that almost become unintelligible, and that would be hospitable and profound enough to receive such late fugitives.[22]

This fascination with the sensual is, of course, in no way exclusive to Nietzsche, Kustodiev or Shostakovich. The positive value of sensuality and its connection to Nature, as well the fascination with its predatory nature – both associated with the concept of the genuine, sincere authenticity of the human self – are a recurring subject in the period between 1890 and 1930, as in the studies of Freud, the art of Henry Rousseau, Paul Gauguin and a considerable part of Picasso's work, Stravinsky's *Rite of Spring*, and Oscar Wilde's *Salomé* (followed by Strauss's opera), to name just a few cultural milestones of that period.

But there is a common ideological thread that passes through Sollertinsky's analysis of Carmen, Shostakovich's interpretation of Leskov's *Lady Macbeth* and Nietzsche's ideas about morality. In fact, Nietzsche regards morality as irrelevant to the basic problems of human existence. In his 1934 article about Shostakovich's *Lady Macbeth*, Sollertinsky refers to the fact that Shostakovich's interpretation of the main protagonist is completely different from Leskov's. He emphasizes that Shostakovich fundamentally rebuilds the basic conception, looking differently at the main roles: 'The victims become executioners; the murderess – a victim.'[23] Katerina is, according to Shostakovich, 'talented', 'affectionate and sensuous', and perhaps (as Volkov reports) also a 'genius in love'. Her most striking feature, however, is that she 'no longer knows anything of good and evil'. Her story, which can be seen as a constant struggle for an independent definition of her own fate (a point that Shostakovich emphasized when writing about the opera), is existential in the Nietzschean sense. She follows her instincts in complete accordance with the philosopher's analysis of the Feminine. However, it is Shostakovich's interpretation of Nietzsche (or perhaps Sollertinsky's, relayed to him) that combines Nietzsche's perception of the Feminine and his ideas about morality. Nietzsche's starting point in his *Genealogy of Morals* (1887) is the classification of humanity into 'slaves' and 'masters', which coincides with their division into 'peasant types' and 'nobles'.[24] Creative minds belong to superior human beings, those that he would consider 'free spirits', who have the courage to celebrate the difficulty and suffering of human life: 'Independence is for the very few; it is a privilege of the strong.'[25] This inherent quality (which could coincide with the term 'talent', used by Volkov's Shostakovich in reference to Katerina) grants 'free spirits' the right to create their own moral standards.[26]

Nietzsche's writings about Carmen, love and Wagner (1889) might have influenced Shostakovich's reported vision of Katerina as a 'genius in love'. It is easy to imagine Sollertinsky and Shostakovich in the early 1930s, both men in their late twenties at the beginning of a conjugal life, fascinated by the following paragraph that combines references to music, love, genius, women and Jews, and relating all these to morality. In this context 'genius' is connected to the concepts of marriage, love, artists, and the symbolic, semi-mythical concept of 'the eternal Jew', doomed to wander but, precisely because of that, eternally free:

> What becomes of the 'eternal Jew' whom a woman adores and *enchains*? He simply ceases from being eternal; he marries, – that is to say, he concerns us no longer. – Transferred into the realm of reality, the danger for the artist

and for the genius – and these are of course the 'eternal Jews' – resides in Woman: *adoring* women are their ruin.[27]

Perceiving geniuses and artists as 'eternal Jews' – those restless souls with no real homeland – whether in a physical or, rather, in a spiritual way, who often are or feel persecuted, surely struck a chord with Sollertinsky and Shostakovich. All these subjects would have perfectly chimed with another subject that interested both friends: Mahler, the Austrian-Jewish composer. Sollertinsky's 1932 book on Mahler, which can be interpreted as an exercise in Marxist apologia, possibly intended to salvage Mahler's music from the fate of other 'bourgeois' composers in Soviet culture, can also be read as an analysis of musical existentialism. Seen as a composer for whom music was inseparable from social and ethical issues, Mahler and his music provided an inspirational model for both Sollertinsky and Shostakovich, who started his 'Mahlerian' Fourth Symphony in the same year. Mahler is quoted in Sollertinsky's book as saying, for example, that the 'Funeral March' in his First Symphony expresses 'heartbreaking, tragic irony', and the Mahlerian grotesque is described as 'the unmasking of Evil on Earth'.[28] Whether Sollertinsky indeed regarded this 'Evil on earth' as represented by 'American Imperialism', or whether his writing so was just a matter of showing a 'correct attitude' according to Soviet standards, is a matter of interpretation.[29] At any rate Sollertinsky later quotes the composer's 'existentialist' letter to Bruno Walter: 'I had already realized that I have to die. – But without trying to explain or describe to you something for which there are perhaps no words at all, I'll just tell you that at a blow I have simply lost all the clarity and quietude I ever achieved and that I stood *vis-à-vis de rien*, and now at the end of life am again a beginner who must find his feet.'[30] Significantly, Sollertinsky notes the influence of Nietzsche and Dostoyevsky on Mahler, clearly regarding the German philosopher, the Russian writer and the Jewish musician as morally akin.[31]

Shostakovich's well-documented fascination with Dostoyevsky, then, was not just based on his avid reading, but most likely also enhanced by his conversations with Sollertinsky, with reference to Dostoyevsky's existentialist writing and, probably, to Nietzsche's ideas as well, since Sollertinsky certainly uses Nietzschean terminology when describing the 'ecstatic dithyrambs' in Mahler's First Symphony.[32]

Existentialism deals with Man's frustrated expectation of congruity in an incongruous universe. Existential *angst*, then, presents a non-ironic message about an ironic subject: the incomprehensibility of the Human Condition. Shostakovich's 'Death' from his *Suite on Verses of Michelangelo Buonarroti*, op. 145 is an example of such a message. Existential *angst* is a condition of extreme emotional strain. Existential irony, on the other hand, is a position that requires some degree of emotional detachment. In other words, Existential irony can *look at* and *comment on* existential *angst*. As such, it can laugh at our deepest source of horror, becoming an act of moral courage, a statement of victory and a reach for immortality. Equally, by openly aspiring towards a superior detached position it exposes its own vulnerability. Existential irony is characterized not only by its structure but also by its specific content (having thus some affinity with the grotesque). In terms of content, any subject related to human existence can operate in an ironic message either as *stimulus* or as *terminus*.[33] An ironic message about existential *angst* creates a special situation, which is complex even in its simplest manifestation, where the concept of existential irony functions as *content* within an ironic *structure*.[34] In such a message irony would appear twice, once within one of its layers and once as the principle dictating the structural inter-layer action. Existential irony as content in music uses correlations of incongruous mental and emotional states, positioning them within one layer (or both) in a structure of incongruity. Existential irony contemplates the irresolvable contradictory aspects of human existence, their reflection in our moral values and their expression through ironic messages. Like many other semantic units, existential irony can have musical correlatives through superimpositions of incongruous 'marked' units.[35] Therefore I propose to interpret some of Shostakovich's works, which ostensibly lack irony, as instances of musical existential irony.

Irony as *stimulus*: satirical existential irony

Existential *angst* itself, or people who experience it, could be subjects for satirical irony as much as people who are unaware of it. 'The Cockroach' from Shostakovich's *Four Verses of Captain Lebyadkin*, op. 146 presents this type of satirical irony (see Ex. 15.1). The main protagonist of this poem is the cockroach flushed down the sink by Nikifor, who, in a mocking parody of Schopenhauer, 'represents Nature'. Perishing at a stroke with the flies that socially rejected him, the cockroach does not complain. The text is an existential ironic allegory about human petty fights that take no notice of our basic helplessness, and about the mute acceptance of the 'human condition'. The banality of this statement is satirically reinforced by the simplistic rhythmic and melodic patterns and the clumsiness of the bass. This simple message, however, includes a subtler self-irony. The bass is built of the same intonation that opens 'Death' in the Michelangelo Suite: two superimposed fourths completing a minor seventh. Shostakovich often uses melodic fourths as a musical correlative

Example 15.1 'The Cockroach', from *Four Verses of Captain Lebyadkin*, op. 146, bars 1–13.
'A cockroach lived upon the earth, a cockroach from childhood, and then it fell into a glass, full of fly-killer.'

of Death. Here the feeling of infinite openness created by superimposing melodic fourths (as in 'Death' of op. 145 or in the Violin Sonata, op. 134) is mocked by the change of their order, creating a grotesquely finite cadence of a false IV–V–I. The rhythmic pattern of two quavers and two crotchets is also a characteristic correlative of dysphoric meanings in the composer's works (as again in the Violin Sonata and the Viola Sonata, op. 147); the three falling minor seconds are an exaggeration of the worn-out 'sigh motif'; furthermore, the first two bars of the vocal line can be heard as a reminder of the grotesque 'funeral march' from Mahler's First Symphony.

Here, however, the theme is composed of small, closed units that are not developed as in Mahler's work, but repeated and then *incongruously interrupted*, only to resume at a higher pitch, *fortissimo*, enhancing the grotesque impression of a pompously inflated, ridiculously pathetic exhibition of self-pity.

The existential irony in 'The Cockroach' is dependent on the text rather than the music. On the other hand, purely musical satirical existential irony may be found in some of Shostakovich's instrumental works. A favourite device for satirical irony is the exaggeration of one or more qualities of the satirized subject. When the chosen subject for satire is *anxiety*, by itself an extreme emotion, identifying *exaggerated anxiety* is difficult; a disparaging, satirical comment on existential *angst* that chooses exaggeration as its main device could easily be interpreted as a non-ironic statement. Although it is obviously impossible to reach a foolproof, absolute interpretation, valuable pointers may be gained by resorting to the context of the composer's style and cultural background, and by looking for affinities between these and other instrumental works.

While Western existentialism is very much occupied with ontological enquiries about existence, Russian existentialism is focused on its moral and ethical aspects. Therefore, while Sartre, for example, asks questions about the intrinsic value of human existence per se, Dostoyevsky's existential query asks what is a *proper* human existence. Dostoyevsky occupies a major role in Shostakovich's cultural background, both socially and personally. The influence of Dostoyevsky's techniques on Shostakovich is discussed and analysed at length elsewhere,[36] but his impact on the composer goes far beyond technical matters. In a letter concerning Yevtushenko, Shostakovich mentions Dostoyevsky (and Mahler) in a list of authors whose message he considered related to ethics and morality. In that letter he also comments: 'To remind us of it [i.e. morality and ethics] over and over again is the sacred obligation of man.'[37]

Ironic reflection on existential *angst* dominates Dostoyevsky's *Notes from Underground*. Yet its exaggerated mix of arrogance and self-loathing are the only sign of irony in this eccentric monologue, considered 'the best overture to Existentialism ever written'.[38] In the introduction to her translation of this work, Jessie Coulson perceptively remarks: 'The hero, or rather anti-hero, as Dostoyevsky calls him, is a man turned in upon himself, a man of heightened awareness and self-consciousness.'[39] A master of self-irony, this anti-hero presents himself by inverse irony: 'I am a sick man … I am an angry man. I am an unattractive man,'[40] and, almost immediately following that: 'What can a decent, respectable man talk about with the greatest pleasure? Answer: himself. Well, so I too will talk about myself.'[41]

The genuine suffering of Dostoyevsky's underground anti-hero is obvious not so much for itself as for the character's awareness of its pointlessness. His double distress is expressed once directly and then in loathing directed towards his own misery. In the following paragraph Dostoyevsky examines toothache as an instance of existential powerlessness:

> People don't suffer *that* in silence, of course, they groan … the groans are an expression, to begin with, of all the pointlessness, which the conscious mind finds so humiliating, of your pain; it's a law of nature, for which, of course, you feel the utmost contempt, but from which you nevertheless suffer, while she doesn't. They express your awareness of the fact that nobody has inflicted the pain on you and yet you feel it, your awareness that … you are utterly at the mercy of your teeth; that if something will it, they will stop aching, and if it doesn't, they will go on aching for another three months; and finally, that even if you still object and try to protest, your only satisfaction will be lashing your own back or running your head even more painfully against your stone wall, and that's absolutely all![42]

The expression of an artist's existential *angst* is a complicated subject, particularly when his medium is music. For example, most interpretations tend to see Shostakovich's Eighth Quartet, for better and for worse, as non-ironic.[43] Taken literally, the Quartet indeed portrays a bleak reality: *all* the musical elements are marked by an unusual accumulation of dysphoric musical elements such as inflected modes and extreme tempi (very fast and very slow) and extreme dynamics (*pianissimo* or *fortissimo*). To these, the extreme dysphoric character of the DSCH motif is added, achieving an allegedly embarrassing instance of an artist's self-pity and lack of emotional restraint. Indeed, it does seem that everything in the work points to such an interpretation, except for the work's context: Shostakovich's other works, written in this period, show nothing of this kind. It is thus hard to believe that the composer of the First Cello Concerto and the Seventh String Quartet, with their inner structural balance and their sophisticated manipulation of ambiguous octatonic modes, and the poignant *Satires* song cycle on texts of Sasha Chorny, all written around the same time, had suddenly become insensitive to exaggerated sentimentality. Given this context and the fact that exaggeration is one of the most obvious markers of irony,[44] I would like to argue that the awkward accumulation of dysphoric devices in the Eighth Quartet is a pointer to irony, in this case self-irony. Positioning oneself within a dense web of musical correlatives of suffering is as self-disparaging as the *Underground* anti-hero's description of toothache. Suffering is, indeed, the basic signifying unit of the Quartet, but its exaggeration supplies a commentary on this very unit, in which Shostakovich satirizes his own compulsion to share his suffering. The exaggerated use of dysphoric devices negates itself: the Eighth Quartet, precisely because of its 'over-explicitness', is not Shostakovich's confession, but his ironic commentary about his own existential powerlessness.

His despair touches the listener not through its explicitness, but because of the tangible, bewildered need to express what tragedy made unspeakable. Like that of Dostoyevsky's Underground Man, Shostakovich's expression of suffering is genuine. However, and still echoing Dostoyevsky's novel, he also expresses self-pity *and* self-disparagement for his self-pity. Sarcastic self-disparagement is a trait common to the following two statements:

> I would have seized every opportunity of first dropping a tear into my glass and then draining it in honour of the best and highest; I would have sought out the best and highest in the nastiest, most unmistakable filth. I should have been as tearful as a wet sponge.[45]

> It is a *pseudo-tragic* quartet, so much so that while I was composing it I shed the same amount of tears as I would have had to pee after half-a dozen beers.[46]

Genuine suffering is unmistakably expressed through the accumulation of dysphoric musical elements in the work. Self-pity and self-disparagement are pointed at by the *exaggerated* amount and quality of these very same musical elements. Still, there is a significant difference between self-deprecation and self-denigration, and Shostakovich's letter is devoid of Dostoyevsky's undertone of cruel hopelessness. In this respect, Shostakovich's self-irony reminds one of Jewish humour, which, while characterized by laughter at one's own tragedy, is also markedly devoid of cruelty.[47]

Irony as *terminus*: non-satirical existential irony

Looking for existential answers in Judaism may be corroborated with reference to Shostakovich's discussions with Sollertinsky about Mahler. Both friends were aware of Mahler's Jewish origins,[48] and his suffering from anti-Semitism is mentioned in both Sollertinsky's article and his book (see notes 33 and 36). The cultural signification of the complex unit that grouped Dostoyevsky, Mahler, irony, existentialism and Jewishness together was, then, a part of Shostakovich's cultural background from as early as 1932, as was, probably, the complex unit that grouped Nietzsche's ideas about morality, courage, genius, artists, and the 'eternal Jew' as an amalgam of doom and freedom. I will argue that Shostakovich accepted, reinforced and expressed these two complex units by using, in his music, existential irony that is marked by Jewish ethos.

Shostakovich's fascination with the Jewish ethos, people and music is well documented, as are his social and professional association with Jewish musicians, writers and artists and his emotional involvement with at least three Jewish women[49] (one of these women, Elmira Nazirova, was not strictly speaking Jewish, but her Jewish relations could nevertheless make her 'Jewish' in the eyes of the composer).[50] His friendship with the actor and director of the Moscow State Yiddish Theatre, Solomon Mikhoels, which started probably in 1943,[51] is most significant, since by the end of that year Shostakovich had started his Second Piano Trio, where he used Jewish musical idioms for the first time.

Solomon Mikhoels had been active in the Russian Yiddish Theatre since 1920 and became its director in 1928. In 1942 he was appointed the head of the Jewish Anti-Fascist Committee that raised funds among world Jewry to support Soviet Russia's effort in the Second World War. After the war he tried to direct the Committee's activities toward the enhancement of Jewish culture in the Soviet Union. In 1948 he was murdered by agents of the regime that he admired and aspired to be part of – a cruel irony that could not escape Shostakovich, who by then was a close friend of the Mikhoels family. Mikhoels's most famous roles were the title roles in Shakespeare's *King Lear* and Sholem Aleichem's *Tevye the Milkman* (better known in its later musical and film adaptations as *Fiddler on the Roof*). Shostakovich loved *King Lear* and in 1941 wrote incidental music to one of its stage productions. It is likely that, in meeting Mikhoels, he would have been interested in the actor's interpretation of the Shakespearian hero, just as it is hard to think that Mikhoels, who was passionate about Jewish culture, would miss pointing out the similarities between the two figures he knew so well. The dispossessed Shakespearian monarch and Sholem Aleichem's down-to-earth folk philosopher are both deeply moving characters who use irony in their struggle with existential questions, and both are characterized by more than a tinge of the grotesque. Shostakovich's insatiable reading habits, his sympathy for Jewish people and the ethical, moral and perhaps existential issues that both composer and actor were interested in would most likely have led Shostakovich to Sholem Aleichem's works.

There are several traits of Tevye that Shostakovich might have found relevant to the questions that bothered him.[52] Like Dostoyevsky's Underground anti-hero, Tevye spends his time talking about himself and to himself, mulling over human life, the concepts of right and wrong, and God's justice. While the Jewish God is 'full of mercy', his main trait, the one that can absolutely be relied on, is justice. The irony of this basic premise is intensified in view of the Jewish fate in general and during the 1930s and 1940s in particular. Tevye expresses this poignantly hurtful irony by addressing the 'compassionate and merciful God' after each misfortune he has to endure, moving from distress to tragedy. However, and in spite of his failed existential query for justice, there is no trace of Russian nihilism in the Jewish milkman's attitude: weighed down by fatal blows, Tevye (whose name means 'the goodness of God'), uses the Jewish ethos to transfigure his suffering into a special kind of existential philosophy: Jewish irony.

When looking at Shostakovich's use of 'Jewish' musical idioms, we must differentiate between his Philo-Semitic interest in Jewish people, culture and thought, and his conscious use of Jewish musical idioms to express general ideas that run beyond any particular ethnic affiliation. Elsewhere I have argued that the composer used these idioms as a source for intrinsically contradictory musical units, thus creating musical correlatives of human existence.[53] Here I will be more specific, suggesting that he used the topic of 'Jewish dance' as a musical correlation with Jewish irony: the ability to dance through tragedy.

Existential irony in the Jewish ethos: musical correlatives

Dancing can employ its euphoric potential as an act of defiance. While in recreational situations it can defy gravitation, in the bleak circumstances of personal tragedy it becomes a moral act that defies, with its constant motion, the boundaries of life, thus becoming an act of existential moral courage. The idea of defying death is not new in Shostakovich's output. In his 'MacPherson's Farewell' (to a text of Robert Burns, from the *Six Romances on Texts of Raleigh, Burns and Shakespeare*, op. 62) he used a quick, duple-metre prancing march to portray MacPherson's mocking of his executioners. Years later he used the same passage in his Thirteenth Symphony to portray an abstract protagonist, Humour, in similar circumstances. In both cases the correlation of the dance-march with courage is direct, and it is mainly the text that transmits the incongruity between the cheerful tune and the macabre subject matter.

There is no such correlation in the finale of the Second Piano Trio, op. 67, nor in the 'Song of Poverty' of *From Jewish Folk Poetry*, op. 79 (1948), composed after the murder of Solomon Mikhoels in the Stalinist post-war purges. In both pieces Shostakovich combines euphoric duple-metre dance idioms with dysphoric inflected modes. Thus, while the topic 'dance' still correlates with 'courage', the inflected modes correlate with *a state of being*. In this respect it is important to note the difference between the assertive, arrow-like directionality of the 'MacPherson theme' with its regular, patterned accompaniment (see Ex. 15.2), and the repetitious, insistent circling of the Trio's finale, in a slightly limping, distorted mumble, but nevertheless – in constant rhythmic motion (see Ex. 15.3).

Example 15.2 'MacPherson's Farewell', from *Six Romances on Texts of Raleigh, Burns and Shakespeare*, op. 62 bars 10–18.'Thus cheerfully, recklessly, he went to the gallows. MacPherson set out for his last hour, for his last dance.'[in the original: 'Sae rantin'ly, sae wantonly, sae dauntin'ly played he / He played a tune and he danced it roon, below the gallows tree']

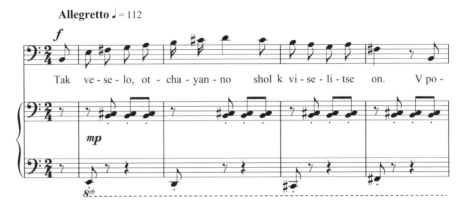

Example 15.3 Finale from Second Piano Trio, op. 67, bars 5–12

While ostensibly it makes sense that *From Jewish Folk Poetry* should express Shostakovich's sympathy for the Jewish people,[54] its deeper meaning may reside in the composer's interest in musical elements that for him correlated with Jewishness *as an attitude*, and in the analogy between the *Jewish ethos* and these musical elements. The rhythmic elements in 'Song of Poverty' correlate with dance, but its mode, register and timbre correlate with disorientation and estrangement. The starting motif repeats and then descends on an octatonic mode, accompanied by a rhythmic dance pattern on an inflected subdominant (see Ex. 15.4). The symmetrical alternation of whole-tone and semitone steps in the octatonic mode does not allow the gravitational hierarchy that a diatonic one would provide. The accompaniment, located in the treble register, lacks the rich overtones of a real bass, and its hovering on the subdominant, moreover an inflected one, builds the whole structure on a shaky environment. Starting from bar 5, the melodic inventory of notes creates a G sharp minor mode without a seventh degree, thus depriving it of any leading-note tensions. The augmented second between the minor third degree and the raised fourth is 'East-European' rather than specifically Jewish (in the latter case the augmented second interval tends to appear between a lowered second degree and a major third). This is significant since Shostakovich clearly prefers the less directional force of the former interval, thus emphasizing the semiotic role of this augmented second: existential disorientation rather than an ethnic pointer.

Shostakovich is not looking for Jewish folklore, it would seem, but for *Jewish ethos*, the Jewish mode of awareness of existence, the inescapable human responsibility to expect justice in a hopelessly unjust world. The incongruity between these two correlations is analogous to the textual one. Suffering, starvation and the death of innocents, condoned by the God of justice, position us in an alienated, awkward, disorienting reality, to which the Jewish ethos responds with incongruent, ironic euphoria.

In the 'Jewish theme' of the Piano Trio's finale (at 66), where the disorientation is portrayed by a series of obsessive repetitions mixing escapism, elation and insanity, passion becomes possession.[55] This melody is the only one of Shostakovich's 'Jewish dance tunes' that has a clear tonal centre. It erupts in the very high register of the piano with a stamping cello part, playing a full four-string C minor chord on each beat. The off-beat chords in the violin add grotesque awkwardness to the dance accompaniment figure. Given the former unclear tonality, this accompaniment could be considered to offer a clear tonal respite, correlating with confidence. However, the effort needed to play four-note pizzicato chords and the obsessive character of this accompaniment figure correlate, in fact, with an ironic 'too much confidence'. When the theme is quoted in the

Example 15.4 'Song of Poverty', *From Jewish Folk Poetry*, op. 79. bars 1–13, 'The roof is sleeping soundly up in the attic under the thatch. In the cradle the child is asleep, without swaddling clothes, stark naked.'

Eighth Quartet, it explodes in the screaming violins after an uncontrollable spiralling (at [20]). The accompaniment figure changes: the chords of the cello are broken into dizzying triplets, played in parallel with the viola, creating the impression of a cataclysmic chaos over which the two violins dance. To regard this thematic reincarnation merely as a 'self-identification with an oppressed community'[56] is, therefore, unconvincing. Jewish euphoric dance is not just a manifestation of courage: in East-European Hassidism (that for Shostakovich was the signifier of Judaism) dance is an act of absolute devotion that is nevertheless acutely aware of its ironic circumstances. The courage in this dance, then, is not an act of defiance but of awareness: it is a musical correlation of existential Jewish ethos. Far from being sarcastic or nihilistic, Jewish ethos is portrayed here as overcoming existential *angst*, by surviving both God's love and His justice.

Notes

Introduction

1. Christopher Norris (ed.), *Shostakovich: The Man and his Music*, London, Lawrence & Wishart, 1982.

2. Robert Stradling, 'Shostakovich and the Soviet System, 1925–1975', in Norris (ed.), *Shostakovich*, p. 207.

3. For a concise summary of major issues involved in these debates, see Pauline Fairclough, 'Facts, Fantasies and Fictions', *Music and Letters*, 86 (2005), 452–60.

4. Laurel Fay, *Shostakovich: A Life*, New York, Oxford University Press, 2000.

5. See Richard Taruskin's and Malcolm Hamrick Brown's descriptions of their own student attitudes in Malcolm Hamrick Brown (ed.), *A Shostakovich Casebook*, Bloomington, Indiana University Press, 2004, pp. 360–83 and 325–45 respectively. See also Gerard McBurney's comments on Pierre Boulez's view of Shostakovich as a 'third pressing of Mahler', in the same volume, p. 288.

6. The chief editor of the new Shostakovich Edition (DSCH Publishing, Moscow) is Manashir Yakubov; the main source for Shostakovich's manuscripts is the Shostakovich Family Archive in Moscow. Any researcher wishing to study original manuscripts requires the personal permission of the composer's widow, Irina Antonovna Shostakovich.

7. Recent publications include *Dmitriy Shostakovich. Issledovaniya i materialï*, vol. 1 [Dmitry Shostakovich. Research and materials], Moscow, DSCH, 2005, and Marina Rakhmanova (ed.), *Shostakovich – Urtext*, Moscow, Deka, for the Glinka State Central Museum of Musical Culture, 2006.

8. *The Golden Age, The Bolt* and *The Limpid Stream*, published in piano score by DSCH Publishers, Moscow, in 1995, 1996 and 1997 respectively, and in slightly cut CD recordings for Chandos prepared by Gennady Rozhdestvensky in 1994, 1995 and 1996.

9. For a recent argument in favour of their place in the twenty-first-century concert hall, see Vladimir Orlov, 'Prokofiev and the Myth of Revolution: The Cantata for the Twentieth Anniversary of the October Revolution', *Three Oranges*, 13 (May 2007), 14–21.

1 Personal integrity and public service: the voice of the symphonist

1. Victor Terras, *A History of Russian Literature*, New Haven, Yale University Press, 1991, p. 519.

2. *Izvestiya*, 3 April 1935, 4.

3. See David Haas, *Leningrad's Modernists: Studies in Composition and Musical Thought, 1917–1932*, New York, Peter Lang, 1998, pp. 167–8.

4. Quoted in Haas, *Leningrad's Modernists*, p. 185.

5. The term *popevka* is here borrowed from Asafyev. See Boris Asafyev, *A Book about Stravinsky*, trans. R. F. French, Ann Arbor, UMI Research Press, 1982, pp. 51 and 62.

6. Lev Grigoryev and Yakov Platek (eds.), *Dmitry Shostakovich – About Himself and His Times*, trans. Angus and Neilian Roxburgh, Moscow, Progress Publishers, 1981, p. 28.

7. See Eric Roseberry, *Ideology, Style, Content and Thematic Process in the Symphonies, Cello Concertos and String Quartets of Shostakovich*, New York and London, Garland Publishing, 1989, p. 515. In his study of Mahler's symphonies, the Soviet musicologist Ivan Sollertinsky made pointed reference to Richard Strauss's comment on the image of 'columns of marching workers' after the first performance of Mahler's Third Symphony. See Sollertinsky, *Gustav Maler*, Leningrad, Gosudarstvennoye muzïkal'noye izdatel'stvo, 1932, p. 29.

8. See Sabinina's scansion in seven sections: miniature polka; scherzo; waltz; march-scherzo; waltz; galop; waltz, in Marina Sabinina, *Shostakovich – Simfonist: Dramaturgiya, estetika, stil'* [Shostakovich – symphonist: dramaturgy, aesthetics, style], Moscow, Muzïka, 1976, pp. 112–13; and Fairclough's divisions in Pauline Fairclough, *A Soviet Credo: Shostakovich's Fourth Symphony*, Aldershot, Ashgate, 2006, p. 198.

9. As is suggested by David Fanning in 'Shostakovich: "The Present-Day Master of the C major Key"', *Acta Musicologica*, 73 (2001), 127.

10. Both David Rabinovich (*Dmitry Shostakovich – Composer*, trans. George Hanna, London, Lawrence & Wishart, 1959, p. 44) and Genrikh Orlov (*Simfonii Shostakovicha*, Leningrad, Muzgiz, 1961, p. 60) refer to a 'difficult' stage in the composer's creative evolution, while Ivan Martïnov

(*Dmitri Shostakovich: The Man and his Work*, trans. T. Guralsky, New York, Philosophical Library, 1947 and New York, Greenwood Press, 1969, p. 59) relegates the work to a non-committal footnote.

11. See Fairclough, *A Soviet Credo*, p. xiv.

12. See Taruskin, 'Shostakovich and the Inhuman', in Taruskin, *Defining Russia Musically*, Princeton, Princeton University Press, 1997, pp. 520–31 where he argues that the *panikhida* – the Russian Orthodox obsequies – permeates the *melos* of this movement.

13. The enduring story of Shostakovich's subtitle to this movement – 'A Soviet artist's reply to just criticism' – is rejected by Fay. See Laurel E. Fay, *Shostakovich: A Life*, New York, Oxford University Press, 2000, pp. 102–3.

14. Taruskin, 'Shostakovich and the Inhuman', *Defining Russia Musically*, p. 518.

15. Shostakovich, 'Dumï o proydyonnom puti' [Thoughts about the path I have taken], *Sovetskaya muzïka* 9 (1956), 14.

16. See Martïnov, *Dmitri Shostakovich*, p. 80; and Hugh Ottaway, *Shostakovich Symphonies*, London, BBC Publications, 1978, p. 33.

17. See Fanning, '"The Present-Day Master of the C Major Key"', 101–40.

18. Arved Ashby, 'Britten as Symphonist', in Mervyn Cooke (ed.), *The Cambridge Companion to Benjamin Britten*, Cambridge, Cambridge University Press, 1999, p. 232.

19. For a full documentary survey of the early reception of the symphony in 1940s America see Christopher Gibbs, '"The Phenomenon of the Seventh"', in Laurel Fay (ed.), *Shostakovich and his World*, Princeton, Princeton University Press, 2004, pp. 59–113.

20. David Haas draws an interesting parallel here with the short oboe cadenza in the first movement of Beethoven's Fifth Symphony. See Haas, 'C Minor Symphony Against the Grain', in Rosamund Bartlett (ed.), *Shostakovich in Context*, Oxford, Oxford University Press, 2000, p. 130.

21. See Sabinina, *Shostakovich – Simfonist*, p. 277.

22. According to the pianist Tatyana Nikolayeva, however, the symphony was finished in 1951. See Elizabeth Wilson, *Shostakovich: A Life Remembered*, new edn, London, Faber, 2006, p. 301. This contradicts Shostakovich's statement in *Sovetskaya muzïka* 1954: 'I worked on the Tenth Symphony last summer and finished it in the autumn.' Cited in David Fanning, *The Breath of the Symphonist*, London, Royal Musical Association, 1988, p. 77.

23. See Nelly Kravetz, 'A New Insight into the Tenth Symphony of Shostakovich', in Bartlett, *Shostakovich in Context*, p. 163.

24. See Fay, *Shostakovich*, p. 257.

25. See Irina Nikolskaya, 'Shostakovich Remembered: Interviews with his Soviet Colleagues', in Malcolm Hamrick Brown (ed.), *A Shostakovich Casebook*, Bloomington, Indiana University Press, 2004, p. 177.

26. See Lev Lebedinsky's account of the Twelfth's composition in Wilson, *Shostakovich*, pp. 387–9.

27. For an account of its treatment by the authorities see Fay, *Shostakovich*, pp. 235–7.

28. See Joachim Braun, 'The Double Meaning of Jewish Elements in Dmitri Shostakovich's Music', *Musical Quarterly*, 71 (1985), 68–80.

29. See letter to Isaak Glikman, 1 February 1969 in Glikman, *Story of a Friendship: The Letters of Dmitry Shostakovich to Isaak Glikman*, trans. Anthony Phillips, London, Faber, 2001, p. 158: 'I am now writing an oratorio for soprano, bass and chamber orchestra' and later (17 February 1969): 'it cannot really be called an oratorio since an oratorio is supposed to have a chorus, and mine doesn't' (pp. 159–60).

30. Anthony Quinton, 'Existentialism', *Fontana Dictionary of Modern Thought*, London, Fontana, 1977, p. 220.

31. For a discussion of the creative relationship between the two composers see Lyudmila Kovnatskaya, 'Shostakovich and Britten: Some Parallels', in Bartlett, *Shostakovich in Context*, pp. 175–89; and Eric Roseberry, 'A Debt Repaid? Some Observations on Shostakovich and his Late-Period Recognition of Britten', in Fanning, *Shostakovich Studies*, pp. 229–53.

32. Grigoryev and Platek, *Dmitry Shostakovich*, p. 291.

33. Shostakovich suggested the metaphor of a toy store for his first movement. See Fay, *Shostakovich*, p. 272.

34. Maynard Solomon, *Beethoven*, London, Cassell, 1978, p. 325.

2 The string quartets: in dialogue with form and tradition

1. For biographical views, see Richard Taruskin, *Defining Russia Musically*, Princeton, Princeton University Press, 1997, pp. 491, 494–5; and Manashir Yakubov, *Proizvedeniya dlya strunnogo kvarteta* [Works for string quartet], programme notes for the Shostakovich International Competition, St Petersburg, 1991, unpaginated (copy held at the Centre Chostakovitch, Paris).

2. For more detail on matters of reception raised in this article, see Judith Kuhn,

'Shostakovich in Dialogue: Form and Imagery in the First Six String Quartets', PhD thesis, University of Manchester (2005).
3. See James Hepokoski, 'Back and Forth from Egmont: Beethoven, Mozart and the Nonresolving Recapitulation', *19th-Century Music*, 25 (Fall/spring 2001–2), 127–54.
4. Theodor Adorno, *Mahler: A Musical Physiognomy*, trans. Edward Jephcott, Chicago, University of Chicago Press, 1992, p. 64.
5. Quoted in M.D., 'Novïye rabotï kompozitora D. Shostakovicha' [New works by the composer D. Shostakovich], *Izvestiya*, 29 September 1938, p. 4 (M. D. was almost certainly Shostakovich's friend, the musicologist Mikhail Druskin); see also Shostakovich, '*O podlinnoy i mnimoy programmnosti*' [On genuine and false programmaticism], *Sovetskaya muzïka* 5 (1951), 76–8.
6. Quoted in M.D., 'Novïye rabotï, p. 4.
7. Shostakovich, letter to Ivan Sollertinsky of 27 July 1938, as translated in Laurel Fay, *Shostakovich: A Life*, New York, Oxford University Press, 2000, p. 112.
8. On 'sixthiness' in nineteenth-century Russian music, see Taruskin, *Defining Russia Musically*, pp. 55–9; Viktor Bobrovskiy, *Kamernïye instrumental'nïye ansambli D. Shostakovicha: Issledovaniye* [Chamber-instrumental ensemble works of D. Shostakovich: studies], Moscow, Sovetskiy kompozitor, 1961, p. 162, n. 1.
9. Leonid Entelis, *Kvartet Dmitriya Shostakovicha* [Dmitry Shostakovich's Quartet], Leningrad, Leningradskaya Filarmoniya, 1939, p. 7.
10. Valentin Berlinsky, interview with the author (Moscow, 25 March 2003); see also Rostislav Dubinsky, *Stormy Applause: Making Music in a Worker's State*, New York, Hill & Wang, 1989, p. 269.
11. The dedication appears on the manuscript but was omitted from published versions until its restoration in the most recent edition (Moscow, DSCH, 2001).
12. See David Fanning, *Shostakovich: String Quartet no. 8*, Aldershot, Ashgate, 2004, pp. 40–1; and Sarah Reichardt, *Composing the Modern Subject: Four String Quartets by Dmitri Shostakovich*, Aldershot, Ashgate, forthcoming.
13. 'S Dmitriyem Mikhaylovichem Tsïganovïm', in Sof'ya Khentova, *V mire Shostakovicha* [In Shostakovich's world], Moscow, Kompozitor, 1996, p. 207; Berlinsky, recorded interview. The composer's fiftieth birthday occurred on 9 September 1956.
14. See Abram Yusfin, *Shestoy Kvartet D. Shostakovicha* [Shostakovich's Sixth Quartet], Moscow, Moskovskaya Filarmoniya, 1960, p. 4.

15. Interview with Tsïganov in Khentova, *V mire Shostakovicha*, pp. 207–8.
16. Letter of 19 July 1960, in Isaak Glikman (ed.), *Story of a Friendship: The Letters of Dmitry Shostakovich to Isaak Glikman*, trans. Anthony Phillips, London, Faber, 2001, pp. 90–3.
17. See Dubinsky, *Stormy Applause*, pp. 283–4; Khentova, *V mire Shostakovicha*, p. 208; Ian MacDonald, *The New Shostakovich*, Oxford, Oxford University Press, 1991, p. 583.
18. See Fanning, *Shostakovich; String Quartet No. 8*, pp. 110-12.
19. See Olga Digonskaya and Olga Dombrovskaya, 'Unfinished Quartet', introductory editorial article accompanying *Dmitry Shostakovich, Unfinished Quartet*, Moscow, DSCH Publishers, 2005.
20. Letter of 21 July 1964 to Isaak Glikman, in Glikman, *Story of a Friendship*, p. 117.
21. Yakubov, *Proizvedeniya*.
22. See Peter Schmelz, 'Shostakovich's "Twelve-tone" Compositions', in Laurel Fay (ed.), *Shostakovich and his World*, Princeton, Princeton University Press, 2004, pp. 303–5.
23. See Schmelz, 'Andrey Volkonsky and the Beginnings of Unofficial Music in the Soviet Union', *Journal of the American Musicological Society*, 58 (Spring 2005), 143–5.
24. Viktor Bobrovskiy, '*Pobeda chelovecheskogo dukha*' [A victory of the human spirit], *Sovetskaya muzïka*, 9 (1968), 33.
25. Interview with Dmitry Tsïganov, in Khentova, *V mire Shostakovicha*, p. 211.
26. This description is from Fyodor Druzhinin, Borisovsky's successor in the Beethoven Quartet, as quoted in Elizabeth Wilson, *Shostakovich: A Life Remembered*, new edn, London, Faber, 2006, p. 499.
27. Shostakovich, letter of 16 January 1973, in Glikman, *Story of a Friendship*, p. 188.
28. *Ibid.*, p. 322.
29. The *Collected Works* edition of the Fourteenth Quartet (vol. 36, p. 227) incorrectly labels this opening theme as a quotation from the composer's opera *The Lady Macbeth of Mtsensk District*: as noted in the text, the quotation from *Lady Macbeth* in fact occurs at ⟨75⟩, in the middle of the movement.
30. See Laurel Fay, 'The Last String Quartets of Dmitri Shostakovich: A Stylistic Investigation', Ph.D. diss., Cornell University, 1978, pp. 48–50.

3 Paths to the First Symphony

1. Arnold Schoenberg, 'Gustav Mahler', in Schoenberg, *Style and Idea*, London, Faber, 1975, p. 468.
2. Specifically, Vladimir Shcherbachov no. 3 (1931), Tikhon Khrennikov no. 1 (1935),

Mikis Theodorakis no. 1 (1943–53), Einar Englund no. 3 (1971), Sambïn Gonchiksumla no. 1.

3. See Ol'ga Dansker, 'Shostakovich v dnevnikakh M.O. Shteynberga' [Shostakovich in the diaries of Maximilian Steinberg], in Lyudmila Kovnatskaya (ed.), *Shostakovich: mezhdu mgnoveniyem i vechnost'yu* [Shostakovich between the moment and eternity], St Petersburg, 'Kompozitor', 2000, p. 102.

4. Details in Manashir Yakubov, 'Dmitri Shostakovich. The First Symphony. Score', in *New Collected Works*, vol. 1, Moscow, DSCH Publishers, 2002, p. 148.

5. For some examples of possible models, see David Haas, *Leningrad's Modernists: Studies in Composition and Musical Thought, 1917–1932*, New York, Peter Lang, 1998, pp. 166–70.

6. See Dansker, 'Shostakovich v dnevnikakh M.O. Shteynberga', p. 98.

7. Dmitry Shostakovich, 'Responses of Shostakovich to a Questionnaire on the Psychology of the Creative Process', in Laurel Fay (ed.), *Shostakovich and his World*, Princeton, Princeton University Press, 2004, pp. 27–41. This supplements the 'Autobiography' Shostakovich produced for official consumption in the same year – first published in French in *La revue musicale*, 170 (1936), 432–3, and in Russian in *Sovetskaya muzïka* (1966/9), 24–5 – and the retrospective published on the occasion of his fiftieth birthday as 'Dumï o proydyonnom puti' [Thoughts about the path travelled], *Sovetskaya muzïka* (1956/9), 9–15, excerpted and translated in Lev Grigoryev and Yakov Platek (eds.), *Dmitry Shostakovich: About Himself and his Times*, Moscow, Progress Publishers, 1980, pp. 176–82.

8. For a list of those in and out of Shostakovich's favour in his later career, as recalled by his pupils, see David Fanning, 'Shostakovich and his Pupils', in Fay, *Shostakovich and his World*, pp. 279–80.

9. For a summary see Fanning, 'Shostakovich, Dmitry', in Stanley Sadie and John Tyrrell (eds.), *The New Grove Dictionary of Music and Musicians*, London, Macmillan, 2001, vol. 23, pp. 280–2.

10. Shostakovich, 'Questionnaire', pp. 33–4.

11. See Lyudmila Mikheyeva, *Zhizn' Dmitriya Shostakovich* [The life of Dmitry Shostakovich], Moscow, Terra, 1997, pp. 20–1.

12. See Grigoryev and Platek, *Dmitry Shostakovich*, p. 178.

13. Described, with musical examples, in Alla Bogdanova, 'Sochineniya D. Shostakovicha konservatorskikh let (1919–1925)' [Shostakovich's compositions from his Conservatoire years], in *Iz istorii russkoy i sovetskoy muzïki* [From the history of Russian and Soviet music], ed. Aleksey Kandinsky, Moscow, Muzïka, 1971, pp. 69–70. The excerpts are scheduled for publication in the *New Collected Works*, vol. 55.

14. Scheduled for publication in the *New Collected Works*, vol. 109.

15. Scheduled for publication in the *New Collected Works*, vol. 146. Examples of some routine harmony, counterpoint and orchestration exercises are also retained in the Family Archives.

16. See Dansker, 'Shostakovich', p. 94, and Ol'ga Digonskaya, 'Pervïy opus Miti Shostakovicha' [Mitya Shostakovich's Opus One], in Marina Rakhmanova (ed.), *Shostakovich – Urtext*, Moscow, Deka, for the Glinka State Central Museum of Musical Culture, 2006, pp. 204.

17. Shostakovich, 'Questionnaire', p. 29.

18. *Ibid.*, p. 30.

19. For the positive side of Shostakovich's thoughts about Steinberg, see Dansker, 'Shostakovich', pp. 85–6.

20. See the extensive correspondence with Yavorsky in Irina Bobïkina (ed.), *Dmitry Shostakovich v pismakh i dokumentakh* [Dmitry Shostakovich in letters and documents], Moscow, Glinka State Central Museum of Musical Culture, 2000, pp. 9–132.

21. Shostakovich, 'Questionnaire', p. 30.

22. See Digonskaya, 'Pervïy opus', pp. 170–205.

23. See *ibid.*, pp. 178–9 (n. 19).

24. USSR Ministry of Culture Symphony Orchestra, Gennady Rozhdestvensky, Melodiya C10 19103 004 [1982], Olympia OCD 194 [1988].

25. A sixth Prelude has recently been rediscovered. See Digonskaya, 'Pervïy opus', p. 198. As a result future publications may need to revise the numbering of the Preludes as used in this paragraph.

26. See Laurel Fay, *Shostakovich: A Life*, New York, Oxford University Press, 2000, pp. 23–4.

27. Shostakovich, 'Questionnaire', p. 30. There is evidence, in addition, that his first awareness of the outlines of sonata form was thanks to a fellow student rather than any of his teachers – see Digonskaya, 'Pervïy opus', pp. 174–5.

28. See Haas, *Leningrad's Modernists*, pp. 4–26, 193.

29. See Fay, *Shostakovich*, pp. 22–3, and *Shostakovich: Symphony No. 1, New Collected Works*, vol. 16, facsimile on pp. 154–9, transcription on pp. 210–15.

30. Yakubov, 'Music Interpretation of the Drafts of Shostakovich's First Symphony', in *Shostakovich: Symphony No. 1, New Collected Works*, vol. 16, p. 169, where, however, the phrase '1923 rather than 1922' is a mistranslation for '1922 rather than 1923'. Another

(or perhaps the same) pre-First Symphony is mentioned in various sources, including Sof'ya Khentova, *Dmitry Shostakovich*, Leningrad, Sovetskiy kompozitor, 1985, vol. 1, p. 529, dated January–February 1924 and supposedly composed in memory of the recently deceased Lenin. However, for authoritative corrections to the information in both sources, see Digonskaya, 'Perviy opus', pp. 180–9.

31. For further affinities, see Haas, *Leningrad's Modernists*, pp. 166–70.

32. Presumably vol. 97 of the *New Collected Works*, whose contents are listed in the advance information as 'Songs', will also include some previously unpublished Juvenilia.

33. For Steinberg's admiration for Shostakovich's performance of these variations, see Dansker, 'Shostakovich', p. 94.

34. Shostakovich 'Questionnaire', p. 34.

35. See facsimile in *New Collected Works*, vol. 16, pp. 115–16, with editorial comments on p. 167. My transcription of the notation, in Ex. 3.3c, differs slightly from Yakubov's (*ibid.*, p. 170).

36. The wide-intervalled melos does have affinities with Skryabin's Third Symphony, however; see Haas, *Leningrad's Modernists*, p. 167.

37. Shostakovich, 'Questionnaire', p. 33.

38. *Ibid.*, p. 32.

4 Shostakovich's Second Piano Sonata: a composition recital in three styles

1. Lev Barenboym's richly informative essay on Nikolayev's pedagogy commences with a chronicle of four decades of misrepresentation. See Barenboym, 'L.V. Nikolayev: osnovopolozhnik leningradskoy pianisticheskoy shkoli' [L.V. Nikolayev: The founder of the Leningrad piano school], in Barenboym (ed.), *L.V. Nikolayev: stat'i i vospominaniya sovremennikov* [L.V. Nikolayev: Articles and reminiscences of his contemporaries], Leningrad, Sovetskiy kompozitor, 1979. Shostakovich and three other protégés had made their protest public in a letter to the editor of *Sovetskaya muzïka*, written in 1961; for commentary, see *ibid.*, p. 19.

2. Quoted in Barenboym, 'Nikolayev', pp. 46, 52.

3. *Ibid.*, p. 49.

4. *Ibid.*, p. 55.

5. Nathan Perelman, cited in: Sofya Moshevich, *Dmitri Shostakovich: Pianist*, Montreal, McGill–Queen's University Press, 2004, p. 50.

6. Erik Tawaststjerna, cited in Moshevich, *Shostakovich*, p. 107.

7. According to Moshevich, Shostakovich performed Nikolayev's Variations on Four Notes in A minor for Two Pianos, op. 14 with Isay Renzin in March 1927, and with

Sofronitsky in February 1938 (*Shostakovich*, pp. 60, 92).

8. The programmes for these recitals are listed in Moshevich, *Shostakovich*, p. 29. Her chronicling of subsequent performances attests to Shostakovich's broad repertoire during his brief career as an interpreter of other composers' music.

9. Leonid Gakkel', *Fortep'yannaya muzïka XX veka* [Piano music of the twentieth century] 2nd edn, Leningrad, Sovetskiy kompozitor, 1990, p. 263.

10. Charles Rosen, *The Classical Style*, New York, Viking, 1971; repr. Norton, 1972, p. 396.

11. Viktor Delson, cited in Gakkel', *Fortep'yannaya muzïka*, p. 263; Alexander Dmitriyevich Alekseyev, *Sovetskaya fortepiannaya muzïka*, Moscow, Muzïka, 1974, p. 179; Moshevich, *Shostakovich*, p. 104.

12. Gakkel', *Fortep'yannaya muzïka*, p. 263.

13. Shostakovich would return to the technique for the finale of his Second Quartet in A major, op. 68 (1944): after a brief introduction, the viola (again!) launches into a variation set with an unaccompanied theme.

14. Yuriy Kholopov, 'Form in Shostakovich's Instrumental Works', in David Fanning (ed.), *Shostakovich Studies*, Cambridge, Cambridge University Press, 1995, pp. 62–3.

15. Gakkel', *Fortep'yannaya muzïka*, pp. 265–6.

16. Barenboym, 'Nikolayev', 31–2. According to Barenboym, Nikolayev avoided imagery because he believed such an approach was too subjective and too confining; he made an exception only in reference to works for which the composer divulged a programmatic intent.

17. Barenboym, 'Nikolayev', 37.

5 'I took a simple little theme and developed it': Shostakovich's string concertos and sonatas

1. The relationship of the sonata to the short, undated (but clearly 1930s) *Moderato* for cello and piano, which remained unplayed and unpublished until 1986, remains unclear: it may represent a rejected fifth movement, a putative replacement for one of the present four movements, or an independent work.

2. In the original edition the tempo markings of the four movements were *Moderato*; *Moderato con moto*; *Largo*; *Allegretto*, but Shostakovich subsequently quickened the indications for movements 1, 2 and 4 to the present *Allegro non troppo*, *Allegro* and *Allegro*.

3. Previous instances of passacaglia form for the slow movement of a violin concerto are nevertheless rare. We can be confident that Shostakovich knew nothing of perhaps the most notable prior example, the Violin Concerto (1934–5) of Havergal Brian, unperformed until 1969, where the slow movement

is an elaborate passacaglia, albeit somewhat freer than Shostakovich's.

4. It is hardly necessary to cite the well-known exceptions, for instance cadenzas linking first and second movements where the first movement is less than a full sonata design (Bruch Violin Concerto no.1, Dvořák Violin Concerto). Small additional cadenzas in other movements, especially the finale, are hardly uncommon, and situating the principal cadenza in the finale became more customary in the early twentieth century (for example, the Elgar, Havergal Brian and Roberto Gerhard violin concertos).

5. In fact as the First Violin Concerto was originally composed, the violin proceeded straight from the cadenza to announce the opening theme of the finale, thus strengthening the continuity in terms of sonority and gesture. It was only at David Oistrakh's request in 1955 that Shostakovich, though retaining the *attacca*, allowed the orchestra to state the theme to give the soloist a short but much-needed respite.

6. Reported by Yevgeny Chukovsky in his description of how Rostropovich first played the Cello Concerto for Shostakovich at the composer's dacha in Komarovo; see Elizabeth Wilson, *Shostakovich: A Life Remembered*, new edn, London, Faber, 2006, p. 369.

7. Benjamin Britten's Symphony for Cello and Orchestra (1963) – also written for and dedicated to Rostropovich – is clearly composed in full knowledge and against a background of Shostakovich's Violin and Cello Concertos (the former perhaps more than the latter), as is shown by the four-movement shape, the placing of the cadenza between slow movement and finale, and the use of passacaglia form (in Britten's case, for his last movement). It could be said to take up and develop the latently 'symphonic' aspects of Shostakovich's two concertos.

8. For the passages in question, see the citations in Wilson, *Shostakovich*, pp. 538–40.

9. Three years earlier (not immediately before, as used to be stated by some authorities) Shostakovich had reorchestrated the Cello Concerto of Robert Schumann for Rostropovich. Once again the tritone relationship with the First Cello Concerto, E flat returning to Schumann's A minor, the key of the First Violin Concerto, is presumably fortuitous.

10. Wilson, *Shostakovich*, p. 444.

11. In addition, a recording exists of a run-through in Shostakovich's apartment, with the composer at the piano, dating from December 1968.

12. The materials from 1945 apparently consist of a draft and a fair copy, but the movement is described as unfinished (Derek C. Hulme, *Dmitri Shostakovich, A Catalogue, Bibliography and Discography*, 3rd edn, Lanham, Md., Scarecrow Press, 2002, p. 445). It is also stated to be in G minor, with the tempo marking *Moderato con moto*. G is indeed the tonal centre of the movement as we have it.

13. Wilson, *Shostakovich*, p. 531.

14. See Malcolm MacDonald, 'Words and Music in Late Shostakovich', in Christopher Norris (ed.), *Shostakovich: The Man and his Music*, London, Lawrence & Wishart, 1982, pp. 141–2.

15. Ivan Sokolov, 'Po napravleniyu k altovoy sonate' [Towards the Viola Sonata], *Muzïkalnaya akademiya*, 3 (2006), 42–8, with revelatory music example on pp. 46–8. Sokolov has not identified a quotation from the Eleventh Symphony between the motifs from the Tenth and Twelfth Symphonies, but it is clearly from bars 3–5 of the first movement. Sokolov's tentative identification of a motif from the Thirteenth is not from a first movement but from that work's fourth, 'Strakhi' [Fears]. It is worth remarking that the bar introducing the whole passage, immediately preceding the First Symphony citation, quotes the opening bar of the Second Violin Concerto.

6 Shostakovich and the theatre

1. 'Deklaratsiya obyazannostey kompozitora' [Declaration of a composer's duties], *Rabochiy i teatr* [The worker and the theatre], 31 (20 November 1931), 6.

2. The works he mentions are opp. 18, 19, 20, 22, 24, 25, 26, 27, 28, 30, 31 as well as the forthcoming op. 32 and two film projects that came to nothing.

3. For a fuller discussion of this episode, see Laurel Fay, *Shostakovich: A Life*, New York, Oxford University Press, 2000, pp. 63–5.

4. Katerina Clark, *Petersburg, Crucible of Cultural Revolution*, Cambridge, Mass., Harvard University Press, 1995.

5. Key steps in the evolution of Socialist Realism were the political and economic changes promulgated at the 17th Conference of the Soviet Communist Party (30 January–4 February 1932), the Central Committee's resolution of 23 April 1932 replacing freewheeling proletarian organizations in the arts with official Unions and other similarly state-controlled organizations, and the first public references to the new aesthetic doctrine in May 1932.

6. See Ol'ga Digonskaya, 'Neizvestnïye avtografy Shostakovicha v GTsMMK' ['Unknown Shostakovich manuscripts in the Glinka State Central Museum of Musical Culture'], in

Marina Rakhmanova (ed.), *Shostakovich –
Urtext*, Moscow, Deka, for the Glinka State
Central Museum of Musical Culture, 2007, p. 145.
7. These versions of Mayakovsky's jokes about
Latin nomenclature are found in Max
Hayward's English translation of the play, in
Patricia Blake (ed.), *Vladimir Mayakovsky:
'The Bedbug' and Selected Poetry*,
Bloomington, Indiana University Press, 1960.
8. *Sovetskiy kompozitor*, Moscow, 1977.
9. Quoted in Fay, *Shostakovich*, p. 51.
10. This reference seems to be to the whole
entr'acte and not just the number from the
suite with the title 'Intermezzo'.
11. Quoted in Fay, *Shostakovich*, p. 51.
12. *Ibid.*, p. 298
13. Clark, *Petersburg*, p. 268
14. *Ibid.*, p. 25
15. These photographs are found in the various Leningrad theatre journals of the time,
most obviously in *Rabochiy i teatr*.
16. See Boris Schwarz, *Music and Musical Life
in Soviet Russia, 1917–1981*, rev. edn,
Bloomington, Indiana University Press, 1983,
p. 53. Deshevov is also remembered for his
opera *Lyod i stal'* (Ice and steel, 1930).
17. This drive towards greater professionalism had begun the previous year with
the staging of an operetta by Deshevov that
was a huge success and ran to 500
performances.
18. See Elizabeth Wilson, *Shostakovich: A Life
Remembered*, new edn, London, Faber, 2006, p. 71.
19. Victor Terras (ed.), *Handbook of Russian
Literature*, New Haven, Yale University Press,
1985, p. 50.
20. See Sof'ya Khentova, *Shostakovich: Zhizn'
i tvorchestvo*, Leningrad, Sovetskiy kompozitor, 1985, vol. 1, p. 244. Marinchik joined
TRAM as an errand boy in the central post
office and some thirty-five years later wrote a
history of the origins of the organization: see
Lynn Mally, 'The Rise of the Soviet Youth
Theater TRAM', *Slavic Review* (Fall 1992), 413.
21. *Rabochiy i teatr*, 4 and 5 (1930).
22. Clark, *Petersburg*, p. 278.
23. Khentova, *Shostakovich*, vol. 1, p. 245.
24. Reproduced in Konstantin Rudnitsky,
Russian and Soviet Theatre, London, Thames
& Hudson, 1988, p. 244.
25. Khentova, *Shostakovich*, vol. 1, p. 246.
26. Clark, *Petersburg*, p. 268.
27. Fay, *Shostakovich*, p. 58.
28. This title is somewhat tricky to translate.
For the present author's performing reconstruction of the score, the author Grigory
Gerenstein suggested the evocative
Hypothetically Murdered. Declared Dead is the
usually accepted academic translation.

29. For this point and others in the following
discussion of op. 31, see Gerard McBurney,
'Declared Dead, but only Provisionally:
Shostakovich, Soviet Music-Hall and *Uslovno
ubityi* [*sic*]', in Neil Edmunds (ed.), *Soviet
Music and Society under Lenin and Stalin*,
London, Routledge Curzon, 2004, pp. 33–66.
30. Rïss was primarily known as a humourist and
children's writer, but Voyevodin had more serious
RAPP connections and had taken an energetic
part in the Collectivization campaign.
31. Edmunds, *Soviet Music*, p. 43.
32. For this and other points, see Laurel Fay,
'Mitya in the Music Hall', first presented as a
lecture at Cornell University, 23 January 1995, and
published in Russian as 'Mitya v myuzik-kholle:
eshchyo odin vzglyad na "Uslovno ubitogo"', in
Muzïkal'naya akademiya, 4 (1997), 59–62.
33. *Sovetskaya muzïka*, 9 (1986), 30, cited in
Fay, 'Mitya in the Music Hall'.
34. Despite the numeration, op. 23 was composed in the first weeks of 1929 and op. 22
begun the following autumn.
35. A portrait drawing of Shostakovich by
Akimov may be found in Khentova,
Shostakovich vol. 1, pp. 448–9.
36. See Rudnitsky, *Russian and Soviet
Theatre*, p. 294.
37. *Ibid.*, p. 270.
38. *Ibid.*, pp. 172–3.
39. See *ibid.*, p. 270.
40. See Wilson, *Shostakovich*, p. 93.
41. *Ibid.*
42. In 1931 Tolstoy and Sukhotin published a
five-act play entitled *This Shall Be* (Èto budet). The
following year Tolstoy was one of the two librett-
ists of Shostakovich's aborted opera *Orango*.
43. See Khentova, *Shostakovich*, vol. 1, p. 398.
44. Vera Ivanovna Prokhorova (b. 1914) in
conversation with the present writer (2000–2).
45. Afinogenov mistakenly transliterates this
name into Russian as 'Lyuchiya', as though it
were Italian not Spanish.
46. Radlov collaborated several times with
Prokofiev, but this was the only occasion on
which he worked with Shostakovich.
47. Khentova, *Shostakovich*, vol. 1,
pp. 435–9.
48. Fay, *Shostakovich*, pp. 79–80.
49. For more on Karmen and his Spanish
films, see Anthony Beevor, *The Battle for
Spain*, London, Weidenfeld, 2006, p. 249.
Beevor includes a photograph of Karmen at
work (pp. 254–5).
50. Research by composer-pianist Alexander
Benditsky, reported by Manashir Yabukov in
'Shostakovich's Fifth Symphony: Assessment
by the Composer and his Critics', in
Shostakovich: New Collected Works, vol. 20,

Moscow, DSCH, 2003, pp. 124–30. See also Wilson, *Shostakovich*, pp. 153–4.

51. Khentova, *Shostakovich*, vol. 1, p. 437.

52. *Ibid.*, p. 438.

53. Clark, *Petersburg*, pp. 179–82.

54. Although no original ballad source for Edgar's line has yet been identified, there are similar ballads and references in, for example, Francis James Child's *English and Scottish Ballads*, 8 vols., London, Samson Low, 1861. It is possible that the text set by Shostakovich is one of these. Samuil Marshak, who translated the Fool's Songs for this same production and could well have provided these verses too, had a wide knowledge of such literature. See Kenneth Muir (ed.), *King Lear*, Arden Edition, London, Routledge, 1972, p. 128, note to line 186.

55. To judge by the numeration given in Derek C. Hulme, *Dmitri Shostakovich, A Catalogue, Bibliography, and Discography*, 3rd edn, Lanham, Md., Scarecrow Press, 2002, pp. 202–3.

56. The translation used for the rest of the play was by the symbolist poet and composer Mikhail Kuzmin (1875–1936) and the poet Anna Radlova (1891–1949).

57. Fay, *Shostakovich*, p. 122.

58. Khentova, *Shostakovich*, vol. 1, p. 521.

59. Fay, *Shostakovich*, p. 315.

60. Meyerhold directed *The Mandate* to great acclaim and was preparing *The Suicide* for production when Erdman was arrested and the play banned. The first production of *The Suicide* in the USSR did not take place until the 1980s.

61. See the entries for Volpin and Erdman in E. D. Uvarova (ed.), *Estrada Rossii XX vek: èntsiklopediya*, Moscow, Olma-Press, 2004.

62. See the chapter on Goleyzovsky in Elizabeth Souritz, *Soviet Choreographers in the 1920s*, London, Dance Books, 1990, pp. 154–215.

63. Souritz, *Soviet Choreographers*, p. 167.

64. Khentova, *Shostakovich*, vol. 2, p. 137.

65. Felix Dzerzhinsky (1877–1926) was the founder of the Soviet secret police.

66. Khentova, *Shostakovich*, vol. 2, p. 137.

67. Hulme, *Shostakovich Catalogue*, p. 255.

7 Shostakovich as opera composer

1. Shostakovich's work in operetta falls outside the purview of the present chapter.

2. Laurel Fay, *Shostakovich: A Life*, New York, Oxford University Press, 2000, p. 9.

3. Manashir Yakubov (ed.), *Dmitriy Shostakovich*: Ledi Makbet Mtsenskogo Uyezda: *Vozrozhdeniye shedevra* [Dmitriy Shostakovich: *The Lady Macbeth of Mtsensk District*: the return of a masterpiece], Moscow, Rossiyskoye Gosudarstvennoye Teatral'noye Agentstvo, 1996, p. 115.

4. *Ibid.*, p. 116.

5. Elizabeth Wilson, *Dmitrij Šostakovič: Trascrivere la vita intera. Lettere 1923–1975* [Dmitry Shostakovich: an entire life of writing: letters 1923–1975], Milan, Saggiatore, 2006, p. 44.

6. See Vladimir Libson, *Bol'shoy teatr SSSR: istoriya sooruzheniya i rekonstruktsii zdaniya* [The Bolshoy Theatre of the USSR: history of its construction and reconstruction], Moscow, Stroyizdat, 1982, pp. 67–72.

7. Anatoliy Yufit (ed.), *Sovetskiy teatr: dokumentï i materialï. Russkiy sovetskiy teatr, 1917–21* [Soviet Theatre: documents and materials. Russian Soviet Theatre 1917–21], Leningrad, Iskusstvo, 1978, p. 87.

8. Boris Schwarz, *Music and Musical Life in Soviet Russia, 1917–1981*, Bloomington, Indiana University Press, 1983, p. 44.

9. See Laurel Fay, 'Shostakovich, LASM and Asaf'ev', in Rosamund Bartlett (ed.), *Shostakovich in Context*, Oxford, Oxford University Press, 2000, pp. 51–66.

10. See Inna Barsova, 'Ranneye tvorchestvo A. Mosolova' [Mosolov's early works], in Barsova (ed.), *A. V. Mosolov: stat'i i vospominaniya* [A. V. Mosolov: articles and memoirs], Moscow, Sovetskiy kompozitor, 1986), pp. 97–9.

11. Levon Akopyan, *Dmitriy Shostakovich: opït fenomenologii tvorchestva* [Dmitry Shostakovich: towards a phenomenology of his work], St Petersburg, Dmitriy Bulanin, for the State Arts Institute, 2004, pp. 77–8.

12. See E. V. Tretyakova, 'Opernïye spektakli S. Radlova' [S. Radlov's operatic productions], in A. L. Porfir'eva (ed.), *Muzïkal'nïy teatr: sbornik nauchnïkh trudov* [Musical theatre: a collection of scholarly articles], St Petersburg, Rossiyskiy Institut Istorii Iskusstv, 1991, p. 223.

13. See Barsova, '… Nigde luchshe ne prinyali moyego "Votstseka", chem v Leningrade' [… Nowhere has my *Wozzeck* been better received than in Leningrad], *Muzïkal'naya akademiya*, 3–4 (1998), 141–4.

14. Fay, *Shostakovich*, p. 39.

15. See E. V. Tretyakova, 'Rozhdeniye teatra' [Birth of the theatre] in L. Delyukin and V. Levtov (eds.), *Sankt-Peterburgskiy Gosudarstvennïy akademicheskiy teatr operï i baleta imeni M. P. Musorgskogo* [St Petersburg State Academic Theatre of Opera and Ballet named after M. P. Musorgsky], St Petersburg, Lik, 2001, pp. 11–35.

16. Valerian Bogdanov-Berezovskiy, *Sovetskaya opera* [Soviet opera], Moscow and

Leningrad, Izdaniye Leningradskogo otdeleniya VTO, 1940, p. 112.

17. Irina Bobïkina (ed.), *Dmitry Shostakovich v pis'makh i dokumentakh* [Dmitry Shostakovich in letters and documents], Moscow, Antikva, for the Glinka State Central Museum of Musical Culture, 2000, p. 475.

18. Fay, *Shostakovich*, p. 39.

19. Igor' Glebov [Boris Asafyev], 'Kompozitorï pospeshite' [Composers, hurry up], *Sovremennaya muzïka* [Contemporary music], 6 (1924), 146–8.

20. See Tretyakova, 'Rozhdeniye teatra', pp. 14–15, and Bogdanov-Berezovsky, *Sovetskaya opera*.

21. See reviews by A-vich and V. Valer'yanov, 'Za krasnïy Petrograd' [For red Petrograd, *Rabochiy i teatr* [Worker and theatre], 18 (1925), 14, and by N. Malkov, 'Za krasnïy Petrograd', *Zhizn' iskusstv*a [The life of art], 18 (1925), 10–11.

22. See, for example, Islamey, 'Sovetizatsiya akoperï' [The Sovietization of Ac[ademic] opera], *Zhizn' iskusstva*, 30 (1926), 17; Islamey, 'Opera i sovremennost'' [Opera and modernity], *Zhizn' iskusstva*, 19 (1927), 7–8; Malkov, 'V poiskakh sovetskoy operï' [In search of Soviet opera], *Rabochiy i teatr*, 42 (1928), 5–6; Viktor Belyayev, 'Eshchyo o sovetskoy opere' [Once again about Soviet opera], *Zhizn' iskusstva*, 15 (1929), 2; Ivan Sollertinsky, 'Problema opernogo naslediya' [The problem of the operatic heritage], *Zhizn' iskusstva*, 18 (1929), 10.

23. Sergey Myatezhnïy, '"Omolozheniye" operï i baleta. Dva cherednïkh subbotnika Modpika' [Making opera and ballet 'young'. Two Modpik subbotniks], *Zhizn' iskusstva*, 10 (1926), 8–10.

24. 'Opernïy "zakat bogov"' [Operatic 'Twilight of the gods'], *Rabochiy i teatr*, 25 (1926), 6.

25. V.B., 'Obnovleniye operï. Na doklade V.R. Rappaporta' [The renewal of opera. At V.R. Rappaport's lecture], *Rabochiy i teatr*, 37 (1926), 12.

26. Yulian Vaynkop, 'Voinstvuyushchaya reaktsiya' [Militant reaction], *Zhizn' iskusstva*, 5 (1925), 5–6.

27. Lev Lebedinskiy, 'Krizis Gos. Akad. Bol'shogo Teatra' [The crisis at the State Academic Bolshoy Theatre], *Sovetskoye iskusstvo*, 5 (1928), 38–43.

28. G. Borovka, 'Akteatrï na perelome (Iz besedï s zam. upr. Akteatrami t. Lyubinskim)' [Actheatres at crisis point (from a conversation with the Deputy Director of Ac[ademic] theatres, Comrade Lyubinskiy], *Zhizn' iskusstva*, 32 (1928), 14; Belyayev,

'Bol'shoy teatr pered perelomnïm sezonom' [The Bolshoy Theatre before the critical season], *Zhizn' iskusstva*, 36 (1928), 4–5.

29. 'Gosteatrï pod udarom!' [State theatres under attack], *Rabochiy i teatr*, 48 (1929), 2; 'Na voyne, na voyne!' [At war, at war!], *Rabochiy i teatr*, 1 (1930), 1; I. Spoluchny, 'Rekonstruktsiya iskusstva' [The reconstruction of art], *Rabochiy i teatr*, 35 (1930), 8–9; M. Yankovskiy, 'Na muzïkal'nom fronte' [On the musical front], *Rabochiy i teatr*, 8–9 (1931), 4–5.

30. Bogdanov-Berezovskiy, *Sovetskaya opera*, p. 113.

31. Levon Hakobian, *Music of the Soviet Age, 1917–1987*, Stockholm, Melos, 1998, p. 76.

32. See Laurel Fay, 'Nose, The', Stanley Sadie (ed.), *The New Grove Dictionary of Opera*, London, Macmillan, 1992, vol. 3, pp. 621–63.

33. Bobïkina, *Dmitry Shostakovich v pis'makh i dokumentakh*, p. 385.

34. Fay, 'Nose, The', p. 623.

35. Tretyakova, 'N.V. Smolich – glavnïy rezhissyor Malegota' [N.V. Smolich – the Main Director of the Malegot [theatre]], *Opernaya rezhissura: istoriya i sovremennost'* [Operatic production: history and modernity], St Petersburg, Rossiyskiy Institut Istorii Iskusstv, 2000, p. 143.

36. Edward Brown (trans. and ed.), *Meyerhold on Theatre*, London, Eyre Methuen, 1969, p. 217.

37. Dmitriy Sollertinskiy (ed.), *D.D. Shostakovich: Pis'ma I.I. Sollertinskomu* [D.D. Shostakovich: letters to I.I. Sollertinskiy], St Petersburg, Kompozitor, 2006, p. 30.

38. Akopyan, *Dmitriy Shostakovich: Opït fenomenologii tvorchestva*, p. 81.

39. Fay, *Shostakovich*, p. 236.

40. A.Y. Trabskiy, 'Protokol rasshirennogo plenuma khudozhestvennogo soveta akademicheskogo malogo opernogo teatra ot 20 maya 1929 goda o rezhissyorskoy ekspozitsii i makete operï D.D. Shostakovicha "Nos"' [Minutes of the extended plenary session of the Artistic Council of the Academic Maly Opera Theatre from 20 May 1929 about the production plan and model for D.D. Shostakovich's opera 'The Nose'], *Opernaya rezhissura: istoriya i sovremennost'*, p. 164.

41. Fay, *Shostakovich*, p. 55.

42. Ivan Sollertinskiy, 'Priblizilis' li mï k sovetskoy opere? "Nos" – orudiye dal'noboynoye' [Have we come near to Soviet opera? 'The Nose' is a long-range weapon], *Rabochiy i teatr*, 7 (1930), 6.

43. S. Gres, 'Ruchnaya bomba anarkhista' [The hand-grenade of an anarchist], *Rabochiy i teatr*, 8 (1930), 17.

44. M. Yankovskiy, '"Nos" v Malom opernom teatre' ['The Nose' at the Maly Theatre], *Rabochiy i teatr*, 5 (1930), 6–7.

45. 'Formalizmu, vkusovshchine, bessistemnosti – konets!' [An end to formalism, tastelessness and unsystematic character], *Rabochiy i teatr*, 7 (1930), 1; 'Na front bol'shevistskogo seva!' [To the front of the Bolshevik sowing!], *Rabochiy i teatr*, 13 (1930), 1; 'Nalyot leningradskikh udarnikov na Moskvu' [The Moscow raid of Leningrad shock-workers], *Rabochiy i teatr*, 14 (1930), 2.

46. Reprinted in Bobïkina, *Dmitriy Shostakovich v pis'makh i dokumentakh*, pp. 493–6.

47. Shostakovich, 'Deklaratsiya obyazannostey kompozitora' [Declaration of a composer's duties], *Rabochiy i teatr*, 31 (1931), 6.

48. Yankovskiy, 'Kto protiv – edinoglasno. Otkrïtoye pis'mo D. Shostakovichu' [Those against – unanimous. Open letter to D. Shostakovich], *Rabochiy i teatr*, 32–3 (1931), 10–11, 'Govoryat kompozitorï' [Composers speak], *Rabochiy i teatr*, 32–3 (1931), 11.

49. For a synopsis, see Fay, 'Lady Macbeth of the Mtsensk District', in Sadie (ed.), *The New Grove Dictionary of Opera*, vol. 2, pp. 1076–9.

50. Fay, *Shostakovich*, p. 69.

51. See Caryl Emerson, 'Shostakovich and the Russian Literary Tradition', in Laurel Fay (ed.), *Shostakovich and his World*, Princeton, Princeton University Press, 2004, pp. 183–226.

52. Yakubov, *Vozrozhdeniye shedevra*, p. 20.

53. Fay, *Shostakovich*, pp. 67–8; Yakubov, *Vozrozhdeniye shedevra*, p. 118.

54. Richard Taruskin, 'Entr'acte: The Lessons of Lady M', in *Defining Russia Musically*, Princeton, Princeton University Press, 1997, pp. 504–5.

55. See, for example, Sheila Fitzpatrick, 'The *Lady Macbeth* Affair: Shostakovich and the Soviet Puritans', in Fitzpatrick, *The Cultural Front: Power and Culture in Revolutionary Russia*, Ithaca, N.Y., Cornell University Press, 1992, pp. 183–215; Fay, *Shostakovich*, pp. 87–93, Leonid Maksimenkov, *Sumbur vmesto muzïki. Stalinskaya kul'turnaya revolyutsiya, 1936–38* [Muddle instead of music: Stalin's Cultural Revolution 1936–38], Moscow, Yuridicheskaya kniga, 1997.

56. Fay, *Shostakovich*, p. 194.

57. *Ibid.*, p. 197.

58. Fay, *Shostakovich*, p. 237.

59. See Laurel Fay, 'Gamblers, The', Sadie (ed.), *The New Grove Dictionary of Opera*, vol. 2, pp. 342–3.

60. Fay, *Shostakovich*, p. 133.

61. Elizabeth Wilson, *Shostakovich: A Life Remembered*, rev. edn, London, Faber, 2006, p. 200.

62. *Ibid.*, p. 517.

63. *Ibid.*, p. 199.

64. Fay, *Shostakovich*, p. 134.

65. Wilson, *Shostakovich*, p. 200.

66. Akopyan, *Shostakovich: Opït fenomenologii tvorchestva*, p. 221.

67. *Ibid.*, p. 136.

68. See Rosamund Bartlett, 'Shostakovich and Chekhov', in Bartlett (ed.), *Shostakovich in Context*, pp. 206–8, and Yelena Silina, 'Veniamin Fleyshman, uchenik Shostakovicha' [V. Fleyshman: Pupil of Shostakovich], in Lyudmila Kovnatskaya (ed.), *Shostakovich: mezhdu mgnoveniyem i vechnost'yu. Dokumentï, materialï, stat'i* [Shostakovich: between the moment and eternity: documents, materials, articles], St Petersburg, Kompozitor, 2000, pp. 346–408.

69. Yakubov, *Vozrozhdeniye shedevra*, p. 116.

70. Fay, *Shostakovich*, p. 56.

71. *Ibid.*, p. 74.

72. See Ol'ga Digonskaya, 'Neizvestnïe avtografy Shostakovicha v GTsMMK' [Unknown Shostakovich Manuscripts in the Glinka Central Museum of Musical Culture], in Marina Rakhmanova (ed.), *Shostakovich – Urtext*, Moscow, Deka, for the Glinka Museum of Musical Culture, 2007, pp. 161–3. The surviving piano score draft reportedly amounts to some forty minutes of music from the first act (or prologue) of the work.

73. Yuriy Dimitrin, *'Nam ne dano predugadat': Razmïshleniya o libretto operï D. Shostakovicha 'Ledi Makbet Mtsenskogo Uezda'* ['It is not given for us to predict': reflections on D. Shostakovich's libretto for 'The Lady Macbeth of Mtsensk District'], St Petersburg, Biblioteka Vsemirnogo kluba peterburzhtsev, 1997, p. 56.

74. See Ol'ga Digonskaya, 'Shostakovich v seredine 1930-x godakh: opernïye planï i voploshcheniya (ob atributsii neizvestnogo avtografa)' [Shostakovich in the middle of the 1930s: operatic plans and realizations (On the attribution of an unknown manuscript], *Muzïkal'naya akademiya*, 1 (2007), pp. 48–60, and Digonskaya 'Neizvestnïye avtografy', pp. 163–8.

75. Fay, *Shostakovich*, p. 310.

76. *Ibid.*, pp. 112–13.

77. *Ibid.*, p. 114.

78. *Ibid.*, p. 311.

79. *Ibid.*, p. 113.

80. Dimitrin, *'Nam ne dano predugadat'*, p. 56.

81. Fay, Shostakovich, pp. 117–18.

82. Dimitrin, *'Nam ne dano predugadat'*, p. 56.

83. Wilson, *Shostakovich*, p. 378.

84. Fay, *Shostakovich*, p. 78.

85. See Rosamund Bartlett, 'Shostakovich and Chekhov', pp. 199–218, and Ol'ga Digonskaya, *Shostakovich i 'Chyornïy monakh': k neosush-chestvlennomu zamïslu operï D. Shostakovicha 'Chyornïy Monakh'. Obrabotka 'Serenadï' G. Braga dlya soprano, mettso-soprano, skrïpki i fortepiano. Partitura* [Shostakovich and 'The Black Monk': on the unrealized plan for Shostakovich's opera 'The Black Monk'. Transcription of G. Braga's 'Serenade' for soprano, mezzo-soprano, violin and piano. Score], Moscow, DSCH, 2006.

8 Shostakovich's ballets

1. Manashir Yakubov, 'The Golden Age: The True Story of the Premiere', in David Fanning (ed.), *Shostakovich Studies*, Cambridge, Cambridge University Press, 1995, p. 189.
2. *Krasnaya gazeta*, 7 January 1929.
3. Sof'ya Khentova, *Shostakovich: zhizn' i tvorchestvo* [Shostakovich: life and works], Leningrad, Sovetskiy kompozitor, 1985, vol. 1, pp. 160–1.
4. Elizabeth Souritz, *Soviet Choreographers in the 1920s*, trans. Lynn Visson, ed. Sally Banes, London, Dance Books, 1990, pp. 280, 282.
5. Fyodor Lopukhov, *Shest'desyat let v balete: vospominaniya i zapiski baletmeystera* [Sixty years in ballet: memories and notes of a bal-letmaster], Moscow, Iskusstvo, 1966, p. 255.
6. Souritz, *Soviet Choreographers*, p. 280.
7. *'Zolotoy vek'. Sbornik statey k prem'ere* [The Golden age. Collection of articles for the pre-miere]. Leningrad, 1931, p. 3.
8. Yuriy Slonimskiy, *Sovetskiy balet* [Soviet ballet], Moscow, 1950, p. 88.
9. Klavdiya Armashevskaya and Nikita Vaynonen, *Baletmeister Vaynonen* [The bal-letmaster Vaynonen], Moscow, 1971, p. 66.
10. Dmitry Shostakovich, 'Nashi tvorcheskiye vstrechi s Leonidom Yakobsonom' [My creative meetings with Leonid Yakobson], in *Leonid Yakobson: tvorcheskiy put' baletmeys-tera, ego baletï, miniatyurï, ispolniteli* [Leonid Yakobson: the creative path of a choreographer, his ballets, miniatures and performers]. Leningrad and Moscow, 1965, p. 11.
11. Aleksandr Gauk, *Memuarï. Izbrannïye stat'i. Vospominaniya sovremennikov* [Memoirs. Selected articles. Recollections of contemporaries]. Moscow, Sovetskiy kompo-zitor, 1975, p. 125.
12. Armashevskaya, *Vaynonen*, p. 67.
13. *Svetlïy ruchey. Sbornik statey k postanovke* [The bright stream. Collected articles for the premiere], Leningrad, 1935, p. 15.
14. Yakobson, 'Zolotoy vek', *Spartak* (1930), 7 November, 6.

15. For a summary of the fates of several operas and ballets at the hands of the militant proletarian factions between 1929 and 1932, see Yakubov, 'The Golden Age', p. 199.
16. Yuriy Brodersen, 'Legalizatsiya prisposo-blenchestva' [The legalization of time-serving], *Rabochiy i teatr*, 60–1 (1930), 8–9.
17. Sekretariat LOVAPM [The Secretariat of the Leningrad Branch of RAPM], 'Burzhuaznuyu ideologiyu v muzïke razobla-chim do kontsa' [The bourgeois ideology in music will be exposed to the end], *Rabochiy i teatr*, 62–3 (1930), 7.
18. The choreographer for the Kiev produc-tion was Ye. Vigilyev, and in Odessa Igor Moiseyev. See Yakubov, 'The Golden Age', pp. 197–8, nn. 24 and 25.
19. See the citation from Shostakovich's letter to Smolich in Wilson, *Shostakovich: A Life Remembered*, rev. edn, London, Faber, 2006, p. 102.
20. Quoted in Yakubov, 'The Golden Age', pp. 203–4.
21. Quoted in Wilson, *Shostakovich*, p. 103.
22. It was revived in February 2005 at the Bolshoy in a new production by Aleksey Ratmansky.
23. B. Rod, 'Lipovïy "Bolt"' [A false 'Bolt'], *Smena*, 87 (1931), 12 April, 4.
24. Rampa, '"Bolt" i BOLTlivïye formalistï' ['The Bolt' and jabbering formalists], *Bïtovaya Gazeta* [Daily Gazette], 20 (1931), 15 April, 2. [The Russian adjective *boltlivïy* means chat-tering, or jabbering; the title is thus a typical example of rather forced Soviet critical word-play.]
25. *Svetlïy ruchey*, pp. 9–10.
26. Fyodor Lopukhov, *Shest'desyat let v balete*, p. 271.
27. *Ibid.*, pp. 272–3.
28. Shostakovich, 'Moy tretiy balet' [My third ballet], in *Svetlïy ruchey*, p. 15.
29. *Ibid.*
30. Ivan Sollertinskiy, *Stat'i o balete* [Articles on ballet], Leningrad, Muzïka, 1973, pp. 115–16.
31. The premiere took place at the Kirov (Mariinsky) Theatre, Leningrad on 14 April 1961.
32. *The Bedbug* was revived in 2001 at the Mariinsky Theatre, St Petersburg on 30 May. It was also performed in the London Coliseum's Shostakovich ballet series in July 2006, together with the *Leningrad Symphony* and *The Young Lady and the Hooligan*.
33. The new production was premiered at the Mariinsky Theatre, St Petersburg, on 28 June 2006.

9 Screen dramas: Shostakovich's cinema career

1. Anon., 'Sumbur vmesto muzïki' [Chaos instead of Music], *Pravda*, 28 January 1936, 3.

2. For a fuller analysis of Shostakovich's cinema career, see John Riley, *Dmitri Shostakovich: A Life in Film.* London, I.B. Tauris, 2005.

3. Dates are those of the film's release, sometimes slightly later than when Shostakovich wrote the music.

4. D. Shostakovich, 'O muzïke k "Novomu Vavilonu"' [On the music to *New Babylon*], *Sovetskiy ekran* [Soviet screen], 11 (1929), 3. For a reproduction of the article see Riley, *Shostakovich: A Life in Film*, p. 8. For an English translation see Marek Pytel, *New Babylon*, London, Eccentric Press, 1999, pp. 24–6.

5. The recently published score (*New Collected Works*, vol. 122, Moscow, DSCH Publishing, 2004) resolves many of these issues, also revealing that the score may not have been lost until several years after the release of the film (pp. 542–52).

6. Yelena Kuzmina, *O tom, shto pomnyu* [About what I remember], Moscow, Iskusstvo, 1989, pp. 251–2.

7. *New Collected Works*, vol. 123, Moscow, DSCH Publishing, 2004, p. 332.

8. Theodore van Houten, *The Films of Leonid Trauberg: Always the Unexpected.* s'Hertogenbosch, Art and Research, 1989, p. 144.

9. Edited by Pierre Luboshutz for two pianos (Leeds Music Corporation, 1945); for four hands by Mikhail Nyurnberg (Sovetskiy Kompozitor, no. 928, 1959) and for piano solo by Lev Atovm'yan (Sovetskiy kompozitor, no. 4565, 1967).

10. Muzgiz, no. 14509, 1935.

11. Yekaterina Khokhlova, 'Forbidden Films of the 1930s', in Richard Taylor and Derek Spring (eds.), *Stalinism and Soviet Cinema*, London, Routledge, 1993, p. 95.

12. S. Kim and A.S. Deryabin (eds.), 'Dïkhaniye voli: dnevniki Mikhaila Tsekhanovskogo' [The breath of freedom: the diaries of Mikhail Tsekhanovsky], *Kinovedcheskiye zapiski* [Cinema notes], 57 (2002), 324.

13. It can be seen on Oksana Dvornichenko, DVD-rom, *Shostakovich*. CHAN 55001, Chandos, 2000.

14. B.S. Ol'khovïy, (ed.), *Puti kino Vsesoyuznoye partinoye soveshchaniye po kinematografii* [Cinematic paths. All-union party conference on cinematogaphy] Moscow, Teo-Kino-Pechat', 1929. For translated extracts, see Richard Taylor and Ian Christie (eds.), *The Film Factory: Russian and Soviet Cinema in Documents 1896–1939*, Cambridge, Mass., Harvard University Press, 1988, pp. 208–15.

15. I am grateful to Yevgeny Dobrenko of the University of Nottingham for pointing this out to me and showing me his manuscript chapter 'Shoots from Underground: Dialectics of Conspiratorial Thinking'.

16. See V. Shcherbina, 'O gruppe estetstvuyushchikh kosmopolitov v kino' [On the group of aesthetic cosmopolitans in the cinema], *Iskusstvo kino* [Film art],1 (January 1949), 14–15.

17. Isaak Glikman, *Story of a Friendship: The Letters of Dmitry Shostakovich to Isaak Glikman*, trans. Anthony Phillips, London, Faber, 2001, pp. 40 and 250.

18. One exception was the wartime pilot Aleksey Maresyev who lost both legs but battled back to fly again. Boris Polevoy's book *The Story of a Real Man* (1946) was adapted for radio (1947) and, in 1948, a film and Prokofiev's opera.

19. He also wrote some music for *Rimskiy-Korsakov* (1952) but this commission eventually went to Georgy Sviridov. Another film with which he had limited involvement was Arnshtam's *The Warmongers* (*Podzhigateli voyní, c.* 1948), which was stopped in production.

20. Letter to Leonid Trauberg, 26 November 1948. Sotheby's Music and Continental Manuscripts Sale (London), 21 May 1998, lot 349. The reference to a running commentary is puzzling, but as the letter was written a year before the film's final release, Shostakovich may have seen an early version, or he may simply have been amplifying the reasons for his outrage.

21. Paul Robeson, who sang the title song, was in an even worse position as he could not leave the USA, and his contribution was overlaid onto a previously recorded orchestral track.

22. Atovm'yan's arrangement for two violins and piano (Sovetskiy Kompozitor, no. 4719, 1975) calls it *Spanish Dance*, while Emanuil Shenykman called his mandolin arrangement *Neapolitan Dance* (recorded on Nonesuch 7 8019).

23. Kozintsev and Trauberg (6 films); Kozintsev alone (4); Arnshtam (5).

24. Shostakovich 'Tragediya-satira' *Sovetskoye iskusstvo* [Soviet art], 16 October 1932, cited in Laurel Fay, *Shostakovich: A Life*, New York, Oxford University Press, 2000, p. 69.

10 Between reality and transcendence: Shostakovich's songs

1. For example, 'Song of the Counterplan', the theme song from the 1932 film *Counterplan*, with words by Boris Kornilov; or the 'Ballad of Cordelia' and the 'Ten Songs of the Jester' from the incidental music to *King Lear* of 1941. On the former see John Riley, 'From the Factory to the Flat: Thirty Years of the *Song of the Counterplan*', in Neil Edmunds (ed.), *Soviet Music under Lenin and Stalin*, London, Routledge Curzon, 2004, pp. 67–80.

2. Dorothea Redepenning, '"And Art made Tongue-tied by Authority": Shostakovich's Song-Cycles', in David Fanning (ed.), *Shostakovich Studies*, Cambridge, Cambridge University Press, 1995, p. 211.

3. Solomon Volkov (ed.), *Testimony: The Memoirs of Dmitri Shostakovich*, London, Hamish Hamilton, 1979, p. 140. The quotation is applied to song analysis in Sebastian Klemm, *Dmitri Schostakowitsch: das zeitlose Spätwerk*, Schostakowitsch-Studien, vol. 4, Berlin, Kuhn, 2001, p. 184, and is implied in Dorothea Redepenning's argument that in Shostakovich's songs 'the poet's words are more important than the music which accompanies them'; see Redepenning, '"And Art made Tongue-tied by Authority"', p. 207.

4. Redepenning, '"And Art made Tongue-tied by Authority"', p. 228.

5. Kadja Grönke, 'Kunst und Künstler in Šostakovičs späten Gedichtvertonungen', *Archiv für Musikwissenschaft*, 53 (1996), 292.

6. Klemm, *Dmitri Schostakowitsch*, pp. 183–4.

7. See Redepenning, '"And Art made Tongue-tied by Authority"', and Bernd Feuchtner, *'Und Kunst geknebelt von der groben Macht': Schostakowitsch, künstlerische Identität und staatliche Repression*, Frankfurt, Sendler, 1986, rev. edn, Kassel, Bärenreiter, 2002.

8. See Ian MacDonald, *The New Shostakovich*, London, Fourth Estate, 1990, p. 132; Richard Taruskin, 'Public Lies and Unspeakable Truth: Interpreting Shostakovich's Fifth Symphony', in Fanning, *Shostakovich Studies*, pp. 43–5; Redepenning, '"And Art made Tongue-tied by Authority"', pp. 205–6; Gerard McBurney, 'Whose Shostakovich?', in Malcolm Hamrick Brown (ed.), *A Shostakovich Casebook*, Bloomington, Indiana University Press, 2004, p. 294. Elizabeth Wilson follows a thought expressed by McBurney in a radio broadcast of 1993 that identifies the melodic shape of the finale's main theme with the first notes of the vocal line in the Pushkin setting – see Elizabeth Wilson, *Shostakovich: A Life Remembered*, new edn, London, Faber, 2006, p. 153. Naturally Soviet commentators have given the connection a very different interpretation – see David Rabinovich, *Dmitry Shostakovich*, London, Lawrence & Wishart, 1959, p. 49.

9. Wilson, *Shostakovich*, p. 296.

10. See Laurel Fay, *Shostakovich: A Life*, New York, Oxford University Press, 2000, p. 169.

11. For further comment see Chapter 3 by David Fanning on the early works.

12. Redepenning, '"And Art made Tongue-tied by Authority"', p. 207.

13. On the meaning of classicism in Stalinist aesthetics, see Marina Frolova-Walker, 'Stalin and the Art of Boredom', *Twentieth-Century Music*, 1/1 (2004), 101–24.

14. Fay, *Shostakovich*, pp. 169–70.

15. Esti Sheinberg. 'Shostakovich's "Jewish Music" as an Existential Statement', in Ernst Kuhn *et al.* (eds.), *Dmitri Schostakowitsch und das jüdische musikalische Erbe*, Schostakowitsch-Studien 3, Berlin, Kuhn, 2001, pp. 92–3; in answer to Fay, *Shostakovich*, p. 170.

16. *Yevreyskiye narodnïye pesni* [Jewish folk songs], ed. Yuriy Sokolov, Moscow, Goslitizdat, 1947.

17. Fay, *Shostakovich*, pp. 168–9.

18. Joachim Braun, 'Shostakovich's Song Cycle *From Jewish Folk Poetry*: Aspects of Style and Meaning', in Malcolm Hamrick Brown (ed.), *Russian and Soviet Music: Essays for Boris Schwarz*, Ann Arbor, UMI Research Press, 1984, pp. 259–86.

19. *Ibid.*, pp. 279–80.

20. See, for example, Richard Taruskin, *Defining Russia Musically*, Princeton, Princeton University Press, 1997, p. 474; Joachim Braun, 'Shostakovich's Song Cycle *From Jewish Folk Poetry*', p. 266.

21. See Nelly Kravets, 'Shostakovich's *From The Jewish Folk Poetry* and Weinberg's *Jewish Songs*, in Kuhn, *Dmitri Schostakowitsch und das jüdische musikalische Erbe*, pp. 279–97.

22. Fay, *Shostakovich*, p. 180.

23. Galina Vishnevskaya, *Galina: A Russian Story*, London, Sceptre, 1986, pp. 281–2.

24. *Ibid.*, pp. 283–4.

25. Caryl Emerson, 'Shostakovich, Tsvetaeva, Pushkin, Musorgsky: Songs and Dances of Death and Survival', in Rosamund Bartlett (ed.), *Shostakovich in Context*, Oxford, Oxford University Press, 2000, pp. 191–8; Caryl Emerson, 'Shostakovich and the Russian Literary Tradition', in Laurel Fay (ed.), *Shostakovich and his World*, Princeton, Princeton University Press, 2004, pp. 183–226.

26. Olga Peters Hasty, *Tsvetaeva's Orphic Journeys in the Worlds of the Word*, Evanston, Ill., Northwestern University Press, 1996, p. 1.

27. *Ibid.*, p. 224.

28. For an extensive commentary on Michelangelo's poetry, see James M. Saslow,

The Poetry of Michelangelo: An Annotated Translation, New Haven, Yale University Press, 1991.

29. See Brown, *A Shostakovich Casebook*, p. 182.

30. Wilson, *Shostakovich*, p. 513.

31. Galina Ustvolskaya, Trio for clarinet, violin and piano, third movement, bars 60–5; quoted in Shostakovich's Fifth String Quartet, first movement, bars 261–82, 421–64, third movement, bars 283–8, 321–43.

32. Wilson, *Shostakovich*, p. 515.

33. Caryl Emerson, 'The Lebiadkin Songs: Bad Poetry, Bad Prose, Bad Politics, Bad Ends', in Fay, *Shostakovich and his World*, pp. 212–20.

34. Isaak Glikman (ed.), *Story of a Friendship: The Letters of Dmitry Shostakovich to Isaak Glikman*, trans. Anthony Phillips, London, Faber, 2001, p. 197.

11 *Slava!* The 'official compositions'

1. See Peter Heyworth, 'Glory and Defeat', *Observer Review*, 9 September 1962, 23.

2. See, for example, Henry Orlov, 'A Link in the Chain', in Malcolm Hamrick Brown (ed.), *A Shostakovich Casebook*, Bloomington, Indiana University Press, 2004, p. 206; Elizabeth Wilson, *Shostakovich: A Life Remembered*, London, Faber, 2006, p. 277; and Ian MacDonald, *The New Shostakovich*, Oxford University Press, 1991, p. 201.

3. *Shostakovich: A Life Remembered*, London, Faber, 1994, p. 247; Wilson omitted this classification in the revised version, London, Faber, 2006, pp. 277ff.

4. Isaak Glikman, *Story of a Friendship: The Letters of Dmitry Shostakovich to Isaak Glikman*, trans. Anthony Phillips, London, Faber, 2001, p. 251.

5. Henry Orlov, 'A Link in the Chain', pp. 203–4.

6. The title, *Torzhestvenniy marsh* is often translated as 'Solemn March', but since the march is anything but solemn, 'Festive March' or 'Ceremonial March' seems a more appropriate translation of the title. In vol. 32 of the *New Collected Works*, Manashir Yakubov dates the march as being written in 1941 (Moscow, DSCH, 2006, p. 159). However, Olga Digonskaya estimates the composition date as 1939 and provisionally suggests that it was commissioned in connection with the Finnish campaign that preceded the Nazi invasion of Russia in 1941. She also observes that in the autograph manuscript of one of the two versions of the march (both are printed in the *New Collected Works* volume), the title was originally 'Torzhestvenniy pokhodniy marsh', with the word 'pokhodniy' [marching]

removed for the first edition in 1941 (personal communication, September 2007). I thank Olga Digonskaya for sharing this information with me.

7. Laurel Fay, *Shostakovich: A Life*, New York, Oxford University Press, 2000, p. 123.

8. Kirill Tomoff, *Creative Union: The Professional Organization of Soviet Composers, 1939–1953*, Ithaca, N.Y., and London: Cornell University Press, 2007, p. 83. Tomoff notes that Shostakovich was among the composers who entered the competition.

9. 'Oath to the People's Commissar' was the original title. After Khrushchev's 'de-Stalinization' campaign the title was changed along with parts of the text that mention Stalin.

10. 'Song of Liberation', adaptation by D.J. Grunes, lyrics Paula Stone. Russian-American Music Publishing Inc., 1944.

11. In conversation with the writer Mikhail Zoshchenko, Shostakovich described this song as a 'chastushka' (a witty poetic genre akin to a limerick). See Sof'ya Khentova, *D.D. Shostakovich v godï Velikoy otechestvennoy voynï* [Shostakovich in the Years of the Great Patriotic war], Leningrad, Muzïka, 1979, p. 35.

12. Derek Hulme gives the date of composition as mid-August 1943, and states that Khachaturyan wrote the first eight bars, while Shostakovich completed and orchestrated the anthem (Hulme, *Dmitri Shostakovich: A Catalogue, Bibliography and Discography*, 3rd edn, Lanham, Md., Scarecrow Press, 2002, pp. 229–30). Fay gives the date of composition as 1942 (Fay, *Shostakovich*, p. 357). The Dolmatovsky song 'Glory to our Soviet Homeland' is printed in vol. 34 of the Shostakovich *Collected Works*, Moscow, Muzïka, 1985, p. 86.

13. Khentova, *D.D. Shostakovich*, p. 176. Khachaturyan's reminiscences about the affair are reprinted in Wilson, *Shostakovich: A Life Remembered* [2006], pp. 208–9.

14. Khentova, *D.D. Shostakovich*, pp. 176–7. One of Khentova's sources for the two 'variants' composed by Shostakovich and Khachaturyan, GTsMMK fo. 32, bit of storage 85 and 86, shows both orchestration and piano versions of a song entitled 'Hymn of the SSSR' by Shostakovich and Khachaturyan, which is a variant of the 1957 song 'We Cherish the October Dawns in our Hearts'. I have not been able to examine her other source, located in TsGALI. I am grateful to Olga Digonskaya for showing me the former manuscript.

15. The song acquired this title after the competition finished in autumn 1943. The first

twenty-four bars are printed in Khentova, *D. D. Shostakovich*, p. 177.

16. The song concludes the arrangement of numbers from the three NKVD shows *Native Country*, op. 63, *Russian River*, op. 66, *Victorious Spring*, op. 72 by Yury Silant'ev, *Rodnaya Otchizna* [My Fatherland] (Moscow, Sovetskiy Kompozitor, 1972). The first twenty-four bars of the song are printed in Khentova, *D. D. Shostakovich*, p. 176 (not to be confused with the song on p. 177).

17. Shostakovich, *Collected Works*, vol. 34, Moscow, Muzïka, 1985, pp. 103–4.

18. Fay, *Shostakovich*, p. 145.

19. Sources vary as to the authors of this song; an alternative composer is Archerov, with text by S. Alimov.

20. I am grateful to Levon Hakobian for his help in identifying these songs.

21. See Khrennikov's comments as recorded by Alexander Werth, *Musical Uproar in Moscow*, London, Turnstile Press, 1949, p. 56.

22. Fay, *Shostakovich*, p. 158.

23. For stenographic reports from the conference, see *Soveshchaniye deyateley sovetskoy muziki v TsK VKP (b)* [Conference of Soviet Music Practitioners at the Central Committee of the All-Union Communist Party], Moscow, 'Pravda', 1948.

24. Hulme, *Shostakovich Catalogue*, p. 297.

25. Fay guesses that the phone call took place in mid- to late February 1949. The Order no. 17 banning performances of Shostakovich's works was revoked on 16 March. See Fay, *Shostakovich*, p. 172.

26. Nelli Kravets, 'Novïy vzglyad na desyatiyu simfoniyu Shostakovicha' [A New Look at Shostakovich's Tenth Symphony] in Lyudmila Kovnatskaya (ed.), *D. D. Shostakovich. Sbornik statey k 90-letiyu dnya rozhdeniya* [D.D. Shostakovich. Collected articles on the 90th anniversary of his birthday], Moscow, 'Kompozitor', 1997, p. 242. See also the English translation 'A New Insight into the Tenth Symphony', in Rosamund Bartlett (ed.), *Shostakovich in Context*, Oxford, Oxford University Press, 2000, p. 170.

27. Fay, *Shostakovich*, p. 175.

28. Kravets, 'Novïy vzglyad', p. 242.

29. Fay, *Shostakovich*, p. 175.

30. Wilson, *Shostakovich*, (1994 edn), pp. 314–15; this part of the reminiscence is omitted from the revised 2006 edition.

31. Glikman, *Pis'ma k drugu*, St Petersburg, 'Kompozitor' and Moscow 'DSCH', 1993, pp. 82–3. For the English translation, see Glikman, *Letters to a Friend*, p. 247.

32. See Werth, *Musical Uproar in Moscow*, especially pp. 82–3.

33. Heyworth, 'Glory and Defeat', p. 23.

34. Werth, *Musical Uproar in Moscow*, p. 83.

35. *Collected works*, vol. 34, 1985, editorial introduction: 'Songs and Choruses from Films'.

36. Quoted in the editorial introduction to *Collected Works*, vol. 34 (no page no.).

37. The year 1959 marks the start of creative renewal after the difficulties of the 1950s, and as such is the logical start of Shostakovich's final creative period, regardless of whether every work from those years merits the poetic description 'late'.

38. For a list of the honours awarded Shostakovich around this time, see Fay, *Shostakovich*, pp. 203–4.

39. See *ibid.*, p. 195.

40. See vol. 11 of the Muzïka *Collected Works*, editor's note, n. 12.

41. See Fay, *Shostakovich*, p. 254.

42. See *ibid.*, p. 266.

43. Quoted *ibid.*, p. 267.

44. Quoted *ibid.*, p. 229.

45. For details of the various trips abroad, domestic duties and capitulation to official pressures, such as the signing of the letter denouncing Andrey Sakharov in his declining years, see Fay, *Shostakovich*, pp. 272–9.

46. *Ibid.*, p. 266.

12 A political football: Shostakovich reception in Germany

1. Rosa Sadykhova, 'Dmitrii Shostakovich: Letters to his Mother, 1923–1927', in Laurel Fay (ed.), *Shostakovich and his World*, Princeton, Princeton University Press, 2004, p. 26.

2. Hilmar Schmalenberg, 'Vorwort des Herausgebers', in Schmalenberg (ed.), *Schostakowitsch in Deutschland*, Berlin, Verlag Ernst Kuhn, 1998, p. ix.

3. Alfred Heuss, 'Musik in Leipzig', *Zeitschrift für Musik* (1930), 55.

4. Karl Westermeyer, 'Das Musikleben der Gegenwart. Berlin, Konzert', *Die Musik* (June 1930), 688.

5. Otto Steinhagen, 'Das Musikleben der Gegenwart', *Die Musik* (February 1931), 362.

6. Eugen Braudo, 'Uraufführungen. Dmitry Schostakowitsch: Die Nase', *Die Musik* (April 1930), 520–1.

7. The first US performance of Shostakovich's Third Symphony took place on 30 December 1932 with the Philadelphia Orchestra under Leopold Stokowski. The Chicago Symphony Orchestra first performed the same work three weeks later at Orchestra Hall on 19 and 20 January 1933, with Frederick Stock conducting. It should be noted that both the Philadelphia and Chicago performances

presented the work without chorus, the texts having been omitted for political reasons. The programme note from the Chicago performance contains the following information: 'The symphony contains an ad libitum chorus (omitted on this occasion) whose text is concerned with the political occasion with which the work is directly concerned.' Following this, there is an English translation of the text. (Information sent to the author by Frank Villella, Rosenthal Archives of the Chicago Symphony Orchestra, 4 and 9 January 2007.)

8. A.L. 'Das Musikleben der Gegenwart: Chicago', *Die Musik* (August 1933), 850.

9. Fred K. Prieberg, *Musik im NS – Staat*, Frankfurt am Main, Fischer Verlag, 1982, pp. 373–4.

10. David Monod, *Settling Scores. German Music, Denazification and the Americans 1946–1953*, Chapel Hill, University of North Carolina Press, 2005, p. 116.

11. Siegfried Borris, 'Ein Künstler neuen Lebenstils', in Karl Laux, *Die Musik in Ru-land und in der Sowjetunion*, Berlin, Henschelverlag, 1958, p. 428. Also cited in Wilfried Brennecke (ed.), *Arbeitshefte der Akademie der Künste der DDR, Sektion Musik, Forum – Musik in der DDR Zweiter Teil*, Berlin, Henschelverlag, 1972, p. 23

12. Klaus Weiler, *Celibidache: Musiker und Philosoph*, Munich, Schneekluth, 1993, pp. 36–7.

13. Carl Friedrichs, 'Zwei Friedenskantaten: Schostakowitsch "Das Lied von den Wäldern" und Vaclav Dobias "Tschekoslowakische Polka"', *Musik und Gesellschaft*, 1/4 (1951), 27–8.

14. Eberhard Rebling, 'Die X. Sinfonie von Dmitri Schostakowitsch', *Musik und Gesellschaft*, 8 (1954), 288–90.

15. The original article appeared as 'Shirokiye massï vernï nastoyashchey muzïke' [The broad masses are faithful to real music], *Sovetskaya muzïka* 11 (1959), 6–9.

16. Dmitri Schostakowitsch, '"Eine Mode ohne Zukunft", Schostakowitsch über den "Warschauer Herbst"', *Musik und Gesellschaft*, 10/2 (1960), 74–6.

17. Theodor W. Adorno, *Philosophie der Neuen Musik*, Frankfurt, Suhrkamp Verlag, 1978, p. 16.

18. Mark Carroll, *Music and Ideology in Cold War Europe*, Cambridge, Cambridge University Press, 2003, pp. 20–1.

19. Klaus Körner, 'Schostakowitschs Vierte Sinfonie', *Archiv für Musikwissenschaft*, 31 (1974), 116–36 and 214–35.

20. Hermann Danuser, 'Dmitri Schostakowitschs musikalisch-politisches Revolutionsverständis (1926–27). Zur Ersten Klaviersonate und zur Zweiten Symphonie', *Melos/ Neue Zeitschrift für Musik*, 4/1 (1978), 3–11.

21. Carl Dahlhaus and Giwi Ordschonikidse (eds.), *Beiträge zur Musikkultur in der Sowjetunion und in der Bundesrepublik Deutschland*, Hamburg, Sikorski and Wilhelmshaven, Heinrichshofen, 1982.

22. Wolfgang Rihm, *Zur Musik von Dmitri Schostakowitsch*, Hamburg, Musikverlag Hans Sikorski, 1985.

13 The rough guide to Shostakovich's harmonic language

1. See Varvara Dernova, *Garmoniya Skryabina*, Leningrad, Muzïka, 1968; Richard Taruskin, 'Scriabin and the Superhuman: A Millennial Essay', in Taruskin, *Defining Russia Musically*, Princeton, Princeton University Press, 1997, pp. 308–59; James M. Baker, *The Music of Alexander Scriabin*, New Haven, Yale University Press, 1986. For Dernova, Skryabin's Mystic Chord and its variants retain vestiges of the dominant sonorities of late Romantic chromatic harmony and thus can be employed in chord progressions of extended tonality. Taruskin spots affinities with the octatonic collection and on this basis argues for Skryabin's increasing preoccupation with invariance as a means of liquidating 'ego-centered' tonality. For Baker, consistency in the employment of non-tonal pitch class sets and subsets both locally and at long range gives theoretical justification for considering the composer's late style to be atonal.

2. L[eonid] Sabaneiev, 'Scriabin's *Prometheus*', in Wassily Kandinsky, Franz Marc and Klaus Lankheit, eds., *The Blaue Reiter Almanac*, New York, Viking Press, 1974, p. 134.

3. Yavorsky's original treatise, *Stroyeniye muzikal'noy rechi* [The structure of musical speech], Moscow, 1908, is difficult to obtain, but the expanded version in book form prepared by his student Sergey Protopopov and edited by Yavorsky is available in translation (Gordon McQuere, '*The Elements of the Structure of Musical Speech* by S.V. Protopopov: A Translation and Commentary', Ph.D. diss., University of Iowa, 1978), as is McQuere's review of its basic aspects and their significance, 'The Theories of Boleslav Yavorsky', in McQuere (ed.), *Russian Theoretical Thought in Music*, Ann Arbor, UMI Research Press, 1983, pp. 109–64.

4. David Haas, *Leningrad's Modernists*, New York, Peter Lang, 1998, pp. 101–2.

5. When the problematic Russian word *lad* is translated as 'mode', certain important connotations are lost. 'Modality' broadens the

meaning from the mere naming and ordering of pitches to the larger concerns of the effects of a given mode on the structure and perception of a mode as its intervallic properties are revealed and utilized in a musical passage.

6. See Aleksandr Dolzhanskiy, 'O ladovoy osnove sochineniy Shostakovicha' [On the modal foundation of Shostakovich's works], in Lyubov' Berger (ed.), *Chertï stilya D. Shostakovicha* [Aspects of Shostakovich's style], Moscow, Sovetskiy kompozitor, 1962, pp. 31–2; Lev Mazel', 'Zametki o muzïkal'nom yazïke Shostakovicha' [Observations on Shostakovich's musical language], in Givi Ordzhonikidze (ed.), *Dmitriy Shostakovich*, Moscow, Sovetskiy kompozitor, 1967, p. 325.

7. Detlef Gojowy, *Neue sowjetische Musik der 20er Jahre*, Laaber, Laaber Verlag, 1980, p. 260.

8. Lev Mazel', *Etyudï o Shostakoviche* [Shostakovich Studies], Moscow, Sovetskiy kompozitor, 1986, p. 4.

9. Mazel', 'Glavnaya tema pyatoy simfonii Shostakovicha i yeyo istoricheskiye svyazi' [The main theme of Shostakovich's Fifth Symphony and its historical links], in *Etyudï o Shostakoviche*, Moscow, Sovetskiy kompozitor, 1986, p. 94.

10. Mazel', 'Glavnaya tema', p. 108.

11. Mazel', 'Zametki', pp. 303–58.

12. *Ibid.*, p. 321.

13. Dolzhanskiy, 'O ladovoy osnove', p. 28.

14. *Ibid.*, pp. 31–2.

15. *Ibid.*, p. 33.

16. *Ibid.*, pp. 40–1.

17. Dolzhanskiy, 'Aleksandriyskiy pentakhord v muzïke Shostakovicha', in Givi Ordzhonikidze (ed.), *Dmitriy Shostakovich*, Moscow, Sovetskiy kompozitor, 1967, p. 414.

18. Ellon Carpenter, 'Russian Theorists on Modality in Shostakovich's Music', in David Fanning (ed.), *Shostakovich Studies*, Cambridge, Cambridge University Press, 1995, p. 90.

19. Yuriy Kholopov, *Ocherki sovremennoy garmonii* [Sketches of contemporary harmony], Moscow, Muzïka, 1974, p. 226.

20. *Ibid.*, pp. 241–3.

21. *Ibid.*, pp. 243–4.

22. Kholopov, 'Form in Shostakovich's Instrumental Works', in Fanning, *Shostakovich Studies*, pp. 57–75.

23. Kholopov, 'Ladï Shostakovicha: strukturï i sistematiki' [Shostakovich's modes: structures and systems], in Yelena Dolinskaya (ed.), *Shostakovichu posvyashchayetsya: Sbornik statey* [Dedicated to Shostakovich: a collection of articles], Moscow, Kompozitor, 1997, pp. 62–77.

24. Norman Kay, *Shostakovich*, New York and London, Oxford University Press, 1971, pp. 75–6.

25. Fanning, *The Breath of the Symphonist: Shostakovich's Tenth*, London, Royal Musical Association, 1988.

26. *Ibid.*, p. 16.

27. *Ibid.*, pp. 16–17.

28. *Ibid.*, p. 18.

29. *Ibid.*

30. *Ibid.*, p. 14.

31. *Ibid.*, p. 20.

32. Fanning, 'Leitmotif in *Lady Macbeth*', in *Shostakovich Studies*, pp. 142–3.

33. Fanning, 'Introduction: Talking about Eggs', in *Shostakovich Studies*, p. 12.

34. Fanning, *Shostakovich: String Quartet No. 8*, Aldershot, Ashgate, 2004, p. 126.

35. *Ibid.*, p. 128.

36. *Ibid.*, p. 131.

37. Patrick McCreless, 'The Cycle of Structure and the Cycle of Meaning: The Piano Trio in E Minor, op. 67', in Fanning, *Shostakovich Studies*, pp. 113–36.

38. Richard Longman, *Expression and Structure: Processes of Integration in the Large-Scale Instrumental Music of Dimitri Shostakovich*, 2 vols., New York and London, Garland, 1989, vol. 1, p. 298.

39. *Ibid.*, p. 300.

40. Eric Roseberry, *Ideology, Style, Content, and Thematic Process in the Symphonies, Cello Concertos, and String Quartets of Shostakovich*, New York and London, Garland, 1989, p. 37.

41. John Moraitis, 'Dmitri Shostakovich's Fourteenth Symphony: Russian Perspectives on the Problem of Genre', MA Thesis, University of Georgia, 1998, pp. 58–87.

42. David Haas, 'Shostakovich and *Wozzeck*'s Secret', in Michael Mishra (ed.), *The Shostakovich Companion*, Greenwood, Conn., Greenwood Press, forthcoming.

43. George Perle, *The Operas of Alban Berg*, vol. 1, '*Wozzeck*', Berkeley, University of California Press, 1980, p. 133.

44. Jason Solomon, 'Under the Masks of Diversity: Unifying Cyclic Procedures in the Twenty-Four Preludes, op. 34', unpublished typescript in Theory Department, Hodgson School of Music, University of Georgia, p. 12.

14 Shostakovich on record

1. Roman Gruber, 'Responses of Shostakovich to a Questionnaire on the Psychology of the Creative Process', in Laurel Fay (ed.), *Shostakovich and his World*, Princeton, Princeton University Press, 2004, pp. 29–30 (translation adapted).

2. See Oksana Dvornichenko, *Shostakovich*, London, Chandos Multimedia, 2000 (CHAN55001 (DVDROM), CHAN 50001 (CDROM)).

3. Formerly available on a mono cassette from Regent Records, MG5020.

4. Elizabeth Wilson, *Shostakovich: A Life Remembered*, new edn, London, Faber, 2006, p. 441.

5. Sofia Moshevich, *Dmitri Shostakovich: Pianist*, Montreal, McGill-Queen's University Press, 2004. This takes into account and surpasses Sof'ya Khentova's identically titled Russian study (Leningrad, Muzïka, 1964). Moshevich's conclusions regarding implications for a new Critical Edition are separately presented in her 'Interpretation and Interpreters', *DSCH* (magazine of the Shostakovich Society) 15 (July 2001), 34–42.

6. For which the most convenient source of information is Wilson, *Shostakovich* (see Index entries under Shostakovich as pianist).

7. Moshevich, *Dmitri Shostakovich: Pianist*, p. 3.

8. *Ibid.*, p. 182.

9. Broadcast interview on BBC Radio 3, 25 June 2004.

10. Moshevich, *Dmitri Shostakovich: Pianist*, p. 20.

11. Moshevich, 'Tempo in Shostakovich Performances of his Own Works', *DSCH* 2 (Winter 1994), 7–17.

12. Noteworthy is Shostakovich's comment to Boleslav Yavorsky that 'the indicated speed has nothing to do with the tempo (*Allegro molto*) but with the spirit and impetus'. Cited in Wilson, *Shostakovich*, pp. 62–3.

13. See Khentova, *V mire Shostakovicha* [In Shostakovich's world], Moscow, Kompozitor, 1996, p. 187.

14. Part of a performance of the First Concerto may be viewed on film, see n. 2 above.

15. For further discussion of pianistic and textual details in the Preludes, see Moshevich, *Dmitri Shostakovich: Pianist*, pp. 70–5.

16. See Wilson, *Shostakovich*, pp. 363–4.

17. See Laurel Fay, *Shostakovich: A Life*, New York, Oxford University Press, 2000, pp. 199, 330 n. 70.

18. The problem is compounded by the extensive discrepancies between the first edition of 1935 and the republications in 1960 and 1971, the two latter edited by Viktor Kubatsky, the first cellist to perform the work, with the apparent approval of the composer. See Moshevich, *Dmitri Shostakovich: Pianist*, pp. 82–7.

19. For a tabulation of tempi in the Cello Sonata see Moshevich, *Dmitri Shostakovich: Pianist*, p. 85.

20. Rostropovich's sleeve-note to the issue on EMI Classics 5 72295–2 comments: 'we took some passages rather on the brisk side; the weather was beautiful and Shostakovich was in a hurry to visit someone in the country.'

For further comment on Shostakovich's penchant for excessively fast tempos, see Valentin Berlinsky in Wilson, *Shostakovich*, p. 280.

21. The CD recording issued in 1991 on the French Vogue label, purporting to be of the composer in 1950 with the Borodin Quartet is in fact identical to the one reliably credited to him with the Beethovens in 1940.

22. Moshevich, *Dmitri Shostakovich: Pianist*, p. 97.

23. See Wilson, *Shostakovich*, p. 279, which also reports Barshai's own, slightly different memory of how the correction came about.

24. For details see Moshevich, *Dmitri Shostakovich: Pianist*, pp. 113–14.

25. Letter of 2 January 1969, in Isaak Glikman, *Story of a Friendship: The Letters of Dmitry Shostakovich to Isaak Glikman*, trans. Anthony Phillips, London, Faber, 2001, p. 158.

26. *Ibid.*

27. Moshevich, 'An Opus 87 Forgery?', *DSCH* 12 (January 2000), 66–9.

28. Moshevich, *Dmitri Shostakovich: Pianist*, pp. 134–7.

29. See *Ibid.*

15 Jewish existential irony as musical ethos in the music of Shostakovich

1. See Esti Sheinberg, *Irony, Satire, Parody and the Grotesque in the Music of Shostakovich*, Aldershot, Ashgate, 2000.

2. *Ibid.*, pp. 313–19.

3. See Levon Hakobian, *Music of the Soviet Age: 1917–1987*, Stockholm, Melos Music Literature, 1998; David Fanning, *Shostakovich: String Quartet No. 8*, Aldershot, Ashgate, 2004.

4. Walter Kaufmann (ed.), *Existentialism from Dostoevsky to Sartre*, New York, New American Library, 1975.

5. The characterization of musical correlatives has benefited immensely from Robert Hatten's application of the theory of markedness to music. For an enlightening explanation of this theory and its applications to music see Hatten, *Musical Meaning in Beethoven*, Bloomington, Indiana University Press, 1994.

6. See Hakobian, *Music of the Soviet Age*, p. 11.

7. Isaak Glikman, *Story of a Friendship: The Letters of Dmitry Shostakovich to Isaak Glikman, 1941–1975*, trans. Anthony Phillips, London, Faber, 2001, p. 197.

8. Lyudmila Mikheyeva, *I.I. Sollertinskiy*, Leningrad, Sovetskiy kompozitor, 1988.

9. *Ibid.*, pp. 26–8, 36.

10. Caryl Emerson, 'Back to the Future: Shostakovich's Revision of Leskov's *Lady Macbeth of Mtsensk District*', *Cambridge Opera*

Journal, 1 (1989), 59–78. Emerson, 'Shostakovich and the Russian Literary Tradition', in Laurel Fay (ed.), *Shostakovich and his World*, Princeton, Princeton University Press, 2004, pp. 183–226.

11. Solomon Volkov, *Testimony: The Memoirs of Dmitri Shostakovich as Related to and Edited by Solomon Volkov*, London, Hamish Hamilton, 1979, p. 108.

12. Ivan Sollertinskiy, '"Karmen" Bize' [Bizet's *Carmen*], in *Istoricheskiye etyudï*, Leningrad, Gosudarstvennoye muzïkal'noye izdatel'stvo, 1963, p. 273.

13. Friedrich Nietzsche, 'The Case of Wagner', in *The Complete Works of Friedrich Nietzsche*, vol. 8, New York, Russel & Russel, 1964, p. 4.

14. Sollertinskiy, '"Karmen" Bize', p. 53.

15. *Ibid.*, p. 55.

16. Nietzsche, 'The Case of Wagner', p. 4.

17. Lev Grigoryev and Yakov Platek (eds.), *Dmitry Shostakovich: About Himself and his Times*, Moscow, Progress Publishers, 1980, p. 38.

18. Friedrich Nietzsche, *Beyond Good and Evil: Prelude to a Philosophy of the Future*, New York, Vintage Books, 1966, p. 90 (para. 153).

19. *Ibid.*

20. *Ibid.*, pp. 169–70 (para. 239).

21. Sheinberg, *Irony, Satire, Parody and the Grotesque*, pp. 251–8; Emerson, 'Shostakovich and the Russian Literary Tradition', pp. 197–201.

22. Nietzsche, *Beyond Good and Evil*, pp. 195–6 (para. 255).

23. Sollertinskiy, 'Karmen', in *Kriticheskiye stat'i* [Critical Essays], Leningrad, Gosudarstvennoye muzïkal'noye izdatel'stvo, 1933, p. 73.

24. Nietzsche, *Beyond Good and Evil*, p. 41.

25. *Ibid.*

26. *Ibid.*

27. Nietzsche, 'The Case of Wagner', p. 8.

28. Iwan Sollertinski, *Gustav Mahler: Der Schrei ins Leere*, Berlin, Ernst Kuhn, 1996, p. 37.

29. For an interesting discussion of this subject see Pauline Fairclough, 'Mahler Reconstructed: Sollertinsky and the Soviet Symphony', *Musical Quarterly*, 85 (2001), 367–90.

30. Gustav Mahler, *Selected letters of Gustav Mahler*, London, Faber, 1979, p. 324

31. Sollertinskiy, *Gustav Mahler*, p. 25, and 'Simfonii Malera' [The Symphonies of Mahler], in *Istoricheskiye Etyudï* [Historical Studies], Leningrad, Gosudarstvennoye muzïkal'noye izdatel'stvo, 1932, pp. 316–34.

32. Sollertinskiy, *Gustav Mahler*, pp. 44–5.

33. Sheinberg, *Irony, Satire, Parody and the Grotesque*, pp. 33–5.

34. *Ibid.*, pp. 57ff.

35. See *ibid.*, pp. 12–14.

36. *Ibid.*, pp. 173ff.

37. Quoted in Fay, *Shostakovich*, p. 229.

38. Kaufmann, *Existentialism*, p. 14.

39. Fyodor Dostoevsky, *Notes from Underground*, London, Penguin Books, 1972, p. 9.

40. *Ibid.*, p. 16.

41. *Ibid.*, p. 17.

42. *Ibid.*, p. 24.

43. See, for example, Richard Taruskin, *Defining Russia Musically: Historical and Hermeneutical Essays*, Princeton, Princeton University Press, 1997, p. 495, and Fanning, *Shostakovich: String Quartet No. 8*, p. 135.

44. See Sheinberg, *Irony, Satire, Parody, and the Grotesque*, pp. 107ff.

45. Dostoevsky, *Notes from the Underground*, p. 28.

46. Letter to Isaak Glikman of 19 July 1960, in Glikman, *Story of a Friendship*, p. 91.

47. Avner Ziv, 'Psycho-Social Aspects of Jewish Humor in Israel and in the Diaspora', in Ziv (ed.), *Jewish Humor*, Tel-Aviv, Papyrus, 1986, 47–71.

48. Marina Ritzarev, 'When did Shostakovich Stop Using Jewish Idiom?', in Ernst Kuhn, Andreas Wehrmeyer and Günter Wolter (eds.), *Dmitri Schostakowitsch und das jüdische musikalische Erbe*, Berlin, Verlag Ernst Kuhn, 2001, pp. 114–30.

49. Nelly Kravetz, 'New Insights into the Tenth Symphony', in Rosamund Bartlett (ed.), *Shostakovich in Context*, Oxford, Oxford University Press, 2000, pp. 159–74; Ritzarev, 'When did Shostakovich stop using Jewish idiom?', pp. 128–9.

50. Marina Ritzarev – personal information.

51. Elizabeth Wilson, *Shostakovich: A Life Remembered*, London, Faber, 2006, pp. 259–60.

52. See Zak, 'Jüdisches und nicht-Jüdisches', pp. 67–9.

53. Sheinberg, *Irony, Parody, Satire and the Grotesque*, p. 318, and 'Shostakovich's "Jewish Music" as an Existential Statement', in Kuhn et al., *Dmitri Schostakowitsch und das jüdische musikalische Erbe*, p. 94.

54. Joachim Braun, *Shostakovich's Jewish Songs*, Tel-Aviv, World Council Yiddish and Jewish Culture and Institute Yad Lezlilei Hashoa, 1989.

55. See Sheinberg, *Irony, Satire, Parody and the Grotesque*, pp. 273–5.

56. Fanning, *Shostakovich: String Quartet No. 8*, p. 81.

Select bibliography

Akopyan [= Hakobian], Levon, *Dmitriy Shostakovich: opït fenomenologii tvorchestva* [Dmitry Shostakovich: a phenomenological examination], St Petersburg, Dmitry Bulanin, for the State Arts Institute of the Ministry of Culture of the Russian Federation, 2004.

Bartlett, Rosamund (ed.), *Shostakovich in Context*, Oxford, Oxford University Press, 2000.

Irina Bobïkina (ed.), *Dmitry Shostakovich v pis'makh i dokumentakh* [Dmitry Shostakovich in letters and documents], Moscow, Antikva, for the Glinka State Museum of Musical Culture, 2000.

Braun, Joachim, 'The Double Meaning of Jewish Elements in Dmitri Shostakovich's Music', *Musical Quarterly*, 71 (1985), 68–80.

Brown, Malcolm Hamrick (ed.), *A Shostakovich Casebook*, Bloomington, Indiana University Press, 2004.

Clark, Katerina, *Petersburg, Crucible of Cultural Revolution*, Cambridge, Mass., Harvard University Press, 1995.

Dombrovskaya, Ol'ga, *Dmitri Shostakovich: Pages of his Life in Photographs*, Moscow, DSCH Publishers, 2006.

Edmunds, Neil (ed.), *Soviet Music and Society under Lenin and Stalin*, London, Routledge Curzon, 2004.

Fairclough, Pauline, *A Soviet Credo: Shostakovich's Fourth Symphony*, Aldershot, Ashgate, 2006.

'The "Old Shostakovich": Reception in the British Press', *Music and Letters*, 88 (2007), 266–96.

Fanning, David, *The Breath of the Symphonist: Shostakovich's Tenth*, London, Royal Musical Association, 1988.

(ed.), *Shostakovich Studies*, Cambridge, Cambridge University Press, 1995.

'Shostakovich: "The Present-day Master of the C-major Key"', *Acta musicologica*, 73 (2001), 101–40.

Shostakovich: String Quartet No. 8, Aldershot, Ashgate, 2004.

and Laurel Fay, 'Shostakovich, Dmitry', in *The New Grove Dictionary of Music and Musicians*, 2nd edn, ed. Stanley Sadie and John Tyrrell, London, Macmillan, 2001, vol. 23, pp. 279–311.

Fay, Laurel, *Shostakovich: A Life*, New York, Oxford University Press, 2000.

(ed.), *Shostakovich and his World*, Princeton, Princeton University Press, 2004.

Glikman, Isaak, *Story of a Friendship: The Letters of Dmitry Shostakovich to Isaak Glikman, 1941–1975*, trans. Anthony Phillips, London, Faber, 2001.

Grigoryev, Lev and Yakov Platek (eds.), *Dmitry Shostakovich: About Himself and his Times*, Moscow, Progress Publishers, 1980.

Haas, David, *Leningrad's Modernists: Studies in Composition and Musical Thought, 1917–1932*, New York, Peter Lang, 1998.

Hakobian, Levon, *Music of the Soviet Age, 1917–1987*, Stockholm, Melos, 1998.

Hulme, Derek C., *Dmitri Shostakovich, A Catalogue, Bibliography, and Discography*, 3rd edn, Lanham, Md., Scarecrow Press, 2002.

Khentova, Sof'ya, *Dmitri Shostakovich: zhizn' i tvorchestvo* [Dmitry Shostakovich: life and works], 2 vols., Leningrad, Sovetskiy kompozitor, 1985, 1986.

V mire Shostakovicha [In Shostakovich's world], Moscow, Kompozitor, 1996.

Kovnatskaya, Lyudmila (ed.), *Shostakovich: mezhdu mgnoveniyem i vechnost'yu. Dokumentï, materialï, stat'i* [Shostakovich between the moment and eternity: documents, materials, articles], St Petersburg, Kompozitor, 2000.

Kuhn, Ernst (ed.), *'Volksfeind Dmitri Schostakowitsch': eine Dokumentation der öffentlichen Angriffe gegen den Komponisten in der ehemaligen Sowjetunion*, Berlin, Kuhn, 1997 (with international bibliography to 1996).

et al. (eds.), Dmitri Schostakowitsch und das jüdische musikalische Erbe, Berlin, Kuhn, 2001.

MacDonald, Ian, *The New Shostakovich*, London, Fourth Estate, 1990, Oxford, Oxford University Press, 1991, rev. and corrected edn, ed. Raymond Clarke, London, Pimlico, 2006.

McQuere, Gordon, (ed.), *Russian Theoretical Thought in Music*, Ann Arbor, UMI Research Press, 1983.

Maes, Francis, *A History of Russian Music*, London, University of California Press, 1996.

Mikheyeva, Lyudmila, *Zhizn' Dmitriya Shostakovich* [The life of Dmitry Shostakovich], Moscow, Terra, 1997.

Mishra, Michael (ed.), *A Shostakovich Companion*, Westport, Ct., Greenwood, forthcoming.

Moshevich, Sofia, *Dmitri Shostakovich: Pianist*, Montreal, McGill–Queen's University Press, 2004.

Norris, Christopher (ed.), *Shostakovich, the Man and his Music*, London, Lawrence & Wishart, 1982.

Rakhmanova, Marina (ed.), *Shostakovich – Urtext*, Moscow, Deka, for the Glinka Museum of Musical Culture, 2007.

Riley, John, *Dmitri Shostakovich: A Life in Film*, London, IB Tauris, 2005.

Schmalenberg, Hilmar (ed.), *Schostakowitsch in Deutschland*, Berlin, Verlag Ernst Kuhn, 1998.

Schwarz, Boris, *Music and Musical Life in Soviet Russia, enlarged edn, 1917–1981*, Bloomington, Indiana University Press, 1983.

Sheinberg, Esti, *Irony, Satire, Parody and the Grotesque in the Music of Shostakovich*, Aldershot, Ashgate, 2000.

Souritz, Elizabeth, *Soviet Choreographers in the 1920s*, London, Dance Books, 1990.

Taruskin, Richard, *Defining Russia Musically*, Princeton, Princeton University Press, 1997.

Tomoff, Kirill, *Creative Union: The Professional Organization of Soviet Composers, 1939-1953*, Ithaca, N.Y., and London, Cornell University Press, 2006.

Volkov, Solomon, *Testimony: The Memoirs of Dmitri Shostakovich as Related to and Edited by Solomon Volkov*, London, Hamish Hamilton, 1979.

Wilson, Elizabeth. *Shostakovich: A Life Remembered*, London, Faber, 1994, new edn, London, Faber, 2006.

Electronic media

Oksana Dvornichenko, *Shostakovich*, London, Chandos Multimedia, 2000
   (CHAN55001 (DVDROM), CHAN 50001 (CDROM)).

Edition

Shostakovich, *New Collected Works* (150 volumes), ed. Manashir Yakubov, Moscow,
   DSCH publishers, 2002–(ongoing).

Index

Cambridge Companions to Music

Topics

The Cambridge Companion to Ballet
Edited by Marion Kant

The Cambridge Companion to Blues and Gospel
Music
Edited by Allan Moore

The Cambridge Companion to the Concerto
Edited by Simon P. Keefe

The Cambridge Companion to Conducting
Edited by José Antonio Bowen

The Cambridge Companion to Electronic Music
Edited by Nick Collins and Julio D' Escriván

The Cambridge Companion to Grand Opera
Edited by David Charlton

The Cambridge Companion to Jazz
Edited by Mervyn Cooke and David Horn

The Cambridge Companion to the Lied
Edited by James Parsons

The Cambridge Companion to the Musical,
second edition
Edited by William Everett and Paul Laird

The Cambridge Companion to the Orchestra
Edited by Colin Lawson

The Cambridge Companion to Pop and Rock
Edited by Simon Frith, Will Straw and John Street

The Cambridge Companion to the String Quartet
Edited by Robin Stowell

The Cambridge Companion to Twentieth-Century
Opera
Edited by Mervyn Cooke

Composers

The Cambridge Companion to Bach
Edited by John Butt

The Cambridge Companion to Bartók
Edited by Amanda Bayley

The Cambridge Companion to Beethoven
Edited by Glenn Stanley

The Cambridge Companion to Berg
Edited by Anthony Pople

The Cambridge Companion to Berlioz
Edited by Peter Bloom

The Cambridge Companion to Brahms
Edited by Michael Musgrave

The Cambridge Companion to Benjamin Britten
Edited by Mervyn Cooke

The Cambridge Companion to Bruckner
Edited by John Williamson

The Cambridge Companion to John Cage
Edited by David Nicholls

The Cambridge Companion to Chopin
Edited by Jim Samson

The Cambridge Companion to Debussy
Edited by Simon Trezise

The Cambridge Companion to Elgar
Edited by Daniel M. Grimley and Julian Rushton

The Cambridge Companion to Handel
Edited by Donald Burrows

The Cambridge Companion to Haydn
Edited by Caryl Clark

The Cambridge Companion to Liszt
Edited by Kenneth Hamilton

The Cambridge Companion to Mahler
Edited by Jeremy Barham

The Cambridge Companion to Mendelssohn
Edited by Peter Mercer-Taylor

The Cambridge Companion to Monteverdi
Edited by John Whenham and Richard Wistreich

The Cambridge Companion to Mozart
Edited by Simon P. Keefe

The Cambridge Companion to Ravel
Edited by Deborah Mawer

The Cambridge Companion to Rossini
Edited by Emanuele Senici

The Cambridge Companion to Schubert
Edited by Christopher Gibbs

The Cambridge Companion to Schumann
Edited by Beate Perrey

The Cambridge Companion to Shostakovich
Edited by Pauline Fairclough and David Fanning